Management Control Theory

History of Management Thought
Series Editor: Derek S. Pugh

Titles in the Series:

Management Control Theory
A.J. Berry, Jane Broadbent & David T. Otley

Entrepreneurship
Sue Birley

International Business
Peter Buckley

Postmodern Management Theory
Marta B. Calás & Linda Smircich

Foundations of Finance, Vols I, II and III
Elroy Dimson & Massoud Mussavian

Contingency Theory
Lex Donaldson

Management Science: An Anthology, Vols I, II and III
Samuel Eilon

Innovation
Jerald Hage

Complex Organizations
Richard H. Hall

Managerial Decision Making
David J. Hickson

Management Education
Robert R. Locke

Historical Evolution of Strategic Management, Vols I and II
Peter McKiernan

Administrative and Management Theory
John B. Miner

Human Relations: Theory and Developments
Lyman W. Porter & Gregory A. Bigley

Comparative Cross Cultural Management
Derek S. Pugh

Critical Perspectives on Organization and Management Theory
Linda Smircich & Marta B. Calás

Managerial Work
Rosemary Stewart

Corporate Governance
R.I. Tricker

Early Management Thought
Daniel A. Wren

Management Control Theory

Edited by

A.J. Berry

School of Financial Studies and Law,
Sheffield Hallam University

J. Broadbent

School of Management,
Royal Holloway, University of London

D.T. Otley

Department of Accounting and Finance,
The Management School, Lancaster University

LONDON AND NEW YORK

First published 1998 by Dartmouth and Ashgate Publishing

Reissued 2018 by Routledge
2 Park Square, Milton Park, Abingdon, Oxon, OX14 4RN
52 Vanderbilt Avenue, New York, NY 10017

Routledge is an imprint of the Taylor & Francis Group, an informa business

Publisher's Note
The publisher has gone to great lengths to ensure the quality of this reprint but points out that some imperfections in the original copies may be apparent.

A Library of Congress record exists under LC control number:

ISBN 13: 978-1-138-39170-3 (hbk)
ISBN 13: 978-1-138-39173-4 (pbk)
ISBN 13: 978-0-429-42255-3 (ebk)

Contents

Acknowledgements ix
Series Preface xiii
Introduction xv

PART I INTRODUCTION

1 Giovanni B. Giglioni and Arthur G. Bedeian (1974), 'A Conspectus of Management Control Theory: 1900–1972', *Academy of Management Journal*, **17**, pp. 292-305. 3

PART II CONTROL AS GOAL-DIRECTED AND INTEGRATIVE

2 Robert N. Anthony and John Dearden (1980), 'The Nature of Management Control', in *Management Control System*, Homewood: Illinois, Richard D. Irwin, Inc., pp. 3-20. 19
3 Tony Lowe and Tony Puxty (1989), 'The Problems of a Paradigm: A Critique of the Prevailing Orthodoxy in Management Control', in Wai Fong Chua, Tony Lowe and Tony Puxty (eds), *Critical Perspectives in Management Control*, Basingstoke: The Macmillan Press Ltd, pp. 9-26. 37
4 Sir Geoffrey Vickers (1958), 'Positive and Negative Controls in Business', *Journal of Industrial Economics*, **6**, pp. 173–79. 55
5 E.A. Lowe (1971), 'On the Idea of a Management Control System: Integrating Accounting and Management Control', *Journal of Management Studies*, **8**, pp. 1–12. 63
6 Adrian Buckley and Eugene McKenna (1972), 'Budgetary Control and Business Behaviour', *Accounting and Business Research*, **3**, pp. 137–50. 75
7 A.E. Mills (1970), 'Management Control and Integration at the Conceptual Level', *Journal of Management Studies*, **7**, pp. 364–75. 89
8 D.T. Otley and A.J. Berry (1980), 'Control, Organisation and Accounting', *Accounting, Organizations and Society*, **5**, pp. 231–44. 101
9 Rick Antle and Joel S. Demski (1988), 'The Controllability Principle in Responsibility Accounting', *The Accounting Review*, **LXIII**, pp. 700–18. 115

PART III CONTROL AS ADAPTATION

10 Stafford Beer (1972), 'Autonomics – Systems One, Two, Three', in *Brain of*

the Firm, Chichester: John Wiley & Sons, pp. 167–80. 137

11 Peter B. Checkland and Michael G. Haynes (1994), 'Varieties of Systems Thinking: The Case of Soft Systems Methodology', *System Dynamics Review*, **10**, pp. 189–97. 151

12 Michael Goold and Andrew Campbell (1987), 'Managing Diversity: Strategy and Control in Diversified British Companies', *Long Range Planning*, **20**, pp. 42–52. 161

13 Robert Simons (1990), 'The Role of Management Control Systems in Creating Competitive Advantage: New Perspectives', *Accounting, Organizations and Society*, **15**, pp. 127–43, and Barbara Gray (1990), 'The Enactment of Management Control Systems: A Critique of Simons', *Accounting, Organizations and Society*, **15**, pp. 145–48. 173

PART IV THE SOCIAL STRUCTURE OF CONTROL IN ORGANIZATIONS

14 Selwyn Becker and David Green, Jr (1962), 'Budgeting and Employee Behavior', *Journal of Business*, **35**, pp. 392–402. 197

15 Michael Schiff and Arie Y. Lewin (1970), 'The Impact of People on Budgets', *The Accounting Review*, **45**, pp. 259–68. 209

16 Peter F. Drucker (1964), 'Controls, Control and Management', in Charles P. Bonini, Robert K. Jaedicke and Harvey M. Wagner (eds), *Management Controls: New Directions in Basic Research*, New York: McGraw-Hill Inc., pp. 286–96. 219

17 Geert Hofstede (1978), 'The Poverty of Management Control Philosophy', *Academy of Management Review*, **3**, pp. 450–61. 231

18 John L.J. Machin (1979), 'A Contingent Methodology for Management Control', *Journal of Management Studies*, **XVI**, pp. 1–29. 243

19 Toshiro Hiromoto (1991), 'Restoring the Relevance of Management Accounting', *Journal of Management Accounting Research*, **3**, pp. 1–15. 273

20 N.B. Macintosh and R.L. Daft (1987), 'Management Control Systems and Departmental Interdependencies: An Empirical Study', *Accounting, Organizations and Society*, **12**, pp. 49–61. 289

PART V THE ORGANIZATION IN ITS ENVIRONMENT

21 David T. Otley (1980), 'The Contingency Theory of Management Accounting: Achievement and Prognosis', *Accounting, Organizations and Society*, **5**, pp. 413–28. 305

22 Vijay Govindarajan (1986), 'Impact of Participation in the Budgetary Process on Managerial Attitudes and Performance: Universalistic and Contingency Perspectives', *Decision Sciences*, **17**, pp. 496–516. 321

23 William G. Ouchi (1980), 'Markets, Bureaucracies, and Clans', *Administrative Science Quarterly*, **25**, pp. 129–41. 343

24 Anthony G. Hopwood (1990), 'Accounting and Organisation Change', *Accounting, Auditing and Accountability Journal*, **3**, pp. 7–17. 357

25 Charles Perrow (1961), 'The Analysis of Goals in Complex Organizations', *American Sociological Review*, **26**, pp. 854–66. 369

26 J.D. Dermer and R.G. Lucas (1986), 'The Illusion of Managerial Control', *Accounting, Organizations and Society*, **11**, pp. 471–82. 383

27 Nils Brunsson (1982), 'The Irrationality of Action and Action Rationality: Decisions, Ideologies and Organizational Actions', *Journal of Management Studies*, **19**, pp. 29–44. 395

28 Peter Miller and Ted O'Leary (1987), 'Accounting and the Construction of the Governable Person', *Accounting, Organizations and Society*, **12**, pp. 235–65. 411

29 Shahid L. Ansari and Jan Bell (1991), 'Symbolism, Collectivism and Rationality in Organisational Control', *Accounting, Auditing and Accountability Journal*, **4**, pp. 4–27. 443

PART VI EPILOGUE

30 Kenneth A. Merchant and Robert Simons (1986), 'Research and Control in Complex Organizations: An Overview', *Journal of Accounting Literature*, **5**, pp. 183-203. 469

Name Index 491

Acknowledgements

The editors and publishers wish to thank the following for permission to use copyright material.

Academy of Management for the essay: Giovanni B. Giglioni and Arthur G. Bedeian (1974), 'A Conspectus of Management Control Theory: 1900–1972', *Academy of Management Journal*, **17**, pp. 292–305.

Administrative Science Quarterly for the essay: William G. Ouchi (1980), 'Markets, Bureaucracies, and Clans', *Administrative Science Quarterly*, **25**, pp. 129–41. Copyright © 1980 Cornell University.

American Accounting Association for the essays: Toshiro Hiromoto (1991), 'Restoring the Relevance of Management Accounting', *Journal of Management Accounting Research*, **3**, pp. 1–15; Rick Antle and Joel S. Demski (1988), 'The Controllability Principle in Responsibility Accounting', *The Accounting Review*, **LXIII**, pp. 700–18; Michael Schiff and Arie Y. Lewin (1970), 'The Impact of People on Budgets', *The Accounting Review*, **45**, pp. 259–68.

American Sociological Association for the essay: Charles Perrow (1961), 'The Analysis of Goals in Complex Organizations', *American Sociological Review*, **26**, pp. 854–66.

Blackwell Publishers for the essays: Sir Geoffrey Vickers (1958), 'Positive and Negative Controls in Business', *Journal of Industrial Economics*, **6**, pp. 173–79; E.A. Lowe (1971), 'On the Idea of a Management Control System: Integrating Accounting and Management Control', *Journal of Management Studies*, **8**, pp. 1–12; A.E. Mills (1970), 'Management Control and Integration at the Conceptual Level', *Journal of Management Studies*, **7**, pp. 364–75; John L.J. Machin (1979), 'A Contingent Methodology for Management Control', *Journal of Management Studies*, **XVI**, pp. 1–29; Nils Brunsson (1982), 'The Irrationality of Action and Action Rationality: Decisions, Ideologies and Organizational Actions', *Journal of Management Studies*, **19**, pp. 29–44.

Decision Sciences Institute for the essay: Vijay Govindarajan (1986), 'Impact of Participation in the Budgetary Process on Managerial Attitudes and Performance: Universalistic and Contingency Perspectives', *Decision Sciences*, **17**, pp. 496–516. The Decision Sciences Journal is published by the Decision Sciences Institute, located in the College of Business Administration at Georgia State University, Atlanta, Georgia.

Elsevier Science Ltd for the essays: Michael Goold and Andrew Campbell (1987), 'Managing Diversity: Strategy and Control in Diversified British Companies', *Long Range Planning*, **20**, pp. 42–52. Reprinted with permission from Elsevier Science Ltd, Oxford, England: D.T. Otley and A.J. Berry (1980), 'Control, Organisation and Accounting', *Accounting, Organizations and Society*, **5**, pp. 231–44. Copyright © 1980 Pergamon Press. Reprinted with permission from Elsevier Science Ltd, The Boulevard, Langford Lane, Kidlington OX5 1GB, UK; Robert Simons (1990), 'The Role of Management Control Systems in Creating Competitive Advantage: New Perspectives', *Accounting, Organizations and Society*, **15**, pp. 127–43. Reprinted with permission from Elsevier Science Ltd, Oxford, England; N.B. Macintosh and R.L. Daft (1987), 'Management Control Systems and Departmental Interdependencies: An Empirical Study', *Accounting, Organizations and Society*, **12**, pp. 49–61. Reprinted with permission from Elsevier Science Ltd, Oxford, England; David T. Otley (1980), 'The Contingency Theory of Management Accounting: Achievement and Prognosis', *Accounting, Organizations and Society*, **5**, pp. 413–28. Copyright © 1980 Pergamon Press. Reprinted with permission from Elsevier Science Ltd, Oxford, England; J.D. Dermer and R.G. Lucas (1986), 'The Illusion of Managerial Control', *Accounting, Organizations and Society*, **11**, pp. 471–82. Reprinted with permission from Elsevier Science Ltd, Oxford, England; Peter Miller and Ted O'Leary (1987), 'Accounting and the Construction of the Governable Person', *Accounting, Organizations and Society*, **12**, pp. 235–65. Reprinted with permission from Elsevier Science Ltd, Oxford, England. Barbara Gray (1990), 'The Enactment of Management Control Systems: A Critique of Simons', *Accounting, Organizations and Society*, **15**, pp. 145–48. Reprinted with permission from Elsevier Science Ltd, Oxford, England.

Geert Hofstede (1978), 'The Poverty of Management Control Philosophy', *Academy of Management Review*, **3**, pp. 450–61. Originally published in *Academy of Management Review*, **3**, 1978, 450–61. Republished in Geert Hofstede, *Uncommon Sense About Organizations: Cases, Studies and Field Observations*, Thousand Oaks CA: Sage Publications, 1994, 154–69. Reprinted with the author's permission.

Institute of Chartered Accountants for the essay: Adrian Buckley and Eugene McKenna (1972), 'Budgetary Control and Business Behaviour', *Accounting and Business Research*, **3**, pp. 137–50.

John Wiley & Sons Ltd for the essays: Stafford Beer (1972), 'Autonomics – Systems One, Two, Three', in *Brain of the Firm*, Chichester: John Wiley & Sons, pp. 167–80. Reproduced by permission of John Wiley & Sons, Ltd; Peter B. Checkland and Michael G. Haynes (1994), 'Varieties of Systems Thinking: The Case of Soft Systems Methodology', *System Dynamics Review*, **10**, pp. 189–97. Copyright © 1994 John Wiley & Sons Ltd. Reproduced by permission of John Wiley & Sons Limited.

Macmillan Press Ltd for the essay : Tony Lowe and Tony Puxty (1989), 'The Problems of a Paradigm: A Critique of the Prevailing Orthodoxy in Management Control', in Wai Fong Chau, Tony Lowe and Tony Puxty (eds), *Critical Perspectives in Management Control*, Basingstoke: The Macmillan Press Ltd, pp. 9–26. Copyright © 1989 Macmillan Press Ltd.

McGraw Hill Companies for the essays: Robert N. Anthony and John Dearden (1980), 'The

Nature of Management Control', in *Management Control System*, Homewood: Illinois, Richard D. Irwin, Inc., pp. 3-20; Peter F. Drucker (1964), 'Controls, Control and Management', in Charles P. Bonini, Robert K. Jaedicke and Harvey M. Wagner (eds), *Management Controls: New Directions in Basic Research*, New York: McGraw Hill Inc., pp. 286–96. Copyright © 1964 McGraw Hill Companies.

MCB University Press for the essays: Anthony G. Hopwood (1990), 'Accounting and Organisation Change', *Accounting, Auditing and Accountability Journal*, **3**, pp. 7–17. Copyright © MCB University Press: Shahid L. Ansari and Jan Bell (1991), 'Symbolism, Collectivism and Rationality in Organisational Control', *Accounting, Auditing and Accountability Journal*, **4**, pp. 4–27. Copyright © MCB University Press.

The University of Chicago Press for the essay: Selwyn Becker and David Green, Jr (1962), 'Budgeting and Employee Behavior', *Journal of Business*, **35**, pp. 392–402.

University of Florida Accounting Research Centre for the essay: K.A. Merchant and Robert Simons (1986), 'Research and Control in Complex Organizations: An Overview', *Journal of Accounting Literature*, **5**, pp. 183–203.

Every effort has been made to trace all the copyright holders, but if any have been inadvertently overlooked the publishers will be pleased to make the necessary arrangement at the first opportunity.

Series Preface

The *History of Management Thought* is based on the assumption that a knowledge of the intellectual history of an academic field is vital for a present day understanding of it. In the past scholars of management as a discipline have tended to ignore or underrate the historical development of their subject. This ignorance has encouraged the 'reinventing the wheel' and 'old wine in new bottles' phenomena which have plagued the subject of management since its birth. The insight that those who ignore history are condemned to repeat it, is surely most true about the development of ideas.

This indifference now appears to be beginning to change, and the history of management and management thought is attracting greater interest. The *History of Management Thought* builds on this development by presenting a number of volumes which cover the intellectual history of the subject. It makes available to a wide range of academics contributions to management thought that have been influential over the years. The volume topics range across the whole field of management studies from early management thought through to post-modern management theory.

Each volume in the *History of Management Thought* is edited by a leading international scholar who gives an introductory analytical historical review of the development of the subject, and then presents a selection of key articles. Many of these articles have previously only been published in journals, often in early volumes which are not generally available. They are now conveniently presented in book form, with each chosen article reproduced in full. They offer an important resource for use by academics and advanced students in the field for increasing their knowledge and understanding of the historical development of the disciplines of management.

DEREK S. PUGH
General Editor
History of Management Thought
Visiting Research Professor of
International Management
Open University Business School, UK

Introduction

This volume of essays is designed to provide an overview of the development of the study of Management Control. Most of the essays are taken from work published in the last 35 years, although the essay by Giglioni and Bedeian (Chapter 1), reviewing the period 1900–1972 provides some roots back to the beginning of the twentieth century. This 35-year window is somewhat arbitrary, but it was a period of considerable change in the range and intent of scholars and researchers in the field.

In order to provide a basic foundation, the introductory Part I contains the review essay by Giglioni and Bedeian (1974). These authors concluded that 'even though control has not achieved the level of sophistication of some other management functions, it has developed to a point that affords the executive ample opportunity to maintain the operations of his firm under check'. Their essay demonstrates that the subject of management control was developed with management accounting at its centre and concerned the patterns of integration to be established and maintained within organizations to assist the attainment of organizational goals. Essentially, the study of management control was rooted in a functionalist paradigm – that is, management control procedures and processes were explained in relation to their function in supporting the management's purposes, without questioning or addressing those purposes. This tradition followed that of management accounting and was primarily concerned with the pursuit of efficiency and effectiveness.

Control as Goal-directed and Integrative

In Part II the theme of efficiency and effectiveness is explored further. These essays are also ones in which consideration of organizational goals is generally taken as given. When these are assumed, control becomes a goal-directed and integrative mechanism. This pursuit of effectiveness and efficiency and the assumption of the existence of unproblematic organizational goals lay at the heart of the now classic definition of management control provided by Robert Anthony (1965) where he claimed that management control was 'the process by which managers assure that resources are obtained and used effectively and efficiently in the accomplishment of the organisation's objectives'. This definition provides the theme for nine editions of his text (written with a number of co-authors) and the essay in Chapter 2 of this volume provides an example of the development of this theme.

Anthony's approach meant that management control was contrasted with the ideas of strategic planning, concerned with setting goals and objectives for the whole organization over the long term, and operational control, concerned with ensuring that immediate tasks are carried out. These three ideas formed a nested hierarchy for control in, and of, an organization. Interestingly, his definition has been adapted in the latest (1998) edition to suggest that management control is 'the process by which managers influence other members of the organization to implement the organization's strategies' (p. 6), which although it now emphasizes the behavioural aspects of control more strongly, still takes strategy as given. It is probably erroneous to assume that Anthony did not know that real organizations did not function with such simple distinctions or that these could not be enacted in practice as watertight compartments. In his writing he is clearly aware of the problem of connection across the three levels of organizational control and he seems to have made space in his thinking for those connections through the organizational cycles of planning and reporting. Indeed, these procedures were seen as the controls which would ensure that control was established and maintained (see Drucker, Chapter 16 in this volume).

Despite this broad intention, the narrow focus of the work does not enable it to fulfil its promise and the emphasis remains one which stresses management accounting control systems to the virtual exclusion of other mechanisms of control.

In Chapter 3 Lowe and Puxty formally examine Anthony's paradigm for management control and restate the criticisms that the hierarchic model do not lead to holistic analysis, and that neither the external environment nor feedforward control mechanisms are explicitly considered. More sharply, these authors consider that, in Anthony's formulation, organizational goals are seen as non-problematic and unambiguous. The complex questions as to the nature of organizational members' goals and their relationship to those of the overall organization are not considered. Thus, Lowe and Puxty's work is not just a behavioural critique of the rational economic theory of the firm implicitly adopted by Anthony, but also a demonstration that the functional epistemological stance of Anthony's model is neither necessary nor always acceptable.

The essay by Vickers (Chapter 4) considers control and its limitations. Whilst focusing on goals he is, nevertheless, careful to remind us that we should be modest in our expectations. Vickers explicitly focuses on control as a means of comparison between a given state and a standard. His analysis thus emphasizes the importance of information about both activities and standards. He notes that controls may be of two kinds: the first, called negative control, sees the standard as a limit which cannot be exceeded; the second, positive control, sees the standard as a norm which is to be sought. In making this distinction he differentiates control and remedial action, thereby allowing three uses of control to be highlighted; first, to indicate whether the operation is reaching norms and limits; second, to compare the actual with forecasts; and, third, to compare activity with targets. Vickers points out that we should beware of overprecise standards, and sees a narrow band as more useful than a single figure. He also recognizes that not all action is 'controllable', making the important observation that the more significant an action is the less likely it is to be controllable. He reminds us that all action is tentative, based on assumptions that may prove mistaken and that managers must still act even when the feedback from control procedures is too slow to be of use.

Lowe (Chapter 5) led the study of management control away from what could be seen as its rather narrow foundations by offering a definition of a management control system as:

> A system of organisational information seeking and gathering, accountability and feedback designed to ensure that the enterprise adapts to changes in its substantive environment and that the work behaviour of its employees is measured by reference to a set of operational sub goals (which conform with overall objectives) so that the discrepancy between the two can be reconciled and corrected for. (p. 67)

In this definition Lowe has broken away from Anthony's hierarchy by conceiving of management control as encompassing the whole organizational problem of goal definition and attainment by adopting a systems perspective. Hence control was now to be studied as a systemic, as well as a systematic, process. Significantly this shifts the control problem from control in a hierarchy to the self-regulation of the organization conceived as a system. Other shifts in focus, in a similar vein, were made by Buckley and McKenna (Chapter 6) and Mills (Chapter 7). Buckley and McKenna's attention is on the relationship of a mode of control (budgets) and managerial behaviour, again linking control to a broader conception of the organizational problem. In similar vein, Mills argues that management control should be a central management discipline, suggesting that it was a more appropriate integrating discipline for general management courses than the common use of business policy or corporate strategy. This viewpoint again stresses the role of management control systems as a major integrative device in organizational functioning.

Otley and Berry (Chapter 8) return to the issue of conceptualizing the problem of control from a more general and abstract standpoint. Building on the ideas of Tocher (1970, 1976) these authors construct a schema for control which links previous ideas into one general model, stressing the connections between the role of expectations, observation and measurement, communication and information flows. In particular, they emphasize the existence of a predictive model through which 'controllers' examine implications of the state of the organization in the environment and consider appropriate courses of action. This work, therefore, provides an important reminder that there are a number of ways to implement actions to reduce the mismatch between actual outcomes and those originally planned, including revising the predictive models or amending the objectives.

Antle and Demski (Chapter 9) also implicitly see control as goal directed, and consider the extent to which managers can be held accountable for achieving particular outcomes. They provide an example of the use of a principal-agent perspective to study the issue of controllability and develop an analysis which assumes that managerial evaluation aims to produce information on the services provided by that manager. They distinguish between controllability and information content. They argue that not only should a manager's performance be evaluated on those items over which they have full control, but also in light of the extent to which they influence the variable in question in the context of other information present (p. 716). At the same time they recognize the difficulty of applying this perspective, leaving us with a problem of how we might apply these insights.

This strand of the management control literature, concerned with adaptation and goal achievement, began with the elegant hierarchic formalism of control in the economically rational firm. It was extended through considerations of systemic modelling to include the environment and the behaviour of actors in varied rationalities. Its epistemological location, in the functionalist paradigm, partly explains why most of the debate had turned upon the nature of knowledge and the implied nature of the role of theory. Perhaps less obvious is why there has been so little empirical examination of Anthony's model.

Control as Adaptation

Part III is concerned with the work of authors who have explored the notion of control as adaptation. An early example of this is the essay by Stafford Beer, reproduced in Chapter 10, who, working within the traditions of operations research and cybernetics sets out to build a model for organizational control that is logically necessary and sufficient. He conceives of a hierarchy of systems which, together, provide the framework for the achievement control. In his schema:

- System 5 is the policy-making system which defines purpose for the organization.
- System 4 is the future responsive system which scans the internal and external world to ensure that the organization's policy and operations are feasible.
- System 3 is the integrator of the policy, future responsiveness and operations and is the locus of managing.
- System 1 contains the individual operating systems.
- System 2 is to manage the oscillations in the interdependence of Systems 1 and 3.

In some ways this model is similar to Anthony's but, in his insistence on System 4, Beer focuses on a significant problem of control – that of adaptation. No longer does the internal world enact the policy or strategic plan; the system must cope with change inside itself as well as outside. The idea of specifying and maximizing particular goals is replaced with a more general objective of survival and effectiveness.

Criticism of Beer's model focused on the fact that, being a logical hierarchy, it was a technical model in an age which saw the continuing development of socio-technical systems. Additionally, the model, being functionalist in nature, attracted the same critique that was levelled at Anthony.

In this same tradition, Checkland and Haynes (Chapter 11) developed what they initially called a 'soft systems methodology' and later came to describe as a modelling process for soft systems. The word 'soft' refers to the inclusion of human and organizational issues alongside the technical operating systems. Again, as Checkland and Haynes were primarily concerned with problem-solving, the issues of change and adaptation were central to their approach. They were setting out to construct a descriptive model of the operations which might then be analysed and modified so that the roots of problems could be identified. From this diagnostic, a further model could be constructed and in turn used for either simulation or prediction.

In a different way Goold and Campbell (Chapter 12) were working on the similar tasks of identifying the characteristics of control strategies used by organizations in various circumstances; their concern was with the fit of control and adaptation to external conditions. Like Beer and Checkland these authors developed their model from a series of field studies. They were concerned with the management of diversification. They found that companies with a 'core business' (set in a few industries) tended to adopt a strategic planning style, with adaptation as a central issue; those with a 'manageable business' (homogeneous in nature, across industries, manageable with short-term financial controls) adopted a financial control style; and those with a 'diverse business' (a portfolio that spreads risk across industries and geography) used a strategic control style. This essay is interesting because it stands apart from the more normative theorizing of the strategy literature and represents an attempt to grapple with the phenomena of control approaches among a small sample of large companies.

Simons (Chapter 13) took a similar interest in practice and asked a sharper question in respect of the consequences of control approaches for organizational performance. Interestingly, Simons offered a further definition of management control systems as 'the formalised procedures and systems that use information to maintain or alter patterns in organisational activity' (p. 128). Starting from the idea that companies design and use management controls to further competitive strategy, Simons undertook a field study of three competing firms over a two-year period, extended to 13 firms at a later stage. The essay reproduced in this volume is built from a comparison of two of these firms. Simons comments that his study underscores the dynamic relationship of the process of strategy-making, competitive strategic positioning and formal procedures. He argues that top managers intervene to monitor the strategic uncertainties which they consider to be critical to achieving organizational goals. In a robust critique of this study Gray (also Chapter 13) notes that the political function served by management controls deserves attention and that it is important for top managers to learn, commenting that Simons' model seems 'to perpetuate an image of top management as an omniscient and omnipotent navigator of the seas of uncertainty (p. 146). She also points out that Simons has neglected to examine how middle-level managers can, and do, influence strategy and are not merely implementors.

What is significant to us about this interchange is that the struggle to connect the normative traditions of management control with careful empirical research does not itself resolve the underlying epistemological stances of the normative model. It seems to us that Simons' excellent contribution is rooted largely in the functionalist tradition while Gray is arguing from an interpretative perspective. Hence they give different significance to phenomena, and it is entirely possible that, although Simons would not demur with Gray's points, he would recognize them as existing in a different frame. However Gray's comments serve as a means for us to move our story forward from the issues of control as adaptation towards the relationship of control and social structure.

The Social Structure of Control in Organizations

Accordingly, the essays in Part IV are concerned with the social structure of control in organizations. With the development of the human relations movement in management and organizational studies scholars began to pay explicit attention to the interplay between people and their work. It was, then, a natural – if perhaps slightly tardy – evolution for scholars to turn to the study of managerial and staff behaviour in relation to accounting practices, especially budgets and budgeting.

A book written by Chris Argyris (1952) alerted us to the impact of budgets on people, and much work followed which took up the challenge of seeking to explore the effects of different approaches to budgetary processes and the adoption of different assumptions about the nature of human behaviour. Becker and Green (Chapter 14) follow this approach and provide an overview of the history of approaches to budget-setting in the twentieth century before moving on to consider the effects of participation in budgetary control processes. They provide an explicit example of an attempt to bring together a technical accounting and a psychological model to enrich understandings of participation in budgetary processes.

Schiff and Lewin (Chapter 15) explicitly take Argyris's position and turn it around to provide a commentary on the effects of people on budgets. In examining the relationship between those who are controllers and those who are controlled they focus on the notion of slack resources – that is, those resources present in the firm in the form of 'invisible' costs.

They are particularly interested in the role of divisional managers in decentralized firms and their role in creating slack. Their remedy is to allow greater participation by managers but, in suggesting this, they assume that slack has no purpose. This latter assumption might well be questioned as might the assumption that top management is right and lower levels wrong. The issue that became clear was the notion of both rationality and obedience to superiors was challenged.

A volume such as this is necessarily constrained and readers might wish to supplement their understandings by reference to other sources. One such collection of essays, Bonini, Jaedicke and Wagner (1964), from which we have chosen an essay by Drucker, testifies to the growing understanding of both the significance of control theory and practice and to how little research had been undertaken. The whole volume repays reading, especially the essays which begin to explore the interrelationship of organization structure and procedures and management control. The earlier essays in Part IV of the present volume tend towards a pyschological approach to managers as individuals, whereas Bonini, for example, in his distinction between control-in-the-small and control-in-the-large pointed to another debate - that of the social and organizational levels of analysis. Interestingly, Bonini came down on the side of the organizational theorist in his claim that the issues of policy, organization structures and work programmes (which define control as a whole) were likely to shape about 85 per cent of a manager's behaviour while the personal issues and views shaped the rest. While this may be a replay of the old battle between sociological and psychological universalism, or indeed European and American perspectives, the recognition that the two might be combined was itself an enriching approach. Drucker's contribution to this volume (Chapter 16) is, as ever, unique and pointed and reminds us of the nature of the social processes and their influence in organizations. He observes that the relationship to the collection of procedures known as controls may or may not actually lead to a state of control - that is, a state of static or dynamic stability. The question that emerges is that which Beer had sought to answer: how do we know what are the procedures that are necessary to a state of control? Drucker takes the opposite point of view by suggesting that actors may be more important than procedures.

Hofstede, having contributed an elegant review of many studies of control and budgeting in his book *The Game of Budget Control* (1967), challenges the rational, mechanical tradition in his essay included here as Chapter 17, especially that informed by the approach of Robert Anthony. Its title, we presume, is borrowed from Popper's *The Poverty of Historicism* - itself an attack on functionalist thinking. Hofstede concludes that much of what was being written about at the time was in the narrow financial and functionalist tradition and neither greatly helped managers nor offered explanations.

There was a sense that scholars in the traditional control field recognized the force of the mounting criticism of which Hofstede was a significant part. Machin's contribution (Chapter 18) based as it is on a wide ranging study of control practices, serves to show how the range of variables being considered in relation to management control systems had expanded to emphasize a much wider rationality. He focuses on the issue of the complex array of expectations of organization members and their role as a diagnostic and problem-solving approach to improve management control design and operation. The essay is included in this part because the contingencies with which Machin was concerned were particularly related to 'expectations' - a notion which was clearly related to social and psychological elements. The concept of contingency, as a move away from universal prescription, has been an important preoccupation of scholars in many management areas. It has also been one which has encountered some criticism, particularly in relation to the use of a contingency approach to management accounting (as the essay by Otley in Part V demonstrates). While it would be true to note that the attack on management accounting did not explicitly include management control, it is not difficult to implicate management control practice in the charge that, in its systematic nature, management accounting and control practices were blinding managers to the systemic and external factors that were rendering their search for efficiency ineffective and rendering uncompetitive their competitive positioning.

The next essay in Part IV picks up on the debate about the relevance of one important control system - management accounting (Johnson and Kaplan, 1987). It also relates to the important question as to whether different nations approach control by different means, in this case linking into a discussion of the influence of Japanese approaches. Japanese practice has attracted much attention recently, and not only has some work in this area demonstrated the clear superiority of Japanese technical procedures, it has also tended to reveal that many of our academic debates have been ignored in Japan. Hiromoto's essay (Chapter 18) suggests a movement towards a behaviour-influencing approach to management accounting, with a market-driven management approach. He stresses the need for a dynamic and team-oriented approach, concluding that 'the most basic element of today's management accounting must be a behavioural focus' (p. 14).

The final essay in this Part provides an initial focus on contingency approaches, looking at the internal contingencies which arguably affect organizations. It can perhaps be seen to provide a bridge to the next section which focuses on contingency approaches, but focuses on external contingencies. The work provides an example of a well developed stream of work which has adopted a behavioural emphasis and which seeks to use statistical approaches to discover relationships between diverse elements within an organization. The assumption is that elements of organizational structure and practice have impact upon individual behaviour and the desire is to find how these interact, with the intention of building the optimal structures and practices. Thus, Macintosh and Daft (Chapter 20) focus on the relationship between departmental interdependence and control system design. The work demonstrates the extent to which the nature of interdependencies between departments affects the role of control systems and as such is also clearly related to and inspired by the contingency work of authors such as Otley (as demonstrated in the next part). As such, the behavioural emphasis in this work is more implicit than in other essays in this part and the essay focuses on the internal structures rather more.

As can be seen from the studies in this Part, the interaction of human behaviour and systems to control them in organizational settings has been of importance and interest over a long period of time. In some studies focus on individual behaviour (psychology, groups and teams), extended through organization procedures (control relevance and utility, structures, work design) to environment (competition, strategy), has produced an attempt to shift from systematic to systemic thinking. This is not to say that this approach has necessarily been dominant and, indeed, its rather narrow organizational focus limits its usefulness because the interrelationships with the environment are underplayed in many ways. The central theme of the next selection of papers is therefore the relationship between the organization and its environment.

The Organization in its Environment

In focusing on the organization in its environment, the first essay in Part V, by Otley (Chapter 21), links to the idea of contingency theory, although in a very different way to Machin as the contingencies discussed are not psychological but related to 'harder' factors such as technology and organizational structure. Otley's emphasis is more on the organization as a whole than on the individual in the organization. In pointing to the difficulty of making sense of the growing literature which adopts a contingency approach, he seeks to develop a framework for evaluation, highlighting the importance of overall organizational effectiveness and, in so doing, notes the broad nature of the organizational control package and the interdependencies of its various elements. The essay both overviews the contingency approach and provides a welcome reminder that the complexity of organizational processes can only be understood through research which recognizes this richness and complexity.

The essay by Govindarajan (Chapter 22) is included because it provides an example of the body of empirical work which develops a statistical analysis to explore contingency relationships. His approach is similar to that in the paper by Macintosh and Daft (Chapter 20), included in the previous section, although it has a rather different focus. This study links internal behaviour to the external context, considering the extent to which participation in budget setting and a propensity to produce budgetary slack were affected by environmental uncertainty. A contingent relationship between the elements is discovered, where high budget participation was found to be useful in contexts of high uncertainty.

In Chapter 23, Ouchi examines the environment of transactions and looks to the structure of their organization using a more economics-based framework. The nature of control in economic relations has long been a matter of debate (for example, Coase, 1937). The question as to whether economic activity should be coordinated by actors in markets or actors in organizations has been a continuing exercise, independent of whether markets can be even approximately perfect. Following Williamson's (1973) essay on markets and hierarchies, Ouchi explores the issue of transaction costs to examine organizational control. He notes that transaction costs are connected to the equity and reciprocity in any exchange process. From consideration as to whether outputs can be easily measured and the degree of understanding as to how inputs are transformed into outputs Ouchi suggested that there may be three ideal-type modes of control. Control through markets is appropriate when outputs are measurable but the transformation process is little understood. Hierarchic (organizational) control may be best when outputs are not easily measurable but the transformation process is well understood. Where outputs are measurable and the transformation process is understood it may be possible to control through either markets or hierarchies. Where the opposite state exists, Ouchi suggests another mode of control – that of clans by which he means self- and social control through the norms and values of the actors. Whilst this suggestion does have the problems of classification which accompany any taxonomic approach it nevertheless has the virtue of suggesting that the simple nostrums are not appropriate.

In looking at organizations in their environment we must also be aware that ideas current in society as a whole may impact on individual organizations and that this may lead to attempts to change them. This provides the rationale for the inclusion of the next essay. Anthony Hopwood has been an important contributor to the continuing exploration of the relationships between accounting control, organizations and society. In Chapter 24 he examines the way in which accounting ideas (and hence control ideas) make visible that which is not otherwise visible, create a possibility of calculating value for concepts, and give a precision and seeming objectivity to economic affairs. These issues are then implicated in processes of organizational change as actors with different value premises push markets deeper into organizations and link the internal and external worlds in new ways. The existence of the visibilities created by control ideas, as well as the use of those ideas to shape meaning and action in the context of shifting technologies, are leading actors to reshape organizations in the image of the ideas - as for example, with the internal market in health and the permeation of education by economic ideas. Hopwood points to the richly textured interplay of control ideas derived from normative and empirical work in the reshaping of new forms of organization which become the new phenomena of research. He also implies that, as Drucker pointed out in Chapter 16, these new organizations are political creations; they are not merely the best solutions of rational men and women to today's circumstances.

Part V of this volume illustrates the emergence of a richer set of control issues in the context of the relationship between the organization and its environment. The essays all have a very different focus but have stressed the richness and diversity of the implications of this relationship. The essence of what we wish to emphasise is its reflexive and dynamic nature. The essays give some insight into these debates and leave us with some need to explore further the social structure of control.

One starting point for this discussion is the idea that all the structures and ideas that we have been considering are human constructs - in other words, organizations, markets, activities and ideas are socially constructed. Whether you wish to see these from an idealist perspective or from a near realist perspective is a personal decision. The final five essays chosen for Part V are recent contributions to the understanding of management control which we see as representing different elements of control relationships which recognize elements of its social structure. Perrow (Chapter 25) provides a starting point with his essay discussing the nature of organizational goals. He argues that they are not necessarily those stated by senior managers or in formal documents but are rather embedded in the daily routines of organizational members. The goals which predominate are those shaped by the particular problems and tasks with which an organization is centrally involved. Perrow sees previous accounts as being overrationalized and, hence, limited in their understandings of organizations and those who work in them.

In Chapter 26 Dermer and Lucas build on the critique that managers can create the illusion of control as they only see the work of the organization through the control procedures. They add a political dimension and turn from seeing the company as a focus of a single rationality (an assumption which they ascribe to the cybernetic approach) to recognizing it as a site of multi-rationality of different actors and different interest groups. In this, they echo Lindblom and Braybrooke's (1963) critique of the rational synoptic model and opt for micro-politics in organizational life - not as an argument, but as an unassailable fact. Order here is not so much imposed as negotiated through shifting patterns of power and influence. But wider than this is the idea that there may be more than one model of reality within what we might still call the organization. Each interest group in an organization pursues its own ends with its own rationality in accordance with its own control capability. Power emerges in their analysis because they consider that it lies at the heart of the uni-rational schema as managers eliminate observed contention through behavioural or political manipulation. Of course, this is to restate the stance of the pluralist political analyst and, to some extent, both happily subverts the idea of organization as unity and extends Cyert and March's notion of dominant coalition to all groups in the domain. Control is now not so much an imposed, as an emergent, phenomena, but given the epistemological stance of Dermer and Lucas that is inevitable.

Brunsson (Chapter 27) approaches similar issues from another direction. He differentiates decision and action rationalities, arguing that it is one thing to make a decision but another to engender action. Whereas decision rationality requires a wide search for possibilities and a need to consider both strengths and weaknesses of each potential course of action, action requires strong commitment which is often the result of considering only the positive aspects of few possibilities. Action, therefore, is often promoted by the ability to act in accord with previously defined or developed ideologies. When ideologies are 'strong', action can be fast, avoiding a great deal of intermediate work as the criteria from the ideology define what is the right thing to do. With 'weak' ideologies there is more room for dissent, more multi-rationality and hence action is more difficult to promote. Of course, should circumstances change, then the holders of a 'strong' ideology may find themselves at a disadvantage of painful and difficult or impossible adjustment. Maybe that is why the weak might be much stronger than they might initially appear! Control in the context of strong ideologies has a reactive nature, while for the others it emerges, as Mary Parker Follett might have put it, from the negotiated activity.

The contribution by Miller and O'Leary (Chapter 28) argues that the effect of a seemingly technically rational approach to efficiency serves a somewhat different purpose: it creates a series of 'governable persons' by stripping them of any identity or meaning other than that imposed by the requirements of the control system. The control system ascribes individual responsibility to each person for a series of actions which will be measured against some predetermined norm. By using accounting measures, control does not need to be immediate; results can be calculated and appraised away from the site of the activity itself and the controlled person has no place to hide from the inspection of the controller. Far from the uni-rationality of economic order of productivity gains, this analysis is suggestive of the dark side of human organizations in the theatre of primitive conflict of one group over another. As Jones and Dugdale (1995) wrote, 'the legacy of seeing people as aggregates of measurable activities and achievements will probably endure for many years' (p. 318).

The final essay in this Part, by Ansari and Bell (Chapter 29) provides a rich description of the extent to which the cultural context in which an organization and its members exist, can impact upon their accounting and control practices. This work is also representative of work which adopts a more qualitative approach, adopting an interpretive anthropological framework. This essay shows how cultural imperatives alongside contextual elements interplay to provide a changing tapestry of accounting and control systems which are called upon selectively to legitimize actions. It provides a reminder of how important cultural and contextual factors are, to understanding how controls develop and are interpreted within organizations.

The essays in Part V illustrate the development of a critical literature about control theory and control practice - literature which may echo debates about the politics and social structure of societies as these authors demonstrate how these same political and social differences are not eliminated by economic rationality but are replicated and extended in economic and other organizations.

Epilogue

As the finale, we include the essay by Merchant and Simons (Chapter 30) as a reflection on the diversities of work and approaches to control. This essay restates the message of this volume, albeit in a different guise and from a particular standpoint, emphasizing that research into control issues is diverse and complex. They seek to wrest some potential coherence and provide a base for more research.

Conclusion

We are only too aware of how oddly limited our selection of essays must seem to the informed reader. However, we have set out in the compass of this volume to present representative essays from the different traditions that have been brought to bear upon the study of management control and also the different traditions that have informed practice. We hope that we have succeeded in giving a flavour of the range and depth of the debates and the research - a picture of how the field has developed and is developing. The reader will find much to follow up in the bibliographies. For a further review of these issues the reader is referred to Berry, Broadbent and Otley (1995), and a further useful collection is available in Emmanuel, Otley and Merchant (1992). The world offers many research opportunities for those who would wish to seek answers to many of the questions which the literature has raised and not answered!

References

Argyris, C. (1952), *The Impact of Budgets on People*, NY: Ithaca, The Controllership Foundation.

Berry, A.J., Broadbent, J. and Otley, D.T. (eds) (1995), *Management Control: Theories, Issues and Practices*, London: Macmillan.

Bonini, C.P., Jaedicke, R.K. and Wagner, H.W. (1964), *Management Controls: New Directions in Basic Research*, London: McGraw Hill.

Coase, R. (1937) 'The Nature of the Firm', *Economica*, **4**, pp. 386–405.

Emmanuel, C.R., Otley, D.T. and Merchant, K. (eds) (1992), *Readings in Accounting for Management Control*, London: Chapman and Hall.

Hofstede, G. (1967), *The Game of Budget Control*, London: Tavistock.

Johnson, H.T. and Kaplan, R.S. (1987), *Relevance Lost: The Rise and Fall of Management Accounting*, Cambridge, Mass.: Harvard Business School Press.

Jones, C. and Dugdale, D. (1995), 'Manufacturing Accountability', in Berry, A.J., Broadbent, J. and Otley, D. (eds) *Management Control: Theories, Issues and Practices*, London: Macmillan, pp. 299-323.

Lindblom, C.E. and Braybrooke, D. (1963), *A Strategy of Decision*, New York: Free Press.

Tocher, K. (1970), 'Control', *Operational Research Quarterly*, June, pp. 159–80.

Tocher, K. (1976), 'Notes for discussion on "Control"', *Operational Research Quarterly*, June, pp. 231-39.

Williamson, O.E. (1973), 'Markets and Hierarchies: Some Elementary Considerations', *American Economic Association*, **63** (2).

Part I
Introduction

[1]

A Conspectus of Management Control Theory: 1900-1972

GIOVANNI B. GIGLIONI
Mississippi State University
ARTHUR G. BEDEIAN
Boston University

A comprehensive review of the literature on control theory, this paper examines the state of the art and provides a basis for rejecting the view that the executive can find very little knowledge to assist him in performing the control function.

Planning, organizing, and controlling are each vital functions in the management process. While management theory provides much information concerning planning and especially organizing, the function of controlling has only recently begun to be analyzed systematically (3, p. 408; 4, p. 317). This, however, is not meant to imply that concern for controlling does not have a long history. Copley states that control was the "central idea" of scientific management (11, Vol. 2, p. 358; cf. 64, pp. 10-11). Taylor considered control to be the "original object" of his experiments. In his Presidential Address before the American Society of Mechanical Engineers, he advocated:

> . . . taking the control of the machine shop out of the hands of the many workmen, and placing it completely in the hands of the management, thus superceding "rule of thumb" by scientific control (82, p. 39).

Control has long been considered "to be one of the most neglected and least understood areas of management activity" (15, p. 42). Its managerial role has often been mistakenly considered to be synonymous with financial control. In such a frame of reference, it has frequently been regarded as the sole domain of the accountant or comptroller and, in turn, completely equated with such techniques as budgets and financial ratios.

Giovanni B. Giglioni (D.B.A.—Indiana University) is Associate Professor of Management and Director of the Manpower Research Center, Mississippi State University, Mississippi State, Mississippi.

Arthur G. Bedeian (D.B.A.—Mississippi State University) is Adjunct Assistant Professor of Management, Overseas Graduate Program, College of Business Administration, Boston University, Boston, Massachusetts.

It is perhaps for this reason that "the word control has the serious shortcoming of having different meanings in different contexts" (47, p. 42). This quality has been noted by such authors as Drucker (30, p. 160; 31, p. 286), Kast and Rosenzweig (48, p. 467), Litterer (56, p. 233), and Luneski (57, p. 593). Each points out that management control may be viewed in two parts. One relates to the achievement of effective control over subordinates through the direction of their activities. The second relates to the evaluation of the desired outcome of an activity and the making of corrections when necessary. This dichotomy has been summarized well by Reeves and Woodward:

> In the literature relating to organizational behaviour there is ambiguity in the use of the word control. The confusion arises largely because to control can also mean to direct. Precisely defined control refers solely to the task of ensuring that activities are producing the desired results. Control in this sense is limited to monitoring the outcome of activities, reviewing feedback information about this outcome, and if necessary taking corrective action (66, p. 38).

As a partial consequence of this confusion, control is considered to be "one of the thorniest problems of management today" (65, p. 30). Although widely discussed, according to some writers it lacks a common area of understanding. It has "scarcely any generally accepted principles, and everyone in the field, therefore, works by intuition and folklore" (2, p. vii; cf. 1). Rowe has noted:

> Although management control is widely discussed, little has been done to formulate a body of principles for use in business system design (72, p. 274).

Furthermore, Jerome has pointed out:

> Principles and procedures and substantive content simply have not been rigorously developed in the area of executive control (47, p. 28).

More recently, Mockler has written:

> In spite of the fact that management control is one of the basic management functions, there is no comprehensive body of management control theory and principles to which executives can turn for guidance in performing their management control functions (59, p. 80).

Having recognized the ambiguity regarding the use of the term control and the alleged lack of control theory, the following definition is set forth. Control will be taken to refer solely to the traditional "constant cyclic-type activity of plan-do-compare-correct" with its "continuous, concomitant system of communication or flow of information" (61, p. 160). In effect, this eliminates from consideration the works of those authors—for example, Follett and Tannenbaum—who have used the word control in their writings to mean "to direct."[1]

Having set this restriction, it is the purpose of this effort to trace the development of twentieth century management control theory and, assessing the scope of this theory, to point out what knowledge the executive can turn to for guidance in controlling.

---

[1] For an anthology of such writings, see Tannenbaum (81).

PIONEER WRITERS AND CONTROL CONCEPTS

Earlier Concepts

Emerson may be credited with the first meaningful contribution to the development of twentieth century management control theory. In his classic work, *The Twelve Principles of Efficiency,* he heavily stressed the importance of control. His "Eighth Principle: Standards and Schedules" was an attempt to stress the use of time standards in achieving increased results from lessened effort. His "Sixth Principle: Reliable, Immediate and Adequate Records" and his "Eleventh Principle: Written Standard-Practice Instructions" both were clearly attempts to achieve control through the comparison of present performance with past achievements. Emerson considered records to have two objectives: (a) "to increase the scope and number of warnings" and (b) "to annihilate time, to bring back the past, to look into the future . . ." (36, p. 206). Emerson's "Ninth Principle: Sandardized Conditions" and "Tenth Principle: Standardized Operations" were efforts to obtain the uniformity necessary for control. While Emerson did not recognize control as an independent function of management, he did provide a framework for its further understanding.

Church also contributed to the development of early management control theory. He identified five "organic functions of administration" (8, p. 28). The third of these functions was "control" and the fourth "comparison." Control was considered to be "that function which coordinates all of the other functions and in addition supervises their work." Obviously, this view of control transcends the concept as defined and includes certain aspects of coordinating and directing. Church's "comparison" function was markedly similar to Emerson's Sixth Principle of "Records." It dealt with "that which concerns itself with the setting up and comparison of standards" (8, p. 81) and was based on "three elements: (a) recognition of what facts are truly significant; (b) accurate record and convenient presentation of these facts; (c) judicious action based on study of the facts" (8, p. 347; cf. 9, p. 859). As is evident, Church may be largely credited with recognition of the main facets of the control process.

Distinguishing between different types of control, Diemer considered control to mean "the methods by which the executive or managing heads of a business carry out their authority to regulate its affairs in accordance with the laws of the organization" (26, p. 2). Later, expanding upon this explanation, he commented:

> Control is that principle of management which demands that the management know what ought to be done and what is being done in all divisions and departments of the business. If what is being done differs from what ought to be done control means knowing why it differs. Control means knowing how to overcome the located defects, shortages or excessive costs and actually remedying them (27, p. 282).

Fayol identified control as one of the five functions of management. He advocated its application to all things within the organization. To

Fayol, control meant "verifying whether everything occurs in conformity with the plan adopted, the instructions issued and principles established" (37, p. 107). It should be noted, however, that some question exists concerning the accuracy of the translation of Fayol's work in this area; see Goodwin (42) and Urwick (91).

The first text devoted entirely to the subject of management control was written in 1920 by Francis M. Lawson. Consisting of six lectures, its purpose was "to set before those who are engaged in organization work the true fundamental laws governing all direction and control . . ." (54, p. v). Lawson held that his work provided a base for scientific management and that only after the laws of control were interpreted could scientific management be applied correctly. His presentation dealt mainly with the preparation of charts and records and was truly a pioneer work in this area.

The lack of application of control theory in the United States during the early period of this century may be discerned from the 1921 national research study, *Waste in Industry*. Over one third of its recommendations for the elimination of waste in industry involved one or more aspects of control. The study's first recommendation, "Improvement of Organization and Executive Control," is especially telling. It reads:

> Planning and control should be adopted as fundamentals of good management. For the most part they have not penetrated the mass of American industry (10, p. 24).

Control was related to planning by Lichtner who believed that "planned control" was "imperative" for successful operation. In defining what was meant by "Planned Control," he explained:

> Planning is the managerial function of working out the best combination of procedures through co-ordinating the requirements with the facilities for carrying out the work of the division. Control is the managerial function of putting these procedures into effect (55, pp. 5-6).

Clearly, Lichtner's concept includes more than just control.

Franklin extensively discussed the relationship between control and records. He presented records of assurance, information and control (39, p. 135). As two of the required specifications of records, Franklin named "Standards or Measuring Rules" and "Comparisons of Results and Trends" (39, pp. 136-37). Both specifications were clearly designed to aid in the control and achievement of results expected.

Dutton presented control as a function of production and subdivided it into planning, supervision, inspection and information (32, p. 7; cf. 33, pp. 24-25; cf. 34, pp. 7-12). In a later work, Dutton stressed the importance of comparison, measurement and standardization (35, pp. 43, 63-67, 93). In doing so he recognized the importance of the control process.

Control was identified by Robinson as the sixth of his "Eight Fundamentals of Business Organization." He described control as

> . . . that fundamental which comprises the means of providing the manager and the executives of an organization with continuous, prompt, and accurate information concerning the efficiency of operation, what the business is doing, what it has done in the past, and what it can be expected to do in the future. A system of control collects the details of operation, segregates them, combines them, and classifies them into a form suitable for use (68, p. 147).

In addition, Robinson identified three principal elements of control: (a) forecasting results, (b) recording of results, and (c) the placing of responsibility for expected results with provision for corrective action (68, pp. 107-08, 137-39, 142, 147).

White identified what he believed to be the elements of control. Referring to them as "subfunctions" of the "function of control," he closely related his discussion to planning (95, p. 113). Williams, in discussing "top control," identified the principal methods of control as general accounting, estimating, cost accounting, budgeting and interpretation (96, 97).

The Beginning of a Framework

The first author to identify a set of control principles may well have been Lyndall F. Urwick. He presented control as being

> . . . concerned with the reaction of persons and materials to the decisions of direction, with the measurement of such reactions in terms of space, time, and quantity, and with methods of securing that the results of such reactions shall be in line with those contemplated by direction (89, p. 163).

The five principles of control Urwick listed were:

1. The Principle of Responsibility
2. The Principle of Evidence
3. The Principle of Uniformity
4. The Principle of Comparison
5. The Principle of Utility (89, p. 179).

By 1943, Urwick had dropped the first two of these principles and had provided the following definitions for the remaining three:

> *The Principle of Uniformity*—All figures and reports used for purposes of control must be in terms of the organisation structure.
>
> *The Principles of Comparison*—All figures and reports used for purposes of control should be in terms of standards of performance required, and, of past performance.
>
> *The Principle of Utility*—Figures and reports used for purposes of control vary in value directly in proportion to the period separating them from the events which they reflect (90, p. 122, see also pp. 107-108).

Davis initially began to construct his philosophy of management control in 1928. He defined control as "the instruction and guidance of the organization and the direction and regulation of its activities" (16, p. 82). He expanded upon these ideas in 1934 (18, p. 67) and by 1940 had largely solidified his understanding of management control. It was at this time that Davis, drawing on an earlier paper (17), popularly identified planning, organizing, and controlling as the three organic functions of management (19, pp. 35-36; cf. 20, pp. 8-10). In line with this, he listed eight control subfunctions: (a) routine planning; (b) scheduling; (c) preparation; (d) dispatching; (e) direction; (f) supervision; (g) comparison; and (h) corrective action (19, p. 109). In a later book, Davis maintained this same framework of analysis with only minor variation (21, pp. 647-52).

Expanding upon the ideas he had presented in an earlier book (12, p. 28), Cornell formulated one of the first listings of the principles of management. The eleventh of his sixteen principles was the principle of control. Cornell stressed the importance of performance standards, performance evaluation, and corrective action. His principle of control reads:

> Planning is of little value unless there is subsequent control to make certain that the plans are carried out (13, p. 212).

Glover and Maze attempted to explain the "instruments and methods" of control and endeavored to emphasize

> . . . the necessity for setting standards and measuring actual accomplishment as a basis for control: . . . to point out the methods for determining causes for variations between planned and actual accomplishment, and . . . [to indicate] the more important causes of such variations as well as their underlying reasons (40, pp. v-vi).

In accomplishing this task, they related managerial control to organization, manufacturing costs, and marketing and administrative costs.

One of the first empirical studies of corporate organization and control was performed by Holden, Fish, and Smith. It reported the top management practices of "thirty-one leading industrial corporations." As one of its conclusions, the study presented control as a prime responsibility of top management (44, p. 3). It further identified control as a process, embracing three elements: (a) Objective—to determine what is desired; (b) Procedure—to plan how and when a task is to be done, organization to determine who is responsible, and standards to determine what constitutes good performance; and (c) Appraisal—to determine how well a task was done (44, p. 77). Clearly, Holden, Fish, and Smith interpreted control very broadly including much of planning. This reflects the interrelatedness of these two functions.

The nineteen-forties were an era of continued interest in management control. Dimock defined control as "the analysis of present performance, in the light of fixed goals and standards, in order to determine the extent to which accomplishment measures up to executive orders and expectations" (28, p. 217). Both Hopf (45, 46) and Schreiber (75) recognized control as a function of management. Rowland associated control with planning by pointing out the relationship existing between the two (73, p. 3). Filipetti identified control as "the most important factor in organization" (38, p. 260). McCaully (58) discussed control for the foreman and supervisor. An earlier text by Schell (74) had analyzed control from the viewpoint of the executive. Both Somervell (77) and Thurston (53,

84, 85, 86) related control to organization and advocated the establishment of company control sections.

In 1948, Brech largely revised his initial framework of management principles. He presented control as the "obverse" of planning and advocated "standards of performance," "continuous comparison of actual achievement or results against these predetermined standards," and a balancing of long- and short-term consequences (6, p. 14). Brech has more recently defined control to mean:

> . . . checking current performance against objectives and targets in terms of predetermined standards contained in the plans, with a view to ensuring adequate progress and satisfactory performance whether physical or financial; also contributing to decision in continuing or changing the plans, as well as "recording" the experience gained from the working of these plans as a guide to possible future operations (7, pp. 13-14).

Control was identified as a process of administration by Newman. He defined control as:

> . . . seeing that operating results conform as nearly as possible to the plans. This involves the establishment of standards, motivation of people to achieve these standards, comparison of actual results against the standard, and necessary corrective action when performance deviates from the plan (63, p. 4).

In line with this definition, Newman presented three essential steps in the control process: (a) setting standards at strategic points, (b) checking and reporting on performance, and (c) taking corrective action (63, p. 408).

Control and Functional Areas

Rose approached control from the position of a managing director. He divided control into three functional "viewpoints": business, trading, and financial. Rose considered his ideas to be the logical extension of the work of Fayol. He defined "higher control"

> . . . as a monthly survey of the functional activities of a commercial undertaking, carried out from the business, trading, and financial viewpoints, and based upon direct trend comparison between the position at the moment and the position at the last financial year (69, p. 67).

Rose further discussed control in a second book (70) and in a third (71) attempted to codify a number of his earlier writings. In the latter of these two works, Rose reentitled his four aspects of control as the business position, the operating position, the profit and loss position, and the financial position.

Dent approached management control from the viewpoint of a budget analyst. He defined budgetary control as "working to a plan to secure the greatest measure of all-round efficiency and teamwork" (24, p. 307; cf. 23). He felt that "budgetary control must be based upon the management principles of planning of activities, delegation of responsibility coupled with authority, definition of authority, and co-ordination of effort" (24, p. 307).

1974 Volume 17, Number 2 299

The writings of Trundle, Goetz, Rice, and Wharton also reflect a similar functional emphasis. Trundle (87, 88) associated control with manufacturing, sales accounting, and industrial relations. Goetz, approaching management control from the viewpoint of the accountant, interpreted control to consist of "securing conformity to plans" (41, p. 3). Rice (67) presented control charts for use by the business executive, and Wharton (93, 94) discussed control in office operations.

MODERN CONTROL CONCEPTS

Principles of Management Textbooks and Control

The nineteen-fifties witnessed the emergence of the first "principles of management" textbooks. The content of these books was basically developed from earlier management thought. Therefore, they presented the control function in a manner similar to pioneer writers such as Fayol and Davis.

A review of these and later texts shows a surprising similarity of presentation. From Terry (83) to Donnelly, Gibson, and Ivancevich (29), a consensus about the essence of controlling is easily discerned. Subjects generally discussed include an identification of the steps in the control process, the requirements of control, the determination of standards, means of measurement, and types of control mechanisms. In relation to the last topic mentioned, budgetary control and the human response to controls are also generally presented. With a few exceptions, the majority of these works take note of the exception principle. However, only three texts—Terry's (83), Koontz and O'Donnell's (52), and Sisk's (76)—identify additional principles of control. Of these three, Koontz and O'Donnell's provides the most complete framework of management control principles.

The widespread reluctance of writers to recognize specific concepts as control principles is indicative of the slow development in this area. While Terry and Sisk each present a few selected principles of control, uncertainty in this area is verified by the fact that Sisk refers the reader to the work of Koontz for a more complete discussion of this topic (76, p. 589n).

Koontz's initial formulation of control principles, showing the influence of Taylor, Urwick, and Goetz, may be traced to his well-known article in the *Academy of Management Journal* (49). Revised the following year, the framework identified fourteen principles of control (50). More recently, Koontz and O'Donnell have limited their framework to twelve control principles (52, pp. 672-76). Thus, thirty years after Urwick's first formulation, Koontz and O'Donnell added to management theory a more comprehensive framework of management control principles.

To date, Koontz and O'Donnell's management control theory as represented by their framework for the principles of control is the clearest and most comprehensive formulation of its kind. Its initial presentation has already been referred to as a "classic of management literature" (14, p. 116).

Research Studies

Research studies in the area of management control have recently been increasing in number. Paik (43, pp. 169-83) has analyzed the control procedures of selected branch banks. Hekimian (43) has reported the control operations of selected life insurance branch offices. Deming (22) has studied the control system of a large electrical corporation. Villers (92) has reported the planning and control practices of selected research and development organizations. Sord and Welsch (78) have studied managerial control problems from the viewpoint of lower-level supervisors. Each of these studies provides useful concepts and understanding about the control function based on empirical findings from the operations of a variety of control systems.

Six recent books, each dealing with various aspects of control, are also indicative of the growing interest in management control theory. Deverell (25) has shown the relationship between the planning and control processes, pointing out their interdependency. He has also presented a discussion of current control techniques. Strong and Smith (80) have dealt with current control techniques and attempted to show the essentiality of control. Taking a different approach, Mundel (61) has dealt mainly with the control concept and its application in the organic areas of production, sales, and finance. Stokes (79) has presented guidelines to aid in installing a "total control program." Viewing control from the vantage point of a top corporate executive, he has presented and discussed areas of critical control performance. Asplund et al. (5) have dealt with materials and production management as special aspects of management control. Mockler (60) has identified and explored each of the steps in the management control process.

Emphasis on Control and Control Models

Authors such as Jerome, Anthony, Koontz and Bradspies, and Muth have recently attempted to solidify the groundwork of management control theory. Jerome has advanced the belief that control is "a subject area with its own distinctive concepts and precepts" (47, p. 27). Anthony (2) has defined and discussed management control from a systems viewpoint and attempted to establish the proper role of control in a firm's operations. Koontz and Bradspies (51), drawing on the field of "systems engineering," have applied the concept of "feed forward" to managerial control problems. Muth, pointing out that "impressive attempts have been made to organize and unify" analytical techniques from various areas into a comprehensive control theory, has provided a "state-space" model for a general control system (62, p. 892).

SUMMARY AND CONCLUSIONS

Twentieth century concern for management control may be traced from the beginning of the scientific management revolution to present-day management thought. Introduced by the work of early writers such as Taylor, Emerson, and Church, the basics of what today may be identified as the control process became well known by the end of the first decade of this century.

While the importance of control was recognized by such authors as Lawson, Franklin, Diemer, Dutton, Lichtner, Cornell, Robinson, Williams, and White, a general lack of management control in the earlier years is attested to by the conclusions of the Federated American Engineering Societies' study, *Waste in Industry*. It was not until 1928 that the first set of control principles was formulated by Urwick.

Early texts, such as those by Rose, Dent, Glover and Maze, and Goetz, were predominantly oriented to accounting and financial control. The 1941 Holden, Fish, and Smith study was the first empirical attempt to explore corporate control. This interest has been revived recently by the works of Anthony, Paik, Hekimian, Deming, Villers, Sord and Welsch. It should also be noted that the interest in control has had a long record of international involvement. This is attested to by the works of Fayol, Lawson, Urwick, Rose, Dent, Brech, Deverell, and Asplund et al.

It has been only in recent years, since the advent of principles of management textbooks, that specific attempts have been made to lay a foundation for the development of a science of management control theory and to develop a unified theory as well as general control models. The Koontz framework of management control principles has been followed by the works of Anthony, Jerome, Smith and Strong, Mundel, Stokes, Mockler, and Muth, among others. Each has attempted to add to the area of knowledge generally referred to as management control. The works of the writers referenced in this conspectus provide a clear basis for rejecting the views of those who believe that executives have little to turn to for guidance in performing their control function. Specifically, executives can use:

A knowledge of the control concept;
A knowledge of the process required to control;
A knowledge of the characteristics of control systems;
A knowledge of the problems likely to occur when controlling and, therefore, a knowledge of what to guard against;
A number of control models, some of which are general and unifying enough to provide systematic control for the firm;
A framework of principles for effective and efficient control;
A set of control techniques.

Even though control theory has not achieved the level of sophistication of some other management functions, it has developed to a point that affords the executive ample opportunity to maintain the operations of his firm under check. Unquestionably, however, continued interest and research in this area are necessary to bring control theory to new levels of sophistication and, above all, pragmatism.

REFERENCES

1. Anthony, Robert N. "Planning and Control Systems: A Framework for Analysis," *Management Services*, Vol. 1 (March-April, 1964), 18-24.
2. Anthony, Robert N. *Planning and Control Systems: Framework for Analysis* (Boston: Division of Research, Graduate School of Business Administration, Harvard University, 1965).
3. Arrow, Kenneth J. "Control in Large Organizations," *Management Science*, Vol. 10 (April, 1964), 397-408.
4. Arrow, Kenneth J. "Research in Management Controls: A Critical Synthesis," in Charles Bonini, Robert K. Jaedicke, and Harvey M. Wagner (Eds.), *Management Controls: New Directions in Basic Research* (New York: McGraw-Hill, 1964).
5. Asplund, Ingemar (Ed.). *Management Control: A Survey of Production and Inventory Control Models in Theory and Practice* (Lund, Sweden: Studentlitteratur, 1969).
6. Brech, E. F. L. *Management: Its Nature and Significance*, 2nd ed. (London: Pitman, 1948).
7. Brech, E. F. L. *Organisation: The Framework of Management*, 2nd ed. (London: Longmans, Green, 1965).
8. Church, A. Hamilton. *The Science and Practice of Management* (New York: Engineering Magazine Co., 1914). Originally serialized in six parts as "Practical Principles of Rational Management," *Engineering Magazine*, Vols. 44-45 (January through July, 1913).
9. Church, A Hamilton, and Leon P. Alford. "The Principles of Management," *American Machinist*, Vol. 36 (May 30, 1912), 857-861.
10. Committee on Elimination of Waste in Industry of the Federated American Engineering Societies (Herbert C. Hoover, chairman). *Waste in Industry* (New York: McGraw-Hill, 1921).
11. Copley, Frank B. *Frederick W. Taylor: Father of Scientific Management*, 2 vols. (New York: Harper, 1923).
12. Cornell, William B. *Industrial Organization and Management* (New York: Ronald, 1928).
13. Cornell, William B. *Business Organization*, Vol. 3 of *Modern Business* (New York: Alexander Hamilton Institute, 1930).
14. Dauten, Paul M., Jr. (Ed.). *Current Issues and Emerging Concepts in Management*, Vol. 1 (Boston: Houghton-Mifflin, 1962).
15. Dauten, Paul M., Jr., Homer L. Gammill, and Stanley C. Robinson. "Our Concepts of Controlling Need Re-Thinking," *Journal of the Academy of Management*, Vol. 1 (December, 1958), 41-55.
16. Davis, Ralph C. *The Principles of Factory Organization and Management* (New York: Harper, 1928).
17. Davis, Ralph C. "The Organic Functions of Management" (Unpublished paper, The Ohio State University, 1934).
18. Davis, Ralph C. *The Principles of Business Organization and Operation* (Columbus, Ohio: H. L. Hedrick, 1934).
19. Davis, Ralph C. *Industrial Organization and Management*, 2nd ed. (New York: Harper, 1940).
20. Davis, Ralph C. *Shop Management for the Shop Supervisor* (New York: Harper, 1941).
21. Davis, Ralph C. *The Fundamentals of Top Management* (New York: Harper, 1951).
22. Deming, Robert H. *Characteristics of an Effective Management Control System in an Industrial Organization* (Boston: Division of Research, Graduate School of Business Administration, Harvard University, 1968).
23. Dent, Arthur G. H. "Budgetary Control Study," *Industry Illustrated* (London), Vol. 2 (May, 1934), 28-30, 36.
24. Dent, Arthur G. H. *Management Planning and Control* (London: Gee, Ltd., 1935).
25. Deverell, Cyril S. *Management Planning and Control* (London: Gee, Ltd., 1967).
26. Diemer, Hugo. *Industrial Organization and Management* (Chicago: La Salle Extension University, 1915).
27. Diemer, Hugo. "The Principles Underlying Good Management," *Industrial Management*, Vol. 67 (May, 1924), 280-83.
28. Dimock, Marshall E. *The Executive in Action* (New York: Harper, 1945).

29. Donnelly, James H., Jr., James L. Gibson, and John M. Ivancevich. *Fundamentals of Management* (Austin, Texas: Business Publications, 1971).
30. Drucker, Peter F. *The Practice of Management* (New York: Harper, 1954).
31. Drucker, Peter F. "Controls, Control and Management," in Charles Bonini, Robert K. Jaedicke, and Harvey M. Wagner (Eds.), *Management Controls: New Directions in Basic Research* (New York: McGraw-Hill, 1964).
32. Dutton, Henry P. *Factory Management* (New York: Macmillan, 1924).
33. Dutton, Henry P. *Business Organization and Management* (Chicago: A. W. Shaw, 1925).
34. Dutton, Henry P. *The Control of Production*. Vol. 2 of *The Shaw Plant and Shop Management Library*, 6 vols. (Chicago: A. W. Shaw, 1927).
35. Dutton, Henry P. *Principles of Organization as Applied to Business* (New York: McGraw-Hill, 1931).
36. Emerson, Harrington. *The Twelve Principles of Efficiency* (New York: Engineering Magazine Co., 1912). Originally serialized in sixteen parts in *Engineering Magazine*, Vols. 39-41 (June 1910 through September 1911).
37. Fayol, Henri. *General and Industrial Management*, translated by Constance Storrs (London: Pitman, 1949).
38. Filipetti, George. *Industrial Management in Transition* (Homewood, Ill.: Irwin, 1946).
39. Franklin, Benjamin A. "Records As a Basis for Management," *Management Engineering*, Vol. 3 (September, 1922), 133-37.
40. Glover, John G., and Coleman L. Maze. *Managerial Control* (New York: Ronald, 1937).
41. Goetz, Billy E. *Management Planning and Control* (New York: McGraw-Hill, 1949).
42. Goodwin, E. Sidney L. "Control: A Brief Excursion on the Meaning of a Word," *Michigan Business Review*, Vol. 12 (January, 1960), 13-17, 28.
43. Hekimian, James S. *Management Control in Life Insurance Branch Offices*, with Appendix: Chei-Min Paik, "Management Controls in Branch Banks" (1963), 169-83 (Boston: Division of Research, Graduate School of Business Administration, Harvard University, 1965).
44. Holden, Paul E., Lounsbury S. Fish, and Hubert L. Smith. *Top-Management Organization and Control* (Stanford University, Cal.: Stanford University Press, 1941).
45. Hopf, Harry A. "New Perspectives in Management—Part IV: Management and the Optimum," *The Spectator: Life Insurance in Action*, Vol. 151 (December, 1943), 4-7, 26-30.
46. Hopf, Harry A. "New Perspectives in Management—Part VII: Instruments Essential to Control," *The Spectator: Life Insurance in Action*, Vol. 151 (March, 1944), 8-12, 45-49. Serialized in fifteen parts, Vols. 151-152 (September 1943 through August 1944 and November 1944 through February 1945).
47. Jerome, William T., III. *Executive Control—The Catalyst* (New York: Wiley, 1961).
48. Kast, Fremont E., and James E. Rosenzweig. *Organization and Management* (New York: McGraw-Hill, 1970).
49. Koontz, Harold D. "Management Control: A Preliminary Statement of Principles of Planning and Control," *Journal of the Academy of Management*, Vol 1 (April, 1958), 45-60.
50. Koontz, Harold D. "Management Control: A Suggested Formulation of Principles," *California Management Review*, Vol. 1 (Winter, 1959), 47-55.
51. Koontz, Harold D., and Robert W. Bradspies. "Managing Through Feed Forward Control," *Business Horizons*, Vol. 15 (June, 1972), 25-36.
52. Koontz, Harold D., and Cyril J. O'Donnell. *Principles of Management: An Analysis of Managerial Functions*, 5th ed. (New York: McGraw-Hill, 1972).
53. Lamperti, Frank A., and John B. Thurston. *Internal Auditing for Management* (Englewood Cliffs: N. J.: Prentice-Hall, 1953).
54. Lawson, Francis M. *Industrial Control* (London: Pitman, 1920).
55. Lichtner, William O. *Planned Control in Manufacturing* (New York: Ronald, 1924).
56. Litterer, Joseph A. *The Analysis of Organizations* (New York: Wiley, 1965).
57. Luneski, Chris. "Some Aspects of the Meaning of Control," *Accounting Review*, Vol. 39 (July, 1964), 591-97.
58. McCaully, Harry J., Jr. *Management Controls for Foremen and Supervisors* (New York: Funk & Wagnalls, 1948).

59. Mockler, Robert J. "Developing the Science of Management Control," *Financial Executive*, Vol. 35 (December, 1967), 80-93.
60. Mockler, Robert J. *The Management Control Process* (New York: Appleton-Century-Crofts, 1972).
61. Mundel, Marvin. *A Conceptual Framework for the Management Sciences* (New York: McGraw-Hill, 1967).
62. Muth, John F. "A Review of Control Theory," in Manfred W. Hopfe (Ed.), *Proceedings of the Fourth Annual Meeting of the American Institute for Decision Sciences* (Atlanta, Ga.: AIDS, 1972).
63. Newman, William H. *Administrative Action* (New York: Prentice-Hall, 1951).
64. Person, Harlow S. "The Origin and Nature of Scientific Management," in Harlow S. Person (Ed.), *Scientific Management in American Industry* (New York: Harper, for the Taylor Society, 1929).
65. Rathe, Alex W. "Management Controls in Business," in Donald G. Malcolm and Alan J. Rowe (Eds.), *Management Control Systems* (New York: Wiley, 1960).
66. Reeves, Tom K., and Joan Woodward. "The Study of Managerial Control," in Joan Woodward (Ed.), *Industrial Organization: Behaviour and Control* (London: Oxford University Press, 1970).
67. Rice, William B. *Control Charts in Factory Management* (New York: Wiley, 1947).
68. Robinson, Webster R. *Fundamentals of Business Organization* (New York: McGraw-Hill, 1925).
69. Rose, Thomas G. *Higher Control* (London: Pitman, 1934).
70. Rose, Thomas G. *Company Control* (London: Gee, Ltd., 1952).
71. Rose, Thomas G., and Donald Farr. *Higher Management Control* (New York: McGraw-Hill, 1957).
72. Rowe, Alan J. "A Research Approach in Management Controls," in Donald G. Malcolm and Alan J. Rowe (Eds.), *Management Control Systems* (New York: Wiley, 1960).
73. Rowland, Floyd H. *Business Planning and Control* (New York: Harper, 1947).
74. Schell, Erwin H. *The Technique of Executive Control*, 4th ed. (New York: McGraw-Hill, 1934).
75. Schreiber, Norman B. *Philosophy of Organization* (Chicago: A. Kroch, 1942).
76. Sisk, Henry L. *Principles of Management: A Systems Approach to the Management Process* (Cincinnati: South-Western, 1969).
77. Somervell, Brehon B. "Organization Controls in Industry," *Organization Controls and Executive Compensation*, General Management Series No. 142 (New York: American Management Association, 1948).
78. Sord, Burnard H., and Glenn A. Welsch. *Managerial Planning and Control*, Research Monograph No. 27 (Austin, Texas: Bureau of Business Research, University of Texas, 1964).
79. Stokes, Paul M. *A Total Systems Approach to Management Control* (New York: American Management Association, 1968).
80. Strong, Earl P., and Robert D. Smith. *Management Control Models* (New York: Holt, Rinehart and Winston, 1968).
81. Tannenbaum, Arnold S. *Control in Organizations* (New York: McGraw-Hill, 1968).
82. Taylor, Frederick W. "On the Art of Cutting Metals," Paper No. 1119, *Transactions* (American Society of Mechanical Engineers), Vol. 27 (1906), 31-350.
83. Terry, George R. *Principles of Management* (Homewood, Ill.: Irwin, 1953); 2nd ed., 1956; 3rd ed., 1960; 4th ed., 1964; 5th ed., 1968; 6th ed., 1972.
84. Thurston, John B. "A New Concept of Managerial Control," *Company Development and Top Management Control*, General Management Series No. 134 (New York: American Management Association, 1945).
85. Thurston, John B. "The Control Unit: Newest Techniques for Controlling Decentralized Operations," *Advanced Management Journal*, Vol. 12 (June, 1947), 74-87.
86. Thurston, John B., Carl Heyel (Ed.), *Coordinating and Controlling Operations. Reading Course in Executive Technique*, Sec. I, bk. ii., 41 vols (New York: Funk & Wagnalls, 1948).
87. Trundle, George T. "Production Control," in William J. A. Donald (Ed.), *Handbook of Business Administration* (New York: McGraw-Hill, for the American Management Association, 1931).

88. Trundle, George T. *Managerial Control of Business* (New York: Wiley, 1948).
89. Urwick, Lyndall F. "Principles of Direction and Control," in John Lee (Ed.), *Dictionary of Industrial Administration*, Vol. 1 (London: Pitman, 1928).
90. Urwick, Lyndall F. *The Elements of Administration* (New York: Harper, 1943).
91. Urwick, Lyndall F. "The Meaning of Control," *Michigan Business Review*, Vol. 12 (November, 1960), 9-13.
92. Villers, Raymond. *Research and Development: Planning and Control* (New York: Financial Executives Institute, 1964).
93. Wharton, Kenneth J. *Administrative Control* (London: Gee, Ltd., 1947).
94. Wharton, Kenneth J. "Administrative Organization and Control," *The Accountant*, August 16, 1947; August 23, 1947; August 30, 1947. Serialized in three parts.
95. White, Percival. *Business Management: An Introduction to Business* (New York: Holt, 1926).
96. Williams, John H. "Top Control," *Bulletin of the Taylor Society*, Vol. 11 (October, 1926), 199-206.
97. Williams, John H. "General Administrative Control," in Harlow S. Person (Ed.), *Scientific Management in American Industry* (New York: Harper, for the Taylor Society, 1929).

Part II
Control as Goal-directed and Integrative

[2]

The nature of management control

In this chapter we describe the nature of control in general and of management control in particular. In order to do this, we distinguish between management control and other planning and controlling processes that are found in organizations, and we also distinguish between the management control function and other functions of management. The chapter concludes with an overview of the management control structure and the steps in the management control process.

THE NATURE OF CONTROL

When the brake pedal is pressed, an automobile slows down or stops. When the accelerator is pressed, the automobile goes faster. When the steering wheel is rotated, the automobile turns. With these devices, the driver *controls* the speed and direction of the vehicle. Without them, the automobile would not do what the driver wanted it to do; that is, it would be out of control. A business company, or indeed any organization, must also be controlled; that is, there must be devices that ensure that it goes where its leaders want it to go. The control of an organization is, however, much more complicated than the control of an automobile. We shall lead up to a discussion of control in organizations by describing the control process in simpler situations.

Control in simple situations

A control system is a system whose purpose is to attain and maintain a desired state or condition. Any control system has at least these four elements:

1. A measuring device which detects what is happening in the parameter being controlled. This is called a *detector* or *sensor*.
2. A device for assessing the significance of what is happening, usually by comparing information on what is *actually happening* with some standard or expectation of what *should be happening*. This is called a *selector*.

4

3. A device for altering behavior if the need for doing so is indicated. This is called an *effector*.
4. A means of transmitting information between these devices. This is called a *communication network*.

The transmission of information from the detector to the control device is called *feedback*.[1]

Collectively, these elements constitute a *system* because any set of interrelated units is a system. The units are interrelated in the sense that each element affects and is affected by the other elements. The bare bones of a control system are diagrammed in Exhibit 1–1. We shall flesh them out by three illustrations: the thermostat, the regulation of body temperature, and human behavior.

EXHIBIT 1–1 Essentials of a control system

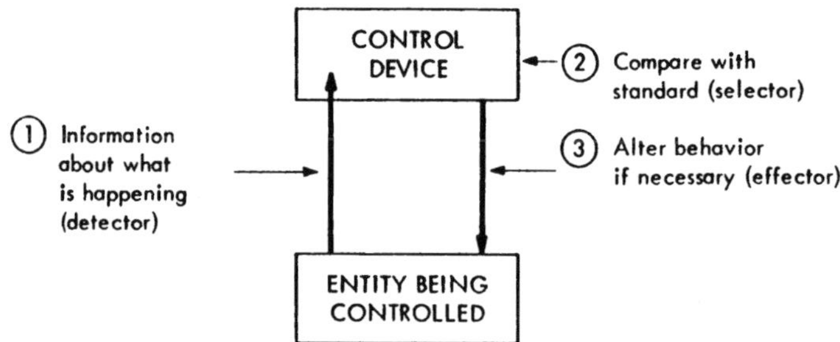

Thermostat. The thermostat that is hooked to a furnace is a control system that has the elements listed above: (1) the thermostat contains a thermometer (detector) which measures the current temperature in the room; (2) the thermostat compares this measurement with a preset standard, the desired temperature (selector); and (3) if the current temperature is significantly below the preset standard, the thermostat causes the furnace to turn on and to send heat to the room, and when the temperature reaches the preset standard, the thermostat causes the furnace to shut off (effector).

Electrical circuits communicate information from the thermometer to the comparison part of the thermostat and convey instructions from the thermostat to the furnace.

Body temperature. Most mammals are born with a built-in standard of desirable body temperature. In humans, it is 98.6°F. The control of body temperature is achieved as follows: (1) sensory nerves scattered throughout the body (detectors) measure the current temperature and transmit information about it to the hypothalamus center in the brain; (2) the hypothalamus compares information on current body temperature with the standard of 98.6° (selector); and (3) if this comparison indicates that the current temperature is significantly above the standard, the hy-

[1]For a more complete discussion, see Norbert Wiener, *Cybernetics* (New York: John Wiley & Sons, Inc., 1948). Cybernetics is defined as "control and communication in man and machine."

pothalamus activates devices to reduce it (panting, sweating, opening of skin pores); and if the current temperature is significantly below the standard, the hypothalamus activates devices to increase it (closing of skin pores, shivering); this is the effector.[2] The control process in this system is called *homeostasis,* which means self-regulating. If the system is functioning properly, it automatically corrects for deviations from the desired state.

Although the control system for body temperature has the same elements as those for the control of room temperature, there are at least two important differences that make an understanding of the body temperature system more difficult than an understanding of the thermostat. First, the system is more complicated: sensors are scattered all through the body, the hypothalamus acts on both plus and minus deviations from normal, and the actions that it takes involve a variety of muscles and organs. Second, although we know *what* the hypothalamus does, we do not really understand exactly *how* this is done.

Human behavior. Consider an automobile driver on a highway where the speed limit is 55 mph. The driver has a control system that acts as follows: (1) the eye observes the speed as stated on the speedometer and communicates this speed to the brain (or perhaps the sense of speed is communicated by a general perception of movement): (2) the brain compares the current speed with the limit of 55 mph; and (3) if this comparison indicates that the speed is too fast, the brain directs the foot to ease up on the accelerator.

Although this control system has the same essential elements as the other two, it has an additional complication: we cannot state with confidence what, if any, action the brain will direct if actual speed exceeds 55 mph. Some people obey the speed limit and therefore will ease up on the accelerator; others act only when the actual speed consistently exceeds 55 mph, and still others obey the speed limit at certain times, but not at other times. In these circumstances, although a control system exists, we cannot predict solely from the characteristics of the system what will happen when the brain receives information about the automobile's speed. Control is not automatic; as a minimum we must also know something about the personality of the driver.[3]

Control in organizations

Control systems in organizations have the same essential elements as those described above. An organization, or any component thereof, has a desired state, which is specified in its goals. Information about the actual state of the organization is compared with the desired state, and if there is a significant difference, action

[2]S. A. Richards, *Temperature Regulation* (London: Wykeham Publications Ltd., 1973).

[3]These examples are arranged in order of increasing complexity. Systems theorists point out that the universe consists of a hierarchy of systems, each higher level system being more complicated than systems of lower levels. One list is: atoms, molecules, crystals, viruses, cells, organs, organisms (e.g., humans), groups (e.g., teams), organizations, societies, and supranational organizations. See L. von Bertalanffy, "General Systems Theory," *Yearbook of the Society of General Systems Research,* 1956.

6

is taken. Control systems for some parts of an organization are practically as automatic as the thermostat. Examples are the process controls in a petroleum refinery, the control of the flow of electricity through a distribution network, and the production controls on an automated assembly line. These control systems, and others that have similar characteristics, are called *operational control systems*. They are described in more detail in the next section.

The control of the organization as a whole, and of the various units of which it is comprised, is much more complicated than that of any of the preceding examples, however. This control is called *management control*, the term implying that the control is exercised through managers. Basic factors causing these complications are as follows:

1. Unlike the thermostat or body temperature, the standard that is used as a basis for assessing the significance of what is happening is not preset. Rather, it is a result of a conscious management process, called planning. In the planning process, management decides what the organization should be doing, and the control process compares actual accomplishments with these plans. Thus, in an organization there is a close connection between the planning process and the control process, so close that for many purposes they should be viewed as a single process.

2. Like human behavior, but unlike the thermostat and body temperature regulation, the system does not operate automatically. Some of the detectors (that is, the instruments for detecting what is happening in the organization) can be mechanical, but important information is often detected through the manager's own eyes, ears, and other senses. There can be automatic ways of comparing reports of what is happening against some standard, but usually a determination of whether or not the difference between actual and standard is significant must be made by human beings, and the action taken to alter behavior also involves human beings. In order to effect change, one manager must interact with another manager. Operations researchers use the term "black box" to describe an operation the exact nature of which cannot be observed and which therefore cannot be expressed in mathematical symbols. A management control system is a black box; a thermostat is not.

3. The connection between the observed need for action and the behavior required to obtain the desired action is by no means as clear-cut as it is in the case of the simple control systems. In the selector stage, the manager may decide "costs are too high," but there is no easy or automatic step, or series of steps, that is guaranteed to bring costs down to what they should be.

4. Management control requires coordination. An organization consists of many parts, and the control system must ensure that the work of these parts is in harmony with one another. This need did not exist at all in the case of the thermostat, and it existed only to a limited extent in the case of the various organs that influence body temperature.

5. Control in an organization does not come about solely, or even primarily, as a result of actions taken by an external regulating device like the thermostat. Much control is *self*-control; that is, managers act the way they do, not primarily

because they are given specific orders by their superiors, but rather because their own judgment tells them the appropriate actions they should take. The persons who obey the 55 mph speed limit do so, not because the sign commands them to do so, but rather because they have consciously decided that it is in their best interests to obey the law.

Thus, control in an organization involves a variety of functions, some of which are not present in the simple situations that often come to mind when the word "control" is used. These include: (1) *planning* what the organization should do, (2) *coordinating* the activities of the several parts of the organization, (3) *communicating* information, (4) *evaluating* information and deciding what, if any, action should be taken, (5) *influencing* people to change their behavior, and (6) *processing information* that is used in the other functions.

PLANNING AND CONTROL PROCESSES

We have mentioned two types of processes that are found in organizations, management control and operational control. In this section, we add a third type of process, called *strategic planning*, and discuss the differences among the three of them. Our purpose is to establish the boundaries of the subject area of interest to us; that is, management control systems. The description of the other two types is brief but adequate to differentiate them from management control. The three are defined as follows:

1. *Management control* is the process by which management assures that the organization carries out its strategies effectively and efficiently.
2. *Operational control* is the process of assuring that specific tasks are carried out effectively and efficiently.
3. *Strategic planning* is the process of deciding on the goals of the organization and on the broad strategies that are to be used in attaining these goals.

Obviously, we do not mean to imply that these three processes can be separated by sharply defined boundaries; one shades into another. Strategic planning sets the guidelines for management control, and management control sets the guidelines for operational control. The complete management function involves an integration of all these processes, and the processes are complementary. The processes are sufficiently distinct, however, so that those who design and use planning and control systems will make expensive errors if they fail to take into account both the common characteristics of a process and the differences between processes.

Management control

We shall explain management control by discussing words and phrases in the definition given above.

Process. A management control system consists of a process and a structure. The process is the set of actions that take place, and the structure is the organizational

8

arrangements and information constructs that facilitate this process. By analogy with the body temperature control system, the way the system regulates temperature is the process, and the neurons, muscles, hypothalamus and other organs are the structure. The word "system" is often used with two overlapping meanings: in one sense, the organization itself is a system; in another sense, management control is a system. The context usually makes clear which sense is intended.

Managers. Management control is a process for the use of managers. It involves the interaction of managers with one another and with subordinates. It is a people-oriented process. Line managers are the focal points in management control. They are the persons whose judgments are incorporated in the approved plans, and they are the persons who must influence others and whose performance is measured. Staff people collect, summarize, and present information that is useful in the process, and they make calculations that translate management judgments into the format of the system. Such a staff may be large in numbers; indeed, the control department is often the largest staff department in a company. However, the significant decisions are made by the line managers, not by the staff.

Since managers are human beings, psychological considerations are dominant in management control. Activities such as communicating, persuading, exhorting, inspiring, and criticizing are an important part of the process.

Goals. The goals[4] of an organization are set in the strategic planning process; in the management control process these goals are generally taken as given. (Occasionally, information obtained during the management control process may lead to a change in goals.) The management control process is intended to facilitate the achievement of these goals. The broad strategies and policies that have been decided on in the strategic planning process are also taken as givens in the management control process.

Efficiency and effectiveness. By *effectiveness,* we mean how well an organization unit does its job; that is, the extent to which it produces the intended or expected results. *Efficiency* is used in its engineering sense; that is, the amount of output per unit of input. An efficient machine is one which produces a given quantity of outputs with a minimum consumption of inputs, or one which produces the largest possible outputs from a given quantity of inputs.

Effectiveness is always related to the organization's goals. Efficiency, per se, is not related to goals. An efficient organization unit is one which does whatever it does with the lowest consumption of resources; but if what it does (i.e., its output) is an inadequate contribution to the accomplishment of the organization's goals, it is ineffective. For example, if a department that is responsible for processing incoming sales orders does so at a low cost per order processed, it is efficient. If, however, the department is sloppy in answering customer queries about the

---

[4]In this book we use the word *goals* for the broad, overall aims of the organization and *objectives* for the more specific statements of planned accomplishments in a given time period. Some people use these two words interchangeably, and others reverse the meanings given above. The words *target* and *aim* are also used as synonyms for either word. Confusion can result if these differences in intended meaning are not understood.

status of orders, and thus antagonizes customers to the point where they take their business elsewhere, the department is ineffective; the loss of a customer is not consistent with the company's goals.

Assurance. The definition states that managers *assure* that the organization carries out its strategies effectively and efficiently, not that managers personally do the work. Managers, when they are acting as managers, do not themselves do the work. Their function is to see to it that the work gets done by others.

System characteristics. Following is a list of the principal characteristics of a management control system:

1. A management control system focuses on *programs* and *responsibility centers*. A program is a product, product line, research and development project, or similar activity that the organization undertakes in order to achieve its goals. A responsibility center is an organization unit headed by a responsible manager.
2. The information in a management control system is of two general types: (a) *planned data,* that is, programs, budgets, and standards; and (b) *actual data,* that is, information on what is actually happening, both inside the organization and in the external environment.
3. Ordinarily, a management control system is an *overall system* in the sense that it embraces all aspects of a company's operation. An important management function is to assure that all parts of the operation are in balance with one another; and in order to coordinate these activities, management needs information about each of them.
4. The management control system is usually *built around a financial structure;* that is, resources and revenues are expressed in monetary units. Money is the only common denominator which can be used to combine and compare the heterogeneous elements of resources (e.g., hours of labor, type of labor, quantity and quality of material, amount and kind of products produced). Although the financial structure is usually the central focus, nonmonetary measures such as minutes per operation, number of employees, and reject and spoilage rates are also important parts of the system.
5. The management control process tends to be *rhythmic;* it follows a definite pattern and timetable, month after month and year after year. In budget preparation, which is an important activity in the management control process, certain steps are taken in a predescribed sequence and at certain dates each year: dissemination of guidelines, preparation of original estimates, transmission of these estimates up through the several echelons in the organization, review of these estimates, final approval by top management, and dissemination back through the organization. The procedure to be followed at each step in this process, the dates when the steps are to be completed, and even the forms to be used can be, and often are, set forth in a policies and procedures manual.
6. A management control system is, or should be, a *coordinated, integrated system;* that is, although data collected for one purpose may differ from those collected for another purpose, these data should be reconcilable with one another. In particular, it is essential that data on actual performance be structured in the

same way—that is, have the same definitions and the same account content—as data on planned performance. If this is not done, valid comparisons of actual and planned performance cannot be made. In a sense, the management control system is a *single* system, but for some purposes it is useful to think of it as a set of interlocking subsystems, one for programming, another for budgeting, another for accounting, and another for reporting and analysis.

Strategic planning

The word *strategic*, in the term "strategic planning," is used here in its usual sense of deciding how to combine and employ resources. Thus, strategic planning is a process having to do with the formulation of long-range policy-type plans that change the character or direction of the organization. In an industrial company, this includes planning that affects the goals of the company; policies of all types (including policies as to management control and other processes); the acquisition and disposition of major facilities, divisions, or subsidiaries; the markets to be served and distribution channels for serving them; the organization structure (as distinguished from individual personnel actions); research and development of new product lines (as distinguished from modifications in existing products and product changes within existing product lines); sources of new permanent capital; dividend policy, and so on. Strategic planning decisions affect the physical, financial, and organizational framework within which operations are carried on.

The need for strategic planning is a fundamental reason why control in an organization differs from the simple control systems illustrated earlier. The thermostat's desired temperature is established by an external agent, the person who sets it. The desired body temperature is an innate characteristic of the organism. In an organization, by contrast, the organization sets its own goals. This goal-setting process does not exist in lower level systems.

Distinctions between management control and strategic planning. Briefly, here are some ways in which the strategic planning process differs from the management control process:

A strategic plan usually relates to some part of the organization, rather than to the totality. The concept of a master planner who constantly keeps all parts of the organization at some coordinated optimum is a nice concept, but an unrealistic one. Life is too complicated for any human, or computer, to do this.

Strategic planning is essentially *irregular*. Problems, opportunities, and bright ideas do not arise according to some set timetable; rather, they are dealt with whenever they happen to be perceived. The appropriate analytical techniques depend on the nature of the problem being analyzed, and no overall approach (such as a mathematical model) has been developed that is of much help in analyzing all types of strategic problems. Indeed, an overemphasis on a systematic approach is quite likely to stifle the essential element of creativity. In strategic planning, management works now on one problem, now on another, according to the needs and opportunities of the moment. Thus, although an organization has a strategic planning *process*, it is unrealistic to describe this as a *system;* the process is essentially unsystematic.

The estimates used in strategic planning are intended to show the *expected* results of the plan. They are neutral and impersonal. By contrast, the management control process and the data used in it are intended to influence managers to take actions that will lead to *desired* results. Thus, in connection with management control it is appropriate to discuss how tight an operating budget should be. Should the goals be set so high that only an outstanding manager can achieve them, or should they be set so that they are attainable by the average manager? At what level does frustration inhibit a manager's best efforts? Does an easily attainable budget lead to complacency? And so on. In strategic planning, the question to be asked about the figures is simply: Is this the most reasonable estimate that can be made?

Strategic planning relies heavily on external information—that is, on data collected from outside the company, such as market analyses, estimates of costs and other factors involved in building a plant in a new locality, technological developments, and so on. When data from the normal information system are used, they usually must be recast to fit the needs of the specified problem being analyzed. For example, current operating costs that are collected for measuring performance and for making pricing and other operating decisions usually must be restructured before they are useful in deciding whether to close down the plant. Another characteristic of the relevant information is that much of it is imprecise. The strategic planner estimates what will probably happen, often over a rather long time period. These estimates are likely to have a high degree of uncertainty, and they must be treated accordingly.

In the management control process, the communication of objectives, policies, guidelines, decisions, and results throughout the organization is extremely important. In the strategic planning process, communication is much simpler and involves relatively few persons; indeed, the need for secrecy often requires that steps be taken to inhibit communication. (Wide communication of the decisions that result from strategic planning is obviously important; this is part of the management control process.)

Strategic planning is essentially applied economics, whereas management control involves both economics and social psychology.

Both management control and strategic planning involve top management, but middle managers (i.e., operating management) typically have a much more important role in management control than in strategic planning. Middle managers usually are not major participants in the strategic planning process and sometimes are not even aware that a plan is being considered. Many operating executives are by temperament not very good at strategic planning. The pressures of current activities usually do not allow them to devote the necessary time to such work. Furthermore, they usually are knowledgeable about only their part of the organization, and strategic planning requires a broader background. (Nevertheless, managers of divisions or other major segments of a business make strategic plans for their own divisions or segments.) Currently, there is a tendency in companies to set up separate staffs to gather the facts and make the analyses that provide the background material for strategic decisions.

These and other differences between management control and strategic planning are summarized in Exhibit 1–2.

Strategic planning and management control activities tend to conflict with one another in some respects. The time that management spends in thinking about the future is taken from time that it could otherwise use in controlling current operations, so in this indirect way strategic planning can hurt current performance. The reverse is also true; many managers are so preoccupied with current problems that they do not devote enough time to thinking about future strategies.

EXHIBIT 1–2 Some distinctions between strategic planning and management control

Characteristic	*Strategic planning*	*Management control*
Focus of plans	On one aspect at a time	On whole organization
Complexities	Many variables	Less complex
Degree of structure	Unstructured and irregular; each problem different	Rhythmic; prescribed procedures
Nature of information	Tailor-made for the problem; more external and predictive; less accurate	Integrated; more internal and historical; more accurate
Communication of information	Relatively simple	Relatively difficult
Purpose of estimates	Show expected results	Lead to desired results
Persons primarily involved	Staff and top management	Line and top management
Number of persons involved	Small	Large
Mental activity	Creative; analytical	Administrative; persuasive
Source discipline	Economics	Social psychology
Planning and control	Planning dominant, but some control	Emphasis on both planning and control
Time horizon	Tends to be long	Tends to be short
End result	Policies and precedents	Action within policies and precedents
Appraisal of the job done	Extremely difficult	Much less difficult

Operational control

As the definition suggests, the focus of operational control is on individual tasks or transactions: scheduling and controlling individual jobs through a shop, as contrasted with measuring the performance of the shop as a whole; procuring specific items for inventory, as contrasted with the management of inventory as a whole; specific personnel actions, as contrasted with personnel management; and so on.

In order to understand the nature of the activities to which operational control is applicable, we need to introduce the idea of *programmed* activities, and this requires an understanding of the terms *outputs* and *inputs*.

Outputs and inputs. Outputs are the goods, services, or other effects created by an organization. Inputs are the resources the organization consumes. Every organization has, or at least is intended to have, outputs, even though they may not be readily measurable or even clearly definable; that is, every organization does something, and that something is its output. In a business, outputs are goods and services. In a school, the output is education; in a hospital, patient care; in a law office, advice and counsel; in a government, service to the public. Similarly, the inputs may range from easily valued items, such as purchased parts, to such intangible items as executive thought.

Moreover, every unit within an organization has outputs. In the case of factories, the outputs are goods. In all other units—personnel, transportation, sales, engineering, administration, and so on—outputs are services. For many of these other units, it may be difficult or impossible to measure the quantity of their outputs. Nevertheless, the outputs exist.

One of the important management tasks in an organization is to seek the *optimum* relationship between outputs and inputs. In many situations, it is rarely, if ever, possible to determine the optimum relationship between outputs and inputs objectively; instead, the choice of a relationship is a matter of subjective judgment. This is true because there is no scientific or objective way of determining how output will be affected by changes in inputs. How much should a company spend for advertising? Are additional fire trucks, or school teachers, or police officers worth their cost? Informed people will disagree on the answers to questions of this type.

The term *discretionary costs* is descriptive of the type of inputs for which there is no objective way of ascertaining the optimum quantity to be employed. An important management function is to make judgments as to the "right" amount of discretionary costs in a given set of circumstances. Such judgments are, by definition, subjective and part of the management control process. Costs whose optimum amount can be estimated objectively are *engineered costs*.

Programmed activities. In other situations, there is at least the possibility that an optimum relationship between outputs and inputs can be found. It is unrealistic to imply that this relationship can ever be determined in an absolute sense, inasmuch as new and better ways of doing things are constantly being developed; therefore, a more realistic meaning of "optimum" is this: The optimum is that combination of resources, out of all *known* combinations, that will produce the desired output at the lowest cost. If the optimum input-output relationship for a given activity can be predetermined, then the inputs that should be employed in a given set of circumstances can be described and reduced to rules; that is, they can be programmed. Operational control is limited to programmed activities.

Distinctions between management control and operational control. As an example of an activity to which operational control is applicable, consider the inventory area. If the demand for an item, the cost of storing it, its production cost and production time, and the loss involved in not filling an order are known, then the optimum inventory level and the optimum production or procurement schedule can be calculated. Even though these factors cannot be known with certainty, sound estimates nevertheless can be made, inventory levels and production or procurement schedules based on these estimates can be calculated, and reasonable people will agree with the results of these calculations. An inventory control system using rules derived from such calculations is an operational control system.

By contrast, consider the legal department of a company. No device can measure the quality, or even the quantity, of the legal service that constitutes the output of this department. No formula can show the amount of service the department should render or the optimum amount of costs that should be incurred. Impressions as to the "right" amount of service, the "right" amount of cost, and the "right" relationship between the service actually rendered and the cost actually incurred are strictly subjective. They are judgments made by management. If persons disagree on these judgments, there is no objective way of resolving the disagreement. Yet the legal department, as a part of the whole organization, must be controlled; the chief counsel must operate within the framework of policies prescribed by top management. The type of control necessary in his situation is management control.

Examples of activities that are susceptible to operational control are automated plants, such as cement plants, oil refineries, and power-generating stations; the direct production operations of most manufacturing plants; production scheduling; inventory control; the order-taking type of selling activity; and order processing, premium billing, payroll accounting, check handling, and similar paperwork activities.

Examples of activities for which management control is necessary are the total operation of most manufacturing plants, which includes such judgment inputs as indirect labor, employees' benefit and welfare programs, safety activities, training, and supervision; most advertising, sales promotion, pricing, selling (as distinguished from order-taking), and similar marketing activities; most aspects of finance; most aspects of research, development, and design; the work of staff units of all types; and, of course, the activities of top management.

The type of control appropriate for the whole of any unit that carries on both programmed and nonprogrammed activities is management control. Thus, the control of one division of a company is management control. The control of the whole accounting department is managment control, even though operational control is appropriate for certain aspects of the work, such as posting and check writing.

Some people believe that the distinction between the two classes of activities described above is merely one of degree rather than of kind; they say that all we are doing is distinguishing between situations in which control is easy and those in which control is difficult. We think the distinction is more fundamental, and hope this will be apparent from the following brief list of characteristics that distinguish management control from operational control.

Management control covers the whole of an organization. Each operational control procedure is restricted to a subunit, often a narrowly circumscribed activity. Just as management control occurs within a set of policies derived from strategic planning, so operational control occurs within a set of well-defined procedures and rules derived from management control.

Control is more difficult in management control than in operational control because of the absence of a valid, objective standard with which actual performance can be compared. A good operational control system can provide a much higher degree of assurance that actions are proceeding as desired than can a good management control system.

An operational control system is a *rational* system; that is, the action to be taken is decided by a set of logical rules. These rules may or may not cover all aspects of a given problem. Situations not covered by the rules are designated as exceptions and are resolved by human judgment. Other than these exceptions, application of the rule is automatic. The rules in principle can be programmed into a computer, and the choice between using a computer and using a human being depends primarily on the relative cost of each resource.

Management control controls *people;* operational control controls *things.* In management control psychological considerations are therefore dominant. The management control system at most assists those who take action; it does not directly or by itself result in action without human intervention. By contrast, the end product of an inventory control system can be an order, such as a decision to replenish a certain inventory item, and this order may be based entirely on calculations from formulas incorporated in the system. (The formulas were devised by human beings, but this is a management control process, not an operational control process.)

In a consideration of operational control, analogies with mechanical, electrical, and hydraulic systems are reasonable and useful, and such terms as feedback, network balancing, optimization, and so on are relevant. It is perfectly appropriate, for example, to view an operational control system as analogous to a thermostat that turns the furnace on and off according to its perception of changes in temperature. These analogies do not work well as models for management control systems, however, because the success of these systems is highly dependent on their impact on people, and people are not like thermostats or furnaces. One can't light a fire under a human being simply by turning up a thermostat.

The management control system is ordinarily built around a financial structure, whereas operational control data are often nonmonetary. They may be expressed in terms of labor-hours, number of items, pounds of waste, and so on. Since each operational control procedure is designed for a limited area of application, it is feasible to use the basis of measurement that is most appropriate for that area.

The information in an operational control system relates to individual transactions: the production order for one lot, the purchase order for one item of inventory, or a requisition for one maintenance job. Most of the information in a management control system consists of summaries of transactions: production costs for a month, the status of groups of items in inventory, and maintenance costs in total. Data in an operational control system are often in real time (i.e., they are reported as the event is occurring), whereas data in a management control system are often retrospective. Computer specialists who do not make such a distinction dream about a system that will display to the management the current status of every individual

16

activity in the organization. Although this *could* be done, it *should not* be done; management does not want such detail. Management does not need to know the time at which lot No. 1007 was transferred from station 27 to station 28; rather, it needs to know only that the process is, or is not, proceeding as planned, and if not, where the trouble lies.

Operational control uses exact data, whereas management control needs only approximations. Material is ordered and scheduled in specific quantities and employees are paid the exact amount due them, but data on management control reports need contain only two or three significant digits and are therefore rounded to thousands of dollars, to millions of dollars, or even (in the U.S. government) to billions of dollars.

An operational control system requires a mathematical model of the operation. Although it may not always be expressed explicitly in mathematical notation, a decision rule states that given certain values for parameters *a, b, . . . n,* action *X* is to be taken. Models are not so important in management control. In a sense, a budget and a PERT network are models associated with the management control process, but they are not the essence of the process.

The formal management control *system* is only a part of the management control *process*, actually a relatively unimportant part. The system can help motivate the manager to make decisions that are in the best interests of the organization, and the system can provide information that aids the manager in making these decisions; but many other stimuli are involved in motivating the manager, and good information does not automatically produce good decisions. The success or failure of the management control process depends on the personal characteristics of the managers, their judgment, their knowledge, their ability to influence others.

In operational control, the system itself is relatively more important. Except in fully automated operations, it is an exaggeration to say that the system *is* the process, but it is not much of an exaggeration. An operational control system ordinarily states what action should be taken; it makes the decisions. As with any operation, management vigilance is required to detect an unforeseen foul-up in the operation or a change in the conditions on which the technique is predicated, and to initiate the necessary corrective action. And management seeks ways to improve the technique. In general, however, the degree of management involvement in operational control is small, whereas in management control it is large.

As new techniques are developed, there is a tendency for more and more activities to become susceptible to operational control. In the factory, the production schedule that was formerly set according to the supervisor's intuition is now derived by linear programming. And although not very long ago it was believed that operational control was appropriate only for factory operations, we now see models and formulas being used for certain marketing decisions, such as planning salespeople's calls and planning direct-mail advertising. This shift probably will continue; it is a large part of what people have in mind when they say, "management is becoming increasingly scientific."

The differences between management control and operational control are summarized in Exhibit 1–3.

EXHIBIT 1–3 Some distinctions between management control and operational control

Characteristic	*Management control*	*Operational control*
Focus of activity	Whole operation	Single task or transaction
Judgment	Relatively much; subjective decisions	Relatively little; reliance on rules
Nature of structure	Psychological	Rational
Nature of information	Integrated; financial data throughout; approximations acceptable; future and historical	Tailor-made to the operation; often non-financial; precise; often in real time
Persons primarily involved	Management	Supervisors (or none)
Mental activity	Administrative; persuasive	Follow directions (or none)
Source discipline	Social psychology	Economics; physical sciences
Time horizon	Weeks, months, years	Day to day
Type of costs	Discretionary	Engineered

OTHER MANAGEMENT PROCESSES

Authors classify the functions of management in various ways. An old classification, which is still widely used, is that of Fayol: planning, organizing, commanding, coordinating, and controlling.[5] It is obvious that the description of management control in the preceding section encompasses several of these functions, for it includes, at least, planning, coordinating, and controlling. The danger exists that the preceding description can create the impression that management control is the *whole* of management. This obviously is not the case; management control is only a part of management.

We have already identified another important management function, strategic planning. An even more important function is the one which Fayol called organizing and which others call staffing, or the personnel function. Managers must make judgments on hiring, promotion, and reassignment; they must decide where a person best fits in the organization, what the person's responsibilities should be, and the relationships of persons to one another; and managers must create an environment that encourages employees to work effectively. Judgments about people are probably much more important to the success of an organization than its control system. Good people can overcome the defects in a management control system, but even

[5]Henry Fayol, *Industrial and General Administration*, trans. J. A. Coubrough (Geneva: International Management Institute, 1929). Originally published in 1916.

the best management control system will not lead to satisfactory results without good people to operate it.

Managers also have an expertise in the particular function they are involved in. The production manager knows about production; the marketing manager knows about marketing. Our discussion of management control does not touch on this functional expertise.

Finally, managers do not spend all their time in the management function itself. The sales manager may close a deal with an important customer. The production manager may "get his hands dirty" with some problem in the plant. The financial vice president personally negotiates credit arrangements.

For these reasons, the discussion of management control in this book is by no means a discussion of the whole process of management, nor is it a description of all that managers do.

OVERVIEW OF MANAGEMENT CONTROL SYSTEMS

A system consists of a structure and a process; that is, what it is and what it does. The structure of a management control system can be described in terms of the units in an organization and the nature of the information that flows among these units. The process is what the managers do with this information.

Structure

The management control structure is described in Chapters 5 through 8. The description focuses on various types of responsibility centers. A *responsibility center* is simply an organization unit headed by a responsible manager. As noted earlier, each responsibility center has inputs and it has outputs. Responsibility centers are classified according to the degree to which these inputs and outputs are measured in monetary terms.

In an *expense center,* inputs are measured in terms of money, that is, costs; but outputs are not so measured. In an *engineered expense center,* the costs are programmed or engineered in the sense described in an earlier section. In a *discretionary expense center,* costs are not programmed; they can be varied at the discretion of the managers involved. The legal department mentioned above, and indeed most staff departments in an organization, are discretionary expense centers.

In a *revenue center,* revenues are measured in monetary terms, but they are not matched with the expenses of the unit. Sales offices are an example.

In a *profit center,* both revenues and the expenses associated with earning those revenues are measured. The difference between revenues and expenses is profit. Thus, in a profit center both inputs and outputs are measured in monetary terms.

In an *investment center,* profit is measured, and in addition the investment, or capital, used in that responsibility center is measured and related to the profit generated by that investment.

Process

Much of the management control process involves informal communication and interactions. Informal communication occurs by means of memoranda, meetings, conversations, and even by such signals as facial expressions. Although these informal activities are of great importance, they are not amenable to a systematic description. In addition to these informal activities, most companies also have a *formal* management control system. It consists of some or all of the following phases:

1. Programming.
2. Budgeting.
3. Operating and measurement.
4. Reporting and analysis.

EXHIBIT 1–4 Phases of management control

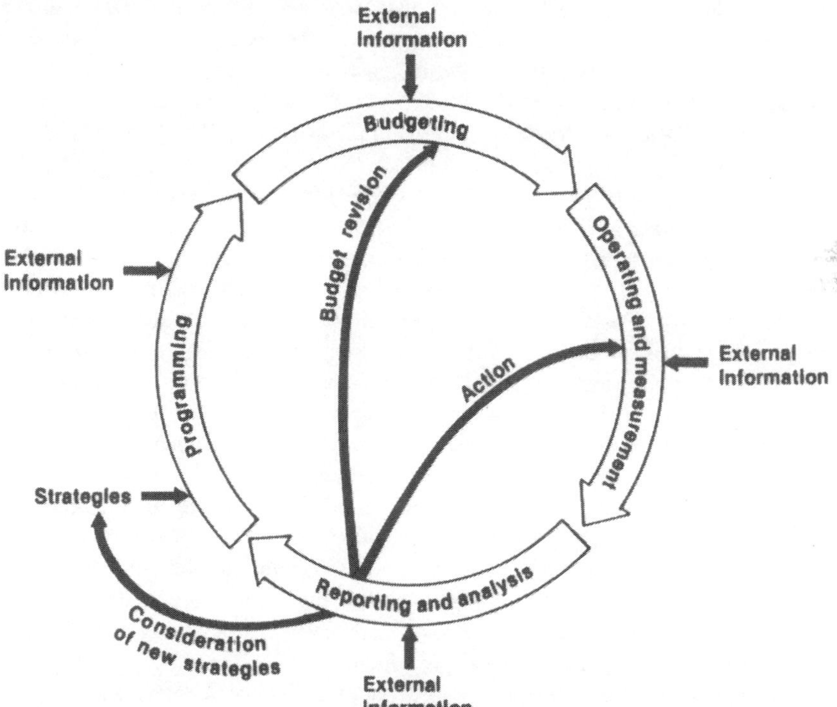

As indicated in Exhibit 1–4, each of these activities leads to the next. They recur in a regular cycle, and together they constitute a "closed loop." These four phases are described briefly below, and are discussed in depth in Chapters 9 through 12.

Programming. Programming is the process of deciding on the programs that the company will undertake and the approximate amount of resources that are to be allocated to each program. Programs are the principal activities that the organization has decided to undertake in order to implement the strategies that it has decided upon. In a profit-oriented company, each principal product or product line is a program. There are also various research and development programs, some aimed at improving existing products or processes, others searching for marketable new products.

Budgeting. A budget is a plan expressed in quantitative, usually monetary, terms that covers a specified period of time, usually one year. In the budgeting process each program is translated into terms that correspond to the sphere of responsibility of each manager who is charged with executing the program or some part of it. Thus, although the plans are originally made in terms of individual programs, in the budgeting process the plans are translated into terms of responsibility centers. The process of developing a budget is essentially one of negotiation between the manager of a responsibility center and his or her superior. The end product of these negotiations is an approved statement of the revenues that are expected during the budget year, and the resources that are to be used in achieving the company's goals for each responsibility center and for the company as a whole.

In addition to the monetary statement of plans, the plan for the year also includes a statement of objectives that are to be accomplished during the year. These objectives are usually expressed in nonmonetary terms.

Operating and measurement. During the period of actual operations, records are kept of resources actually consumed (i.e., costs) and of revenues actually earned. These records are structured so that cost and revenue data are classified both by programs and by responsibility centers. Data classified according to programs are used as a basis for future programming, and data classified by responsibility centers are used to measure the performance of responsibility center managers. For the latter purpose, data on actual results are reported in such a way that they can be readily compared with the plan as set forth in the budget.

Reporting and analysis. The management control system serves as a communication device. The information that is communicated consists of both accounting and nonaccounting data, and of both data generated within the organization and data about what is happening in the environment outside the organization. This information keeps managers informed as to what is going on and helps to ensure that the work done by the separate responsibility centers is coordinated.

Reports are also used as a basis for control. Essentially, such reports are derived from an analysis that compares actual performance with planned performance and attempts to explain the difference. Based on these formal reports, and also on information received through informal communication channels, managers decide what, if any, action should be taken. They may, for example, decide to change the plan as set forth in the budget, and this leads to a new planning process. It is for this reason that the phases shown in Exhibit 1–4 are depicted as a closed loop with one phase leading to the next.

[3]

The Problems of a Paradigm: A Critique of the Prevailing Orthodoxy in Management Control

Tony Lowe and Tony Puxty

The genesis of management control is difficult to trace – perhaps because, in the manner of Humpty Dumpty, different writers use the term to mean what they want it to mean. Giglioni and Bedeian (1974) see the earliest writings in the area being those of Emerson, Church and Diemer, who were writing in 1912, 1914 and 1915 respectively. Already at that date, the link between accounting and the control of the enterprise was being forged: they emphasised the importance of adequate records, of comparison with standards, and with the adequacy of those standards. Giglioni and Bedeian quote Church as follows:

> [the comparison is based on] three elements: (a) recognition of what facts are truly significant; (b) accurate record and convenient presentation of these facts; (c) judicious action based on study of the facts.

The modern development of management control as a subject within the field of accounting must however be credited to Robert Anthony and his colleagues at the Harvard Business School. Management control was intended to be a broadening out of the more technical kinds of accounting which were then taught – the mechanics of costing and bookkeeping methods.[1] Through this, it was felt, one of the essential functions of accounting could be applied in its context, and at the same time be enriched by the findings of other management researchers where they impinged on accounting. Until then the sole link between accounting and other disciplines had been economics, and the development of income theory had already reached a considerable degree of sophistication. Law, of course, has also been important to accounting history because of the significance accorded to accounting information in corporate legislation. But by the early 1960s it was becoming evident that other disciplines could throw light on the relevance of accounting to the firm: and chief among these was social psychology.

The link between accounting and social psychology can probably be traced at its earliest to the pioneering work of Chris Argyris (1952) who researched the effects budgeting systems had on middle management and supervisory grades. Development of the link, of the evident enrichment which could come from the insights social psychology could add to the accounting process, were at first slow. But they gained momentum throughout the decade, and the 1960s academics could base their research on a growing body of knowledge at the level of the individual: in particular, the effects of budget systems on motivation.

This body of knowledge was of course known at Harvard: but they were also able to add insights from the rapidly growing area of organisation theory. This had been fragmented, the interest of a minority of sociologists and industrial psychologists: but perhaps the turning point may be traced to publication of March and Simon's classic book *Organisations* (1958).[2] Here, perhaps for the first time, the particular characteristics of the organisation were being looked at within a coherent framework of their own. No longer did the reader have to turn to the (fragmented) translations of Max Weber (whose orientation was in any case very different from his own, interested as Weber was essentially in the interrelation between organisation type and societal development) or the mechanical prognostications of Frederick Taylor, or the equally mechanical if broader writings of practical businessmen such as Fayol, Urwick and Brech. A basis now existed for a theoretical and rigorous approach to the analysis of organisations.

With these as sources, a body of knowledge known as 'management control' could be tentatively developed. It can be seen from the first edition of Anthony, Dearden and Vancil's *Management Control Systems* (1965) just how tentative they were at the time. The opening essay of the book laid down the essential differences between strategic planning and management control: in particular, the 'source disciplines' of these two topics were said to be 'economics' and 'social psychology' respectively. Little of social psychology is seen in the rest of the book, however: apart from some implicit social psychology in the discussion of ideas such as decentralisation and the expense centre/financial performance centre/investment centre distinction, the book turns out to be concerned in the main with information and financial assessment. This has changed to some extent by the fifth edition (Anthony, Dearden and Bedford, 1984). By now the readings have gone, to be replaced by a more integrated text: and the text itself includes a 28-page essay entitled 'Control and Organizational Behaviour'. The structure of the book is also more assured, being divided into four parts entitled 'An Overview', 'The Management Control Structure' (which includes the material on different types of accounting centre) 'The Management Control Process' and 'Special Management Control Situations'. It might be said, therefore, that in the Harvard perspective at least, management control has come of age, and its subject matter and the way in which it should be approached are agreed upon. The influence of the approach can be seen in later works such as those by Dermer (1977) and Euske (1984).

The approach taken by these writers (which we shall describe in more detail in the next section) might still be said to be the ruling paradigm of management control, both in the eyes of management teachers and in the eyes of practical businessmen. Yet the insights available from the disciplines marshalled – principally, as we have said, social psychology – are limited in their applicability. Other disciplines can add much (such as general systems theory, sociology and cybernetics) and we shall discuss ways in which we feel that the approach taken by the classic authors is now incomplete and thus, as a managerial prescription, misleading. In taking these authors as our touchstone we are not questioning the value of the orientation which they have given to accounting, in helping it to move from a technical perspective to a more useful organisational perspective:[3] rather, we are choosing the latest edition of Anthony and his colleagues' work as a subject for critique precisely because of its authority. We begin by outlining our understanding of its approach and subject-matter.

THE ARCHITECTURE OF A PARADIGM

The book opens by outlining the general nature of control as it is understood by the authors. This is done in terms of negative feedback: of a process, a comparison with standard, and an effector to change the process if necessary to maintain its performance as near as possible to the standard. It is, therefore, essentially cybernetic, although a very simple kind of cybernetics. On page 6 a reference is given to Norbert Wiener and his book *Cybernetics* (1961): the term does not appear in the index however, and we must assume that the science of cybernetics itself is not considered relevant to the authors' purposes. From this general discussion of control they then consider its nature specifically in the organisation and, after noting certain differences between other control processes and organisational control they move on to consider management control and its characteristics as contrasted with strategic planning and task control.

It is at this stage that they define management control in the context of strategic planning which they have defined immediately previously:

> management control is the process by which management assures that the organization carries out its strategies.
>
> (Anthony, Dearden and Bedford (1984) p. 10)

In this way they make the distinction between planning and control quite clear. Strategic planning sets the strategies: management control checks they are being pursued appropriately. Their distinction between management control and (on each conceptual side) strategic planning and task control is given considerable prominence at this stage, and is seemingly done to assure the reader of the precise subject-matter of the rest of the book. By means of their definition they explain who carries out these functions, their nature (in such terms as time horizon and appraisal of the function's proper execution) and, as already mentioned, the source disciplines used. It is important for our later discussion to appreciate the restrictions placed on the nature of management control in these pages: it is programmed (in Simon's terms), concerns line and top management, involves large numbers of people, is concerned with administrative procedures, which are effected by 'persuasion', tends to have a short time horizon and is rather easier (although not 'easy') than strategic planning to appraise when done. We should like to emphasise here that it is concerned essentially with the control of *people rather than events*.

To close the introductory chapter, the authors give their phases of the process of management control. These are

1. Programming
2. Budgeting
3. Operating and Measurement
4. Reporting and Analysis

These are explicated in detail in Part III of the book.

The rest of Part I of the book consists of three chapters. The first, entitled 'Control and Organization Behaviour' outlines some elementary ideas of corporate structure in terms of managerial hierarchies – in fact, in common with the literature of organisational behaviour, structure is considered to be synonymous with the hierarchy of the people in the organisation; it considers a few characteristics of the individual which are seen as relevant to management, in particular, motivation: and the chapter ends with some comments on the function of the controller in the organisation. The second looks at goals and strategies. The third considers quite briefly some characteristics of information transmission in organisations.

Part II, which concerns structure (which, as we have already explained, means managerial structure), centres around the idea of reporting centres: and the characteristics of revenue and expense centres, and profit centres are explored in one chapter each, a separate chapter being devoted to transfer pricing. It is of course true that the organisation of the enterprise is being made congruent with the organisation of the management; the fact that a manager is responsible for a particular area of the enterprise has implications for the actual operation (as is shown by the classic case of Birch Paper Co.). Finally, there is a chapter on investment centres.

Some perhaps fairly obvious points should be mentioned at this stage about the implicit model of man presented here as a manager. He is, basically, expected to be in favour of the success of the total enterprise, although he is also self-interested, and will tend to put himself first when any conflict of interest arises. He is not expected to be wholly self-disciplined: procedures of accountability are intrinsic to the hierarchical structure of the responsibility-centre system, and externally imposed standards are there to ensure that he does not slip back. Despite these faults, he does not allow any matters extrinsic to the organisation to affect his orientation to his job: the control procedures of the firm take no account of his features other than as a 'managerial hand and mind'.

When we turn to Part III we find a discussion of the process of management control. This is based on the five headings of Programming; Budget Preparation; Analysing and Reporting Financial Performance; the Profit Budget in the Control Process; and Executive Compensation Plans. Each of these is the subject-matter of one chapter. The first two of these are heavily rationalistic, proposing procedures which are/should be gone through by management (the normative is not distinguished from the positive, so it is not always possible to tell to what extent the authors are describing what they believe to be business reality and the extent to which they are prescribing 'good' procedures). To the extent that social psychology is considered, it is only implicit, so that, for example, certain procedures are expected to motivate; other procedures recognise cognitive limits: and so on. There is no explicit discussion of human behaviour. The third chapter of this section is entirely devoted to variance analysis, and is similar to cost accounting textbooks.

The fourth chapter appears to reflect the philosophy of such management writers as Koontz, O'Donnell and Weihrich (1980) in its discussion of budget problems and performance appraisal. The fifth chapter, taking it for granted that bonus plans will 'encourage high performance by allowing managers to participate financially in the results of their accomplishments' (p. 585), discusses the different kinds of scheme available.

Part IV is concerned with special kinds of problems: multinational corporations, service organisations, non-profit organisations, and projects. Since it is essentially an application of the philosophy of the rest of the book to these areas it will not be considered further.

We have felt it necessary to go rapidly through the structure of Anthony, Dearden and Bedford's book despite the fact that this paper is not intended to be a book review but rather, as we stated earlier, because its very structure tells us the message behind its approach. We can now proceed to an evaluation.

AN EVALUATION

Before we consider our specific criticisms of this approach in detail, it is perhaps useful to clarify our contrasted approach to that of Anthony by means of diagrammatic representation. Anthony (1965) gives Figure 2.1 as a guide to his thinking. Anthony and Dearden (1976) give Figure 2.2. A better understanding of their approach as it now stands might however be depicted as in Figure 2.3. This

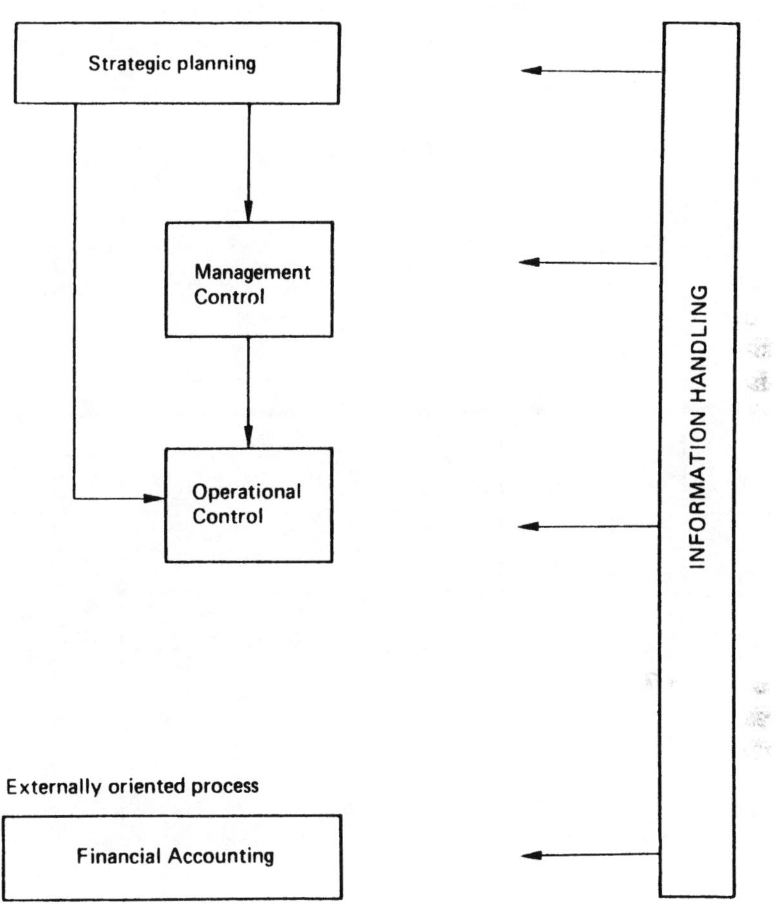

Figure 2.1

gives, specifically, a clarification of their ideas concerning the domain of strategic planning, management control, and task control.

We might suggest that a better approach is that shown in Figure 2.4. There is still a tripartite division; but it is now based specifically on an environmentally-founded typology. The environment is given prominence, as is the feedback loop which has effect coterminately with the environment. Above all, the difference between this approach and that of Anthony is that here, all decision functions are accommodated within the idea of management control, and contrasted with the subject matter of decisions made for control – namely financial funds and the physical subsystem.

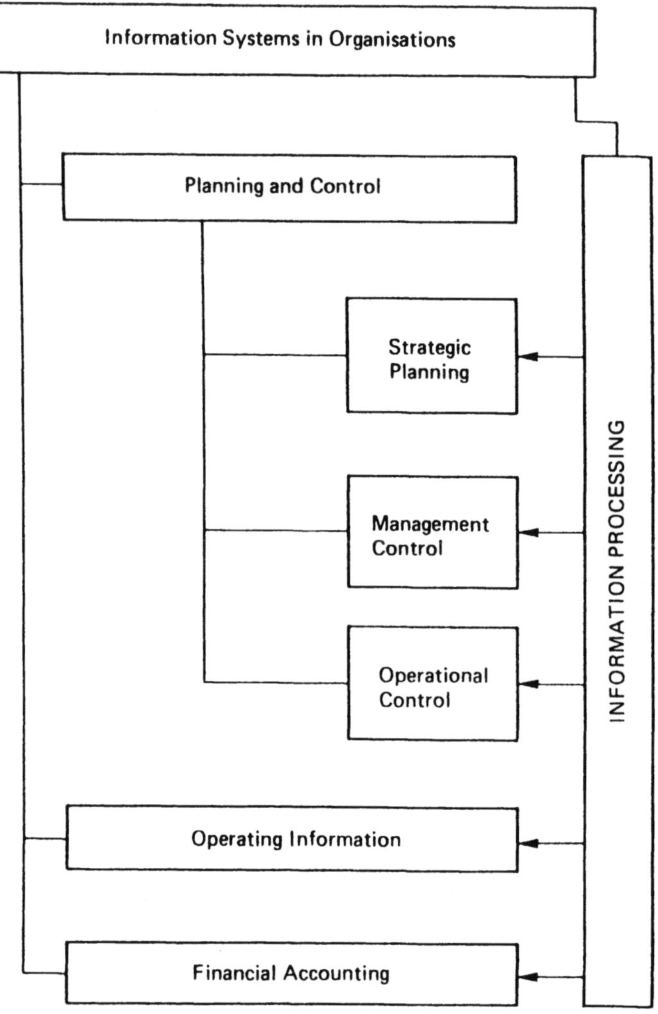

Figure 2.2

We now turn to an examination of the specific subject-matter of Anthony, Dearden and Bedford's book. We consider our objections to their scheme under seven headings.

The Environment and the Organisation

It is generally recognised in much recent literature that the environment of an organisation has a critical role in the determination of

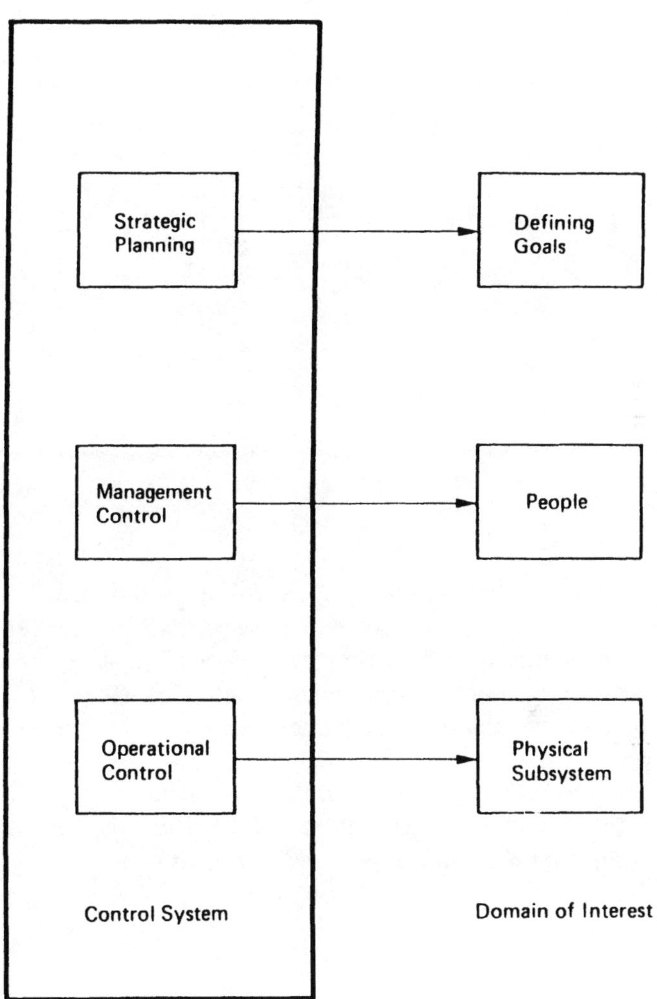

Figure 2.3

the organisation's success. The organisation exists because there is a need for it within the environment: and conversely, the organisation is dependent on its environment for resources. Much research has analysed this interdependence between the organisation and its environment (for example Rhenman, 1973; Lawrence and Lorsch, 1967; Duncan, 1972; Terreberry, 1968; Aldrich, 1979; Karpik, 1978; Pfeffer and Salancik, 1978). The most basic message of cybernetics and general systems theory is that control of an organisation is

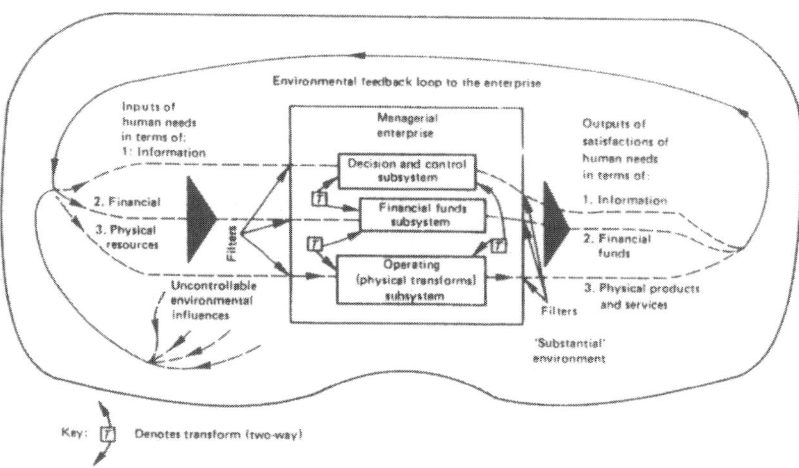

Figure 2.4

dependent on its being able to control its relationship with its environment (Lowe, 1971; Lowe and McInnes, 1971). Yet in the whole of the approach advocated by Anthony's paradigm, we find little acknowledgement of the environment.[4] Instead of relating control to the environment it is defined as

> (1) *planning* what the organization should do, (2) *co-ordinating* the activities of the several parts of the organization, (3) *communicating* information, (4) *evaluating* information and deciding what, if any, action should be taken, (5) *influencing* people to change their behaviour, and (6) *processing information* that is used in the other functions.
>
> (p. 6)[5]

The whole emphasis of this is on internal processes: on actions to be taken within the organisation. It is of course true that these actions will affect the relationship of the organisation to its environment, but this relationship is not made explicit and the specific ways in which it should be governed are not discussed. The result is an inward-looking philosophy of control which, by concentrating on a small part of the control process, ignores the most important part.

Control as Feedback

As a result, control is seen as a feedback process only. Just as Anthony, Dearden and Bedford take as their starting point for comparison the thermostat (a discrete regulator) and the body's homeostat (a continuous regulator) so they consider the control process as a feedback process only.

The result is that the reader is led to expect that control can only take place after the event. This is of course exemplified in the variance analysis of cost and budget statements. The understanding of the concept 'control' is thus imprisoned in the idea of the time-lagged regulator. Yet this is, in fact, the least effective and least efficient type of regulator. Consider Figure 2.5 (Lowe, Puxty and Tinker, 1979).

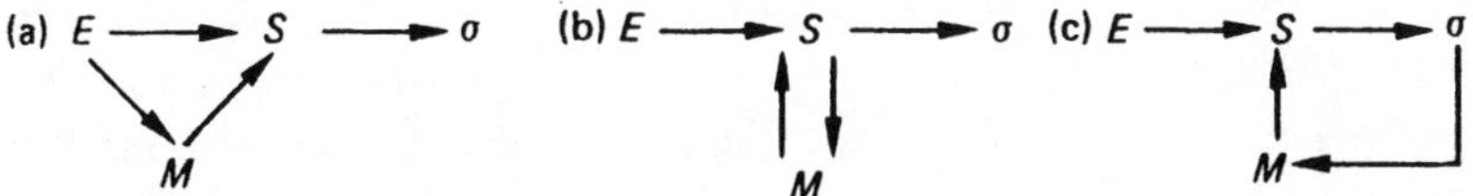

E = environmental variety
S = system
M = regulator
σ = effect upon system

Figure 2.5

In the first case, M forms a perfect regulator: it is able to sense the coming environmental variety and counter it in such a way that the state of the system S is preserved and there is no change in σ. In the second case the regulator is imperfect, and attempts to counter disturbances by sensing their immediate effects on the system. The third case is the error-controlled regulator: only after the system has been disturbed does it take remedial action. It is this third case that is exemplified by cost-variance analysis.

Now it is quite true that this traditional approach to management control recognises future control: it calls it planning. However, the very fact that planning is supposed to be *different* from control acts as a barrier to its integration into the total concept of the control system.

Planning and Control

Intuitively obvious, it is this dichotomy that appears to have hidden the true meaning of planning. Instead of the emphasis being placed on its role as a tool for controlling the future, emphasis is put on its relation to what orthodoxy restricts under the heading of control. *First* plans are made: *then* control takes over and ensures that plans are, so far as possible, adhered to. Now it cannot be denied that certain planning processes are discrete, and take place at specified intervals (such as a year) in a very formal way. Yet they are only a part of a much more general process which is taking place at all levels of the organisation all the time: the process of trying to foresee the next move in the organisation's relationship to its environment and take such action as will minimise disruption caused by any change.

Plans are formalisations of the process, and are useful in the total control process. Yet planning should be seen as a part of control rather than a prior but distinct process. As the framework stands, it seems to imply that if certain bureaucratic routines are kept to, control will result. This ignores the work of Burns and Stalker (1961) and Lawrence and Lorsch (1967) which suggest that in dynamic environments, the best organisation structures are those that are more prepared to adapt and which design their structure so as to facilitate this adaptation. Reliance on predesigned procedures will not do this: and as such, the emphasis we find here is positively misleading as a prescription, since environments are, in general, becoming more and more dynamic (cf. Emery and Trist, 1965). Remarkably, Anthony, Dearden and Bedford acknowledge contingency theory (pp. 46–7) while in most of the book continuing to put forward universal propositions.

A similar rigidity is to be seen in Anthony's distinction between strategic planning, management control and task control.

The Three-Way Distinction

As we have seen in our description of their framework, Anthony Dearden and Bedford consider this three-way distinction to be of great importance in defining their topic. Considerable detail is given to ensure that there is no confusion among the three levels. Despite the authors' assurance that 'we do not mean to imply that the three planning and control processes can be separated by sharply-defined boundaries; one shades into another' there is no disguising the fact that by designating the 'middle ground' of control as management control, and specifying that it is essentially psychologically-based, an opportunity is lost to emphasise the holistic nature of control. By creating this distinction they ensure that the general control problem – that which, in Beer's (1981) terminology would be systems 4 and 5 – is not to be confused with 'management control'. They ensure that the reader's attention is moved also from the more routine day-to-day control problems which are designated 'task control'. Of course, they do not deny that these are control processes: but the very act of shunting them off to a different world leaves one without an integrating framework to see how the three 'levels' fit in and interrelate in the achievement of control.

A particularly unfortunate result of this, then, is the lack of a holistic framework once again: a lack of recognition that the control problems interrelate in such a way that action to improve control in one area of the organisation will almost certainly have repercussions on other aspects of the organisation.

This causes another conceptual difficulty: because in defining the predictive function as the task of top management (that is, within the province of strategic planning) they fail to make it clear to the middle manager (supposedly particularly concerned with their concept of management control) that a predictive function as to future actions in his environment is essential to his effectiveness as a manager. Instead, there is an emphasis on the feedback function: on corrections of the past. Yet prediction, as part of the control process, is central to all kinds of control continuously at all levels of the organisation. It is particularly interesting that management control under Anthony's definition is claimed to be 'total control': because when it comes to a definition of that concept, the closed system nature of traditional thinking becomes plain:

> a management control system is a *total organizational system* in that it embraces all aspects of organization operations.
>
> (p. 13)

The Management Control Structure

When we turn to look at Part II of Anthony, Dearden and Bedford's book, we find that the structure of management control is concerned with responsibility centres of various kinds. Responsibility is a human concept: which brings us to the interesting observation that management control is being defined as control over people rather than control over or for an organisation as such. Control the people, the argument seems to suggest, and you have achieved control over the organisation. It will be seen how this links in to the social-psychological basis which, it is claimed, underlies management control.

Yet a proper understanding of control, as has already been suggested, is predicated on an understanding of the necessary relation between an organisation and its environment. Control over the people within the organisation in the very restricted sense is not control in a true sense. In the first place, it assumes a relation between the people 'controlled' and the actual operating system which interacts with the organisation's environment: and in the second place, it ignores one crucial feature of organisational control: the extent to which the organisation can dominate its environment (Rhenman). Being able to ensure that the managers controlled do as the plans require is a very different concept from being able to ensure that the organisation adapts, or dominates so as to reduce the need for adapting, to its environment. This match between the organisation's capabilities and the environment's demands is crucial: but a myopic insistence on profit-achievement will not ensure this in the long run.

Reification: Deification?

The nature of the relationship between the organisation and the society in which it is embedded has already been briefly discussed. The nature of the organisation's relation to its environment and of its goals cannot be understood except in the context of its relations with its wider social context. Equally, it is necessary to understand this context in order to understand the relation of the organisation to those who make it up: in particular, those who work for it.

In speaking of an organisation in this way, we are implicitly reifying it. To reify an organisation in isolation from its context however is a dangerous analytic approach.

Anthony, Dearden and Bedford do not analyse the social context of the organisation at all: and in such an omission they allow themselves to imply that, not only is the organisation a significant entity in itself (which is as may be) but it can do 'what it wishes': and it has 'goals' which appear from nowhere and then become imperatives upon the managers who must try to satisfy those goals.

> A management control system ... is tailored to the particular goals of and the particular strategies of the organization ... the systems designer should insure that the control system is consistent with the organization's goals, whatever they are ... we use the term *goals* to mean broad, fairly timeless statements of what the organization wants to achieve.

'Wanting to achieve', we suggest, is simply not on. The goals of the organisation cannot be considered in isolation from the context in which it exists: and that context will constrain the organization – it will imbue the organisation through the fact that the members of the organisational coalition are also members of the environment – in such a way that, although not preordained, the goals cannot be considered as decidable 'by' the organisation. This is not achieved by the acknowledgement that 'goal changes may have to be made when the conditions of survival and growth imposed by a changed environment demand them' (p. 95) because there is still an unacceptable degree of voluntarism, rationality and intentionality implicit here.

Moreover, this approach distances the participants from the organisation. An organisational system is certainly more than the sum of its parts: but nevertheless it does consist of those parts, and it is misleading to treat it as some kind of deity that is to be served by those who happen to be its managers.

Structural Invariance

Finally, we must consider the way in which a school of thought such as this views organisational structure. Any organisation does indeed have a real structure but that structure is not the one which appears on organisation charts, or on the basis of which accounting systems are set up which allocate responsibility on the basis of responsibility centres. The true structure of an organisation is a renegotiation through a continuous process, and it is continually changing in subtle ways (see, for example, Murray and Puxty, 1981). The formal structure is a 'wish' by certain 'designers' of the organisation: it is in reality merely one more constraint on the way in which the real structure comes into being and changes over time.

This real structure is not considered by the traditional 'rationalist' school at all. Instead, the 'formal', planned structure is treated as if it were the real and only structure; and it is considered as *invariant*.[6]

Despite any evidence that organisations do change their structures (both real and formal) and despite the evidence of researchers that structure must be changed as other circumstances alter (see the considerable literature which treats structure in relation to environment, technology and size) no mention is made of changes, and in fact, the very treatment in the book we have been considering – in which various kinds of responsibility centre are treated in one chapter each, as if they were essential for all organisations at all times – gives an impression of such a narrow focus.

This is particularly dangerous when one considers the influence such a book has. It is intended as a manual to teach management control. It is concerned particularly with case studies, as a result of which the student is intended to come to conclusions as to the 'best' solution to adopt. If (s)he is constrained from adopting a solution of structural change, his or her mental set will become imbued with the notion that structure is and should be invariant: the structural change solution is not one that will even be considered (see Puxty and Chua, this volume).

CONCLUSION

It is particularly unfortunate that at a time of rapid change and development in our understanding of organisational processes (see, for example, the work of Hage, Aiken, Pennings, Aldrich, Weick and Karpik) a myopic approach to control can still be taught as legitimately useful: and indeed still considered the standard work on its topic. It is quite possible that in certain organisations in certain circumstances in certain cultural milieux the approach advocated by Anthony, Dearden and Bedford might be effective. But even in these circumstances it is being effective on the basis of a partial truth: one which, moreover, acknowledges no contingency of essential variables other than that implicit in those authors' last part (non-profit organisations and so on).

It is even more unfortunate when alternative schemas are becoming available. Despite Hofstede's (1975) misgivings, there is no poverty of management control philosophy. Open systems approaches to organisations are fruitful; cybernetics is not merely a matter of negative feedbacks (as Hofstede seems to imagine): and the understanding we already have of organisational processes, although certainly still fragmented, is sufficient to give a beginning to a new route that is still unmapped by Anthony, Dearden and Bedford.

Notes

1. This broadening out was also to be seen in other areas at the same time: see in particular the emergence of 'business policy' as a subject.
2. This is not to suggest that this work was a sudden efflorescence: its roots may be seen in the earlier work by Simon, *et al.* (1954).
3. Indeed, Anthony recognised early on the role of a preliminary framework: '. . . development of a framework or a conceptual scheme often has led to progress, *even though the framework turns out to be wrong*' (his emphasis) (Anthony, 1965).
4. One page of discussion is provided of 'Externally Oriented Organization Theory' (pp. 41–2). It mentions none of these authorities, however.
5. This succinct definition is taken from Anthony and Dearden (1976). The philosophy in the latest edition, though less tightly defined, is otherwise quite similar.
6. We are indebted to John Machin for pointing this out.

References

H. E. Aldrich, *Organizations and Environments* (Prentice-Hall, 1979).

R. N. Anthony, *Planning and Control Systems* (Harvard, 1965).

R. N. Anthony, J. Dearden and R. F. Vancil, *Management Control Systems* (Irwin, 1965).

R. N. Anthony and J. Dearden, *Management Control Systems* (3rd edn: Irwin, 1976).

R. N. Anthony, J. Dearden and N. Bedford, *Management Control Systems* (5th edn: Irwin, 1984).

C. Argyris, *The Impact of Budgets on People* (Controllership Foundation, 1952).

S. Beer, *Brain of the Firm* (2nd edn: Wiley, 1981).

T. Burns and G. M. Stalker, *The Management of Innovation* (Tavistock, 1961).

J. Dermer, *Management Planning and Control Systems* (Irwin, 1977).

R. B. Duncan, 'Characteristics of Organizational Environments and Perceived Environmental Uncertainty', *Administrative Science Quarterly* 17 (1972) pp. 313–27.

F. Emery and E. Trist, 'The Causal Texture of Organizational Environments', *Human Relations* 18 (1965) pp. 21–32.

K. J. Euske, *Management Control: Planning, Control, Measurement and Evaluation* (Addison-Wesley, 1984).

G. B. Giglioni and A. G. Bedeian, 'A Conspectus of Management Control Theory: 1900–1972', *Academy of Management Journal* (June 1974) pp. 292–305.

G. H. Hofstede, 'The Poverty of Management Control Philosophy', Working paper 75–44 (Dec. 1975); European Institute for Advanced Studies in Management.

L. Karpik, *Organization and Environment* (Sage, 1978).

H. Koontz, C. O'Donnell and H. Weihrich, *Management* (7th edn: McGraw-Hill, 1980).

P. R. Lawrence and J. W. Lorsch, *Organization and Environment* (Harvard, 1967).

E. A. Lowe, 'On the Idea of a Management Control System', *Journal of Management Studies* (Feb. 1971) pp. 1–12.

E. A. Lowe and J. M. McInnes, 'Control in Socio-Economic Organizations: A Rationale for the Design of Management Control Systems (Section 1)', *Journal of Management Studies* (May 1971) pp. 213–27.

E. A. Lowe, A. G. Puxty and A. M. Tinker, 'Improving the Accounting Function for Society: Proposals for a GST-Based Newcomer to Social Science', *Proceedings of the Silver Anniversary Meeting of the Society for General Systems Research* London (Aug. 1979).

J. G. March and H. A. Simon, *Organizations* (Wiley, 1958).

G. Murray and A. G. Puxty, 'An Action Approach to Control Systems', *Managerial Finance*, vol. 6, no. 1 (1981) pp. 9–19.

J. Pfeffer and G. Salancik, *The External Control of Organizations: A Resource Dependence Perspective* (New York: Harper and Row, 1978).

A. G. Puxty and W. F. Chua, 'Ideology, Rationality and the Management Control Process' this volume.

E. Rhenman, *Organization Theory for Long Range Planning* (Chichester: Wiley, 1973).

H. A. Simon, H. Guetzkow, G. Kozmetsky and G. Tyndall, *Centralization and Decentralization in Organizing the Controller's Department* (Controllership Foundation, 1954).

S. Terreberry, 'The Evolution of Organizational Environments', *Administrative Science Quarterly* (March 1968) vol. 12,4, pp. 540–613.

N. Wiener, *Cybernetics* (2nd edn: MIT Press, 1961).

[4]

POSITIVE AND NEGATIVE CONTROLS IN BUSINESS

by Sir Geoffrey Vickers

I. DEFINITIONS

I use the word control throughout this paper in an exact and rather narrow sense. By a control I intend a means of comparing any state, actual or hypothetical, with a standard. The building contractor plots on charts against time the projected course of many interdependent operations; and against these courses he plots, week by week, the progress actually achieved. Thus he is able continually to compare what is with what ought to be; and this is the essence of control.

Some of the standards which the contractor plots are limits which must not be transgressed. Others will give cause for concern if the actual diverges from the standard in either direction. It does not matter, for example, how quickly planning permission is obtained, so long as it is obtained before he wants to begin to build; but it does matter if one phase of building is completed so much ahead of time that the labour cannot be at once deployed on the next phase. The first type of control I refer to as negative control and I call the standard a limit. The second I refer to as positive control and I call the standard a norm.

When performance transgresses a limit or diverges from a norm, the damage which ensues varies with the amount of the divergence but not in any constant way. Within certain limits it may be negligible. Thereafter, the damage may be acute at first and may then accrue more slowly; or (more usually) it may accrue at an accelerating rate. In either case, there is likely to come a point beyond which dramatic and irreversible changes occur. For example, shortage of cash causes progressive embarrassment, as it becomes more acute; but if it reaches the point at which the bank refuses to meet the weekly wages cheque, its effect suddenly overflows and brings the whole operation to a standstill. Beyond each limit and on either side of each norm there usually exist points such as this, which cannot be passed without effecting radical and irreversible change. These points of no return I call thresholds.

I invite you then to regard a business and the processes which compose it as a system of variables, which can maintain itself only so long as the values and mutual relations of the variables are kept within certain thresholds. Within these limits management at all levels operates. When management can compare what is happening with standards defining what should or should not be happening if its plans are to be realized, it is exercising control.

The comparison of the actual with the standard (be it norm or limit) gives a signal, conveniently called a 'mis-match' signal. If control is to be effective, this signal has to release the right sort of action, that is, action which will bring the situation back towards the norm or away from the limit. Often, at least in English, the word control covers the remedial action as well as the eliciting of the signal. Sometimes it is used simply of the remedial action. For example, a skidding car is said to be out of control, whether the driver realizes all too well the difference between what is and what ought to be or whether he is too drunk to know that anything is the matter. In French and German the corresponding word is kept much more carefully for the sense in which I am using it and this is desirable, especially when we are talking about the kind of controls which I have in mind. If we were talking only about thermostats and safety valves – equally, examples of positive and negative controls – the distinction would not be important, for the way in which a thermostat or a safety valve recognizes deviation from a norm or arrival at a limit is inseparable from the remedial action which it takes. But with the controls which I have in mind, the question – 'What is the position?' is distinct from the question – 'What do we do about it?' and we must have separate words for them. I am keeping the word control for the first half of the process.

The deviation which a control registers has a time dimension. The building contractor is concerned to know not merely that an operation is *x* days behind schedule but also that it is running *y* per cent more slowly than schedule. The rate at which it is deviating from a norm or approaching a limit is at least as important as the amount of the current deviation or the current safety margin as the case may be.

I do not apologize for beginning with this careful and arid definition of terms, for the word control is one of the most confused words in the English language and in business it has collected so many emotional overtones that in some quarters it is hardly usable. Yet it is fundamental to management whether of money, materials, processes or men. It is equally essential to the idea of self-control and hence to all discussion of decentralization.

2. USES AND DANGERS OF CONTROL

Control serves three different purposes. It provides means to compare performance (*a*) with norms and limits which are given by the nature of the operation, (*b*) with forecasts reflecting the expected results of policies, and (*c*) with targets representing goals for attainment. The first shows whether the system is approaching an objectively defined limit, e.g. exhaustion of cash resources or moving favourably or otherwise according to objectively defined indices of efficiency such as profitability or rate of turnover. The second shows whether the system is following the course forecast as most probable on the basis of its policy and thus checks whether current plans are being realized and provides a basis for future planning. The third provides a measure of success.

The second and third differ in that they use slightly different norms and limits. For most planning purposes the estimate should be as realistic as possible, i.e. it should be as likely to be too high as too low. For some, e.g. for controlling the margin of cash resources and in other controls related to thresholds, it should be extremely conservative. By contrast, where the standard is used as a standard of success, it should be as high as will give a reasonable chance of its being attained. It is thus seldom possible to make one set of standards serve both purposes.

This difficulty is accentuated by two factors which today are more troublesome than they need be. The first is the tendency for standards to become too precise. It is seldom possible to estimate what should be without a large margin of error. These margins tend to disappear on paper and there is always a danger that the resultant figure will acquire a sanctity which it does not deserve, the assumptions on which it is based being forgotten.

This difficulty is partly technical. It is easy to express estimates as a figure with a margin of error. It is inconvenient to aggregate margins of error but it is not impossible; simple mathematical techniques are available. It would be welcome, if accountants would devise acceptably simple methods of preserving margins of error in our estimates. Meantime, it is not surprising that business men often prefer to derive norms and limits from their inner consciousness, rather than allow themselves to be forced into the unreal rigidity of a figure.

If all standards could be represented as bands, rather than as precise figures, this difficulty would disappear and it would become easier to use the same standards for target and for forecast. The top of the bracket would represent the target, the mean would be the forecast and the bottom would be the threshold.

The second difficulty springs from the need to include in forecasts an allowance for uncontrollable contingencies, whilst targets for success need to be related as closely as may be to factors under the control of the authority whose success is to be measured. These allowances can of course be distinguished within the composition of the standard; but the larger they bulk, the harder it becomes to reconcile effectively the standards of forecast and target.

No information is useful which cannot be compared with a standard in one of the three senses mentioned above. Very little information is useful which cannot be compared with forecasts or targets.

The virtue of formalizing control in this way is that it makes the standards of comparison precise and explicit. It thus ensures that they shall be formulated with due care. It reveals inconsistencies between one standard and another and between the standards of one user and another. It makes standards public and fosters common and realistic views of what is, and common and realistic expectations of what should be. These are benefits of the greatest value. To secure them is a major responsibility of management.

The main dangers of control, as we at present know it, are that it is liable to focus attention too exclusively on fields where control can be established; to magnify errors which are built in to the control system itself; and to withdraw awareness from the wide and important fields where action is not in fact controllable.

3. THE ORGANIZATION OF CONTROLS

Control is used to guide action. It must therefore be available at each level where action is taken and the guidance it supplies at each level must be relevant to the action which is taken *at that level.*

Control systems are often more elaborate at higher than at lower levels of an organization. The only justification for this — and it is at best an inadequate and partial one — is that higher levels are blind without organized controls whilst lower levels are more directly aware of what is going on. There is in fact no level, not even the individual level, at which we are aware of *all* that is going on. Selection is involved even in individual perception. At every level we have to choose what indices to watch and it is useful to make the choice explicit.

Furthermore, remedial action depends largely on people at each action level being directly aware of what is going wrong and hence of what is required of them. They should need direction from a level above only when the action required is related to some situation which can only be seen from the level above — as when the overall financial position of the undertaking limits what would otherwise be appropriate action by one section of it.

In a large organization it is necessary and proper to insist that indices which need to be recorded and used centrally, are recorded and used in the same way at lower levels. Given this, it should scarcely ever occur that information required at a higher level has not already been collected and examined at a lower level or that an inquiry arising at a higher level has not already been asked and answered at a lower level. The only proper exceptions are those rare ones when the information sought is only relevant when it has been aggregated. With this sole exception, if a lower level has to prepare information or answer questions specially at the request of a higher level, the fact is itself prima facie evidence that the lower level has neglected its job or that the higher level has asked an irrelevant question.

Generally speaking, the indices of control become less significant and less useful at progressively higher levels. At every aggregation, significance is lost. Control at any level cannot be more effective than it is at the levels below. If top management can ensure adequate control at operating levels, control at higher levels will present no difficulties.

Since the 'lowest' – and thus the most important – 'level' is the individual, it is worthy of note that these foregoing principles apply equally to the self-control of the individual, both generally and in the doing of his job in business. Individuals also control their own behaviour by comparing its results with positive and negative standards (norms and limits) which they have somehow established. Ineffective human conduct is more often due to deviance in the setting of the norms and limits (the 'ought to be' and the 'ought not to be') or to failure to appreciate the relevant situation (the 'is') than to inability to act on the mis-match signal. It follows that the effective control of a business depends absolutely (amongst other things) on the ability of each individual man and woman in it to recognize what the situation requires of him or her and to act accordingly.

4. THE LIMITATIONS OF CONTROL

Not all action is 'controllable'. The more important it is, the less controllable it is likely to be. This is, unhappily, inherent in the nature of control.

The helmsman derives from the compass card a continuous stream of signals, showing the divergence of the ship's head from the appointed course. His response is expressed in a movement of the rudder within seconds after he receives the visual signal; and the result of the rudder movement is fed back to him, again within seconds, by the further movement of the ship's head, reflected in the compass. Conditions of control are thus almost optimal. Yet even in this brief time lag many effects of wind and sea, some of them more potent than the rudder, have added their quota to the movement of the ship's head. What the helmsman sees, in the movement of the ship's head, is not the result of his helm movements alone but the result of many forces, of which his helm movements are only one. He gets sufficient guidance to steer by only because most of these other forces are fairly regular and of those which are not — such as an exceptional sea on the bow — he is usually directly aware.

In the control of human affairs, information about the current position and current trends is usually intermittent, partial and sometimes greatly in arrear, whilst the results of our responses may not return for judgment for months or years; by which time they may have become mixed with many more potent variables, perhaps unpredictable or even unknown and may furnish neither validation of the past nor guide for the future. The field of control is strictly limited.

It is important therefore —

to extend the field of control as widely as may be;

to recognize its limitations;

to understand the principles of action outside the field of control and to have the courage to act on them.

The field of control is limited primarily by the length of time which elapses before the results of action return for judgment and by the nature of variables which by that time have intervened to mask its results.

Within these general limitations, it is limited further by the degree of precision with which we can measure the actual and define the standard with which the actual should be compared.

Whether the conditions of control exist or not, human behaviour, whether in business or out of it, is basically rule-governed. It is guided by applying to the situation, as perceived, rules which take one of two forms. They may take the form — 'To achieve this, do that' or — 'To avoid this, do that'. Alternatively, they may take the more general form 'In these circumstances, do this'; or 'In these circumstances, avoid doing that'. Since whatever we do has far more effects than we intend or can foresee, we act on rules of the second more general pattern more often and more justifiably than we realize.

When the conditions of control are present, we can check the results of our rule-governed behaviour and revise our rules or the application of them — or, more probably, our view of the situation in which we are acting — in accordance with our experience. This is of the greatest value, the more so because the conditions of control are so often not present.

Moreover, the existence of control, even in a limited field, reminds us that all action is tentative, based on assumptions which may prove to be mistaken. This helps to prevent us becoming more blind than we need be.

It is equally important that the use of controls, where they are available, should not spoil our nerve or our skill in those more numerous and more important situations where decisions must be taken at times when we are denied the reassurance of control, either because the feedback is too slow to be useful or because 'bad visibility' obscures the actual or the norm or both.

LONDON

[5]

ON THE IDEA OF A MANAGEMENT CONTROL SYSTEM: INTEGRATING ACCOUNTING AND MANAGEMENT CONTROL

BY

E. A. Lowe

The Need for a System

The need for a planning and control system within a business organization flows from certain general characteristics of the nature of business enterprises, the chief of which are as follows: firstly, the enterprise has (by definition) organizational objectives, as distinct from the separable and individual ones of the members constituting the 'managerial coalition';[1] secondly, the managers of the sub-units of the enterprise must necessarily be ambivalent in view of their own personal goals, as well as have a good deal of discretion in deciding how they should behave and in formulating their part of any overall plan to achieve organizational objectives; thirdly, business situations (and people's behaviour) are full of uncertainty, *internally* as well as externally to the business enterprise; fourthly, there is a necessity to economize, in human endeavours we are invariably concerned with an allocation of effort and resources so as to achieve a given set of objectives using the minimum amount of total economic resources and effort; or alternatively put, to achieve a maximum amount of objective attainment, given a specified amount of resources and effort.

Purpose of a System

The purpose of a unified management control system is to ensure that actions are in accordance with the firm's plans to achieve its objectives. Hence, planning and controlling are inseparable parts of an overall effective management control system and looked at in this way such a system is primarily concerned with the construction of an organization and with long range planning. Looked at from a functional viewpoint it is an attempt to enforce the integration of separate control devices[2] and of the separate functional areas of the firm (marketing, production, product development, personnel, accounting, etc.) into one information-for-control network so as

[1] As defined in Cyert, R. M., and March, J. G., *A Behavioural Theory of the Firm*, Englewood Cliffs, N.J.: Prentice-Hall Inc., 1963.

[2] For a formidable list of such separate control devices used, see for instance Rathe, A. W., 'Management Controls in Business', in Malcolm, D., and Rowe, A. J., (*eds*), *Management Control Systems*, New York: Wiley, 1960.

to improve upon present decision rules and decision-making. Different decision procedures have complicated interactions throughout an enterprise and since these inter-relations are complex and indirect it is important to attempt to consider the whole enterprise as one model (or system) so that the effect of, or implications of, any one decision or decision procedure can be traced throughout the whole enterprise. Decision-making will thus be improved through an integrated management control system largely through the systems ability to identify and incorporate within one system conflicting signals and provide mechanisms through which unrequired redundancies can be eliminated, as well as conflicts resolved.

Looked at from yet a further viewpoint it should ideally be an attempt to bring together the various disciplines most relevant to business enterprise, particularly economics, accounting, cybernetics, systems theory and analysis, behavioural science and organizational theory, so as to produce an inter-disciplinary (and more realistic) model of business decision-making.[3]

The vital part of the control aspect of the system is an information feed-back designed so as to reveal: firstly, the magnitude of the discrepancy, relative and absolute, between actual and planned performance;[4] secondly,

[3] This inter-disciplinary approach to control is not the traditional one of course. In the past heavy reliance has been placed upon purely accounting models of control — for a description of which, see any good accounting text, e.g. Shillinglaw, Gordon, *Cost Accounting: Analysis and Control*, Homewood, Ill.: Irwin, 1961; Horngren, C. T., *Cost Accounting: A Managerial Emphasis*, Englewood Cliffs, N.J.: Prentice-Hall Inc., 1962. The newer, more comprehensive, models built upon the modern organization theory are propounded in Barnard, Chester I., *The Functions of the Executive*, Cambridge, Mass.: Harvard University Press, 1938; in Simon, Herbert A., *Administrative Behaviour (2nd Ed.)*, New York: MacMillan, 1957; and in March, J. G., and Simon, H. A., *Organizations*, New York: Wiley, 1960; and Cyert in the former book, and in Cyert, R. M., and March, J. G., *A Behavioural Theory of the Firm*, Englewood Cliffs, N.J.: Prentice-Hall Inc., 1963. Pioneering and interesting work on these kinds of models has been carried out by Forrester, Jay W., *Industrial Dynamics*, New York: MIT Press and Wiley, 1961; in Bonini, C. P., *Simulation of Information and Decision Systems in the Firm*, Englewood Cliffs, N.J.: Prentice-Hall, 1963; in Sprowls, R. Clay, and Asimov, M.,'A Computer Simulated Business Firm', see Malcolm, D., and Rowe, A. J., op. cit.; in Rowe, Alan J., 'A Research Approach in Management Control', see Malcolm, D., and Rowe, A. J., op. cit., and by business games researchers; for example Buchin, S. I., in 'The Harbets Simulation Exercise and Management Control', in Bonini, C. P., Jaedicke, R. K., and Wagner, H. M., (*eds*), *Management Control, New Directions in Basic Research*, New York: McGraw-Hill, 1964, describes an interesting experimental investigation on these lines, and Cohen K. J., and Rhenman, E., in 'The Role of Management Games in Education and Research', *Management Science*, Vol. 7, No. 2, 1961, discuss the possible management research uses of business games or exercises. A piece of research by Woodward, Joan, and Eilon S., entitled 'A Field Study of Management Control in Manufacturing Industry' (presented at the International Conference on Operational Research and the Social Sciences, at Cambridge, England, Sept. 1964), has produced concrete evidence of some of the unfortunate consequences of a number of functional control systems operating in parallel rather than in unison, and emphasizes the need for integrated and inter-disciplinary control systems.

[4] For these purposes one would doubt whether, for instance, standard costing variance analysis has the sensitivity and methodology to give feedback information at the 'strategic' level necessary for management control.

and more crucially, whether plans should be modified in the light of events and performance so as to better achieve objectives.

The flows within such an information system are primarily those about the management of production and marketing systems and their economic environments so that typically the flows concern: revenues, costs, inputs, outputs, stock levels, competitors, demand, relevant general economic variables, technological changes, etc. However it is also necessary to emphasize that behavioural and sociological variables are important ingredients of management planning and control systems, for two reasons, amongst others. Firstly, management control is a process of ensuring that what in some senses 'ought' to be done is done and of detecting when it is. Clearly 'ought' implies a system of values, and control is therefore concerned with determining a system of work values for all members of an enterprise and therefore with social norms about work and effort; with recruitment; with promotion; and with training. But operationally 'ought' cannot be simply a metaphysical matter and within the organizational situation it must be argued that it is also a matter of responsibility and authority; nevertheless, it well behoves the planner and controller to take notice of these sociological aspects of the systems design.[5] Secondly, an information-for-control system has a large human element within it and therefore we need to take account of the observed characteristics of human behaviour within organizations. Thus concepts of an economic-behavioural theory of the firm such as information bias, organizational slack, aspiration levels, pressure, conflict, etc. are likely to be highly relevant.[6]

Control-in-the-Large and in-the-Small

In order to emphasize the concept of a 'Management Planning and Control System' that is a *total* business systems approach, it may be useful to distinguish between two distinct concepts of control. For want of a better name, the total systems approach has sometimes been referred to as *Control-in-the-Large* to distinguish it from *Control-in-the-Small.*[7]

Control-in-the-Large implies a specified decision-making system to achieve organizational objectives and involves the design of a total system of policies, procedures, decision rules, internal pricing for resources allocation, etc., for all functions, which take into account the interactions of all parts of the system. A further crucial element is that the decision procedures of the total

[5] See Baldamus, W., *Efficiency and Effort*, London: Tavistock, 1962.

[6] See Argyris, C., *The Impact of Budgets on People*, New York: Controllership Foundation, Inc., 1952; McGregor, D., 'The Role of Staff in Modern Industry', in Schultz, G. P., and Whisler, T. L., (*ed.*), *Management Organization and the Computer*, Glencoe, Ill.: The Free Press, 1960; Stedry, A. C., *Budget Control and Cost Behaviour*, Englewood Cliffs, N.J.: Prentice-Hall, 1960.

[7] As for instance discussed by Bonini in 'Simulation of Organizational Behavior', in Bonini, C. P., Jaedicke, R. K., and Wagner, H. M., (*eds*), *Management Control: New Directions in Basic Research*, New York: McGraw-Hill, 1964.

system approach must constitute a complete programme. That is it must be possible to specify what decision is to be made for each and every situation (in a flow-charting sense). For example, how much stock is to be carried, how many workers hired, what prices should be, what advertising expenditure should be, what production would be, etc., in any given situation, at particular decision points in time. Each of the above decision variables, is viewed as a function of a whole series of other variables. Collectively these variables constitute the means of describing managerial situations.[8]

Control-in-the-Small on the other hand lays emphasis upon the separate parts of the enterprise. Each sub-unit manager is viewed as being concerned primarily with his own unit and not so much with the effects of his decisions upon the whole enterprise. Also each manager is not given anything like a complete set of decision procedures for all circumstances (i.e. a complete programme). The viewpoint is usually that individual managers are paid to use their judgment not follow rules. There is of course one very good reason why most control procedures are of the 'in-the-Small' variety, that is to say, we generally do not yet know enough about how the business actually works (or how it should work) to be able to programme for the total set of possible or probable decision situations. Also we need to consider whether a total enterprise model would not also be too complex and difficult to handle by traditional analytical methods; however, simulation techniques offer more promise in this respect. A further fundamental question concerns what kind of managers (as human beings) do we want and how would they be affected by the nature of such kinds of control systems. Such matters concerning 'management philosophy' are highly relevant to the design of a control system but will not be discussed here any further.

A good example of this narrower notion of control, Control-in-the-Small, is a budgetary cost control system. Generally costs are allocated and apportioned to each of the sub-units to give the individual manager information about the working efficiency of his unit in isolation. Little or no information is usually given to him by the costing system about the effects of his decisions upon other sub-units and upon the firm as a whole and where it is given it is often highly misleading.[9] Perhaps this is primarily because accounting method has little to offer about the subtle input-output relations within the organization. This is not to say of course that accounting systems do not fulfil adequately a multitude of control purposes — the financial accounting

[8] For a complete description of one version of such a model see Bonini, C. P., *Simulation of Information and Decision Systems in the Firm*, Englewood Cliffs, N.J.: Prentice-Hall Inc., 1963.

[9] This may not be thought by some to be strictly true. The purpose of allocating general overheads to individual departments in accounting control systems is intended to do precisely this. However, it is difficult to take these (usually) arbitrary procedures seriously in this context of discussion.

system is, in fact, the most effective control-in-the-large system in general use at present.

The budgetary control system serves to illustrate another characteristic of present control-in-the-small systems: that is their general neglect of communication and behavioural aspects of the control problem. As Stedry[10] has pointed out 'management by exception' tends to make superior subordinate relations revolve around things that have gone wrong thus making their communications generally about criticism and punishment. One implication is that control systems should also attempt to distribute rewards as systematically and positively as they do punishments. Reward should not be seen as an absence of punishment if managers are to be motivated so as to best achieve organization objectives.

Towards the Design of a Management Control System

A management control system might be briefly defined as a system of organizational information seeking and gathering, accountability, and feedback designed to ensure that the enterprise adapts to changes in its substantial environment and that the work behaviour of its employees is measured by reference to a set of operational sub-goals (which conform with overall objectives) so that the discrepancy between the two can be reconciled and corrected for.

Decision-making is the basic concept in a modern approach to the study and analysis of an organization and the idea of a 'decision' provides a possible basis for a control system design. Organizational theorists see the enterprise as a bounded collection of information and decision centres (with information links between them) acting upon a derived set of decision rules. Almost invariably each centre is neither purely an information-processor or decision-maker but partly one and partly the other.

The principal elements of the system might be as follows:[11]

Decision Centres

Each consists of an individual or a group (or possibly a machine!) with a specified role and scope of action, charged with selecting one course of action from the total set of specified alternative courses of action in any given situation, according to a given decision rule.

Decision Rules

A decision rule consists of a specific procedure (or programme) for selecting an action from the total set of possible alternative actions. The rule will

[10] Charnes, A., and Stedry, A., 'Exploratory Models in the Theory of Budget Control', in Cooper, W. W., Leavitt, H. J., and Shelly II, M. W., (*eds*), *New Perspectives in Organization Research*, New York: Wiley, 1964.

[11] These elements are those of Bonini's analysis, see Bonini, C. P., op. cit.

also include the underlying premises which must be specified in order to operate the rule. For example the production decision for any given period might be to take the higher of the sales figures for the three preceding periods. A pricing decision for a given period might be to add 20 per cent to the defined average cost of last period's output. These rules assume as premises the last three periods sales figures and the last period's average cost, respectively. The parameters of these decision rules, namely 20 per cent, one period, and three periods could be changed (without changing the basic decision rule) as circumstances change.

The above are examples of 'objective' or factual type premises but a model might also take account of subjective-type assumptions, such as the personal values, ability to bias information, aspirations and professional allegiances of the decision-makers within decision and information centres and the organizational pressure (and slacks), punishments and rewards as developed by Cyert and March, with others.[12]

Information Centres

It is conceptually useful to distinguish between decision centres and information centres but in the real world all decision centres must be information centres, *ipso facto* (since they at least must inform about decisions), and *vice versa* (since they must decide upon what information to gather and what to pass on). Information centres collect, analyse, store and transmit information about the internal operations of the enterprise and/or its external environment. More usually it will be quantitative type data but it may simply be advice or decisions or other qualitative information.

Information Links

Each information link consists of a flow-line for a certain specified type or types of information from one decision/information centre to another. Again the model of the organization can be more or less behavioural. We can choose to include only 'factual' information or we can also consider behavioural attributes of information flows relating to conflict between sub-units, felt pressures, information bias, etc.

Management Decision System

The decision system consists of the complete collection of decision rules and since decision rules imply the information premises underlying them, it also embraces the rest of the information system.

[12] Cyert, R. M., and March, J. G., *A Behavioural Theory of the Firm*, Englewood Cliffs, N.J.: Prentice-Hall Inc., 1963. Such behavioural factors might, for instance, be formally included by adjusting for their model effect on the information flows within the model. Bonini's index of felt pressure is an example; see Bonini, C. P., op. cit.

The actual model derived by simulation methods from the actual system must specify the decision rules in each part of the system and the underlying information premises. The first step in constructing a management control system might therefore be a comprehensive systems analysis using the conceptual framework discussed above. That is to say identifying the main decision and information centres of the system, then identifying their decision and information collecting and transmitting rules to arrive at a total description of the decision system. If possible the methods of economics, accounting, cybernetics, systems theory and analysis, organizational theory and behavioural science should be used to identify the important variables present.

A central assumption is that the important elements of an actual functioning system can be represented in a meaningful and coherent fashion preferably as a mathematical model and that the system's decision-making can be optimized. It is perhaps relevant to note here the obvious but important point that it is not possible to optimize two functions simultaneously.[13] The importance of this fact becomes evident when we attempt to elucidate the objectives of a real-world business enterprise. Unlike the firm of classical economic theory, which has an unconstrained objective of profit maximization, we are likely to find that the real-world enterprise 'cares' about a great many things (i.e. has multiple strategies, values and goals) such as, 'we don't want to lay-off workers', 'we want our total asset structure to grow at a certain rate', 'we want a certain liquidity ratio', etc. The obvious procedure is to write such goals or objectives into our models as constraints. Moreover, operationally this is much to be preferred when constructing a model of a system.[14] Asking managers about the objectives of their firms in the abstract is not likely to produce very helpful answers. However, in the course of investigating the detailed decision rules of the enterprise one is likely to come across these secondary goals in a 'natural' way.

The literature of economics is full of very general arguments that such constraints can be derived from a pure (unconstrained) long-run profit maximizing objective.[15] However, nobody seems to be able to produce empirical evidence to show that these multiple goals (usually described as

[13] Unless we do so in some necessarily approximate manner, such as constructing a super-functional which is a weighted sum function of a set of criteria functions.

[14] For a general discussion on this aspect of model building, see Simon, Herbert A., 'On the Concept of Organizational Goal', *Administrative Science Quarterly*, June 1964; Charnes, A., and Cooper, W. W., 'Chance-Constrained Programming', *Management Science*, Vol. 6, No. 1, 1959; Charnes, A., and Cooper, W. W., 'Deterministic Equivalents for Optimizing and Satisficing Under Chance Constraints', *Operations Research*, Vol. 11, No. 1, 1963. See also, for description of certain classes of multiple goal models, Charnes, A., and Stedry, A., 'Investigations in the Theory of Multiple Budgeted Goals', in Bonini, C. P., Jaedicke, R. K., and Wagner, H. M., (*eds*), op. cit.

[15] For a discussion of the various views of economists, see Lipsey, R. G., *An Introduction to Positive Economics*, London: Weidenfeld and Nicolson, 1963, pp. 257–65.

being of a short-run nature although they are not necessarily so) derive from an explicit long-run profit maximizing objective and yet it is possible to find a good deal of evidence which suggests otherwise. It seems that businessmen do not see their business in this respect as an academic economist does. Alternatively one may simply dismiss the economist's profit maximizing theory as unscientific in Popper's terms.[16]

Relation of the Management Decision System to Control

The main justification for a control system within an enterprise is built upon the relation between information and behaviour. Behaviour which is not in accordance with the plan of action may be modified with the feedback given about such behaviour and it is the purpose of a control system to generate such information and use it so as to modify the plan in some realistic manner and/or bring about a closer correspondence between a plan and the execution of the plan. Within a complex organization information may well have different behavioural effects due to the circumstances of timing, method of presentation and linkings in the information system. Hence, stress is laid upon a comprehensive model based upon a detailed simulation of the system's interdependencies and interactions so that not only first but also second order effects can be traced. Clearly a rational correcting mechanism can only be forthcoming if in fact the basic causal patterns can be identified or inferred. This of course is where the traditional accounting control system is often found to be deficient. Accounting has no refined methods for identifying the basic causes of departures from a plan. A simulation model holds out much more hope in this respect but in a rather different way. That is to say control by simulation models is more concerned with redesigning the management decision system to better achieve the organization's objectives. The programme of decision procedures is an organizational plan as well as a control mechanism for controlling the execution of the plan.

From the control viewpoint, the important thing that the model will allow us to do, once it is complete, is to make hypotheses about the factors which influence the behaviour of the firm and thus trace the important variables and inter-relationships within an enterprise. In this sense we can learn to control the enterprise better by using the simulation model as a predicting device when important variables in the model are experimentally changed.

[16] See Cyert, R. M., Dill, W. R., and March, J. G., 'The Role of Expectations in Business Decision Making', *Administrative Science Quarterly*, Vol. 3, No. 3, 1958; Baumol, W. J., *Business Behaviour, Value and Growth*, New York: MacMillan, 1959; Williamson, D. E., *The Economics of Discretionary Behaviour*, Englewood Cliffs, N.J.: Prentice-Hall Inc., 1964, for some interesting observations and theory on this matter. Williamson in particular puts forward a model for testing hypotheses based upon the discretionary power of managers. See also Popper, K. P., *The Logic of Scientific Discovery*, London: Hutchinson, 1959.

These variables may of course relate either to internal factors (and therefore directly controllable by management) or to external ones, not directly controllable by management. However the latter variables are still the responsibility of top-management in the sense that they are required to predict their behaviour, measure their effect on organizational objectives, and take appropriate action.

In addition we can by simulation methods also examine the way in which control devices used in an enterprise, e.g. standard costing systems, quality control methods, inventory control procedures, etc., affect the likely behaviour of the enterprise viewed *as an entity*, by second order as well as first order effects, as well as individual and group behaviour *within* the enterprise. This is of course one of the important possible uses of Bonini's ideas for improving upon the design and use of actual control systems in practice.

The Validity of a Simulation Model

A most important question is that concerning 'how do we know whether any model derived by simulation methods is valid in the sense of being a real-world representation of the enterprise?' Simulation is really a reasoning by analogy and raises all the questions about a correct analogue. The simulation could of course never be in any sense an exact replica but it must be reasonably so according to some acceptable criteria. But with simulations of organizations the problem is likely to be much more acute. It may well be very difficult to evaluate exactly how useful the representation really is. It seems evident, for instance, that the present state of statistical methodology is not sufficiently advanced to allow a proper validation of these kinds of models which have numerous and complex interacting parts. Some measure of 'systems fit' is needed to help in analysing organizational simulations and thus building better, more realistic, simulations. One check, a rather weak one perhaps, is to use the model to trace out the path through time of characteristics of overall enterprise behaviour and possibly of the behaviour characteristics of parts of the enterprise. Bonini for instance in his work uses statistical experimental design to test his model of an hypothetical firm.

A major point to recognize about simulation techniques, as applied to large and complex man-machine systems, such as a business enterprise represents, is that it is largely experimental and untried but at the same time is interesting and full of possibilities. This may still mean that this application is only yet suitable for basic management research and not operational research within a business enterprise. But in any case looking at control in terms of simulation of the total enterprise always provides a valid way of thinking about the problem of management control and moreover of providing a set of criteria for analysing and judging the efficiency of actual control systems in use.

Developments in Accounting Approaches to Control

It is, of course, important to consider whether approaches other than the total systems simulation approach to the problem of control systems are likely, on balance, to be more suitable for enterprise control purposes. In general terms, it is reasonable to suggest that approaches which are basically of the Control-in-the-Large variety are preferable. An accounting type model has many advantages in this respect partly because the total accounting system of an enterprise is the best developed information system of the Control-in-the-Large kind, now in use despite the naivety of certain aspects of present practices as valid representations of economic and enterprise behaviour and as realistic control mechanisms.[17]

There are two main lines of current thought developing out of accounting models:

1. *The construction of quasi-decentralized control* by the use of accounting system values to construct internal quasi-markets through the use of transfer prices. The basic question posed by this approach to the control problem is 'under what conditions and circumstances can internal accounting, administrative-type, prices be attached to goods and services, which are the subject of internal transactions as between partially autonomous sub-units, so as to simultaneously maximize the profits of the whole enterprise and yet leave sub-unit managers to behave as if they were in business for themselves?'

   This line of thinking has been developed from a number of other viewpoints, as well as from accounting where the problem has generally been seen in terms of the concept of cost to be used when transferring goods and services as between supplying and receiving departments or divisions, for cost accounting purposes.

These other viewpoints are:

(a) Welfare economics, where the question has been 'whether a freely competitive market pricing system achieves the "best" allocation of resources within an economy?' The economist has naturally extended his interest from macro-systems to looking at micro-systems such as firms.[18]

[17] However one must always distinguish between the general power of *accounting method* and present *practices of orthodox accountancy* at any point in time.

[18] See Arrow, K. J., 'Optimization Decentralization and Internal Pricing in Business Firms', in *Contributions to Scientific Research in Management*, Los Angeles: Univ. of California, 1959; Gould, J. R., 'Internal Pricing in Firms When There are Costs of Using an Outside Market', *The Journal of Business*, January 1964; Hirshleifer, Jack, 'On the Economics of Transfer Pricing', *The Journal of Business*, Vol. 29, 1956; Hirshleifer, Jack, 'Economics of the Divisionalized Firm', *The Journal of Business*, Vol. 30, 1957.

(b) Organization theory where the idea has been explored in terms of the 'centralized versus decentralized management' controversy.[19]

It seems clear from the argument in the literature referred to above that the transfer pricing approach cannot be completely satisfactory as a solution to the control problem. On the other hand it has the great advantage that a price conveys a good deal of information and exerts a great deal of pressure in a most economical way. There are clear limits to its usefulness in general: firstly, every transaction as between sub-units could not be negotiated by means of transfer prices because negotiating costs would become too high; secondly, there is the important aspect of the matter that the consequences of a large number of decisions extend quite far into the future and an internal price system therefore would have to include a system of prices for future supply. This might well tend to make decision-making unnecessarily rigid. It seems clear that there must be co-ordination as between the sub-units of an enterprise other than by way of prices and that therefore transfer pricing ideas could not be applied generally and exclusively. But in any case it seems absurd to expect that any quantitative-type control model can and should be the only necessary control device; in contrast to the use also of direct person-to-person behavioural type rules, sanctions, pressures and relations.

2. *The use of the accounting system as a centralized planning device by means of the application of mathematical programming to accounting budgets.*

Ijiri's[20] work implies observation of the budgeting decision processes (particularly the budget meetings and supporting economic-accounting type documents produced) with the purpose of formulating an accounting type model of the firm's periodic budget as a linear programme. The primal solution to the programme may be interpreted as the optimal set of accounting transactions to be carried out by the firm for the budget period, given the criteria and constraints suggested by the behaviour of management. The dual solution indicates to the firm's management the opportunity costs, in terms of the criteria function, of relaxing each of the constraining factors. The model implies the inclusion of economic, production, technological and behavioural type factors, incorporated in terms of their accounting attributes and the use of the dual evalutors to suggest to the management ways in which the firm's economic performance might be improved. Ijiri's discussion of

[19] See Cook, P. W., Jnr., 'Decentralization and the Transfer-Price Problem', *The Journal of Business*, Vol. 28, 1955; Shubik, M., 'Incentives, Decentralised Control, the Assignment of Joint Costs and Internal Pricing', *Management Science*, Vol. 8, 1962; Whinston, A., 'Price Co-ordination in Decentralized Systems', *ONR Research Memorandum, No. 99*, Graduate School of Industrial Administration, Carnegie Institute of Technology, 1962.

[20] Ijiri, Y., *Management Goals and Accounting for Control*, Amsterdam: North-Holland Pub. Co., 1965.

extensions to his basic model so as to incorporate capital investment decisions by a linking of short-term period models into one longer-term model provides some basis for developing his model into a more comprehensive management control system; such a development would require the inclusion of the important variables relating to longer-run achievement of objectives. In part these factors might be incorporated into Ijiri's system by means of a comprehensive cost of capital model which was less 'introverted' than most of those to be found in the present literature; that is to say it should take account of those environmental economic factors which significantly affect the enterprise but which are beyond management's control.[21] In order to reflect alternative investment opportunity expectations outside the enterprise moreover the cost of capital would have to be one of a truly opportunity cost variety.

Conclusion

The ideas of an integrated systems approach to management control require a great deal of development before they are operationally useful. Nevertheless they are clearly important now in the current research and development work, in both the academic and business spheres, directed towards the construction of management control (and information-for-control) systems. Moreover they have an importance now in serving as 'a way of thinking' about our control problems at the organizational level. By the same token they give to accountants a suggested framework both for the improvement of accounting thought about the structure of accounting controls and their relationship to organizational control, of which they can only be a part. It seems moreover that accounting controls can only be justified in terms of this conceptual framework, and from a pedagogical viewpoint that in developing thinking about accounting control we should commence with a framework on the lines of the discussion of this paper.

However accountants need not be faint of heart for they surely possess a good basis (perhaps the only one) for the development of an integrated management control (and information) system provided that they extend their thinking in the application of that powerful tool-accounting method.

[21] The work of Lerner and Carlton is a notable exception in this respect and may be classified as truly extrovert! See Lerner, E. M., and Carleton, W. T., *A Theory of Financial Analysis*, New York: Harcourt, Brace and World, 1966.

Budgetary Control and Business Behaviour

Adrian Buckley and Eugene McKenna

Nowadays most companies of any size employ some of the techniques of management accounting. Probably the most widely used is budgetary control.

The process of budgeting consists of planning, controlling, co-ordinating and motivating through money values, members, and departments within an organisation. In a nutshell, the budget is a plan – usually for one year ahead – in quantitative terms. The control follows by means of comparing actual performance against the performance standard and taking corrective action where necessary. The key features of budgetary control are as follows:

the system is a yardstick for comparison. The planned performance is meant to be perceived by management as a target that should motivate managers towards achievement of the goal implied by the budget.

the system transfers information in quantitative terms.

it isolates problems by focusing upon variances.

The identification of variances makes the system an early warning for management action.

it should identify and highlight performance items as opposed to non-performance items (non-performance items include cause and effect outside the control of the company, e.g. a strike in a tyre supplier will affect Ford sales, but Ford cannot be said to be to blame).

it is a tool of management, not a policing mechanism.

it should be a formalised system culminating in management action.

The sinews of the budgeting process – and indeed of most other management control systems – are the influencing of management behaviour by setting agreed performance standards, the evaluation of results and feedback to management in anticipation of corrective action where necessary.

Since most management controls are conceived and operated by accountants, it is relevant to question whether accountants in general are aware of the impact upon people of these control systems. For there is a body of research findings which is highly critical of accounting control procedures. But, at least in this country, the accounting literature appears only to have given marginal coverage[1] to this most important topic and the syllabuses and examination questions of all the bodies of accountants make little reference to behavioural science. This may be because, as Tricker[2] points out 'the accountant is sometimes suspicious of the emphasis in management studies on people. People are difficult to quantify', but 'the understanding of management planning and control systems hinges on an understanding of people. Organisational theory has a place in the accountant's background knowledge.' However, the Association of Certified Accountants has recently announced a proposed new examination syllabus which includes a paper on Human Relations.

Control and company objectives

Most management control systems are assumed to operate as part of a series of devices designed to enable the company to achieve its corporate objective. Budgetary control is in addition a monitor of actual outturns in the light of short-term estimates of performance. But given that management controls aim to help the achievement of the corporate objective, it is pertinent to ask what most meaningfully constitutes a corporate objective.

When accountants examine this problem they invariably think in terms of maximising profit. A study by Caplan[3] showed that 75 per cent of accountants viewed this as the key business objective, whilst of a sample of non-accounting general managers only 25 per cent saw this as the primary business objective.

The traditional economic theory of the firm

explains the behaviour of 'economic man' in pursuit of maximum profit. The theory views the entrepreneur as confronted with:

a demand function, in which the prices of the commodities he sells are given by the market

a cost function, in which the prices of the factors of production which he purchases are given by the market

a production function, which is essentially a statement of engineering technology.

In this situation the entrepreneur's behaviour is assumed to be predicted by his desire to maximise economic profits. This theory of business behaviour is based on the following set of assumptions:

complete knowledge of alternative courses of action

unlimited cognitive capacity

perfect knowledge of outcomes

total rationality in decision choice.

The modern theory of financial management takes a view near to economic theory in suggesting that: 'the operating objective for financial management is to maximise wealth or net present value'[4] of the owners.

But neither of these views is endorsed by research findings in this area, and it is doubtful whether the concept of profit maximisation is relevant to any but the most entrepreneurial of businesses.

Indeed most economists would view the economic theory of the firm as an abstraction which hardly simulates today's business world. Ideas of rationality and perfect knowledge are inconsistent with the realities of uncertainty and limited reasoning. There is also substantial opinion which questions the profit maximising desire of the firm. Some writers, having observed the development of the modern corporate entity, and the divorce of ownership and control, assert that managers, with minimal equity stakes in the company, are less motivated than the owner-manager.[5] Others[6] have suggested that economic survival may be the primary goal of a business. Alternatively, some firms[7] may appear to maximise sales provided that a satisfactory return on invested capital is earned.

This approach is well in line with the concept of 'satisficing' developed by Herbert Simon[8] from his observations of the workings of administrative systems. Instead of economic man, Simon talks of 'administrative man'. Whilst economic man maximises – selecting the best course of action available – administrative man satisfies – that is, he selects a course of action which is satisfactory or good enough. In business terms, administrative man seeks adequate profit rather than maximum profit; a fair price rather than maximum price.

Another concept of the role of the company sets out somewhat ideological goals, i.e. conducting[9] 'the affairs of the corporation in such a way as to maintain an equitable and working balance amongst the claims of the various directly interested groups – stockholders, employees, customers and the public at large'. How this compromise is achieved may vary from one firm to another, but the existence of a balance presupposes a conflict with profit maximisation which is solely a shareholder objective.

The interpretation of the firm's goals as the various interacting motives of the interested parties is endorsed by the research of Cyert and March,[10] who argue: 'that the goals of a business firm are a series of more or less independent constraints imposed on the organisation through a process of bargaining among potential coalition members and elaborated over time in response to short-run pressures. Goals arise in such a form because the firm is, in fact, a coalition of participants with disparate demands, changing foci of attention, and limited ability to attend to all organisational problems simultaneously.' 'In the long run, studies of the goals of a business firm must reflect the adaptation of goals to changes in the coalition structure.' This concept, the behavioural theory of the firm, implies that it is meaningless to talk of a single organisational goal. It is the participants who have personal objectives, and organisational goals can only mean the goals of the dominant members of the coalition.

A similar picture has been suggested in the theory of managerial capitalism:[11] 'top management, owning little or no equity in the firm, has three main motives: growth, because growth provides job satisfaction, job expansion, higher salaries, higher bonuses and prestige; continuity of employment, which means for the management team as a whole, avoidance of involuntary takeover; and reasonable treatment of shareholders and generally good relations with the financial world.'[12]

Samuel Richardson Reid[13] has suggested that the concern of management for such factors as security, power, esteem, income and advancement within the firm may result in emphasis on growth of size rather than profit maximisation.

In summary, economic theory views the firm as an entrepreneur rather than as an organisation, and, assuming perfect knowledge of all market conditions, stresses profit maximisation. The behavioural theory, based on observations of how modern complex business enterprises function, sees a series of goals – the goals of the key individual members of the managerial coalition – as motivating decision making. As pointed out by Caplan,[14] 'most attempts to explain, predict, or motivate human behaviour on the basis of economic factors alone are likely to be notably unsuccessful'.

The roots of management control

The underlying rationale of most business control procedures is traceable to authoritative styles of management, although this leadership pattern is gradually being superseded by a more enlightened, democratic form which is inversely opposite to its nineteenth century forerunner. But it is questionable as to whether, in general, control procedures are changing in sympathy with more participative styles of management.

In this area Rensis Likert[15] distinguishes four styles of management. System 1, the exploitive authoritative type uses fears and threats, communication is downwards, superiors and subordinates are psychologically distant and almost all decisions are taken at the apex of the organisational pyramid. System 2, the benevolent authoritative style is where management uses rewards to encourage performance, upward communication flow is limited to what the boss wants to hear, subservience to superiors is widespread and, whilst most decisions are taken at the top, some delegation of decision-making exists. System 3, the consultative type, is where management uses rewards, communication may be two-way although upward communication is cautious and limited, by and large, to what the boss wants to hear, some involvement is sought from employees and subordinates have a moderate amount of influence in some decisions – but again broad policy decisions are the preserve of top management only. System 4, the participative style, gives economic rewards and makes full use of group participation and involvement in fixing high performance goals and improving working methods. Communication flows downward, upward, with peers and is accurate; subordinates and superiors are psychologically close and decision-making is widely done throughout the firm by group processes. Various personnel in the organisation chart overlap – they are members of more than one group – and thereby link members in the firm. The system 4 style of leadership is said to produce greater involvement for individuals, better labour/management relations and higher productivity.*

System 4 managers exercise 'general rather than detailed supervision, and are more concerned with targets than methods. They allow maximum participation in decision-making. If higher performance is to be obtained, a supervisor must not only be employee-centred' (as opposed to job-centred) 'but must also have high performance goals and be capable of exercising the decision-making processes to achieve them'.[16]

Closely associated to Likert's concepts is Douglas McGregor's postulation of Theory X and Theory Y behaviour within organisations. Theory X behaviour, as observed in the traditional concept of administration suggests that:[17]

> 'the average human being has an inherent dislike of work and will avoid it if he can'.
>
> 'because of this human characteristic of dislike of work, most people must be coerced, controlled, directed, threatened with punishment to get them to put forth adequate effort toward the achievement of organisational objectives'.
>
> 'the average human being prefers to be directed, wishes to avoid responsibility, has relatively little ambition, wants security above all'.

Because this philosophy of management behaviour became less prevalent in organisations which were moving towards industrial democracy, McGregor proposed alternative explanations for human behaviour in business – namely Theory Y. The assumptions behind Theory Y behaviour are:[18]

> 'the expenditure of physical and mental effort in work is as natural as play or rest'.
>
> 'man will exercise self-direction and self-control in the service of objectives to which he is committed'.
>
> 'the average human being learns, under proper conditions, not only to accept but to seek responsibility'.

The corollaries of Theory Y are important. They are that many more people in the firm are able to contribute constructively towards the solution of problems; second, that the main reward in the work situation is the satisfaction of the individual's self-actualisation needs (see also our reference to Maslow, below); third, the potential of the average person in the organisation is not being fully tapped.

---

* But whilst this may generally be true, Fiedler's findings (Fred E. Fiedler, *A Theory of Leadership Effectiveness*, McGraw-Hill, 1967) suggest that styles of leadership other than system 4 can be perfectly effective. According to Fiedler in any situation cognisance must be taken of the extent of job structuring, power vested in the leader, and the relationship between leader and group member.

McGregor makes the point that whilst staff departments exist essentially to control the line (as is postulated by Theory X), conflict will exist between staff and line management. This conflict may be eliminated if the role of the staff specialist is perceived as being that of providing professional aid to all levels of management, i.e. a supportive relationship.

It should be noted that an investigation undertaken by Caplan[19] indicated that there were definite indications of cost accounting systems being based on the assumptions of the authoritative and Theory X models of behaviour. Thus, whilst management leadership styles have been evolving from System 1 through towards System 4, the management accounting system has not moved with the rest of the organisation.

For budgetary control purposes, Likert's findings suggest that the more participative the process of setting budgets, the more effective they are likely to be in terms of committing personal motivation towards their achievement. This view was confirmed by Coch and French[20] in a study of the effectiveness of participative versus non-participative budgets. Similarly Hofstede[21] tested the hypothesis that higher participation leads to higher budget motivation and found a positive correlation between these factors. In support of this, Bass and Leavitt[22] found that employees participating in setting standards performed better than those who did not.

But beware budget biasing and pseudo-participation. In connection with budget biasing – which is discussed in some depth later – managers may inflate costs or reduce revenue at the budget stage, thus making the budget standard more readily achievable; this is clearly easier to do in a participatory system. However, the problems inherent in this situation may be reduced[23] by an in-depth review during the process of developing the budget. In connection with pseudo-participation there can be no better example than the following, quoted from research findings by Chris Argyris.[24] 'The typical controller's insistence on others' participation sounded good to us when we first heard it in our interviews. But after a few minutes of discussion, it began to look as if the word "participation" had a rather strange meaning for the controller. One thing in particular happened in every interview which led us to believe that we were not thinking of the same thing. After the controller had told us that he insisted on participation he would then continue by describing his difficulty in getting the supervisors to speak freely. For example:

> "We bring them in, we tell them that we want their frank opinion, but most of them just sit there and nod their heads. We know they're not coming out with exactly how they feel. I guess budgets scare them; some of them don't have too much education. . . . Then we request the line supervisor to sign the new budget, so he can't tell us he didn't accept it. We've found a signature helps an awful lot. If anything goes wrong, they can't come to us, as they often do, and complain. We just show them their signature and remind them they were shown exactly what the budget was made up of. . . .'

'Such statements seem to indicate that only "pseudo-participation" is desired by the controller. True participation means that the people can be spontaneous and free in their discussion. Participation, in the real sense of the word, also involves a group decision which leads the group to accept or reject something new. Of course, organisations need to have their supervisors accept the new goals, not reject them; however if the supervisors do not really accept the new changes but only say they do, then trouble is inevitable. Such half-hearted acceptance makes it necessary for the person who initiated the budget or induced the change, not only to request signatures of the "acceptors" so that they cannot later on deny they "accepted", but to be always on the lookout and apply pressure constantly upon the "acceptors" (through informal talks, meetings and, "educational discussions of accounting").'

Budget motivation

The accountant generally perceives the budget as being a commitment, in quantitative terms, of future performance. As Robert Anthony[25] says 'by agreeing to the budget estimates, the supervisor in effect says to management: "I can and will operate my department in accordance with the plan described in the budget".' Hofstede[26] summarises this position by saying that 'budgets and cost standards act as incentives for motivating the budgetees'. However, this view is not necessarily universally accepted by authorities. Gordon Shillinglaw[27] says 'what is not commonly understood is that the budget itself is not intended to act as a motivating force'. But there is evidence that the budget can be a motivator. Is this generally true? Does motivation vary from tight budgets to loose budgets? What happens if the agreed budget becomes patently unachievable?

In examining the question of whether the budget is a stimulus or not, it is first necessary to look at some of the general concepts of motivation in business. For, as Hofstede[28] observes, 'there is no reason to assume that the basic needs of the budgeted manager will be any different from the basic needs of other people'.

SPRING 1972 141

The theories of three of the leading writers – Maslow, Herzberg and McClelland – on the subject are therefore summarised.

Maslow, Herzberg and McClelland

Maslow[29] conceives of the individual as striving to satisfy a hierarchy of basic needs represented in the pyramid in Exhibit I below.

Exhibit I Maslow's Hierarchy of basic needs

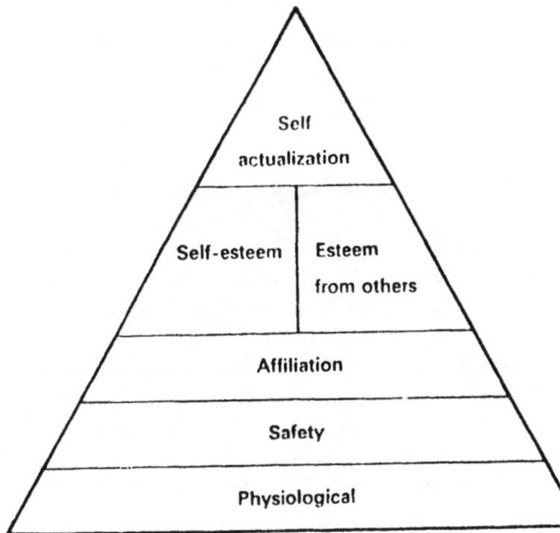

The foot of the pyramid represents the most basic need and the individual strives to move upwards through the hierarchy towards the apex of self-actualisation. Maslow observes[30] that 'man is a wanting animal and rarely reaches a state of complete satisfaction except for a short time. As one desire is satisfied, another pops up to take its place'. Thus only if the lower needs are satisfied will the higher needs appear. Physiological needs include food and rest. Safety needs include job security, a modestly comfortable and predictable routine and a desire for fair treatment and justice from supervisors in the job situation. Frustration of the safety needs lies at the root of resistance to change. Higher than safety needs come affiliation needs – social contacts, belonging to a group, love, etc. Maslow's next level is esteem, divided between self-esteem – the desire for achievement, competence, autonomy, strength, adequacy, mastery – and esteem from others – appreciation of performance, status, recognition. Desire for power also probably belongs in the esteem category. Self-actualisation, at the apex of Maslow's pyramid, implies fulfilling one's ultimate desires, or doing what one is truly fitted for.

Maslow's concept has been tested empirically* and is widely accepted, for example by McGregor,[31] and in terms of explaining actions seems intuitively appealing. How it affects budget motivation is discussed below.

The second motivational theorist looked at here is Fred Herzberg.[32] His concept is empirically based – although there are dissentient views[33] to his total concept – and is built on the principle that people are motivated towards what makes them feel good and away from what makes them feel bad. Herzberg's research identifies the following factors as producing good feelings in the work situation:

achievement

recognition

the work itself

responsibility

advancement.

All of these are real motivators. By contrast Herzberg suggests that the following factors arouse bad feelings in the work situation:

company policy and administration

supervision

salary

inter-personal relations

working conditions.

These latter factors are clearly concerned with the work environment rather than the work itself. Herzberg calls these 'hygiene factors', and they differ significantly from motivators inasmuch as they 'can only prevent illness, but not bring about good health'. In other words, lack of adequate 'job hygiene' will cause dissatisfaction, but its presence will not, of itself, cause satisfaction; it is the motivators that do this. The absence of the motivators will not cause

* For example D. T. Hall and K. E. Nougaim, 'An Examination of Maslow's Need Hierarchy in an Organisational Setting', *Organisational Behaviour and Human Performance*, 1968, No. 3, find support for the hierarchy in a field study based on the success of management trainees over a five-year period in the American Telephone and Telegraph Co. R. Pellegrin and C. Coates, 'Executives and Supervisors: contrasting definitions of career success', *Administrative Science Quarterly*, 1957, No. 1, observe that whilst executives tend to see success as career accomplishment, first line supervisors viewed success in terms of security and income. Similarly, L. Porter, 'Job attitudes in Management', *Journal of Applied Psychology*, 1963, No. 4, found that top executives are more concerned with esteem and self actualisation than managers occupying lower levels in the organisation.

dissatisfaction, assuming the job hygiene factors are adequate, but there will be no positive motivation. Herzberg's findings are summarised in Exhibit II below.

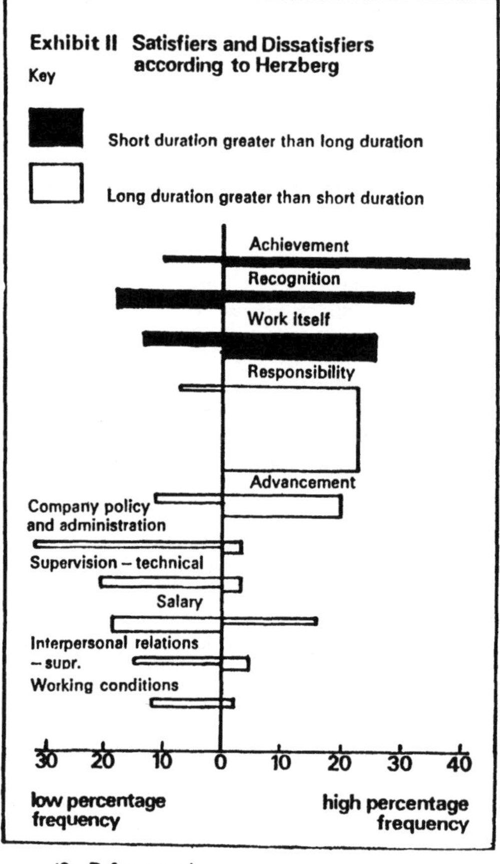

(See Reference 34.)

As Herzberg[35] explains, referring to the above diagrams, 'the length of each box represents the frequency with which the factor appeared in the events presented. The width of the box indicates the period in which the good or bad job attitude lasted, in terms of a classification of short duration and long duration. A short duration of attitude change did not last longer than two weeks, while a long duration of attitude change may have lasted for years.' It will be noted that the length of the salary bar is such that it is both satisfier and dissatisfier. In fact, in the Herzberg experiment it was the most ambiguous of all of the factors highlighted although the negative element tended to predominate.

It is axiomatic in Herzberg's approach that job satisfaction and job dissatisfaction are not opposites. The opposite of job satisfaction is not job dissatisfaction but no job satisfaction; the opposite of job dissatisfaction is lack of job dissatisfaction. The essence of Herzberg's message to business is that employee motivation is a function of challenging work in which responsibility can be assumed. Towards this end he prescribes various methods of 'job enrichment'.

As Hofstede[36] says, in setting Herzberg's motivation, i.e. hygiene factors in the context of Maslow's hierarchy of basic needs 'although some of the hygiene factors, like salary, may be related to several basic needs (e.g. safety, affiliation, and esteem needs), the general tendency of the above list is that the motivators are related to needs considerably higher in the pyramid . . . than the hygiene factors'. Hofstede goes on to point out that 'in Western countries physiological needs are almost universally satisfied; safety needs to a greater extent; on the other hand, the standard for satisfaction of, for example, achievement needs will be much higher in the case of some occupational groups, for example scientists, than for others, for example assembly line workers.' We attempt below to put the Herzberg approach into the framework of budget motivation.

The third major contributor to motivation theory considered here is D. C. McClelland.[37] He suggests that two major needs can be discerned; these are:

- the need for achievement, which should be thought of as achievement identifiable with one's own efforts. In complex working organisations this is often very difficult.
- the need for power, which is not just limited to power over others, but includes also power over one's own liberty of action. Again, in work organisations, a person's liberty of action obviously has to be constrained. Whilst constraints are necessary in the organisation, unnecessary ones convert motivation to frustration.

Building in Maslow's hierarchy implies that achievement and power become dominant drives when the physiological needs are satisfied.

In developing his concept of the 'achievement motive', McClelland focuses upon the drive of people to be challenged and to be innovative and he found that the drive for achievement varies in individuals according to their personality and cultural background. Classifying people as 'high achievers' and 'low achievers', he suggests that high achievers make more successful managers than low achievers. According to McClelland, high achievers relish responsibility and seek out problems which offer challenge; he tends to set himself standards that stretch him and he derives satisfaction from their achievement. The need for positive feedback as a barometer of his performance is important to the high achiever. But with targets set too low, no challenge exists and hence no satisfaction is derived from achievement; at the other extreme, standards set too high tend not to motivate because of the high risk of failure. The high achiever is generally less directly concerned with money than the low achiever – because satisfaction flows from accomplishment – however, money reward may have significance in terms of being seen to be held in esteem. To the high achiever the opportunity for personal satisfaction from successfully accomplishing tasks is of essence. Clearly the need to identify the personal characteristics of the high achiever and the low achiever is essential, in the context of both the budget and general management, if the best is to be got out of people.

Maslow, Herzberg and McClelland in the context of budget motivation

Having summarised each of the above experts' theses, it is necessary to place their findings within the overall framework of budget motivation. Maslow's motivational hypothesis would suggest the need to stress those factors near the apex of the hierarchy of basic needs. Hofstede[38] interprets this theory with reference to the budget as follows. 'In the case of our budgeted managers, we can expect their . . . need fulfilment to be fairly high on the . . . pyramid. Therefore, attempts on budget motivation by building on the lower level needs for these people will be likely to have either no effect, or possibly a negative one. Positive budget motivation will only be possible by trying to fulfil the higher needs; esteem from others, self-esteem, and possibly some kind of self-actualisation.'

The implications of Herzberg's findings are evidently the need to stress, in the budget system, the presence of motivating factors and an adequate level of hygiene factors.

The relevance of McClelland's approach lies in the fact that the budgeted manager should seek challenge from the setting of budget standards.

But there are additional guidelines that can be gleaned from the rules of Maslow's and Herzberg's approaches to motivation. Rewards, in terms of salary increments, promotion, etc. are often based upon performance relative to budget – although this generally operates in parallel with superiors' interpretation of the level set in the budget. However, given Herzberg's findings that salary is generally either neutral or a dissatisfier – although Maslow's and McClelland's views of salary as fulfilling esteem desires must not be overlooked – it may be logical to sever the connection of budget performance and salary review. Ross[39] has shown that separating evaluation and control improves communication. This would tend to diminish feelings of injustice relative to budget performance. If salary and promotion are based, even in part, upon performance versus budget these injustice feelings may arise because of the varying subjective standards which managers set for themselves in the budget situation. Examples of varying standards include new managers, or managers setting their first budget standards, who may desire to achieve their initial budget, and set standards accordingly; managers who have regularly achieved budget may set increasingly demanding targets; and managers who, because they have frequently failed to reach budget, set increasingly more difficult – even fantasy–budget standards. These behavioural patterns are considered further later in this paper.

In the budget situation, Maslow's affiliation needs may be met by budgetees tending to develop informal groups who will resist budget pressures exerted by the controller's department. This sort of occurrence most often happens in an authoritative management environment, or where the control system is of an authoritative type (see the discussion of Likert's work earlier in this paper). Argyris[40] observed this tendency in a study of employee behaviour in relation to budgets.

Maslow's esteem needs, and Herzberg's recognition and achievement desires are relevant to the budget because managers obviously wish to succeed and be seen to succeed. Similarly Herzberg spotlights responsibility as one of the key motivators of managers – this suggests, for budgets, the need to stress participation in setting standards.

Other motivational theorists

Many other investigators have developed formulations to explain the behaviour of people and their business motivation.

> Vroom[41] is one example. His basic model is as follows:
>
> Motivation = f (Valence × Expectancy)
>
> in which the concepts are defined as follows:
>
> Motivation: the force to perform a certain act.
>
> Valence: the orientation (preference of attainment above non-attainment) of a person towards a certain outcome of his act.
>
> Expectancy: the degree to which a person believes a certain outcome of his act to be probable.

In the budget context the Vroom formula becomes:

Budget motivation =
f [Valence of attaining budget
× Perceived influence on results
+ Σ (Valences of other effects of actions
× Expectancies of these other effects)].

in which the concepts mean the following:

Budget motivation: the force to take actions necessary to attain the budget.
Valence of attaining budget: the preference of attaining the budget above not attaining it.
Perceived influence on results: expectancy of the effect of one's action on budget results.
Valences of other effects of action: the preferences for these other effects.
Expectancies of other effects: the degree to which the budgetee believes these other effects to be probable.

Becker and Green[42] present precepts not dissimilar to McClelland. They accept that the level of aspiration of employees is related to their performance, and go on to show that the business firm may be highly influential in affecting levels of aspiration of employees. This, of course, would be confirmed by Herzberg.

Stedry[43] is also concerned with aspiration levels in budgeting. He set out to probe the impact of budget level on performance. He showed that aspiration level formation played a big part in actual performance, and that highest results were achieved by those with highest aspiration levels. Stedry's study affirmed the adage that budgets should be 'attainable but not too tight'. In a subsequent study with Kay[44], Stedry looked at the effect of more than one aspiration level. Goals were set either at a normal level (achievable 50 per cent of the time) or a difficult level (achievable only 25 per cent of the time). The findings of the researchers are interesting. Difficult goals appear to lead either to very good or very bad performance in comparison with performance with normal goals. In the case of the good results it appeared that the formal goal had become an aspiration level. But where very bad performance followed the difficult goal, the budgetee evidently perceived his target as being impossible, he failed to set an aspiration level and began to show withdrawal symptoms. Thus where the difficult goal was seen as a challenge (as it tended to be with the 'high achievers' and also with the younger participants), actual performance was better than target. But where the difficult goal was viewed as impossible, performance fell below even the normal goal.

With regard to aspiration levels, Child and Whiting[45] have determined that:

success generally leads to a raising of the level of aspiration, and failure to a lowering,

the stronger the success, the greater is the probability of a rise in level of aspiration; the stronger the failure, the greater is the probability of a lowering.

shifts in level of aspiration are in part a function of changes in the subject's confidence in his ability to attain goals.

effects of failure on level of aspiration are more varied than those of success.

They also found some evidence to the effect that failure is more likely than success to lead to withdrawal in the form of avoidance of setting an aspiration level. We are sure that this is in line with many accountants' experience.

Hofstede's[46] research confirms many of the above findings. Defining aspiration level as that 'level of future performance in a familiar task which an individual, knowing his level of past performance in that

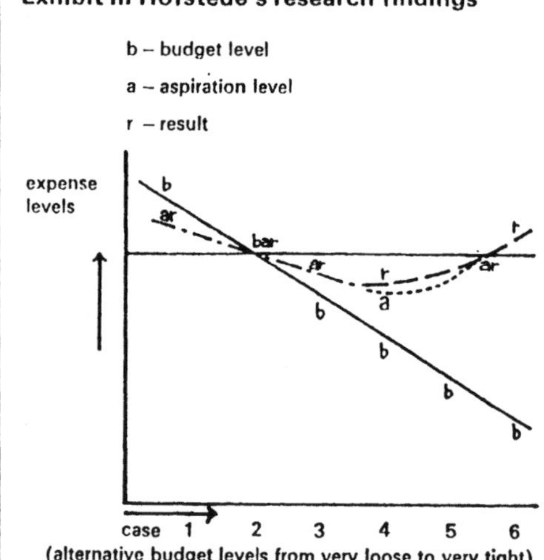

Exhibit III Hofstede's research findings

task explicitly undertakes to reach', he tests the effect on outturn of varying degrees of 'tightness' in the budget. His findings are summarised in Exhibit III, which shows the level of expense on the vertical axis and the degree of 'tightness' of the budget on the horizontal axis going from very loose on the left to very tight on the right.

It can be seen that as budgets become tighter the budgetee adapts his aspiration level to the budget level. In case three the actual results coincide with the aspiration level and although the budget has not been achieved, the actual results are better than normal. The budget in case four is much tighter, and although the employee was motivated and aspires to higher levels, his actual results fail to rise. After this point his aspiration and results fall because the budgetee no longer believes it possible to reach the budget level. In case six the budgetee looks upon the budget as being utterly impossible, and this creates negative motivation and performance deteriorates in sympathy.

The key findings of Hofstede's study are that performance improves when the following features are present in the budget process:

participation in the setting of the budget

frequent communication about cost and budget variances with the boss

knowing exactly which costs one is responsible for

frequent group meetings of the boss with subordinates.

Obviously different managers and supervisors will have different aspiration levels. It may be that controllers can affect actual performance by ensuring that high achievers are set challenging targets. But there is a difference between the challenging target and the impossible. What is challenging to one manager may be impossible to another, and it is our contention that the controller must be sympathetic to the aspiration goals of his managers if he is to achieve full effectiveness.

Budget biasing

As mentioned above, Child and Whiting showed that past budgeting performance affected aspiration levels. Lowe and Shaw[47] have also shown how past results *vis-a-vis* budget can influence the level at which future budgets are set. As would be anticipated, where budgetees 'are allowed to take part in a bargaining type process for fixing their own budget standards they tend to bias information according to the way in which they perceive themselves to secure greatest personal benefit'. Generally managers saw it in their personal interest to agree lower rather than higher budget standards. Similarly Schiff and Lewin[48] observed a tendency for managers in a participatory budget environment to bias budget costs upwards and revenues downwards. As Lowe[49] points out 'the rational economic behaviour of individual managers will be motivated by a desire to strike a balance between present security in retaining their job, and increasing future income. A manager in the budgeting process, may reason that a conservative forecast increases the likelihood of achieving a favourable budget performance in the coming budget period, and therefore his superior's approval then, but at the cost of possibly disappointing his superior now with the size of his present forecast. Where a manager has little or no goodwill left because of poor past budgeting performance he may well be tempted to make extravagantly high forecasts now in order to maintain his superior's present acceptance despite the possible dire consequences later. . . . In contrast the manager who has plenty of such goodwill stored up with his superior may well find it possible to temper his forecasts now with a view to obtaining more goodwill later.' Sometimes genuine over- or underestimation occurs. Here Lowe and Shaw[50] observed for level of sales budgeted that 'when sales . . . are rising there is a tendency to underestimate and when falling there is a tendency to overestimate the level'.

Budget communication

The direction of flow of budgetary control information within an organisation may have critical repercussions for its efficiency. The situation in which information flows from the budget controller's department upwards first to more senior management – a characteristic of the authoritative control systems referred to above – is clearly in breach of the control principles of Likert's system 4 democratic style of management in which communication is downwards, upwards, and with peers and is accurate.

In these circumstances the manager will, as McRae[51] observes, 'tend to feed up the kind of information he thinks his superior likes; and this will probably be information which causes least stress and tension.' As Argyris[52] says 'playing it safe is a way to keep the road to advancement open'.

Miles and Vergin[53] have appreciated the communications failure of traditional control systems and they have summarised their findings and precepts for a behaviourally sound control system as follows: 'The principal flaw in the traditional theory of control according to the behavioural scientists, is the assumption that control is exercised downwards in the organisation – by superiors or subordinates charged with carrying out detailed organisational assignments. In the traditional control model, its critics argue, the organisation is pictured as essentially machine-like. Control procedures are designed to monitor the machine's performance along a number of dimensions and to despatch various reports to upper level officials. Management, in this model, stands at the "control panel" alert to evidence of negative deviation from pre-established standards and procedures and ready to pull switches and twist dials to enforce compliance at any point at which such deviation may occur.'

'The behaviouralists grant that management may gather information on discrepancies and attempt to restore conformance. But, they argue, it is the individual organisational member who actually exercises control – who accepts or rejects standards, who does or does not exercise care in the performance of his duties, or who accepts or resists efforts to change his behaviour to achieve some objective or goal.'

'While behavioural scientists have generally not translated their criticism into detailed prescriptions for the design of control systems, it is possible to abstract from their statement some conditions which they feel must be present in the organisational environment and some requirements which they believe must be met by management control systems.

Standards must be established in such a way that they are recognised as legitimate. This requires that the method of deriving standards must be understood by those affected, and that standards must reflect the actual capabilities of the organisational process for which they are established.

The individual organisation member should feel that he has some voice or influence in the establishment of his own performance goals. Participation of those affected in the establishment of performance objectives helps establish legitimacy of these standards.

Standards must be set in such a way that they convey "freedom to fail". The individual needs assurance that he will not be unfairly censured for an occasional mistake or for variations in performance which are outside his control.

Feedback, recognised as essential in traditional control designs, must be expanded. Performance data must not only flow upward for analysis by higher echelons, but they must also be summarised and fed back to those directly involved in the process.'

It has also been shown,[54] in support of the desirability of downwards communication, that knowledge of results influences favourably future performance.

On other aspects of communication, is the budget account free from criticism? In our opinion the answer is no. The marketing maxim that the seller should use the tone of voice and the words that the consumer understands applies no less in the context of a budgeting framework. The budget accountant should be aware that non-accountant managers prefer to look at management information in terms other than a matrix of figures.

As Robert Townsend says[55] 'statements comparing budget to actual should be written not in the usual terms of higher (lower) but in plain English of better (or worse) than predicted by budget. This eliminates the mental gear changes between income items (where parens are bad) and expense items (where parens are good). This way reports can be understood faster'. Becker[56] suggests that accountants should look to the coding and receiving processes of the individuals to whom information is transmitted. This view is endorsed by Bruns,[57] Dyckman[58] and Birnberg and Nath.[59] All refer to the tendency of non-accountants to look literally at the title of an accounting document – for example a profit and loss account – and perceive it as just that. But they fail to appreciate how differences may arise by virtue of accounting treatments of say stock valuation, depreciation, profit on long-term contracts, etc. Solving the questions raised by this 'functional fixation' is outside the scope of this article but all accountants must be aware of its existence if they are to provide line management with the full support that it expects from finance men.

The budget system – punitive or supportive?

Both McGregor and Likert suggest that for the modern organisation to be wholly effective it is necessary that employees should see themselves as having supportive relationships to other employees. In this (perhaps Utopian) situation, the boss gives support to the employee as he wants the employee to be effective. From this it can be deduced that control systems would have the role of helping to make the manager more effective – that is, they would support him. But it has been suggested by Chris Argyris[60] (see below) that the way in which accountants operate budgetary control systems is punative rather than supportive.

Budgets and people

The major study of the effect of budgets on people – by Chris Argyris[61] – was undertaken some 20 years ago. Nonetheless, the findings are relevant now if, as for example, Caplan[62] believes, cost accounting systems are still based on the assumptions of an authoritative model of behaviour. Argyris set out to examine the effects of budgets on people in organisations. He observed that budget staff viewed their role as essentially one of criticism. They perceived themselves as watchdogs looking for and reporting to top management deviations from plan. The budget staff looked upon the budget as being a means of applying pressure and offering a challenge to line employees. Line supervisors objected to the method of budgetary control in the organisation because:

it merely reported results without commenting on reasons for the results.

the accountants were considered inflexible.

the budget staff were always increasing pressure by increasing targets. This was resented because it implied that they (the line) lacked adequate interest in their job and would not be interested were it not for the budget.

the budgets were always set unrealistically high.

Supervisors suggested that these problems could be overcome if accountants saw the other person's point of view; and further realised that budgets were only opinions and were not final. Argyris reports an astounding degree of aggression against the budget department, which is perhaps not surprising given first that the budget system in Argyris' study appeared to be a policing mechanism, and second that 'success for the budget supervision means failure for the factory supervisor'.[63] Some of the supervisors' comments about accountants were indicative of a control system that was anything but supportive. 'Most of them are warped and they have narrow ideas.' 'They don't know how to handle people.'[64]

In the jargon of the 'managerial grid', the average budget accountant is a truly 9, 1 manager. What is

Exhibit IV The managerial grid

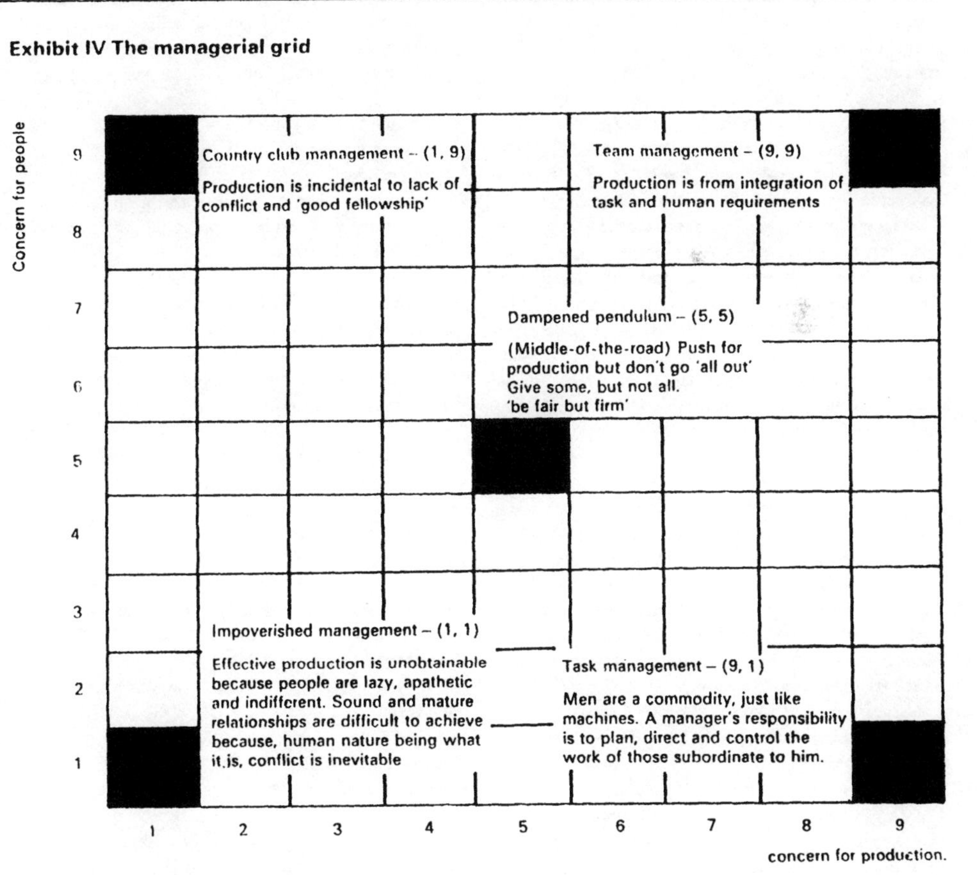

(See Reference 66.)

meant by this is explained by a brief examination of Blake and Moulton's[65] thesis. Their initial assumption is that management should aim to foster environmental attitudes conducive to efficient performance and in so doing they must stimulate creativity, innovation, experimentation and enthusiasm for the job. The managerial grid combines the two key elements of business behaviour, namely concern for production and concern for people. In this context 'concern for' is associated wih the management style of the executive. 'Production' is not limited to factory manufacturing techniques, but may refer to any task of management – excluding the management of people, which falls into the other heading – for example research and development, level of sales, the logistics of depot locations, etc. Concern for people encompasses all aspects of human relations, personal motivation and inter-personal contact.

With these two concerns – for production and for people – on axes as shown in Exhibit IV, it is comparatively easy to summarise a manager's style in relation to the maximum possible of 9.

Thus 9,1 management, or 'task management', focuses wholly upon production and the manager in this category can generally be said to have acute problems in dealing with people, but to be exceptionally competent technically. The 9,1 management style is entirely geared to high level productivity – at least in the short term. Superiors make decisions, subordinates carry them out without question. But this system has inherent weaknesses because subordinates will be working in an environment where none of Herzberg's motivators are present – achievement, recognition, responsibility and advancement will probably be absent and the nature of the work will not stimulate. Such factors as company policy and administration, salary, interpersonal contacts and working conditions must therefore all be acceptable if industrial strife is to be avoided. Shop floor conditions in the motor industry are a good example of the 9,1 management style, and the fact that its record of industrial relations is punctuated with disputes is indicative of the shortcomings of the task management style. It is also possible that this style of leadership is a major contributor to the polarisation of superior and subordinates, which results in the 'Them' and 'Us' thinking[67] which is at the root of so many industrial disputes.

By contrast the 1,9 style, or 'country club management', emphasises people to the exclusion of their performance. People are encouraged and supported, but their mistakes are actually overlooked, because they are doing their best – the maxim of 'togetherness' applies. Direct disagreement or criticism of one another must be avoided at all costs and hence production problems are not followed up. This style of management can easily evolve when competition is limited, for example, the mature oligopoly.

The ideal of the managerial grid is to move towards the 9,9 style, and Blake and Moulton advocate a phased organisational development programme with this as the goal.

On the evidence presented here the budget accountant falls into the 9,1 category; it is hoped that this paper may help him to increase his concern for people and thereby move upwards in the managerial grid.

Conclusions

We now bring together our examination of available research findings into a series of guidelines which we would regard as being indicative of good budgeting practice given the implications of behavioural science. They are:

in terms of setting standards, maximum participation should be sought. As Robert Townsend[68] says 'budgets must not be prepared on high and cast as pearls before swine. They must be prepared by the operating divisions. Since a division must believe in the budget as its own plan for operations, management cannot juggle figures just because it likes to. Any changes must be sold to the division or the whole process is a sham.' But the need for an in-depth review of budgets prepared on a participatory basis is paramount.

information flow should be downwards, upwards and with peers; *not* just upwards.

frequent communication about cost and budget variances with the boss

managers should know exactly which costs they are responsible for

frequent group meetings of the boss with his subordinates

performance is clearly of essence in giving salary and promotion rewards. But in making these assessments of how well managers have performed it may be wise to leave the budget outside the appraisal

budget accountants should communicate in the language of the person with whom they are dealing

budget accountants should be prepared to be humble in explaining their presentations. They must remember that non-accountants may not appreciate how variations may arise through different stock valuation methods, different depreciation methods, etc. In other words the non-accountant literally believes the title of the document – for example profit and loss account – with which he is presented.

everything should be done to make the budget – and indeed any control system – supportive rather than punitive; the aim should be towards self-control rather than a policing mechanism

the budget should not be used to pressurise line management

the budget accountant must be sensitive to the reactions of management and supervisors to his control mechanisms

focus should be on efficiency variances. Variances that arise purely from accounting treatment should be omitted.

budgets which are attainable but not too tight are the best motivators.

It is also of essence that the budget accountant understands the ways in which managers play the game of budget control, for instance:

'difficult' budget goals may lead either to very good or very bad results compared with budgets set at a 'normal' level. The difficult budget may either be perceived by the high achiever, to whom it represents an aspiration level, as a challenge, or by the low achiever as impossible

managers like to achieve budget since in so doing they fulfil esteem and achievement needs

success generally leads to a raising of the level of aspiration, and failure to a lowering

the stronger the success, the greater the probability of a rise in level of aspiration; the stronger the failure, the greater is the probability of a lowering

shifts in level of aspiration are in part a function of changes in the subject's confidence in his ability to meet goals

effects of failure on level of aspiration are more varied than those of success

failure may lead to withdrawal in the form of avoidance of setting a level of aspiration. This withdrawal, if failure persists, may lead to a complete breakdown in communications, and personal and industrial relations problems.

managers may bias standards conservatively in order to ensure that they achieve budget, arguing that superiors' short-term dissapproval at a conservative budget will be compensated by approval when their budget is more than achieved. This tendency to play it safe more frequently occurs in an authoritative organisation

when a manager has a poor track record of budget performance he may be tempted to make extravagantly high forecasts in order to gain short-term approval, despite probable dire consequences later

when sales levels are rising there is a tendency to underestimate sales outturns; when falling the tendency is towards overestimation.

What we have tried to do in this paper is to summarise some of the findings of behavioural science on the topic of the budget. Necessarily our approach has been brief and all of the theories and research work to which we have referred clearly say much more than we have reported here. However, we hope that we have made readers aware of some of the ways in which employees react to budgets. We further hope that we have shown that budgets are powerful behavioural tools and if their use is to result in consistently desirable results it is important that accountants in budget departments should be aware of their behavioural implications.

References

[1] See, for example, E. A. Lowe, 'Budgetary Control – An Evaluation in a Wider Managerial Perspective', *Accountancy*, November 1970; T. W. McRae, 'The Behavioural Critique of Accounting', *Accounting and Business Research*, No. 2, Spring 1971; I. Gibson, 'Management by Objectives', *Management Accounting*, May 1970; R. I. Tricker, *The Accountant in Management*, Bastford, 1967.

[2] R. I. Tricker, ibid.

[3] Edwin H. Caplan, *Management Accounting and Behavioural Science*, Addison-Wesley, 1971.

[4] Ezra Solomon, *The Theory of Financial Management*, Columbia University Press, 1963.

[5] For example, Thorstein Veblen, *Absentee Ownership*, Macmillan, 1923.

Adolf A. Berle and Gardner C. Means, *The Modern Corporation and Private Property*, Macmillan, 1932.

Robert A. Gordon, *Business Leadership in the Large Corporation*, The Brookings Institution, Washington, 1945.

Edith T. Penrose, *The Theory of the Growth of the Firm*, Oxford University Press, 1959.

[6] K. W. Rothschild, 'Price Theory and Oligopoly', *Economic Journal*, September 1947. Peter F. Drucker, 'Business Objectives and Survival Needs: Notes on a Discipline of Business Enterprise', *The Journal of Business*, April 1958.

[7] William J. Baumol, *Business Behaviour, Value and Growth*, Macmillan, 1959.

[8] Herbert A. Simon, *Administrative Behaviour*, Macmillan, 1960.

[9] Frank Abrams quoted in E. S. Mason, 'The Apologetics of Managerialism, *Journal of Business*, January 1958.

[10] Richard M. Cyert and James C. March, *A Behavioural Theory of the Firm*, Prentice-Hall, 1963.

[11] Robin L. Marris, *The Economic Theory of Managerial Capitalism*, Macmillan, 1964.

[12] Robin L. Marris, 'Profitability and Growth in the Individual Firm', *Business Ratios*, Spring 1967.

[13] Samuel Richardson Reid, *Mergers, Managers, and the Economy*, McGraw-Hill, 1968.

[14] Edwin H. Caplan, *op. cit.*

[15] Rensis Likert, *New Patterns of Management*, McGraw-Hill, 1961.

[16] D. S. Pugh, D. J. Hickson and C. R. Hinings, *Writers on Organisations*, Penguin, 1971.

[17] Douglas McGregor, *The Human Side of Enterprise*, McGraw-Hill, 1960.

[18] Douglas McGregor, ibid.

[19] Edwin H. Caplan, *op. cit.*

[20] L. Coch and J. R. P. French, 'Overcoming Resistance to Change', *Human Relations*, Vol. 1, 1948.

[21] G. H. Hofstede, *The Game of Budget Control*, Tavistock Publications, 1968.

[22] B. M. Bass and H. J. L.Leavitt, 'Some Experiments in Planning and Operating', *Management Science*, No. 4, 1963.

[23] M. Schiff and A. J. Lewin, 'The Impact of Budget on People', *The Accounting Review*, April, 1970.

[24] Chris Argyris, 'Human Problems with Budgets', *Harvard Business Review*, Jan.–Feb., 1953.

[25] Robert N. Anthony, *Management Accounting*, Richard D. Irwin, 1964.

[26] G. H. Hofstede, *op. cit.*

[27] Gordon Shillinglaw, 'Divisional Performance Review: An Extension of Budgetary Control', in C. P. Bonini *et al.*, *Management Controls*, McGraw-Hill, 1964.

[28] G. H. Hofstede, *op. cit.*

[29] Abraham H. Maslow, *Motivation and Personality*, Harper and Row, 1954.

[30] Abraham Maslow, ibid.

[31] Douglas McGregor, *op. cit.*

[32] F. Herzberg, *Work and the Nature of Man*, World Publishing Co, 1966.

[33] See for example, J. R. Hinrichs and L. A. Mischkind, 'Empirical and Theoretical Limits to the Two-Factor Hypothesis of Job Satisfaction', *Journal of Applied Psychology*, Vol. 51, No. 2, 1957; Paul F. Wernimont, 'Intrinsic and Extrinsic Factors in Job Satisfaction', *Journal of Applied Psychology*, Vol. 50, No. 1, 1966; V. H. Vroom and N. R. F. Maier, 'Industrial School of Psychology', *Annual Review of Psychology*, No. 12, 1961.

[34] F. Herzberg, B. Mausner and B. Snyderman, *The Motivation to Work*, Wiley, 1959.

[35] F. Herzberg, *op. cit.*

[36] G. H. Hofstede, *op. cit.*

[37] D. C. McClelland, *The Achieving Society*, The Free Press, New York, 1967; D. C. McClelland, J. W. Atkinson, R. A. Clark and E. L. Lowell, *The Achievement Motive*, Appleton-Century-Crofts, 1953.

[38] G. H. Hofstede, *op. cit.*

[39] I. C. Ross, 'Role Specialisation in Supervision', *Doctoral Dissertation*, Columbia University, 1952.

[40] Chris Argyris, *The Impact of Budgets on People*, The Controllership Foundation, 1952.

Chris Argyris, 'Human Problems with Budgets', *Harvard Business Review*, Jan.–Feb., 1953.

[41] V. H. Vroom, *Work and Motivation*, John Wiley, 1964.

[42] S. Becker and D. Green, 'Budgeting and Employee Behaviour', *Journal of Business*, October, 1962.

[43] A. C, Stedry, *Budget Control and Cost Behavior*, Prentice Hall, 1960.

[44] A. C. Stedry and E. Kay, *The Effects of Goal Difficulty on Performance: A Field Experiment*, Sloan School of Management, Massachusetts Institute of Technology, 1964.

[45] I. L. Child and J. W. M. Whiting, 'Determinants of Level of Aspiration: Evidence from Everyday Life', in Brand (ed) *The Study of Personality*, John Wiley, 1954.

[46] G. H. Hofstede, *op. cit.*

[47] E. A. Lowe and R. W. Shaw, 'An Analysis of Managerial Biasing: Evidence from a Company's Budgeting Process', *Journal of Management Studies*, October 1968; E. A. Lowe and R. W. Shaw, 'The Accuracy of Short-Term Business Forecasting: An Analysis of a Firm's Sales Budgeting', *Journal of Industrial Economics*, Summer 1970.

[48] M. Schiff and A. Y. Lewin, *op. cit.*

[49] E. A. Lowe, *op. cit.*

[50] E. A. Lowe and R. W. Shaw, *op. cit.* (1970).

[51] T. W. McRae, *op. cit.*

[52] Chris Argyris, *Integrating the Individual and the Organization*, John Wiley, 1964.

[53] R. E. Miles and R. C. Vergin, 'Behavioural Problems of Variance Controls', *California Management Review*, Spring 1966.

[54] N. R. F. Maier, *Psychology in Industry, A Psychological Approach to Industrial Problems*, George G. Harrap, 1955.

[55] Robert Townsend, *Up the Organization*, Michael Joseph, 1970.

[56] S. W. Becker, 'Discussion of the Effect of Frequency of Feedback on Attitudes and Performance', Empirical Research in Accounting: Selected Studies, 1967, supplement to Vol. V of *Journal of Accounting Research*, University of Chicago, 1968.

[57] William J. Bruns Jr, 'Inventory Valuation and Management Decisions', *The Accounting Review*, April 1965.

[58] Thomas R. Dyckman, 'The Effects of Alternative Accounting Techniques on Certain Management Decisions', *Journal of Accounting Research*, Spring 1964.

[59] Jacob G. Birnberg and Raghu Nath, 'Implications of Behavioural Science for Management Accounting', *The Accounting Review*, July 1967.

[60] Chris Argyris, *op. cit.* (1952).

[61] Chris Argyris, ibid.

[62] Edwin H. Caplan, *op. cit.*

[63] Chris Argyris, *op. cit.* (1953).

[64] Chris Argyris, ibid.

[65] Robert R. Blake and Jane S. Moulton, *The Managerial Grid*, Gulf Publishing, 1964.

[66] Robert R. Blake and Jane S. Moulton, 'The Managerial Grid', *Advanced Management Office Executive*, Vol. 1, No. 9, 1962.

[67] Michael Shanks, *The Stagnant Society*, Pelican, 1961.

[68] Robert Townsend, *op. cit.*

[7]

MANAGEMENT CONTROL AND INTEGRATION AT THE CONCEPTUAL LEVEL

BY

A. E. Mills

1. *Preliminary Considerations*

The articles of Mr. B. W. Denning and of the class of the Manchester Business School[1] will, I hope, add momentum to the study of the wide range of concepts used by teachers, consultants, and managers, and to the process of integrating thinking among these groups.

The work is urgent for several reasons. First, the structural and procedural moves occurring within the civil service, the large private organizations in industry and commerce, the nationalized industries, and in the military services call for broad horizons in administrators. Yet the breadth must not be at the expense of depth since superficiality leads to ignorance and error. This rare quality of mind, simultaneous breadth and depth, is desired not only in tomorrow's managers undergoing integrative courses in business schools, but more urgently in the innumerable specialists, managers and researchers who cannot get time off for courses and who need to cooperate in their present tasks across conceptual frontiers.

It is required with no less urgency among the technologists pouring out of our universities and technical colleges. Traditional curricula are being slowly modified. Attempts are being made to give technologists an insight into the full range of managerial relationships and the interaction between their environment and the firms which employ them. The traditional arid approach to management studies in our colleges is at last being abandoned, along with its false premises and assumptions, and replaced by up-to-date methods.[2]

Again, the pressures on managers are being felt far and wide across the world, in firms owned by citizens of developing countries as well as those

[1] Denning, B. W., 'The Integration of Business Studies at the Conceptual Level', *Journal of Management Studies*, Vol. 5, No. 1, 1968, and, Manchester Business School Graduate Students, 'Integrated Organizational Strategy', *Journal of Management Studies*, Vol. 6, No. 1, 1969. These articles are not the first published work in this area. The present writer evolved a pattern of concepts in the *Dynamics of Management Control Systems* (April 1967) which had not come to the attention of the writers of the articles.

[2] The writer, in association with Mr. J. P. Edwards, has initiated a new approach to management studies for specialists, with selected case studies. See Mills, A. E., and Edwards, J. P., *Management for Technologists*, London: Business Publications Limited, 1968.

with parent companies in the developed ones. The kind of fragmented theory so far available for the training of these managers has obstructed rather than enhanced their competence in solving their problems. Integration at the conceptual level is necessary not only to allow specialists in the developed regions to assist each other, but also to allow managers in different environments across the continents to learn from each other's experience and thought.

So much for aims. A word now on those who seek to achieve them. The fact that Mr. Denning and the Manchester class have set off the dialogue in this Journal might give readers the impression that students of business policy, particularly of planning, are best equiped to carry out the integrative task. This is not, I think, necessarily so. In my experience, persons interested primarily in planning do not penetrate far enough into the territory where the interdisciplinary thinking most needs to be done. They tend to ignore or overlook many of the finer points of disagreement among specialists, particularly those concerned with evolving organization structures and the intricate pattern of resistances to change.

The area of *control* would seem to be a more favourable one. Preoccupation with the control as distinct from the planning of operations concentrates the mind particularly upon the contributions of the behavioural scientists to the quantitative elements in managers' decisions. It is here that the major need for integrative thinking exists. Planning and control are closely related functions in today's dynamic environment; they may indeed be considered a single function.[3] But they remain separable decision activities, and individuals can be preoccupied with one or the other and so know more of one than of the other. Control, I have found, predisposes a person to focus effort on the more truculent areas of divergence in both concepts and interests. This is probably important today, as mergers and technological ingenuity force the pace of organizational adjustment and change.

In this article I shall abandon the constraint voluntarily set upon their study by the Manchester Business School class and go beyond analysis of the firm's strategy and tactics within its environment. Like Mr. Denning I shall consider internal organization, innovation, and control. My purpose is to develop a more refined and practicable model for integrating control with behavioural effectiveness (leadership) and with planning (strategy and tactics) which was the primary concern of the Manchester class.

2. *Devising the Model*

The planning function is preoccupied with the forces underlying and determining the strategy and tactics of the organization. It is primarily

[3] Mills, A. E., *Dynamics of Management Control Systems* (*Introduction*, p. xvii), London: Business Publications Limited, 1967.

concerned with the relation between objectives and resources, the analysis of the company's markets, its technological strengths and weaknesses, and the acquisition of company inputs, particularly the knowledge and skills of its managers, specialists, and operatives.

The control function, on the other hand, is designed to effect corrective action where targets are not being achieved. It focusses attention on the factors determining performance, rather than on the objectives and targets which are the criteria for judging performance.

Both planning and control depend on the flow of information to the decision-takers. There is however a difference in the kind of question asked about this flow of information by the planners and the controllers respectively. The planners consider the source and range of the information. They wish to know which types of information are available, and which might be made available, for them to be able to determine appropriate objectives and targets. Planners therefore tend to concentrate attention on the external environment and on its interaction with the company.

The controllers, by contrast, tend to direct attention to the internal context, to the problems of monitoring performance, to the factors which provoke suppression or distortion of information, to the processing of information for purposes of corrective action, and to the conditions which delay or prevent corrective action from being taken when it is called for. These problems are largely human problems, concerned with the pattern of attitudes among the various groups of managers, specialists, and operatives, and therefore focus attention on the interaction between the economic and technical elements of activity on the one hand and the social and psychological elements on the other. Research into problems of management control is primarily concerned with the ways in which the behavioural aspects of activity interact with the economic and technical aspects in determining performance. It is in this type of research that greatest insight into problems of integration at the conceptual level is being acquired.

We shall now build up a simple model from an actual case study to throw light on the working of a company management control system.

The company we shall briefly consider for the purpose, the Murray Engineering Company,[4] was engaged in manufacturing precision instruments. It had traditionally produced mechanical and electrical instruments, but, in the early 'fifties, began to design and produce electronic devices to keep abreast of the market. It developed an R & D department to design the new instruments and produce the prototypes, but it met difficulty both in marketing the new line and in establishing smooth working relationships between the design and development staff and the production staff. In the

[4] For a detailed account of this case study, see Mills, A. E., and Edwards, J. P., op. cit., Ch. 5.

factory, operatives were retrained and transferred from the old to the new line as the prototypes acquired approval for production, but the process was fitful and prolonged, gave rise to intense feelings of insecurity, and resulted eventually in a strike. Long before this crisis, the finances of the company were already under strain. Inventory of the old lines piled up and could not be sold, but at the same time even the new instruments, when they appeared, frequently could not be sold because the selling staff lacked the technical knowledge to convince potential clients of their value. The chief executive felt somewhat at a loss in dealing with these problems. Information to enable him to control performance did not reach him, though his accountant could have furnished him with a good deal of it, had he been encouraged to do so. Barriers between design and development staff and production staff persisted and hardened year by year as the position worsened, and led to increasing costs. The problem of marketing the new line similarly persisted: though the sales manager tried to grasp electronics, he did not succeed, and even the personal support in the field of the chief executive failed to improve sales. It required the intervention of a consultant to solve these problems and establish an effective system of management control.

As a first step in devising a model to help the chief executive to understand his problems, the consultant portrayed the company graphically as an open system on two levels, the physical level and the decision level. He explained how the chief executive's lack of control stemmed from his failure to ensure that he had information to determine long-range and short-range targets and to monitor performance, to know where corrective action was called for.

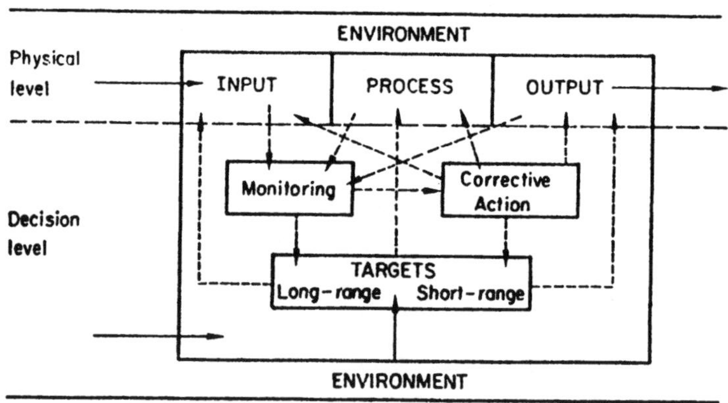

FIG. 1. THE CONTROL SYSTEM

This simple model, however, could not serve to explain to the chief executive the type of actions he should take to secure the information. The consultant reminded him that information reached him not only directly from the work flow but through the managers and other employees whose relationships were shaped by the organization structure of the company. This structure had grown up haphazardly over the years and had faults, but it could be modified by the chief executive.

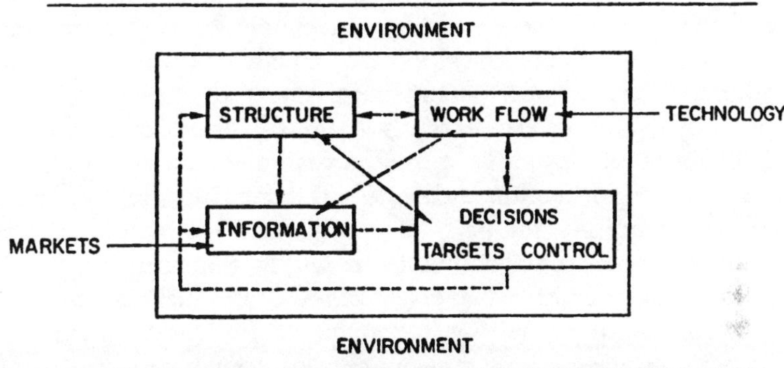

FIG. 2. ELABORATION OF THE INTERNAL CONTEXT

Sceptically the chief executive enquired how he should modify the organization structure. The consultant now had to make up his mind which of the considerable variety of analyses of organization structure available in the literature[5] he should select for this task of elucidation. The books offer typologies of 'activities' or 'processes' or 'variables' or 'imperatives' or 'functions', according to the preference of the researcher or writer.

Having this particular chief executive in mind, the consultant's choice was a classification of three major functions: innovation, control, and leadership. Managers in a changing environment, like those in Murray Engineering, have to innovate to survive. Innovation is a function they can perform only through the other two functions, control and leadership. The basic control function he had already outlined using Fig. 1. The leadership function, he went on to explain, embraced the behavioural elements in the internal context, and dealt particularly with organization structure, motivation, and perceptions.

Joan Woodward's research,[6] he went on, has made us aware that technology is one powerful determinant of structure, one among several, while Burns and Stalker[7] have suggested a typology of structures (mechanistic/

[5] E.g. Parsons, T., *Structure and Process in Modern Societies*, New York Free Press, 1960; Mullen, J. H., *Personality and Productivity in Management*, New York: Temple University Press, 1966; Bakke, E. W., 'The Concept of Social Organization', in Haire, M. (*ed.*), *Modern Organization Theory*, New York: Wiley, 1959; Smelser, N. J., *The Sociology of Economic Life*, New Jersey: Prentice-Hall, 1963; Mills, A. E., op. cit.

[6] Woodward, J., *Industrial Organization: Theory and Practice*, London: Oxford University Press, 1965.

[7] Burns, T., and Stalker, G. M., *The Management of Innovation*, London: Tavistock Publications, 1961.

organismic) related to the pace of change in the environment. The Human Relations School, and the host of sociologists, psychologists and organization theorists who have contributed to the seminal work of this School, have analysed the needs (basic and sophisticated, personal and social) underlying employees' behaviour. All these variables — technology, type of organization structure, motivation of employees — are moulded into a socio-technical system (of greater or less cohesion and effectiveness) by the style of management adopted by the top level of executives and to a lesser extent those below that level. The way each employee perceives his immediate environment and the breadth of his vision within and outside the company are also factors of importance in integrating the parts of the system. Training is one means among many by which information from within the firm and outside it permeates the behaviour of managers, occasionally influencing the style of management (but usually requiring the catalytic aid of consultants to do so). Where the existing management style fails to inspire the degree of cohesion required to survive competition, pressure from the environment (e.g. in the form of a take-over bid or of nationalization) usually comes to enforce a change. The quantity and quality of information flowing into the decision-taking centres are therefore the resultant of a pattern of variables all interacting simultaneously in a complex socio-technical system.

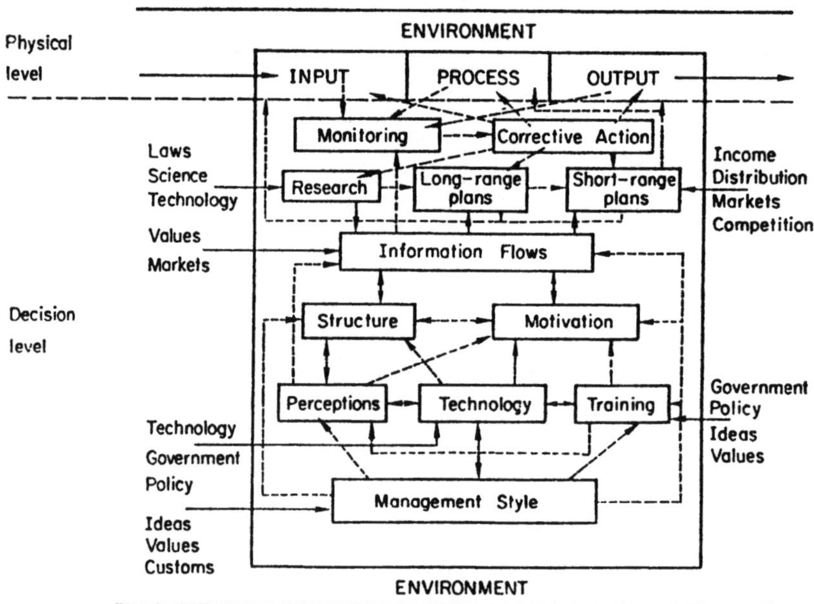

FIG. 3. A COMPREHENSIVE MODEL

3. *Management Style and the Control System*

In the rest of this paper we shall discuss just two of the variables in this model; management style and the level of perception in the individual employee.

The typologies of management style in the literature are as numerous as those of organization structures. It has been customary to classify leadership as authoritarian or democratic, and there have been many research investigations indicating that economic performance is correlated one way or the other with each type. The trend has been in favour of methods of participation and delegation of initiative and against coercion. The results are inconclusive, for the reason that this classification of the types of organization is not based on the factors which in effect determine norms of behaviour and the values underlying them. Democracy is a political concept implying that views of everyone in a society have been given expression, either directly or through representation, and that this process resolves conflicts of view and interest in the society by reflecting the general will. The legitimacy of democracy lies in its affecting behaviour by a political process establishing a consensus of view, which is used to endow an executive with power.

This process may, or may not, influence personal behaviour; it usually does influence behaviour, but there is no indication, if it influences behaviour, in what way it will do so. It does not always achieve the results expected of it. Similarly, autocracy seeks its justification, not in the general will, but in a high principle or interest. It may be God, the rights of property, those of labour or of the intellect. The divine right of kings, fascism, communism, the meritocracy can all be excuses for autocracy. Yet the superior value of whatever principle or interest is proclaimed may not be accepted as an adequate basis of the legitimate exercise of power; and we cannot tell how autocracy affects behaviour in different institutions or countries. It does not explain how personal or group behaviour is determined. We have to look at norms and values for this.

A seemingly acceptable classification of organizations is Burns and Stalker's, based on the distinction between mechanistic and organismic types. The first type tends to have a rigid division of the organization into levels of authority and functional departments, while the second allows a more fluid arrangement of relationships and communication. This classification is certainly useful for understanding why organizations function effectively or not in the modern technically-dynamic environment in which we work. But like the dichotomy between authoritarian and democratic types, the distinction between mechanistic and organismic systems does not go to the roots of the problem. It does not explain clearly why these types of organization affect behaviour and how. It is therefore not adequate for our purpose.

What we seek is a classification based on the factors determining values and norms of behaviour. To discover these factors we have to investigate the sources of psychological security to the organization members.[8] Basically there are three sources each giving rise to a style of command.[9] Though in any actual organization we find manifestations of two or even all three of the styles in the various sub-systems, for analytical purposes it is essential to separate them and explore the nature of each and its ramifications upon factors determining performance. The three sources of psychological security are the person, the rule, and the task. The styles of command associated with them we may call the 'boss-centred', 'rule-centred' and 'task-centred' styles of command or of management.

In 'boss-centred' command the source of security is in the power and personality of the owner or manager, and criteria of performance stem from his personal values as to what activities or objectives have priority over others. Where his personal preferences lead to priorities inconsistent with company objectives, or where he distributes status and favours erratically, the effects on achievement can be destructive. This type is particularly important in the early stages of growth of small businesses, but it is also important in medium and large concerns, at top level and in departments, in branches and on the shop-floor. Its effect is to divert employees' attention away from the task and on to the attitudes of the boss.

In the 'rule-centred' style, the sources of security lie in the pattern of rules, regulations, procedures and policies which are accepted by the entire body of employees, from chief executive down. This is the kind of organization frequently referred to as bureaucracy, common in very large institutions such as government departments, public corporations, and not unknown in private business. It tends to divert employees' attention away from the task and on to the rules and procedures. Tradition is treasured as a safeguard against change and the upheavals change provokes. Innovation becomes stifled.

In the 'task-centred' style of command, security arises from the tasks to be performed, from the demands of the work situations and the contribution each individual or group makes to the joint effort. The organization structure is based on the nature of the work-flow, which is broken down into units of work, each consisting of a number of closely-related operations, and an individual is given a target as his responsibility for his part of the work-flow. Concentration on task targets tends to bring people together into teams around the operations, and authority arises from the work situation. The creativeness, enthusiasm, and drive that arise from a highly developed team-spirit are the valuable features of this style of command. They contrast with the frigidity, frustration, resentment that characterize attitudes among

[8] Meigniez, R., *Pathologie Sociale de l'Entreprise*, Paris: Gauthiers-Villars, 1965.

[9] Mills, A. E., op. cit., Chs. 3 and 10.

individuals and groups in so many 'boss-centred' and 'rule-centred' organizations.

The flow of information conditioning the control system depends on the degree of integration of the parts of the firm into an effective system, which in turn depends crucially on which of the three styles of management prevails throughout the organization.

4. *Level of Perception and Management Control*

We return to Murray Engineering to illustrate the importance of level of perception. The consultant was at pains to explain how management style interacted with organization structure to influence the flow of information through the company. He referred to the chief executive's own style of management which had been largely negative and arbitrary because of his unfamiliarity with the interplay of variables within the system. He referred also to the 'rule-centred' style of the production manager whose addiction to rules and regulations was a form of self-defence against the encroachments of the design and development staff in production of the new line.

To explain the link between style of management and flow of information, the consultant found he had to introduce the concept of level of perception. A manager within the system exercised control over the flow of information within the limits of his influence among his colleagues. Information can be a weapon, and there was evidence that the production manager had so used it first to protect his influence and later to extend it. It was clear that an important factor was the manager's attitude towards his colleagues; he could treat them as associates or as rivals. He could co-operate, refuse to co-operate, and even struggle aggressively with them. What explained his attitude?

Here the consultant emphasized the level of perception of the manager. He classified these levels as 'self-centred' or 'egocentric', as 'group-conscious', or as 'systems-conscious'. The 'self-centred' person saw only his own interest and acted accordingly. The 'group-conscious' person was aware of the interests of his immediate group (gang, section, or department) and sought these alone. The 'systems-conscious' person was aware, not only of the interests of the group of which he was a member, but also of the interests of the other groups and of the company as a whole. In Murray Engineering most operating managers had been 'group-conscious'. The chief executive had had a broad company view, but had had no inkling of how to encourage the same broad view among his managers. The engineers, both designers and production men, had been guided by their professional values, and had sought to do a job which met the technical standards of their profession. Their interests had thus coincided with those of the company, but they had been quite thwarted and frustrated by the political machinations of their line superiors. The result had been a pattern of departmental strife where barriers across the organization had led to distortion and suppression of information indispensable to effective control.

In his experience the consultant had found that there was a large degree of correlation between styles of management and levels of personal perception. The 'self-centred' vision is characteristic of the 'boss-centred' style of management, though we do find 'group-conscious' individuals in 'boss-centred' organizations. Similarly we find mainly 'group-conscious' persons in 'rule-centred' organizations; the evidence is strong in the civil service, in private business concerns and in nationalized industries. It is rare to find 'systems-conscious' persons in other than 'task-centred' organizations, those in which the basis of security for employees is in their concentration upon performance of the task, and not in the person of the employer or in the body of company regulations. The reason is that their needs are not met in 'boss-centred' or 'rule-centred' firms and they therefore seldom stay long in them. The 'task-centred' style of management tends to mould 'systems-conscious' vision among employees.

The consultant's diagnosis of the situation in Murray Engineering led him to suggest that the marketing problem could be solved by destroying departmental barriers and making the design head responsible for marketing the products; this man had the technical knowledge. The responsibility would make him aware that, after all, the purpose of designing the products was to sell them. In this way the marketing information would pass directly to the designers, and simultaneously the designers would have an incentive to sell what they designed.

Next the consultant advised the chief executive to create an organizational mechanism to permit the flow of information among senior managers and specialists. This could be a single management committee, or it could be a dual mechanism, a policy-making or planning committee and an operating committee. The co-option of specialists on to these committees could not only improve the information available to managers, but also help to overcome barriers between persons and departments. Regular discussion would help to develop a broader range of perceptions among managers, which would influence their attitudes and behaviour. The process would have to be reinforced by creating a team-based method of working in contrast with the previous departmental method which had called for external co-ordination by the chief executive — co-ordination which he had signally failed to effect. In other words the consultant aimed at creating a new flexible pattern of style of management, organization structure, and personal perceptions which would be consistent within itself and would release a flow of reliable information in all directions. The result would be more effective control at the levels of both the chief executive and his juniors.

We may incidentally note the relevance of this typology of levels of perception to the area of *planning* as distinct from control.

The 'egocentric' type of perception corresponds, at the level of top management, to a 'firm-centred' vision, i.e. one focussed on the interests of the firm. It sees no common interests between the firm and the other firms in the same market context. It has in the past characterized some exceptionally enterprising individuals who have achieved resounding success: the Fords, Carnegies, Nuffields, Rockefellers. But the survival of the business empires they created has depended usually on their handing over to men of a more sophisticated type of perception, more far-seeing, less egocentric, less arbitrary and erratic.

The 'group-conscious' vision is one still focussed on the firm but aware of common interests between the firm and others in the same market context. This kind of vision leads to co-operative action on a limited scale, such as co-operative research institutions, trade associations to share information services, determine price and output policies, and to agree on common policies in dealing with special labour or political situations. Their links and understanding do not, however, extend beyond those firms within their own industrial grouping, and behaviour as a result tends to be more often restrictive than expansive.

The 'systems-conscious' type of vision is broad enough to understand the objectives of the whole economy, to perceive how one firm can be concerned in activities or institutions far beyond its own product markets, and base actions on these broader, more subtle, and more far-reaching relationships associated with joint objectives. It is this kind of perceptiveness which leads firms to inquire into scientific, technological, and marketing developments far beyond those occurring in their own particular industries and within their own national boundaries. Their managers are aware that innovations in one field have repercussions in others. It is this kind of inquisitiveness which provokes managers to watch research findings wherever they occur, overseas as well as at home, and to try to foresee how and where new innovations might impinge on the firm's present product-mix, channels of distribution, range of markets, and on its internal organization, recruiting and training programmes, and capital investment projects. It is this imaginativeness which has characterized entrepreneurs who have built great business and industrial empires all over the world.

There is usually, though not necessarily, some correspondence between the type of market context and the type of vision. We seldom find any but the 'firm-centred' type of perception in firms in the little developed market context where business units are small and communications rudimentary.[10]

[10] For analyses of types of environment, see Emery, F. E., and Trist, E. L., 'The Causal Texture of Organizational Environments', *Human Relations*, Vol. 18, No. 1, 1965, and also Mills, A. E., op. cit., Ch. 2.

We find it too alongside 'group-conscious' vision in the more developed market context where clusters of firms of all sizes exist, where there is a slow rate of innovation, and communications are more advanced. In Britain the context is marked by a rapid rate of innovation, by the important role of large industrial groups, and by a highly developed pattern of communications. This requires among its managers 'systems-conscious' perception. Yet we find almost entirely 'group-conscious' vision; the Restrictive Practices Registrar appointed under the Act of 1956 received details of innumerable restrictive agreements in almost every industry in the economy. The Act served to advise the business community that 'group-conscious' attitudes and vision are inconsistent with the objectives of a closely integrated system. In every advanced economy where the closely integrated economic and social context is becoming common, we still find the great majority of managers with the 'group-conscious' type of perception. Their limited knowledge and understanding is reflected through their policies and behaviour, above all their unimaginative marketing and passive, almost defeatist, industrial relations.

5. *Conclusion*

The Murray Engineering case study is one illustration of how study of the control function enhances integrative thinking. It does so to a degree greater than that usually produced by studies of the planning function, and this is because it has to focus on the behavioural variables in the internal context and their influence on the informational elements in decisions. The concepts outlined in this article have been found useful in a large number of industrial and commercial concerns, some of which have been written up in the writer's published books referred to earlier. They have also been found relevant in other types of organization — in the civil service, in military establishments, in schools and universities — where pressures from the modern dynamic environment are exacting greater flexibility of operation and greater sophistication of mind among managers to achieve control.

What are the implications of this analysis for teaching in business schools? They are that, where business policy courses are being used as the primary device for promoting integrative thinking, more time and attention should be given to study of management control as an integrative discipline. There is indeed an argument for a course on control separate from the business policy course, whose syllabus naturally gives little weight to control because it concentrates on strategy and tactics and the policies associated with them. A separate course can ensure that the integrative thinking receives specialized treatment and the emphasis it deserves in students' minds.

[8]

Accounting, Organizations and Society. Vol. 5, No. 2, pp. 231–244.

CONTROL, ORGANISATION AND ACCOUNTING*

D. T. OTLEY

University of Lancaster

and

A. J. BERRY

Manchester Business School

Abstract

Organisation control is a subject of fundamental importance to the designer of accounting control systems. Yet discussions of accounting control tend to take place against a back-cloth of incomplete and outmoded theories of organisation and simplistic and authoritarian concepts of control. In this paper, the applicability of a cybernetic model of control to the control of human organisations is explored, with particular reference to the role of accounting information systems. The analysis uncovers a number of issues that require resolution before the model can be applied to accounting information system design. Some directions for research on accounting controls are discussed.

Organisation control is a much neglected subject. That is, the study of the ways in which organisations manage and regulate their affairs so as to remain viable and to achieve their chosen ends or objectives has received comparatively little attention. Organisational theorists have tended to emphasise the exercise of power, authority and influence within organisations, and have given little consideration to how viable patterns of behaviour are achieved; those concerned with control theory have tended to ignore the special characteristics of human organisations which distinguish them from other systems, with the consequence that inappropriate control models have been suggested. Accounting researchers have paid scant attention to either body of thought and have tended to make control recommendations in a theoretical vacuum based on incomplete and outmoded ideas of both organisation and control. In this paper, cybernetic concepts of control are applied in an organisational context to the design of accounting information and control systems with the aim of generating a coherent theoretical basis for future accounting research.

"Control" is a term with more different shades and nuances of meaning than almost any other in the English language, with Rathe (1960) listing "57 varieties" of its connotations. The most common idea it suggests is that of dominance; the domination of one individual or group by another through the exercise of power. However, there is a second strand of meaning that emphasises the idea of regulation and the monitoring of activities. This latter use of "control" is more in keeping with the original French term meaning "inspection", and comprises the main connotation in several

---

*An early version of this paper under the title "Control and Organisation" was presented at the Workshop "Information and Control Systems" held at the European Institute for Advanced Studies in Management, Brussels, September 1977.

European languages (Hofstede, 1968). Business usage commonly incorporates both of these ideas, as is indicated by Webster's Dictionary definition:

Application of policies and procedures for directing, regulating and co-ordinating production, administration and other business activities in a way to achieve the objectives of the enterprise.

In this paper the term "control" will be used in its full cybernetic sense of both monitoring activities and then taking action in order to ensure that desired ends are attained.

CONTROL AND ORGANISATION

The study of organisation and the study of control have been closely interrelated in the sense that control is a central and inescapable feature of all human organisations. For example, McMahon & Ivancevich (1976) state that "there is practically universal agreement that organisation implies control", a view which had received earlier support from Tannenbaum (1968) when he claimed that "organisation without some form of control is impossible". Despite a degree of ambiguity and lack of definition in both the terms "organisation" and "control", it is clear that control processes are a fundamental part of organisational activity. Both the exercise of power by individuals and groups and its relationship to the overall maintenance of the organisation are central issues.

Indeed, organisation can itself be viewed as a control process, occurring when groups of people feel the need to co-operate in order to achieve purposes which require their joint action. Following Etzioni's (1961) definition that "organisations are social units deliberately constructed to seek specific goals" then it is vital that control over the goal achievement process is established and maintained. However, such a functional definition of organisation would not be accepted by all, and, as March & Simon (1958) earlier observed, "it is easier and probably more useful to give examples of formal organisations than to define the term". In this way certain features of formal organisations can be made apparent, such as those outlined by Silverman (1970).

Silverman notes that organisations, unlike some other social arrangements, are perceived as *artefacts*, constructed to serve certain purposes (although such initial purposes may subsequently be displaced). As an artefact, the patterning of relationships within an organisation will be less taken for granted by organisational participants than that accepted by actors in other social roles. Organisations thus possess an unusual consciousness about their own behaviour, essentially seeking to modify it to meet both internal and external situational demands. This natural concern with the processes of organisational control is an important characteristic of organisational behaviour.

The recognition that goals or purposes can be displaced emphasises that the control process includes the adaptation of the organisation to meet new situations. Control is thus importantly related to purposes, co-ordination and change, a categorisation that closely parallels Parson's (1951) description of the functions of an organisation as being goal-directed, integrative and adaptive. A full description of organisational control procedures must therefore include an analysis of those procedures which act to maintain viability through goal achievement, those concerned with the co-ordination and integration of differentiated parts, and those which promote adaptation to both internal and external change.

As an example it can be observed that the planning procedures of an organisation can be used in ways that serve each of the three functions identified above. Much planning is concerned with goal-setting with a view to subsequent monitoring and control (e.g. budgetary planning and control); other planning activity is concerned mainly with ensuring adequate co-ordination between different departments engaged on parts of a larger task (e.g. project planning); finally, some planning is specifically oriented towards modifying the stance of the organisation toward its environment (e.g. corporate strategic planning). Planning is thus an important aspect of organisational control, for as Wildavsky (1973) pithily summarises, "planning is future control". It is unfortunate that everyday usage distinguishes between planning (future-oriented) and control (present-oriented), for the only meaningful distinction is perhaps that where planning uses expectations to trigger action, one type of control (feedback control) uses information on actual occurrences to trigger a reaction. We shall continue therefore to use the term control to cover both the feedback and feedforward (anticipatory) connotations and thus to include both planning and control. The extensive literature on management planning and control systems and on corporate strategy is but one indication of the perceived importance of control processes in.

economic organisations. However, it is notable that most of this literature pays only the most limited attention to organisation factors.

Control has been defined as the process of ensuring that the organisation is adapted to its environment and is pursuing courses of action that will enable it to achieve its purposes. Thus, in order to operate such an organisational level of analysis it is necessary to consider the existence and nature of organisational purposes. Etzioni (1961) has suggested that organisations may be categorised into three main types, based on the degree of commonality that exists between individual and organisational objectives.

In a *normative* organisation there is a wide area of agreement on and commitment to organisational goals; in an *instrumental* organisation individual goals are neutral towards organisational goals; in a *coercive* organisation, many if not most individual goals are opposed by organisational goals, with the goals of a dominant group being taken as those of the organisation, as illustrated in Fig. 1.

Type of organisation	Goal alignment	Example
Normative		Religious order Charitable organisation Professional bodies 'Crusade' army
Instrumental	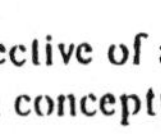	Industrial and business organisation Travel clubs Mercenary army
Coercive	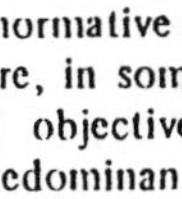	Prison Slavery Conscript army

Fig. 1. Types of involvement in organizations.

The idea of an objective of an organisation is of most obvious use as a conceptual tool in analysing control systems in normative organisations, where overall objectives are, in some sense, an aggregation of individual objectives. In instrumental organisations the predominant pattern is one of an exchange of inducements by the organisation to gain contributions from individuals (Barnard, 1938). However, certain basic objectives may still be agreed upon (often for a limited period) as being in the interests of all participants, such as the survival of the organisation as a means of providing sought-after inducements. Such an approach has close parallels with a stake-holder view of the enterprise with each stake-holder's interest being maintained at a satisfactory level (Simon, 1957).

Instrumental organisations are likely to be characterised by periods of conflict during which compromise agreements are reached between stake-holder groups as to the distribution of inducements followed by periods of apparent consensus during which the agreements are implemented. Objectives thus have a different nature depending upon whether one is analysing activity during the periods of consensus or during periods of conflict. Finally, a coercive organisation can exist only because of the use of power which overwhelms the ability of most of the participants to pursue their own goals. Thus the interests of a majority of the participants are irrelevant to the functioning of this type of organisation, although the counter-sources of power and influence open to them should not be overlooked [see for example Mechanic (1962), Roy (1955)].

Although business organisations have been typified as being primarily instrumental in nature this over-simplifies a situation which will differ both within and between organisations. Within a single organisation the type of involvement will differ from person to person, with hierarchical level often being a major factor. For example, those at senior management levels tend to exhibit, at least publicly, a normative involvement, whereas at shop floor level an instrumental involvement is perhaps more typical with elements of a coercive involvement being apparent in certain occupations. Thus a spectrum of forms of control is defined ranging from self-regulation in pursuit of common objectives to the imposition of constraints by a dominant group acting to maintain its own self-interest.

Although organisational theorists have expressed an interest in the study of organisation control, they appear to have devoted much of their effort towards studying the impact of "controls" on organisational participants, rather than in assessing their appropriateness to organisational "control" [to use Drucker's (1964) distinction]. Control is concerned with overall organisational effectiveness, yet it is in this area that both theoretical and empirical work is weak. Although contingency theories of organisational functioning have received widespread attention recently, it is notable that very few studies follow through their chain of logic to establish the circumstances in which one form of organisation is more effective than another, rather than stopping short at observing that it exists (Otley, 1979). Again it is to be expected that those concerned with corporate strategy would have shown an interest in organisation control, but the implications of the fact that the subject is concerned with the behaviour of human organisations are precisely those most neglected in this field. Thus the organisational literature, with a few notable exceptions (e.g. Vickers, 1973) has shown little concern with the idea of overall organisational control.

The neglect of control by organisational theorists has been paralleled by the neglect of organisation by control theorists. Cybernetics has been defined (Weiner, 1948) as "the science of communication and control" but relatively little work has been applied to the control of human economic organisations, although that of Beer (1959, 1966, 1973) is an important exception.

Beer (1966) notes that "our whole concept is naïve, primitive and ridden with an almost retributive idea of causality. Control to most people is a crude process of coercion." In contrast his analysis begins by assuming that organisational systems are complex, non-deterministic and homeostatic (that is, containing a considerable ability for self-regulation). However, although this approach allows escape from the narrow assumptions of mathematical cybernetics and mechanistic analogies, the replacement analogy is usually that of a living organism [Beer (1973), Katz & Kahn (1966)]. Even then there are considerable difficulties in the transfer of concepts and it is by no means evident that the analogies used have more than very limited validity. Cybernetics has yet to demonstrate that it can provide useful insight into the design of organisational control systems.

It is thus argued that the control literature has used over-simple or poorly validated models of organisation and the organisational literature has shown only a limited concern with the idea of overall organisational control. In this paper an attempt is made to bring together these two bodies of work and to review their implications for the design of accounting control systems.

Accounting procedures are one of the few integrative devices in an organisation which have an explicit model into which activities may not only be drawn together but also integrated in a quantitative manner. These procedures serve as a control system by providing both a language and a set of procedures for establishing quantitative standards of performance and in measuring actual performance in comparison with such standards. They can thus be highly effective at generating mis-match signals indicating deviations of actual performance from that which was projected, thus fulfilling Simon *et al.* (1954) attention-directing function. However, accounting procedures tend to be much less useful in providing information on which the predictions necessary for control can be made and thus fulfilling Simon's function of problem-solving. The type of variable used in predictive models of organisational performance are traditionally considered outside the scope of the accounting structure for two reasons. Firstly they often require information from sources external to the firm other than financial markets and secondly many of the variables necessary for prediction are difficult to measure in quantitative or objectively verifiable terms. Both reasons have led to the belief amongst accountants that provision of such information lies outside the scope of accounting procedures, although studies of the information requirements of managers indicate that it is often required in practice (e.g. Mintzberg, 1975).

It is becoming evident that there is a need to match accounting information and control procedures to the type of organisations in which they operate. Yet the development of accounting appears to have lagged behind developments in organisation theory. The tradition of cost accounting and responsibility accounting is based on bureaucratic and scientific management models of organisations (see for example Parker's (1977) summary critique of the role of control in corporate budgeting). Meanwhile theories of organisation have developed through a Human Relations phase into what has been variously described as a Systems view (Kast & Rosenzweig, 1974) or Behavioural science approach (Filley *et al.*, 1976) and currently, the Contingency Theory of organisational design. The accounting literature has lagged significantly behind, with development in this area only beginning to surface [but see Gordon & Miller (1976), Ansari (1977) and Hayes (1977)] possibly as the objections to contingency theory gain strength (Hopwood, 1978). Indeed, a survey of the literature on control systems in organisations (Lawler, 1976) concluded that very little research had been performed on why organisations end up with the control systems they have. In particular, the management control literature has neglected not only organisational factors but also the crucial role of predictive models in the control process.

There is thus a need for the construction of accounting control models appropriately related to organisation theory. The value of such an approach has long been recognised, for as Horngren (1972) states:

> Ideally, the organisation itself and its processes must be thoroughly appraised, understood and altered, if necessary, before an (accounting control) system is constructed. That is the design of a system and the design of an organisational structure are really inseparable and interdependent.

But little attempt has been made to work through the implications of such a statement in the design of control systems for organisations. Accounting controls still appear to be designed on the basis of strictly hierarchical organisations, with well defined responsibilities at each level and where the top of the organisation is the focus of all knowledge and control. Although something approximating to such an organisation structure may be appropriate where an organisation faces a stable technology and environment, it also represents the situation where accounting controls are of least use (Hopwood, 1974).

A body of literature which claims to have tackled the problem of the relevance of accounting to organisational control has done so under the general title of management control and the classic definition of management control is that of Anthony (1965) who defines management control as "the process by which managers assure that resources are obtained and used effectively and efficiently in the accomplishment of the organisation's goals". Despite its initial plausibility, this definition by which management control is distinguished from strategic planning and operational control raises significant problems. Firstly the problem of defining organisational goals is explained away by relegating it to the realm of strategic planning. Secondly the issue of ensuring that desired activities occur is left to operational control. The purpose of this simplication is to define an area of study which can ignore the great differences in organisation that occur due to technology and environment, so as to be able to discover a universal system of management control. Having done this leaves an emaciated concept of management control which may have been valuable as an initial strategy, but is a present embarrassment in implying an over-narrow view of the management control process. A wider view is put forward by Lowe (1971) where he defines a management control system as

> a system of organisational information seeking and gathering, accountability and feedback designed to ensure that the enterprise adapts to changes in its substantive environment and that the work behavior of its employees is measured by reference to a set of operational sub-goals (which conform with overall objectives) so that the discrepancy between the two can be reconciled and corrected for.

Although accounting research is only beginning to address the issues raised by such a definition, it is now clear that such problems are a proper focus of attention and that attempts are now being made to implement Horngren's exhortation [e.g. Waterhouse & Tiessen (1978), and Hedberg & Jönsson (1978)].

The remainder of this paper is addressed to examining some of the issues that are raised when ideas of control which stem from a cybernetic approach are applied to human organisations and a consideration of their implications for the design of accounting systems.

A MODEL OF THE CONTROL PROCESS

Cybernetic approaches such as those of Ashby (1956) and Beer (1973) have a quite different focus to those of the organisation theorists. The cyberneticians are primarily concerned with inner structures of variety, probability and logic which may be used to characterise organisations. They tend to accept the risk of reifying their constructs in the search for a widely applicable generality. For example the nine levels of the General Hierarchy of Systems of Bertalanffy (1956) and Boulding (1956) are derived from an implicit distinction of complexity. These nine levels are:

(1) static frameworks
(2) dynamic systems with pre-determined motions
(3) closed loop control or cybernetic systems
(4) homeostatic systems, such as biological cells
(5) the living plant
(6) animals
(7) man
(8) organisations
(9) transcendental systems

The mechanistic or engineering control theory which was developed for systems of levels 2 and 3 is not simply transferable to the higher levels, not only because of the difference in complexity of the levels but also because of the shifting nature of the systems both in regard to the issue of probability and the values underlying risk preferences and choices. However, to argue that ideas are not simply transferable does not mean that they are irrelevant. The cybernetic tradition has produced a general definition of control (Tocher, 1970, 1976) which possesses some interesting and useful properties when applied to the control of organisations.

It may be deduced from Tocher's definition that at least four necessary conditions must be satisfied before a process can be said to be controlled. These state that there must exist:

(1) an objective for the system being controlled
(2) a means of measuring results along the dimensions defined by the objective
(3) a predictive model of the system being controlled
(4) a choice of relevant alternative actions available to the controller

A control system containing these elements is shown in Fig. 2, annotated with Vickers (1967) terminology.

In this model the four necessary conditions for control are articulated. Firstly control can only exist when knowledge of outcomes is available; with no feedback on actual performance, improvement (and even continued success in changing conditions) is possible only by chance. However, such knowledge of the true state of the real world is not always easy to come by and is called by Vickers the making of a "reality judgement". Secondly, control requires an objective; without an aim, activity can be described only as aimless. This process of deciding upon appropriate directions for activity is essentially that of making value judgements. Thirdly, having compared actual and desired outcomes and generated a mis-match signal by noting any discrepancy between the two, a control action has to be determined. This requires a predictive model of the process being controlled, that is, a means of forecasting the likely outcomes of various alternative courses of action. To the extent that such a model is non-existent or defective, then control is impossible and attempted control actions may well be counter-productive. It is noteworthy that many elementary descriptions of control processes completely omit the central position of predictive models. Finally, a selected action requires to be

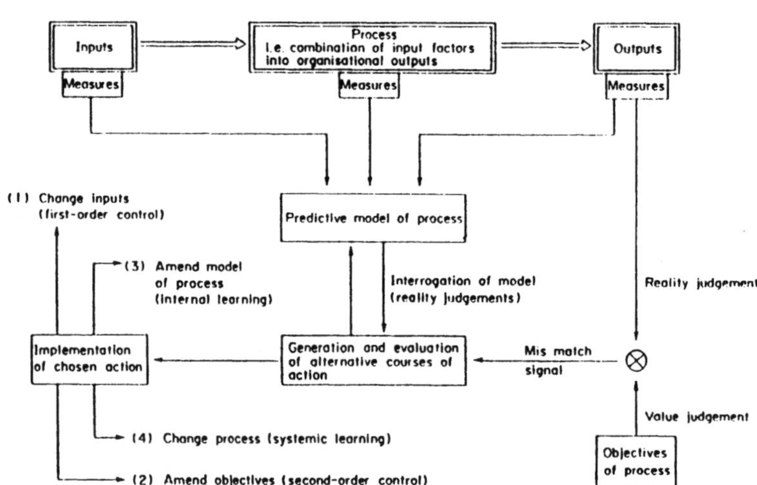

Fig. 2. Outline scheme of necessary conditions for a controlled process.

implemented. This may do one or more of four things. It may adjust the system inputs (first-order control); it may alter system objectives (second-order control); it may amend the predictive model on the basis of past experience (internal learning) and it may change the nature of the process itself (systemic learning).

Such a conception of control is recursive in nature. That is, it may be applied to any level of system and therefore to any sub-system within an overall system. It may be used to analyse an individual's control of his own activities, a group of people controlling each other's behaviour (social control), an organisation controlling its internal activities in response to the environment in which it operates (organisational control) or a society controlling the activities of organisations, groups and individuals within it (societal or governmental control), although the specific features of the model will obviously differ for each level of resolution. At each of the higher levels, one immediately obvious problem of control is that for each control action the response of sub-systems is often likely to be one of minimising the effects of the control action, as each self-controlling sub-system adapts its behaviour so as to continue to achieve and modify its own objectives. There is thus no assumption of consensus in using such a control model; it may be used to examine situations of conflict.

Perhaps the most fundamental problem that is faced in transferring such a cybernetic or homeostatic model of control to an organisational level of analysis is the apparently inevitable division of labour between controllers and those who are controlled, that is the distinction between the dominator and the dominated. Even when one separates out the control exercised within organisations by managers as an interest group in their own right (and a powerful one by reason of their access to information and power over the distribution of resources and rewards), the primary function ascribed to the task of management is that of organisation control. That is, their role is to ensure that the organisation continues to cohere in a form that keeps all interested parties satisfied enough to continue to support the organisation's activities.

In a normative organisation the task of management is not primarily one of dominance, rather it is one of encouraging self-regulation; in an instrumental organisation limited or partial authority is ceded to management to legitimise its control actions; in a coercive organisation control rests primarily on dominance. The middle ground of the business organisation is thus one where many differing styles of control might be expected to be observed.

The prior discussion has proceeded along very general lines and has viewed the organisational control process as a correlate of organisation *per se*, without considering the locus and form of the control function. Much discussion of control in an organisational context has either taken the position of a particular agency or interest group (e.g. workers' control as against owners' or managers' control) or has concentrated on the effects of particular "controls" on various groups within the organisation. In business organisations authority and influence (Tannenbaum *et al.*, 1974) are a function of participants' expectations and national culture. In the typical western European and American business organisation, the stereotype of which is to be found in many accountancy text books, the control function is located at the top of the hierarchy. This position is reinforced in the accounting literature with its normative assertions of profit maximisation and the present legal position which establishes a bias in favour of the providers of capital (Nichols and Beynon, 1977). There is some evidence that this balance of power might be shifted with the advent of increased worker participation and of changes such as the introduction of two-tier boards. However, the mere existence of any group charged with the responsibility of organisational control seems to lead to its perceived superiority over other organisational participants (although this does not follow absolutely as, for example, hospital administrators are not usually viewed as the superiors of consultants). Such a differentiation of status is reinforced by the nature of control decisions. A control decision requires that organisational participants take actions other than those which they would have taken in the absence of the control decision (for otherwise it would not be necessary to take an explicit decision). These actions, although designed to lead to the overall good, may not be aligned with the immediate interests of those who have to implement them. On the assumption that the original actions were in their own best interests, then the control instruction is likely to reduce the benefits they receive from the organisation. Control in general, and the controllers in particular are likely to be unpopular, and methods of clarifying the connection between control activities and overall organisational welfare are designed to reduce this unpopularity.

Accounting and accountants are very much caught up in the process of controlling the behaviour of others, as they constitute an agency of what Lowe & Tinker (1978) infelicitously term the "central authority". Indeed, many of the findings of the behavioural studies of the role of accounting and accountants in relation to managers stem from the interaction of their mutual roles. Because of these factors the integration of accounting controls into the process of overall organisational control is subject to severe limitations. We now turn to an examination of the problems posed by such an integration, through a consideration of the four necessary conditions for control derived in this section.

APPLICATION TO ORGANISATIONAL CONTROL

In the original development of his control framework Tocher (1970) was evidently thinking in terms of the control of a system by an external agency, and it is no doubt appropriate to analyse the control of organisations from this point of view (e.g. the control of business organisations by governmental actions). However, this paper is concerned with a different level of resolution, namely the self-control exerted by organisations themselves so that they may better achieve their objectives in the face of external (and internal) circumstances. It is of interest to note that in his subsequent discussion Tocher (1976) observes that attempts were made to apply his concepts in situations where no external agency was apparent. That is, we are considering a self-regulating system where control is exercised by agencies within the system itself. Human organisations evidently exhibit features of self-regulation and this section is concerned with examining the applicability of the four necessary conditions for a controlled system in self-regulating economic organisations.

Objectives

The very idea of an objective for an organisation as distinct from the objectives of the individuals involved is problematic (Simon, 1964). As Arrow (1951), following a long sociological tradition, has pointed out, even if it can be assumed that individuals have well-defined and transitive preferences there is no non-arbitrary method of deriving a group preference function from the individual preferences. A decision can, of course, be made but different decision rules give different results. Although the application of utility theory may seem appropriate, it is still necessary to combine inter-personal utilities and there is no accepted method of doing this. Thus, although use of a decision rule will give a result, such a result is essentially arbitrary, and depends for its effectiveness on its acceptance by those involved. More realistically, in such a situation, political bargaining and negotiation will occur, and a process of coalition forming and breaking takes place until the issue is resolved by the application of an accepted decision rule, be it managerial decree or democratic vote.

The consequence for the analysis of control is that considerable care has to be taken in defining objectives and assessing their status. Logically one is comparing benefits given to disparate groups of people and the satisfactions that are given by these benefits. Each group is in a different bargaining position with respect to changes and the task of the control procedures is to arrange a balance between the rewards given to competing interest groups in a changing environment. To the extent that involvement is instrumental rather than normative, control may be achieved in part by the design of reward structures which influence individuals to act in an agreed manner by pursuing their own self-interest. That is the control of the instrumental organisation is achieved by means of processes within the organisation which structure the distribution of valued rewards in return for compliance.

To the extent that an instrumental organisation can be said to have objectives, they may be characterised as multiple, partially conflicting and subject to change in response to environmental changes. These objectives are perhaps better regarded as constraints defining a feasible region for activities (Simon, 1964). As objectives or constraints change over time so then will the feasible region change. The task of the control process is to keep actual activity within such a dynamic feasible region; that is to keep each individual and interest group satisfied enough to continue to provide their necessary support towards ensuring that appropriate activities are carried out.

Accounting systems play a significant role in both the process of objective formulation and of identifying feasible regions for organisational activity. For example, budgetary standards and targets often represent the outcome of bargaining processes where agreed expectations are negotiated. In addition, the master budget itself may be treated as an organisational model (admittedly of a very simple kind) with which the effects of alternative courses of action are evaluated. Accounting information is itself of use in the bargaining process and the provision of such information to representatives of various interest groups (e.g. trade union officials, customers on certain types of contract) is part of the negotiation activity. For example, trade unions now often use accounting information to define a company's "ability to pay", which is their assessment of one boundary of the feasible region.

Whatever approach is adopted, it is necessary to engage with the issue of authority in organisations. As Berry (1979) has argued, accounting thrives in a culture of dependence, and that culture can be powerfully destructive. The concept of a central authority as a locus of control as developed by Lowe & Tinker (1978) is not necessarily embedded in a social hierarchy; it can be a meeting of a group of members and in this sense represent a focus of mutual responsibility. There is no doubt that the role of controller is immensely powerful, which gives all the more reason to attempt to ensure that those who fulfil such a role are held accountable to those whom they control.

Predictive models

The major purpose of the predictive model is to enable answers to questions of the form: if a certain course of action is taken, then what consequences will follow; in particular, how will the achievement of objectives or avoidance of constraints be affected? Two features of predictive models for the behaviour of organisations are immediately apparent. Firstly the available models are usually imprecise and inaccurate so that predictions made from them are likely to be at odds with actual events. Because of this, actions designed to assist control may actually turn out to hinder it because of unanticipated consequences [Forrester (1961) simulates many such systems]. When relevant reality is only imperfectly modelled it may be wise to proceed in small, incremental steps where some degree of prediction is possible, rather than by making radical changes whose effect is largely unpredictable [Lindblom (1959); Wildavsky (1973)]. Secondly within organisations there are usually multiple and partially conflicting predictive models rather than a single holistic model (e.g. separate models relating to employment of labour, production processes, marketing and finance). This situation is due to both a relatively undeveloped understanding which generates small partial models as a first step and also to the fact that organisations consist of individuals in roles, each of whom will apply his own models, insights and understandings. In addition one also finds the use of over-simple but apparently general models, often tinged with an ideological basis (e.g. the perfectly competitive economic model), in circumstances where the model's fit with reality is poor.

It is important to consider how models might be improved. If an organisation remains in control by taking only those actions where reasonable prediction is possible, all is well in the short-term. However, the wider applicability of the model may need to be tested, especially as time horizons lengthen and the range of variables to be considered is extended. By taking actions whose outcomes are not as accurately predictable, the range of applicability of the model can be examined. The stimulus to learn about the model and its applicability takes place by detecting differences between expected outcomes and actual outcomes (i.e. making mistakes).

While there is clearly a role for a development activity on models the existence of environmental uncertainty must preclude an exact specification. There is again a close parallel here between the design of control processes and the design of organisations. Bureaucratic organisations can lead to efficient performance of a well specified task in a stable environment, but such organisations cope poorly with unexpected changes; organismic organisations are relatively inefficient for well specified tasks but have a greater adaptive capacity (Burns & Stalker, 1961). This insight may be extended to the models in a control process. The control model must evolve in use with due attention to the problems of immediate goal attainment (efficiency) and the attainment of future gaols (adaptation and experimentation). It is ironic that those organisations which most need to experiment and improve their adaptive capability are those where present circumstances define such necessities as luxuries. [Wildavsky (1975) gives a parallel from national planning and budgeting.]

In attaining overall organisation control, the

predictive model used by the control system must include a representation of the models used by individuals and groups within the organisation who are attempting to control outcomes to their own advantage. For in order to predict the consequences of a given action, it is necessary to predict how relevant others will seek to affect events. In turn, the models used by the others concerned will include models of the behaviour of the organisational control system. Thus part of the difficulty in attaining overall organisational control is the interdependent nature of the models used where each attempts to include the other. (Wage bargaining negotiations provide a vivid example of this phenomenon as does the process of bias and counter-bias in the setting of budgets.)

The implications for accounting are clear enough. An accounting or financial model of an organisation is only partial and contains insufficient variety for organisational control. However, the accounting model is important and necessary even though insufficient; necessary because it relates to a relevant environment, insufficient because the range of variables included is only partial and because other relevant environments are not considered. This is not to say development and improvement cannot take place; indeed, the provision of appropriate information to allow prediction of a wider range of relevant outcomes is perhaps the most important extension of an organisation's accounting system that can be envisaged. In a similar vein, Lowe (1971) concludes that

> accountants need not be faint of heart for they surely possess a good basis (perhaps the only one) for the development of an integrated management control (and information) system provided they extend their thinking in the application of that powerful tool – accounting method.

This implies that the accountant must be prepared to include within his remit the collection of information concerning a far wider range of variables than has traditionally been the case, and to develop the necessary skills for collecting such information.

Measures

Two distinct sets of variables require measurement. Firstly activity requires to be monitored along those dimensions defined as objectives. Thus, for example, if long-run survival requires the generation of a certain level of profitability then this requires measurement and comparison with the defined standard. Secondly, as the predictive models used contain an array of variables which are necessary to predict behaviour and performance, these predictor variables must also be measured.

Accounting procedures have traditionally been designed in response to the need for the first kind of measurement. Thus they stress the components of objective-oriented measures such as production, cost and profit. Although influenced heavily by shareholder objectives, they are compatible with measuring partial objective achievement for other groups (e.g. price for customers; wages for employees etc.). Indeed, it may be argued that certain income measures, for example, residual income, are surrogates for measures of overall enterprise viability, rather than serving the interests of any particular stakeholder group (Emmanuel & Otley, 1976). But such measures possess little predictive power. The second purpose is partially served by systems which allow causes for deviations from standard to be deduced (e.g. the calculation of cost accounting variances), but even these systems have very limited predictive ability.

One particular difficulty in providing information for predictive models is that they are concerned both with processes internal to an organisation and with the interaction between an organisation and its environment. Thus factors of interest will include external circumstances as well as internal responses. It would seem that most organisations are less well developed in formally monitoring their external environment than their internal state, although there is evidence that informal networks carry some information about external phenomena.[1] But even internally some variables (e.g. cost) are better dealt with than others (e.g. job satisfaction).

Thus the variables that it is necessary to measure for an effective set of processes are those defined by the objectives of the controlled process and those utilised in the predictive model. It appears that relatively little attention has been paid to the development of information systems to serve the needs of predictive models in contrast to the measurement of objective-oriented factors. This may be a further reason for the often observed lack of use of many management

[1] Management Control Research Project Reports 1–4, Manchester Business School.

information systems (Mintzberg, 1975). The typical structure of accounting procedures is such as to leave aside the required measures of environment. Whether accounting should be redefined to include such measures or whether its claims should be re-assessed is a matter that will be taken up in the final section.

Choice of action

A final requirement for control is that a choice of action is available. If no relevant inputs to a system can be changed then control cannot be exercised. Four different types of action can be distinguished any, or all, of which can be implemented. Firstly there are actions which change the inputs to the system being controlled and cause its behaviour to alter (i.e. first-order control). Secondly there are actions which change the objectives, or at least the level of the standards which it is deemed necessary to reach (i.e. second-order control). Thirdly there are actions which amend the predictive model of the system being controlled and the measurement and communication processes associated with it; this may be described as internal learning. Fourthly there are actions which change the system itself and hence its inputs, outputs and associated predictive models; this may be described as adaptation or systemic learning.

An organisation acts only by way of the actions of the individuals who comprise it. Thus for organisational control to be effective, not only must feasible control actions be possible but individuals must also be persuaded to implement the required actions. At a minimum this requires the communication of the desired action or of other information from which an appropriate action may be deduced. Such communication alone may be sufficient in normative organisations where the goal alignment of individuals may produce sufficient motivation to act; in instrumental or coercive organisations some reward or penalty structure is likely to be required. Finally, the individual who is in a position to know what needs to be done, and who is motivated to take action, must have access to adequate resources to implement the requisite action.

The type of information that indicates control actions are necessary (i.e. attention-directing information) does not usually indicate what actions should be taken (i.e. it does not assist with problem-solving). As well as an innovative input which can suggest apt courses of action, a predictive model is necessary in order to evaluate the likely outcomes of proposed alternative actions. It is evident yet again that without prediction there is no control, and that a predictive model must contain variables outside the traditional scope of accounting systems.

CONCLUSIONS

Formal organisations continue to cohere only when the benefits they yield to each individual and group connected with them exceed the contributions to the organisation required from them and when this net balance of benefits exceeds what is perceived to be available elsewhere when transition costs are taken into account. It is therefore in the interests of organisational participants to establish procedures for organisational control which are designed to help ensure that such benefits continue to be produced, notwithstanding the sectional interest of each participant to influence the distribution of benefits in his own favour. Control procedures are thus essential features of organisations.

However, it has been noted when the control process is considered at an organisational level of analysis, there are significant weaknesses in the ability of organisations to regulate their own behaviour on each of the four major dimensions identified. Firstly, organisational objectives are often vague, ambiguous and change with time. They are often set by ill-defined processes, and are multiple and partially conflicting. In addition they are congruent to only a varying extent with the objectives of various interest groups associated with the organisation. Secondly, in this situation, measures of achievement are possible only in correspondingly vague and often subjective terms. Thirdly, predictive models of organisational behaviour are partial and unreliable, and furthermore different models may be held by different participants. Finally, the ability to act is highly constrained for most groups of participants, including the so-called "controllers", by virtue of the limited range of possible actions open to them. A fundamental problem is that there is still a need for the overall regulation of the organisation, although the complexity and uncertainty inherent within it may make the possibility of control very limited. In addition, the nature of control actions is such that they are perceived as undesirable in relation to the immediate interests of at least some participants. The task of the control procedures is therefore to balance the differing requirements of the various parties associated with the well-being of the enterprise, to ensure the continued satisfaction of those requirements. The strategies available for the design of control procedures should be studied in this light.

IMPLICATIONS FOR ACCOUNTING RESEARCH

The limitations shown up by this examination of the role of accounting information in organisational control are limitations caused by a lack of variety in the accounting system so that it in no way matches the complexity of the organisation being controlled. However, no control system will ever be able to match the variety of an organisation unless it is of an equal complexity itself (e.g. in the way that a football team may be "controlled" by an equally skilful team of opponents). Control in a full cybernetic sense will never be achieved in the context of a human organisation, although this is not to deny that existing techniques of attempting to gain control cannot be improved. However, the contrast between approaches to control in organisation theory, cybernetics and accounting is such as to raise the fundamental question of the usefulness of an approach to control which has such limitations. By means of a somewhat different argument Hofstede (1975) came to the conclusion that the philosophy of management control (by which he meant the tradition following Anthony and other authors who concentrate on accounting control) was impoverished.

But we cannot leave the matter there, for in the preceding analysis it has been recognised that accounting at least provides an appropriate language for examining the relationship between an organisation and its financial environment. What is at issue is whether there is an holistic approach to organisational control and, if so, whether accounting models provide an appropriate framework for their development. It is our belief that it is important to attempt to develop such an holistic approach, for the control of such important artefacts as human organisations is of vital importance to the welfare of society. Further, although accounting control procedures are admittedly inadequate for the task, they nevertheless appear to provide the best framework that is currently available. This final section therefore considers some ways forward in improving accounting systems so that they may better serve their control function.

There has been a tendency in the literature of management science and financial management, if not in practice, towards the development of elegant mathematical models for non-problems against the development of heuristics or crude models for real problems. The insistence upon an objective function to be optimised is perhaps symptomatic of this malaise. It would appear to be a logical and positive extension to the role of the academic accountant for him to be concerned with the construction of predictive models incorporating a wider range of variables than has traditionally been the case. In such a role he would concern himself with the definition and measurement of those variables which are of significance in influencing the successful operation of an organisation, and with the design of procedures to report this information to those who can take action based upon it. This is not intended to replace the financial control role of accountants, but to be additional and complementary to it.

The central issues involved in the control of organisations are of great importance and insights from a variety of academic disciplines are essential in developing improved understanding. A number of approaches are possible. Firstly following Caplan (1966) it would be possible to analyse the assumptions of modern (contingent) organisation theory and to compare these with the assumptions made in accounting theory and practice, noting that the latter two may well differ. To some extent this work has been begun, but it requires extension into the re-working of the design of accounting structures so that they "fit" better the requirements of organisations. Secondly it might be appropriate to neglect the current accounting framework as being so far removed from the issue of interest as to make it inappropriate. Such a departure would require an attempt to synthesise an integrated theory of organisational control from cybernetics, general systems theory and organisation theory. [Amey (1979) makes a partial start to such an endeavour.] However, even if this were to be successful in terms of providing a tidy and perceptive theoretical structure there would be considerable problems of application to particular organisational control issues. A third approach would be to leave the problem of theoretical synthesis unresolved and to concentrate on understanding how specific organisations actually go about controlling their activities. Whilst recognising that no observation is value- or theory-free this approach might take such limited theory as has been developed and demand that the researcher develop explanations for phenomena which actually occur. This would have the advantage of not prejudging the role and relevance of accounting control procedures.

Following the argument of this paper, a sensible choice between alternative courses of action requires a predictive model of outcomes. In terms of the effectiveness of alternative research strategies to build improved theories of organisational control, we have little knowledge of the likely outcomes. The little we have suggests that the third approach, which concentrates on the structured and intensive observation of the operation of the whole range of control activities undertaken by specific organisations, offers the most hope of being fruitful in the long term.

BIBLIOGRAPHY

Amey, L. R., *Budget Planning and Control Systems* (London: Pitman, 1979).

Ansari, S. L., An Integrated Approach to Control Systems Design, *Accounting, Organizations and Society* (1977), pp. 101–112.

Anthony, R. N., *Planning and Control Systems: A Framework for Analysis* (Boston, Mass.: Graduate School of Business Administration, Harvard University, 1965).

Arrow, K. J., *Social Choice and Individual Values* (New York: Wiley, 1951).

Ashby, W. R., *An Introduction to Cybernetics* (London: Chapman and Hall, 1956).

Barnard, C., *The Functions of the Executive* (Cambridge, Harvard University Press, 1938).

Beer. S., *Cybernetics and Management* (London: E.U.P., 1959).

Beer, S., *Decision and Control* (New York: Wiley, 1966).

Beer, S., *Brain of the Firm* (Harmondsworth, Middx.: Allen Lane, 1973).

Berry, A. J., Policy, Accounting and the Problem of Order, *Personnel Review* (1979).

von Bertalanffy, L., General System Theory, *General Systems, Yearbook of the Society for the Advancement of General System Theory* (1956), pp. 1–10.

Boulding, K. E., General Systems Theory: The Skeleton of Science, *General Systems Yearbook of the Society for the Advancement of General System Theory* (1956), pp. 11–17.

Burns, T. & Stalker, G. M., *The Management of Innovation* (London: Tavistock, 1961).

Caplan, E. H., Behavioural Assumptions of Management Accounting, *Accounting Review* (1966), pp. 496–509.

Drucker, P., Control, Controls and Management, in Bonini, C. P., *et al., Management Controls: New Directions in Basis Research* (New York: McGraw-Hill, 1964).

Emmanuel, C. R. & Otley, D. T., The Usefulness of Residual Income, *Journal of Business Finance and Accounting* (Winter, 1976), pp. 43–51.

Etzioni, A., *A Comparative Analysis of Complex Organisations* (New York: Free Press, 1961).

Filley, A. C., House, R. J. & Kerr, S., *Managerial Process and Organizational Behavior* (2nd ed.; Glenview, Illinois: Scott, Foresman and Co., 1976).

Forrester, J. W., *Industrial Dynamics* (Cambridge, Mass.: M.I.T. Press, 1961).

Gordon, L. A. & Miller, D., A Contingency Framework for the Design of Accounting Information Systems, *Accounting, Organizations and Society* (1976), pp. 59–69.

Hayes, D. C., The Contingency Theory of Managerial Accounting, *Accounting Review* (January, 1977), pp. 22–39.

Hedberg, B. & Jönsson, S., Designing Semi-confusing Information Systems for Organisations in Changing Environments, *Accounting, Organizations and Society* (1978), pp. 47–64.

Hofstede, G., *The Game of Budget Control* (London: Tavistock, 1968).

Hofstede, G., The Poverty of Management Control Philosophy, Working Paper 75-44 of the European Institute of Advanced Studies in Management, Brussels, December 1975.

Hopwood, A. G., *Accounting and Human Behaviour* (London: Haymarket Publishing, 1974).

Hopwood, A. G., Towards an Organisational Perspective for the Study of Accounting and Information Systems, *Accounting, Organizations and Society* (1978), pp. 3–13.

Horngren, C. T., *Cost Accounting: A Managerial Emphasis* (3rd edition; Englewood Cliffs, N.J.: Prentice-Hall, 1972).

Katz, D. & Kahn, R. L., *The Social Psychology of Organisations* (New York: Wiley, 1966).

Kast, F. E. & Rosenzweig, J. E., *Organization and Management: A Systems Approach* (2nd edition; New York: McGraw-Hill, 1974).

Lawler, E. E., Control Systems in Organizations, in Dunnette, M. D. (ed.), *Handbook of Industrial and Organization* (Rand-McNally, 1976).

Lindblom, C. E., The Science of "Muddling Through", *Public Administration Review* (Spring, 1959), pp. 79-88.
Lowe, E. A., On the Idea of a Management Control System, *Journal of Management Studies* (February, 1971), pp. 1-12.
Lowe, E. A. & Tinker, A., Some Empirical Evidence related to the case of the Superordinate Integrator, *Journal of Management Studies* (February, 1978), pp. 86-105.
McMahon, J. T. & Ivancevich, J. M., A Study of Control in a Manufacturing Organization: Managers and Nonmanagers, *Administrative Science Quarterly* (March, 1976), pp. 66-83.
March, J. G. & Simon, H., *Organizations* (New York: Wiley, 1958).
Mechanic, D., Sources of Power of Lower Participants in Complex Organisations, *Administrative Science Quarterly* (1962), pp. 349-364.
Mintzberg, H., *Impediments to the Use of Management Information* (New York: N.A.A., 1975).
Nichols, T. & Beynon, H., *Living with Capitalism* (London: Routledge and Kegan Paul, 1977).
Otley, D. T., Towards a contingency theory of management accounting: a critical assessment, Accounting Research Workshop Papers, University of Glasgow, May 1979.
Parker, L., A Reassessment of the Role of Control in Corporate Budgeting, *Accounting and Business Research* (Spring 1977), pp. 135-143.
Parsons, T., *The Social System* (New York: Free Press, 1951).
Rathe, A. W., Management Controls in Business, in Malcolm, D. G. and Rowe, A. J. (eds.), *Management Control Systems* (New York: Wiley, 1960).
Roy, D., Efficiency and the "Fix": Informal Intergroup Relations in a Piecework Machine Shop, *American Journal of Sociology* (1955), pp. 255-266.
Silverman, D., *The Theory of Organisations* (London: Heinemann, 1970).
Simon, H. *et al.*, *Centralisation versus Decentralisation in the Controllers' Department* (New York: Controllership Foundation, 1954).
Simon, H., *Administrative Behaviour* (2nd edition; New York: Macmillan, 1957).
Simon, H., On the Concept of an Organisational Goal, *Administrative Science Quarterly* (June, 1964), pp. 1-22.
Tannenbaum, A. S., *Control in Organisations* (New York: McGraw-Hill, 1968).
Tannenbaum, A. S., Kaveic, B., Rosner, M., Vianello, M. & Weiser, G., *Hierarchy in Organisations* (San Francisco: Jossey-Bass, 1974).
Tocher, K., Control, *Operational Research Quarterly* (June, 1970), pp. 159-180.
Tocher, K., Notes for Discussion on "Control", *Operational Research Quarterly* (1976), pp. 231-239.
Vickers, G., *Towards a Sociology of Management* (London: Chapman and Hall, 1967).
Vickers, G., *Making Institutions Work* (London: Associated Business Programmes, 1973).
Waterhouse, J. H. & Tiessen, P., A Contingency Framework for Management Accounting Systems Research, *Accounting, Organizations and Society* (1978), pp. 65-76.
Weiner, N., *Cybernetics* (Cambridge, Mass.: M.I.T. Press, 1948).
Wildavsky, A., If Planning is Everything Maybe Its Nothing, *Policy Sciences* (1973), pp. 127-153.
Wildavsky, A., *Budgeting: A Comparative Theory of the Budgetary Process* (Boston: Little, Brown and Co., 1975).

[9]

THE ACCOUNTING REVIEW
Vol. LXIII, No. 4
October 1988

EDUCATION RESEARCH

Frank H. Selto, Editor

The Controllability Principle in Responsibility Accounting

Rick Antle and Joel S. Demski

ABSTRACT: The purpose of this paper is to examine controllability: the notion a manager should be evaluated based on that which she or he controls. We embed the managerial evaluation problem in a principal-agent setting and ask whether the optimal agency solution bears any logical relation to a casual definition of controllability. It does not. More to the point, the agency framework compels us to look at information content. This information content perspective, upon reflection, agrees with our intuition, with our anecdotal impressions of practice, and with the dictates of the principal-agent model. Moreover, there is a well-defined relation between information content and a notion of control. Thus, the information content perspective may be thought of as offering a precise definition of controllability.

SHOULD a manager be evaluated as the head of a cost center or a profit center? Our familiar and intuitive analysis of this perennial question focuses on whether the manager *controls* cost and revenue. If so, the manager should be evaluated as the head of a profit center. If the manager only controls cost, a cost center evaluation is appropriate. If the manager only controls revenue, a revenue center evaluation is appropriate.

Analyzing this wisdom requires two specifications. First, we must be precise about what it means for the manager to "control" cost or revenue. Second, we must be precise about what it means to evaluate the manager "correctly" or in the "best possible manner."

We use a principal-agent model to

Helpful comments of Froystein Gjesdal, Bob Kaplan, Rick Lambert, Krishna Palepu, Frank Selto, anonymous reviewers, and seminar participants at Harvard Business School, McMaster University, and Michigan State University as well as financial support from the National Science Foundation are gratefully acknowledged.

Rick Antle and Joel S. Demski, Yale University.

Manuscript received May 1986.
Revisions received March 1987 and January 1988.
Accepted April 1988.

Editor's Note: In compliance with a resolution of the Executive Committee of the American Accounting Association, no new manuscripts have been considered by Education Research since June 30, 1987. Editor Frank Selto indicates that this manuscript is the last to be published in Education Research. On behalf of the readers, reviewers, and authors of Education Research, I wish to thank Frank for his three years of exceptional service as Editor of the section.

provide a coherent framework for the evaluation exercise. This gives a setting where a nontrivial control problem is present, where evaluation of the manager can be explicitly modeled, and where managerial evaluation can be endogenously specified. In this way a control problem is modeled as an exercise in motivating a particular behavior by the manager, and performance evaluation as producing information relevant to the question of whether the desired behavior was supplied. The focus is on control of inputs, not outputs. Managerial evaluation, then, becomes framed in terms of inferring this supply of input.

In turn, we specify what it means for the manager to "control" an evaluation statistic, such as cost or revenue, by asking whether his or her supply of inputs is able to affect the probability distribution of the output statistic. For example, if cost is characterized as a probability distribution, can the manager affect this distribution by altering her or his managerial inputs?

This particular definition is highly stylized, but expositionally convenient. A result is that the principal-agent analysis leads to a focus related to, but distinct from, this notion of controllability. In particular, the principal-agent analysis leads us to ask whether the manager can affect the probability distribution of the output statistic *conditioned on whatever other information is present*. The intuition for this conclusion is best developed by beginning with a stylized notion of controllability, and then refining it to match the principal-agent conclusion. In this way the principal-agent paradigm is used to infer a formal definition of controllability. For exposition purposes, we refer to the performance evaluation dictates of the principal-agent model as the *information content* approach and the casual controllability definition as the (traditional) *controllability* approach.[1]

The paper is organized as follows: In Section I we present three numerical examples that explore the traditional controllability notion in a principal-agent setting. In Section II we introduce the information content perspective and use it to explain the anomalies in the earlier examples. In Section III we illustrate this perspective with a brief analysis of tournaments. Conclusions are offered in Section IV.

I. Some Examples

Basic Model

Consider a setting where an individual, termed a principal, owns a production function that offers uncertain cash flow prospects. Three items of cash flow are identified: cash inflow from customers (revenue), cash outflow for materials and overhead (cost), and cash outflow to compensate the supplier of labor (wage). The revenue and cost amounts depend on which state of nature obtains as well as whether labor supply is "LOW" or "HIGH." There are three equally likely states of nature. The possibilities are described in Table 1 (000 omitted).

The principal faces two options, whether to input labor supply HIGH or LOW. She is risk neutral and, therefore, evaluates the options in terms of the expected value of the net profit they promise. To complete the analysis, we must specify the labor cost, or wage.

Labor is supplied by a second individual, termed an agent (or manager). Three characteristics of this second indi-

[1] We emphasize our particular controllability rhetoric is designed to build intuition. Earlier authors, such as Ferrara [1967], were not as narrow in their conception of controllability. On the other hand, we use the formality of the principal-agent paradigm to propose a precise notion of controllability.

TABLE 1
REVENUE, COST, AND GROSS PROFIT FOR EXAMPLE 1

		State		
		s_1	s_2	s_3
LOW Labor Supply:	Revenue	800	1000	1000
	Cost, exclusive of labor	400	500	500
	Profit, exclusive of labor cost	400	500	500
HIGH Labor Supply:	Revenue	800	1000	1000
	Cost, exclusive of labor	400	400	500
	Profit, exclusive of labor cost	400	600	500

vidual are important. First, he is strictly risk averse, and values his wage compensation according to the expected value of $[\text{wage}]^{1/2}$. In this way, both individuals are important in the production process. The agent supplies labor, while the risk neutral principal supplies risk carrying capacity.[2]

Second, labor supply by the agent is personally costly. He prefers LOW to HIGH. In fact, his preference for wage (w) and labor supply (l) is given by the additive function $[w]^{1/2} - V(l)$, with $V(\text{LOW}) = 0$ and $V(\text{HIGH}) = 50$. In this way the supplier of labor is not an indifferent automaton. He and the principal are in conflict. She prefers HIGH, while he prefers LOW, other things equal.[3]

Third, the agent is not being held captive. He is free to work for the principal, or to work "elsewhere." Working elsewhere nets the agent an expected utility of 250 utiles. (For example, it offers a wage of $(250)^2$, and $V(\cdot) \equiv 0$.) The principal must match this to secure the agent's employment.

With these details in place, we can calculate the cost of labor. If the agent is to supply $l = \text{LOW}$, he must face a wage, denoted w_L, such that $[w_L]^{1/2} - 0 \geq 250$. Otherwise, he does better by working elsewhere. This implies $w_L \geq (250)^2 = 62{,}500$. Similarly, to provide $l = \text{HIGH}$, the principal must offer a wage, denoted

[2] Risk is noxious to the agent and a matter of indifference to the principal. Efficiency dictates the principal shoulder the risk. In this way we view the principal as a loose caricature of a capital market.

More specifically, contrast the agent's thoughts about receiving \$500 for certain or flipping a fair coin where with probability 1/2 he "wins" 1000 and with probability 1/2 he "wins" nothing:

$$[500]^{1/2} = 22.36 > 1/2[1000]^{1/2} + 1/2[0]^{1/2} = 15.81$$

Concavity of $[\cdot]^{1/2}$ guarantees the agent will reject fair gambles. He considers risk noxious. The principal, however, is indifferent between the two options:

$$500 = 1/2[1000] + 1/2[0].$$

[3] The idea is the two individuals face some conflict in the employment relationship. In a larger model this might arise over human capital concerns, over taste for a particular style of administration or set of products, or whatever. The most straightforward way is to assume some type of nonpecuniary cost befalls the agent. We further model this in a separable manner, so the conflict does not interact with the agent's wage. While unrealistic, this allows us to examine the controllability dictates in a transparent setting.

w_H, such that $[w_H]^{1/2}-50\geq 250$. This implies $w_H\geq(300)^2=90{,}000$.[4]

The principal, of course, will pay what the "market demands." Combining these labor cost calculations with the earlier (gross) profit data, we conclude with the following analysis of the principal's decision (000 omitted).

	Labor Supply	
	LOW	*HIGH*
E(Revenue)	933.33[5]	933.33
Less *E*(Cost)	466.67[6]	433.33[7]
E(Gross profit)	466.67	500.00
Less Wage	62.50	90.00
E(Net profit)	404.17	410.00

Evaluation Context

To this point there is little interest in evaluating the agent. The principal prefers labor supply HIGH, while the agent prefers LOW. But we have implicitly assumed the agent, in exchange for appropriate compensation, supplies the agreed upon amount. If this assumption is accurate, there is no interest in verifying the agent's labor supply.

Now move to the opposite extreme and assume the agent operates in his self interest. Further assume only the realized cost (exclusive of labor payment) and revenue are jointly observable and verifiable. Thus, the contract with the agent can call for payment as a function of the gross profit, but not as a function of the labor input actually supplied. The actual labor input is not verifiable and, therefore, not available as a basis for contracting.

This final verifiability assumption is important because it allows the agent room to maneuver in exploiting the natural conflict between principal and agent. In particular, suppose the principal offers a guaranteed wage of $w_H=90{,}000$ in exchange for supply of input HIGH. The agent can supply HIGH, with a resulting utility measure of $[90{,}000]^{1/2}-50=250$ or supply LOW with a resulting utility measure of $[90{,}000]^{1/2}-0=300>250$. In short, supply of HIGH under this compensation arrangement is not incentive compatible.

Our original analysis, in other words, does not provide a practicable resolution of the labor contracting problem in this setting of self interested behavior coupled with limited observability and verifiability. We seek labor input, but cannot verify its supply. Only labor output, cost and revenue here, is observable and verifiable. Thus, we use the output to infer the input. We evaluate the agent, so to speak, based on his output. In this way output serves two roles: it is a source of *value* in the production process and it is a source of *information* for the control problem of motivating the self interested manager. This gets to the basic question: how should we use the information provided by output; do we want to use cost, revenue, or cost and revenue to evaluate the manager?[8] The question is interesting because the value and information components of the output are not coextensive. We cannot unambiguously infer the one from the other.

[4] It is efficient to compensate the agent with a constant wage. Otherwise, his payment is at risk while risk is noxious to him but not to the principal.

[5] $(1/3)(800)+(2/3)(1000)=933.33$.

[6] $(1/3)(400)+(2/3)(500)=466.67$.

[7] $(2/3)(400)+(1/3)(500)=433.33$.

[8] We sketch the story in terms of cost, revenue, or cost and revenue to provide a caricature of an institutional setting. The typical cost center setting would, however, focus on cost and physical output, as with a flexible budget. So the available information is perhaps better framed in terms of cost, physical output, and revenue rather than cost and revenue. The addition of an explicit output descriptor, though, needlessly complicates our setting. Similar comments apply to variances.

EXHIBIT 1
AGENT'S DECISION TREE
COST OBSERVABLE

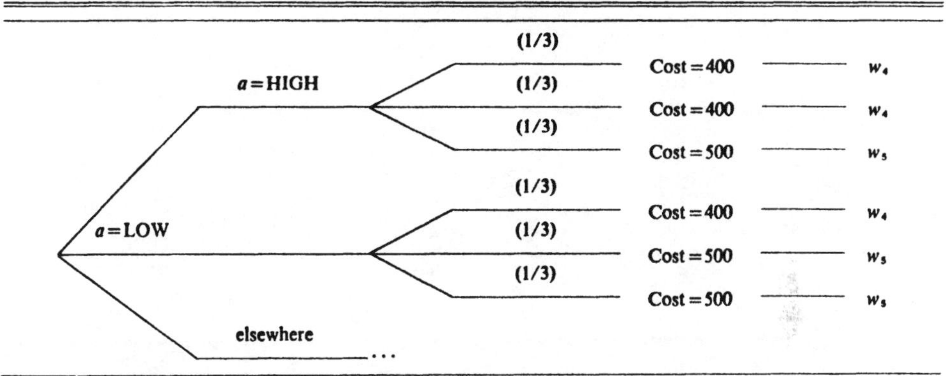

Controllability Answer

Consider the controllability prescription. If an output statistic such as revenue is used in the agent's evaluation then the agent should be able to control that statistic. Return to the data in Table 1. The revenue depends on which state nature supplies, but not the labor input. Conversely, the cost depends on both the state and labor. The agent, through conscious behavior, can influence the cost probability or lottery. The revenue probability or lottery is totally independent of what the agent does. We conclude, using this notion of controllability, our particular agent is best evaluated as the head of a cost center. He controls cost, but not revenue.

Model's Answer

Now ask the agency model the same question. First, suppose we observe only the cost outcome. What is the best way to contract for supply of HIGH? The trick is to design the agent's decision tree so his self interested behavior mirrors the principal's wishes. Let w_4 denote the agent's wage if cost=400 is realized and w_5 if cost=500 is realized. The agent's decision tree is shown in Exhibit 1. Goal congruence demands the agent prefer HIGH to the other options. Thus, we must engineer *the agent's* decision tree so HIGH is preferred. This requires:

$$2/3[w_4]^{1/2}+1/3[w_5]^{1/2}-50\geq 250,$$

and

$$2/3[w_4]^{1/2}+1/3[w_5]^{1/2}-50 \geq 1/3[w_4]^{1/2}+2/3[w_5]^{1/2}-0.$$

The first inequality forces HIGH to be as good as "go elsewhere...." The second forces HIGH to be as good as LOW. In this way self interest on the agent's part leads to choice of HIGH. Goal congruence is a constraint in designing the control system. We design the system so the preferred behavior is in the agent's self interest.

But achieving goal congruence is only part of the principal's problem. Another concern is the cost of aligning the agent's behavior. Naturally, the principal will select the $w_4\backslash w_5$ combination that is least expensive. With the principal risk

EXHIBIT 2
AGENT'S DECISION TREE
REVENUE AND COST OBSERVABLE

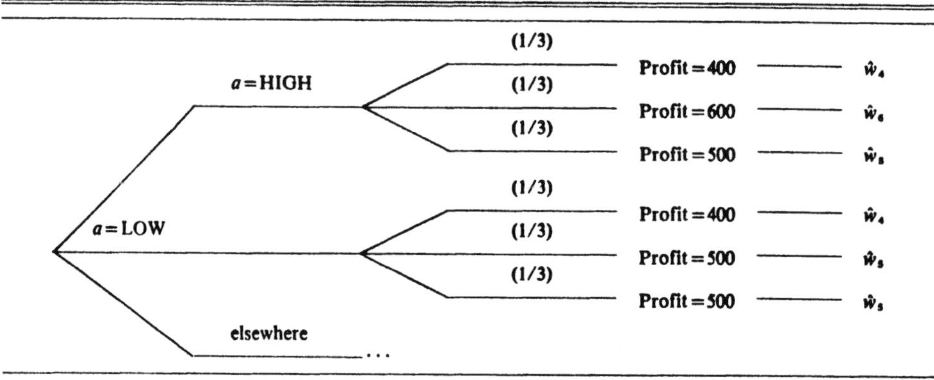

neutral, least expensive means least expected payment to the agent when he is motivated to supply HIGH. The best combination is, therefore, located by the following program:

$$\min_{w_4, w_5} \quad 2/3w_4 + 1/3w_5$$

subject to

$$2/3[w_4]^{1/2} + 1/3[w_5]^{1/2} - 50 \geq 250$$
$$2/3[w_4]^{1/2} + 1/3[w_5]^{1/2} - 50$$
$$\geq 1/3[w_4]^{1/2} + 2/3[w_5]^{1/2} - 0$$
$$w_4, w_5 \geq 0.$$

The solution is $w_4 = 122{,}500$ and $w_5 = 40{,}000$.[9] The principal's evaluation is now:

	Labor Supply	
	LOW	*HIGH*
E(Revenue)	933.33	933.33
Less *E*(Cost)	466.67	433.33
E(Gross profit)	466.67	500.00
Less *E*(Wage)	62.50[10]	95.00[11]
E(Net profit)	404.17	405.00

Contrast this with use of revenue and cost in the agent's evaluation. Recalling

[9] This solution can be developed in the following intuitive fashion. Suppose only the first constraint is binding. This is the setting where we have to induce the agent to work for the principal, without any concern for selecting HIGH over LOW. With the principal risk neutral intuition correctly suggests $w_4 = w_5 = 90{,}000$. But the second constraint is violated. Conversely, using only the second constraint requires $[w_4]^{1/2} - [w_5]^{1/2} = 150$. Minimizing the expected payment implies $w_5 = 0$ and $w_4 = 22{,}500$, which violates the first constraint. By implication both constraints are binding. Solving two equations in two unknowns provides $[w_4]^{1/2} = 350$ and $[w_5]^{1/2} = 200$, or $w_4 = 122{,}500$ and $w_5 = 40{,}000$.

Alternatively, let $v_4 = [w_4]^{1/2}$ and $v_5 = [w_5]^{1/2}$. Substituting, our program is

$$\min_{v_4, v_5} \quad 2/3v_4^2 + 1/3v_5^2$$

subject to

$$2/3v_4 + 1/3v_5 - 50 \geq 250$$
$$2/3v_4 + 1/3v_5 - 50 \geq 1/3v_4 + 2/3v_5 - 0$$
$$v_4, v_5 \geq 0.$$

This is a quadratic objective function with linear constraints and can be analyzed with standard optimization routines, such as LINDO. Alternatively, direct numerical methods using standard software packages, such as Borland's Eureka, can be used.

[10] The earlier solution of $w_4 = w_5 = 62{,}500$ satisfies both constraints because there is no lower labor supply than LOW.

[11] $(2/3)(122{,}500) + (1/3)(40{,}000) = 95{,}000$.

the data in Table 1, we see the possible (gross) profit realizations are 400, 500, and 600. Let $\hat{w}_4$ denote the agent's compensation if a profit of 400 is realized, $\hat{w}_5$ if a profit of 500 is realized, and so on. The agent's decision tree is shown in Exhibit 2. Engineering the agent's tree requires

$$1/3[\hat{w}_4]^{1/2}+1/3[\hat{w}_6]^{1/2}+1/3[\hat{w}_5]^{1/2}-50 \geq 250,$$

and

$$1/3[\hat{w}_4]^{1/2}+1/3[\hat{w}_6]^{1/2}+1/3[\hat{w}_5]^{1/2}-50 \geq 1/3[\hat{w}_4]^{1/2}+2/3[\hat{w}_5]^{1/2}-0.$$

The principal's program becomes

$$\underset{\hat{w}_4,\hat{w}_5,\hat{w}_6}{\text{Min}} \quad 1/3\hat{w}_4+1/3\hat{w}_6+1/3\hat{w}_5$$

subject to

$$1/3[\hat{w}_4]^{1/2}+1/3[\hat{w}_6]^{1/2}+1/3[\hat{w}_5]^{1/2}-50 \geq 250$$

$$1/3[\hat{w}_4]^{1/2}+1/3[\hat{w}_6]^{1/2}+1/3[\hat{w}_5]^{1/2}-50 \geq 1/3[\hat{w}_4]^{1/2}+2/3[\hat{w}_5]^{1/2}-0$$

$$\hat{w}_4, \hat{w}_5, \hat{w}_6 \geq 0.$$

The solution is $\hat{w}_4=90{,}000$, $\hat{w}_5=50{,}625$, $\hat{w}_6=140{,}625$.[12] The principal's evaluation is now:

	Labor Supply	
	LOW	*HIGH*
E(Revenue)	933.33	933.33
Less *E*(Cost)	466.67	433.33
E(Gross profit)	466.67	500.00
Less *E*(Wage)	62.50	93.75[13]
E(Net profit)	404.17	406.25

The principal is strictly better off using cost and revenue, as opposed to just cost, in the agent's evaluation. The agent, however, is indifferent. In either case his expected utility is 250. Revenue is a useful evaluation statistic, despite the controllability-based conclusion it is not controllable and, therefore, useless in the evaluation exercise.[14]

A Second Example

Now consider a slight variation on this example. Everything is identical except the revenue structure is altered in Table 2 (000 omitted).

This makes the revenue lottery dependent on the agent's behavior. So a controllability approach would imply revenue is a useful evaluation statistic because the agent is able to influence which revenue result obtains. Further observe the revenue structure is constructed so a cost realization of 400 always is accompanied by a revenue realization of 1000; and a cost realization of 500 always is accompanied by a revenue realization of 800.[15] Working through

[12] Some may be troubled by the non-monotonicity of this contract, which calls for a higher payment to the manager for achieving a profit of 400 than a profit of 500. Before concluding this does not accord with schemes in practice, the following reinterpretation should be considered. The manager's contract is equivalent to a salary of 50,625, with a bonus of 39,375 for holding costs to 400. If costs are "controlled" (i.e., held to 400) while revenue is "maintained" at 1000, the bonus is increased to 90,000.

[13] (1/3)(90,000)+(1/3)(50,625)+(1/3)(140,625) =93,750.

[14] Two important assumptions should be recalled. First we carefully chose an illustration in which the relationship between revenue and cost and revenue less cost is one to one. Otherwise, the precise pair of realizations is important, not just their algebraic difference. Second, we assume the principal is risk neutral. The agent, therefore, has no comparative advantage at carrying risk. If this were not the case we would always prefer a profit center evaluation simply because efficient risk sharing would dictate the principal and agent each have income at risk. Here, however, we focus exclusively on control considerations in examining how best to evaluate the agent. This is accomplished by neutralizing the demand for risk sharing with the agent. See Demski [1976].

[15] This extreme case of a one-to-one association between cost and revenue makes the analysis transparent, but is not necessary for the point to hold. As is discussed later, the important feature is that the *distribution* of revenue conditional on cost does not vary with the agent's behavior. The distinction is one of equivalence in (conditional) distribution, not of "equality" in the guise of a one-to-one association. Of course, the latter implies the former.

TABLE 2
REVENUE, COST, AND GROSS PROFIT FOR EXAMPLE 2

		State		
		s_1	s_2	s_3
LOW Labor Supply:	Revenue	1000	800	800
	Cost, exclusive of labor	400	500	500
	Profit, exclusive of labor cost	600	300	300
HIGH Labor Supply:	Revenue	1000	1000	800
	Cost, exclusive of labor	400	400	500
	Profit, exclusive of labor cost	600	600	300

the details of the agency framework will produce the following conclusions: (1) the principal prefers to implement a HIGH supply of labor; (2) the most efficient contracting arrangement is use of the cost outcome, accompanied by $w_4 = 122{,}500$ and $w_5 = 40{,}000$; and (3) revenue is of no use in evaluating the agent.[16] Thus, we have a case where a controllability focus implies revenue is an important evaluation statistic while an agency analysis implies it is superfluous.

A Third Example

For a final example, change the revenue structure in our setting as described in Table 3 (000 omitted). As in the second example, revenue now depends on the agent's behavior and a controllability focus implies it is best to hold the agent responsible for the cost and revenue (or profit) outcomes. In turn, working through the details of the agency framework reveals: (1) the principal prefers to implement a HIGH supply of labor; and (2) the most efficient contracting arrangement is use of cost and revenue with payment to the agent of $\hat{w} = 0$ when a profit of 200 obtains and $\hat{w} = 90{,}000$ otherwise.

In this setting, a profit of 200 signals unmistakably the agent has supplied LOW. So the contract "penalizes" the maximal amount by paying 0 (dismissal?). This threat allows for an equilibrium payment of 90,000. We, thus, have an illustration where the controllability and agency analyses agree.

II. SOME INTUITION

These examples, taken together, give settings where a non-controllable item is useful, where a controllable item is useless, and where a controllable item is useful. The important question is what explains this schism between the common sense of the controllability notion and the deductive sense of the principal-agent exercise. The answer is to be found in the probabilities of the revenue and cost outcome.

[16] More precisely, knowledge of cost implies knowledge of revenue and vice versa. So using only cost, using only revenue, or using cost and revenue are identical evaluation schemes. Also notice HIGH is preferred here because we have the same cost structure along with less revenue prospects under LOW.

TABLE 3
REVENUE, COST, AND GROSS PROFIT FOR EXAMPLE 3

		State		
		s_1	s_2	s_3
LOW Labor Supply:	Revenue	800	700	1000
	Cost, exclusive of labor	400	500	500
	Profit, exclusive of labor cost	400	200	500
HIGH Labor Supply:	Revenue	800	1000	1000
	Cost, exclusive of labor	400	400	500
	Profit, exclusive of labor cost	400	600	500

To develop this point, notice the common structure in the above examples centers on two facts: First, there is inherent conflict because the principal wants to implement one labor supply (HIGH) while (other things equal) the agent wants to implement a different labor supply (LOW). Second, informational asymmetry is present since the cost and revenue outcomes do not necessarily reveal exactly what input the agent has supplied. Put differently, the principal seeks input from the agent, but cannot directly observe input. As a result, the parties contract on observable and verifiable output. In short, output is used as an imperfect indicator of input, and the *information content* of output becomes of concern.[17]

Information Content

Information content is a subtle notion in this setting. We use the cost and revenue outcomes as indicators of what input was supplied. In particular, we use the statistical pattern of these outcomes. But since we are concerned about the agent's supply of input, we contrast the statistical pattern under the assumption he supplies the desired input with the statistical pattern under the assumption he supplies some other input.

To develop this theme, we contrast two probability statements: (1) the probability of revenue $=R$ under inputs a $=$HIGH and $a=$LOW; and (2) the probability revenue $=R$ under inputs a $=$HIGH and $a=$LOW conditioned on cost $=C$. Let $f(R|a)$ denote the probability revenue $=R$ when the agent supplies input $=a$. Also, let $f(R|C,a)$ denote the probability revenue $=R$ when cost $=C$ has been observed and when the agent supplies input $=a$. These probabilities, for the three examples, are displayed in Table 4.[18] Notice, in particular,

[17] As mentioned earlier, the productive output provides value (here in the sense of profit) and information. In an extended setting, we would then design the productive process to balance these two types of output. As a result, we do not model the setting as one of finding the least costly control system to implement the otherwise most efficient production arrangement. The design problem does not separate.

[18] The easiest way to replicate these calculations is to construct the joint probabilities, $f(R,C|a)$. These are displayed in the Appendix. By the laws of probability, we have $f(C|a)=f(700,C|a)+f(800,C|a)+f(1000,C|a)$ and $f(R|C,a)=f(R,C|a)/f(C|a)$.

TABLE 4
MARGINAL AND CONDITIONAL PROBABILITIES

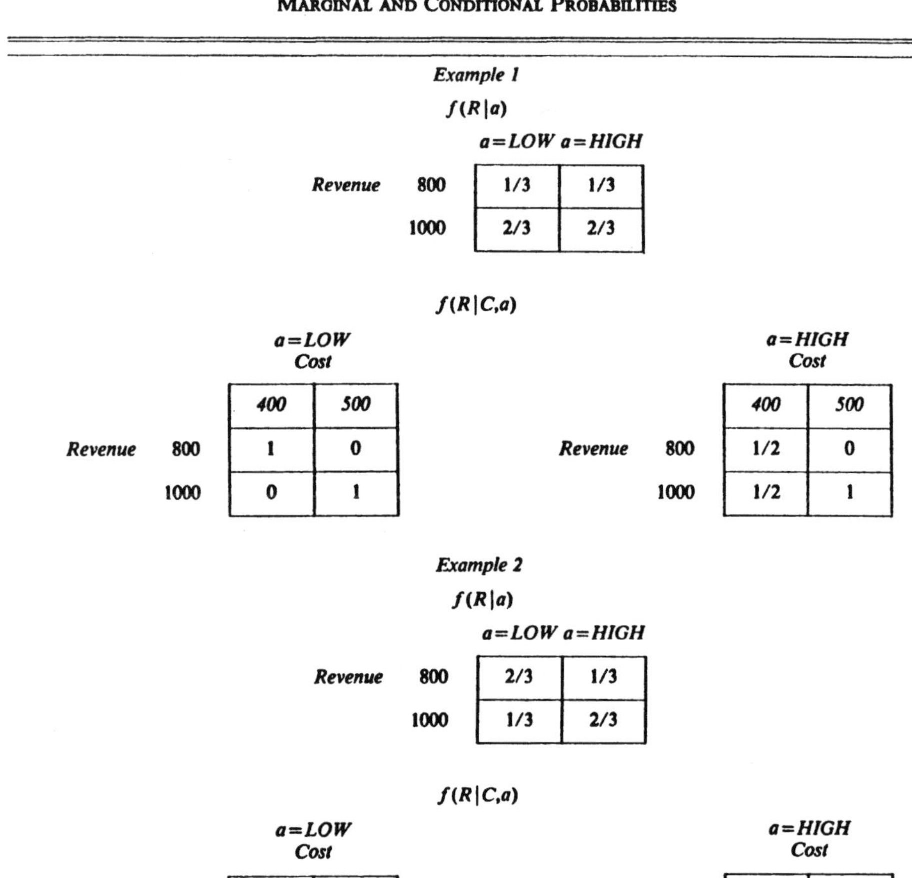

Example 1

$f(R|a)$

Revenue		$a=LOW$	$a=HIGH$
	800	1/3	1/3
	1000	2/3	2/3

$f(R|C,a)$

$a=LOW$

Revenue	Cost	400	500
	800	1	0
	1000	0	1

$a=HIGH$

Revenue	Cost	400	500
	800	1/2	0
	1000	1/2	1

Example 2

$f(R|a)$

Revenue		$a=LOW$	$a=HIGH$
	800	2/3	1/3
	1000	1/3	2/3

$f(R|C,a)$

$a=LOW$

Revenue	Cost	400	500
	800	0	1
	1000	1	0

$a=HIGH$

Revenue	Cost	400	500
	800	0	1
	1000	1	0

the following differences among the three examples:

example one:

$$f(R|\text{HIGH})=f(R|\text{LOW}) \text{ and } f(R|C,\text{HIGH})\neq f(R|C,\text{LOW})$$

example two:

$$f(R|\text{HIGH})\neq f(R|\text{LOW}) \text{ and } f(R|C,\text{HIGH})=f(R|C,\text{LOW})$$

example three:

$$f(R|\text{HIGH})\neq f(R|\text{LOW}) \text{ and } f(R|C,\text{HIGH})\neq f(R|C,\text{LOW}).$$ [19]

[19] Two other points should be noted. First, an example where revenue is simply noise would provide a setting with $f(R|\text{HIGH})=f(R|\text{LOW})$ and $f(R|C,\text{HIGH})=f(R|C,\text{LOW})$. Second, there is nothing pathological about the examples. The data for example 2, for instance, exhibit perfect correlation between cost and revenue. But as mentioned in footnote 15, this is done to keep

TABLE 4—*Continued*

Example 3

$f(R|a)$

		a=LOW	a=HIGH
Revenue	700	1/3	0
	800	1/3	1/3
	1000	1/3	2/3

$f(R|C,a)$

a=LOW

		Cost 400	Cost 500
Revenue	700	0	1/2
	800	1	0
	1000	0	1/2

a=HIGH

		Cost 400	Cost 500
Revenue	700	0	0
	800	1/2	0
	1000	1/2	1

Consider $f(R|a)$, the marginal probability revenue $=R$ under input supply a. $f(R|\text{HIGH}=f(R|\text{LOW})$ in the first example, while $f(R|\text{HIGH})\neq f(R|\text{LOW})$ in the second and third examples. By conscious choice of input, the agent controls the revenue probabilities (or revenue lottery) in the latter two examples, but not in the first. This is the basis on which we applied the controllability notion.

definition: The agent *controls* revenue if $f(R|a)$ is a nontrivial function of a.

That is, we say the agent controls revenue if he is able to affect the marginal probability of revenue through his behavior (i.e., his supply of labor input).[20]

Now consider the use of revenue (or cost) in the compensation arrangement. We say the parties use the revenue measure if the agent's compensation depends on the actual revenue realization. Let the agent's compensation be denoted $w=I(R,C)$. If revenue of R and cost of C are realized the agent is paid amount $w=I(R,C)$. If for some value of C different values of R lead to different payment amounts, we then say the agent is held responsible for revenue.

definition: The agent is *held responsible* for revenue (cost) under $I(R,C)$ if $I(R,C)$ is a nontrivial function of revenue (cost).[21]

the illustration uncluttered. Consider a setting where revenue is either 1000 or 800. Let the revenue lottery depend only on cost, and be such that $R=1000$ is more probable with one cost realization than another. This will ensure $f(R|\text{HIGH})\neq f(R|\text{LOW})$ and $f(R|C,\text{HIGH})=f(R|C,\text{LOW})$. See the extended example that begins in footnote 26.

[20] A similar statement can be made about controlling cost and $f(C|a)$.

[21] By nontrivial we mean for some value of C, say $\hat{C}$, we have distinct R^1 and R^2 such that $I(R^1,\hat{C})\neq I(R^2,\hat{C})$.

From here we articulate the controllability notion as saying the agent should be held responsible for revenue if he controls revenue, for cost if he controls cost, and for profit if he controls revenue and cost.[22] By this principle, the agent should be held responsible for cost in each of the three examples, and for revenue (and, therefore, profit) in only the latter two.[23]

Conditional Probabilities

The conclusion above does not agree with the principal-agent solutions, where we find revenue a useful evaluation measure in the first and third examples.[24] This discrepancy arises because information content and controllability are not coextensive. In the second example, for instance, the agent controls revenue, but revenue tells us nothing about the agent's input, provided we already are observing cost. In this case, $f(R|C,a)$ depends only on cost; we may write $f(R|C,a) \equiv f(R|C)$. Given we are already using cost to evaluate the agent, the *conditional* probability of revenue, $f(R|C,a)$, cannot be influenced by the agent.

In contrast, the agent does influence the conditional probability of revenue in the other two examples. $f(R|C,a)$ is a nontrivial function of input a in these two cases. The explanation is, perhaps, more clear if we factor the probability construction:

$$f(R,C|a)=f(R|C,a)f(C|a).$$

If $f(R|C,a)=f(R|C)$, we have a case where the random variation in revenue *that is not explained by cost* cannot be influenced in any way by the agent's behavior. Stated differently, if $f(R|C,a) = f(R|C)$ the random variation in revenue not explained by cost tells us nothing whatever about whether the agent supplied a=LOW or a=HIGH. Given we know cost, revenue has no information content in terms of inferring what the agent supplied. If this is the case, holding the agent responsible for revenue and cost is inefficient. It merely "noises up" the evaluation. Revenue variations are, in the presence of cost, pure noise. This suggests the following:

> *definition*: Revenue has *information content* in the presence of cost if $f(R|C,a)$ is a nontrivial function of a.

To understand this definition, suppose we already know cost and focus on the conditional distribution of revenue, $f(R|C,a)$. If the agent cannot influence this conditional distribution, we say revenue has no information content in the presence of cost. But if the agent can influence this conditional distribution, we say revenue has information content in the presence of cost. Note well, information content is related to our concept of control over revenue. The difference is we now acknowledge the information content of cost. The focus is influence over the distribution of revenue *given*

[22] Stated differently, the idea is the agent should be held accountable for revenue if he controls revenue. Held accountable, in turn, translates into $I(R,C)$ is a nontrivial function of revenue in this setting.

[23] Observe that the controllability principle can be applied sequentially. If we are considering three variables, say labor cost, raw material cost, and revenue, we can assess whether the manager controls each of these variables without reference to the others. In this way, one form of textbook exercise consists of the specification of the individual's position within the organization and a list of potential performance measures. The student is then asked to proceed down the list and suggest whether each variable is controllable by the identified individual. In this way, the student supposedly identifies the best subset of variables for evaluating the individual in question.

[24] More precisely, we are indifferent between use of revenue or cost in the second example, but strictly prefer use of both variables in the first and third examples. As noted, the second example has a one to one relation between revenue and cost. An expanded version of the example, as sketched in footnote 26, would have cost strictly preferred to revenue, along with revenue being useless in the presence of cost for evaluation purposes.

cost is known. The key is $f(R|C,a)$, not $f(R|a)$.

Model Interrogation

This shift in focus has intuitive appeal. Marginal and conditional distributions are not the same, and it seems we should focus on what we learn conditioned on what we are already observing. Moreover, the principal-agent analysis reinforces this intuition.[25]

> *Claim*: Suppose the agent is held responsible for revenue in the optimal solution to the principal-agent problem. Then revenue has information content.

The assertion is nontrivial use of revenue (given cost is being used to evaluate the manager) can only arise in the principal-agent solution if revenue has information content. To explore the formal reasoning, suppose, to the contrary, we have a case where the agent is held responsible for revenue even though $f(R|C,a)$ does not depend on input a. In our specialized setting, this means we have some $I(R,C)$ compensation scheme that satisfies the following constraints:[26]

$$\Sigma_{R,C}[I(R,C)]^{1/2}f(R,C|\text{HIGH}) - V(\text{HIGH}) \geq \bar{U},$$

and

$$\Sigma_{R,C}[I(R,C)]^{1/2}f(R,C|\text{HIGH}) - V(\text{HIGH}) \geq \Sigma_{R,C}[I(R,C)]^{1/2}f(R,C|\text{LOW}) - V(\text{LOW}).$$

The first constraint, recall, requires the agent weakly prefer accepting the contract terms and supplying HIGH to his other alternative, with a utility value of $\bar{U}$. The second requires the agent weakly prefer accepting the contract terms and supplying HIGH to accepting the contract terms and supplying LOW. Now, since revenue does not have information content in the presence of cost, factoring the probability provides:[27]

[25] Holmstrom [1979] and Shavell [1979] developed the generic argument that use of a monitor in the principal-agent setting implies the monitor's conditional distribution is a nontrivial function of the agent's input. Subsequent studies, such as Baiman and Demski [1980], Baiman [1982], and Demski and Sappington [1986], have applied it to specific accounting questions. Baiman and Noel [1985] examine a multiperiod setting where noncontrollable capital cost is useful as a proxy for anticipated capacity choices by the principal when the agent is induced to alter his input as a function of this proxy.

Further recall we assume the principal is risk neutral. This means the agent is never used for risk sharing purposes. (By analogy, risk sharing is accomplished in the capital, not the labor, market.) If the principal were also risk averse here, simple risk sharing would dictate the agent always be held responsible for revenue and cost, since profit is at risk.

[26] To illustrate, consider a setting identical to that in our earlier examples, except for the following relationship among states, acts, revenue, and cost (000 omitted):

	s_1	s_2	s_3	s_4	s_5	s_6	s_7
probability	2/16	1/16	2/16	1/16	6/16	2/16	2/16
LOW labor supply:							
Revenue	800	800	800	800	1000	1000	1000
Cost	400	500	500	500	400	500	500
Gross Profit	400	300	300	300	600	500	500
HIGH labor supply:							
Revenue	800	800	800	1000	1000	1000	1000
Cost	400	400	500	400	400	400	500
Gross Profit	400	400	300	600	600	600	500

Further assume the agent is held responsible for revenue and cost under the following $I(R,C)$ payment arrangement:

$$I(1000,400)=160{,}000,$$
$$I(1000,500)=40{,}000,$$
$$I(800,400)=40{,}000, \text{ and}$$
$$I(800,500)=10{,}000.$$

This payment arrangement meets the agent's required utility constraint (of 250 utiles). It also induces the agent to supply the HIGH labor input. Using the construction that follows in the text, however, we can show this is a wasteful arrangement because it ties the agent's pay to revenue, which has no information content in the presence of cost. Subsequent notes trace this construction.

[27] In the example in the previous footnote we have:

$$f(800,400|\text{LOW})=f(800|400,\text{LOW})f(400|\text{LOW}) =(.25)(.50)=.125,$$
$$f(800,400|\text{HIGH})=f(800|400,\text{HIGH})f(400|\text{HIGH}) =(.25)(.75)=.1875,$$
$$f(800,500|\text{LOW})=f(800|500,\text{LOW})f(500|\text{LOW}) =(.50)(.50)=.25, \text{ and}$$
$$f(800,500|\text{HIGH})=f(800|500,\text{HIGH})f(500|\text{HIGH}) =(.50)(.25)=.125.$$

Note, $f(800|400,\text{LOW})=f(800|400,\text{HIGH})=.25$ and

$$f(R,C|a)=f(R|C,a)f(C|a)$$
$$=f(R|C)f(C|a).$$

With this factoring, we rewrite the constraints as follows:

$$\Sigma_{R,C}\{[I(R,C)]^{1/2}f(R|C)\}f(C|\text{HIGH}) - V(\text{HIGH}) \geq \bar{U},$$

and

$$\Sigma_{R,C}\{[I(R,C)]^{1/2}f(R|C)\}f(C|\text{HIGH}) - V(\text{HIGH}) \geq \Sigma_{R,C}\{[I(R,C)]^{1/2}f(R|C)\} f(C|\text{LOW}) - V(\text{LOW}).$$

Each term enclosed within the $\{\cdot\}$ brackets is identical. This allows us to express the constraints in the following fashion:[28]

$$\Sigma_C\{\Sigma_R[I(R,C)]^{1/2}f(R|C)\}f(C|\text{HIGH}) - V(\text{HIGH}) \geq \bar{U},$$

and

$$\Sigma_C\{\Sigma_R[I(R,C)]^{1/2}f(R|C)\}f(C|\text{HIGH}) - V(\text{HIGH}) \geq \Sigma_C\{\Sigma_R[I(R,C)]^{1/2}f(R|C)\} f(C|\text{LOW}) - V(\text{LOW}).$$

From here we replace the common term with a payment that depends only on cost:[29]

$$\Sigma_R[I(R,C)]^{1/2}f(R|C) \equiv [\hat{I}(C)]^{1/2}.$$

$\hat{I}(C)$ is that payment the agent would gladly exchange for the $I(R,C)$ lottery. Since the agent is held responsible for revenue, we know $I(R,C)$ is a nontrivial function of R. But $\hat{I}(C)$ does not depend on R. For each cost realization, the agent is indifferent between receiving $\hat{I}(C)$ for certain or engaging in the nontrivial $I(R,C)$ compensation lottery. But since the agent is strictly risk averse, he is willing to pay a premium to unburden himself of this revenue risk:

$$\Sigma_R I(R,C)f(R|C) > \hat{I}(C).$$

In this way, the principal is able to replace $I(R,C)$ with $\hat{I}(C)$. This replacement does not hold the agent responsible for revenue, has lower expected cost to the principal, delivers the same expected utility to the agent, and induces the agent to supply HIGH.[30] Put another way, the $\hat{I}(C)$ construction is possible because we are "filtering out" needless noise in the evaluation process.

From Controllability to Information Content

Thus, any solution that holds the agent responsible for revenue when revenue has no information content in the presence of cost can be improved. The key

---

$f(800|500,\text{LOW})=f(800|500,\text{HIGH})=.50$. We also have $f(1000|\text{LOW})=10/16$ and $f(1000|\text{HIGH})=11/16$.

[28] In the continuing example, these constraints become:

$$\{400(3/4)+200(1/4)\}(3/4)+\{200(1/2)+100(1/2)\}(1/4) - 50 \geq 250,$$

and

$$\{400(3/4)+200(1/4)\}(3/4)+\{200(1/2)+100(1/2)\}(1/4) - 50 \geq \{400(3/4)+200(1/4)\}(1/2)+\{200(1/2) + 100(1/2)\}(1/2) - 0.$$

[29] Continuing the example, we have the following constructions:

$$[400(3/4)+200(1/4)]=350=[\hat{I}(400)]^{1/2}, \text{ or } \hat{I}(400)=122{,}500;$$

and

$$[200(1/2)+100(1/2)]=150=[\hat{I}(500)]^{1/2}, \text{ or } \hat{I}(500)=22{,}500.$$

This is, in fact, the optimal payment schedule to motivate choice of HIGH in this example. It has an expected labor cost of 97,500. In contrast, the original $I(R,C)$ arrangement has an expected labor cost of 103,750.

[30] By construction we have:

$$\Sigma_{R,C}[I(R,C)]^{1/2}f(R,C|\text{HIGH}) - V(\text{HIGH}) = \Sigma_C[\hat{I}(C)]^{1/2}f(C|\text{HIGH}) - V(\text{HIGH}) \geq \bar{U},$$

and

$$\Sigma_{R,C}[I(R,C)]^{1/2}f(R,C|\text{HIGH}) - V(\text{HIGH}) = \Sigma_C[\hat{I}(C)]^{1/2}f(C|\text{HIGH}) - V(\text{HIGH}) \geq \Sigma_{R,C}\{[I(R,C)]^{1/2}f(R|C)\}f(R|\text{LOW}) - V(\text{LOW}) = \Sigma_C[\hat{I}(C)]^{1/2}f(C|\text{LOW}) - V(\text{LOW}).$$

insight is we use the agent's output (revenue and cost here) to infer his input. This inferential exercise compares the statistical properties of the agent's input when he supplies the desired input with those that arise when he supplies some alternative input. Given cost is already observed, an informative revenue output means the (conditional) statistical properties differ according to the agent's behavior. But an uninformative revenue output means the (conditional) statistical properties are independent of the agent's behavior. Holding the agent responsible for revenue in such a case has no effect other than making his compensation subject to purely random noise. In other words, the information content of revenue is signaled by the conditional probability being controllable. Use of an uninformative output statistic merely subjects the agent to noise. The definition of information content tells us precisely when we would want to "filter out" this noise in the agent's evaluation.

In this manner we conclude from the principal-agent analysis that any use of revenue in the agent's evaluation implies revenue has information content in the presence of cost. Conversely, with additional regularity assumptions (as in Holmstrom [1982] or Demski and Sappington [1986]), we could provide a setting where information content of revenue necessarily implies the agent should be held responsible for revenue. The important message, though, is no use of revenue is called for by the model unless revenue has information content in the presence of cost.

The intuition for this conclusion parallels that for the original controllability notion. The single variation in the logic is to take account of what other information we already are observing. The key, in other words, is to define controllability in terms of the conditional probability of the output statistic, thereby taking account of the available information.

III. Application

Stepping back from the examples and analysis somewhat, we are focusing on a setting where a list of performance variables is present and asking which elements on the list should be used in evaluating the manager (or agent) in question. Applying the controllability notion, we are led to a focus on marginal probabilities. Can the manager, through action, control the probability distribution of the variable in question. If so, the manager should be held responsible for that variable. Control begets responsibility in this framework.

Adopting a more explicit information perspective, we ask what it is the manager is supposed to be doing and why we want to evaluate his performance. Moving to an agency setting, the answers are the manager is to supply personally costly labor inputs, the supply of this input is not observable, and we must use output (including the output of various performance statistics) as a noisy indicator of input. This allows us to be precise about the information content of an evaluation measure. The key principle turns out to be information content, a close cousin of controllability but one that adjusts for what other information is already being used. Controllability does not imply information content and information content does not imply controllability.

Going still further, we now ask whether this insight of distinguishing controllability and information content helps us solve or understand real problems as opposed to numerical examples. This is not an easy task, because the information perspective demands we think in terms of probabilities and take explicit account of what other information is being processed.

A ready illustration is provided by tournaments. Familiar examples are sports bonus clauses (e.g., for achieving some type of all-star status) and sales contests (e.g., sales person of the year recognition).[31] Grading on a curve is a common practice. Relative performance evaluation of high level executives, where compensation depends on performance relative to that of a peer (e.g., industry) group, is another illustration. In each case a primary consideration in the agent's evaluation is performance of a peer agent. When viewed from a controllability perspective this is perplexing. The agent in question has no control over the performance of the peer. When viewed from an information content perspective, this practice is far from perplexing. It is easy to imagine performance of another agent in similar circumstances could possess information content.[32] Each agent's performance is affected by the common environment. The peer's performance tells us something about that environment and, thus, indirectly something about the performance of the agent in question.

Suppose two students take a common examination. The second student's score tells us nothing about the first student's performance. But the second student's score in conjunction with the first student's score typically does, by indirectly telling us something about the common environment. For the sake of argument, suppose the score of student i is determined by

$$score_i = effort_i + noise_i + instrument$$

where $effort_i$ is the effort of the student in question, $noise_i$ is randomness in the examination environment that is idiosyncratic to our student, and *instrument* is randomness associated with the examination instrument. Clearly, student $i=1$ cannot control $score_2$. But $score_1 - score_2$ is an interesting statistic, because the instrument randomness has been factored out. In this way, $score_2$ becomes useful in the evaluation of student $i=1$, given we already know $score_1$.[33]

As another illustration, suppose we have two agents, each working in the environment described by Table 1. One agent's output tells us something about the state and, therefore, something about the other's environment and, indirectly, something about the other's input. In fact, agents working in perfectly correlated environments, an admitted extreme, is a case where one agent's output is unusually informative about the other agent, given we know that agent's output.

IV. Conclusions

This paper offers a refined version of the controllability principle. The argument rests on the assumption managerial evaluation is aimed at producing information that reports on the managerial services or inputs supplied. If the manager can affect the statistical pattern of some particular variable, the manager controls that variable. If the manager can affect the statistical pattern condi-

[31] Halberstam [1986] describes extensive use of sales contests in the domestic automobile industry.

[32] Baiman and Demski [1980] and Holmstrom [1982] formalize this intuition in a principal-agent setting. Dye [1984] provides a general discussion of problems generated by tournaments. Antle and Smith [1986] provides an empirical investigation, based on high level executive compensation practices.

[33] This vignette hints that an extension of our argument would have the agent's labor supply more generally characterized in terms of quantity and quality. Alternatively, in this particular setting the student's performance would depend on effort, skill, and luck. We then proceed as before, but in a manner aimed at information content with respect to quantity and quality of input, as opposed to quantity of input.

tioned on whatever else we know, the variable carries information content about the manager's behavior. The concept of information content falls out of a principal-agent analysis as being a central feature of valuable monitoring or evaluation information. In this sense, we offer the information content perspective as a refined version of the controllability principle. Whether the manager controls the variable in question is immaterial. Whether the manager controls (or influences) the variable in question, conditioned on whatever other information is present, is the key notion. That is, information content is a precisely defined controllability notion that accounts for other sources of information.

The darker side to this refined principle is the added demand it places on the identification of a control problem. With the traditional controllability notion, we need only ask whether the manager can control the variable in question. With the conditional or information content notion, we must first specify what other information is being used in the evaluation process. Once this source of information is accounted for, we ask whether any new information is produced by the variable in question.[34] This manifests itself in the manager's conditional control of the variable in question.

In short, we find the intuition of the information content perspective appealing, but we also recognize assessing information content is likely to be a difficult task.

[34] Recent field studies by Merchant [1987] and Dent [1987] illustrate this difficulty. Each study reports violations of the controllability principle. This is accomplished by documentation of various uncontrollable phenomena that are used in the evaluation process. In contrast, the information content perspective is not so amenable to investigation. It demands assessing information content in light of all information being used in the evaluation process. The field investigator's task is dramatically complicated by the importance of identifying the conditioning information.

Appendix
Joint Probabilities
$f(R,C|a)$

Example 1

a=LOW

		Cost 400	*Cost* 500
Revenue	800	1/3	0
	1000	0	2/3

a=HIGH

		Cost 400	*Cost* 500
Revenue	800	1/3	0
	1000	1/3	1/3

Example 2

a=LOW

		Cost 400	*Cost* 500
Revenue	800	0	2/3
	1000	1/3	0

a=HIGH

		Cost 400	*Cost* 500
Revenue	800	0	1/3
	1000	2/3	0

Example 3

a=LOW

		Cost 400	*Cost* 500
Revenue	700	0	1/3
	800	1/3	0
	1000	0	1/3

a=HIGH

		Cost 400	*Cost* 500
Revenue	700	0	0
	800	1/3	0
	1000	1/3	1/3

REFERENCES

Antle, R., and A. Smith, "An Empirical Investigation of the Relative Performance Evaluation of Corporate Executives," *Journal of Accounting Research* (Spring 1986), pp. 1–39.

Baiman, S., "Agency Research in Managerial Accounting: A Survey," *Journal of Accounting Literature* (Spring 1982), pp. 154–213.

——, and J. Demski, "Economically Optimal Performance Evaluation and Control Systems," Supplement to *Journal of Accounting Research* (1980), pp. 184–220.

——, and J. Noel, "Noncontrollable Costs and Responsibility Accounting," *Journal of Accounting Research* (Autumn 1985), pp. 486–501.

Demski, J., "Uncertainty and Evaluation Based on Controllable Performance," *Journal of Accounting Research* (Autumn 1976), pp. 230–245.

——, and D. Sappington, "Line-Item Reporting, Factor Acquisition, and Subcontracting," *Journal of Accounting Research* (Autumn 1986), pp. 250–269.

Dent, J., "Tensions in the Design of Formal Control Systems: A Field Study in a Computer Company," in W. Bruns and R. Kaplan, Eds., *Accounting and Management: Field Study Perspectives* (Harvard Business School Press, 1987), pp. 119–145.

Dye, R., "The Trouble with Tournaments," *Economic Inquiry* (January 1984), pp. 147–149.

Ferrara, W., "Responsibility Reporting versus Direct Costing—Is There a Conflict?" *Management Accounting* (June 1967), pp. 43–54.

Halberstam, D., *The Reckoning* (Wm. Morrow, 1986).

Holmstrom, B., "Moral Hazard and Observability," *Bell Journal of Economics* (Spring 1979), pp. 74–91.

——, "Moral Hazard in Teams," *Bell Journal of Economics* (Autumn 1982), pp. 324–340.

Merchant, K., "How and Why Firms Disregard the Controllability Principle," in W. Bruns and R. Kaplan, Eds., *Accounting and Management: Field Study Perspectives* (Harvard Business School Press, 1987), pp. 316–338.

Shavell, S., "Risk Sharing and Incentives in the Principal and Agent Relationship," *Bell Journal of Economics* (Spring 1979), pp. 55–73.

Part III
Control as Adaptation

[10]

Autonomics — systems one, two, three

The principles of an autonomic system were discussed at length in Part II. Essentially we are dealing with the evolutionary answer to the bogus dichotomy of centralization versus decentralization. As in the previous chapter, I shall take the whole of that earlier discussion for granted.

We need to know first of all how System One really works — in the eyes of the corporation. Remember that it has to control a division, in response to policy directives and over-riding instructions from above, in reaction to the direct demands of the external world upon it, and in awareness of the needs of other divisions.

There has first of all to be a divisional directorate, which was depicted in Figure 27. It lies on the vertical command axis, reports to the corporate management from which instructions are received, and is responsible for managing the division. Essentially this means that it in turn controls activities in a 'line' sense; but from the corporate standpoint this responsibility is routine. What really matters is that the divisional directorate assumes responsibility for programming, planning by objectives, and normative planning throughout the division.

Its management tool is the divisional regulatory centre (marked in Figure 27 with a triangular symbol). Here the monitoring and filtering functions for input data, and the strategic planning and tactical programming functions for output data, jointly reside. (Then this part of the *corporate* System One constitutes the *divisional* System Three — the operations directorate of the division.) This organ, the regulatory centre, explicitly models the spinal ganglion in relation to the vertebral segment of the cord.

Notes on the Operation of System One

In view of the arguments advanced in the last chapter, we shall take it that basic information about performance is to be generated for corporate use in terms of pure numbers — the achievement indices. At once an opportunity occurs to classify divisional operations on a better basis than is normally attempted in orthodoxy.

People normally classify activities according to their manifest appearance to the world at large. They may be classified by their location, by the nature of the processes they employ, by the nature of the things which they produce, by the sort of people who undertake them, or even by the geographical destiny of the output. But since management is interested in efficiency, and since a particular measured level of performance now attaches to each of these activities, a more managerially sophisticated and practically useful classification system may be developed.

What matters to management about two entirely different products is not whether they look alike but whether they are profit-earners or not. Two very similar-looking products may perform quite differently; two dissimilar products may display the same performance. Then we should use the pure numbers we have generated to classify what is going on in the firm by these measures of achievement.

The tool to use here is applied statistics. Assume that pure numbers are now flowing out of the division, and along the input line to the divisional directorate. It is a function of the divisional regulatory centre to cause these numbers to fall into convenient heaps (technically: Gaussian distributions), whereby probability theory may be used to determine to which family of performance a particular number belongs. There is no prior judgement here from historicity, nor from manifest appearance. The criterion is straightforwardly the shape of the 'achievement profile', determined by the absolute value of the performance index and the balance within that index of its constituent latency and productivity.

All this is very easy to arrange on a computer, because there are simple and robust tests for statistical normalcy, and extremely familiar tables of the integral under the curve of the two tails of the normal distribution. Technical note: the ratios, which have an upper bound of unity, cannot be used as raw data immediately for these tests, because they generate skewed distributions. Some adjustment will be necessary: I have always found the inverse sine transformation of the raw score to be quite effective, but there are other possibilities. However, this is a matter for the statistician member of the implementation team. We need not be delayed here by considerations of technical detail.

The point is that we should no longer classify the firm's activities according to convention, apply cost measures to these activities because they are the only measures we understand, and then aggregate the answers. We should instead apply the measures of performance we have designed to the activities, and demand that the information system classifies the operational world on our behalf. The brain does this for us in ordinary life through its pattern-recognition capability, and produces the classification by manifest appearance with which we normally wish to work. As managers, however, we are seeking to detect other patterns — those of significance to the business — and that means classifying by achievement.

The input to the classification machine at the divisional regulatory centre consists of raw data emanating from divisional operations. These data need to be collected and organized ready for processing, and then passed on to the divisional regulatory centre. This is a synaptic function, and it is depicted in Figure 27 as a very tiny circle on the input transmission line. The synapse itself is shown in the more detailed drawing of Figure 30, depicting System One — it is Step 2. Initially, the whole of the data will be collected so that the classification system may be created. We shall need to store quite simple models of potentiality and more complicated models of capability which have been evolved by operational research. Then, as data about actual operations flow in, from Step 1 transducers and through the synaptic Step 2, we shall need to compute the achievement indices — and arrange them in statistically homogeneous groups (Step 3). Thereafter, however, it will be necessary to transmit only organized samples beyond the Step 2 synapse — for checking against the population characteristics of the group.

Here we encounter the first filtering process of the divisional regulatory centre. This also is based on the application of very easily handled statistical techniques — exactly like those used in Quality Control applications. A set of activities belonging to Class X builds up a data potential at the Step 2 synapse, and (on reaching an intensity threshold) fires the whole sample into the regulatory centre. Here (Step 3) the data are applied to stored models, and the appropriate achievement indices are formed. These values are compared with the stored parameters of the appropriate achievement group (Class X), to see whether any statistically significant information has been evolved. If it has not, the filter suppresses the information. If it has, the filter passes it on.[1]

The regulatory system as so far described is capable of detecting the movement of members of the population out of that population and into another; it is capable of detecting movements in both the mean and the variance of the population itself as a time trend; and (practical experience shows) it can do both these things long before human observers have detected any significant change. Thus the classification system is made continuously adaptive to the events of the real world, and the divisional directorate is simultaneously alerted to any change that has occurred (this is Step 4 in Figure 30).

[1] A detailed account of the cybernetics of this whole process is given in Chapter 13 of *Decision and Control* (see Bibliography), together with an historical case study showing the results achieved.

Key to corporate system one

A. Directoral function to receive over-riding corporate instructions.
B. Directoral function to report back.
C. Normative planning function (divisional Systems Four and Five).

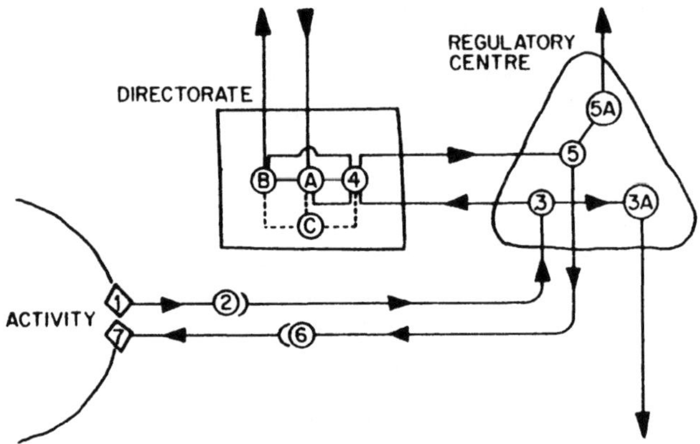

Operations control (divisional System Three)

1. Sensory transduction (codifying actuality on continuous basis).
2. Input synapse (transmitting samples at given threshold of intensity).
3. Achievement monitor (calculating, classifying, filtering indices).

3A. Information relay to other divisions.

4. Directoral function to respond (endorsing routine, initiating special action).
5. Continuous planning (strategic) and programming (tactical) generator.

5A. Information relay to corporate regulatory centre.

6. Output synapse (transmitting programme).
7. Motor transduction (determining action).

Figure 30. Organization of divisional management — System One

Here is the managerial trigger of the reflex arc which responds to the sensory input so far classified, monitored and filtered. To understand what happens next (at Step 5) it is vital to realize that basic procedures for controlling activities are already settled. For example, we know the process routes for all products, or we know the list of retailers on whom salesmen must call. The purpose now, therefore, would be wrongly regarded as the 'creation' of a plan and a programme, because they already exist in shadow form. Rather Step 5 is a dynamic process of adjustment, which *selects* particular plans for implementation, and *quantifies* the required programmes in a feasible form for the present epoch.

Planning therefore consists of the arrangement, within these known procedures, of a number of building blocks which are forecast actualities. Note that the directorate may gear itself to normative plans, and also (particularly in collaboration with other divisions) strive towards those harmonious and synergistic relationships which will raise the whole level of actual achievement to the level of capability. But in the short run, in responding at Step 5 with motor output to a sensory input, the governing required must needs be based on an accurate assessment of what will actually happen. It is now clearer than ever why the provision of massive data bases will not achieve these ends. Every possible variant on every possible programme cannot be evaluated in advance, and cannot be stored; that is our standard argument. Still less, we can now see, would it be possible to update all these features from epoch to epoch in the light of whatever time trends were affecting productivity. The alternative is to generate the quantities required, as they are required, by the following method.

There is a general model of capability in store, which was not too difficult to construct nor too expensive to record — because it is idealized. We may then select the required features of our programme from this model, just as if we intended to issue an idealized programme based on capability. But before putting the building blocks of the programme together, we adjust or weight each item by the reciprocal of its current productivity index.

For example, suppose that the time required to do a certain job comes out in capability terms as two hours. If the mean productivity currently attaching to the class to which this item belongs is one half, then the forecast actual time for use in the programme will be four hours. Now suppose that, as a result of turning this particular set of programmes into an activity, the division succeeds in effecting radical and permanent improvements in its methods of production. This will be detected in the next epoch, and Steps 2 and 3 of the sensory input will detect and measure the change. To take an extreme case, suppose the productivity rises from a half to four-fifths. The filters will at once alert the directorate, which (assuming it can satisfy itself as to the change) will approve the new coefficient at Step 4. That means, that in this next epoch, Step 5 will be computing the same element in its programme as follows. The basic model of capability will continue to supply a time of two hours. But now this will be multiplied by the reciprocal of four-fifths instead of a half, and the forecast actual time will emerge as $2 \times 5 \div 4 = 2\frac{1}{2}$ hours.

Here is what is happening:

$$\text{actuality} = \text{capability} \times \frac{1}{\text{Productivity}} \qquad \text{...we said}$$

$$\text{Now Productivity} = \frac{\text{capability}}{\text{actuality}} \qquad \text{...by definition}$$

$$\text{So} \quad \frac{1}{\text{Productivity}} = \frac{\text{actuality}}{\text{capability}}$$

So what we said amounts to:

$$\text{actuality} = \frac{\text{capability}}{1} \times \frac{\text{actuality}}{\text{capability}} = \text{actuality again.}$$

172

As we saw in Figure 29, the productivity equation, depending on the measurements used, may be 'the other way up'. But in that case, the rest of the above argument is also inverted. It makes no difference. In either case we are confronted by a circular argument, an algebraic tautology. It must be right, then, but why undertake it? The answer is: *ease of control.* We are taking actuality to have one constant and one variable component. The constant is easy to store; the variable is easy to control. To try and handle the whole thing in one go would take us straight back to the massive data banks which have been repudiated.

Programmes for action within the division, continuously generated in this fashion at Step 5, will be assembled for issue to the operating centres as required at the synaptic Step 6. As a typical example of this Step, we may think of the preparation of a complete shift's work of job cards, which will be transduced into a production shop (Step 7) by whatever means is customary for their distribution.

It will be appreciated that the approach we are using decouples the control variables (which are pure numbers) from the managerial parameters of the system. These parameters may be expressed in terms of machine occupancy, time taken, number of men employed, and so forth as required — and as determined in advance by the general idealized model. In that case, we should treat the cost variable in precisely the same way. Actual costs may be associated with every resource used at the idealized (capability) level. This means that the model can at once generate an idealized cost for which a given activity *could* be undertaken. But the components of this cost will each be modified (along with every other feature of the activity) according to the appropriate productivity classes which become invoked in the programming process. Hence we shall generate forecast actual costs for all activities *as a by-product.* Moreover when the work has been completed, we shall of course be able to generate an historical cost from the final measured productivity which the specific activity, in the event, procured.

Notes on the Operation of System Two

System Two is the metasystem subsuming all Systems One. Throughout this book its existence has been diagrammatically indicated by the tall thin rectangular box drawn round the column of boxes which are themselves the System One. However, the mechanics of System Two are found in the interlinking of the divisional regulatory centres, and in the corporate regulatory centre, as shown in Figure 31. So it would be correct, and even helpful, to think of System Two as an elaborate interface between Systems One and Three. It partakes of both.

The need for a System Two was explained at some length as being the only means whereby uncontrolled oscillation between the divisions could be prevented. Consider now exactly how this works. An example from any kind of operation will do, since all operations are measured and monitored in terms of achievement indices. Suppose that Division B receives a raw material from Division A which is, for A, a finished product. Note that the physical stuff will be transferred from A to B down the squiggly pipeline which joins their two circles in Figure 27. The requisition of the raw material, however, and its acknowledgement, progressing and invoicing, are all information transfers which will occur on the vertical paravertebral chains shown in Figure 31.

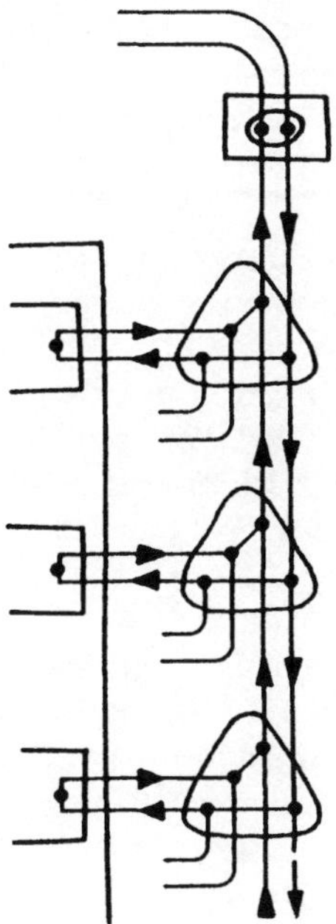

Figure 31. System Two

How, first of all, is the 'requisition' placed? In most firms, an actual internal order for the raw material is originated by B and sent to A. Yet in most instances (although one can think of exceptions) this is a silly procedure, a ritual which people think must be undertaken for the sake of sound accounting in the office. It is contrary to the notion of *continuous* planning and control developed throughout this book. In fact, Division A knows very well that a volume of this particular raw material flows to Division B, and it currently produces what B currently consumes — unless, that is, an interdivisional stock of the stuff is held. In that case, more complicated rules may be used to govern A's output to suit B's input. But in general, and over a period, actuality is the same for A as for B in relation to this material. If it were not so, the stock (or queue, as we call a stock we do not like) would become infinitely large, or else B would have idle capacity for lack of supplies.

Then we start with the notion of a material flow which, however governed to suit the two divisions, is understood to exist and to be adjusted to B's actuality — which varies with its own order book. Here we have a simple error-controlled feedback system. Now suppose that for complex reasons A's capability falls. Its productivity will then be affected. Suppose it is so affected that the measure of achievement for the production of this material leaves its statistical achievement group. In Division A this will be detected at Step 3, and a replanning process will take necessary action through Steps 4, 5, 6, and 7 to make sense of the production programme. The directorate will be alerted, so that its members (the B and C functions of Figure 30) do what they must do to investigate matters — hopefully to restore productivity to its former level.

The next question concerns the impact of all this on Division B, whose supplies are now in jeopardy. In an orthodox system, it is a moot point whether or when B will be officially informed. The supplying management may be too proud, too optimistic or too forgetful to alert the consuming management. If not, what is actually to be said? 'We are having a bit of trouble in the annealing, old man,' will alert Division B, whose managers will then try to discover what this remark means. Will the material be late, and if so, how late? How much stock is there? Should they go outside for supplies? And so on.

Now complicate this example one little bit. Suppose that not only Division B, but Divisions E, F, and G also use A's product. Perhaps B could borrow from the E, F, or G stocks. But these divisions are threatened too. Suddenly we are in a competitive situation instead of a collaborative one, and experience shows that this is where communications break down. For an element of gamesmanship is introduced into an already complicated situation. The fact that all of this can happen (has happened, often happens) leads to a new result. The consuming divisions adopt a cautious policy about their stocks, and try to build them up; the financial authorities become alarmed (the performance of investment is being adversely affected), and they intervene; meanwhile all concerned devise rules and procedures for handling the situation which are supposed to be fair, supposed to be collaborative, supposed to be optimal. But by now people are playing poker with the situation; trust is lost, informal rules are adopted at the divisional level which are intended to secure local satisfaction ... and oscillation has set in.

The intention behind System Two is twofold. First, the change in productivity in Division A is automatically relayed to the other divisions by Step 3A. The change notified is neither fuzzy nor emotive: it is a statistical statement couched in achievement numbers. The regulatory centres in other divisions can immediately evaluate the effect on their production plans and programmes, and look to the performance measures of their own stocks. Secondly, the corporate regulatory centre, receiving all this information, is enabled to take a higher-order view of the total consequences. It will report to System Three, which (be it remembered) is on the vertical command axis — and can take managerial action invoking, if necessary, the authority of System Five. The corporate regulatory centre, it can be seen, is acting *vis-à-vis* System Three very much as the input synapse on the horizontal command axis acts *vis-à-vis* System One.

Perhaps the main point of this whole arrangement is its automatic simplicity, and therefore its speed. The message that 'something has changed, and like this' goes simultaneously from the divisional regulatory centre to (i) the divisional directorate, (ii) other regulatory centres, and (iii) the corporate regulatory centre — whence onward to System Three if required. The job of the divisional directorate is first and foremost to discover what went wrong, what made this happen, and to devise measures to put it right. Meantime, everyone else has other fish to fry. The change is, for this epoch at least, a fact, and one which must be coped with. So the divisional regulatory centre has re-programming to do. The other divisions have consequences to draw, and reports to make quickly to the corporate regulatory centre. That centre itself has to take fast corrective action, either through its regulating machinery, or (if managerial prerogatives are involved) via System Three and the command axis.

Contrast this with the orthodox procedures with which we are acquainted. The matter is not referred to the corporate level, if it ever is referred, until the oscillation has set in. This generates a difficult problem in terms of control theory, quite apart from human attitudes. But by the time these too have degenerated into suspicion and defensiveness there is an appalling management problem of a social and psychological sort as well. Small wonder that these fundamental oscillatory mechanisms in the firm (and in government and society at large) prove so very damaging. They are a curse of our age — because our age has produced so many large-scale organizations without a System Two. Most of the successful ones I have observed have been entirely unofficial and largely unrecognized.

The corporate regulatory centre, then, is both a monitor and co-ordinator of divisional centres, and also an input filter on the path into System Three, to which we now turn.

Notes on the Operation of System Three

Here is the highest level of autonomic management, and the lowest level of corporate management. Its function is primarily to govern the stability of the internal environment of the organization. The neurophysiological model of the process was advanced in Chapter 8, and its managerial analogue was discussed in Chapter 9.

There are three kinds of information system converging on System Three. The first belongs to the vertical command axis. System Three is part of corporate management, and therefore a transmitter of policy and special instructions to the divisions. It is also a receiver of information about the internal environment, which it handles in three ways: 1. as a metasystemic controller *downwards,* 2. as the most senior filter of somatic news *upwards,* and 3. as an algedonode. Secondly, System Three is the only recipient of information filtered upwards from System Two — the mechanics of this process have just been discussed. Thirdly, System Three handles the parasympathetic information circuits which are antithetic to those of the sympathetic (System Two) circuits.

The first task now is to examine this third informational component more carefully, and this is done in the recollection of earlier explanations. The key to an understanding of the parasympathetic component of the model (the left-hand chain of Figure 27) is the limitation of the sympathetic (System Two) component. All along we have insisted on the on-going nature of routine control. We do not suppose that a firm is virgin territory, over which we may trample — making plans — ready for the day when something will happen. The firm is happening now; the firm's activities are well understood; its regulators at System One and System Two *are* regulators, i.e. they are error-controlled feedback servos. It follows that there are models of standard behaviour enshrined in the control mechanisms we have so far discussed — they are the paradigms against which 'error' is measured.

From the viewpoint of corporate management, however, and in this case of System Three, such paradigms assume too much. They take no account of the external environment of the organism as a whole — only of the external environment of their own divisions. They may be regulators of *local* homeostasis, then, but System Three is the only competent regulator of *organic* homeostasis, since it alone has a System Four input. What we have so far (Systems One and Two) created, it follows, is a way of handling divisional control, and a way of handling interdivisional interaction — on the assumption that the divisions between them know all there is to know about the adaptation and growth of the total organism. This they do not.

In fact, it is easy enough to propose examples of total behaviour which (because they are novel, heuristic, evolutionary) cannot be adequately represented within System Two, with its paradigmatic models, although they may be communicated to System One by the direct somatic system. Divisional directorates will understand these latter messages, of course, because they are themselves masters of the company's operations. The trouble is that their local regulatory centres are not organized to handle what is not routine. In particular, they are not organized to represent — to attend to, to measure, to transduce — other than what locally happens. This is a problem of requisite variety.

The answer, learned from the autonomic nervous system, is a direct parasympathetic access to the divisional operations themselves. There, under the local supervision of the divisional directorate, antithetical modes of control may be established. These are antithetical precisely in the sense that they handle aspects of affairs not handled via System Two. Remember the cholinergic and adrenergic chemistries of the parasympathetic and sympathetic systems. The distinction between them is not absolute, any more than our diagrams are absolutely correct in dividing the autonomic system as a whole into quite separate parts. But the main architecture and chemistry is clear — and useful.

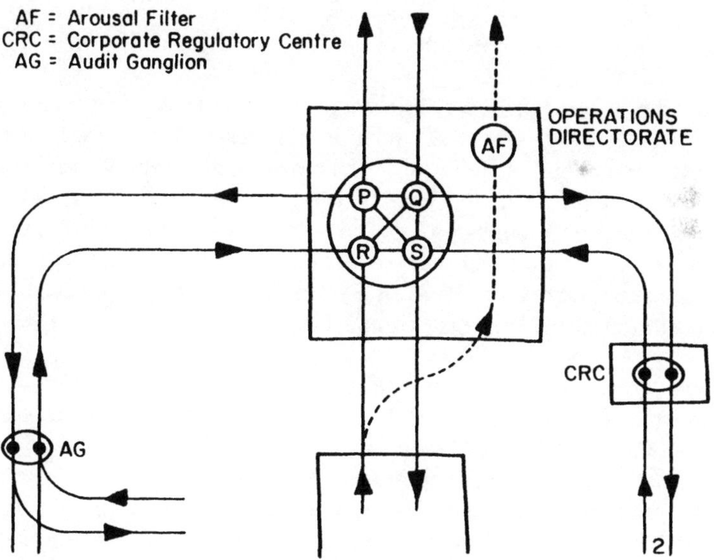

Figure 32. System Three

Looking at Figure 32, we see how system Three is intended to work. Routine information about internal regulation is always available from the corporate regulatory centre. Point S constantly receives filtered news; point Q may request any further data generated by System Two. The complex Q-S is filtering information down to the divisional directorates, while the complex R-P is filtering information up to the senior management. The entire complex P-

178

Q-R-S is the machinery for controlling internal homeostasis; point P is enabled to interrogate divisional operations themselves, which respond to inquiries at point R.

All of this is a corporate management structure, which constitutes the operations directorate of the firm. Since the R-P complex is intended to report upwards, its right to information should be carefully noted, and the role of its direct access (parasympathetic) channels must be properly understood. Remember: somatic information ascending the main vertical axis will be *divisional* information, coalesced to be called corporate information — for no better reason than that all the divisional operations taken together apparently exhaust the corporation's operations. The information ascending through the corporate regulatory centre is already more than this — it is genuinely about the synergy of the divisions. However, its limitation is its stereotyped nature; the structure of its mechanisms is paradigmatic. With the third type of reporting, both problems are overcome. Point P is instigating a kind of internal audit (though not simply financial, nor even necessarily office-based). This is a corporate activity, having short-term synergistic objectives (the Systems One have not) which are paradigm-free (and System Two is not).

In the diagram, the acquisition of information in this form is seen as mediated through special ganglia — centres which do not merely transmit information, but process it too. Thus each division has its own audit ganglion, reporting to the operations directorate, and dealing wholly with the corporate synergy. These ganglia will be brought into action solely for this synergistic purpose, and because every other kind of reporting upward must always fail to comprehend the information needs of System Three which arise beyond the pre-arranged routines of Systems One and Two.

This book deals nowhere with the established techniques of scientific management in any detail, but we should observe in passing how most of them will be applied by a competent System Three. The P-Q-R-S complex is ideally placed to use every kind of optimizing tool in its direction of current operations, from inventory theory to mathematical programming. A dynamic, current model of the firm's internal working must in fact emerge at this level, and offers the ideal management tool for the control of internal stability.

The final point to note about System Three is the existence of the arousal filter which models the reticular formation of the brain stem. The collateral fibres feeding the algedonic system are clearly shown in Figure 32, and the purpose of this system has been dealt with at some length already. We shall return to it when we reach the algedonode in System Five.

The arousal job at the third level is in fact the usual filtering job. Statistical criteria must be established to ensure that ascending algedonic information on the vertical axis, of whatever kind, is not simply absorbed by the P-Q-R-S homeostat in the performance of its own function, for it would then be lost in the upward reports from point P — which, after all, will be about the effective functioning of the homeostat and not about discrete internal events. Those are the ones we seek, algedonically, to monitor.

Notes on the Problems of Systemic Interfaces

There are evidently three interfaces between the three systems so far considered. The systemic interaction between Systems Two and Three presents no special problem since each is managerially controlled by the same authority, the corporate operations directorate. But Systems One are managerially controlled by chief executives of autonomous divisions, to whom the principle of accountability applies. They accept the policy-making of the corporation, which impinges on their activities down the central command axis. But their reaction to other kinds of 'interference', at the interfaces between their own Systems One and the corporate Systems Two and Three, may be very different.

Here then is a major snag; it is the hoary old problem of central control, written in a new form. Let this much, however, be clear at once: the snag is endemic to large-scale organization — it has not been invented here. All the cybernetic model has done is to identify the precise nature of the snag. It apparently has two components.

Firstly, there is the One/Two interface. This has to do with recognizing that there are other autonomous divisions than my own, and that they have rights as well. Especially, these others have the right not to be undermined by me, however pure my own motives are. Secondly, there is the One/Three interface. This has to do with recognizing that my own autonomous division is part of a corporation, and that it too has rights. Especially, sad as it seems, the corporation has the right to inhibit and if necessary to liquidate my autonomous division. The first component is about interdivisional collaboration; the second is about corporate synergy.

The problem will not vanish because of cybernetics. It will not be resolved by shouting. But there is a temporary solution: to declare roundly that the divisions are *not,* after all, autonomous, and that the firm has been wholly centralized. Then divisional executives who cannot stomach this edict resign, and for a while the monolithic firm runs on. It does not work; the whole of this book is dedicated to showing it *cannot* work. So the pendulum swings. The next temporary solution is ready-made: to declare roundly that the firm has been wholly *de*centralized. Then those who have been working at the centre for synergistic policies see that their work is doomed, they resign and for a while

180

the fragmented firm runs on. This does not work either. It cannot work. The pendulum must either swing again, or the corporation blows apart in a series of takeovers.

There is no solution to this problem independent of common sense. (Pathetically enough, collaborative common sense becomes scarcer the higher one goes in an organization — for psychological reasons which are not obscure.) Cybernetics identifies this problem, and specifies where it lies. Cybernetics illuminates the problem, indicating the solutions towards which nature itself has evolved. Cybernetics provides a language sufficiently rich and perceptive to make it possible to discuss the problem objectively, without heat.

There are people (whom the gentle reader will not know) who find it much more fun to fight it out across the spurious frontiers of their own ambition.

[11]

Varieties of systems thinking: the case of soft systems methodology

Peter B. Checkland and Michael G. Haynes

A number of ways of intervening rationally in human affairs are based on systems thinking: understanding real-world complexity via systems ideas. This article reviews the development of systems thinking and focuses on one of the systems approaches: Soft Systems Methodology (SSM). It indicates how SSM embodies systems thinking by giving an account of the crucial steps in the thinking as SSM developed. Issues in current work are reviewed by setting out a number of experientially derived generalizations. These concern: SSM as an ideal-type process that the user suitably adapts on each occasion of use; the fact that SSM's systemicity lies primarily in the process of inquiry; the fact that its focus is the interaction between theory and practice; the implicit belief behind SSM that learning is axiomatically good; and the belief that SSM is best used participatively.

We are gregarious animals, and we join (and are born into) various tribes. As members of these, we live our professional and private lives. Our tribal experiences are frequently confusing, and it is an intuitive truism that human affairs are intrinsically complex and unpredictable. So, necessarily, are our responses to human situations. We may respond in various ways: by instinct, emotionally, by random thrashing about (never a shortage of that in human affairs), or by the application of our ability to reason. It is the use of reason to direct intervention in human affairs that is our concern here. More specifically, we are concerned with a particular intellectual construct or metaphor that may be enlisted in the reasoning process—that of 'system' and its incorporation into systems thinking.

The core system idea is that of the adaptive whole, the whole entity that may adapt and survive in a changing environment. This concept is an epistemological device, that is, a construct in terms of which what counts as knowledge may be defined. The concept of a system has been found over the last 50 years to be a powerful intellectual device, and there are many different ways in which it has been employed. These different uses of the notion 'system' collectively constitute systems thinking, which encompasses any use of the core idea of an adaptive whole to understand or intervene in the complexities of human affairs.

In particular, we focus here on one kind of systems thinking, that embodied in Soft Systems Methodology (SSM). This approach to tackling complex real-world problems has been developed in a 25-year program of action research at Lancaster University. It has developed steadily as experience of its use has been gained, and it continues to be developed and refined. Its evolution is covered in several hundred papers, three books from Lancaster (Checkland 1981; Wilson 1984; Checkland and Scholes 1990), and a burgeoning secondary literature. (The secondary literature, often aimed at a student audience, may be sampled via Schäfer 1988; Waring 1989; Avison and Wood-Harper 1990; Patching 1990; Davies and Ledington 1991; Flood and Jackson 1991; and Hicks 1991.)

The aim here is very simple: to set out the intellectual position embodied in SSM after a quarter century of development in order to make a contribution to ongoing debate about the many varieties of systems thinking and the often differing assumptions that they embody.

System Dynamics Review Vol. 10, nos. 2–3 (Summer–Fall 1994): 189–197 *Received January 1994*

190 System Dynamics Review Volume 10 Numbers 2–3 Summer–Fall 1994

Peter Checkland was for 15 years a manager concerned with innovation in the manufactured fiber industry. Then he joined Lancaster University, where he has led the action research program which developed Soft Systems Methodology. *Address:* Department of Management Sciences, Lancaster University, Lancaster LA1 4YX, U.K.

Mike Haynes worked for 15 years as a senior engineering manager in various public service organizations. After a period of midcareer study, he established an independent management consultancy (Creative Strategies and Systems for Management—CSSM), the practice of which is based on SSM.

The development of systems thinking

About 70 years ago, in arguments about the nature of biology and the best way to tackle its problems, one school of thought argued against a reductionist approach. They advocated developing ideas relevant to what they took to be the unit of concern: the organism as a whole. They were known as the organismic biologists, and about 50 years ago one of their number, the Austrian Ludwig von Bertalanffy, began to argue that the ideas they had developed (concerning, for example, processes of growth, development, and decay) could be applied to wholes of any kind, which he referred to as *systems*. (Gray and Rizzo 1973 give a panoramic view of Bertalanffy's work.)

Bertalanffy was setting the scene for the emergence of what became known as General Systems Theory (GST), and in 1955 he took part in organizing the Society for General Systems Research (SGSR, now ISSS—the International Society for the Systems Sciences) together with an economist (Boulding), a physiologist (Gerard), and a mathematician (Rapoport). This multidisciplinary group sought to promote the unity of science by improving the communication between specialists, this to be achieved by the development of GST as a language in which the problems of many disciplines could be expressed and thus shared.

Inevitably the overarching theory envisaged by the founders of GST has been slow to emerge. GST must pay for its generality with lack of content, and workers in diverse fields have been extremely reluctant to acknowledge GST as relevant to their particular problems. On the other hand, many disciplines (including economics, geography, and sociology) do contain some systems thinkers. The rethinking of physical geography in systems terms is a particularly interesting example of systems thinking in action. Chorley and Kennedy (1971) reconceptualize physical geography as a study of systems of four kinds: "morphological systems," which are characterized by shape; "cascade systems," in which things, like water, fall down; "process-response systems," a combination of the two preceding kinds; and (the unfortunately named) "control systems," interventions by human beings in the natural environment, for example, the building of groynes on beaches.

In general, the core systems concept of the adaptive whole has been put to use in many different fields (including engineering, ecology, the management sciences) and in many different ways. A "map" of the systems movement (Checkland 1971; 1981) divides its work, as in Figure 1, into (1) the study of systems ideas as such, and (2) the application of systems thinking in other disciplines. Category (1) is split into (1.1) theoretical development, and (1.2) problem solving in real-world problems. Category (1.2) is further divided into (1.21) work in "hard" systems, (1.22) aid to decision making, and (1.23) work in

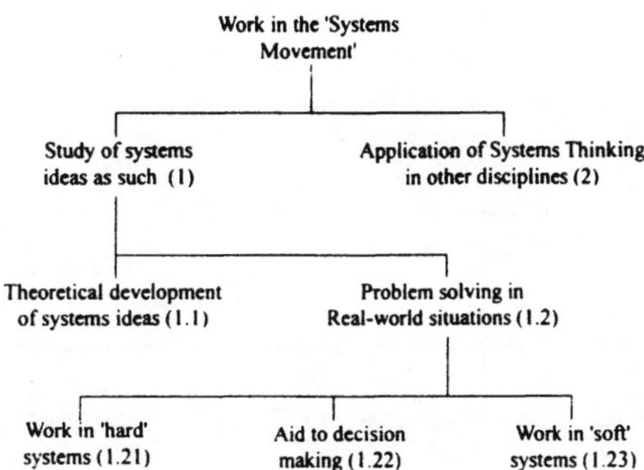

Fig. 1. Varieties of systems thinking in the systems movement

"soft" systems. Examples are then given of varieties of systems thinking: (1.1)—cybernetics, hierarchy theory, control theory, information theory; (1.21)—systems engineering, computer systems analysis; (1.22)—RAND systems analysis, classical operations research; (1.23)—soft systems methodology. System dynamics, though not used as an illustration, would, as it was originally developed, be a part of category (1.21)

These many versions of systems thinking are not unreasonably referred to collectively as "the systems movement," on two counts. Their very variety suggests a broad movement rather than any more focused unitary program; and the reasonable degree of coherence of that movement stems from the common factor that they all make use of the concept 'system': an adaptive whole, an entity having emergent properties, a layered structure, and processes of communication and control that allow adaptation in a changing environment (Checkland 1981, ch. 3).

In this connection it is interesting, not to say disconcerting, to find recent uses of the phrase *systems thinking* which imply that it applies narrowly to the method of system dynamics, as if this were the only embodiment of systems thinking.

Given the history of the systems movement, this is wholly unconvincing, whether used with reference to the simplistic version of system dynamics that Senge (1990) offers to managers or to the qualitative stages of a conventional system dynamics study as Wolstenholme (1993) describes them. It is reassuring to find Lane (1993) writing within the field of system dynamics that

> . . . SD is an element of the broad field of systems thinking. Yet usage of the term "systems thinking" is spreading in the SD community with an enthusiasm which verges on the hegemonic. The employment of this term to describe our own

> single methodology is virtually to deny the existence of any other. If we use that term for our one discipline, we are putting ourselves in a mental prison. (p. 24)

Happily we note that Lane detects that "an expansion of the SD community's definition of systems thinking is occurring"; so this semantic aberration may soon disappear.

In recent years, the most active part of the systems movement has been the one concerned with the development of systems-thinking-based methods of intervening in real-world problem situations. The rest of this article is devoted to one of those methods: Soft Systems Methodology (SSM).

The development of SSM: steps in the thinking

As described elsewhere (e.g., Checkland 1981; Checkland and Scholes 1990), SSM was developed in the 1970s in an action research program that began by investigating whether the by then well established methodology of systems engineering could be applied in problematical management situations. The systems engineering approach assumes that the system of concern can be named unequivocally and that its objectives can be defined with precision, allowing it to be engineered to achieve the objectives, using a range of well-tested techniques.

The questions, What is the system? and What are its objectives? were found to be too naive in typical management situations, where the inability to define unequivocally the objectives or even the area of concern was very often what caused the situation to be thought of as problematic. Management problem situations were, more often than not, ones in which the crucial need was to find accommodation between (permanently) conflicting viewpoints and interests rather than consensus on goal seeking. SSM emerged as a total reconceptualization of systems-thinking-based intervention; it can now be seen as a clear process through which such accommodation can be sought.

In reaching that definition of SSM, the mature form of which is described in Checkland and Scholes (1990, ch. 2), the pattern of the development was marked by four significant ideas, which together shape SSM. The first was the recognition that all problematical human situations can be thought of as situations in which people are trying to define and take useful purposeful action. The idea of purposeful activity was therefore taken seriously as a systems concept, and ways of building models of so-called human activity systems based on the idea of a transformation process were developed. (Such models consist of structured sets of activities linked logically together to make them capable of achieving a purpose, together with a monitoring and control subsystem, which ensures that adaptation is possible.) Such abstract objects, which are holons (Koestler 1967), embody the ideas that constitute the concept 'system'—emergent properties; layered or hierarchical structure; processes of communication and control (Checkland 1981, ch. 3).

Following the idea of models of human activity systems as abstract holons, a second significant idea was that a coherent model of this type could be built only if the worldview with respect to the transformation process embodied in the model were unequivocally stated. This stems from the fact that human observers are always capable of making many different interpretations of purposeful activity. One observer's "freedom fighting" is another's "terrorism," for example; and purposeful models relevant to real-world university activity could focus on its teaching and research or on its hotel-like character.

It followed from this that after an explicit process of finding out about a problematical situation (for which methods are described in Checkland and Scholes 1990, ch. 2) a number of models of purposeful activity systems, based on different worldviews, would be built. These models are thought of as relevant to exploring the situation; they do not purport to be models of any part of the real world, although the secondary literature on SSM often gets this crucial point wrong. They are epistemological devices, intellectual devices in terms of which what counts as knowledge concerning the problem situation and how to improve it will emerge. Methodologically this is done by using the models as sources of questions to ask of the real world in SSM's "comparison stage." The models thus structure a debate (which ought to be participative) about taking action to improve the problem situation.

This leads to the third crucial idea in the development of SSM: that SSM is itself a learning system, a process for acquiring knowledge about and taking action in a human situation thought of as problematical (see Fig. 2) (Checkland and Scholes 1990, Fig. 1.3). SSM thus happens to build holons that are systemic in nature, but the process of learning could still be executed using other kinds of models than system models (or, for that matter, other kinds of system models); the most important systemicity in SSM lies in making the process of inquiry into an organized system. That marks the distinction between hard and soft systems thinking (Checkland 1983). Hard systems thinking (including, for example, systems engineering, RAND-style systems analysis, classical operations research, and classical system dynamics) assumes that systems exist in the world; SSM provides an example of soft systems thinking, in which systemicity is shifted from the world to the process of inquiry into the world.

The fourth crucial step in the development of SSM will not be pursued here; it was the realization that models of human activity systems could be used to work out what information support was appropriate to purposeful activity. This took SSM into the field of information strategy and information systems

Fig. 2. The shape of SSM

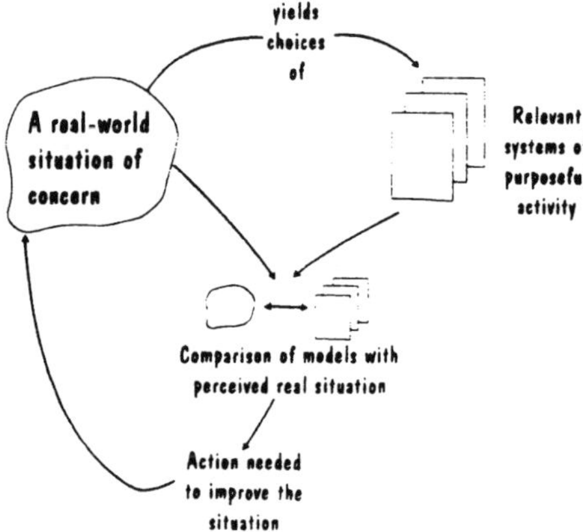

but is not relevant in the present context. Here, the final section describes some current issues and concerns in SSM development, and its fundamental assumptions.

SSM: issues and fundamental assumptions

Generalizing about any methodology is a hazardous venture. Any methodology, which is, as the word indicates, the *logos* of a method rather than simply the method or technique, is not independent of its users. Rather, the users must make their own judgments about both what to use of the methodology and how to use it in their particular situations. Hence, every use of a methodology will be in at least some sense unique, and generalizations about SSM are likely to be difficult to defend. This does not deter the writers of the secondary literature from making such generalizations, although they are unwise, in a scholarly sense, to do so. (Forbes 1989 finds that commentators on SSM are usually writing about the mid-1970s version, seemingly unaware of the developments in the second decade of development.)

With this warning concerning the dangers of generalizing about SSM, we may now make a few experientially derived generalizations from our own thinking about, and use of, SSM. The authors are a university-based teacher and researcher who has worked on the development of SSM in action research for 25 years, and a management consultant whose practice is SSM-based. What follows derives from our experience with the approach.

The first generalization we can make with confidence derives from what has already been said. Ontological statements of the kind "SSM is..." are virtually never defensible. Such statements need to indicate carefully whether they refer to SSM as words on paper or SSM as a process in use; and in either instance they need to locate the statement with respect to time, place, and users.

Behind this lies a second justifiable generalization, namely, that SSM is not in fact the name of a prescriptive procedure but rather the name of an "ideal type": the name of a framework for thinking about, making sense of, and finding ways of improving real-world situations that are perceived as problematical. The "constitutive rule" that has to be followed if one wishes to claim to be using SSM is broad: one need only be able to give an account of what one did (or is doing) by using in a precise way the language of SSM, whether or not SSM language was (is) used in actually doing the work. (See Checkland and Scholes 1990, 284–289, for a careful statement of SSM's crucial semantic concepts.) What was done in a situation might be near to use of SSM as an explicit prescriptive seven-stage process (what is called in Checkland and Scholes 1990, "mode 1" use) or, at the other extreme, use of SSM to make sense of what is being done in a problem situation (what is now called "mode 2" use). Mode 1 and mode 2 use of SSM are of course themselves ideal types, and the ten studies that Checkland and Scholes describe in detail in the 1990 book are themselves placed on a spectrum from mode 1 to mode 2 (p. 283). Each actual use is a unique mixture of the two modes, as ideal types.

Reflecting upon our experiences of the process of using SSM in many different ways in different situations, we are left with the view that at a broad level the essence of SSM lies in five related concepts.

First, there is the point that the process as described on paper is an ideal type, which users must mold to their own purposes in specific circumstances.

Second, the prime systemicity, according to SSM, lies in the process of inquiry rather than in the world, as is assumed in hard systems thinking, which attempts to model the real world. In SSM the models of human activity systems are holons used as devices to structure coherent debate.

Third, the focus of the approach is on the interaction between theory and practice rather than on either element on its own. Thus, the concepts of systems theory in SSM guide practice, which is itself the source of modified theory, and so on, in a learning process that is in principle never-ending.

Fourth, part of the worldview underlying SSM is that learning is a good thing and that the process enacted using SSM can generate continual learning about human situations, the intentions that arise in them, and the realization of those intentions through accommodations between conflicting interests.

The fifth point follows from this: although it is not the only way to use these concepts, in our experience the most stimulating and fruitful way to use them is participatively, with the people in the problem situation themselves building models and conducting the debate.

Conclusion

Any version of a systems approach to rational intervention in human affairs ought to be clear about exactly how it incorporates systems thinking into its process. This entails being clear about both its systemic epistemology and about how it generates knowledge in use. Most approaches of systems thinking have simply assumed that the world is systemic. Since SSM shifted systemicity to the process of inquiry into the world, its developers have been especially conscious of the need to think out these issues. This article, by setting out some of SSM's fundamental features and assumptions, has sought to contribute to the debate about the many different varieties of systems thinking and what they can contribute to rational intervention in human affairs.

References

Avison, D. E., and A. T. Wood-Harper. 1990. *Multiview: an Exploration in Information Systems Development*. Oxford: Blackwell.

Checkland, P. B. 1971. A Systems Map of the Universe. *Journal of Systems Engineering* 2 (2): 107–114.

———. 1981. *Systems Thinking, Systems Practice*. Chichester, U.K.: Wiley.

———. 1983. OR and the Systems Movement: Mappings and Conflicts. *Journal of the Operational Research Society* 34 (8): 661–675.

Checkland, P. B., and J. Scholes. 1990. *Soft Systems Methodology in Action*. Chichester, U.K.: Wiley.

Chorley, R. J., and B. A. Kennedy. 1971. *Physical Geography: A Systems Approach*. Englewood Cliffs, N.J.: Prentice Hall.

Davies, L., and P. Ledington. 1991. *Information in Action: Soft Systems Methodology*. London: Macmillan.

Flood, R. L., and M. C. Jackson. 1991. *Creative Problem Solving: Total Systems Intervention*. Chichester, U.K.: Wiley.

Forbes, P. 1989. The Development and Dissemination of Soft Systems Methodology. Ph.D. dissertation, Lancaster University, Lancaster, U.K.

Gray, W., and N. D. Rizzo, eds. 1973. *Unity Through Diversity: A Festschrift for Ludwig von Bertalanffy*. New York: Gordon and Breach.

Hicks, M. J. 1991. *Problem Solving in Business and Management*. London: Chapman and Hall.

Koestler, A. 1967. *The Ghost in the Machine*. London: Hutchinson.

Lane, D. C. 1993. With a Little Help from Our Friends: How Third-Generation System Dynamics and Issue-Structuring Techniques of "Soft" OR Can Learn from Each Other. In *System Dynamics 1993*, ed. E. Zepeda and J.A.D. Machuca, 235–244. System Dynamics Society, 49 Bedford Rd., Lincoln, MA 01773, U.S.A. Published in expanded form as City University Business School Discussion Paper ITM/93/DCL2.

Patching, D. 1990. *Practical Soft Systems Analysis*. London: Pitman.

Schäfer, G., ed. 1988. *Functional Analysis of Office Requirements*. Chichester, U.K.: Wiley.

Senge, P. 1990. *The Fifth Discipline*. New York: Doubleday/Currency.

Waring, A. 1989. *Systems Methods for Managers*. London: Blackwell.

Wilson, B. 1984. *Systems: Concepts, Applications, Methodology*. Chichester, U.K.: Wiley.

Wolstenholme, E. 1993. A Case Study in Community Care Using Systems Thinking. *Journal of the Operational Research Society* 44 (9): 925–934.

[12]

42 Long Range Planning, Vol. 20, No. 5, pp. 42 to 52, 1987
Printed in Great Britain

0024-6301/87 $3.00+.00
Pergamon Journals Ltd.

Managing Diversity: Strategy and Control in Diversified British Companies

Michael Goold and Andrew Campbell

Many large companies today operate in a range of different businesses. These companies need to fine tune their management styles to the specific requirements of each business in their portfolio. But they also wish to avoid unmanageable organizational complexity, and, as far as possible, to operate with a single, consistent, widely understood corporate culture throughout the company. Managing diversity therefore causes particular problems and conflicts. This article puts forward three alternative philosophies for managing diversity that the authors have encountered in extensive research on this topic with 16 large U.K. companies. It brings out the advantages and disadvantages of each philosophy and discusses the results that companies following each approach achieve.

> We are in a range of different businesses. We regard this diversity as a source of strength. It spreads our risks and gives us the opportunity to switch resources from low growth, low return areas to fund expansion in opportunity areas. But we do pay a penalty in the complexity of the management task this creates. Whether our degree of diversity is manageable, I'm not sure.

This concern, voiced by the planning director of a major U.K. company, must strike an echo in the board rooms of many multibusiness companies.

For senior managers at the corporate headquarters of most large companies, diversity is a fact of life. The portfolios of these companies frequently include businesses from several industries, at different stages of maturity, with different growth options and different financial performance. Understanding and controlling each of the businesses in a portfolio of this sort is a severe test of corporate management.

During the last 3 years we have undertaken research with a cross-section of 16 large U.K. companies to examine how different companies cope with this problem of managing diversity.[1] We began by examining the ways in which the corporate centre relates to its subsidiaries. This led us to distinguish three main different central management 'styles': Strategic Planning, Strategic Control and Financial Control. (A fuller description of these styles is provided at the end of this article, in a separate section, which describes the nature of the research which we undertook.) We believe that each style is more or less appropriate in different business circumstances. For example a stable and mature business such as London Brick (part of Hanson Trust's porfolio) may respond well to a centre that stresses control of financial results—the Financial Control style. But in the oil exploration business, or in information technology, a combination of long lead times, large investments and technological complexity requires a central style with more stress on prior planning of strategy—the Strategic Planning style.

It follows that different businesses in a diverse portfolio may respond best to different styles, and hence that the centre may need to adjust or fine tune its relationship with each subsidiary or group of subsidiaries. Furthermore, as businesses change —encountering new competitors, breaking into new markets, employing new technologies—the centre's style may need to change with the changing environment.

Courtaulds, for example, includes within its portfolio small, national clothing businesses, with short lead times, fragmented competitors and a need for

---

Michael Goold and Andrew Campbell are Senior Research Fellows at the London Business School Centre for Business Strategy. They were previously strategy consultants working in Europe and the United States. Michael Goold was Vice-President and Director with the Boston Consulting Group's London Office. Andrew Campbell was a consultant with McKinsey in London and Los Angeles. Together they are setting up an Institute for Strategic Management to focus on research into the management of diversified companies. Their book *Strategies and Styles: The Role of the Centre in Managing Diversified Corporations* will be published by Basil Blackwell (Oxford) in the autumn 1987.

careful financial control; and also an international marine paint business that requires global co-ordination across markets, state-of-the-art research into new coatings and a willingness to invest for long-term competitive advantage. These businesses each require rather different handling by the centre.

As another example, STC grew up as a subsidiary of ITT, with most of its business in the supply of telecommunications equipment to the British Government. This was a stable and comparatively protected competitive situation. ITT's emphasis on meeting budget was appropriate. In the early 1980s ITT reduced its shareholding to a minority interest, British Telecom was privatized, liberalizing its purchasing to include overseas suppliers, and the technologies and markets of telecommunications, data processing and computing began to converge rapidly. STC found itself in a different business environment. It began to create a new management style with greater emphasis on long-term planning to cope more effectively with the dramatic changes in the nature of its business circumstances.

Ideally, therefore, corporate management need to be flexible in the styles they adopt for different parts of the portfolio, and to fine tune those styles as businesses change.[2] But, given a large and diverse portfolio, is this a feasible requirement?

In our research we found that companies tend to employ a uniform style across most of their businesses, and that changes in style occur seldom. When they do come, they normally involve the trauma of extensive senior management (and chief executive) turnover. We found few examples of the central team adopting a radically different style with different parts of the portfolio.

We believe that this is no coincidence. It reflects the importance of simplicity and consistency in organizational structures and systems.[3] With a single style across all businesses it is easier for the centre to communicate its priorities and intentions to subsidiary management. It can also ensure that information systems, organization charts, incentive and career development systems are supportive of the underlying style. Whereas with flexible or changing styles, clarity of communication is harder, and subsidiary management can more easily be confused about the signals they are receiving. We all now appreciate the power of a shared corporate culture;[4] flexible or multiple styles are at odds with any such unifying values.

Even more fundamentally, we noted in our research that companies' styles almost always reflect the personality and views of their chief executives. The style is an embodiment of the beliefs and attitudes of the CEO. As such, flexibility in style calls for a degree of schizophrenia that is rare amongst the strong individuals who are typically found at the top of large organizations.

Diverse businesses that require different styles are therefore hard to reconcile with the need to maintain simple organization structures and systems within a unified corporate culture. This means that building and managing a successful corporate portfolio encounters some intractable problems:

☆ how to handle a diversity of business types without running into unmanageable organizational complexity

☆ how to maintain organizational simplicity without encountering major problems of style mismatch

☆ how far, and in what circumstances, diversification should be sought or avoided.

In our research we have encountered three main philosophies for building and managing a diverse portfolio. These broadly correspond to the three most popular strategic management styles.

They are:

- Core Businesses (Strategic Planning style)
- Diverse Businesses (Strategic Control style)
- Manageable Businesses (Financial Control style).

Core Businesses

In its 1984 Annual Report, Cadbury Schweppes stated its Group objectives in these terms:

> The Group will concentrate on its principal business areas. . . . Our objective is to maximize the use of existing assets rather than to diversify into unrelated areas.
>
> In confectionery we at present hold a 5 per cent share of the world chocolate market and are ranked as the fifth largest company in it. We intend to increase that share and to climb the league of international chocolate companies.
>
> In soft drinks, we are currently number three in the market outside the U.S.A., but fifth in the world overall. Our aim is to become the world's leading non-cola carbonated soft drinks company.

During the year following this statement, Cadbury's divested itself of two major divisions, Beverages and Foods and Health and Hygiene, to concentrate more exclusively on the core areas of confectionery and soft drinks.

This is classic 'Core Businesses' thinking. The company commits itself to a few industries (usually two or three), and sets out to win big in those industries. Growth is through organic development of the businesses in these industries, and through related acquisitions that help to strengthen and extend the core businesses. A push into international markets is often a feature. More peripheral (non-core) businesses are starved of funds or divested. The organization structure of the typical Core Businesses portfolio is shown in Figure 1. The CEO has strong central functional support, and the businesses oper-

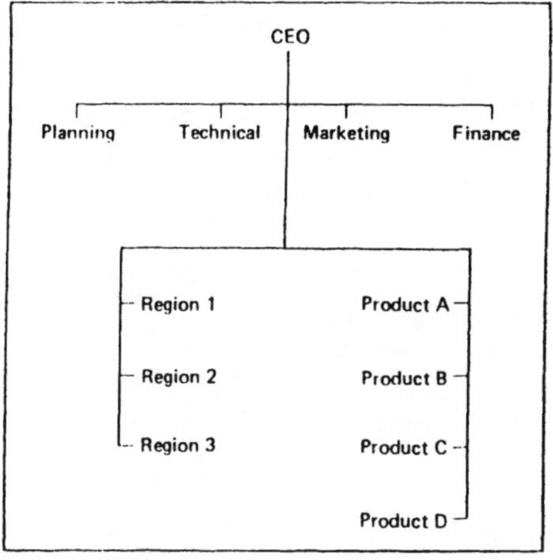

Figure 1. Core businesses' organization structure

ate in some form of product–geographic matrix, to ensure global co-ordination of strategy. Examples of companies from our research adopting the Core Businesses philosophy were Cadburys, BOC, Lex and STC (see Table 1).

In a Core Businesses portfolio, the Strategic Planning style works best. Limited diversity means that the centre can be knowledgeable about each of the core businesses, and can make constructive suggestions about their strategies. Furthermore they can provide co-ordination between businesses where this is needed. At STC we were told: 'For our approach to succeed, the centre must understand the businesses well to be able to challenge the management companies on the quality of their proposals. Our limited size and diversity allows us to do this.'

The core businesses are selected, in part, because they offer opportunities for major growth, and hence strategies for the core businesses often involve big, bet-your-company decisions. To reach agreement on these decisions close corporate involvement and sponsorship is needed. The pay-off to these decisions is sought in the long term, and it is accepted that there may be hiccoughs along the route to building up the core businesses. Lex would probably not have plunged so heavily into the wholly new business of electronic component distribution without strong corporate sponsorship for the move; nor would they have weathered the storms in the business during the last 2 years without continuing corporate support.

A Strategic Planning style—close central involvement in strategy development and flexible strategic controls—is therefore generally appropriate to the portfolio and to the ambitions associated with this philosophy. If applied consistently across the whole portfolio, it causes few serious problems of mismatch.

The strengths of the philosophy are, therefore, that it gives industry focus, making it easier for the centre to add value; it provides growth opportunities within the core businesses; and it can be managed with a single style, thereby permitting shared values and organization simplicity.

There are, however, weaknesses in the philosophy.

☆ Lack of diversity across industries provides less spread of risks. The downturn in the electronics industry left both STC and Lex exposed. Moreover reliance on the core industries for growth creates problems when those industries go ex-growth, as companies in the tobacco and oil businesses have found.

Table 1. Companies adopting core business philosophy

Company	Core business	Recent investments, acquisitions (1980–1985)	Recent disposals, closures (1980–1985)
BOC	Gases Healthcare Carbon products	Japanese and S. American gases acquisitions Healthcare acquisitions Major investment in carbon graphite electrode business	Computer services division Welding interests Variety of smaller businesses
Cadbury's	Confectionery Soft drinks	Joint company with Coca-Cola for U.K. soft drinks Various soft drinks acquisitions in U.S. and Europe Investments to increase share of U.S. and European confectionery	Beverages and food division Health and hygiene division
Lex	Vehicle distribution Electronic component distribution	Nine electronic component distribution companies in U.K., U.S. and Europe	Transportation interests Hotel division
STC	Information technology	IAL ICL (computers) Major component investments	(Several since 1985)

☆ Changes in the business environment can make the Strategic Planning style less generally appropriate, leading eventually to the need for a difficult change in style. In the mid-1970s, Courtaulds began to feel that the linkages between their textile businesses were less important than flexibility and responsiveness. But it took a further 7 to 8 years before a move to a Strategic Control style was fully established.

☆ Non-core businesses that remain within the portfolio tend to feel unloved and constrained in their strategies. These problems were brought out forcibly by the managing director of a non-core business in one of the Strategic Planning companies.

> They were not particularly interested in the strategy of the division. What knowledge at the centre there was of the business tended to be based on past personal experience of people who had worked in the area, often several years earlier at a time when circumstances were quite different. The central contribution to strategy has been mainly negative as a result of all this. One never knew from day to day when someone was going to come in and want to try to sell part of the business.

This is no atmosphere in which to plan and execute strategy.

Manageable Businesses

Like Cadbury Schweppes, Hanson Trust spells out its objectives and philosophy. In 1984, Lord Hanson, the Chairman, stated his objectives ('determined 21 years ago') as:

> To invest in good quality basic businesses providing essential goods and services for the consumer and industry and to obtain an improving return for shareholders by maximizing earnings per share and dividend growth . . . . Those in the operating companies have clear responsibility for running their businesses.

The notable points about this statement are that it is consistent with diversification into a wide range of industries, and that goals are essentially financial in nature. This is in sharp contrast to Cadbury Schweppes's objectives.

In the period since this statement of objectives, Hanson has entered a range of new industries through the acquisitions of SCM in the United States and Imperial Group in the United Kingdom. These acquisitions have taken Hanson from 55th place in the Times 1000 largest British companies in 1983 into the top 10 in 1987.

But underlying the aggressive, acquisitive growth of Hanson, there is a strong sense of the types of industries ('basic businesses providing essential goods and services') that will respond best to Hanson's management style. Acquisitions in high tech, rapidly changing or capital intensive businesses are avoided, and any subsidiary which began to show these characteristics is liable to be divested. We were told about a Hanson business that made turbochargers which had come up with an investment plan, indicating several years of negative cash flow to get established in a new and developing field of technology. 'This worried us a lot. We sold the business shortly afterwards.' The emphasis is therefore on selecting businesses for the portfolio which can be effectively managed using short-term financial controls. Hanson Trust is in this way a typical example of the 'Manageable Businesses' philosophy.[*] Other examples of the Manageable Businesses philosophy from our research are BTR and Tarmac (see Table 2).

The qualities that make businesses in different industries 'manageable' have been articulated by Hanson and BTR managers:

Table 2. Manageable Businesses philosophy

Company	Style	Business
BTR	Financial Control	Construction, engineering, electrical distribution, valves, pipes, control systems, transportation, healthcare, sporting goods, ceramics, materials, laminates, agricultural equipment, cleaning devices, conveyor belting, polymeric fabrications, power transmission, automotive carpets, automotive components, radiators, reinforced plastics, safely equipment, paper machine clothing, publishing, dental supplies, hospital equipment, rehabilitation products, hosiery, furniture and insurance
Hanson Trust	Financial Control	Department stores, batteries, bricks, electrical and automotive, yarns and threads, engineering, machine tools, control systems, construction equipment services, fabrics, textile finishing machinery, soft furnishings, apparel, footwear, housewares, artificial flowers, meat processing, office and home furniture and furnishings, kitchen cabinets, vanities, fasteners, garden and industrial hand tools, wood mouldings, windows, building materials, lumber, energy equipment, engineering products and services, lighting fixtures and fittings, tobacco, brewing, restaurants, retailing, hotels, catering, snacks, frozen foods, sauces
Tarmac	Financial Control	Stone, sand, gravel, concrete, asphalt, bricks, tiles, installation of building materials, construction, design and management for building work, civil engineering, gas and oil engineering, house building, development of commercial and industrial property, oil and gas exploration, bitumen refining

☆ 'We avoid areas of very high technology. We do not want to be involved in businesses which are highly capital intensive and where decision making has to be centralized.' Lord Hanson, Hanson Trust.

☆ 'We are a fairly low risk organization. We avoid businesses that require major, risky outlays with long payback periods.' Clive Stearnes, Group Chief Executive, BTR.

☆ 'We don't like mass production. We like niche situations that involve customer problem solving.' Lionel Stammers, Joint Chief Executive, European Region, BTR.

There may be extensive diversity in terms of industries, but there is homogeneity in the nature of the businesses and, hence, in the required style of management—the Financial Control style. In practice, this means that the businesses should have few linkages with each other, should be in relatively stable competitive environments, and should not involve large or long-term investment decisions.

Growth is achieved mainly through acquisitions that add new, manageable businesses to the portfolio. Financial Control is less suitable for fast growth, unstable environments and does not encourage aggressive initiatives to achieve organic growth.

Figure 2 is an organization chart for a typical Manageable Businesses company. The headquarters is slim, supported only by a strong finance function. Underneath, there are layers of general management, but prime profit responsibility is pushed right down to the lowest level. It is the high degree of decentralization of strategy and responsibility that allows the extensive diversity to be manageable.

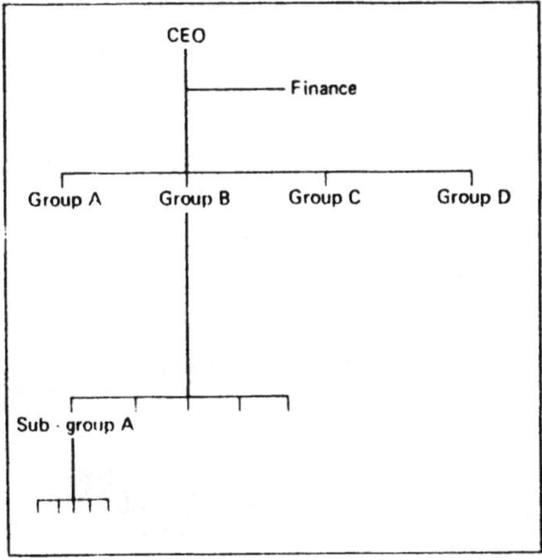

Figure 2. Manageable businesses organization structure

This philosophy therefore achieves a strong culture based on the pursuit of short-term financial objectives despite a high degree of diversity across industries. It avoids mismatches between this style and its businesses by selecting and rationalizing the portfolio with 'fit' in mind. At Tarmac, we were told that they had disinvested from their North Sea oil holding with some relief, since the size and timescale of exploration activities had been uncomfortable for them. And, at BTR, one central manager argued that one of the best decisions they made was to get out of tyres in the 1960s. 'To continue in tyre manufacture we needed to make a large capital investment. However, the business wasn't producing the sort of return we expected and we couldn't see the picture changing.' Portfolio selection and rationalization of this type greatly simplifies the management of diversity. As such, the philosophy has considerable strengths.

However, there are also weaknesses. The philosophy does not lead to much organic growth, and is liable to result in piling up excess cash from a whole range of profitable, mature, cash cows. Fresh acquisitions both create growth and use up the cash. But, when a company reaches the size of a Hanson or a BTR, finding new acquisition targets big enough to maintain the momentum of growth becomes difficult.

The Financial Control style is also vulnerable to aggressive competitors. When the going gets tough, management will typically retrench or divest. Selective tactical withdrawals may be fine, but a general willingness to retreat can be exploited by a well-resourced and ambitious opponent.

Lastly, the philosophy creates small, more specialist, 'niche' businesses rather than global players in big international businesses. From a corporate perspective, this may be no bad thing given the intensity of competition on the major international battlefields. But from a national perspective there is a need for at least some companies who can compete successfully in international industries such as information technology, oil, automobiles and pharmaceuticals.

Diverse Businesses
In the Diverse Businesses philosophy, the emphasis is on diversity rather than focus. The centre seeks to build a portfolio that spreads risk across industries and geographic areas, as well as ensuring the portfolio is balanced in terms of growth, profitability and cash flow. Resources are allocated to grow (or acquire positions in) competitively strong businesses in attractive industries; and there is a willingness—even a desire—to extend the portfolio into a range of different markets, technologies and competitive situations.

Although confident and aggressive diversification of this kind was in vogue during the 1960s and early

1970s, the more recent fashion for sticking to the knitting has meant that few, if any, of the companies in our research sample now wholeheartedly embrace the Diverse Businesses philosophy. The obvious problems in understanding and managing wide diversity have greatly reduced corporate enthusiasm for 'new legs' for the portfolio.

Nevertheless, there were a number of highly diverse companies in our sample, who did seem to be moving towards a distinctive philosophy for managing their portfolios. This philosophy entails creating groups of more homogeneous businesses, and delegating much of the strategy responsibility to those groups. Each group can then adopt its own, perhaps different, style for dealing with its businesses. Figure 3 is a schematic representation of how such a company might be structured.

This sort of structure, with strong and largely independent groups or divisions, allows a portfolio with real diversity to be 'chunked' into more manageable pieces. The divisions can grow organically at their own rates—and new divisions can be added, by acquisition or subdivision, as appropriate.

Companies that appear to be adopting a philosophy of this sort include ICI, where each division has extensive freedom to manage itself as it sees fit, and Courtaulds, which has recently split the company into two groupings, Textiles and Chemical & Industrial, in the belief that each grouping needs a different type of management.

The central style in these companies tends to be Strategic Control. Only Strategic Control is likely to be flexible enough to accommmodate different divisions, each with its own style. The old adage that its hard to have a longer time horizon than your boss

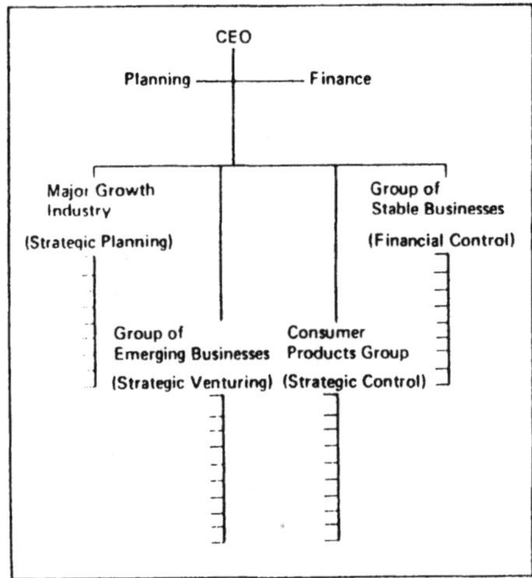

Figure 3. Diverse businesses organization structure

suggests that a corporate style of Financial Control will preclude Strategic Planning or Strategic Control at the divisional level; while a corporate desire to adopt a Strategic Planning style forces divisional line managers to do likewise in order to satisfy headquarters planning requirements.

With Strategic Control, the centre is, in Chris Hogg of Courtauld's words, simply 'a sympathetic and knowledgeable 100 per cent shareholder', allowing the divisions to go their own way in terms of style. By structuring the divisions right, the centre can create homogeneous groupings of businesses, where few mismatches occur, and can adjust the composition of divisions over time, as businesses change.

The Diverse Businesses philosophy, then, appears to be a way of managing diversity with a single central style, and without creating mismatches between business circumstances and central style. But there is a price to be paid. The centre must be willing (and able) to play a chameleon role, adopting a low profile relative to divisional management. This is not likely to be comfortable for a strong CEO, and also raises questions concerning the value-added by the centre. If the centre is so low key, and the divisions have so much autonomy, why would the divisions not be better as independent companies without the corporate overhead?

But an even more difficult issue arises from the cultural complexity implied by different styles in each division. Is it really possible for different styles to flourish side by side, or will certain divisions become second-class citizens? One company that purports to adopt the Diverse Businesses philosophy told us:

> We adapt our style to the different companies in our portfolio. We use Strategic Planning where we are building businesses with a 5–10 year payback. Strategic Control is our normal style and an active strategic dialogue takes place between the Group and the operating companies. And we use Financial Control for our 'dog' companies, when we are sorting out and preparing for disposal operations which do not fit our long term requirements.

It is evident that the Financial Control divisions in these circumstances are a sort of 'sin bin' and face a very different situation to their counterparts in Hanson Trust or BTR.

Cultural complexity is also liable to create succession problems when the existing CEO retires. Candidates from the different divisions may have radically different approaches to management, and each may well find the low-key central role incompatible with their styles. Moreover, if a new more positive central style emerges, it will be hard to preserve the divisional autonomy of style that characterizes the Diverse Businesses philosophy.

Results

Each of these management philosophies represents a

48 Long Range Planning Vol. 20 October 1987

viable managerial alternative. But none is ideal; they all have both strengths and weaknesses. This is illustrated by considering the results that companies pursuing each philosophy have achieved.

In terms of underlying profitability, all the companies that we have mentioned have achieved relatively high levels of return on capital through the period 1981–1985 (see Figure 4). The companies classified as following the Diverse Businesses philosophy (Courtaulds and ICI) have seen a lower average level of profitability but have enjoyed particularly rapid improvements in returns in recent years. (Figure 5).

The differences between companies are more marked when we turn to eps (earnings per share) and share price growth (Figure 6). Here the acquisitions and portfolio rationalizations carried out by the companies following the Manageable Businesses philosophy have yielded dramatic growth in eps and, especially, share price. By contrast, the companies following the Core Businesses philosophy have underperformed on these measures. This reflects problems and set-backs that companies such as STC, Cadbury Schweppes and Lex have encountered in their aggressive strategies to build up their core businesses.

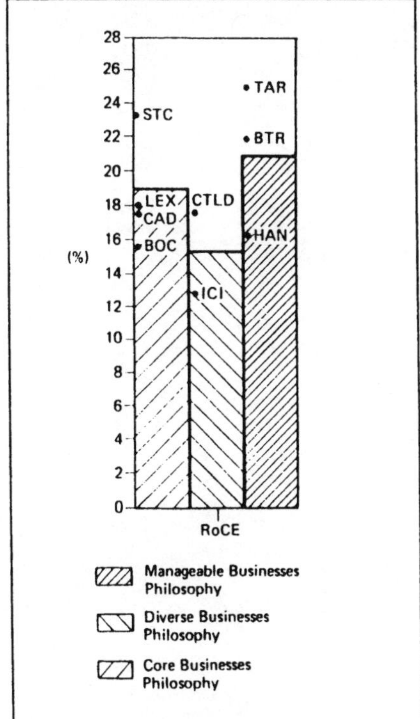

Figure 4. Four-year profitability averages, 1981–1985

In terms of portfolio growth, the Manageable Businesses group appears to have delivered spectacular rates of sales increase (Figure 7), while the Diverse Businesses group has shown little real growth. This overall picture is, however, somewhat misleading, since it combines organic and acquisition growth. In Figure 8[7] we break out growth in fixed assets between these two sources, and find that the vast bulk of the growth in the Manageable Businesses category is attributable to acquisitions. BTR and Hanson Trust have actually shown negative rates of real, organic growth through this period. For organic growth, it is companies such as STC, Cadbury Schweppes and BOC, who follow the Core Businesses philosophy, that have performed best.

The number of companies in our sample is clearly too small to provide the basis for any firm generalizations in terms of performance. However, it would appear that the Manageable Businesses companies have shown the highest rates of profitability and acquisition-based growth; that the Core Businesses have grown fastest organically, though with some setbacks to profitability; and that the Diverse Businesses companies have achieved rapid improvements in profitability, but with little real growth in sales. It is possible to see these differences in results as a consequence of the different emphases in each management philosophy.

Review

Ideally, a company's approach to managing its portfolio will achieve:

☆ enough diversity across industries and geographic areas to spread the risks of sudden changes;

☆ enough balance in types of businesses to ensure an even profit and cash flow profile;

☆ a close match between the nature of the businesses in the portfolio and the strategic management style;

☆ organization and cultural simplicity;

☆ a means of generating growth and regeneration for future portfolio development.

Table 3 summarizes the ways in which each philosophy copes with the problems of managing and growing a diverse portfolio. Each represents an internally consistent, but different, approach to the task. Our research suggests that there are successful companies pursuing each approach, although the Diverse Businesses philosophy has few committed adherents. But we have also found that each philosophy has certain drawbacks. These drawbacks do not represent fatal flaws, but are best seen as contingent liabilities. They are problems which may

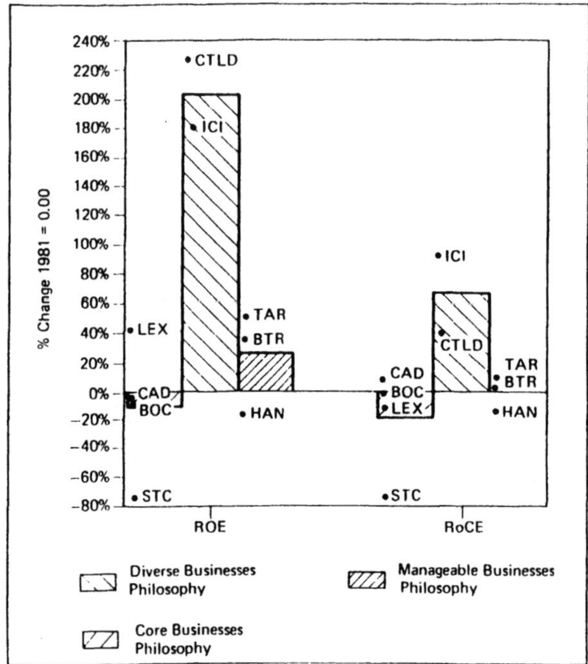

Figure 5. Change in profitability ratios, 1981–1985

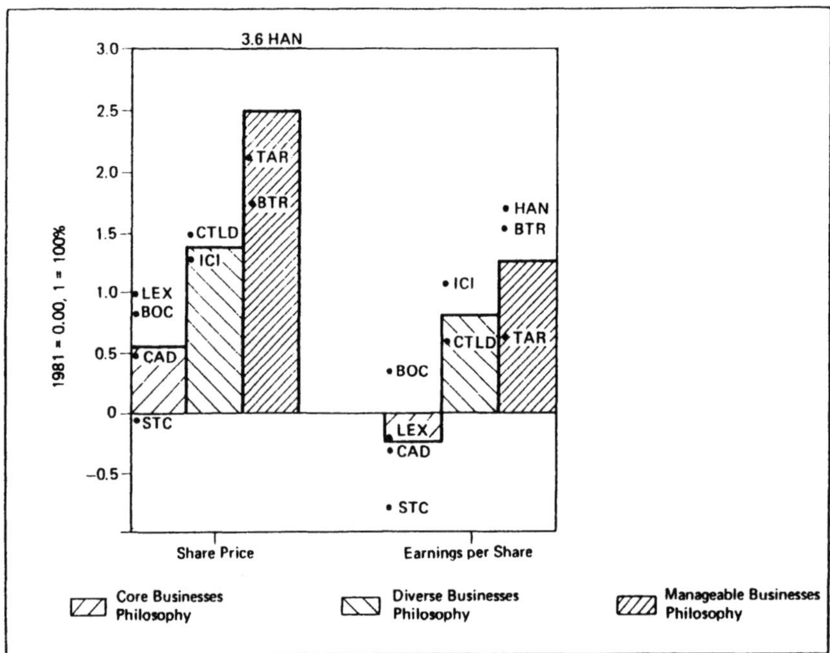

Figure 6. Four-year growth indices, 1981–1985 (real values)

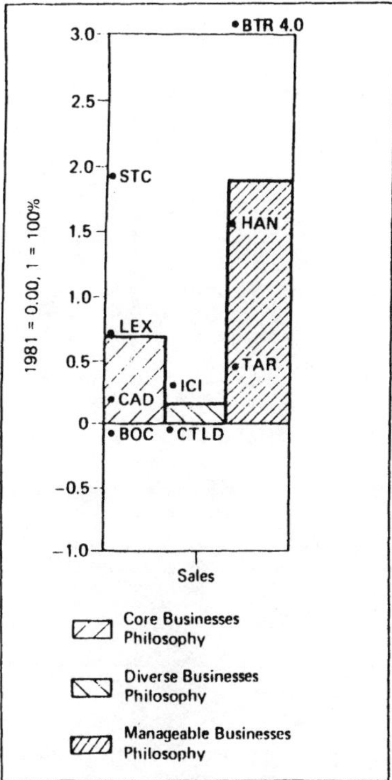

Figure 7. Four-year growth indices, 1981–1985 (real values)

be avoided for long periods of time, but which can come home to roost under certain circumstances. In terms of the results they achieve, each philosophy achieves success on certain measures of performance, but is weaker on other dimensions.

Perhaps most surprisingly, we have found that in most companies the philosophy for managing diversity remains implicit. There may be an approach which approximates one of our philosophies, but it is not normally explicitly articulated and examined. In consequence, the ways in which the philosophy can be reinforced and strengthened are less clearly perceived, and the risks and drawbacks of the approach may not be adequately recognized. We are confident that improvements in performance can be achieved by companies that create a clearer focus on these issues, and make a more conscious choice of their portfolio-building philosophy.

The Research

Our research has involved detailed work with a cross-section of leading British firms. We carried out open-ended interviews with corporate, divisional and business management to determine the range of current practices, to identify major issues as perceived by different levels within the firms, and to relate the strategic decision-making processes of those firms to the results they achieved. In this way we hoped to have some empirical basis for conclusions about what corporate strategic management is, and how the corporate level adds value.

In the event we received co-operation from the 16 companies listed in Table 4. These companies are all publicly quoted, with headquarters in the United Kingdom. They cover a range of manufacturing and service sectors, although we have excluded financial services and retailing. Their main common characteristics are size, diversity and success.

In these companies we conducted interviews with anything from five to 20 senior managers, including in almost all cases the chief executive. In addition we have gathered data from within the company,

Table 3. Management of a diverse portfolio

	Philosophies		
	Core businesses	Manageable businesses	Diverse businesses
Diversity across industries	Low	Very high	High
Diversity across types of businesses	Fairly low	Low	High
Style at centre	Strategic Planning	Financial Control	Strategic control
How mismatches avoided	Core businesses mainly responsive to Strategic Planning	Portfolio selection and retention of 'manageable' businesses	Structure into homogeneous groups
Growth	Mainly organic	Mainly acquisition	Organic and acquisition
Drawbacks	—Limited industry diversity —Maturation of core businesses —Non-core businesses	—Limits to acquisition-based growth —Vulnerable to aggressive competition —Does not build	—Low key centre —Limited central added value —Cultural complexity

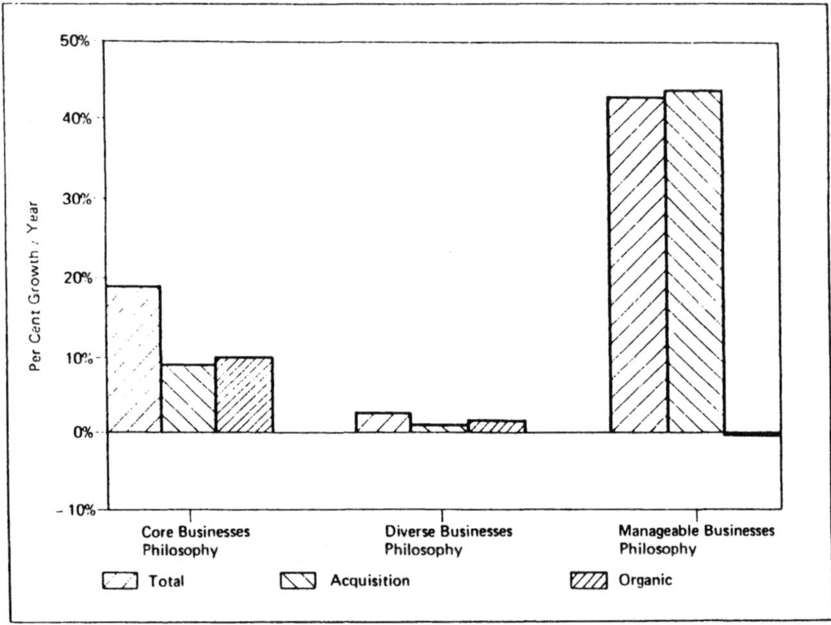

Figure 8. Average yearly fixed asset growth, 1981–1985

usually via the head of planning, concerning formal aspects of the company's strategic decision-making process, and have assembled published information on company results. Our conclusions are based on what we have learned about the advantages and shortcomings, the successes and failures of strategic decision-making in these 16 organizations.

Table 4. Participant companies

Company	Main activity	Sales (£m) 1985	Rank in Times 1000
BP	Oil	47,156	1
ICI	Chemicals	10,725	4
GEC	Electricals	5222	14
Imperial	Tobacco, food, drinks	4919	15
BTR	Diversified	3881	18
Hanson Trust	Diversified	2675	33
Courtaulds	Textiles and chemicals	2173	45
STC	Electronics	1997	48
BOC	Gases and healthcare	1901	54
Cadbury	Confectionery, Soft drinks	1874	56
UB	Foods	1806	60
Tarmac	Construction	1536	72
Plessey	Electronics	1461	76
Lex	Distribution	1041	110
Vickers	Engineering	611	159
Ferranti	Electronics	568	169

Source: The Times 1000, 1986–1987, Times Books Limited, London (1986).

In the research we identified three main styles of corporate strategic management: Strategic Planning, Strategic Control and Financial Control.

Corporate management in *Strategic Planning* companies believe that the centre should participate in and influence the development of business unit strategies. Their influence takes two forms: establishing a planning process and contributing to strategic thinking. In general, they place rather less emphasis on financial controls. Performance targets are set flexibly, and are reviewed within the context of long-term progress. Participant companies who showed these characteristics were BOC, BP, Cadbury Schweppes, Lex Service, STC and UB.

The centre of *Strategic Control* companies is concerned with the plans of its business units. But it believes in autonomy for business unit managers. Plans are reviewed in a formal planning process. The objective is to upgrade the quality of the thinking. But the centre does not want to advocate strategies or interfere with the major decisions. Control is maintained by the use of financial targets and strategic objectives. These are agreed with the centre, and business unit managers are expected to meet the standards. Companies with these characteristics are Courtaulds, ICI, Imperial Group, Plessey and Vickers.

Financial Control companies focus on annual profit targets. There are no long-term planning systems and no strategy documents. The centre limits its role to approving investments and budgets, and monitoring performance. Targets are expected to be stretching and once they are agreed they become part of a contract between the business unit and the centre. Failure to deliver the promised figures can lead to management changes. The Financial Control companies from our sample are BTR, Ferranti, GEC, Hanson Trust and Tarmac.

These styles, the results they achieve and the value that they add, are more extensively described in Michael Goold and Andrew Campbell *Strategies and Styles: The Role of the Centre in Managing Diversified Corporations*, Basil Blackwell (1987).

References

(1) For a full description of the work, see Michael Goold and Andrew Campbell, *Strategies and Styles: The Role of the Centre in Managing Diversified Corporations*, Basil Blackwell, Oxford (1987).

(2) This point is well made in Jay W. Lorsch and Stephen A. Allen III, *Managing Diversity and Interdependence*, Harvard University Graduate School of Business Administration Division of Research (1973).

(3) See, for example, Thomas J. Peters and Robert H. Waterman, Jr, *In Search of Excellence*, Harper & Row, London (1982).

(4) See Terence E. Deal and Alan A. Kennedy, *Corporate Cultures*, Addison-Wesley, Reading, MA (1982).

(5) See, for example, Robert H. Miles, *Coffin Nails and Corporate Strategies*, Prentice-Hall, Englewood Cliffs, NJ (1982), which gives an account of how the U.S. tobacco companies have tried to cope with maturity and decline in their core business area.

(6) The idea that top management groups put together their portfolio around businesses that they feel comfortable managing has also been proposed by C. K. Prahalad and R. A. Bettis: The dominant logic: a new linkage between diversity and performance, *Strategic Management Journal* (November–December 1986).

(7) Breaking out acquisition and organic growth from published information is hard. We have used information on fixed asset growth in published accounts as a proxy for overall growth, supplemented by our own estimates where this information was not available. Fuller details of the methodology are available from the author.

[13]

Accounting, Organizations and Society, Vol. 15, No. 1/2, pp. 127–143, 1990.
Printed in Great Britain

0361–3682/90 $3.00+.00
Pergamon Press plc

THE ROLE OF MANAGEMENT CONTROL SYSTEMS IN CREATING COMPETITIVE ADVANTAGE: NEW PERSPECTIVES*

ROBERT SIMONS
Harvard University Graduate School of Business Administration

Abstract

For the last two decades, management control systems have been conceptualized in terms of implementing a firm's strategy. This view fails to recognize, however, the power of management control systems in the strategy formulation process. Based on a 2 year field study, a new model is presented to show how interactive management control systems focus organizational attention on strategic uncertainties. This process is examined in two competing firms to illustrate how top managers use formal systems to guide the emergence of new strategies and ensure continuing competitive advantage.

We know surprisingly little about the effects of strategy on management control systems or, alternatively, about how these systems affect strategy. How do top managers actually use planning and control systems to assist in the achievement of organizational goals? What formal processes are emphasized at top management levels where responsibility rests for strategy formulation and implementation? Does the strategy of the firm affect the administrative systems used to set competitive policies?

Most writing on this subject has been normative and not based on analysis of organizational practices; as a result, the function of management control described in accounting literature has changed little since Anthony (1965) defined management control in terms of assuring that organizational objectives are achieved. During the 1960s and 1970s, researchers built on Anthony's work and that of others by attempting to develop the best way to design and use formal systems to help organizations implement their strategies and objectives.

Meanwhile, new directions were emerging in the strategy field. While early normative research had focused on the processes used by managers to develop successful strategies, descriptive research in the 1970s and early 1980s began to identify patterns and commonalities in the ways that firms compete in different industries (e.g. Mintzberg, 1973a; Utterback & Abernathy, 1975; Miles & Snow, 1978; Porter, 1980). The identification of patterns in strategic activity posed a new question for management control researchers: what is the relationship, if any, between the way a firm competes and the way that it organizes and uses its management control systems?

The few recent studies that have addressed this question indicate that there are systematic differences in management control systems among firms that compete in different ways (e.g. Miller & Friesen, 1982; Govindarajan & Gupta, 1985; Simons, 1987a). But these large sample, cross-sectional studies reveal little about the process of management control in these firms. The studies begin to provide answers to "how" management control systems differ among firms, but not to "why" they differ.

As part of a broader research program

*For comments on an earlier draft of this paper, I wish to thank my colleagues Robert Anthony, Chris Argyris, Joseph Bower, C. Roland Christensen, Evelyn Christiansen, Robert Eccles and Howard Stevenson. I also thank the participants of the Harvard Business School Control Workshop, especially Charles Christenson, Rajib Doogar, Julie Hertenstein, Robert Kaplan, Jean-Francois Manzoni, Kenneth Merchant and Richard Vancil. Last, but not least, I thank Anthony Hopwood for encouragement and suggestions.

(Simons, 1987b,c), the present study seeks to address this question directly by focusing on management *process* as it relates to management control and strategy. The familiar normative approach to management control describes a feedback process of planning, objective setting, monitoring, feedback and corrective action to ensure that outcomes are in accordance with plans. Two attempts have been made in the past to link this framework with strategy. The first is Anthony's (1965, 1988) — strategies are taken as given and management control systems motivate, monitor and report on their implementation. Another attempt to couple strategy and management control can be seen in the concept of strategic control. Strategic control has been described as a system to assess the relevance of the organization's strategy to its goals, and when discrepancies exist, to highlight areas needing attention (Lorange & Scott Morton, 1986, p. 10). Although strategic control has been identified as an important topic of strategic management (Schendel & Hofer, 1979, p. 18), the area has yet to generate a vigorous research program (Shrivastava, 1987). This failure is due in part to a lack of understanding of the relationship between management control systems and strategy.

The view of management control presented in this paper differs from the traditional framework. My research indicates that management control systems are not only important for strategy implementation, but also for strategy formation. I define management control systems, therefore, to recognize that these systems are more than devices of constraint and monitoring: management control systems are the formalized procedures and systems that use information to maintain or alter patterns in organizational activity. Using this definition, these systems broadly include formalized procedures for such things as planning, budgeting, environmental scanning, competitor analyses, performance reporting and evaluation, resource allocation and employee rewards (Simons, 1987a).

Although most strategy theorists correctly recognize that strategy formulation and strategy implementation are interrelated (Andrews, 1980, p. 24), researchers still tend to conceptually separate strategy implementation from strategy formation. This split has contributed to a lack of understanding of the nature of management control. Separating strategy formulation and implementation results in an artificial dichotomy that equates strategic planning with formulation and management control with implementation. The findings from the current study underscore the shortcomings of this approach by demonstrating the power of management control systems in empowering organizational learning and interactively influencing strategy.

I have three objectives in the discussion to follow. The first is to review the limited cross-sectional studies that have uncovered systematic relationships between management control systems and a firm's strategy. This literature suggests that the identification of these patterns remains an important agenda for management control research. Second, based on extensive field research, a dynamic process model is introduced to describe the use of management control systems at the top level of the firm. In this model, systems are used by top managers to set agendas for the discussion of uncertainties that arise as the firm attempts to create competitive advantage. Management control systems are used not only to monitor that outcomes are in accordance with plans, but also to motivate the organization to be fully informed concerning the current and expected state of strategic uncertainties. This general model may provide insight in explaining the fragmented relationships noted in previous empirical studies. Finally, a research agenda is outlined that may provide further knowledge about the relationship between management control systems and strategy. This leads to a discussion of some of the methodological issues that have to be addressed in future research.

STRATEGY, COMPETITIVE ADVANTAGE AND MANAGEMENT CONTROL

Before attempting to discuss the relationship

between management control and strategy, we must first differentiate among a number of interrelated concepts in the strategy literature: strategy as process, strategy as competitive position, strategy at the business level and corporate strategy.

Strategic process describes the managerial activity inherent in shaping expectations and goals and facilitating the work of the organization in achieving these goals. Many influential writers from Barnard (1938) through Andrews (1980) have considered how business leaders should manage organizational processes to gain competitive advantage.

A firm's strategic position, by contrast, refers to how the firm competes in its markets, i.e. the product and market characteristics chosen by the firm to differentiate itself from its competitors and gain competitive advantage. Unlike the process analysis, the positional approach examines the strategic choices made by firms independent of the management process by which those choices were made; patterns in business unit strategic action are the unit of analysis.

Patterns in strategic actions have been identified at both the business level and the corporate level of the firm. Business strategy refers to how a company competes in a given business and positions itself among its competitors (Andrews, 1980, p. 18). Defining strategy as patterns of action (Mintzberg, 1978; Mintzberg & Waters, 1985), this vein of research has de-emphasized the link between observed strategies and prior, explicit managerial intentions. Research has concentrated instead on uncovering recurring patterns in the way that firms deliver value to customers.

These recurring patterns have been identified empirically and clustered into strategic archetypes (Table 1 provides a summary of four illustrative studies that identify and describe strategic archetypes).[1] Strategic archetypes demonstrate that firms can compete successfully in a variety of ways: for example, superior value can be offered to customers through new product features, high service levels, outstanding quality or low cost (Porter, 1985).

Other research has investigated patterns in strategic activities at the corporate level of diversified firms. Corporate strategy is concerned with determining what business(es) the organization chooses to compete in and the most effective way of allocating scarce resources among business units (Schendel & Hofer, 1979, p. 12). Patterns have been identified using typologies that describe the operating and financial characteristics of the divisions in diversified firms. These typologies are exemplified by the portfolio approach to corporate strategy popularized by U.S. consulting firms in the 1970s and reviewed in Hamermesh (1986, pp. 9–17).

The research discussed in this paper focuses on the relationship between business strategy (i.e. how a firm achieves competitive advantage) and the firm's use of management control systems. The analysis considers the importance of both strategic process and strategic position in understanding the role of formal systems. The relationship between control and corporate strategy, while not a focus of this research, is addressed briefly in the conclusion of the paper.

Previous studies of strategy and management control

If firms compete in identifiable but different ways, e.g. low cost or product uniqueness, what are the opportunities to design management control systems in accordance with the strategy of the firm? Three strategy researchers, Miles & Snow (1978) and Porter (1980), for example, agree that overall cost leadership and Defender strategies require sophisticated cost controls. Other than this simple observation, the strategy studies that have identified strategic archetypes offer little insight into how management control systems might be designed in different strategic situations.

Studies in other areas, however, are beginning to illustrate how these systems may differ among firms following different strategies. Khandwalla

[1] Other studies that have attempted to identify strategic archetypes include Miller & Friesen (1978), Wissema *et al.* (1980), Galbraith & Schendel (1983) and Herbert & Deresky (1987).

TABLE 1. Illustrative studies of strategic archetypes

Study	Identified archetypes	Features
Mintzberg (1973a)	Entrepreneurial	Opportunity seeking, founding CEO, bold decisions, growth-oriented, high uncertainty.
	Adaptive	Reactive, incremental goal setting, relative certainty in decision-making.
	Planning mode	Analysis dominates decisions, integrated strategies, placid environment.
Utterback & Abernathy (1975)	Performance-maximizing	Uncertain environment, offers unique products, searches for new opportunities.
	Sales-maximizing	Standardized products, more stable environment, high level of competition, some product differentiation.
	Cost-minimizing	Standard product, extreme price competition, high efficiency, low innovation, sophisticated control techniques.
Miles & Snow (1978)	Defender	Stable environment, limited product range, competes through low cost or high quality, efficiency paramount, centralized structure.
	Prospector	Always seeking new product and market opportunities, uncertain environment, flexible structure.
	Analyzer	Hybrid. Core of traditional products, enters new market after viability established, matrix structure.
	Reactor	Lacks coherent strategy, structure inappropriate to purpose, misses opportunities, unsuccessful.
Porter (1980)	Overall cost leadership	Low price, high market share focus. Standardized product, economies of scale, tight cost control.
	Differentiation	Product uniqueness brings brand loyalty, emphasis on marketing and research.
	Focus	Focus on defined buyer group, product line or geographic market. Niche strategy.

(1972, 1973), in the first study of its kind, focused on the relationship between formal accounting-based control systems and the type of competition in an industry. He concluded that increased competition leads to increased use of management control procedures. This relationship was strongest for product competition, moderate for marketing competition and weakest for price competition. This study, like others focusing on the relationship between formal control systems and external environments of the firm (e.g. Gordon & Narayanan, 1984; Ewusi-Mensah, 1981; Hedberg & Jönsson, 1978), did not consider the strategies of the firm, but did suggest that control system design was sensitive to the way that the firm competes.

Miller & Friesen (1982) studied the relationship between two strategic archetypes, which they labelled "entrepreneurial" and "conservative", and the use of control systems.[2] The firms in their sample were split into two strategic groups based on ratings of innovation and risk taking. The conservative subsample possessed many of the attributes of Miles & Snow's (1978) "Defenders" and Mintzberg's (1973a) "Adapters": low differentiation, homogeneous markets and stable environments. The second subsample was the entrepreneurial firm, similar to Miles &

[2] In the Miller & Friesen (1982) study, "controls" was a single variable among a set of 13 variables. The 13 variables measured organizational attributes such as environment, information processing, structure, and decision making. The "controls" variable was calculated by averaging the scores of six Likert-type scales that related to the comprehensiveness of controls, and the use of cost and profit centers, statistical quality control practices, variance analysis and formal personnel appraisals.

Snow's "Prospector" and Mintzberg's "Entrepreneurial" firms. These firms experienced more hostile environments and competed through product differentiation.

Miller & Friesen's analysis indicates that the strategy of the firm affects the way that management controls are used to either encourage or discourage innovation. Control was positively correlated with innovation for conservative firms and negatively correlated with innovation for entrepreneurial firms. The authors speculated that conservative firms use formal control systems to signal market opportunities and/or declining results; as a result, innovation increases. For entrepreneurial firms, however, control systems flag innovative excess and result in less innovation.

Govindarajan & Gupta (1985) studied the relationship between corporate strategy and one aspect of management control — bonus remuneration. The research focused on corporate-level, portfolio strategies in diversified firms (e.g. build market share, maximize cash flow, prepare to liquidate business). Govindarajan & Gupta concluded that long run evaluation criteria and subjective, non-formula bonus calculations are effective for businesses following a "build" strategy, but detrimental to business units pursuing a "harvest" strategy.

Building on the Miles & Snow (1978) typology, Simons (1987a) studied firms classified as either Prospectors or Defenders to determine whether management control systems differ between the two groups. Using concepts derived from the management control literature, factor analysis was used to reduce questionnaire scales to ten dimensions of management control.[3]

Statistical analysis and interview data indicated that control systems differ systematically between Prospector and Defender firms. Successful Prospectors use a high degree of forecast data in control reports, set tight budget goals and monitor outputs carefully. Cost control is reduced. Moreover, large Prospectors emphasize frequent reporting and use uniform control systems that are modified frequently. These results led to speculation that Prospectors use their mangement control systems intensively to monitor uncertain and changing environments. Defenders, by contrast, use management control systems less actively. Negative correlations were calculated between profit performance and attributes such as tight budget goals and the monitoring of outputs. Defenders, operating in stable environments, emphasize bonus remuneration based on achieving budget targets and report little change in their control systems over time.

A CLOSER LOOK AT STRATEGY AND MANAGEMENT CONTROL SYSTEMS

The studies cited in the preceding section suggest that there is a link between the way that firms achieve competitive advantage and the design and use of their management control systems. Little is known, however, about how this association should be conceptualized to increase our knowledge and improve our predictive ability.

The research which provides the basis for the present analysis, conducted over a 2 year period, focuses on the use of management control systems by top management — those responsible for ensuring that strategies are formulated and implemented. (In some organizations, top management refers to one individual; in large complex organizations, top management commonly refers to an operating committee, comprising heads of businesses or sectors, chaired by a CEO.) The concepts and model presented in the paper were developed during a series of field studies in a single U.S. industry. The first stage of the project involved in-depth interviewing and

[3] The ten factors developed and used in the Simons (1987a) study were tightness of budget goals, extent of external scanning, monitoring of results, use of cost control, use of forecast data, extent to which goals relate to output measures, reporting frequency, use of formula-based remuneration, extent to which control systems are tailored and the degree of changeability of control systems.

document review in three competing companies in this industry. The concepts reported in this paper were developed from this work and were then tested by expanding the sample to include an additional 13 firms in the industry. In all, over 70 interviews (augmented by reviews of relevant documentation and, in some cases, observations of company meetings) with top managers, each of approximately 2 hours duration, were conducted in the sixteen firms that agreed to participate in the study.

The subsequent analysis focuses on how two competing firms in this industry organize their management control systems at top management levels. The strategy of each firm is described followed by a brief overview of selected aspects of their management control systems. The control system aspects described are those identified by top managers of these firms as important to the way they manage their business. If a particular aspect of management control was identified as important by the managers in one firm, then a description is also provided of how the competing firm uses this aspect of management control. After this brief description, a conceptual model is presented to explain the differences in control system configuration between the two firms.

Company A and company B compete in the same industry; each company employes over 30,000 people and both companies are successful. Over the last 10 years, both companies have recorded compound growth rates of approximately 10% in sales and earnings and each has outperformed industry averages in terms of growth in sales, earnings, and cash flow. The shares of both company A and company B are rated by market analysts as high quality investments. Each company, however, follows a distinctly different strategy.

Company A competes in its various markets through cost leadership and customer service. Its products are a diverse group of well-known, mature products concentrated in high volume, low price categories. The company specializes in offering products that heighten efficiency and cut costs for the customer. Some of its intermediate products are licensed from competitors. Compared to competitors, the company has done historically little R&D (approximately 4% of sales in 1986) and is ranked as the lowest R&D spender in the industry.

"We are now definitely the low-cost producer in the markets we serve," observes the CEO of company A. "However, once in a while, by serendipity, we come across something promising. We have a habit of seizing on products the pack has scored". Company A rarely introduces revolutionary new products, although existing product features evolve over time to take advantage of new technology and perceived customer needs. In terms of the strategic archetypes described in Table 1, company A might be described as a "Defender" (Miles & Snow, 1978), an "Adaptive firm" (Mintzberg, 1973), an "Overall Cost Leader" (Porter, 1980), or as a "Cost-Minimizing" firm (Utterback & Abernathy, 1975).

The company is organized into approximately 100 divisions which are grouped into four major sectors. *Business Week* magazine reports that company A is "considered to be one of the best-managed firms in the industry."

In contrast, company B competes through product inovation and marketing. Its products are premium priced and have advanced features. Products are developed internally and the features of most products are updated and improved on a regular basis. Marketing is intensive, using both media and sales representatives. The company has been successful in developing new markets through research-based product development. The company is widely regarded within the industry as an innovation leader. Most of the company's R&D effort is concentrated on product development; in 1986 company B spent approximately 10% of sales on R&D, making it the largest spender on R&D in its industry.

Company B differentiates its products on quality and innovativeness. The company attempts to achieve market leadership by aggressively marketing new products and enhancing its leadership image. Since it is often developing new markets, it competes in rapidly changing environments. Its Statement of Strategic Direction states, in part, "We are dedicated to profitable high growth. To achieve this, we must be well positioned in growth markets. Each management must be aggressively innovative, willing to take risks, and strive to grow faster than the markets in which it competes". This company could be described as a "Prospector" (Miles & Snow, 1978), a "Differentiation firm" (Porter, 1980), "Performance-maximizing" (Utterback & Abernathy, 1975), or "Entrepreneurial" (Mintzberg, 1973).

The company is decentralized. It is structured into three sectors with over 100 operating companies worldwide that manufacture and sell over 20 basic product categories. *Fortune* magazine's annual survey recently rated this company as one of the most admired companies in America.

Management control systems in the two companies

Given that these two highly-regarded competitors follow different strategies, what are the differences in the way they organize their management control systems? Companies of this size and complexity are bound to have many differences; the analysis is limited, therefore, to the use of management control systems at top management levels, since it is this group of individuals that has ultimate responsibility for strategy making and implementation. At this level, the differences in management control systems

TABLE 2. Comparison of competitive characteristics and top-level management control systems used at two companies

	Company A	Company B
Competitive characteristics		
Miles & Snow (1978)	Defender	Prospector
Mintzberg (1973a)	Adaptive	Entrepreneurial
Porter (1980)	Overall cost leader	Differentiation
Management control systems at top management levels		
1. Strategic planning review	Sporadic. Last update 2 years ago. Does not motivate a lot of discussion in the company.	Intensive annual process. Business mangers prepare strategic plans for debate by top management committee.
2. Financial goals	Set by top management and communicated down through organiization.	Established by each business unit and rolled up after a series of review and challenge meetings.
3. Budget preparation and Review	Budgets prepared to meet financial goals. Budgets coordinated by Finance Dept and presented to top management when assured that goals will be met.	Market segment prepares budgets with focus on strategy and tactics. Intensive debate at presentations to top mangement committee.
4. Budget revisions and updates	Not revised during budget year.	Business units rebudget from lowest expense levels three times during year with action plans to deal with changes.
5. Program reviews	Intensive monitoring of product- and process-related programs. Programs cut across organizational boundaries and affect all layers of company.	Programs limited to R&D which is delegated to local operating companies.
6. Evaluation and reward	⅔ of bonus based on contribution to generating profit in excess of plan. ⅓ based on personal goals (usually quantified).	Bonus based on subjective evaluation of effort. MBO system used throughout organization.

between the two firms (highlighted in Table 2) are striking.

Company A. Company A has a 5-year strategic plan that has not been revised for over 2 years. The plan is prepared by operating managers with the assistance and coordination of head office staff groups and presented to the top managers who comprise the Office of the Chief Executive (OCE). These managers report that the plan is for informational purposes and is not used actively in running the business.

Based on prior operating performance and market expectations, profit goals are established each year by the CEO and President of company A and communicated to division heads. Each division then prepares an annual budget to meet these goals. After the finance department verifies that the consolidated budget will meet corporate profit goals, the completed budgets are submitted to top management for approval. Annual budget presentations to top management are characterized by the CEO as "show and tell"; problems and issues have been identified and worked out in person with the CEO and President prior to the meetings. Once approved, budgets are never changed.

Budget reviews by top management during the year are limited to monthly reports to the OCE of sales, gross margin percentages, total operating expenses, tax rates and earnings per share.

Top management pays extremely close attention to a series of ongoing programs: these programs are established for the review of new product technologies, changes in existing product features and a variety of "value improvement" efforts. Since programs are designed to explore new ways of doing things, they often cut across organizational boundaries and involve many people at different levels of the company.

Each program is reviewed regularly (at least once every 6 weeks and often more frequently) using formal reports and presentations to the highest level of management. Goals are established for all individuals working with each program and achievement against goals is measured on a regular basis. The ongoing review process generates product and process ideas throughout the organization that are tested and ultimately implemented. New programs are often established from ideas generated during existing program review.

Bonuses at company A are received by a relatively small group of middle and senior managers (the management group eligible for bonuses is 2.5% of total employees). Bonuses range from 15% to 50% of salary and are allocated to employees based on corporate performance against budget (⅓), operating unit performance against budget (⅓) and individual objectives that are negotiated with superiors (⅓).

Company B. Company B invests heavily in long range planning. All planning, however, is done by operating managers; there are no planning staff groups. Long range plans are based on 5 and 10 year forecasts and are updated each year by comparison with the plan prepared the year before. All changes in estimates require proposed tactics to deal with the changed environments. Included in the plans for each operating company are forecasts of competitive environments, *pro forma* income statements by product category for each major competitor, as well as an analysis of each competitor's perceived strategy.

Long range plans are debated heavily in the organization and must ultimately be sent, in summary form, to the CEO. The final debate and approval of long range plans takes place annually in an Executive Committee meeting which comprises the CEO, President and key sector heads and company group chairmen.

In company B, budgets, as well as a second-year forecast, are prepared annually by operating managers throughout the organization. Budgets are formally revised three times during the year; each revision requires a full re-estimation of all budget items and programs. Budgets are the focus of a great deal of debate among operating managers and are used, not as purely financial documents, but rather as agendas to discuss tactics, new marketing ideas, and product development plans throughout the organization and ultimately at the top management level. To focus the debate on strategies rather than financials, the plans and budgets are reduced at the top management level to four numbers only (estimated unit sales, revenues, net income and ROI) and to the tactics that will be used to achieve these numbers.

Profit goals are established on a bottom-up basis as managers throughout the organization set personal and business unit goals based on perceived corporate needs. These goals are challenged rigorously at all levels in the organization during a series of profit planning meetings held at various times during the year. Once the review process at lower levels is complete, top management rarely makes a formal request to operating managers to reconsider their budget to deliver more profit.

Unlike company A, the use of programs is generally limited to the R&D area, which is decentralized to operating companies. Programs are therefore managed at the local level and are not typically an agenda for top corporate management.

Bonuses at company B are entirely subjective and are based on effort and innovation rather than performance against predetermined targets. Managers throughout the organization spend a great deal of time each year discussing and reviewing suggestions concerning appropriate bonus levels for subordinates. Bonus recommendations for all managers with salaries in excess of $95,000 are reviewed by the Executive Committee. Below the executive committee level, all managers are eligible for annual bonuses, the amount of which is determined subjectively by operating company presidents. After bonuses have been awarded, the Executive Committee also uses a "post audit" to review the reasons for unusually high or low bonus awards throughout the organization. Through a special bonus plan for entrepreneurial accomplishment, the company distributes additional bonuses in excess of $1 million annually; recommendations for these special bonuses, which typically represents 10–50% of an individual's salary, are reviewed and acted upon by the Executive Committee.

A PROCESS MODEL

Casual observation suggests that all large, complex organizations have similar types of management control systems. Short and long range plans, financial budgets, capital budgets, variance analyses and project reporting systems are commonplace tools in virtually every large, professionally managed corporation. But the illustrative example presented above shows that there are distinct differences in the way that management control systems are used at top management levels in different firms. How can we explain the differences in management control systems between company A and company B? How do these differences relate to their strategies?

The answer lies in how and why top managers choose to personally monitor certain management control systems and to delegate other aspects to subordinates. Four concepts are used to develop the model: limited attention of managers; strategic uncertainties; interactive management control; and organizational learning.

Limited attention

Interviews conducted during this research reveal that managers have neither the time nor the capacity to process all the information available to them. Two concepts, well established in the literature, support this observation. First, managers are rational only within cognitive boundaries (Simon, 1957). Mind is a scarce resource (Williamson, 1986, p. 5) and must be viewed as a constraint on the information processing capabilities of managers. Second, top managers must engage in many concurrent activities. Mintzberg (1973b) argues that top managers have ten working roles including that of figurehead, leader, liaison, monitor, disseminator, spokesman, entrepreneur, disturbance handler, resource allocator and negotiator. Decision-related activities represent only a subset of the activities of top managers; interpersonal and informational roles are equally important.

The concept of limited attention has important implications for management control. A multitude of activities demand attention — appearing at outside functions, speeches to employees, reading reports, making and ratifying decisions, evaluating employees, planning for succession — and daily choices must be made. Thus, only limited subsets of the organization's formal management control process can have the attention of top management; most areas of management control are delegated, by necessity, to subordinates.

Strategic uncertainties

Because of these attention constraints, top managers report that they implicitly rank the set of activities they monitor from most critical to least critical: this ranking allows top managers to attend to strategic uncertainties — uncertainties that top managers believe they must monitor personally to ensure that the goals of the firm are achieved.[4]

Although firms competing in the same industry face the same set of potential uncertainties (changes in government regulation, intensity of competition, advance of new technologies, nature of customers and suppliers, product life cycles and diversity in product lines), the strategy of the firm strongly influences which uncertainties are critical to the achievement of chosen objectives.[5] For example, managers in company A believe that they can only sustain their low cost position if their products evolve to offer superior efficiency to users. The strategic uncertainties that top managers in company A monitor personally, therefore, relate to potential changes in product technology that yield superior cost-in-use benefits to customers.

Although company B faces the same set of potential uncertainties as company A, its strategy has resulted in different strategic uncertainties. Top managers in this firm monitor the choice of appropriate competitive responses for its various operating companies that compete through aggressive marketing tactics and new product introductions.

Interactive management control

Top managers must decide which aspects of management control systems to use interactively and which aspects to program (Simons, 1987b). Management controls become interactive when business managers use planning and control procedures to actively monitor and intervene in ongoing decision activities of subordinates. Since this intervention provides an opportunity for top management to debate and challenge underlying data, assumptions and action plans, interactive management controls demand regular attention from operating subordinates at all levels of the company. Programmed controls, by contrast, rely heavily on staff specialists in preparing and interpreting information. Data are transmitted through formal reporting procedures and operating managers are involved infrequently and on an exception basis.

Modern companies have many different types of management control systems. How do top managers decide which systems to make interactive and which to program? Top managers will choose to make a management control system interactive if the system collects information about strategic uncertainties. The selected interactive system can then be used by top managers for three functions: signalling, surveillance and decision ratification.

Signalling is the use of information to reveal preferences (Spence, 1974; Meyer, 1979). Signalling is necessary since top managers cannot always know when or where the impetus for important policy decisions will originate, how or why a decision will be made, or by whom. The decision process is diffuse with inputs from multiple actors over a protracted time period (Pinfield, 1986; Leifer & White, 1986; Burgel-

[4] Strategic uncertainties are different than the concept of critical success factors that was popularized by business consultants in the 1960s and is taught in business schools today (Daniel, 1966). Critical success factors are the distinctive competencies that the firm must possess to sustain current competitive advantage (e.g. manufacturing efficiency for a strategy of overall cost leadership; research and development productivity for a strategy of new product introduction).

[5] A critical uncertainty for all firms is the ability to internally generate profit to provide resources to fund business strategies (Donaldson, 1984, p. 12). Thus, top managers always monitor personally the profit-generating ability of the firm.

man, 1983; Mintzberg *et al.,* 1976; Cohen *et al.*, 1972). For this reason, top managers do not know *ex ante*, and often not even *ex post*, who in the organization initiates and fosters important policy decisions. By using interactive management controls to monitor stratagic uncertainties, top managers reveal their values and preferences to the many individuals in the organization who have input in decision processes.

Surveillance is the search for surprises; interactive management controls provide guidance to organizational members as to where to look for surprises and what types of intelligence information to gather. Feldman & March (1981) describe this function:

> Organizations, as well as individuals, ... gather information that has no apparent immediate decision consequences. As a result, the information seems substantially worthless within a decision-theory perspective. The perspective is misleading. Instead of seeing an organization as seeking information in order to choose among given alternatives in terms of prior preferences, we can see an organization as monitoring its environment for surprises (or for reassurances that there are none). The surprises may be new alternatives, new possible preferences, or new significant changes in the world (p. 176).

Finally, decision ratification by top managers (as distinct from decision making) is necessary when any strategic policy decision commits the organization and its resources (Mintzberg, 1973b, p. 87; Bower, 1986, pp. 64). Interactive management controls allow top managers to be fully informed about such decisions throughout the organization.

Organization learning

The final concept needed to complete the analysis is organizational learning. Organizational learning describes the ways that organizations adjust defensively to reality and use knowledge to improve the fit between the organization and its environment (Hedberg, 1981, p. 3). Comprehensive reviews of the concept of organizational learning are found in Argyris & Schön (1978) and Fiol & Lyles (1985).

I have argued that the personal involvement of top managers, the defining characteristic of interactive control, influences strongly the incentives to produce and share information. Moreover, this focusing of organizational attention and the interactive exchange of information stimulates learning throughout the organization about the strategic uncertainties that are perceived by top management. By focusing attention throughout the organization, top managers use interactive management control to influence and guide the learning process — understanding that individual ideas and initiatives will emerge over time in unsystematic ways. By emphasizing select management controls and making them interactive (and programming and delegating others) top managers ensure that the organization is responsive to the opportunities and threats that the firm's strategic uncertainties present.

The four concepts presented above can now be summarized and integrated: the intended business strategy of a firm creates strategic uncertainties that top managers monitor. While all large companies have similar management control systems, top managers make selected control systems interactive to personally monitor the strategic uncertainties that they believe to be critical to achieving the organization's goals. The choice by top managers to make certain control systems interactive (and program others) provides signals to organizational participants about what should be monitored and where new ideas should be proposed and tested. This signal activates organizational learning and, through the debate and dialogue that surrounds the interactive management control process, new strategies and tactics emerge over time.

The recursive nature of the model (Fig. 1) illustrates why management control systems should be considered as an important input to strategy formation. We know that strategies can be both intended and emergent (Mintzberg, 1978). This model illustrates, moreover, that emergent strategies can be influenced and managed — serendipity can be guided by top managers who use formal process to focus organizational attention and thereby generate new ideas, tactics and strategies. Management control processes, which have been characterized solely as tools for implementing goals, can be instrumen-

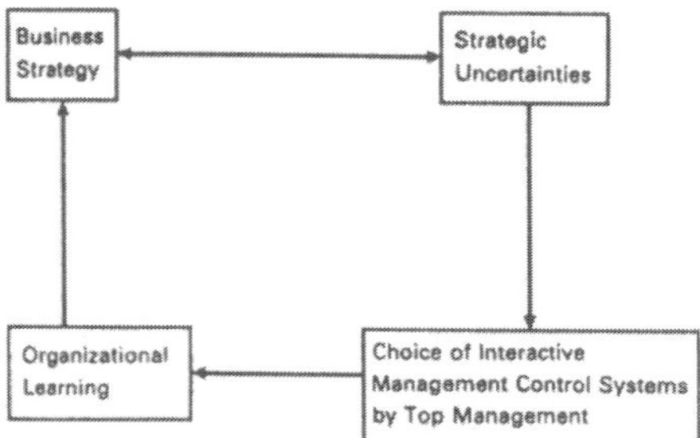

Fig. 1. Process model of relationship between business strategy and management control systems.

tal in allowing the organization to learn and adapt over time.

Applying the model

Since company A and company B compete in the same industry, each firm faces the same set of potential uncertainties (Fig. 2). From this set of potential uncertainties, top managers of each firm have identified strategic uncertainties that relate to their company's individual strategy. From interviews at company A, it is clear that top managers believe that the major strategic uncertainty facing the firm is new product technologies or attributes that could shift existing low cost advantage. They recognize that company A's success derives from continually providing customers with products that offer low end-use cost: new, more efficient product technologies of competitors and changes in buyer needs are potential threats.

To manage these strategic uncertainties, top management has made a limited subset of management controls interactive and programmed other controls. The program review system, which operates from the lowest organizational level to the CEO's office, is an example of an interactive management control system that is a major information source for both top management and all operating managers in the company. Programs focus on ways to improve value for customers ("cost improvement with equal or better quality"), new technologies that build on existing product lines and product enhancements to help customers be more efficient. Programs typically have the potential of affecting a wide range of the company's products and therefore cut across formal organizational boundaries.

Managers in company A know, by the emphasis that top management puts on the review of selected programs, which aspects of the business are considered critical to long term organizational success. For each program, information is continually gathered throughout the organization, agendas are set to review progress and new information, and changes and surprises are rapidly communicated. The organizational

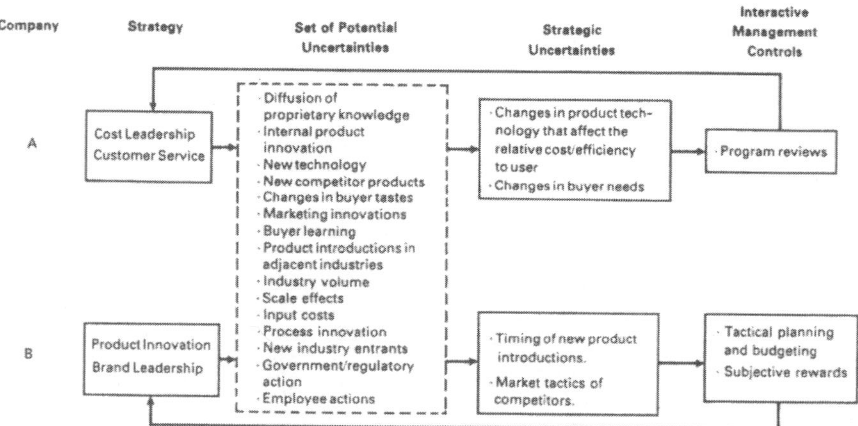

Fig. 2. Summary of interactive process model in two firms.

learning engendered through the interactive management control system is a powerful influence on strategy making.

The CEO of company A described how new strategies emerge from the process, "I really work those programs. Everyone understands how important they are. New initiatives are not decided as part of the planning process, but as part of the program review process. The Capital Expenditure Committee is not doing strategic thinking about programs — they just say "yes" when a proposal is developed out of a program review and someone comes to them asking for money. In fact, many of our new programs arise out of the review process. As we sit and discuss these things, someone will have a bright idea for product enhancement or a new way of doing something. This often leads to new programs which can eventually take us into new technologies or open up a whole new group of products."

Top management at company A pays little day-to-day attention to aspects of the firm's management control systems that do not relate to strategic uncertainties. Long range planning is programmed and is not an agenda item for top management: strategies throughout the firm are clear and consistent. Profit planning and budgeting, an annual event orchestrated by staff departments, are not interactive because the environment is relatively stable and well understood; top managers do not need to rely on these systems to motivate the organization to constantly scan changes in the market. The rewards system is also programmed since bonuses are determined largely by reference to quantitative targets and require minimal attention from top management. Even aspects of management control systems that are associated with the success of current strategies, i.e. so-called "critical success factors", are programmed and delegated to staff specialists.

The programming of critical success factors is apparent in the way that top management at company A deal with manufacturing and logistical operations — clearly critical success factors for this low cost producer. Every Wednesday at 10:00 a.m., a 20 minute meeting is held with 15 key managers, chaired by a member of the top management group. Conversation focuses on one sheet of paper that reviews twelve product categories in terms of unit sales, inventory levels, backorders, service levels and quality control release times — all against target. The chairman described the meetings, "we run the day-to-day operations by focusing on things off track. If there is a problem, the individual had better have the answer before he walks in. In this way, we can review the entire business in twenty minutes each week. We have become very good at understanding what we were looking at so we can just do it."

Because company B follows a different strategy, its top managers focus on different strategic uncertainties. By competing through product innovation rather than price and efficiency, top managers want their organization to focus on marketing tactics that can exploit new product development and thereby build market share or open new markets. Top managers perceive strategic uncertainties that relate to the timing of new product introductions and the defensive actions of competitors. Accordingly, the top management of company B has chosen to make planning and budgeting highly interactive and tactical.

The development and discussion of 5 and 10 year plans, for example, is an important agenda for top management and, by implication, for all operating managers in company B. Each year, plans for each operating unit are revised with reference to the previous year's plan; product life cycles are carefully monitored. All anticipated changes are coupled with action plans that focus on marketing tactics and the timing of new product introductions — both strategic uncertainties for company B. These plans, which are based on environment, competitor and technology assessments, are prepared, challenged and debated over a period of several months each year by successive levels of operating managers until they are debated at the Executive Committee level. Staff units play no role in this process. The highly interactive nature of long range planning results in intense organizational learning about changes in the competitive product markets and ideas on how to react offensively to these threats and opportunities. From these discussions, new strategies emerge.

Top management has also made profit planning and budgeting interactive at company B by focusing attention, almost continuously during the year, on budget changes and action plans to deal with changed conditions. Managers use this bottom-up process not as a financial exercise, but rather to set agendas to debate current and future product/market strategies in the company's changing markets. Budget discussions throughout the year revolve around unanticipated changes in the competitive environment, marketing tactics to preempt competitor actions, and the type and timing of new product developments. Managers point out that they are planning and budgeting so frequently and with so much discussion about appropriate tactics and targets that it is unnecessary to formally issue corporate goals. One top manager elaborated, "the feeling that we are forever planning is due to the fact that you never have the luxury of putting the plan on a shelf—it forces you to continually look at your mistakes and learn how to do better next time."

The reward system at company B has been made interactive and thus also demands a great deal of attention from managers throughout the organization. Managers cannot rely on a formula, but must rather attempt to subjectively assess each individual's contribution in rapidly changing market environments. Rewarding effort rather than results requires evaluators to understand competive business environments, potential opportunities and constraints, and the range of action alternatives available to subordinate managers. This information gathering process generates learning about strategic uncertainties and about possible new tactics and strategies.

Like company A, the top managers at company B are not normally involved in controls that do not focus on strategic uncertainties. The review of detailed cost information is programmed and is not an agenda for top management. Efficiency programs are typically overseen by staff groups. As a top manager stated, "I leave the analysis of variances, etc., to the financial people. I let them bring any problems to me. I don't check it or get involved in it myself." Even programs for new product development, a critical success factor, are managed at the local operating company without regular attention from top mangement; given limited attention, top management chooses to focus instead on the strategic uncertainties that arise from the actions of competitors.

Managers in each of these firms have made certain management controls interactive and programmed others. This phenomenon is not limited to these two companies, but was observed also in the other 14 companies in the sample. One CEO captured the spirit of the phenomenon, "we can have all the formal processes in the world and some of these, frankly, I don't give a damn about and others I do. And everyone understands the difference."

DISCUSSION AND CONCLUSION

The model presented in this paper departs from the traditional analysis of "fit" between formal systems and critical success factors. Instead, new concepts are introduced to link management control systems with competitive advantage. The research underscores the importance of the dynamic relationship between formal process and strategy: competitive strategic positioning, management control and the process of strategy-making play one upon the other as the firm evolves and adapts over time. The analysis shows that interactive management control processes can be used to manage emergent strategy: rather than focusing on what the organization already understands and does well, these systems direct organizational attention to emerging threats and opportunities.

Theories of information provide additional perspective to the ideas presented in this paper. Language theorists differentiate between rules that constrain and those that open up new realms of activity (Campbell, 1982, p. 128). The latter type of rule is capable of generating variety, novelty, and surprise. This distinction is analogous to that between programmed and interactive controls. Campbell (1982) illustrates the power of fixed rules in producing unpredictable amounts of complexity as information and meaning is generated. The necessity of structure to produce meaning, a concept fundamental to theories of information and language, is echoed in the way that managers use structured, formal process interactively to motivate organizational learning. "Structure and freedom," summarizes Campbell, "like entropy and redundancy, are not warring opposites, but complementary forces" (p. 264).

Top managers use formal process to gain maximum advantage from these forces. These managers know that decisions and actions affecting current strategies will emerge from all corners of the organization; their primary job is to provide guidance, resources and incentives to motivate the organization to gather and interpret new information so that the organization can respond and adapt. Energy is channelled and directed by the interactive process; formal management control systems provide a common language. The organization is energized: momentum is created to exploit existing strategies and to anticipate strategic uncertainties. Information is shared and interpreted. Action plans are tested. New strategies emerge.

Our analysis suggests that caution is necessary in interpreting previous studies that have focused on strategy and control. Cross-sectional studies such as Khandwalla (1972, 1973) and Miller & Friesen (1982) were conducted using a single measure for control that was computed as the simple average of the importance of various aspects of a firm's administrative controls system. Thus, scores to represent the use of cost control and variance analysis, formal appraisal of personnel, capital budgeting techniques and flexible budgeting were averaged to produce one summary index. The process model developed here, however, suggests that it is not the mean value that is of importance, but rather the distribution of management attention among the various control subsystems.

Studies that have decomposed control systems into constituent elements support the process model presented in this paper. Govindarajan & Gupta (1985) noted that subjective bonus systems were beneficial for emerging businesses following "build" strategies, but detrimental to businesses in a "harvest" mode. Interactive reward systems based on subjective evaluation of effort are appropriate for firms that need to motivate organizational learning in rapidly changing environments and where rewarding team effort is important — typical conditions of firms in a growth phase. This approach is costly, however, and generally uneconomic for businesses in slow decline.

Simons (1987a) found that Prospectors generally use a lot of forecast data, set tight budget goals, monitor outputs carefully and emphasize frequent reporting with uniform control systems. Like company B, the prototypical Prospector faces strategic uncertainties owing to rapidly changing product or market conditions; interactive management control systems such as planning and budgeting are used to set agendas to debate strategy and action plans in these rapidly changing conditions. Defenders, by contrast, use planning and budgeting less intensively. Like company A, which operates in a relatively stable environment, many aspects of the business that are important in terms of current competitive advantage are highly controllable and managers need only focus on strategic uncertainties — often related to product or technological changes that could undermine current low cost positions.

Further research must also be sensitive to the unit of analysis. This study has focused on business strategy. But what are the process relationships between management control systems and corporate strategy? Recently, the portfolio management approach that has been the cornerstone of corporate strategy has been strongly criticized (Porter, 1987). The ability of diversified firms to add value through portfolio techniques is argued to be increasingly limited in today's efficient capital markets. In terms of the process model presented here, a strategic uncertainty for the diversified firm is the appropriate allocation of resources among diverse business units. Given the scarce attention of top mangement, focusing attention on portfolio allocations may limit the attention that can be accorded to business-related aspects of management control to the detriment of organizational learning and effective strategy making.

This research offers a new perspective for understanding how and why firms make the design choices that we observe in practice. But tnere are many other questions to be answered. How do managers identify strategic uncertainties? What types of interactive management controls are used by managers in different organizations? Do patterns exist among firms following similar strategies? Are strategic uncertainties unique to each firm or do patterns exist across firms? Research to answer these questions is ongoing and some further results are reported in Simons (1987c).

Management theoriests must strive to understand better the dynamic relationship between strategy and management control processes. This means not only recognizing that strategy formation and implementation are intertwined, but also opening up the meaning of management control to a broader notion that builds upon guidance rather than coercion, and on learning as well as constraint. We need, in fact, a better language to describe management control processes. Control systems are used for multiple purposes: monitoring, learning, signalling, constraint, surveillance, motivation and others. Yet, we use a single descriptor — mangement control systems — to describe these distinctly different processes. Eskimos use precise words to describe different types of snow and sailors have specialized words for ropes that perform different functions. Management control theorists also need a precise vocabulary to develop and communicate the concepts necessary to describe complex organizational phenomena.

BIBLIOGRAPHY

Andrews, K. R., *The Concept of Corporate Strategy* (Homewood, IL: Irwin, 1980).

Anthony, R. N., *Planning and Control Systems: a Framework for Analysis* (Boston, MA: Graduate School of Business Administration, Harvard University, 1965).

Anthony, R. M., *The Mangement Control Function* (Boston: Harvard Business School Press, 1988).

Argyris, C. & Schön, D. A., *Organizational Learning* (Reading, MA: Addison-Wesley, 1978).

Barnard, C. I., *The Functions of the Executive* (Cambridge, MA: Harvard University Press, 1968; originally published 1938).

Bower, J. L. *Managing the Resource Allocation Process: a Study of Corporate Planning and Investment*, 2nd Edn (Boston, MA: Harvard Business School Press, 1986).

Burgelman, R. A., Corporate Entrepreneurship and Strategic Management: Insights from a Process Study, *Management Science* (1983) pp. 1349–1364.

Campbell, J., *Grammatical Man: Information, Entropy, Language, and Life* (New York: Simon & Schuster, 1982).

Cohen, M. D., March, J. D. & Olsen, J. P., A Garbage Can Model of Organizational Choice, *Administrative Science Quarterly* (1972) pp. 1–25.

Daniel, R., Reorganizing for Results. *Harvard Business Review* (November–December, 1966) pp. 96–104.

Donaldson, G., *Managing Corporate Wealth* (New York: Praeger, 1984).

Ewusi-Mensah, K., The External Organization Environment and Its Impact of Management Information Systems, *Accounting, Organizations and Society* (1981) pp. 301–316.

Feldman, M. S. & March, J. G., Information in Organizations as Signal and Symbol, *Administrative Science Quarterly* (1981) pp. 171–186.

Fiol, C. M. & Lyles, M. A., Organizational Learning, *Academy of Management Review* (1985) pp. 803–813.

Galbriath, C. & Schendel, D., An Emprical Analysis of Strategy Types, *Strategic Management Journal* (1983) pp. 153–173.

Gordon, L. A. & Narayanan, V. K., Management Accounting Systems, Perceived Environmental Uncertainty and Organization Structure: an Empirical Investigation, *Accounting, Organizations and Society* (1984) pp. 33–47.

Govindarajan, V. & Gupta, A. K., Linking Control Systems to Business Unit Strategy: Impact on Performance, *Accounting, Organizations and Society* (1985) pp. 51–66.

Hamermesh, R. G., *Making Strategy Work: How Senior Managers Produce Results* (New York: John Wiley, 1986).

Hedberg, B., How Organizations Learn and Unlearn, in Starbuck, W. H. and Nystrom, P. C. (eds) *Handbook of Organizational Design* pp. 3–27 (New York: Oxford University Press, 1981).

Hedberg, B. and Jönsson, S., Designing Semi-Confusing Information Systems for Organizations in Changing Environments, *Accounting, Organizations and Society* (1978) pp. 47–64.

Herbert, T. T. & Dereksy, H., Generic Strategies: an Empirical Investigation of Typology Validity and Strategy Content, *Strategic Management Journal* (1987) pp. 135–147.

Khandwalla, P. N., The Effect of Different Types of Competition on the Use of Management Controls, *Journal of Accounting Research* (Autumn 1972) pp. 275–285.

Kandwalla, P. N., Effect of Competition on the Structure of Top Management Control, *Academy of Management Journal* (1973) pp. 285–295.

Leifer, E. M. & White, H. C., Wheeling and Annealing: Federal and Multidivisional Control, in Short, J. F. (ed.) *The Social Fabric* (New York: Sage, 1986).

Lorange, P., Scott Morton, M. F. & Ghoshal, S., *Strategic Control Systems* (St Paul, MN: West, 1986).

Meyer, M. W., Organizational Structure as Signalling, *Pacific Sociological Review* (1979) pp. 481–500.

Miles, R. E. & Snow, C. C., *Organizational Strategy, Structure, and Process* (New York: McGraw–Hill, 1978).

Miller, D. & Friesen, P. H., Archetypes of Strategy Formulation, *Management Science* (1978) pp. 921–933.

Miller, D. & Friesen, P. H., Innovation in Conservative and Entrepreneurial Firms, *Strategic Management Journal* (1982) pp. 1–27.

Mintzberg, H., Strategy Making in Three Modes, *California Management Review* (Winter 1973a) pp. 44–53.

Mintzberg, H., *The Nature of Magerial Work* (New York: Harper & Row, 1973b).

Mintzberg, H., Patterns in Strategy Formation, *Management Science* (May 1978) pp. 934–948.

Mintzberg, H., Raisinghani, D. & Théorêt, A., The Structure of "Unstructured" Decision Process, *Administrative Science Quarterly* (June 1976) pp. 246–275.

Mintzberg, H. & Waters, J. A., Of Strategies, Deliberate and Emergent, *Strategic Management Journal* (1985) 257–272.

Pinfield, L. T., A Field Evaluation of Perspectives on Organizational Decision Making, *Administrative Science Quarterly* (September 1986) pp. 365–388.

Porter, M. E., *Competitive Strategy* (New York: The Free Press, 1980).

Porter, M. E., *Competitive Advantage* (New York: The Free Press, 1985).

Porter, M. E., From Competitive Advantage to Corporate Strategy, *Harvard Business Review* (May–June, 1987) pp. 43–59.

Schendel, D. E. & Hofer, C. W. (eds), *Strategic Management* (Boston, MA: Little, Brown, 1979).

Shrivastava, P., Rigor and Practical Usefulness of Research in Strategic Management, *Strategic Management Journal* (January–February 1987) pp. 77–92.

Simon, H., *Models of Man* (New York: John Wiley, 1957).

Simons, R., Accounting Control Systems and Business Strategy: an Empirical Analysis, *Accounting, Organizations and Society* (1987a) pp. 357–374.

Simons, R., Planning, Control, and Uncertainty: a Process View, in Bruns, W. J. Jr and Kaplan, R. S. (eds), *Accounting and Management: Field Study Perspectives*, (Boston, MA: Harvard Business School Press, 1987b) pp. 339–362.

Simons, R., Implementing Strategy: Configurations in Management Control Systems. Paper presented at the 1987 annual meeting of the Strategic Management Society held in Boston, 14–17 October (1987c).

Spence, M., *Market Signalling* (Cambridge, MA: Harvard University Press, 1974).

Utterback, J. M. & Abernathy, W. J., A Dynamic Model of Product and Process Innovation, *Omega* (1975) pp. 639–656.

Williamson, O. E., Economics and Sociology: Promoting a Dialogue, Yale School of Organization and Management, Working Paper Series D no. 25, August 1986.

Wissema, J. G., Van der Pol, H. W. & Messer, H. M. Strategic Management Archetypes, *Strategic Management Journal* (1980) pp. 37–47.

Accounting, Organizations and Society, Vol. 15, Nos. 1/2, pp. 145–148, 1990.
Printed in Great Britain

0361–3682/90 $3.00+.00
Pergamon Press plc

THE ENACTMENT OF MANAGEMENT CONTROL SYSTEMS: A CRITIQUE OF SIMONS

BARBARA GRAY
Department of Management and Organization, Pennsylvania State University

Abstract

Simon proposes a contingency relationship between a firm's strategy and its management control systems. However, his model underspecifies the relationship between strategic uncertainties and management controls, underplays the recursive impact of management controls on strategy formulation, and ignores the potential influence of managerial characteristics on control system design.

The major focus of Simons' paper is on the link between strategy and management control systems. More specifically, Simons asks, "What is the relationship, if any, between the way a firm competes and the way that it organizes and uses its management control systems?" The paper posits a process model of strategy and control in which top management regulates strategic uncertainties through its choice of strategy and the institutionalization of a management control system. In his Fig. 1, Simons depicts the relationship among four key variables (business strategy, strategic uncertainties, management controls and organizational learning) as a cyclic one.

The paper makes two important contributions to the literature on strategic planning. First, it provides a rich description of management control systems in two firms within the same industry. Second, in addition to representing the effect of strategy on the design of management controls, it acknowledges the recursive effects of strategic controls on subsequent strategy formulation. I believe, however, that Simons' model does not go far enough. That is, it underspecifies the relationships between strategy, strategic uncertainties and management controls and underplays the impact of management controls on strategy formulation. Furthermore, the analysis gives short-shrift to the learning step which completes the loop between management control systems and strategy and to the mechanisms by which strategic change is induced when the strategy fails.

MANAGING STRATEGIC UNCERTAINTIES

It is difficult to discern from the paper whether strategic uncertainties for Simons refer to objective threats and opportunities the firm encounters or to an environment which management perceives or to an enacted environment which management creates. Management theorists differ in their depictions of the environment as determined (Hannan & Freeman, 1978; Aldrich, 1979), perceived through the eyes of less-than-perfect observers (Duncan, 1972; Downey *et al.*, 1981; Lorenzi *et al.*, 1981) or created through acts of interpretation and action (Weick, 1979; Smircich & Stubbart, 1985).

> What people refer to as their environment is generated by human actions and accompanying intellectual efforts to make sense out of these actions. The character of this produced environment depends on the particular theories and frameworks, patterns of attention, and affective dispositions supplied by the actor-observers (Smircich & Stubbart, 1985, p. 726).

Regardless of which school one adopts, however, they all seem to agree that there are boundaries which limit managerial discretion. These limitations are not explictly considered in Simons' model. Instead, it appears from his application of the model to the two cases that managers are always able to temper or forestall the effects of uncertainty through design of an appropriate control system. For example, Hrebeniak & Joyce (1985) distinguish contexts in which firms can adapt by design from those in which they adapt by chance or adapt within constraints or may not be able to adapt at all. It seems reasonable to assume that management control systems would be designed differently to correspond to each of these contexts.

A brief discussion of the limited attention of managers suggests that Simons is more comfortable with conceiving of managers as interpreters. Theorists consistent with this perspective also differentiate strategic contingencies according to the degree of threat or opportunity they invoke (Dutton & Duncan, 1987; Dutton & Jackson, 1987) or by the adjudged ability of the firm to respond (Wartick & Christy, 1986). Thus, the nature of strategic contingencies themselves as interpreted and acted upon by top management could be expected to require different management controls. Consideration of how differences in interpretation of strategic contingencies shape management control systems would enrich Simons' model.

THE INFLUENCE OF MANAGEMENT CONTROLS ON SUBSEQUENT STRATEGY-MAKING

Learning, for Simons, is described as a process by which management signals to subordinates about its strategic intentions. I cannot help but wonder, then, if learning is only for the lower levels of the organization? What about the mechanisms by which top management also learns? The model seems to perpetuate an image of top management as an omnicient and omnipotent navigator of the seas of uncertainty. What happens, for example, if an unanticipated strategic uncertainty strikes, such as a hostile takeover attempt or a major accident such as Three Mile Island or Bhopal?

An alternative model imagines managers as co-participants in the enactment of their strategic environments (Pfeffer & Salancik, 1978; Weick, 1979; Smircich & Stubbart, 1985). Not only do they interpret strategic contingencies, but they construct the environment with which they will have to navigate in the future (Giddens, 1979; Gray *et al.*, 1985). They create the context within which the next round of strategic decisions will be made.

> . . . organized people often struggle within the confines of their own prior enactments. Patterns of enactment rooted in prior personal, organizational and cultural experiences powerfully shape ongoing organizational and cultural options. Starbuck (1983) calls these patterns "behavior programs" and emphasizes how past thinking gets concretized into standard operating procedures, job specifications, buildings, contracts, and so on that take on the aura of objective necessity (Smircich & Stubbart, 1985, p. 732).

Applying this to Simons' model, enactment occurs precisely through the choice of which management controls to make interactive. That structures subsequent organizational learning and delimits what top management will and will not attend to. Thus, the choice of control systems imposes a "mindset" or a set of blinders on the organization which reinforces existing interpretations and discourages novel interpretations. Research on cognition confirms that people pay attention to behaviors and events that are consistent with their existing frameworks for sense-making and tend to discredit conflicting evidence (Kiesler & Sproull, 1982; Gray & Allen, 1987). This leads to persistence in a course of action, often beyond its usefulness (Staw, 1976).

That brings us back then to questions concerning how top management learns and how a change in strategy is introduced. Burgelman (1983) argues that a major consequence of the structural context is a reduction in the variation in proposals for strategic change which emerge. He contends that a second track of autonomous strategic behavior is needed in order to introduce new initiatives. These initiatives arise from the lower and middle levels of the organization, but require the use of political tactics in order to induce any modifications in the existing strategy. Political pressure is needed to overcome the inertia created by existing control systems which, according to Burgelman, "impound the learning of the firm over time" (p. 68). Miller & Friesen (1982) seem to be making a similar argument with their findings that management controls utilized in prospector firms discourage, rather than encourage innovation.

Simons seems oblivious to the need for political maneuvering to induce strategic change. While he acknowledges a role for debate over planning and budgets, the acceptance of strategic initiatives by middle and lower levels is taken for granted. It seems curious that the interviewees in companies A and B did not report any resistance to strategic directives created by inertial forces and vested interests in the status quo (Miller & Friesen, 1980; Quinn, 1980; Gray & Ariss, 1985). Simons does, however, acknowledge top management's resistance to entertaining proposals which deviate from its current strategic course. Clearly the political function served by management controls deserves exploration in subsequent work.

MANAGERIAL CHARACTERISTICS

One final set of factors which influence strategic decisions may help explain why different firms institute different systems of control. Recent work by Hambrick & Finkelstein (1987) and Miller & Droge (1986) speculate that top management characteristics (e.g. aspiration level, tolerance for ambiguity, need for achievement, political acumen, etc.) influence strategic choices and the exercise of discretion and control in the organization. If the additional 14 cases in Simons' research do not correspond to the Prospector/Defender prototypes illustrated by companies A and B, some explanation for the deviations may be found in top management attributes such as these.

BIBLIOGRAPHY

Aldrich, H. E., *Organizations and Environments* (Englewood Cliffs, NJ: Prentice-Hall, 1979).

Burgelman, R., A Model of the Interaction of Strategic Behavior, Corporate Context, and the Concept of Strategy, *Academy of Management Review* (1983) pp. 61–70.

Downey, H. K., Hellriegel, D. & Slocum, J. W., Jr, Environment Uncertainty: The Construct and its Application, *Administrative Science Quarterly* (1975) pp. 613–629.

Duncan, R. B., Characteristics of Organizational Environment and Perceived Environmental Uncertainty, *Administrative Science Quarterly* (1972) pp. 313–327.

Dutton, J. E. & Duncan, R. B., The Creation of Momentum for Change Through the Process of Strategic Issue Diagnosis, *Strategic Management Journal* (1987) pp. 279–295.

Dutton, J. E. & Jackson, S. E., The Categorization of Strategic Issues by Decision Makers and its Link to Organizational Action, *Academy of Management Review* (1987) pp. 76–90.

Giddens, A., *Central Problems in Social Theory* (Berkeley, CA: University of California Press, 1983).

Gray, B. & Allen, R. G., Cognitive and Group Biases in Issues Management: What You Don't Know Can Hurt You, in Marcus, A. A., Kaufman, A. M. and Beam, D. R. (eds) *Business Strategy and Public Policy* pp. 195–208 (Westport, CT; Greenwood Press, 1987).

Gray, B. & Ariss, S. S., Political and Strategic Change Across Organizational Life Cycles, *Academy of Management Review* (1985) pp. 707–723.

Gray, B., Donnellon, A. & Bougon, M. G., Organizations as Constructions and Destructions of Meaning, *Journal of Management* (1985) pp. 83–98.

Hambrick, D. C. & Finkelstein, S., Managerial Discretion: A Bridge Between Polar Views of Organizational Outcomes, in Staw, B. M. and Cummings, L. L. (eds) *Research in Organizational Behavior* (Greenwich, CT: JAI Press, 1987).

Hannan, M. T. & Freeman, J., The Population Ecology of Organizations, *American Journal of Sociology* (1977) pp. 929–964.

Kiesler, S. & Sproull, L., Managerial Response to Changing Environment: Perspectives on Problem Sensing from Social Cognition, *Administrative Science Quarterly* (1982) pp. 548–570.

Lorenzi, P., Sims, H. P. & Slocum, J. W., Jr, Perceived Environmental Uncertainty: An Individual or Environmental Attribute, *Journal of Management* (1981) pp. 27–41.

Miller, D. & Droge, C., Psychological and Traditional Determinants of Structure, *Administrative Science Quarterly* (1986) pp. 539–560.

Miller, D. & Friesen, P. H., Momentum and Revolution in Organizational Adaptation, *Academy of Management Journal* (1980) pp. 591–614.

Miller, D. & Friesen, P. H. Innovation in Conservative and Entrepreneurial Firms, *Strategic Management Journal* (1982) pp. 1–27.

Pfeffer, J. & Salancik, G. R. *The External Control of Organizations: A Resource Dependence Perspective* (New York: Harper and Row, 1978).

Quinn, J. B., *Strategy for Change: Logical Incrementalism* (Homewood, IL: Irwin, 1980).

Smircich, L. & Stubbart, C., Strategic Management in an Enacted World, *Academy of Management Review* (1985) pp. 724–736.

Starbuck, W. H., Organizations as Action Generators, *American Sociological Review* (1983) pp. 91–102.

Staw, B., Knee-deep in the Big Muddy: A Study of Escalating Commitment to a Chosen Course of Action, *Organizational Behavior and Human Performance* (1976) pp. 27–44.

Wartick, S. L. & Christy, D. P., Issues Management: An Empirical Study of the Link Between Issues Identification and Issues Analysis, paper presented at the Academy of Management Meeting, Chicago (August 1986).

Weick, K. E., *The Social Psychology of Organizing* (Reading, MA: Addison-Wesley, 1979).

Part IV
The Social Structure of Control in Organizations

[14]

BUDGETING AND EMPLOYEE BEHAVIOR*

SELWYN BECKER† AND DAVID GREEN, JR‡

WRITING in *Number, the Language of Science*, Tobias Dantzig observed: "The concrete has ever preceded the abstract. . . . And the concrete has ever been the greatest stumbling block to the development of a science. The peculiar fascination which *numbers as individuals* have exerted on the mind of man from time immemorial was the main obstacle in the way of developing a *collective* theory of numbers, i.e., an arithmetic; just as the concrete interest in individual stars long delayed the creating of a scientific astronomy.[1]

And so it has been with budgeting, where for some there is still question on whether or not a theory has developed. Business budgeting is a twentieth-century innovation; its development has been characterized by a fragmentary literature and an emphasis on technique. A review of its history indicates that progress has largely been through learning from mistakes—a "cut-and-try" approach. In this paper we will review this history as a background toward an understanding of the relation of the budget to the motivations of those who effect and are affected by it. In a sense this will be an excursion—an attempt to determine "what the behavioral scientists can tell us or find out for us about . . . the impact [of budgets] on people and on their aspirations."[2] In the process, we will point out that the attempt to make use of motivational factors in the budgeting construct raises many difficult and imperfectly understood problems. Further, we will attempt to explain why the style of managerial leadership is of critical importance in the choice of budget procedures—an issue largely overlooked. Also, we will consider the role played by the communication of performance results and the timing of budget revisions.

In the United States, budgeting by state and local government started with the municipal reform movements around the turn of the century. At the outset, the budget was viewed as an instrument of control—"control over the officers . . . of administration by placing limitations on their authority to spend."[3] These early budgets were, and for the most part still are, authorizations to spend—appropriations—for particular "objects of expenditure" such as personal services, commodities, travel, and the like. The appropriation was the "upper limit" much like a thermal control on a furnace—when the limit is reached the fuel, or, in the fiscal sense, the money is stopped. The upper limit was imposed through the approving of the budget by the gov-

* The authors are indebted to the members of the Workshop in Accounting Research, Institute of Professional Accounting, Graduate School of Business, University of Chicago for helpful comments—especially Charles T. Horngren and George H. Sorter.

† Assistant professor of psychology, Graduate School of Business, University of Chicago.

‡ Associate professor of accounting, Graduate School of Business, University of Chicago.

[1] 4th ed.; New York: Macmillan Co., 1956, chap. iii.

[2] David Solomons, "Standard Costing Needs Better Variances," National Association of Accountants Bulletin, XLIII, No. 4 (December, 1961), 30.

[3] Frederick A. Cleveland, *Chapters on Municipal Administration and Accounting* (New York: Longmans, Green & Co., 1909), p. 72.

erning body—the board, the council, the legislature, etc.

These governmental budgeting procedures provided for a second type of control—a restraint control. Each claim presented had to be approved for payment by the chief financial officer. The question of "what is a legal or bona fide obligation?" was resolved by considering (1) whether the budget document provided for such an expenditure, (2) whether sufficient funds were left in the appropriation to pay the claim, and (3) whether the necessary documents were on hand. To know if the remaining appropriation was sufficient, fairly elaborate records were maintained. To these were posted the dollar amounts of issued purchase orders as well as the specific expenditures. Both types of transactions reduced the "available" balance. This was a practice of *clerical* control—a technique employed to insure the completeness of record and one that is still unique to governmental accounting (with the possible exception of retail "open-to-buy" records). To the extent that interim reports were prepared and distributed to department heads, rudimentary *communicative* control was practiced.

Governmental purposes were served well enough by these budget procedures. Revenue and expense forecasts were relatively simple. Because changes were not contemplated, the budgets were for fixed amounts for the designated time period. Where actual revenues fell short of the estimates, unilateral demands to cut expenditures by a designated percentage were issued—sometimes by resort to payless paydays.

Early business budgeting largely imitated governmental practice and technique. It began with "imposed" budgets[4] and the obvious controls—limit, restraint, clerical and communicative. During the early and middle 1930's, it became fashionable to speak of "budgetary control" and to view the budget as both (1) a financial plan and (2) "a control over future operations."[5] Also in the Thirties, the inadequacies of the static budget became obvious when business activity took a sharp downturn and profits disappeared.[6]

A budget form that provided for intra-period changes in the level of sales or manufacturing was introduced and was called a flexible or variable budget. It attempted to provide "bench mark" numbers for a range of contemplated activity.

Primarily, budgetary control has been the attempt to keep performance at or within the acceptable limits of the predetermined flexible plan. In a sense the plan controls—but for how long? And how is the plan to be modified?

BUDGET PERIODICITY

The recurring cycle of early governmental and business budgets was simple. The budgets were imposed, there was performance, and the comparison of the performance against the budget influenced the next budget. The cycle could be depicted as follows:

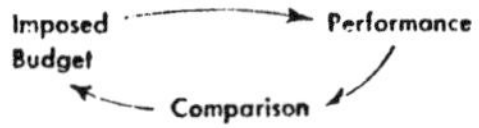

[4] Imposed budgets have been characterized as ones "dictated by top management without the full participation of the operating personnel" (R. N. Anthony, "Distinguishing Good from Not-So-Good Accounting Research," in *Proceedings of the 22nd Annual Institute on Accounting* [Columbus: Ohio State University, 1960], p. 68).

[5] Eric Kohler, *A Dictionary for Accountants* (Englewood Cliffs, N.J.: Prentice-Hall, Inc., 1957), p. 75.

[6] F. V. Gardner, "How About That 1935 Operating Budget?" *Factory Management and Maintenance*, November, 1934; C. E. Knoeppel and E. G. Seybold, *Managing for Profit* (New York: McGraw-Hill Book Co., 1937), p. 206.

Ordinarily, the budget period was one year or two. The comparison of performance and budget often had curious results on the subsequent budget. Where expenditure was less than budget, there was a tendency to revise the subsequent budget downward. As a result, managers would engage in a spending spree the last few weeks of an appropriation year to avoid being cut down next year.

The budget period in business has also been calendar oriented—the quarter or twelve-week period extended twelve or fifteen months. Ordinarily, budget revisions are restricted to future periods. Later in the paper we will discuss reasons for cycling budget revisions on a basis other than the calendar.

BUDGET MODIFICATION

By 1930 it was recognized in business circles that imposed budgets "resulted in some dissatisfaction and advice was given to prepare them in the departments and have them revised or edited in the central offices."[7] Thus *participation* was introduced into the budgeting construct. It has been said that the "real values of participation at all management levels . . . , aside from better planning are the psychological values that accrue as the result of participation. A high degree of participation is conducive to better morale and greater initiative"[8]

There is some evidence of the extent (and degree) to which participation is currently employed in business. Sord and Welsch interrogated managements of thirty-five companies to determine the level at which principal budget objectives were developed. No companies said they used totally imposed budgets. Six firms (17 per cent) prepared objectives at higher levels and allowed subordinate managers to consider and comment on them before final adoption. Twenty-nine firms (83 per cent) said they requested subordinate managers to prepare their own goals and objectives for review and approval at higher levels.[9]

Theirs obviously was a very small sample. Furthermore, it is questionable that the interrogatories used did, in fact, investigate participation. As Chris Argyris discovered, there is such a thing as "pseudo-participation." "That is, participation which looks like, but is not, real participation."[10]

Participation may have great value in improving budgets by drawing together the knowledge diffused among the participants, although we do not treat this objective here. Our interest is in participation as a useful technique for dealing with the psychological problems of employee satisfaction, morale, and motivation to produce; that is, the belief that increased participation can lead to better morale and increased initiative. The evidence supporting this belief will be evaluated, as well as other psychological effects associated with participation that may be of even greater importance. But first the question: What is participation? We will use the following definition: Participation is "defined as a process of joint decision-making by two or more parties in which the decisions have future effects on those making them."[11]

A collateral question: how does the

[7] *Budgetary Control in Manufacturing Industries* (New York: National Industrial Conference Board, 1931), p. 52.

[8] B. H. Sord and G. A. Welsch, *Business Budgeting* (New York: Controllership Foundation, Inc., 1958), p. 97.

[9] *Ibid.*, p. 95.

[10] *The Impact of Budgets on People* (New York: Controllership Foundation, Inc., 1952), p. 28.

[11] J. R. P. French, Jr., J. Israel, and D. As, "An Experiment on Participation in a Norwegian Factory," *Human Relations*, XIII (1960), 3.

introduction of participation affect the budget cycle? At first glance, it seems that the chart would appear as follows:

However, we believe this is too simple. Participation adds a separate "psychological path." Participation is ***not*** a single-value variable but rather is a concept encompassing several explicit variables. (Instead of a simple cycle we have a sequence that might be depicted as follows:

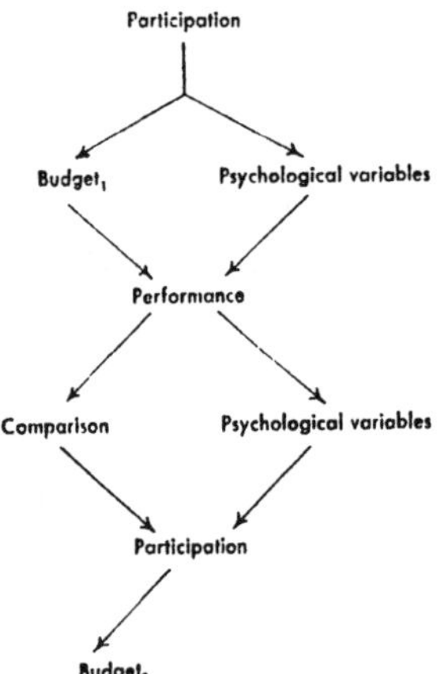

In paragraphs that follow we will attempt to identify these unspecified psychological variables by examining what we consider to be the relevant available research results. Before proceeding it is imperative to make one fundamental point: ***Participation is not a panacea.***[12] Indeed, there is evidence to suggest that it is inappropriate in certain "environments." When participation is employed, the concept of control, as outlined above requires modification. Instead of the budget being the plan to which performance is conformed, compared, and evaluated irrespective of changes in environment (other than those provided for in the flexible budget), the plan is influenced, at least in part, by the environment. That is, control limits and informs those operating under the budget; in turn, they determine and limit the succeeding budget.

PARTICIPATION, MORALE, AND PRODUCTIVITY

In an industrial setting Coch and French investigated the effects of prior participation on production after work changes were introduced.[13] Difficulty of work and percentage of work changes were equated for a no-participation group (NP); for participation by representation (PR); and for a total participation (TP) group. With a prechange standard of sixty units per hour, after relearning, the NP group reached a level of fifty units per hour; the PR group sixty units per hour; and the TP group sixty-eight units per hour, or an improvement of about 14 per cent over the standard rate. Another important finding was that 17 per cent of the NP group quit their jobs in the first forty days after the change, and the remaining members of the group filed grievances about the piece rate, which "subsequently was found to be a little 'loose.'" There was one act of aggression against the supervisor from the PR group, none from the TP group, and no quits in either the PR or TP groups.

If employee turnover and stated griev-

[12] A useful discussion—"Participation in Perspective"—appears as chap. ix in *The Human Side of Enterprise* by Douglass McGregor (New York: McGraw-Hill Book Co., Inc., 1960).

[13] L. Coch and J. R. P. French, Jr., "Overcoming Resistance to Change," *Human Relations*, I (1948), 512–32.

ances can be taken as a measure of morale, then it seems clear that the two groups that participated in the initiation of change were better disposed toward their job situations than was the no participation group.

Based only on this study one cannot decide if participation directly increased incentive to produce, as measured by subsequent productivity, or only improved morale, which in turn led to increased motivation. This is a point worth considering since morale is not perfectly correlated with productivity.

An inference about this relationship can be drawn after examination of a study by Schachter *et al.* on group cohesiveness and productivity.[14] (Group cohesiveness is usually defined as attraction to the group—desire to become or remain a member—and reluctance to leave the group. Another way of looking at cohesiveness might be the amount of "we" feeling generated in an individual as a result of his association with others.) Schachter and his associates experimentally created high and low cohesiveness in two groups. A task was chosen in which output could be easily measured. In half of each group subjects were individually given instructions designed to induce production at a high rate; the other half instructions designed to induce production at a low rate. It was found that group cohesion and acceptance of induction were significantly related. The high-cohesive groups more frequently accepted induction than did the low-cohesive groups. This was especially true of the negative induction, or "slow-down" situation.

The Coch and French study suggests that morale and/or productivity are enhanced as a result of employee participation in the initiation of change. The Schachter *et al.* study suggests that with participation held constant (all groups worked under constant conditions) change in productivity is related to group cohesiveness. Cohesiveness, it can be seen from the definition, is related to morale. Morale is most frequently defined as satisfaction with one's job, supervisors, and working associates. It has also been defined as the *degree* to which an employee identified himself as part of the organization. In either case morale and cohesiveness with a group imply some similar reactions and attitudes toward an organization or group.

Since participation affects morale (cohesiveness) and productivity, but cohesiveness without participation affects production, the most likely conclusion is that cohesiveness is dependent on participation but that changes in productivity are more directly related to cohesiveness.

ELEMENTS OF PARTICIPATION: PROCESS AND CONTENT

Let us consider participation as conceptually divisible into process and content. Process means the *act* of participating with the possible consequences stemming from the act, content is the *discussion topic* toward which are generated the positive or negative attitudes. The *act* of participating enables the participants to know one another, communicate and interact with one another—conditions that easily can lead to increased cohesiveness. As we have seen, however, increased cohesiveness also can result in lower production if that is the sentiment of the cohesive group. Thus it becomes clear that the content of participation is an important determinant of final pro-

[14] S. Schachter, N. Ellertson, D. McBride, and D. Gregory, "An Experimental Study of Cohesiveness and Productivity," *Human Relations*, IV (1951), 229-38.

duction levels. What should the content consist of and what should it accomplish? These questions can be answered on the basis of some data on group decision-making collected by Kurt Lewin and his students.[15] One experiment was designed to induce housewives to use previously unused foods (sweetbreads, etc.). Positive communications describing the foods were presented to two groups; one by the lecture method, the other by a group-discussion method. A subsequent check revealed that 3 per cent of the women who heard the lectures served one of the meats never served before, whereas after group discussion, 32 per cent served one of the meats. This experiment was repeated with a different leader, different groups, and a different food—milk—and yielded essentially similar results.

As compared to individual instruction and the lecture method, group discussion was superior in inducing change—a result attributed to the hesitancy of individuals to accept goals that depart from the group standard. (Psychological non-acceptance of a goal by an individual virtually precludes its attainment by him.) The group-discussion method allows the group member to assess the standards of all other members so that, if the group apparently accepts a change, he too can accept it and retain his group membership.

It is clear that the content of participation should be directed toward setting a new goal with discussion of a sort sufficient to enable each participant to realize that the goal is accepted by the others in the group. The fulfilment of these conditions could serve as a definition of successful participation by (1) providing the opportunity for enough interaction so that a cohesive group can emerge and (2) directing the interaction so that each participant's analysis of the content will enable him to accept as his own those goals adopted by the group. Thus, we can see that the process and content of a participation program interact, and that such interaction can lead to one of several outcomes:

a) High cohesiveness with positive attitudes (goal acceptance), a condition of maximally efficient motivation;
b) Low cohesiveness with positive attitudes, an unlikely but possible condition that probably would result in efficient performance;
c) Low cohesiveness and negative attitudes, a condition resulting from unsuccessful participation that would tend to depress production within the limits of the integrity or conscience of each individual; and
d) High cohesiveness and negative attitudes, the occurrence most conducive to a production slow-down.

Level of aspiration and performance.—Ideally, in the budgeting process, participation results in a plan of action including a proposed amount of accomplishment and an estimate of the costs to achieve it. If participation has been successful, then these proposed levels of cost and accomplishment are accepted as goals by the participants. In effect, these projected levels of achievement become the levels of aspiration of the managers of the organization. (In a smoothly running organization the managers induce acceptance of the same levels of aspiration in the members of their departments.)

Level of aspiration has been defined in the psychological literature as a goal that, when just barely achieved, has associated with it subjective feelings of success; when not achieved, subjective

[15] "Studies in Group Decision" in D. Cartwright and E. Zander (eds.), *Group Dynamics* (Evanston, Ill.: Row Peterson & Co., 1956), pp. 287–88.

feelings of failure.[16] From an extensive review of the literature Child and Whiting summarize many findings into five conclusions:

1. Success generally leads to a raising of the level of aspiration, failure to a lowering.
2. The stronger the success the greater is the probability of a rise in level of aspiration; the stronger the failure the greater is the probability of a lowering.
3. Shifts in level of aspiration are in part a function of changes in the subject's confidence in his ability to attain goals.
4. Failure is more likely than success to lead to withdrawal in the form of avoiding setting a level of aspiration.
5. Effects of failure on level of aspiration are more varied than those of success.[17]

Recently Stedry has utilized this psychological variable in an attempt to establish some relations between level of aspiration, imposed budgets, and subsequent performance.[18] Stedry, not a psychologist, may have overlooked some of the relevant psychological literature. Seemingly he selected an inaccurate method of measuring aspiration level which weakens his several conclusions and recommendations. For his measure of level of aspiration, Stedry asked his subjects to express what they "hoped to achieve" on the next set of problems. Festinger found that the *D* score (the difference between performance and aspiration) was greater between performance and expressions of "like to get" than between performance and expressions of "expect to get."[19] Diggory found the correlation between "hope" statements before and after failure significantly higher than statements of expectations before and after failure.[20] In other words, "hope" and "expect" represent different attitudes. Since level of aspiration is defined as the goal one explicitly undertakes to reach rather than the goal one hopes to achieve, it seems clear that Stedry's conclusions are based on an inaccurate measure of his major variable. Subsequently, Stedry has indicated his belief, based on questionnaire information, that his "subjects appeared . . . to have given the right answer to the wrong question." [21] In any event, his attempt is valuable heuristically because it highlights a possible relation between budgets, budgeting, and human motivational performance.

We have already hypothesized a relationship between participation and the formation of levels of aspiration. There remains a specification of the effects of level of aspiration on the remaining segments of the budget cycle.

After the budget has been adopted, the attempt to translate it into behavior constitutes the performance part of the cycle. The degree of effort expended by members of the firm as they attempt to achieve budgeted goals is partially dependent upon their levels of aspiration. Maximum effort will be exerted to just reach an aspired-to goal. In fact, according to level of aspiration theory if, for example, five units of effort are required

[16] K. Levin, T. Dembo, L. Festinger, and Pauline Sears, "Level of Aspiration," in J. McV. Hunt (ed.), *Personality and the Behavior Disorders*, I (New York: Ronald Press Co., 1944), 333–78.

[17] J. L. Child, and J. W. M. Whiting, "Determinants of Level of Aspiration: Evidence from Everyday Life," in H. Brand (ed.), *The Study of Personality* (New York: John Wiley & Sons, 1954), pp. 145–58.

[18] Andrew C. Stedry, *Budget Control and Cost Behavior* (Englewood Cliffs, N.J.: Prentice-Hall, Inc., 1960).

[19] L. Festinger, "A Theoretical Interpretation of Shifts in Level of Aspiration," *Psychological Review*, XLIX (1942), 235–50.

[20] J. C. Diggory, "Responses to Experimentally Induced Failure," *American Journal of Psychology*, LXII (1949), 48–61.

[21] Stedry, "Aspiration Levels, Attitudes, and Performance in a Goal-oriented Situation," *Industrial Management Review*, III, No. 2 (Spring, 1962), 62.

to reach goal $x - 3$, ten units to reach goal $x - 2$, fifteen units to reach goal $x - 1$, and twenty-five units to reach goal x, the level of aspiration goal, an individual will expend the disproportionate amount of energy to achieve at level x to derive that subjective feeling of success. Thus we can see how a budget that is partially derived through a successful program of participation can result in greater expenditure of effort on the part of employees to reach goals specified in the budget.

Such expectations are not without foundation, of course. Bayton measured the levels of aspiration of three hundred subjects of roughly equivalent ability prior to their performance on seven arithmetic problems. He found that subjects with higher levels of aspiration followed with higher performance.[22] From a finding of this sort one cannot conclude that greater motivation to achieve is associated with the level of aspiration goal, but it is well known that increased motivation leads to increased effort, a condition usually followed by an increase in performance. We can thus find indirect support for our contention. Another bit of evidence may illustrate the point further. Siegel and Fouraker set subjects to bargaining under bilateral monoply conditions.[23] With no control of levels of aspirations, the subjects maximized their joint profits and split the profits nearly equally. However, when high and low levels of aspiration were induced into the bargaining pairs (despite the fact that a better bargain meant more money for the subject), those with a low level of aspiration gained only about one-third of the joint profits. Thus, it seems clear that level of aspiration not only describes a goal for future attainment, but also it partially insures that an individual will expend a more-than-minimum amount of energy, if necessary, to perform at or above that level.

Depending, then, on the conditions under which a budget is drawn the budget can act as a motivating force and can induce better performance from the members of the organization. On the other hand, the budget can specify aims and goals so easy of attainment that the organization's members will be induced to produce at less than their usual capacity.

After the performance phase of the cycle a comparison is made between the costs and income previously predicted in the budget and the actually attained income and costs. We are not here concerned with how the comparison is made but rather with its utilization, since that may have considerable effect on employee behavior and morale.

Much has been written on the effect of communication within an organization. With reference to the comparison, or control, function of the budget, the use or misuse of communication can be critical especially when viewed in the context of participation and level of aspiration.

First and foremost, it is imperative for each participant to know whether he should feel subjective success or failure. If he is not informed of the results of the comparison he cannot know whether his striving for a particular level was worthwhile or not. Nor can he, in turn, pass on the word to his subordinates in whom he induced specific levels of aspiration. They, too, will not know whether to feel success or failure. We can see that communicating knowledge of results acts,

[22] J. A. Bayton, "Interrelations between Levels of Aspiration, Performance and Estimates of Past Performance," *Journal of Experimental Psychology*, XXXIII (1943), 1-21.

[23] S. Siegel, L. Fouraker, *Bargaining and Group Decision Making* (New York: McGraw-Hill Book Co., 1960).

in this case, as reward or punishment. It can serve either to reinforce or extinguish previous employee behaviors. Where subjects were given a learning task and provided knowledge of results, learning increased; but when knowledge of results was withheld performance fell, that is learning not only stopped but performance was decreased.[24] In discussing these results, Munn argued that "the rapid drop in performance which followed this point may be attributed to the loss of motivation which came with withdrawal of knowledge of results, not from forgetting what had been learned up to this point."[25]

Failure to communicate knowledge of results adversely affects not only performance but also morale. Leavitt and Mueller, in an investigation of effects of varying amounts of feedback, found that task accuracy increased as feedback increased. They also found that zero feedback is accompanied by low confidence and hostility while free feedback is accompanied by high confidence and amity.[26]

The question may now be asked: "So what if the employees don't know how they did? They already performed and the profit is recorded." The answer obviously concerns the effects this lack will produce on subsequent behavior and, more specifically, on the goals to be set in the succeeding budget.

The next budget will be affected because omitting feedback not only precludes certainty regarding a previous level of aspiration but also affects the subsequent level of aspiration. Most generally an individual will raise his level of aspiration after success and lower it after failure.

In the budgeting cycle, after the comparison phase, the new budget is started. The participating supervisors bring to the new participation situation all their new aspirations resulting from past feelings of success or failure. If they have been deprived of a rightfully achieved feeling of success, their subsequent aspirations are likely to be lowered. This could result either in a less efficient budget, that is, lower goals than could easily be achieved or, after disagreeable argument, an imposed budget from an adamant management. In the first case succeeding performance will be unnecessarily low; in the second, participation will be ineffectual with the possible result of poor performance and, almost certainly, lower morale. The *proper* budget cycle then is really a dual, interacting sequence of budgeting and psychological events. It can be depicted as follows:

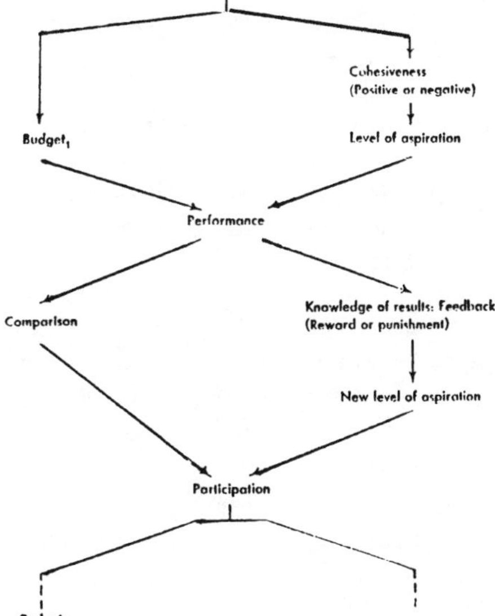

[24] J. L. Elwell and G. C. Grindley, "The Effect of Knowledge of Results on Learning and Performance," *British Journal of Psychology*, Vol. XXIX (1938).

[25] N. L. Munn, *Psychology* (Boston: Houghton Mifflin Co., 1946).

[26] H. J. Leavitt and R. A. H. Mueller, "Some Effects of Feedback on Communication," *Human Relations*, IV (1951), 401–10.

A successful participation budget does two things: (1) it induces proper motivation and acceptance of specific goals, and (2) it provides information to associate reward or punishment with performance. These lead to new aspirations and motivations that set the stage for the next participation budget.

CONCLUSIONS

An understanding of the psychological variables stemming from participation is valuable, perhaps, for its own sake, but it is hardly likely to provide concrete assistance in a decision to institute such a program. We have seen that participation can lead to either increased or decreased output. It is not unlikely that the setting in which participation occurs is one determinant of the production outcome. Some organizations can be characterized as operating under relatively authoritarian leadership. By definition, participation is essential to democratic process and very probably is antithetical to an authoritarian organization. To illustrate the latter, assume that the various department heads participate in the decision-making process, prepare a budget, only to have it rejected by upper management without explanation other than that a more satisfactory budget is necessary. The best prediction here is that the participating group will be highly cohesive and hold negative attitudes toward management, a precondition to lowered output.

It is also likely that under authoritarian management status differences will be rigidly adhered to. If the participants in the budgeting process occupy different status levels influence on decisions will be directly related to status—the more status the more influence. Status differences would probably mitigate against high cohesiveness. Presumably status differences that did not affect the decision-making process would not preclude either a cohesive group or positive goal acceptance, especially if the occupants were secure in their positions or perceived the possibility of upward mobility.[27]

We do not wish to enter the controversy over the relative merits of various styles of leadership but merely wish to point to some possible limitations on the use of participation. In order to be successful, the participants must participate, that is, must have influence on the adopted decisions. If participation can be achieved under more or less authoritarian conditions, it is likely to be effective, just as it can be undermined (by disregard) with democratic leadership. Only management itself can determine whether it is worthwhile to initiate or continue the participation segment of the budgeted cycle.

At any rate, presuming an organization has determined that it can benefit from participation, are the psychological effects such that participation simply can be "grafted" onto existing procedures or are other changes necessary? Or indeed, if no changes are necessary, are there any that can be made so that efficiency, motivation, and productivity will be enhanced?

Suggested changes in budgeting are not difficult to find. Stedry, recognizing the possible motivating forces produced by budgets, seems to suggest that "phony" budgets be prepared while the real budget is kept secret.[28] The "phony" ones would be designed to induce maximum motivation through a manipulation of level of aspiration. This plan would require different phony budgets

[27] Harold H. Kelley, "Communication in Experimentally Created Hierarchies," *Human Relations*, IV (1951), 39–56.

[28] *Budget Control and Cost Behavior*, pp. 5, 17, 41–42, and 71. Stedry does not use the term "phony."

for each department and, indeed, for each individual. If different budgets are viewed as discriminatory and unfair devices, company morale might suffer. Further, if already disgrunted employees learn that they were striving to attain phony goals the effectiveness of future budgets, real or phony, might be seriously impaired.

A knowledge of the effects of level of aspiration may lead to changes designed to increase employee motivation and output. The budget cycle characteristically is tied to an arbitrary time schedule. Even with no other information, this is defensible logically and perhaps economically as well. If, however, the budget is to be used as a control device (in the sense of prohibiting excessive expenditures) as well as a motivating device, then it clearly should be tied to the level of aspiration cycle rather than to a time schedule. We know that success leads to a rising level of aspiration and, generally, failure to a lowering. Failure can also result in "leaving the field," that is, psychological or physical withdrawal from the goal-oriented environment.

It is suggested here that much more frequent comparison of performance and budget be made, including feedback to the employees of the results of the comparison. This recommendation is made for the following reasons: (*a*) If the performances meet or slightly exceed expectation, then level of aspirations will rise and budgets can and should be revised; otherwise employees will perform at the budget level when they could be performing at a higher budget level. Maximum efficiency can only be achieved by revising the budget upward. (*b*) If performances are just slightly below the budget expectations, budget changes are not necessary, but feedback is so that employees will continue to strive for the budget goals. (*c*) If performances are well below the budget, it may be well to revise the budget downward. If such revision is not made, employees' level of aspiration will fall, the budget will be viewed as unattainable, and output will fall. The danger here is that levels of aspiration and output may fall much more than is necessary. If the budget is revised downward just enough so that it is perceived as being attainable, then maximum output will be achieved again.

[15]
The Impact of People on Budgets

Michael Schiff and Arie Y. Lewin

In the past decade budgets have become widely accepted as the key element in the corporation's planning and control system. This is evident both from the extensive writings on the subject and from a random sampling of current textbooks in management in which the discussion of operational planning and control centers about the role and use of financial budgets.[1]

Financial budgets represent the firm's plans for the coming year summarized in projected financial statements. Because financial budgets are plans they become the criteria by which managerial performance is measured and therefore the basis of the control system. Indeed, whereas budgets have this dual role, of being plans and performance criteria, they are generally viewed as synonymous with control and not with planning.[2] Moreover, it is their use as control devices that has made budgets the focus of much criticism by behavioral scientists who view them as a coercive instrument used by top management to "enforce" its objectives on the participants of the organization.

It is the purpose of this article to review the role of financial budgets in the corporate planning and control process by reexamining the relationship between the controller and the controlled.

The Traditional Accounting Model of the Firm

The most prevalent management accounting model of the firm is founded on classical economic theory of the corporation and the traditional Tayloristic model of the organization. The main features of this model are the emphasis on authority, accountability and control and the assumption that the organization members are passive participants. Indeed, most existing control practices assume the controlled to be passive elements within the controller-controlled relationship. As Caplan in his comparison of the behavioral decision-making model of organizations and the traditional model notes, the two models differ in their treatment of the role of humans in organizations.[3] In the behavioral model, humans are viewed as being goal directed, constrained by the cognitive limits on their rationality and possessing individual personalities. The emphasis is on the individual, his goals and aspirations and how he achieves them.[4]

[1] See for example the extensive bibliography presented in Y. Ijiri, J. C. Kinard, and F. B. Putney, "An Integrated Evaluation System for Budget Forecasting and Operating Performance with a Classified Budgeting Bibliography," *Journal of Accounting Research*, Vol. 6, No. 1, (Spring 1968), pp. 11–28.

[2] For an excellent summary and review on the applications of budgets, see G. H. Hofstede, *The Game of Budget Control*, (Van Gorcum and Comp. N. V. Assen, 1967), pp. 8–103.

[3] E. H. Caplan, "Behavioral Assumptions of Management Accounting," The Accounting Review, Vol. XLI, (July 1966), pp. 496–509.

[4] *Idem.*

Michael Schiff and Arie Y. Lewin are Chairman of the Department of Accounting and Assistant Professor of Management and Behavioral Sciences, respectively, at New York University.

The Tayloristic model of organizations has been further criticized by the participative advocates of organizations. These writers,[5] accept the view that organization members have aspirations and individual personalities, but firmly believe that organizations must provide the environment within which each individual can satisfy his needs as well as achieving the organization goals. According to the participative view, existing organizations are coercive systems along the lines of the Tayloristic model because of their insistence on accountability and control. Moreover in their view it is the use of imposed budgets which is instrumental to achievement of control and conformity.[6]

The emphasis on budgeting by the critics of traditional organizations derives from their equating control with coercion and from their belief that only in a participative environment is it possible to maximize organization effectiveness and individual satisfaction. As Leavitt points out, it is naive to describe organizations as "unhuman."[7] Indeed, many features of traditional organizations which are anathema to participative beliefs, such as division of labor, are necessary for the effective functioning of organizations.

It seems to us that the participative advocates of management, just as the traditionalists before them, fail to consider the goal-directed nature of human behavior. The Taylorists neglected humans altogether, whereas the participative practitioners believe that all humans in organizations should be able to self-actualize.

A More Pragmatic View of Organizations

Clearly, as Leavitt has pointed out, organizations do not fit the Tayloristic model and cannot be identified as being either coercive or unhuman.[8] The main characteristic of real organizations is that they have to achieve complex tasks and objectives through the many efforts of their diverse participants. Indeed, Fayol was quite correct when he stated that:

> The managerial function finds its only outlet through the members of the organization (body corporate). Whilst the other functions bring into play material and machines the managerial function operates only on the personnel.[9]

Dale in his discussion of management and the organization concludes that "Management is getting things done through other people."[10]

Whereas the organization may have specific objectives, activities and work flows which need to be achieved, it necessarily relies on humans who differ in their aspirations, perceptions, personalities, and capabilities to achieve them. Indeed, we need to understand why individuals join a particular organization, why they stay in or leave it, and what are the principle processes around which organizations revolve.

March and Simon have shown that the individual's decision to join, stay, or leave any organization depends on the interaction of a number of personal and situational variables.[11] Basically the individual seeks an organization which in his estimation will be instrumental to the achievement of his personal goals while he is furthering the organization goals. It is

[5] See for example the writings of H. A. Shepard, "Changing Interpersonal and Intergroup Relations in Organizations," in J. G. March, (ed) *Handbook of Organizations*, (Rand McNally & Co., 1967), pp. 1115–1144.
R. Likert, *The Human Organization: Its Management and Value*, (McGraw Hill, 1967).
D. McGregor, *The Human Side of Enterprise*, (McGraw Hill, 1961).

[6] This point is particularly emphasized by C. Argyris, *The Impact of Budgets on People*, (The Controllership Foundation, 1952), p. 25.
S. Becker and D. Green, "Budgeting and Employee Behavior," *Journal of Business*, Vol. 35, pp. 392–402.

[7] H. J. Leavitt, "Unhuman Organizations," *Harvard Business Review*, (July-August 1962), pp. 90–98.

[8] *Idem*.

[9] H. Fayol, *General and Industrial Management*, (Pitman, 1949), p. 19.

[10] E. Dale, *Management: Theory and Practice*, (McGraw-Hill, 1965), p. 4.

[11] J. G. March and H. A. Simon, *Organizations*, (Wiley, 1958), pp. 84–110.

clear that this does not imply a consistency between the individual's goals and the organization goals. Indeed, it suggests that some degree of latent conflict is always present within organizations. This conflict may occur between individuals and/or between sub-units of the organization and/or between individuals and their sub-units. These conflicts, as Cyert and March point out, revolve around the organization resource allocation processes, and are reflected in its continuing problem solving and decision making activities.[12]

Williamson has similarly observed that managers are motivated to achieve two sets of goals—the firm's goals and their personal goals. Personal goals, according to Williamson, are directly related to income (salary plus bonuses), size of staff, and discretionary control over allocation of resources. Williamson's conclusion was that managers can best achieve both their personal goals and the firm goals in a slack environment,[13] suggesting that managers will attempt to influence the budget process and obtain slack budgets.

The traditional budget and control system, however, operates on the principle of management by exception. Since budgets are the criteria for measuring performance, and management participates in their formulation, it clearly serves management's interests to influence the performance criteria incorporated in the budget. Lower level management, therefore, can be expected to strive for a budget which it feels is attainable and, at the same time, to meet top management's requirement for a desirable net income.

Thus, rather than viewing the organization as a coercive system, it is perforce quite participative, involving a dynamic interlevel bargaining process over goals, objectives and the means to these objectives (resource allocations). The budget preparation process satisfies the need for planning the operations of the firm, and the resulting budget serves as a mutually agreed upon control device for monitoring the activities of the various sub-units. Furthermore, the process of preparing the budget is highly instrumental in resolving the conflict among the various participants about organizational goals and resource allocation commitment and at the same time is precedent dependent.

Cyert and March defined organizational slack as the difference between the total resources available to the firm and the total necessary to maintain the organization coalition.[14] These slack resources arise from the imperfection of the resource allocation process and become available as additional payments to the organization participants. By comparison the resource allocation process of the firm in conventional economics allows for no slack under equilibrium conditions. Slack, furthermore, may be widely distributed or undistributed.[15] As the term implies, undistributed slack refers to resources which are recognizable and have not been distributed, such as idle cash and securities. Distributed slack refers to resources present in the firm in the form of "invisible" costs spread through the organization and hence not readily ascertained. In this paper we are concerned with the latter type of slack.

In a very real sense, then, every firm operates with slack resources which, in theory at least, are distributed in some way to all the participants of the organization. Thus, for example, shareholders may be paid dividends in excess of those required to keep them from selling their shares. Similarly workers may be paid excessive wages and executives may receive

[12] R. M. Cyert and J. G. March, *The Behavioral Theory of the Firm*, (Prentice Hall, 1963), pp. 26–127.
[13] O. E. Williamson, *The Economics of Discretionary Behavior: Managerial Objectives in a Theory of the Firm*, (Prentice Hall, 1964), pp. 28–37.
[14] Cyert and March, *op. cit.*, pp. 36–38.
[15] *Ibid.*, pp. 36–38, 279.

incentive compensation, services and luxuries beyond the minimum required to secure their continued participation in the organization.

Clearly, many more instances of distributed slack in the Cyert and March terms can be described. Our concern, however, is manager oriented. We have seen that slack exists and that managers possess the necessary motives to desire to operate in slack environment. For most corporations this environment is embodied in the budget document, and therefore it should not be surprising if managers attempted to influence the budget process and bargain for slack budgets. Stated differently, managers will create slack in budgets through a process of *understating revenues and overstating costs.* The last statement is an operational definition of slack.

A search of the literature, however, reveals that the problem of slack in budgets has not received much research attention although it is implicitly recognized throughout the budget literature. Stedry, on the basis of a laboratory experiment on levels of aspiration, suggests that the workers' aspirations affect their performance and that the budgetary process can be employed to impart to the worker higher aspirations resulting in a commitment to higher performance levels.[16] Lowe and Shaw report on downward bias introduced in sales forecasts by line managers aimed at assuring good performance where rewards were related to forecasts.[17] Dalton reports various examples of department managers who allocated resources to what they considered justifiable purposes which were not authorized in their budgets.[18] Shillinglaw notes that budgets can be extremely vulnerable when used to measure divisional performance because of the great control that division management exercises in the preparation of the budget and on the reporting of results.[19]

Williamson studied the slack content in the budgets of three companies over a period of time in which the companies passed from profitable to significantly less profitable states. In his report he identifies the actions of top management (incumbent or new) in controlling and reducing costs. Based on his analysis there emerges a close correlation between the type of cost reductions undertaken and the expense categories in which slack would accumulate. Thus Williamson reports that the cost reduction programs would result in decreases in employment, decreases in overhead, decreases in corporate staffs, decreases in R&D expenditures, etc.[20]

Whereas the data reported by Williamson is clearly supportive of the occurrence of slack, it does not detail the role of managers in this process and does not relate it specifically to the annual budget process. A detailed description of how managers build slack into their budgets by understating revenues and overstating costs was reported by Schiff and Lewin[21] in their study of the budget process of three divisions, parts of multi-division companies. The study involved a two year budget sequence and detailed the process whereby managers satisfied personal aspirations through the use of slack in "good years" and reconverted slack into profits in bad years. Schiff and Lewin reported that division management generally created slack in their budgets by underestimating gross

[16] A. C. Stedry, *Budget Control and Cost Behavior*, (Prentice Hall, 1960).

[17] A. E. Lowe and R. W. Shaw, "An Analysis of Managerial Biasing: Evidence from a Company's Budgeting Process," *The Journal of Management Studies*, Vol. 5, No. 3, (October 1968) pp. 304–315.

[18] M. Dalton, *Men Who Manage*, (Wiley, 1959), pp. 36–38.

[19] G. Shillinglaw, "Divisional Performance Review: An Extension of Budgetary Control," In C. P. Bonini, R. K. Jaedicke, and H. M. Wagner, (eds) *Management Controls: New Directions in Basic Research*, (McGraw-Hill, 1964), pp. 149–163.

[20] Williamson, *op. cit.*, pp. 85–126.

[21] M. Schiff and A. Y. Lewin, "Where Traditional Budgeting Fails," *Financial Executive*, Vol. XXXVI, No. 5, pp. 51–62.

revenue, inclusion of discretionary increases in personnel requirements, establishment of marketing and sales budgets with internal limits on funds to be spent, use of manufacturing costs based on standard costs which do not reflect process improvements operationally available at the plant, and the inclusion of discretionary "special" projects.

Understating gross revenue was generally accomplished by understating potential unit sales and average expected unit prices. This normally was more than sufficient in accommodating expected top management requests for higher profits at budget review sessions.

Examples of discretionary budgetary allocations included increases in the budgeted personnel positions. These positions, however, were staffed progressively as the year's operating results met expectations. In other words, the additional personnel positions under adverse conditions would not be staffed and the savings in budgeted salaries would appear as increases in divisional net income. The same basic procedure was observed in regard to advertising budgets, promotional programs, sales meetings, training programs and allocations to special projects.

The observations that the introduction of operationally available process improvements in the manufacturing process was a discretionary managerial decision is quite significant. Based on the observations of Schiff and Lewin it would appear that standard manufacturing costs may include slack in terms of unincorporated process improvements. In the example cited by Schiff and Lewin such process improvements were introduced by management, again only under adverse conditions and were kept on the "shelf" otherwise.

The research reviewed here clearly raises the issue of the influence which various managerial levels have on the outcome of a company's financial budget, particularly in terms of the slack which they strive to build into it. This slack may be quite significant and according to estimates by Schiff and Lewin may account for as much as 20–25 percent of a division's budgeted operating expenses. Similar estimates can be derived from the data reported by Williamson.

The Role of the Controller

The type of control system employed by the corporation may also be a factor in how slack is created within a division and how it is managed. For some time corporations have tended to decentralize their control system, partly in response to the participative critics of the traditional coercive organizations but mainly in the hope of improvements in the decision making process and in anticipation of tighter control over costs. The main feature of the decentralized control system is the creation of control positions on the division and subdivision level (sometimes down to the plant level) staffed with controllers who are directly responsible to the corporate controller.[22]

It appears, however, that in the decentralized companies the divisional controller, while formally responsible to the corporate controller, is in fact a key member of the division top management, and is closely involved in achieving division objectives. Thus Schiff and Lewin report that the divisional controller appears to have undertaken the task of creating and managing divisional slack and is most influential in the internal allocation of this slack.[23]

This apparently unexpected behavior may be due to a number of causes. Generally in the decentralized company the divisional controller and the division man-

[22] D. Solomons, *Divisional Performance: Measurement and Control*, (Financial Executives Research Foundation, 1965).

[23] Schiff and Lewin, *op. cit.*, pp. 51–62.

agement are spatially removed from corporate headquarters. This physical removal leads to infrequent interaction between the divisional controller and the corporate controller while it increases the interaction between the divisional controller and the division management. This increased interaction arises from the divisional controller's participation in the everyday problem-solving and decision-making activities of the division. As a result we find the formation of personal relationships, and more importantly the sharing of goals and objectives. Finally, it is clear that the achievement of the controller's personal goals depends on his active participation in the division's affairs and to a much smaller extent on his nominal superior, the corporate controller.

It is therefore not surprising that the divisional controller, with his intimate knowledge of the budget and its underlying elements, becomes the division's general manager's right-hand man in establishing division goals, presenting them to corporate management and overseeing their achievement. It is the achievement of the division plans which earns the controller both corporate and divisional recognition represented by his share of salary bonuses (normally tied to divisional earnings above plan), increased staff and discretionary control over allocation of slack resources.

Slack, however, occurs in a centralized company to the same extent as in the decentralized one. In a centralized company, however, slack created at the divisional level would exist in a less disguised form, primarily because the central controller is removed from the day-to-day problems of company divisions and personally not involved in creating budgetary slack. Indeed, in the centralized system, being part of corporate management requires the corporate controller to be mainly concerned with monitoring the implementation of plans and controlling costs.

The observations of Schiff and Lewin support this contention. In the two decentralized divisions, the controllers were intimately familiar with day-to-day operations and had very sophisticated procedures for managing division slack. In the case of the division operating within a group of divisions with control centralized at the group level, the group controller was uninformed about the extent of slack in the budgets of the various divisions in the group. Furthermore, within the group, division management lacked tight control over slack and, by comparison with controllers of the decentralized divisions, was rather unsophisticated in its efforts to manage slack. Indeed, lower levels of management of the centralized company including plant managers had significant influence in creating and appropriating this slack.

Thus it appears that *ceteris paribus*, the location and form of slack in the budget is also dependent on the type of control system employed. Specifically it appears that in a decentralized company, slack is concentrated at the divisional management level. Moreover, the divisional controller is intimately involved in the creation and "husbanding" of slack. Conversely, in a centralized company with a weaker control system, slack is diffused through all management levels of the division.

Top Corporate Management and Slack

Top management role in the budgetary process is generally exercised in the divisional budget review sessions. Although top management has the formal power to accept or reject the budgets proposed, it is generally at a disadvantage, because it lacks the detailed information regarding makeup of items and underlying analyses which the divisional management has. Thus, while top management can be assumed to be aware of "padding" and "sandbagging" practices, it finds itself trying to guess at what a reasonable increase in profit requirements should be. Indeed, the fact that such higher profit targets are often achieved affirms the existence of slack. Yet slack can be a major problem for top management and can be viewed as representing lost opportunities to the firm and in the long run increasing its cost function.

The organization reward structure, by overreacting to under-achievement of objectives, is one of the causes of managerial desire for slack. This suggests that managers view slack as a means of avoiding the stigma normally attached to under-achievers. It may be that a reward structure based on an objective reporting system and which places equal emphasis on over-achieving as on under-achieving could lessen managerial uncertainty avoidance. However, as Birnberg and Nath point out, such a system has not been achieved yet, and to the best or our knowledge exists only as a hypothetical model.[24] Furthermore, we have noted that uncertainty avoidance is only one factor in management's motivation for slack. Managers we noted, possess personal goals and aspirations whose achievement depends on the existence of slack, under their control. Thus we feel that devising new objective reporting systems and restructuring the reward system, though important to the problem of assessing performance, will not by itself solve the problem of slack.

Indeed, as long as people are the corporation we must expect occurrence of dysfunctional behaviors such as the desire for and creation of slack. It would be feasible, however, for top management to influence the budget process in a constructive way, if it had the information base on which to make decisions.[25] Clearly top management cannot have any significant impact on a budget at the terminal review sessions, when it can only make aggregate demands for higher profits and improved return on investments. Similarly *ex post facto* analyses like those proposed by Thiel[26] or internal audits would not get at the basic problems which revolves around the actual budget formulation process.

Theoretically it can be argued that if top management could evaluate and review the budget at key points during the budget preparation process it could also be more successful in countering the tendency toward the creation of slack. Stedry[27] has shown that imposed aspirations which exceed self-set aspirations often will be achieved and that their achievement depends on whether the subordinate accepts them as reasonable.

Thus, the problem for top management is first one of information—how to develop the information necessary to impose reasonable goals? Second, it is one of organization design—how to institutionalize top management's active participation in the budget process.

Some examples of pragmatic approaches to dealing with the problem of slack creation follow. It must be stressed that they are suggestive and would require further research before implementation.

Influencing the Budget: In-Depth Reviews

As a first step, the evaluation and review of the budget would be shifted from the termination of the process to points *during* the process. This should not be confused with standard reviews of tentative or completed budgets or with budget audits which are performed *ex post facto*. Instead, top management should focus on examining the basic elements of the budget as they are quantified and assembled. Some of

[24] J. G. Birnberg and R. Nath, "Implications of Behavioral Science for Managerial Accounting," The Accounting Review, Vol. XLII. No. 3. pp. 468–479.

[25] A similar point is made by Lowe and Shaw, *op. cit.*, pp. 312–315.

[26] H. Theil, "How to Worry About Increased Expenditures," The Accounting Review, Vol. XLIV, No. 1, pp. 27–37.

[27] Stedry, *op. cit.*, pp. 61–90, 144–154.

these key elements occur in the formation of the following estimates:

1. Market shares
2. Sales
3. Unit selling prices
4. Standard costs
5. Marketing expenses
6. Personnel needs
7. Other expenses

To influence the budget process at its critical formative stages, top management must question the information base underlying the formulation of specific estimates. For example, sales projections can be reviewed by examining, among other variables, the inputs from marketing research, competitive intelligence, the economic environment and the company's own long range plans. Additionally, the critical reviews could involve staff and operating managers in manufacturing, engineering, marketing and administration and not merely the division president, his controller and their staffs. For example, when standard cost estimates are being reviewed, the factory cost accountant, the factory engineering staff concerned with process improvements and engineering studies, as well as the factory personnel manager could be involved. What should be stressed are questions of the "why" and "what if" variety along with the "how" type of questions.

The objective of top management is not to "second guess" divisional management or deny their decision-making prerogatives but rather to force them to ***rethink*** their previously unquestioned assumptions and long standing standard operating procedures. Such constant probing of basic assumptions will lead to a minimal slack environment and approach conditions of optimal performance.

The extensive reviews urged here should not be done in every division every year. Several divisions may be selected each year and the effect of the review will carry over for a number of years. The characteristic of slack is that it builds up over cumulative successful operating periods and levels off in poor years. Furthermore, as slack builds up it becomes largely irretrievable in the long run. This suggests that the appropriate time to perform the in-depth budget reviews could be after a division has experienced a sequence of ***successful*** operating years. Whereas this recommendation seems to contradict the principles of management by exception it really augments it. Clearly top management must attend to problem divisions; however, successful divisions can be made even more effective.

Institutionalizing In-Depth Reviews

So far we have not dealt with the problem of implementing the proposed in-depth budget reviews. Clearly this is a task for top management. It is equally clear, however, that top management does not have the resources (time and personnel) to do the job. Since such in-depth reviews must be done periodically throughout the corporation and since it is important that different approaches be employed each time, it appears that special task groups directly reporting to the president might be best suited for this assignment. The staffing of these task groups is the determining factor in the success of these reviews and the following are three staffing strategies representing different approaches to the problem.

i) Senior Managers

Task groups composed of company senior managers—vice presidents of divisions and corporate staff members—probably would be top management's first choice for the review assignments. The senior managers are intimately familiar with company procedures and history. In the review process they often would be able to prescreen alternatives which have been tried in the past and failed. The same senior managers, however, are to a large extent prisoners of their own prior preconceptions derived from history and, therefore, may be reluctant to propose or accept new ideas. Furthermore, the reviews are likely to raise past issues in which they may have been personally involved, thus introducing personal biases which could clearly affect the outcome of the problem under review. Finally, the senior managers themselves may be the target of reviews at some other point in time, and this in itself could undermine the effectiveness of the periodic review procedures.

ii) Outside Consultants

Staffing the task groups with outside consultants clearly solves many of the disadvantages associated with the use of in-house senior managers teams. The outside consultants are not hampered by corporate precedents and history and would be inclined to approach the reviews with greater objectivity. They bring to the reviews broader backgrounds and interdisciplinary skills. Moreover, new groups of outside consultants can be used each time.

Corporations, however, can be expected to resist the use of outside consultants on budget reviews primarily because of a confidence gap. The budget, after all, reveals in detail the company short-term plan and the budget process itself may highlight various conflicts, all of which top management may prefer to keep in-house. Furthermore, the consultant takes what he has learned to his next job, thus increasing the likelihood of exposing confidential information.

iii) Whiz Kids

The "whiz kids" in this case would be recently hired top-flight MBA's. Like the outside consultants, they are free of corporate bias and will approach problems with greater objectivity. Unlike the consultants they have no broad prior background but instead are trained in the current state of the art of management, have an understanding of the behavioral aspects of management decision-making, are highly motivated to think creatively and are eager to question established standard operating procedures. Furthermore, the assignment to the budget review task groups provides them with a superb training period to learn about the company prior to their assignment within the company. Finally, unlike the consultant who takes what he has learned to his next job, the "whiz kids" approach has a carryover effect in terms of total organizational learning, on-the-job training of the "whiz kids" and in terms of accelerating the diffusion of innovative ideas in management decision making.

Summary

In this paper we have reexamined the relationship between the controller and the controlled within the organization. We have argued that this relationship revolves around the budget process and that the "controlled" exercise significant influence on the outcome of their budgets. This influence manifests itself in the amount of slack which managers (and all other participants) can incorporate into their budgets.

The theoretical rationale for such dysfunctional behavior has been previously stated by a number of writers. However, except for the exploratory studies by Schiff and Lewin and Lowe and Shaw, there exist no observations or empirical evidence on how and why managers create slack. Decentralized control was expected to increase organization effectiveness due to the increased participation in decision making created on the local level and because the divisional controller was formally responsible to the corporate controller. Assuming, however, as we did, that financial budgets are no more than a mutually agreed upon control device, then the whole notion of control needs to be reexamined, particularly the role of the decentralized controller who appears to act as the divisional slack manager.

Finally, if managerial desire for slack and the attendant dysfunctional consequences must be taken as given then the implications for top management actions must be reconsidered. We have suggested a pragmatic approach aimed at increasing the participation of top management in the budget process on a selective basis. Specifically we have discussed the problem of how top management could impose reasonable goals[28] through constructive reviewing of the budget at critical points during the budget preparation process. We have also recognized that top management is severely limited in its ability to undertake on such a task. We have, therefore, proposed the creation of budget task groups, directly under the president, which will in effect participate in the budget preparation process. The success of these task groups clearly depends on their staffing and mode of operation within the organization. Whether the approach outlined here will work will require extensive further experimentation in the field.

[28] Lowe and Shaw, *op. cit.*, pp. 312–315.

[16]

CONTROLS, CONTROL AND MANAGEMENT

PETER F. DRUCKER
New York University

SECTION I

In the grammar of social institutions the word *"controls"* is not the plural of the word "control." Not only do more "controls" not necessarily give more "control"—the two words, in the context of social institutions have different meanings altogether. The synonyms for "controls" are measurement and information. The synonym for "control" is direction. "Controls" pertain to means, "control" to an end. "Controls" deal with facts, that is with events of the past. "Control" deals with expectations, that is with the future. "Controls" are analytical and operational, concerned with what was and is. "Control" is normative, concerned with what ought to be, with significance rather than with meaning.

We are rapidly acquiring great capacity to design "controls" in social institutions, based on a great improvement in techniques, especially in the application of logical and mathematical tools to events of this social universe, and in the ability to process and analyze large masses of data very fast. What does this mean for "control?" Specifically what are the requirements for these greatly improved "controls" to give better "control" to management? For, in the task of a manager, "controls" are purely a means to an end; the end is "control."

That here is a problem, ordinary language and its use makes abundantly clear. The man in a business who is charged with producing the "controls" is the "controller." But most, if not all executives, including most controllers themselves, would consider it gross misuse and abuse of controllership were this "controller" to use his "controls" to exercise "control" in the business. This, they would argue would actually make the business be "out of control" altogether.

The reasons for this apparent paradox lie in the complexity, both of human beings and of the social task. I do not intend to go into metaphysics, nor is this necessary. I am willing to grant that both, the human being and society are actually completely determined. But there are so many determinants, and their form and impact are so varied, that, at least on the microcosmic level on which we operate—and on which even the basic policy decisions of great powers are being made—there is so much complexity as to result in a genuine "uncertainty principle" insofar as the relationship between "controls" and "control" is concerned. A genuine feed-back is not possible.

If we deal with a human being in a social institution, "controls" must become personal motivation to lead to "control." Instead of a mechanical system, the control system in a human-social situation is a volitional system. That we know very little about the will is not even the central point. A translation is required before the information by the "controls" can become ground of action—the translation of one kind of information into another which we call *perception*.

In the social institution itself there is a second complexity, a second "uncertainty principle." It is almost impossible to pre-figure the responses appropriate to a certain event in a social situation. We can, and do, build a control into a machine which slows down the turning speed whenever it exceeds a certain figure. And we can do this either by mechanical means or by instrumentation which shows a human operator what the turning speed is, and which gives him the specific, unambiguous instruction to turn the speed down when the indicator reaches a certain point. But a control reading "profits are falling" does not indicate, with any degree of probability, the response "raise prices" let alone by how much; the control—reading "sales are falling" does not indicate the response "cut prices," and so on. There is not only a large—a very large—number of other equally probable responses—so large that it is usually not even possible to identify them in advance. There is no indication in the event itself which of these responses is even possible, let alone appropriate, not to mention its being right. The event itself may not even be meaningful. But even if it is, it is by no means certain what it means. And the probability of its being meaningful is a much more important datum than the event itself—and one which is almost never to be discerned by analyzing the event.

In other words what is needed in the social situation is a decision based on assumptions—and essentially assumptions not in respect to the recorded event but in respect to the future, that is expectations which know no probability but can only be judged according to plausibility. For there are no "facts" in the future in a social universe in which periodicity—at least on our minuscule scale—cannot be assumed, must indeed rather be considered quite unlikely.

There are at least parts of such a situation which resemble the phenomena of the physical universe. We can in other words "simulate," that is, pretend that we deal with physical events rather than with social events. And such "simulation" is indeed highly fruitful as we have learned these last ten years or so. But we should never forget the fact that this is "simulation"—and therefore something completely different from the symbolic representation of reality which the physicist's formula represents. It is always based on assumptions regarding volition, perception and expectations which need constant re-appraisal.

SECTION II

Does this mean that "controls" are unimportant? Does it mean that they are misleading? The opposite actually follows. Precisely because we deal with such a complex subject, we need control very badly. And precisely because we find ourselves in constant uncertainty as managers in such a situation, "controls" tend to have tremendous impact. In fact both the need and the impact are so great that the wrong "controls" can be exceedingly misleading and dangerous. It is, therefore, important today when our capacity to design and to manipulate controls is increasing so fast, to think through what controls in a social institution and in particular in the business enterprise have to be and have to do, and also what they cannot be and must not attempt to do.

There are four major characteristics of "controls" in business enterprise—two pertain to all social institutions and reflect the fact that business enterprise is a social institution. One of these characteristics pertains to institutions within a society of which business enterprise is one. And the fourth and last one is specifically a characteristic of business enterprise as an economic institution.

1. When we measure the rate of fall of a stone, we are totally outside the event itself. By measuring we do not change the event; and measuring the event does not change us, the observers.

Measuring is both objective and neutral.

In a wide range of natural phenomena, however, especially on the microcosmic level, the act of measuring interferes with the event measured—whether the events are nuclear, microbiological or psychological. The observer in these events becomes a part of the situation. Measurement is still objective but no longer neutral.

In a perceptual situation of complexity, that is in any social situation of the kind we deal with in business enterprise, the act of measurement is, however, neither objective nor neutral. It is subjective and of necessity biased. It changes both the event and the observer. For it changes the perception of the observer—if it does not altogether create his perception. Events in the social situation acquire value by the fact that they are being singled out for the attention of being measured. No matter how "scientific" we are, the fact that this or that set of phenomena is singled out for being "controlled," signals that it is being considered to be important. Everybody who ever watched the introduction of a budget system has seen this happen. For a long time—in many companies forever—realizing the budget figures becomes more important than what the budget is supposed to measure, namely economic performance. This goes often so far that managers, upon their first exposure to a budget system, deliberately hold back sales and cut back profits rather than be guilty of "not making the budget." It takes years of experience and a very intelligent budget director to restore the balance. And there is any number of otherwise perfectly normal research directors who act on the conviction that it is a greater crime to get research results for less than the budgeted amount than not getting any research results at all while spending all the "proper" budget money.

"Controls" in a social institution, in other words, are goal-setting and value-setting. They are not "objective." They are of necessity moral. The only way to avoid this is to flood the executive with so many "controls" that the entire system becomes meaningless, becomes mere "noise." From that point of view maybe the gross abuse of our new data processing capacity, namely as a tool for grinding out huge quantities of totally meaningless data—the abuse of which every early computer user is guilty—is a blessing after all. But it is hardly the right way to use our capacity to provide "controls." This must start out with the realization that "controls" create vision. That is they both affect the events measured and the observer. They endow events not only with meaning but with value.

And this means that the basic question is not "How do we control?" But "What do we measure in our control system." That we can quantify something is no reason at all for measuring it. The question is: "Is this what a manager should consider important?" "Is this what a manager's attention should be focused on?" "Is this a true statement of the basic realities of the enterprise?" "Is this the proper focus for "control," that is for effective direction with maximum economy of effort?"

If these questions are not being asked in designing "controls," we will end up by making business essentially uncontrolled—for then we will simply have no remedy except to proliferate control information to the point where it does not register at all.

2. Because "controls" have such an impact it is not only important that we select the right ones. To enable controls to give right vision and to become the ground for effective action, the measurement must also be appropriate. That is it must present the events measured in structurally true form. Formal validity is not enough.

Grievances coming out of a work force are commonly reported as "five grievances per thousand employees per month." This is formally valid. But is it structurally valid? Or is it misdirection?

The impression this report conveys is first that grievances are distributed throughout the work force in a random matter. They follow, the report seems to say, a U-shaped Gaussian distribution. And secondly—a conclusion from the first impression—they are a minor problem especially if we deal with five grievances per thousand employees per month.

It is almost certain, however, that this, while formally valid, completely mis-represents and mis-informs, let alone mis-directs. Grievances are a social event. Physical nature knows no such phenomena. And social events are almost never distributed in the "normal distribution" we find in the physical world. The "normal distribution" of social events is almost always exponential—with the hyperbola the typical curve. In other words, the great majority of departments in the plant, employing ninety-five per cent of the work force, normally does not even have a single grievance during one year. But in one department, employing only a handful of men, we have a heavy incidence of grievances—so that the "five per thousand" may well mean (and in the actual example from which I took these figures, did mean) a major grievance per man per year. If this department is then the final assembly through which all the production has to pass, and if the workers in this department go out on strike when their grievances are being neglected by a management which has been misled by its own "controls," the impact can be shattering. In the case I quoted it bankrupted the company which is no longer in existence.

Similarly 90 per cent of the volume of a business is usually represented by 2 to 5 per cent of the number of its products. But 90 per cent of the orders by number cover, typically, only 4 or 5 per cent of the volume—but account for 90 per cent and more of the costs. And so it goes. A modern strategic bomber may have a million parts. But 90 per cent of its cost is represented by a very small number of parts, maybe fifty or so—and so is 90 per cent of the upkeep it need though, unfortunately, the 90 per cent of the dollars and the 90 per cent of the upkeep-needs rarely comprise the same parts.

Practically all the innovations in a research laboratory, no matter how large, come out of the work of a very small percentage of the research people. And invariably, 80 per cent of a company's distributors move, at best, 20 per cent of its output, while 10 per cent or fewer of the distributors move two-thirds to three quarters of total sales.

This, unfortunately, very few managers know. The traditional information systems, especially accounting, conceal rather than highlight this fact. (In particular the allocation of overhead tends to obscure the "normal distribution" of economic and social phenonema).

At the same time knowledge of this fact and understanding of it are pre-requisites for effective control. For control is above all a principle of economy. It means allocation of efforts where they can produce the most results with the minimum of energy. This means allocation of efforts to the small number of phenomena which in any social situation account for the great bulk of results.

Without controls that bring out sharply what the real structure of events is, the manager not only lacks knowledge. He cannot, normally expect to do the right thing. On the contrary, all the weight of the daily work pushes him towards allocating energies and resources in proportion to the *number* of events. There is a constant drift towards putting energies and resources where they can have the least results, that is on the vast number of phenomena which, together, account for practically no effects.

Any sales organization I have ever seen, has the bulk of its salesmen—and especially the good men—working on the 90 per cent of the customers who, together, buy 10 per cent of the output, or on the 90 per cent of products by number which, together produce 10 per cent of the company's revenue and markets, and so on. Any technical service force—one of the most expensive and most valuable resources of a company—in the absence of the right information regarding market structure and customers, will put its best men on the smallest and least valuable accounts, if only because these are the people who have the least technical competence themselves and therefore seem to need technical help the most. In fact this constant drift towards the irrelevant and unproductive is so great, and the weight behind it so heavy, that a "controls" system which did nothing but focus attention on the central events—the events which under normal probability statistics are not seen at all—would give any manager a great deal more control and very much better performance and results than the most elaborate simulation and quantification can possibly produce.

To bring out the structure of economic and social events should be a major contribution of our new approaches to "controls." We now have the logical and mathematic tools available for the job. Indeed it is in this area that the new methods have been most productive. Of course not everything there is to be measured, conforms to the "normal distribution" of social events. After all we also deal with physical events in business enterprise. And one of the most important and least understood areas of operation are those where events following the "normal distribution" of the physical universe have to be coupled with events following the "normal distribution" of the social universe, for instance, where we have to bring together the physical flow of materials through a plant with an order pattern.

Here in other words is an area of very great contribution. But the new tools and methods will not make this contribution, will indeed miss their greatest opportunity, unless it is realized that how we measure is as important as what we measure—and that the question: "What is the proper measurement and the proper scale" is infinitely more important in social events than it is in the physical universe—precisely because perception is an integral part of the events themselves.

3. The third characteristic important for the design and use of controls in business enterprise is that business is an institution of society. It exists to contribute to economy, society and individual.

In consequence *results* in business exist only on the outside—in economy, in society and with the customer. It is the customer only who creates a "profit". Everything inside a business, manufacturing, marketing, research and so on, creates only costs, is only a "cost center."

In other words the "managerial" area is concerned with costs alone. *Results are always entrepreneurial.*

Yet we do not have adequate, let alone reliable information regarding the "outside." They are not only by far the hardest to get—to the point where no organization for the acquisition and collection of meaningful outside information could really be set up—the job is much too big. Above all we simply lack the necessary entrepreneurial concepts. The job itself has never been thought through—at least not so far. And the century of patient analysis of managerial, inside phenomena, events and data, the century of patient, skillful work on the individual operations and tasks within the business, has no counterpart in respect to the entrepreneurial job.

To put it differently, we can easily record and therefore quantify efficiency, that is, efforts. We have very few instruments to record and quantify effects, that is, the outside. But even the most efficient buggy whip manufacturer would no longer be in business. It is of little value to have the most efficient engineering department if it designs the wrong product. The Cuban subsidiaries of U.S. companies were by far the best run and, apparently, the most profitable—let alone the least "troublesome"—of all U.S. operations in Latin America. And it mattered little, I daresay, during the period of IBM's great expansion in the last ten or fifteen years how "efficient" its operations were; it's basic entrepreneurial idea was the right, the effective one.

It is not only that the outside, the area of results, is much less accessible than the inside. It is at the same time much more remote as well. The central problem of the executive in the large organization is his—necessary—insulation from the outside. This applies to the President of the United States as well as to the President of United States Steel. What today's organization therefore needs, above all, are synthetic sense organs for the outside. If modern "controls" are to make a contribution, it would be above all here.

Yet this is exactly the area where we do not put to work the new technology of control. We tend—as people with a new tool kit always do—to go to work where it is easy. These are the inside, the managerial events. We should, however, go to work where we can make the greatest contribution. On the outside, we cannot indeed hope to come up with anything of such beautiful precision as a Queuing Theory inventory system. But we may come up with something which (unlike some fancy inventory systems I have seen) is actually useful and may even be used. In other words a new approach, a new technology, a new set of tools should always be put to work on the difficult rather than the easy, on the things the old tools could not do at all rather than on the things they did passably well. It should give new power rather than be frittered away on improvements. And unless we use the new approaches for an understanding and ordering of the outside, the entrepreneurial world of business enterprise—even though all we can produce there for the time being are insights rather than quantitative statements—we are not going to make the new technology truly useful. We are going to abuse it for the gratification of the technician's virtuosity rather than for the satisfaction of an urgent need of business and society.

4. Finally, in terms of specifications for effective quantitative controls, we should look at business enterprise as something separate, that is as business as a meaningful sphere of human action by itself. As such it presents a unique appearance to people interested in controls and control. Business, unlike all natural and mechanical systems, exhibits a wide range of events and results that are of profound importance and yet cannot easily be quantified within any meaningful system of measurement. But business, also, unlike any other social system, has a wide range of events and results which can be quantified. Business is the only system we know which has both quantifiable and non-quantifiable results and events, both equally important.

This gives business a unique opportunity for controls, but also a unique problem.

Any experienced executive knows companies or industries which are bound for extinction because they cannot attract or hold able people. This, every experienced executive also knows, is a more important fact about a company or an industry than last year's profit statement. Any logical positivist who were to tell an executive that this statement, being incapable of unambiguous definition is a "non-statement" dealing with a "non-problem," would be quickly—and correctly—dismissed as an ass. Yet the statement cannot be defined clearly let alone "quantified." It is anything but "intangible;" it is very "tangible" indeed (as anyone ever having to do with such a business quickly finds out.) It is just "non-measurable." And the results, while exceedingly measurable, will not show up for a decade.

But business also has measurable and quantifiable results of true meaning and significance. These are all those that have to do with past economic performance. For these can be expressed in terms of the very peculiar measurement of the economic sphere, money.

This does not mean that these are "tangibles." Indeed most of the things we can measure by money are so totally "intangible"—take depreciation for instance—that they outdo any Platonic Idea in that nothing corresponds to them in any reality whatever. But they are measurable.

That they are abstractions the "management scientist" with his background in physics or engineering often has to learn the hard way. Far too few management scientists for instance realize that practically every single definition of accounting is based on assumptions of high metaphysical content—and that any accountant worth his salt, can convert any profit figure into a loss figure, or vice versa, if given control of the accounting definitions, all unquestionably, "within the limits of proper accounting practice."

This does not alter the fact that there are important measurable events. And then, to say it again, there are equally important events that cannot be measured.

To this comes the fact that the measurable results are things that happened, they are in the past. There are no "facts" about the future. To this comes secondly that the measurable events are primarily inside events rather than outside events. The important developments on the outside, the things which determine that the buggy whip industry disappears and that IBM becomes a big business—let alone that Cuban subsidiaries of American companies are confiscated—are not measurable until it is too late to have "control."

A balance between the measurable and the non-measurable is therefore a central and constant problem of management. In many ways it is *the problem* of management and the true decision area.

Measurements which do not spell out the assumptions in respect to the non-measurable that are being made—as parameters if you please or in any other form—misdirect therefore. They actually misinform. Yet the more we can quantify the truly measurable areas, the greater the temptation to put all out emphasis on those—the greater, therefore, the danger that what looks like better "controls" will actually mean less "control" if not a business out of control altogether.

SECTION III

There is one more important thing to be said. There is a fundamental, incurable, basic limitation to "controls" in a "social institution." This lies in the fact that a "social institution" is both a true entity and a complete fiction. As an entity it has purposes of its own, a performance of its own, results of its own—and a survival of its own. These are the areas of which we have been speaking so far. But a social institution is comprised of persons, each with his own purpose, his own ambitions, his own ideas, his own needs. No matter how "totalitarian" the institution, it has to satisfy the ambitions and needs of its members, and do so in their capacity as individuals but through institutional rewards and punishments, incentives and deterrents. The expression of this may be quantifiable—such as a raise in salary. But the system itself is not quantitative in character and cannot be quantified.

Yet here is the real "control" of the institution, that is the ground of behavior and the cause of action. People act as they are being rewarded or punished. For this, to them, rightly, is the true expression of the values of the institution and of its true, as against its professed, purpose and role. Employment selection and promotion decisions are the real "controls." In the employment selection an institution decides what kind of people it wants altogether. In the promotion decisions it makes operational its true and actual values and its real performance standards. A company that tells its foremen that the job is human relations but which then promotes the foreman who best does his paper work, makes it very clear to even the dumbest man in the shop that it wants paper work rather than human relations. And it will get paper work.

A system of "controls" which is not in conformity with this true, this only effective, this ultimate "control" of the organization which lies in its people-decisions, will therefore at best be ineffectual—as most are. At worst it will cause never-ending conflict and will push the organization out of control. Unfortunately this is only too often the situation where economically focused controls are imposed upon a research organization which professes dedication to "scientific values." Either promotions are then being made according to economic criteria—which violates the profession of the research group. Or promotions are being made according to scientific criteria—which destroys the credibility and acceptance of the economic "controls."

In designing "controls" for a business one therefore has to understand and analyze the actual "control" of the business, its personnel decisions especially in respect to promotion. Otherwise one designs a system of "controls" which does not lead to "control." One secondly has to think through the actual "control" system, the personnel decisions, to see whether it really is in agreement with the true needs of the business. Otherwise there is no economic performance.

But finally one has to realize that even the most powerful "instrument board" complete with Computers, Operations Research, and Simulations is secondary to the invisible, qualitative control of any human organization, its systems of rewards and punishments, of values and taboos—as it expresses itself in the ultimate decision, the personnel decision.

The new controls technology has tremendous scope and power. There is tremendous need for new and better controls, and especially for controls that are quantitative and therefore not just matters of "opinion." But the new "controls" have this power and satisfy this need, precisely because they are not "objective," are not "neutral," precisely because they change both the events they record and observe and the men to whom they report and whom they inform. What is needed therefore for those who are the designers of these "con-

trols" is an attitude very different from that of the physical scientist or the instrument maker. Theirs is much greater power- but also much greater limitation. They have to know that they can do much less—and have to know what they cannot do. But they also have to know that what they can do means much more- and have to impose on themselves the responsibility appropriate to this power.

[17]

The Poverty of Management Control Philosophy

GEERT HOFSTEDE
European Institute for Advanced Studies in Management

The ineffectiveness of many management control systems is attributed to the cybernetic philosophy on which they are based. A distinction is made between routine industrial-type processes, for which a homeostatic paradigm is more suitable, and non-routine, non-industrial-type processes, for which a political paradigm is recommended. Attempts at enforcing a cybernetic paradigm on the latter processes, like Program-Planning-Budgeting System and Management-By-Objectives, are bound to fail.

Ja, mach' nur einen Plan!
Sei nur ein grosses Licht!
Und mach' dann noch 'nen Zweiten Plan,
Geh'n tun sie beide nicht
Bertolt Brecht, Die Dreigroschenoper. [1]

Anthony and Vancil (1. p. 5) define Management Control as "the process by which managers assure that resources are obtained and used effectively and efficiently in the accomplishment of the organization's objectives." Others narrow this definition down and distinguish "planning" (the setting of goals) from "control" (living up to the goals that were set). Whether we use the wider or the more limited definition, management control is the domain *par excellence* of formalized systems in organizations, and these systems tend to be designed according to a cybernetic philosophy.

Geert Hofstede (Ph.D. — University of Groningen, the Netherlands) is Professor of Organizational Behavior at the European Institute for Advanced Studies in Management, Brussels, Belgium, and at INSEAD, Fontainebleau, France.

Received 9/27/76; Revised 3/1/77; Accepted 7/27/77; Revised 10/13/77.

1 Brecht's Beggars Opera may exist in an English translation but I have not been able to locate it. My own imperfect translation of these German lines is:

"Just try to make a plan
for which you pick your brain
and after that, another plan:
your toil will be in vain".

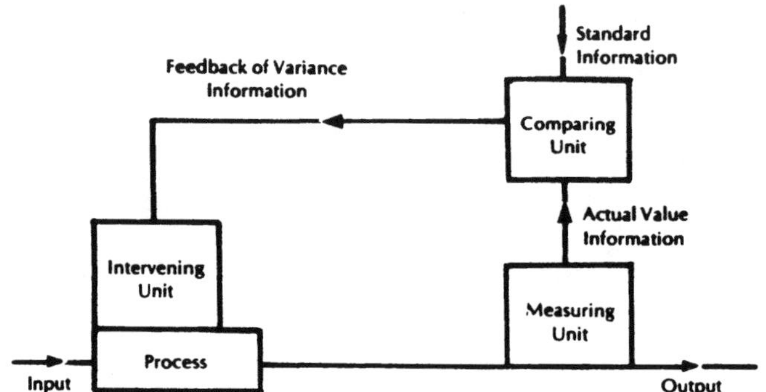

FIGURE 1. Technical Control Model of an Organizational Control System.

Source: G. Hofstede, *The Game of Budget Control* (Assen: Van Gorcum, and London: Tavistock, 1967), p. 84.

By "cybernetic" is meant a process which uses the negative feedback loop represented by: setting goals, measuring achievement, comparing achievement to goals, feeding back information about unwanted variances into the process to be controlled, and correcting the process. This is a much narrower use of the term "cybernetic" than that advocated by Wiener who coined it to deal with the transfer of messages in the widest sense (17), but it corresponds more closely to its present use in practice. In spite of (or maybe owing to) its simplicity, the cybernetic-in-the-narrow-sense feedback loop has attained the status of a proper paradigm in a wide area of systems theory including, but not limited to the management sciences (15). A review of nearly 100 books and articles on management control theory issued between 1900 and 1972 (4) reflects entirely the cybernetic paradigm.

In the cybernetic view, a management control process in its most simplified form is similar to a technical control process, for example, control of the heat of a room by a thermostat (see Figure 1).

The model in Figure 1 uses only first-order feedback. More sophisticated models for which technical analogues also can be found use higher order feedbacks to control the lower order controllers. Another possible control model used in technical devices is "feed-forward", sometimes presented as an alternative for management control. Feed-forward, however, assumes that interventions are programmable in advance as a known function of environmental disturbances — a condition unlikely to be fulfilled in most management control situations.

All cybernetic models of control have to assume that:

1. There is a standard, corresponding to effective and efficient accomplishment of the organization's objectives.
2. Actual accomplishment can be measured. In Figure 1, the "measuring unit" is connected to the output of the process, but the measuring may include data about the input, or about the ratio between output and input. For example, in an industrial production process, the quantity of various inputs (labour, materials, energy) for a given quantity of output may be measured.
3. When standard and measurement are compared and variance information is fed back, this information can be used to

intervene in the process so as to eliminate unwanted differences between measurement and standard for the next round.

There is no doubt that the cybernetic model of control has been eminently successful in the design of machines, electronic circuits, or similar technical systems, but management control in an organization is a social process in a social, or maybe socio-technical system. The "units" (see Figure 1) in this case are people, or even groups of people. This subjects the use of the cybernetic model to severe limitations because:

1. In many organizational situations, one or more of the three above-mentioned basic assumptions necessary for the validity of the cybernetic model are not justified: standards do not exist, accomplishment is not measurable, feedback information cannot be used. This is particularly the case for indirect (service) activities in industrial organizations and for all non-industrial organizations, such as schools, hospitals, and public bodies. I became painfully aware of this when discussing classical industrial-type management control (12) with a group of experienced management consultants working in non-industrial settings. After finding out that the cybernetic paradigm did not apply to these consultants' daily practice, we even started to wonder to what extent it *really* applies in many industrial settings.
2. The three assumptions of the presence of a standard, the measurability of accomplishment, and the usability of feedback are most justified for routine, industrial-type processes: industrial production and sales: the supplying of routine services to clients. But even these relatively machine-like processes are in reality social: the cybernetic control process as pictured by the model is only one of many interpersonal processes going on among the same people at the same time. Other processes — some of them by-products of the control system — may interfere with the control process, and sometimes may even lead to an outcome which is the opposite of what was intended by the designers of the system (6).

One remarkable fact about control processes in organizations which has become associated with the cybernetic paradigm is that they are usually tied to a division of labor — different units in the model correspond to different people who are specialized in their tasks. Measuring and comparing are often done by "staff" personnel of a controller's department, standards are set by higher "line" management, intervening is the task of lower line management, while the actual process to be controlled is carried out by operating personnel (workers). In the last resort, it is usually these workers' response to the control process which determines whether the control has been effective.

Proper functioning of the control process presupposes *communication* (17): the necessary messages should be sent and correctly received between the various specialized actors; it also presupposes that all will feel *motivated* to act according to the model (6). Already the proper sending and receiving of the necessary messages poses many problems, as the various persons involved have different types of education, work experience, and hold different values. The latter also affects their motivation pattern.

A difference in values between people in controllers' departments and line management is evident to anyone familiar with organizational folklore; moreover, it is illustrated by research. For example (6, p. 236), controllers' department personnel in five Dutch companies felt more than line managers that working does not come naturally to most people and that people therefore need to be controlled and prodded (a "Theory X" point of view); they also showed themselves more concerned with the method of measuring performances than with the content of what was measured. In another study of an international group of middle management personnel (8), those in accounting and control departments, compared to others, showed low concern for the efficiency and effectiveness of their actions but high concern with orderliness, following a systematic approach, and doing things according to a schedule. Both studies quoted suggest that people in control departments would tend to stress *form* where those in line roles would rather stress *content*.

In most cases, the controller's department is responsible not only for measuring and comparing, but also for design of the entire control system. An excessive stress on form rather than content explains why, at close scrutiny, many management control systems do *not* supply real control, but only "pseudo-control". Pseudo-control is a state of affairs in which a system is under control on paper (the figures look right) but not in reality. There are several ways to achieve pseudo-control, for example, by correcting the standards (rather than the process) whenever an important variance occurs, by choosing one's measures of performance so as to reflect the desired result (there are many ways to bend the figures without actually cheating), or by adjusting one element in the process at the expense of another which does not show up in the figures (reducing cost at the expense of quality).

The value differences between controller's department personnel and line management are just one type of social communication barriers in the system. We can also think of the way in which rank-and-file workers, with their particular education, work experience, and value systems, tend to react to control measures. We all know these are often met with considerable suspicion and resistance, going counter to the desired motivation, but control systems designers have been extremely slow to take account of these facts. As far back as 1953, Jonas (11, p. 188) signalled the tendency among cyberneticians to apply two kinds of doctrine — one to the people in their models, who are taken as robots, and another one to themselves: "he (the cybernetician) considers behavior, except his own; purposiveness, except his own; thinking, except his own". People usually dislike being taken as robots, and they will resist an organization built on such a double doctrine.

An Alternative Paradigm: Homeostasis

While the cybernetic paradigm, by distinguishing various "units" in the control process, has undoubtedly contributed to the division of labor in control process tasks, there can be cybernetic control without division of labor. Division of labor in control of production tasks may have been a productive innovation in the days of F. W. Taylor who advocated ". . . taking the control of the machine shop out of the hands of the many workmen, and placing it completely in the hands of the management, thus superseding 'rule of thumb' by scientific control" ("On The Art of Cutting Metals", 1906, p. 39; 4). It is recognized now that the separation of tasks and specialization which Taylor defended can go too far. What, among other factors, has changed since Taylor's days, at least in developed countries, is the worker. Today's worker is better educated, and to escape from starvation is no longer his or her primary work motive, but he or she can afford to look for a task with some intrinsic reward to it. Entrusting measuring, comparing, and intervening to specialized staff and line personnel implies an assumption that the operating personnel themselves cannot or do not want to adequately perform these tasks. This assumption, which is reinforced by the "Theory X" attitude found among certain people in controlling roles, may no longer be justified in many cases.

A fully documented example is available from a typewriter assembly workshop in Amsterdam (7). Up to 1969, assembly took place in long lines of 60-70 operators each. The process was controlled by specialists in various ways. Engineers calculated time standards and divided the total assembly job into individual tasks of as equal as possible duration. For control purposes, the lines were further divided into five sections of 12-14 operators. Each section had its quality inspector to check the section's production; quality inspectors produced computerized defect lists for the line manager, and specialized repair men repaired the defects. Five foremen, each assisted by a charge hand, supervised the five sections of two parallel assembly lines, so that each foreman was specialized in the supervision of one particular part of the assembly process. Foremen allocated workers to places, gave instructions, and watched over presence and absence; another computerized list showed the production and the various kinds of unproductive time for each worker. Specialized "dispatchers" provided the assembly operators with the parts they needed.

After extensive experiments, the department was reorganized in 1971 into semi-autonomous groups of 20 operators each. Operators divided the total assembly task among themselves according to each person's real capacities rather than based on a general standard. Quality defects were reported verbally within the group and corrected immediately; repair men became superfluous and switched to production. Operators started ordering their own parts instead of waiting for the dispatcher. The foreman's task changed drastically; it now demanded less technical, more social leadership, representing the group to the rest of the organization. Operators arranged among themselves replacement for temporary absences, and the production recording was reduced to counting the number of finished machines at the end of the day. The various computer lists were discontinued. Productivity increased by 18 percent in two months and continued improving: in the two-and-a-half years following the reorganization the total gain was 46 percent, and quality improved.

The new situation also posed new problems. At the worker level, training time for new operators increased. As groups rather than individuals had become the basic elements in the production system, stability of group composition became much more of an issue than before. For these reasons, rapid extension, change and reduction of production programs and levels posed more problems under the new system. The number of constraints for planning had increased, the process had become less flexible. An explosive production volume increase in 1974 led to severe productivity and quality problems in 1975. Another difficulty was that the new structure was limited to the worker level and was not reinforced by corresponding changes in structure and philosophy at higher levels in the hierarchy and in staff departments. People at the interface between the classical and the re-structured part of the organization, such as supervisors found their roles extremely difficult. As a result, the organization of the department moved back to more classical management control procedures in later years, although the small working groups with their aspect of job enlargement (work cycles of about ten minutes instead of three minutes in 1969) were retained.

The case shows that, under favorable circumstances, semi-autonomous groups were created and took over most of the management control roles previously fulfilled by superiors and specialists. All tasks within the classical cybernetic control loop — measuring, comparing, feedback, intervening — were carried out within the group itself. Its links to the organization's needs were mainly established through the *standards* set by others in the organization for the group's tasks. Quality standards were given by the quality control department based on sales and customer service requirements; delivery programs by the production control department; productivity standards were present in the form of past production records. Rather than cybernetic, I would call such a control process *homeostatic*. Its analogy is not a technical device like a thermostat but a biological element represented by a *living cell,* which is equipped with internal processes capable of maintaining an equilibrium in a changing environment, provided that the environmental conditions do not become too unfavorable.

Like the word' "cybernetic", "homeostatic" can be used to mean different things; the term is used here because of its predominantly biological connotation. Homeostatic processes are composed of cybernetic elements, but without the division of labor between controlling and controlled units; control is exercised within the system itself. We could also call these processes "self-regulating" (14).

The switch from a technical to a biological paradigm also explains one other aspect of homeostatic control processes which was illustrated in the typewriter assembly case: whereas a technical control device can quickly be put together and can be repaired if it breaks down, a cell must grow (which takes time), and it can die. Homeostatic control processes, therefore, are more vulnerable than cybernetic processes.

The transfer from cybernetic to homeostatic management control systems will demand a drastically changed control philosophy, especially with regard to the traditional division of labor tied to the cybernetic model. Those in controllers' departments involved in the design and introduction of control systems will have to widen their outlook to include a broad view of the socio-psychological processes going on between people in an organization. The homeostatic approach needs a new type of controllers. It may also need a new type of information systems. Considerable efforts are put today into developing and improving management information systems, but here again the designers' basic assumptions about socio-psychological processes are often remarkably simplistic and shallow.

Non-Cybernetic Processes

So far, we have dealt with control situations for which the three main conditions of the cybernetic model were fulfilled: a standard exists, accomplishment is measurable, feedback can be used for corrective intervention. If we consider the full range of human organizations in which control processes occur, those that satisfy the conditions for the cybernetic model tend to be the more structured ones, those which more or less fit a machine analogue. In a criticism of the cybernetic paradigm in system theory in general, Sutherland (15) makes applicability of cybernetic control dependent on the determinedness of a system. If phenomena are completely determined, cybernetic control is obviously superfluous. It becomes useful for moderately stochastic phenomena. When phenomena are severely stochastic, cybernetic control becomes either technically or economically unfeasible. When phenomena are completely undetermined, cybernetic control has become meaningless. Translated in terms of everyday organization activities, Sutherland's moderately stochastic phenomena are the more structured ones: the routine industrial-type processes referred to before. In many other organizational situations (indirect departments in industrial companies, public bodies, schools, hospitals, voluntary associations), we are in Sutherland's area of severely stochastic or even completely undetermined phenomena, and we meet with great problems in applying the cybernetic model. What we notice in practice when we try to follow a cybernetic approach is: (a) Objectives may be missing, unclear, or shifting; (b) Accomplishment may not be measurable; and/or (c) Feedback information may not be usable. Each of these three conditions is illustrated below.

1. *Objectives are missing, unclear, or shifting* — If there is to be a standard, there should be objectives from which this standard is derived. Setting of standards presupposes clarity about the organization's objectives. Now social scientists have often stressed that to speak of "an organization's objectives" is unallowable; organizations cannot have objections, only people can. We can speak of an organization's objectives only to the extent that there is either virtually complete consensus between all organization members about what should be done (for example, in a voluntary fire brigade); or a dominant coalition of persons within the organization

with sufficient power to impose their objectives on all others, and with consensus among themselves (as in many business enterprises); or a single power-holder whose objectives count as the organization's objectives (as in a small owner-controlled business firm).

Many organizations do not satisfy any of these three conditions, and their objectives are therefore ambiguous. Examples are:

— Democratic institutions such as the city governments in most Western countries — In this case, power is deliberately distributed among several persons or coalitions who hold different objectives for the entire organization; moreover, power is partly held by elected representatives, partly by permanent civil servants; the two groups differ considerably in their involvement with and expectations from the organization.

— Universities — Perhaps the extreme case of organizations in which power is widely distributed and different power groups hold very divergent views about objectives.

— Business organizations or parts of business organizations in which dominant coalitions are not unanimous about objectives — Business employees know that objectives may shift from one day to another, depending on who has the upper hand. This becomes even more likely where societal changes, such as attempts at establishing industrial democracy, bring new coalitions of organization members into the objective setting process.

In such cases, decisions, if they are consciously taken at all, are based on processes of negotiation and struggle and cannot be derived from any prior organizational objective. Objectives may forever remain unclear. This may even be true if someone in the organization publishes eloquent espoused objectives for public relations purposes — like those sometimes expressed in company charters. The objectives in use in the real-life situation of the organization's members are not necessarily the same as the published ones.

2. *Accomplishment is not measurable* — Even in cases where objectives are clear to all involved, it is often not possible to translate them into unambiguous, quantitative output standards against which performance can be measured. How should we measure the output of a police department? One of its final objectives is definitely to prevent crime, so we might consider the decrease of crime rates as an output measure. This assumes that other influences on crime rates can be neglected (which is not true) and that crime rates themselves can be measured objectively (whereas in fact they are partly derived from police reports; low reported crime rates could also mean administrative incompetence of police personnel to adequately register crimes). In such cases, organizations often resort to *surrogate* measures of performance (2), measures which are less directly tied to the organization's objectives but which are more easily measurable. In the case of the police department, the number of people arrested or the amount of fines levied could be such surrogate measures.

For many organizations or activities within organizations, outputs can only be defined in qualitative and vague terms; the only thing really measurable about such activities is their inputs — how much money and other resources will be allotted to them. These include most management and indirect activities in industrial organizations, like advertising, personnel departments, control activities in headquarters, research; most public bodies, like municipal and government services; most activities in schools, universities, hospitals and voluntary associations. In all these cases, the sole control of management exists at the time of resource allocation, but the criteria for resource allocation to this and not to that activity are judgmental. The essence of the process is negotiation, a political process in which many arguments other than the effective and efficient use of resources usually play a role — status of the negotiator, amount of support among influential persons which he/she might mobilize, personal relationship between negotiators, and sometimes nepotism.

One frequently used control device is whether similar funds allocated last year were really spent; its main effect is the spending of unnecessary funds. Skillful negotiators have many "ploys" at their disposal, and skillful resource allocators have many counter-ploys (2, p. 249). This is a part of the game of management control which has little to do with either effectiveness or efficiency of the organization — not because of anybody's evil intentions but simply because nobody is able to predict what resource allocation corresponds to maximum effectiveness.

3. *Feedback information is not usable* — The cybernetic model presupposes a recurring cycle of events: variance information is used to correct the present state of affairs to eliminate unwanted variances for the future. The model basically does not apply to one-time projects, like most investment projects, whether in private or in public organizations. As the project in its present form never returns, even large differences between planned and actual cost and performance have no effect on future projects.

It is remarkable that many organizations do not even attempt to do any project cost accounting to check whether predictions at the time of proposal were really fulfilled, and this can hardly be justified solely on the technical grounds that the benefits of one single project are difficult to disentangle. Once a proposal is accepted, the resources allocated to it become "sunk costs" and it is good management practice not to bother about such costs. However, this state of affairs stresses the negotiation element in the allocation of resources to investment projects even more. It is often hardly important whether the project's forecasted costs and performances are realistic — it is important that they "look good" to the person or persons who decide about the allocation. Once the decision is taken, few people worry about real outcomes. This leads to deliberate underestimation of costs. A common practice in the game of investment budgeting is, for example, to budget for the price of a machine but not for its installation costs, auxiliary tools, or spare parts; once the machine is bought, the organization is forced to spend on these other items to get it going.

A few organizations do use regular evaluation studies of past investment projects; Hägg (5) studied these investment reviews and claims as one of their potential effects a "symbolic use". There is no change impact as far as planning of future projects is concerned. But managers use the review procedure by, for example, referring to it as a sign of progressive management. They can do this when asked questions about capital investment activities by researchers or superiors. The review procedure can also be looked upon as "institutionalized", as part of a tradition or a myth in the organization (5, pp. 58-59). Of course, it is also possible that reviews do have a change impact, or that they have no impact at all, not even a symbolic one. Hägg notes a general lack of interest by managers in the reviews; in cases where reviews could reveal outright failures in investment decisions, we could expect them to be unpopular among those who proposed and took these decisions.

Enforcing a Cybernetic Model

With all its weaknesses, management control in situations which do meet the three basic conditions for applying the cybernetic model (presence of standards, measurable accomplishment, usable feedback) has still had a fair amount of success. In the developed countries of our world, an increasing part of the national income is spent on activities which do *not* meet these conditions — indirect departments in private organizations and all kinds of public activities, including education and health care.

Responsible managers have attempted to

find ways to control the considerable resources spent on such activities. The success of the cybernetic model in other situations has led them to try to enforce a cybernetic approach for indirect and public activities, as well. In practice, this has been done by calling successful industrial consultants (McKinsey!) to propose reorganizations for non-industrial organizations — reorganizations which rarely have been carried out and even more rarely been successful. The transfer of Robert McNamara from the Ford Corporation to the Secretary of Defense in the sixties began a movement in U.S. public agencies towards a "Planning/Programming/Budgeting System" which became widely known as PPBS or (PPB). PPBS has a number of objectives, but among these is control which it tries to execute by enforcing the cybernetic model, and in its most ambitious form it claims to apply to any organization. Reactions and experiences have been mixed. In 1967, C. L. Schultze, former Director, U.S. Bureau of the Budget, before a U.S. Senate Subcommittee, stated:

> I look forward to substantial improvements next year in terms of schedule, understanding of the role and desired character of the Program Memoranda, and, perhaps more important, in terms of their analytic content. Analytic staffs have been assembled and have had a chance to shake down; a number of data collection efforts and long term study efforts should reach fruition; and we are learning how to state program issues in a way that facilitates analysis and comparison. We have not yet by any means achieved my expectations for the system. That is partly because I have such high expectations for it. Ultimately I expect we will realize these expectations (1, p. 702).

However, Wildavsky noted:

> PPBS has failed everywhere and at all times. Nowhere has PPBS (1) been established and (2) influenced governmental decisions (3) according to its own principles. The program structures do not make sense to anyone. They are not, in fact, used to make decisions of any importance. Such products of PPBS as do exist are not noticeably superior in analytic quality or social desirability to whatever was done before" (18, pp. 363-364).

The fundamental problem of an approach like PPBS — which has spread to other countries in spite of its ambiguous results in the U.S.A. — may be precisely that it extrapolates a cybernetic philosophy derived from industrial production and sales situations to organizations of a very different nature and that it never asked the basic question whether and when this extrapolation is justified. Within the public system there are activities which meet the criteria for a cybernetic control approach, such as quantifiable public services: garbage collection, public transport, the Post Office. Other activities miss one or more of the fundamental conditions for the cybernetic model, and no amount of trying harder, setting up analytic staffs (with all the value conflicts involved), and data collection will overcome this.

There is a certain parallel between PPBS in public administration and another popular technique of the sixties mainly used in private organizations: *Management By Objectives* (MBO). MBO is also based on a cybernetic philosophy (15): objective setting (jointly between the employee, who is often himself a manager, and his superior), performance review, and corrective action. Not unlike PPBS, MBO is supported by believers but also heavily attacked. Levinson calls it "one of the greatest management illusions" and "industrial engineering with a new name" (13). Few cases of successful implementation of MBO have been reported — that is, cases in which others than the one responsible for the implementation claim it has been successful in improving performance. Ivancevich (9), besides reviewing the rare literature on research about MBO, reports on a 3-year longitudinal study on the introduction of MBO in two out of three plants of one U.S. manufacturing company. The results were mixed, with one plant showing significant long-term improvement in performance, and the other not. His study dealt with production workers and salesmen, organization members whose accomplishment is to some extent measurable. In these cases enforcement of a cybernetic control model by MBO may not be too difficult and, if the program is well managed, it may lead to performance improvement. However, MBO is also advocated, and applied, for indirect jobs, in medical institutions, school systems and government agencies. In these cases, accomplishment is much less measurable, and it is rare to find surrogates acceptable to both parties. If a commonly agreed measurement of accomplishment is lacking, the cybernetic model again does not apply, and MBO is simply bound to fail. A second reason why MBO may fail, even if the cybernetic model does apply, is that MBO is based on simplistic and mechanistic assumptions about the relationships among the people involved: it uses a reward-punishment psychology (13). There is more going on between people than cybernetic objective setting and feedback alone.

Political Control

Blanket application of a cybernetic philosophy to non-cybernetic organization processes can only do more harm than good. This does not mean that the advantages of the cybernetic approach *to those cases where it applies* have to be dropped. Within most organizations, even indirect and public ones, there are activities which *can* be controlled in a cybernetic way: those which are mechanized so that individuals play no role in them; those where individuals play a role, but where there is consensus about what this role should be; but it is necessary that performance be measurable so that standards can be set. In these cases, a cybernetic control philosophy — or preferably even a homeostatic philosophy — can make a real contribution. But often these cybernetic cases will be the exception. The more typically human and less mechanistic an activity, the less the chance that the conditions for a cybernetic approach will be met.

The essence of the non-cybernetic situations is that they are *political*; decisions are based on negotiation and judgment (as an employee of a Dutch city government expressed it: on enlightenment by the Holy Spirit). Decisions often deal with *policies*. There is a well-known slogan: "There is no reason for it. It's just our policy." What this means is that policy is not merely composed of rational elements; its main ingredients are *values*, which may differ from person to person, and *norms*, which are shared within groups in society but vary over time and from group to group (16). It makes little sense to speak of control processes here, at least in the formal sense in which such processes are described in cybernetic situations. It does make sense to speak of a control *structure*, taking into account the power positions of the various parties in the negotiations. Within this structure, we may study the control *games* played by the various actors (3). Once resources are allocated, there is no automatic feedback on the effectiveness of their use; the only controls possible are whether the resources were really spent and if no funds were embezzled. Beyond that, it is a matter of trust in those in charge of carrying out the programs; the real control takes place through the appointing of a person to a task. Activities once decided upon will tend to perpetuate themselves; corrective actions in the case of ineffective or inefficient activities are not automatically produced by the control system but ask for a specific evaluation study; deciding upon such a study is in itself a political act which may upset an established balance of power.

As an example of a control aid that is still feasible in such a situation, Wildavsky (18, Ch. 19) describes the Public Expenditure Survey Committee (PESC) in the U.K. The PESC is an interdepartmental group which establishes a yearly report, showing the future cost of existing government policies, if these policies remain unchanged, over the next five years. The product of PESC is not planning or management control as such; it does not try to measure or evaluate outputs. It only presents an educated forecast of already committed inputs, as a base line for governmental planning and policy making. PESC does not assume any cybernetic model.

Conclusion: The Use of Models

In thinking about organizations, we cannot escape from using models. To see why this is so, I find it helpful to refer to the General Hierarchy of Systems which was first formulated in different ways by Von Bertalanffy and Boulding (10, pp. 7-9). In the General Hierarchy of Systems, nine levels of complexity of systems are distinguished:

1. Static frameworks,
2. Dynamic systems with predetermined motions,
3. Closed-loop control or cybernetic systems,
4. Homeostatic systems like the biological cell,
5. The living plant,
6. The animal,
7. Man,
8. Human organizations, and
9. Transcendental systems.

Every next level adds a dimension of complexity to the previous one.

So we find organizations at Level 8, where the complexity is overwhelming. As the individual is at Level 7, it is fundamentally impossible for the human brain to grasp what goes on at Level 8. In order to think about organizations, we have to simplify: we use lower-level systems which we can understand as models for what we cannot understand. Early thinkers about organizations focussed on the organization chart, a first-level model. Scientific management was often concerned with procedures, second-level models. The cybernetic control process is already a more complex, third-level model, and the homeostatic "cell" model is found at the fourth level.

One consequence of the use of lower-level systems as models for organizations is that we automatically consider the people in the system (at least all except ourselves — see the quote from Jonas above), as if they were things — as means to be used; the goals are supposed to be given. But in fact, all organization goals derive from people: in the hierarchy of systems, the source of organization goals is at Level 7, with the individual. In an organization, the individual is *both goal and means;* but the use of lower level models implies dealing with people as means. We may do this only when there is consensus over goals, or goals can be imposed — so we see these are not just conditions for the applicability of the cybernetic model, but for any lower-level model, including biological ones.

In political situations, there is no consensus about goals, and replacing the organizational reality by a model which treats people as means is no longer allowed. Using a cybernetic model — such as PPBS — in such a case means a covering up of the real issues and will be perceived rightly by most people involved as an attempt by a technocratic coalition to impose their implicit goals on all others.

REFERENCES

1. Anthony, R. N., J. Dearden, and R. F. Vancil. *Management Control Systems: Text, Cases and Readings,* rev. ed. (Homewood, Ill.: R. D. Irwin, 1972).
2. Anthony, R. N., and R. Herzlinger. *Management Control in Nonprofit Organizations* (Homewood, Ill.: R. D. Irwin, 1975).
3. Crozier, M. "Comparing Structures and Comparing Games," in G. Hofstede and M. S. Kassem (Eds.), *European Contributions to Organization Theory* (Assen: Van Gorcum, 1976), pp. 193-207.
4. Giglioni, G. B., and A. G. Bedeian. "A Conspectus of Management Control Theory: 1900-1972," *Academy of Management Journal,* Vol. 17 (1974), 292-305.
5. Hagg, I. "Reviews of Capital Investments," in S. Asztely (Ed.), *Budgeting och Redovisning som Instrument for Styrning* (Stockholm: P. A. Norstedt, 1974), pp. 53-68.
6. Hofstede, G. *The Game of Budget Control* (Assen, Van Gorcum, and London: Tavistock Publications, 1967).

7. Hofstede, G. "Deux Cas de Changement," in H. C. de Bettignies (Ed.), *Maitriser le Changement dans l'Entreprise* (Paris: Les Editions d'Organisation, 1975), pp. 175-199.
8. Hofstede, G. "Nationality and Espoused Values of Managers," *Journal of Applied Psychology*, Vol. 61, No. 2 (1976), 148-155.
9. Ivancevich, J. M. "Changes in Performance in a Management by Objectives Program," *Administrative Science Quarterly*, Vol. 19 (1974), 563-577.
10. Johnson, R. A., F. E. Kast, and J. E. Rosenzweig. *The Theory of Management of Systems* (New York: McGraw-Hill, 1963).
11. Jonas, H. "A Critique of Cybernetics," *Social Research*, Vol. 20 (1953), 172-192.
12. Juran, J. M. *Managerial Breakthrough: A New Concept of the Manager's Job* (New York: McGraw-Hill, 1964).
13. Levinson, H. "Management by Whose Objectives?" *Harvard Business Review*, Vol. 48, No. 4 (1970), 125-134.
14. Sandkull, B. "The Discontinuity of Modern Industry: A Quest for an Alternative Principle of Organizational Control," *Research Report No. 31* (Linkoping: Department of Management and Economics, Linkoping University, 1975).
15. Sutherland, J. W. "System Theoretical Limits on the Cybernetic Paradigm," *Behavioral Science*, Vol. 20 (1975), 191-200.
16. Vickers, G. *Making Institutions Work* (London: Associated Business Programmes, 1973).
17. Wiener, N. *The Human Use of Human Beings: Cybernetics and Society*. 2nd rev. ed. (Garden City, N.Y.: Doubleday, 1954).
18. Wildavsky, A. *Budgeting: A Comparative Analysis of the Budgetary Process*. (Boston: Little, Brown, 1975).

[18]

A CONTINGENT METHODOLOGY FOR MANAGEMENT CONTROL

BY

JOHN L. J. MACHIN

Introduction

THE purpose of this article is to describe the design and mode of use of a new management control system which has been developed and tested over the last four years with the assistance of over 1500 managers from more than thirty-five organizations. The actions, reactions, and expressed support of the managers who have been involved in the development and use of the system operationally, indicate that it has immediate, practical, managerial usefulness and the potential for further operational development. Managers ascribe the former to the basic simplicity of the system, whilst their support for the latter appears to be derived from the contingent nature of both the system's design and the way in which managers have used it.

This article is not designed to report findings on a case-by-case basis or to describe what has been discovered about operational and individual effectiveness in the many organizations which have participated in the system's development, but rather by describing the system's design and the way in which managers have used it, to show that it is both practically viable and conceptually sound. It seeks to explain, in other words, what led an engineering director of a multinational company to write recently, after having used the system with some of his colleagues, 'I believe this new approach to be one of the best management systems we have met in recent years'.

Key Design Decisions

One of the key questions which any systems designer has to face is 'What do I include in, and what do I exclude from, the system?' For the management control system designer that decision has been particularly difficult, given the complexity of most managerial jobs and the variety of information which he uses to perform effectively. It has long been recognized that a manager in the course of day-to-day management is more dependent on situationally derived information for his success than on system-supplied information.[1] A detailed situational analysis would indicate that in one or more respects each manager's job is unique, whilst a systems analysis at the appropriate level of abstraction would show that all managers' jobs contain many identical elements. Recent developments in the field of contingency theory have

[1] Dalton, G. W. and Lawrence, P. R., *Motivation and Control in Organizations*, Homewood, Ill.: Irwin, 1971.

sharpened the focus of attention on two key questions in respect of management control.[2]

1. *Who should define the system's boundaries and content?* The choice would appear to be between the users as a group, each user individually, or a system designer. The goal of the contingency theorists is clear. 'The overall goal of a contingency theory of management would be to match quantitative, behavioural and systems approaches with appropriate situational factors.'[3] The only person who can adequately determine which situational factors are appropriate in a given managerial situation is the manager concerned and, therefore, it follows that if a system is to be truly contingent, each individual user must be able to control and specify both the boundaries and the content of his part of the system.
2. *Who should decide on the most effective way of using the system once it is developed?* Once again the choice appears to be between the users as a group, each user individually or the system designer. In response to this question General Systems Theory (G.S.T.) offers the most positive guide to a solution. Whilst each manager is the person most fully aware of the key contingent variables in the situation which he is managing, that situation is merely one of many such situations in the total organization. It follows that if the parts of an organization are to cooperate and coordinate their activities effectively the management control system must be used systematically and consistently by all the system users.

The system which has evolved provides a fruitful link between G.S.T. and contingency theory. Each user individually controls the boundaries and content of his part of the system. The methodology of using the system as a means of helping users to manage more effectively has been developed by user groups deciding on how they will use it and then agreeing to use it consistently.

System Development

The system was developed to provide a manager with the information which he feels he needs to do his job effectively, and is therefore concerned with relationships as well as roles. The complex patterns of interrelationships and interlocking behaviour which form the usual environment for managerial

[2] For additional insight into this subject, the reader is referred to Newstrom, John W., Reif, William, E. and Monczka, Robert M., *A Contingency Approach to Management: Readings*, New York: McGraw-Hill, 1975.

[3] Luthans, Fred, 'The Contingency Theory of Management: A Path Out of the Jungle', *Business Horizons*, June 1973, pp. 67–72.

activity make it very difficult for most managers to get an accurate perception of the total detail of their jobs. A major part of this difficulty stems from problems associated with managerial communication. It is supposed to be a two-way process though research has shown that all too often it is two-way only in the sense that poor communication of what is expected is matched by inadequate and/or inaccurate perception of what has been communicated.[4] The reasons for this are fairly clear. Communication channels to or from any one manager may be vertical, horizontal, or diagonal relative to organization structure. They may be formal or informal and will usually be large in number. Apart from other factors which influence communication accuracy, the sheer multiplicity of channels[5] in respect of a manager's job tends to lead to breaks in communication links that go unnoticed and, therefore, unmended. The information being carried by them may become misdirected, diffused, altered, misinterpreted, or simply lost in the noise of the system.

As the managerial environment becomes more dynamic and complex it is increasingly important to develop sensitive, responsive, controls which enable mangers to cope with and enjoy the challenges which that dynamic complexity poses to them. In the context of management control that means

> that the manager should be neither over nor under-informed, and it is essential that the information he receives is relevant. This condition requires that the information is focused on what the manager himself can manage, on what he can control.[6]

It also means, of course, that the unit of information chosen for a management control system must be relevant to *any* kind of managerial input or output. This obviously ruled out an accounting unit in the opinions of the managers involved in the design of the system, and they decided to choose a unit of communication as the basic unit.

The unit chosen was an '*expectation*'. Managers found that they were able to express their input needs and output objectives most easily and clearly in terms of expectations; first, in terms of the expectations which other people hold of them, and which they are trying to meet and, secondly, in terms of the expectations they hold of others in respect of, for example, support, information, cash or decision-making, without which they could not do their own jobs satisfactorily.

The existence of expectations and, perhaps more appropriately, the

[4] Machin, John L. J., 'Management Applications of the Expectations Approach: Management Summary Report', U.K.S.C. 0077, Peterlee, Co. Durham: I.B.M., U.K. Ltd., September 1975.

[5] Ference, T. P. 'Organizational Communication Systems and the Decision Process', *Management Science*, Vol. 17, No. 2, October 1970, pp. B 83–96.

[6] Sihler, William H., 'Toward Better Management Control Systems', *California Management Review*, Vol. 14, No. 2, Winter 1971, p. 38.

interpretation of expectations in an organizational setting, has been an important area of focus in many earlier research studies. Katz and Kahn[7] noted that characteristics of the organization as a whole, of its subsystems, and of the location of particular positions, act to determine the expectations which managers will hold and communicate to each other. Whilst the holding and sending of such expectations is personal and direct, their content is nevertheless shaped by systemic factors.

An 'expectations analysis' has been seen as a potentially useful approach in that it could provide a better basis for communicating job content information and focus on the existing state of interpersonal relationships in a given situation. Parsons and Shils[8] discussed role expectations in terms of universalistic–particularistic dimensions and this approach is useful in helping to understand the focal person's primary relationships with his work associates. Kahn *et al.*[9] have studied the normative expectations of persons engaged in an organization. They hold the view that a norm consists of expectations held in common and usually shared by all (or nearly all) members, but that many expectations for a role may each be held by only a single role-sender. This latter view indicates that some, if not all, role-related expectations will be contingent upon the personal attributes and attitudes of the role holder.

Clearly most people do not have the resources to meet each and every expectation which is held of them in either their working or their societal roles. Each person has, therefore, to choose which expectations he or she will attempt to meet. The process of choosing is complex because there are many, frequently conflicting, criteria which may be used to assess the relative importance, relevance, usefulness, or difficulty of an expectation, or the differing degrees of personal satisfaction which would be derived from successfully meeting different expectations.

For the purposes of system design, therefore, the role of a manager was defined as one of 'meeting the expectations appropriately held of him in connection with his work by other people within and outside the organization by which he is employed'.[10]

Clearly no manager is a system closed unto himself. A thorough review of the key literature in the management control field and the subsequent

[7] Katz, Daniel and Kahn, Robert L., *The Social Psychology of Organizations*, New York: Wiley, 1966.

[8] Parsons, Talcott and Shils, Edward (Eds.), *Toward a General Theory of Action*, Cambridge, Mass.: Harvard University Press, 1954.

[9] Kahn, R. L., Wolfe, D. M., Quinn, R. P., Snoek, J. D. and Rosenthal, R. A., *Organizational Stress: Studies in Role Conflict and Ambiguity*, New York: Wiley, 1964.

[10] Machin, John L. J., 'Measuring the Effectiveness of an Organization's Management Control Systems — The Expectations Approach', *Management Decision*, Vol. 11, No. 3, Winter 1973, pp. 260–79.

development of a framework for empirical studies[11] made it clear that a contingent methodology must avoid substituting a larger closed system for a smaller one. Contingent factors will come and go, and change in their situational importance and relevance, and the system had to exhibit both the robustness and flexibility necessary to cope with the fluid reality of the managerial role.

The choice of an 'expectation' as the basic unit of information within the management control system had the additional result of producing a system which incorporates the attributes described by Lowe and McInnes,[12] *i.e.* the system can operate effectively at any 'resolution level' from that of the whole organization to that of the individual manager.

Organizations are formed to meet the expectations of a range of other organizations, groups and individuals. The survival and development of an organization depends on its ability to anticipate, and/or adapt to, changes in the content and pattern of expectations held by the substantive environment (or stakeholders) and changes in the relative importance of different expectations and expectation-holders. An organization must choose appropriately which expectations it will plan to meet and recognize that there will be many different ways of managing the generation of the necessary output.

At the organizational level the process is called strategic planning, but the rationale of the process is equally relevant for an organization, a department or subgroup. What changes is not the rationale of the basic system assumptions, it is the degree of detail which appears in the relevant appropriate expectations. Since the unit of communication which managers chose to form the basis of the management control system was an 'expectation', it is not surprising that the managers who have worked with it over the last four years have given it the colloquial title of the 'Expectations Approach'.

The 'Expectations Approach' Management Control System Elements

The system has been developed and modified by a large number of users and whilst it has already reached an advanced state of flexible usefulness, the pattern of regular improvement over four years probably means that the system's evolution is not yet complete. Managers in different organizations have often developed organization-specific ways of using the system, but the basic elements of the system have remained constant and are described in the following statements:

[11] Nelson, Edwin G. and Machin, John L. J., 'Management Control: Systems Thinking Applied to the Development of a Framework for Empirical Studies', *Journal of Management Studies*, Vol. 13, No. 3, October 1976, pp. 274–87.

[12] Lowe, E. A. and McInnes, J. M., 'Control in Socio-Economic Organizations: A Rationale for the Design of Management Control Systems', *Journal of Management Studies*, Vol. 8, No. 2, May 1971, pp. 1–12.

A. An expectation can be generated only by a person (not a thing) and therefore every expectation has an identifiable 'subject', namely the person who holds the expectation.

B. A specific expectation can be met only by a person (not a thing) and therefore every expectation must have an 'object', namely the person of whom the expectation is held.

[Two points of clarification are needed here about the 'object'. Frequently a manager holds an expectation that a particular department (say 'Accounts') will supply him with something (say 'accurate, monthly, budget variance reports on the controllable costs in his responsibility centre within eight days of the end of the month'), but does not know, and probably does not even care, which person within that department will produce the information. He therefore specifies the head of the department as the 'object' of the expectation. Secondly, many managers hold one or more generalized expectations of a number of people. In every case these have been initially expressed as a number of identical expectations, each with an individual manager as the object.]

C. There are two kinds of expectations — 'actual' and 'perceived'. 'Actual' expectations are the expectations which a subject manager holds of others in connection with his job (*i.e.* the inputs he needs to generate his own output). 'Perceived' expectations are the expectations which a manager thinks (or perceives) others to hold of him (*i.e.* the outputs which other people want from him).

D. Expectations vary in importance both to an individual manager and to the organization as a whole, so it is important to be able to record the priority of an expectation.

E. Expectations vary in type (*e.g.* content or function) and it is important for senior management to check to see that key organizational processes or procedures are being implemented satisfactorily. It is therefore necessary to be able to identify the volume, direction and content of communication of a particular kind — *e.g.* management development, or procurement, or customer creditworthiness, *etc.*

F. Expectations are not always met! It is important therefore both for the achievement of organizational purpose and for individual performance appraisal that expectations are performance-rated either in terms of the extent to which they have been met (feedback) or the extent to which a manager believes they will be met (feedforward).

G. Expectations are contingent on the situation being managed. Each manager can express as many or as few expectations as he believes to be necessary to enable him to do his job both efficiently and effectively.

H. Expectations are contingent on the individual's personality, experience, and commitment. Therefore each manager may express his expectations in his own way, in his own language.

None of these eight statements is either new or contentious. The existence and importance of the distinction between actual and perceived expectations, for example, has been discussed frequently enough in the literature on organizations.[13] What is new is that user managers have seen fit to incorporate all eight elements into a single, operational, management control system. The result is a system whose design owes much to contingency theory, and whose use by managers has been contingent on the particular needs and objectives of particular groups of managers.

The remainder of this article outlines the methodology which managers have developed for using this new contingent management control system. What follows is a 'composite' methodology for using the 'Expectations Approach' management control system based on observations of how managers in over thirty-five organizations have used it. (The details of the mechanics of the system, data-collection forms, managerial reports, procedures and computer programs are fully documented elsewhere.[14] Any reader wishing to use the system may obtain copies of the specified references from the author.)

A Methodology for Using the 'Expectations Approach' Management Control System

Observation of managerial use of the system has provided many examples of individually different choices of how best to use the system to meet the personal needs of a manager facing specific situational problems, or the specific needs of an organization. Researchers have, however, identified three basic phases in the methodology of managerial use. Not all of the organizations researched have used every phase of the methodology, and not all of the organizations which have used a given phase have used each of the elements of the phase described in the remainder of this article. What is presented is the current stage of developed use of a system whose methodology for use has evolved under the control of managers who were also specifying the developments in the design of the mechanics of the computer supported system itself.

[13] Lawrence, P. R. and Lorsch, J. W., *Developing Organizations: Diagnosis and Action*, Reading, Mass.: Addison-Wesley, 1969, p. 17; also, Beckhard, R., *Organization Development: Strategies and Models*, Reading, Mass.: Addison-Wesley, 1969, p. 34.

[14] Machin, John L. J., 'Annotated Index to Expectations Approach Working Paper Series', Durham University Business School Expectations Approach Working Paper 1, Durham, England, 1978.

Note: This Working Paper series contains papers by both managers and researchers on different uses of the Expectations Approach and user manuals for the programs which are currently available in PLI, Fortran and Cobol.

The three phases identified are:

1. Clarification of what is wanted by whom and from whom.
2. Planning job inputs and outputs.
3. Performance reporting.

The processes observed in the last two phases were not significantly different *in concept* from those found in connection with other management control systems such as budgetary control or M.B.O., but the *practical managerial activity of implementing those processes* when using the E.A. management control system were as different from the activities involved in respect of budgets or an M.B.O. programme as they are from each other.

Two of the more important causes of those differences are the contingent nature of the information which the system uses and the methodology whereby that information is collected and clarified. For this reason the methodology which managers have developed for Phase 1 is of particular interest and relevance.

Phase 1. Clarification of What is Wanted by Whom and from Whom

Since the management control system was based on data different from that used by any control system with which the managers were familiar, and since it was designed to enable the user to decide on the layout and content of the planning and control reports he or she wanted, it seemed likely that the system, simply by being different, would give rise to different methodologies of use from those associated with systems with which the managers were familiar. The very first report which managers called for demonstrated to many of them the justification for, and the importance of, the increasing concern which is being expressed about the quality of planning and control communications within organizations.

Most managers when reading their first reports (see table I) found that they themselves were not always communicating sufficiently clearly to others what they expected from them, and the report showed that the intended recipients of such communication sometimes perceived it less clearly and occasionally failed to perceive it at all.

Since the E.A. management control system was found to offer a basis on which a methodology could be developed for dealing with this problem contingently at the very start of the planning and control process, it may be helpful to the reader to be presented initially with a scheme (figure 1) of the steps in the methodology which managers have developed for handling Phase 1 of the use of the system.

Clearly, in respect of those requirements where the actual expectation is unambiguous, where the perceived expectation is perfectly matched (*i.e.*

TABLE I. Initial report before any interpersonal discussion has taken place

Expectations which manager E.N.J. actually holds of manager P.D.B.	*Expectations which manager P.D.B. perceives manager E.N.J. to hold of him.*
—Arrange the purchase of all materials as directed by authorized managers. —Arrange the provision of all services as directed by authorized managers. —Negotiate supplier contracts as directed. —Compile any necessary information requested by authorized managers. —Directly supervise buying office staff. —Provide requested information for cash flow control. —Regular briefing on current events in buying office. —Support agreed administrative policies and procedures. —Maintain buying records as agreed. —Arrange efficient scrutiny of purchase invoices prior to passing for payment. —Ensure sufficient information is presented to facilitate accurate analysis of purchase invoices.	—To supply information regarding present and future trends in obtaining materials. —To carry out purchasing function to maximize profitability of company. —To supply written reports on projects together with accurate costings and recommendations to allow decisions to be made. —To supply information on fluctuations or alterations in supply costs at earliest possible time. —To carry out purchasing function in such a manner as to enhance the company's reputation with suppliers. —To supply accurate information regarding expenditure to assist in forecasting cash flow. —To vet all requisitions and obtain goods at the most reasonable cost. —To maintain accurate purchase records to assist in the passing of invoices. —To accurately check and verify all invoices and pass to allow payment by accounts department. —To prepare accurate sales invoices for origination.
Expectations which manager E.N.J. perceives manager P.D.B. to hold of him	*Expectations which manager P.D.B. actually holds of manager E.N.J.*
—Regular briefing on current management policies. —Give or obtain decisions when requested. —Authorization for certain purchases. —Advice on personal decisions. —Advice on personnel matters concerning buying staff. —Clear understanding of personal duties. —Support for departmental policies.	—To make impartial assessment of staff problems and take remedial action. —Give backing to assist in carrying out purchasing policy. —Advise on areas to be improved upon in department. —To improve knowledge of day-to-day working of buying department. —To give advice on financial matters affecting purchasing policy. —To advise on company policy affecting purchasing department. —Advise areas which you consider I may improve myself. —To assist in establishing lines of communication. —To give advice where I need to make a decision.

Notes:

1. This table is part of a typical report produced by the 'Expectations Approach' system for a manager.
2. In this table the subject manager is E.N.J. and it depicts his working relationship with manager P.D.B.
3. On the left hand side are the expectations produced by E.N.J. and on the right hand side are those expectations produced by manager P.D.B. The two sides may be directly compared to assess the match of communication.

Figure 1. Clarification of what is wanted by whom and from whom: An outline of steps in the Phase I methodology

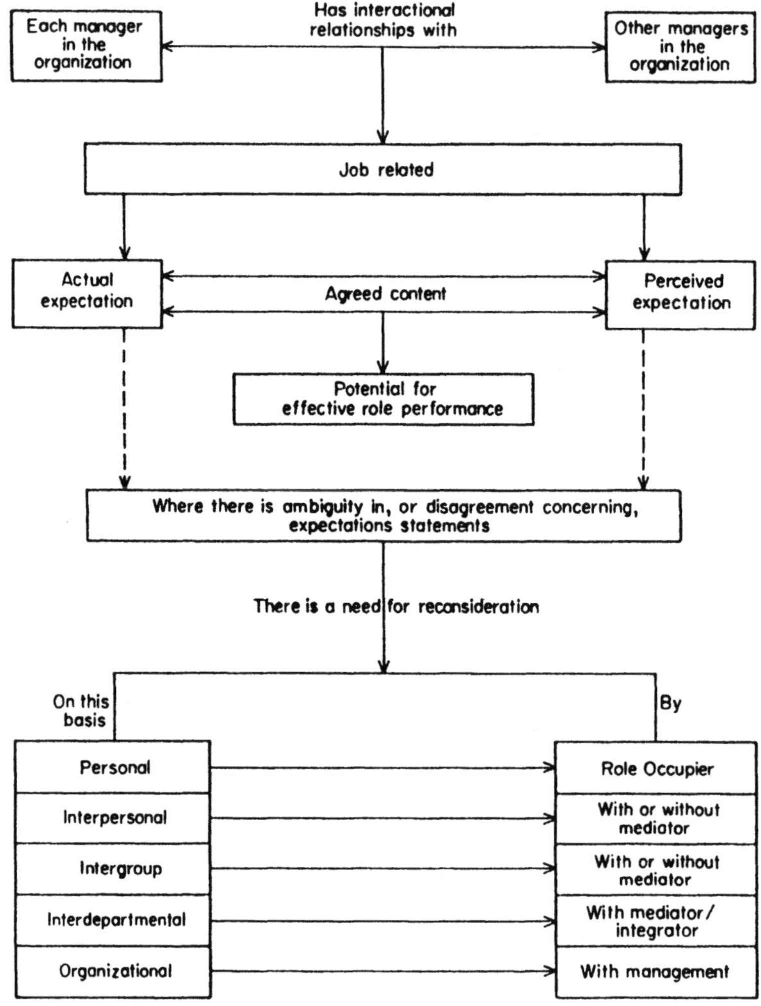

[Figure 1 was developed by Nurur Rahman when undertaking research at Durham University Business School.]

accurately communicated), where the contents are likely to contribute to the achievement of known organizational goals, and where the 'object' manager concerned agrees to try to meet what is required of him, there is the potential for effective role performance.

When there is ambiguity in the statement of what is required, or poor communication, or disagreement about either the organizational relevance of the requirement or whether the 'object' manager could, should, or will, try to meet that requirement, then equally clearly there is the danger of ineffective role performances.

The scale of the problem can be illustrated by taking as an example some data in respect of the use of the E.A. management control system recently used by thirty directors and senior managers in a multinational organization. Their initial reports contained 3826 expectations. After following the Phase 1 methodology outlined below they individually and collectively decided that it was necessary and/or desirable to add, delete or modify a total of 718 expectations.

The volume and complexity of the communication channels involved and the need to maintain the situational relevance of the content of the communication are both factors with which managers are familiar from normal day-to-day experience. Presented with a system which enables them to cope with those factors in a methodical and controlled manner managers have developed a methodology for using that system which is based on gradual and sequential review and discussion aimed at clarifying ambiguity and then either resolving or accepting disagreement.

The first step in the methodology which managers use is invariably self-appraisal. Managers have consistently reported that the first thing that has struck them when reading their first reports is that they have often been far from clear or precise when expressing their requirements of colleagues. Clarifying in their own minds what they really need from others is obviously a highly personal process for the managers involved, but it leads fairly naturally to the next step of checking to see how accurately their colleagues perceive what is wanted from them and, thence, to the final step of checking to see how well they in their turn are perceiving accurately what their colleagues want from them. The initial step in the methodology is personal analysis of the first report.

Phase 1, Step 1. Personal analysis. The range of expectations set down by managers in connection with their own jobs is notable for the diversity of content which is covered. The traditional approach of dividing management into organizing, motivating, planning and controlling is far too simplistic a selection of topics from the wide range of expectations which managers hold of each other in connection with their jobs. Table I showed the range of expectations carried by one dyadic channel in a medium-sized profit-seeking organization, but the following examples will give readers a feel for the range of actual expectations which find their way into the system:

1. To visit customers to sort out their problems especially packaging machine ones.

2. Award an immediate increase in my salary of 50 per cent.
3. To supply information about any work on the autoweigh plant required to be carried out by his department.
4. To improve working conditions by at least 10 per cent per year.
5. That your subordinates will provide me with routine information on serious customer complaints.
6. To see that customers are advised of company holidays.
7. To listen to constructive ideas and react.
8. To satisfy himself that newly opened accounts are progressing satisfactorily.
9. Take an enthusiastic interest in special assignments.
10. To ensure board and delivery lead times and price increases are advised to salesmen.
11. To expect and ask for progress reports from salesmen.
12. To seek out new accounts and secure orders.

The above selection of examples was chosen exclusively from subject managers' actual expectations *which were not perceived at all* by the specified object managers in the initial report. Such ostensibly broken (*i.e.* unreceived) communication attempts clearly matter to the managers concerned though the existence of imperfect communication is understandable when set in the context of a typical manager's report. In one company where all the managers are currently using the Approach the 'average' manager's report covered twenty communication channels and contained approximately 350 expectations (approximately 160 perceived and 190 actual). Given the number of communication channels, the volume of communication and the sheer breadth of kinds or 'types' of expectations, it is hardly surprising that very few managers have claimed to find a 'perfect match' between actual and perceived expectations in their first communication reports.

Almost every manager, as he read his first expectation report, has been led to reflect on the material which he himself provided. Sometimes a manager has found that the expectations expressed about his own job by some of his colleagues are clearer than those he put down himself, but usually the reverse is the case.

Managers often find views expressed in expectation statements with which they disagree more or less strongly, and discover the absence from their report of expectations which they feel should have been there.

The first process of clarification is usually done by the role-occupier on his own. He can step outside his job and compare his view of it with the way that others see it. In particular managers have tended to differentiate between three categories of expectations because the process of clarification is likely to be different for each.

A. Relationship expectations. Many expectations carry statements about the personal relationships that exist between managers. These expectations are concerned with the relationships that two specified individuals have, the nature of those relationships, and the extent to which one or other person would choose to see them changed and improved. These expectations are contingent on the individual personalities, attributes and experience of the people performing their roles and on the situations within which they manage. These expectations change when role-incumbents change and can really only be negotiated by the individual managers involved.

B. Role expectations. The second identifiable category of content constitutes expectations about the role that is being performed by each individual, and are role-related in the sense that they are not related to the personality or individualism of the person performing that role. Managers identify within this category those expectations which would not change if a different individual were to replace the role-incumbent. The quality of these expectations is often contingent on the effectiveness of the organizational process of developing job descriptions.

C. Regulation expectations. The third category of content incorporates those expectations that are concerned with regulations surrounding the operation of the role. These expectations relate to authority, responsibility, and accountability, and the manner in which those three elements will be handled. Frequently there is considerable disparity between the formal expression of such expectations represented by say the organizational structure, the way in which authority, responsibility and accountability are actually operated and the way in which different managers feel they should be operated. Regulation expectations are contingent because they are expressed in a form which represents one or other of the last two viewpoints.

The specific clarification process for the role-occupier to undertake on his own is to reconsider the content of the actual and perceived expectations in his report and to determine which of them are ambiguous or unmatched.

If an expectation is to stand much of a chance of being met in the manner which the holder desires, it needs to have four elements:

1. Content — a precise description of what is expected.
2. Quality — a precise statement of the quality that is required.
3. Quantity — a precise statement of how much is wanted.
4. Timing — a clear statement of when the expectation should be met.

It is predictable that in organizations of any real size or complexity, a significant body of expectations will not be accurately communicated and accurately perceived, and experience has shown that some of these can be important.

There is a proven need, therefore, for each role-occupier to refine some of the statements he has made in respect of his own expectations and to identify those of the expectations expressed by his colleagues, which he finds either ambiguous or unsatisfactory. Thus each manager identifies the specific matters which he wishes to clarify in a way which will ensure that when he discusses the communication of expectations with other managers, he is clear in his own mind what he hopes to achieve.

It is at this stage that managers demonstrate the individuality which is made possible by the fact that the 'Expectations Approach' allows each individual manager to participate in developing and controlling *his own* information system, to meet *his own* situational needs. By simply stating the expectations that he holds he can describe and define the basic interaction patterns and working groups involved with his own job, and do so in a way which can form the basis for resolving areas of misunderstanding and opening new, clear lines of communication, thereby increasing both individual effectiveness and personal satisfaction. No longer is the individual manager trying to operate at the intersection point of a number of general purpose systems; he becomes the focal point of a process of mutual interactivity based on a management control system whose data-base can be controlled by him to support the clarification of his role and relationships, in as open a manner as he himself chooses.

The first step in clarifying ambiguity and mismatch is therefore an individual and personal review of both the content of the communication report and the attitude which the individual will take towards the remaining elements in the process as outlined in the scheme in figure 1. This starts with interpersonal discussion aimed at resolving the ambiguities in the report and seeks to discover whether disagreements on the content or even the existence of job related expectations is a function of oversight or intention.

Phase 1, Step 2. Interpersonal discussion. Managers' priorities in initiating interpersonal discussion have varied widely, though most have used the first discussion of the communication report with another manager to sort out quickly those ambiguities or apparent disagreements which are the result of oversight (not as frequent as one might at first imagine) or poor communication, from those which represent genuine disagreement. Most of the former can be dealt with pretty easily and the necessary additions, clarifications, or deletions made to the data-base, whilst genuine disagreements, once identified, tend to be left for a second, arranged, meeting.

Differences in managerial style are readily apparent in this part of Phase 1 of using the system. Since each manager may have communication with anything up to twenty or thirty other people in his report, he has the opportunity of either planning the order in which he will approach them or just leaving it to the next suitable informal meeting. Some managers seek to arrange discussions first with all the more senior managers who feature in their report, others concentrate initially on clarifying communication with their immediate subordinates, and yet others have just carried their reports around in their briefcases and discussed the contents with each person as and when a suitable occasion presented itself.

It is in this stage of Phase 1 that the implications of the contingent nature of the system become fully apparent to the managers themselves or to an outsider or researcher for that matter. It is virtually impossible to generalize about either the contents of the communication reports or the ways in which managers seek to use them. The degree of openness, clarity of expression and desire for recognition vary enormously within a given group, as do the relative influences of hierarchical position, functional training or geographic separation. In their initial discussions, managers have to cope with this using not only the formal communication links indicated by, say, the organizational structure, but also such of the vital links or mazeways of informal communication as each individual manager has seen fit to include in his part of the expectations data-base. In almost every organization which has used the approach, the volume of diagonal or lateral communication has been appreciably larger than the vertical communication ascending or descending the lines of authority depicted on an organization chart. Since the communication of job-related requirements other than those between superior and subordinate had never been systematically documented on a person to person basis before in any of the organizations using the Approach, there were no established formal processes for resolving ambiguity or disagreement which was diagonal or lateral.

The manner in which ambiguity or apparent disagreement in the contents of expectations between superior and subordinate were resolved reflected the established relationships between them. Some subordinates merely copied the precise wording of their superior's expectations in an absolute acceptance of the latter's authority and/or clearer knowledge of what was needed, whilst other superior–subordinate discussions produced negotiated agreement on a precise wording for disputed expectations which represented significant change from either person's original intention or wording. What of course was rarely in dispute was whether job-related requirements expressed in expectations either did or should exist between the two people concerned.

Initial interpersonal discussions, in respect of ambiguity or apparent disagreement in diagonal and lateral communication of job requirements, were usually directed at resolving any conflict of views about which-inter personal communication should take place. A specific, and not atypical example taken from the first report of a profitable organization, with twenty-five managers and an annual turnover of approximately £3 million will serve to illustrate the nature and scope of the problem.[15] All twenty-five managers were using the system. The works director had expressed expectations of eight of his colleagues whereas fourteen people had expressed expectations of him. In total fifteen people featured in his report but in respect of only seven of them was there reciprocated recognition that communication took place between them. In respect of eight people out of the fifteen there was only one way communication, which represents 53 per cent unconfirmed membership of the works director's working group. Such a situation is obviously unsatisfactory, both from the point of view of organizational effectiveness and personal satisfaction. The works director's position can be set in the context of the equivalent position for each of his twenty-four colleagues (see table II).

Table II. Unconfirmed membership of the twenty-five subject manager working groups (before any discussions)

Subject no.	*Percentage mismatch*	*Subject no.*	*Percentage mismatch*	*Subject no.*	*Percentage mismatch*
1	20	10	50	19	33
2	75	11	29	20	64
3	4	12	53	21	54
4	39	13	73	22	20
5	14	14	56	23	67
6	39	15	53	24	46
7	36	16	50	25	71
8	64	17	47		
9	53	18	75		

Mean of the percentages = 47·36, S.D. of the percentages = 19·59.

It must be emphasized that the situation presented in table II is typical of managers' first attempts to use a contingent system. Members of an organization will vary in the extent they wish to make informal relationships in some sense formal, by including them in their expectation data-base. Lateral and diagonal discussion includes reaching agreement on those requirements and communications which should be included in the system.

The high level of unconfirmed membership of individual subject managers' working groups can be caused by poor communication, inadequate percep-

[15] The data and the research on which comments are made in the text in respect of this example are presented in the following unpublished M.Sc. dissertation: Parker, T. J., *Research into Uses and Applications of the 'Expectations Approach'*, Durham University Library.

tion or a conscious decision by the object manager not to acknowledge the expectations which are actually held of him.

One of the advantages of the expectations system is that it does not ascribe blame to any of the managers concerned. The fact that manager 'A' does not set down that he perceives manager 'X' to expect something of him and the fact that manager 'X' has in fact set down an actual expectation of manager 'A', highlights the need for the two of them to discuss and decide whether a reciprocated recognition of an accepted requirement should exist between them, but it does not automatically presuppose either 'A's poor perception or 'X's poor communication.

Where the subject manager's desired communication has been unacknowledged in the first report because of oversight or previously poor communication, the object manager has usually been happy to add the necessary expectations to the data-base, thereby acknowledging the existence and the reasonableness of the expectations concerned.

Experience shows that the resolution of this form of interpersonal lack of acknowledgement, effectively a one-sided refutation of a desired working relationship, is best handled on a two-person basis whenever possible.

The acknowledgement and acceptance by one individual of a statement implying a desire to establish a working relationship made by another individual carries with it a number of recognitions that are both personal as well as organizational. Whilst in the majority of cases, discussion has shown that the lack of recognition of a working relationship has been due to poor communication, there have been many situations in which the lack of recognition of a working relationship in practice has been due to interpersonal attitudes or feelings rather than failures to perceive or communicate.

Where this situation is either discovered, or formally recognized as a result of the initial communication report, then whether it is caused by interpersonal friction, or just by differing perceptions of the desired relationships between the two managers concerned, some third, mediating person can often make a positive contribution during discussions aimed at improving the situation. At this early stage of Phase 1 the mediators chosen have usually been colleagues, or neutrals such as consultants, researchers, or members of an O.D. or Personnel Department, to help in the discussion rather than to decide which of the two who disagree is right. Obviously if disagreements cannot be mutually resolved and are likely to affect individual or group effectiveness, then, later in the use of the system, someone with the necessary acknowledged authority will need to be involved in its resolution.

In the process of clarifying expectations there is obvious scope for conflict because there is no doubt that the process of clarification requires a gradual refining of different peoples' views about both their jobs and their relationships. It is therefore frankly surprising that there have been so few reported examples of conflict having been generated during this stage of using the system. When asked about this managers have pointed to the contingent nature of the system and claimed that because the data are under their control, there is greater scope for resolving and clarifying conflict than for actually creating it. An inadequately worded expectation in the past may very well have led to a tremendous amount of effort, pointlessly directed at an undesired end product. This is immensely frustrating if, subsequently, each manager maintains that his earlier communication had been clear, even though it had given rise to two manifestly different expectations on the part of the giver and the receiver.

Managers point out that one of the advantages of the system is that it offers the scope for this kind of conflict to be identified and resolved, and future potential points of conflict avoided, if the clarification process is handled in a systematic and supportive manner.

It need scarcely be reiterated for, no doubt, the thousandth time, that any managerial system or process is successful in direct proportion to the interest and support given openly by top management in respect of it. Therefore in the initial use of this approach, senior management have made it abundantly clear to those using it that there will be misperceptions of working relationships, that these are reasonably to be expected, and that the use of this approach is to try to help each manager become more effective as the result of having a written, visual, legible communication map of the contingent complexity of his particular job. It has also, however, to be pointed out that it is most unlikely that interpersonal discussion alone will resolve all disagreements or ensure organizational effectiveness. Whilst interpersonal discussion can ensure situational relevance in a contingent manner, each individual's job must be set in the context of group and organizational needs. Interpersonal discussion usually resolves some but not all differences of opinion as can be demonstrated by showing the unconfirmed membership of the working groups of the twenty-five managers mentioned previously at the end of their interpersonal discussions (see table III).

A great deal had obviously been achieved, but a number of genuine disagreements still remained for group discussion and decision-making to resolve.

Phase 1, Step 3. Intergroup discussion. Where there is disagreement or uncertainty about who should meet a given expectation, group discussions have been directed towards finding who has the necessary skills and available resources, as well as checking to see that the expectations which form the basis of disputes are actually organizationally justifiable. Sometimes organizational clients of a staff department are uncertain to whom they should

Table III. Unconfirmed membership of the twenty-five subject manager working groups (after interpersonal discussion)

Subject no.	*Percentage mismatch*	*Subject no.*	*Percentage mismatch*	*Subject no.*	*Percentage mismatch*
1	14	10	18	19	38
2	25	11	18	20	42
3	8	12	8	21	38
4	44	13	50	22	0
5	8	14	33	23	44
6	18	15	40	24	36
7	31	16	0	25	62
8	36	17	25		
9	36	18	73		

Mean of the percentages = 29·84, S.D. of the percentages = 18·40.

Note 1: A comparison of the means and S.D.'s of the two tables indicates a clear tendency towards concordance.

Note 2: A comparison of individual subjects in the two tables, indicates that although, by and large, the tendency is towards greater agreement, in some cases, especially where concordance was high in the first table, agreement fell.

go to obtain a particular service. For example in the Personnel Department of a multinational motor manufacturer the departmental members formed a group with a very wide range of skills. They themselves had not completely analysed and mapped the skills available within the department, and it was therefore not surprising that managers outside Personnel, who had occasion to have dealings with them, were not always aware of the most highly skilled, or most relevant person to form the object for a given expectation. It was discovered in the first communication report that a wide range of subject managers had expressed as the object manager, for a given expectation, the head of the Personnel Department. This was not done for structural reasons, but because the holders of the expectations were simply unaware of which person in the departmental group had the necessary skills to meet that expectation and, as described earlier, had used the head of department's code, as the obvious starting point for discussions.

This form of ambiguity about a statement, namely uncertainty about the most appropriate object manager for a given expectation, in that kind of situation can be resolved best by intergroup discussion. There is obviously a very wide range of potential ways of handling this situation. At one end of the spectrum is a directive approach where the departmental head, exercising his authority to do so, specifies the individual person within his department who will form the object for a given expectation. At the other end of the spectrum is an open, participative discussion, where the group concerned separate out the tasks that need to be performed on the basis of those who either currently are most skilled in a given area, or those who are seeking to develop a given skill and will happily accept the responsibility for meeting an expectation, because it gives them a vehicle for both acquiring, and then subsequently testing, the necessary skill.

Another form of uncertainty, which has consistently featured in group discussions, has been the situation where an individual perceives accurately that an expectation is held of him by one or more people, but feels that he lacks either the necessary skills or knowledge to meet the expectation. An example occurred recently in a matrix-structured multinational. Managers were both members of a functional department and members of multi-functional project teams. A project-team's existence depended on the life of a particular contract which varied from six months to several years. Some managers expected their functional boss to appraise their performance and help with their personal career development, whilst other managers expected their project leader to perform these tasks. In the course of group discussion, most project leaders and some functional bosses pointed out that they lacked the necessary information to perform the tasks satisfactorily and the entire group referred the problem to top management with the request that the firm's approach to performance appraisal should be re-examined and classified.

This and other examples from the same organization confirmed Knight's[16] research findings that matrix structures have been poorly served by management control systems designers, whose traditional assumption of sole authority, responsiblity and accountability held by one manager is demonstrably out of place in a matrix organization.

The senior managers who were using the approach found it particularly helpful in defining key roles clearly and over 90 per cent of them saw the system as providing the additional information processing required for effective management control within matrix structures.

In intergroup discussions, one of the most effective forms of resolution has been the result of the group concerned meeting with a chairman selected from amongst themselves, and pursuing free discussion on the basis of the specific part of the communication report needing to be clarified.

Groups vary significantly, however, in their capacity for handling open discussion on matters which affect some or all of them. Apart from anything else, it is a process which needs regular use, if it is to achieve a high level of success, and many groups have chosen to invite an outsider to act as a trusted mediator in the first round of group discussions. In the early days of the system's development, the researcher was often invited to perform this role, but now that the system is operational, either an outside consultant or a member of an internal staff function may be called in.

[16] Knight, K., 'Matrix Organization — A Review', *Journal of Management Studies*, Vol. 13, No. 2, May 1976, pp. 111–30.

In a recent application in a medium-sized engineering company, the Managment Development Manager was invited to chair the discussion in a group made up exclusively of Managing Directors of the holding and subsidiary companies. They chose him because they felt he was the best equipped to chair those meetings in which they were discussing both their relationship as well as their role expectations.

Disagreements within a group can ultimately always be resolved if not by discussion, then by the exercise of authority. When the group discussion part of Phase 1 concludes, the disagreements which are still left are those which lie between departments. Since interpersonal discussion has not resolved them previously, they tend to be disagreements which are fairly important both organizationally and to the people concerned. In most organizations there has been a recognition that such disagreements have reached the stage where decision-making is at least as important as negotiation.

Phase 1, Step 4. The resolution of interdepartmental disagreement. If at this advanced stage of role negotiation disagreement still exists between two people in different departments, there are basically two questions which have to be posed and resolved — preferably reasonably objectively, and in a way which is likely to contribute to achieving cooperation between the two people subsequently, if that is the final decision.

1. *Subject manager.* The first question is whether the subject manager has the right to hold the expectation that he has actually stated. Does he need what he has asked for? For what purpose is he seeking that particular input to his work? Can he justify the requirement as appropriate to his particular role within the organization?
2. *Object manager.* The second question is to decide whether the object manager, appropriately within the role as specified within the structure of the organization, should use some of the resources which he has at his command to meet that particular expectation.

In many organizations the million-dollar question was 'Who does the resolving?', and managers eventually came up with a simple solution which was programmed into the system's reporting procedures. The subject manager and the object manager could each indicate the person they thought had the sole authority to resolve the disagreement and a report would be sent to the nominated official asking him to do so, either with or without discussion with the parties concerned. In the first organization where this approach was adopted, the results startled the managers themselves. In over half the cases of interdepartmental disagreement, the subject and object managers specified different managers as having 'the sole authority'. Later when all these managers received reports nominating them to resolve the disagreements, the majority claimed not to have the necessary authority and indicated someone else as the appropriate person. The company concerned was young and had expanded very rapidly but, even so, senior management were surprised by the difference between the way in which authority was actually exercised, and the way it seemed authority should be exercised if one looked at the organization chart. In other organizations the disparity has not proved to be so great, but interdepartmental disagreements have frequently uncovered the fact that one of the causes of such disagreement is the lack of a person with the accepted authority to resolve them. *What has become clear is that a contingent system has the scope to go from situational disagreement to the point where ultimately someone is found to resolve it.* Interestingly, it has not always been the traditional 'shared boss', sometimes a person has been nominated who is believed to have the requisite ability, knowledge, and experience to resolve disagreement in the light of an integrated understanding of the needs of the organization as a whole.

The role of such an 'integrator' has been outlined by Lawrence and Lorsch.[17] It is unnecessary here to repeat their description of this role but it is important to point out that in their article there was no reference to the need for access to information that would enable the integrator's role to be proactive rather than reactive. It will be apparent that the expectations report for the organization as a whole enables a perceptive integrator to start looking for interdepartmental ambiguity, or areas where there is potential interdepartmental conflict, in the light of the needs of the organization for effective integration.

It is natural at departmental level that the prime concern of departmental heads should be for functional or line differentiation. The pattern of information flow and work-related interaction that is shown by an analysis of the expectations placed in the data-base by managers, provides a clear analogue of the formal and informal interactions within the organization. By seeking through analysis to anticipate interdepartmental conflict or duplication of effort, the integrator can begin to take a more active and, potentially, more proactive role.

By analysing communication patterns departmentally, the integrator can check to identify the unbroken transmission of key elements in the purpose of the total organization, and relate the pattern of such communications with the pattern envisaged when the organization's structure was designed. It is in this 'seeking' role that an integrator can bring into the consideration of the contingent reality of interdepartmental conflict and ambiguity, the

[17] Lawrence, Paul and Lorsch, Jay, 'New Management Job: The Integrator', *Harvard Business Review*, Vol. 45, No. 6, November/December 1967.

broader perspective of the needs of the organization as a whole. In a recent application, a senior manager in the personnel function, whose career within the organization had included production management experience, was chosen to perform precisely this role. Whilst he has been able to bring about the resolution of many disagreements, some key disagreements remain concerning, for example, details in the corporate plan or problems at the interface between sales and production. The responsibility for the resolution of such organizationally critical disagreements has invariably been seen as a senior management responsibility.

By this stage of using the system, however, most managers reports have changed considerably. The manager who had received the first report shown in table I had by this stage refined it to the point shown in table IV.

Phase 1, Stage 5. Planning to resolve organizational ambiguity and disagreement. Corporate planning is undertaken to produce a set of time-related objectives for an organization, sufficiently clearly articulated that structure and systems can be designed to facilitate the achievement of those objectives.

Much has been written on the degree of specificity of the definition of most organizations' purpose. The reality in most of the organizations which have used the Expectations system, has been that the purpose was diffuse, multivariable, expressed in quite a high level of abstraction, concerned with different time periods, and it included both measurable and unmeasurable elements.

Any large organization is seeking, normally with difficulty, to mediate between the expectations held of the organization by individuals and groups in the substantive environment, those held by employees and those held by people who supply the organization with resource in a variety of forms. It is quite impossible to produce a *single* purpose from that multiplicity of individual motivations and expectations.

There is, therefore, considerable scope for genuine disagreement about the best way to structure the organization, whether to use flexi-time, what marketing policy to adopt in a recession, *etc.*, and discussion and decision about such matters really must be linked to medium and longer term strategic considerations.

In deciding how such matters will be resolved, both regarding the way in which the decision is made, and the decision itself, the managers concerned are making conscious decisions about the future and determining the environment in which individual managers can and must set work objectives. A strategic plan can never be as detailed as a blueprint, so organizations experience difficulty in tracing the links between planned purpose and action. The expectation data-base can provide corporate planners, directors, or first-line supervision with an easily accessible way of checking those

Table IV. Revised report at the end of interpersonal discussion phase

The expectations which manager E.N.J. actually holds of manager P.D.B.
—Negotiate supplier contracts as directed.
—Compile any necessary information requested by authorized managers.
—Directly supervise buying office staff.
—Provide requested information for cash flow control.
—Regular briefing on current events in buying office.
—Support agreed administrative policies and procedures.
—Maintain buying records as agreed.
—Ensure sufficient information is presented to facilitate accurate analysis of purchase invoices.
—To carry out purchasing function to maximize profitability of company.
—To accurately check and verify all invoices and pass to allow payment by accounts department.
—To supply written reports on projects together with accurate costings and recommendations to allow decisions to be made.
—To carry out purchasing function in such a manner as to enhance the company's reputation with suppliers.
—To act firmly and fairly with suppliers who are not giving required service.
—To vet all requisitions and obtain goods at the most reasonable cost.
—To prepare accurate sales invoices for origination work prior to being typed.

The expectations which manager P.D.B. perceives manager E.N.J. to hold of him.
—To carry out purchasing function to maximize profitability of company.
—To supply written reports on projects together with accurate costings and recommendations to allow decisions to be made.
—To carry out purchasing function in such a manner as to enhance the company's reputation with suppliers.
—To vet all requisitions and obtain goods at the most reasonable cost.
—To accurately check and verify all invoices and pass to allow payment by accounts department.
—To prepare accurate sales invoices for origination work prior to being typed.
—To act firmly and fairly with suppliers who are not giving required service.
—Negotiate supplier contracts as directed.
—Compile any necessary information requested by authorized managers.
—Directly supervise buying office staff.
—Provide monthly stock position of board — current and spare — and clarifoil.
—Regular briefing on current events in buying office.
—Support agreed administrative policies and procedures.
—Maintain buying records as agreed.
—Ensure sufficient information is presented to facilitate accurate analysis of purchase invoices.

The expectations which manager E.N.J. perceives to be held of him by manager P.D.B.
—Regular briefing on current management policies.
—Give or obtain decisions when requested.
—Authorization for certain purchases.
—Advice on personal decisions.
—Advice on personnel matters concerning buying staff.
—To make impartial assessment of staff problems and take remedial action.
—Give backing to assist in carrying out purchasing policy.
—Advise on areas to be improved upon in department.
—To improve knowledge of day-to-day working of buying department.
—To give advice on financial matters affecting purchasing policy.
—Advise areas which you consider I may improve myself.
—To assist in establishing lines of communication.

The expectations which manager P.D.B. actually holds of manager E.N.J.
—To make impartial assessment of staff problems and take remedial action.
—Give backing to assist in carrying out purchasing policy.
—Advise on areas to be improved upon in department.
—To improve knowledge of day-to-day working of buying department.
—To give advice on financial matters affecting purchasing policy.
—Advise areas which you consider I may improve myself.
—To assist in establishing lines of communication.
—Regular briefing on current management policies.
—Advice on personal decisions.
—Give or obtain decisions when requested.
—Authorization for certain purchases.
—Advice on personnel matters concerning buying staff.

Note: This table should be compared with table I.

links between the decisions about company purpose and the actions that are being undertaken in an attempt to achieve that purpose.

In one small organization some junior managers disagreed about a pattern of working which they felt was inefficient. The managing director was able to show them on a computer-linked visual display unit how customers' expectations of the organization were best served by that pattern of working, by tracing the activity through the organization.

This real-time availability of an integrated expectation data-base enables planners to identify the results of planning, as well as it enables junior managers to gain the perspective of why the need for coordination can impose constraints on individual units.

Phase 1. Conclusion. Extensive discussion has been given to this phase of using the 'Expectations Approach' management control system because what follows is naturally consequential upon this phase.

Each individual in a working group has nominated all the members of his working group, has then contacted them to make sure that they accept such nomination, has then negotiated as precise an expression of what each expects from the other as can be agreed, and where agreement cannot be easily reached has sought to find where within his working group, or elsewhere within the organization, ways can be found of resolving such disagreements.

Experience shows that managers vary widely: in their use of the system; in the degree to which they not only tolerate but in some cases seek ambiguity; and in the degree to which they care about resolving disagreement. The process described in Phase 1 cannot force a person to be more effective, but it has provided managers who wish to be more effective with both a methodology and a data-base system which can materially help them to be so.

Phase 2. Planning Job Inputs and Outputs

At the start of Phase 2 each individual has a report of all the inputs he has negotiated from his colleagues, and all the outputs he has agreed to supply to others.

At regular intervals it is customary in most organizations for individuals to be called on to think through what they are doing and why and to whether it is possible or desirable to plan for the future in such a way that either different work is done, or present work is done more effectively. Priorities may change either temporarily because of a crisis, or more permanently because of a change of policy.

Managers who have had experience of using Management by Objectives have identified the following differences when using the 'Expectation Approach'. Discussions about objectives:

1. Can cover lateral and diagonally directed output.
2. Can cover the necessary inputs as well as outputs for the job.
3. Can be checked with the specified 'object' manager to make sure he still wants it (output) or is still prepared to produce it (input).
4. Can deal with the detail of a job and not just the Key Results Areas.
5. Can cover the input–output relationship.
6. Can be done easily, quickly, and whenever changes seem desirable because the relevant detailed information is available to both superior and subordinate instantly from the computerized data-base where the expectations are held on a visual display unit or within twenty-four hours or less in printed form.

The fact that each individual can control his use of the system means that the dynamics of the methodology are contingent on his perception of need. There is no presupposition that the expectations data-base will achieve and maintain a stable state, indeed the reverse is the case. Individual and group expectations change for many reasons. Some can be predicted. For example, when a new manager is appointed to replace another person, many, if not all the relationship expectations held of the previous incumbent by his colleagues will be changed immediately and new ones gradually developed, as uncertainty about the new man gives way to trust, support or hostility. In many organizations the regulation expectations have been altered for the first few months in respect of the new man performing the role, and then modified and altered if his performance justifies increased delegation of authority by his superiors, or encourages greater according of authority by his subordinates and colleagues. Role-related expectations changed little if at all in this situation.

Some expectations can and do change in ways which cannot always be foreseen. A competitor may enter the market with a new product, a problem with the organization may call for a short-term project team to be established, or a supplier may notify inability to deliver on time – or at all! In such circumstances expectations in parts of the organization will change dramatically. Usually in these cases it has been people's role expectations that have been modified whilst the relationship and regulation expectations have not been disturbed.

The advantage therefore of the contingent nature of the system is to provide such flexibility that when any manager realizes he can improve his own personal effectiveness by changing input or output objectives, he can immediately use the appropriate Phase 1 stage to ascertain whether such changes will create or resolve problems for others.

The frequency of review and, if necessary, change of the data-base is contingent on the needs of individual managers or groups of managers and therefore neither has to wait for the annual review nor happen unnecessarily just because there is need for change in another part of the organization. One obvious trigger mechanism to reconsider objectives is when performance is consistently varying from the expected level.

Phase 3. Performance Reporting

Since every expectation has both a subject manager and an object manager, it is technically easy for both the supplier and the recipient of a given managerial output to rate the output as above, at, or below the expected level. The system has been developed to provide just this facility and reports can be produced showing the role-incumbent's rating of his own performance, expectation by expectation, and the rating of his performance in respect of the same expectation by his colleagues.

Though technically easy, this process represents quite a challenge psychologically to traditional views of accountability, authority and status. Individual managers hold expectations of many people, some senior, some junior, some colleagues in their own departments and some people in other departments. A subordinate rating the extent to which his boss, or for that matter any more senior manager, has met his expectations is not a common phenomenon of management control. The contingent nature of the 'Expectations Approach' methodology does not *demand* that this be done, it just makes it as easy technically to assess performance upwards as downwards. It is the decision of the managers who use the system to determine the appropriate way to use it and it can be used in different ways, in different parts of the organization. A participative manager may encourage his own subordinates to rate his performance, whilst in the same organisation, another manager may refuse to allow his subordinates or colleagues to rate his performance – a truly contingent methodology.

This form of control reporting was first used in a profit-seeking organization in 1975, by the senior managers and directors of an engineering company. Contrary to the fears of the researcher[18] concerned, the managers said they had neither inhibitions nor embarrassment in rating their own as well as their colleagues' achievements. Nor was the process a whitewash. Those supplying output to others rated themselves as having met 85 per cent of the expectations which were held of them. Those who held the expectations, however, rated only 72 per cent as having been met. Since those differences could be traced to individually rated expectations, the managing director said, 'Now we know what we have to concentrate on to be more effective'. In that organization it worked well, but that was contingent on the managerial climate within the group. In a recent use of the methodology in a

[18] Tai, C. H. S., *A System and 'Expectations Approach' to Planning and Control in an Industrial Subsidiary*, unpublished M.Sc. Dissertation, Durham University Business School, 1975.

major public utility,[19] over 70 per cent of the managers questioned felt that this was an excellent way of assessing individual effectiveness. Interestingly enough, it was the more senior managers who were lukewarm or hostile to its use. They stated that it might undermine their authority if subordinates were given the opportunity to rate their bosses' performance.

So far, very few organizations have used the performance rating modules of the system. As one vice-president said, 'Phases 1 and 2 represent an enormous conceptual leap from where we are now with our present systems. It will take us five to ten years to get up the confidence to use Phase 3.' Some *have* used it, but their satisfaction with doing so undoubtedly owes more to their commitment to achieving effective performance than to the system which helped them to do so.

Conclusion

The vast majority of the hundreds of managers who have now used the 'Expectations Approach' management system have reported that the time taken writing down their expectations, reading their own individual communication reports and then working to remove ambiguity has been worthwhile. They point to the system's usefulness in enabling them to raise the justifiable level of confidence they bring to their job. The results to date certainly support Paul's findings that 'managerial satisfaction is positively correlated with role clarity'.[20] The use of this method will produce a report for each manager which incorporates the complexity of the interactions necessary to perform his job effectively, and the specific clear content of what is expected in respect of each of those interactions. It enables him, in short, to manage his own job in a way that previously has just simply not been possible. A manager can now choose how to allocate that most valuable resource, his time, in the light of the certain knowledge of what is actually expected of him.

Clearly, if a manager is to manage his own job effectively, rather than find himself reacting under the pressure to meet the next demand on his time and, in a sense, ending up out of his own control, he needs a clear and concise map of the expectations that are held of him by others in connection with his work and the 'Expectations Approach' produces precisely what is needed.

Perhaps the most important element in this approach is that it has been user designed and is user controlled. As a result it allows each manager to handle his own job in his own way, at his own pace, whilst dealing with the contingent complexity of his managerial position.

[19] Byrne, J. D., Mason, D. M. and Webster, P. F., 'The Expectations Approach' to Management, Northern Gas, Killingworth, 1978.

[20] Paul, R. J., 'Role Clarity as a Correlate of Satisfaction, Job Related Strain and Propensity to Leave — Male vs. Female', *Journal of Management Studies*, Vol. 11, No. 3, October 1974, pp. 233–45.

In a dynamic and relative situation, regular adjustment is necessary if there is to be any hope of effective performance. This 'Expectations Approach' provides a means for this end, since it takes people seriously and realistically, by acknowledging their individuality. In so doing, the 'Expectations Approach' is believed to represent a positive attempt to respond to Peery's call for 'A systems design formulation which shows real appreciation of intra-organizational conflict, diversity of values, and political action within organization',[21] and he shares Sorenson's view that the appropriate way of identifying new approaches to control is 'within a contingency framework'.[22]

If self-awareness is the gift of the age, self-expression the sign of the age and self-satisfaction the need of the age, then the individual can be effective only through the fullest exchange of expectations.

The 'Expectations Approach' makes value awareness and goal congruence both the responsibility and the opportunity of every individual in a human organization.

[21] Peery, Jnr., N. S. 'General Systems Theory Approaches to Organizations: Some Problems in Application', *Journal of Management Studies*, Vol. 12, No. 3, October 1975, pp. 266–75.

[22] Sorenson, Jnr., P. F. 'Control and Effectiveness in Twenty-seven Scandinavian Voluntary Organizations', *Journal of Management Studies*, Vol. 13, No. 2, May 1976, pp. 183–90.

[19]

Restoring the Relevance of Management Accounting

Toshiro Hiromoto
Hitotsubashi University

Abstract: In our internationally competitive business environment, the path to take to restore the relevance of management accounting is sought by many. This article is based on the author's intensive field studies at successful Japanese manufacturing firms in several major industries, including automobiles, semiconductors, and consumer electronics. Four case descriptions are included. Today's innovative management accounting systems are designed to support continuous innovation, which is a new common theme of management accounting systems design. The four elements of the new theme are: A Behavior Influencing Focus, Market-Driven Management and A Dynamic and Team-Oriented Approach. In the past, management accounting has tended to focus on optimization with respect to a given set of parameters. Today's manufacturers, however, need a new system that would promote strategic management and focus on motivating employees to act strategically.

We are now in a period of innovation. A global innovation race is on. Innovation existed and was important in other ages as well, but what is being seen today is "continuous innovation,"[1] and in our internationally competitive environment, corporate excellence depends a great deal on whether the process of innovation can be effectively managed. As a result, yesterday's management accounting has lost relevance. The management accounting being performed by top Japanese manufacturers today shows a new common focus or theme that represents a departure from what was observed in the past. They are showing us a path to take to restore the

[1]Continuous innovation is close to "kaizen" as described by Imai [1986]. Both are incremental or evolutionary processes, not revolutionary. And both are customer oriented. However, the Japanese term "kaizen" implies that focus is on the factory activities. Continuous innovation is applied to all corporate activities.

I am indebted to Professor William L. Ferrara (Stetson University) for his helpful suggestions and comments. I also wish to thank Professor Emeritus Robert N. Anthony (Harvard University), Professors Charles T. Horngren (Stanford University), H. Thomas Johnson (Portland State University), Robert S. Kaplan (Harvard University), Kenneth A. Merchant (University of Southern California), Frances Moss (The Polytechnic of Central London) and Kiyoshi Okamoto (Hitotsubashi University), and Professor Emeritus David Solomons (University of Pennsylvania) for many editorial and thoughtful comments on earlier versions of this article. I also acknowledge the encouragement of Professors Jonathan B. Schiff (Fairleigh Dickinson University) and John K. Shank (Dartmouth College). The usual caveat applies that they are not responsible in any way for remaining errors, inconsistencies, omissions, or faulty interpretations.

relevance of management accounting. Their management accounting systems reinforce a top-to-bottom commitment to process and product innovation.

In today's rapidly changing business environment, innovation is the key to a company's survival and competitiveness, and the strategies that determine the direction of that innovation have become crucial to corporate management. In Japan, management accountants work hard to link their management accounting systems to their companies' strategies for innovation. Faced with the need to simultaneously realize low cost, high quality, and timely delivery, they have been attempting more frequent use of nonfinancial measures. Cost allocation systems have been modified to promote automating factories, standardizing parts, and shortening lead time. And management accounting systems are also being redesigned so as to function better in an environment of restructuring and globalization. Moreover, given the importance of managing customer preferences, market-driven management systems are also being designed. All these innovations center around a single theme: *the design of measurement and control systems for continuous innovation.*

This paper will look at the relevance of this new theme and four elements within it, following which will be some examples of innovative practices that have developed from it.

A REEXAMINATION OF THE PURPOSE AND ROLE OF MANAGEMENT ACCOUNTING

In order to restore the relevance of management accounting, some changes are needed. The aim of this section is not to oversimplify traditional management accounting and try to bash it entirely. Rather I do believe most of the basic concepts of traditional management accounting are still relevant and sound. I would like just to suggest that some perspectives of traditional accounting should be worth rethinking, e.g.,

1. Management accounting should play an "information for decision-making" role.
2. Management accounting should help obtain the optimal activities with regard to the current conditions.

Overemphasis on "Information for Decision-Making" Role

Management accounting has had not only a decision-making but also a behavioral focus. As Ferrara [1990] indicated, accounting research of a behavioral nature has long been observed in U.S. literature. Anthony [1957] and Bedford [1957] described a behavioral focus as early as 1957. Schiff and Lewin [1968] were also cognizant of behavioral factors. Horngren also has increasingly emphasized the motivational effects of the choices of accounting systems since the 1970s [Horngren, 1989].

However, it is a fact that there has been an overemphasis on a decision-making focus. As Horngren [1989, p. 23] noted, motivation was mentioned, but the emphasis was on which accounting quantifications would lead toward wiser economic decisions. Research tended to focus on accounting data for management decision making [Horngren, p. 22; Johnson and

Kaplan, 1987, p. 162]. That accounting is a system for providing information useful for economic decisions has been the widespread view, and it still is. In fact, some are going so far as to say that western management accountants "are brought up to believe that numbers must above all be right to enable managers to make informed decisions" [*Financial Times* of London, 11/18/88]. They want to provide information as inputs to decision-theoretical models and give correct answers and optimal solutions. They would stress the relevance and accuracy of accounting figures and pursue the conditional truth, trying to build an accounting system that permits measures and analyses of costs in relation to a particular decision.

Overemphasis on Constrained Optimization

Kaplan [1983] pointed out that management accountants normally assumed a stable corporate environment when considering a company's cost or managerial accounting system. Johnson [1990] discussed the shift in management accounting thinking from "taking constraints as given" to "moving constraints."

The basic managerial problem apparently assumed by conventional companies was to accept the current production environment as a given and implement policies that are optimal with respect to these existing conditions. In this kind of situation, cost accounting could contribute to management appropriately by following the consumption of resources precisely and computing the optimal policy with respect to a given set of parameters.

Scientific management also assumed known characteristics and a stable technology, as when manufacturers mass-produced and marketed mature standard products. The most prominent single element in scientific management was the task idea. It consisted very largely in preparing for and carrying out tasks based on engineering design, bills of material and time-and-motion study. Employees were expected just to succeed in doing their individual tasks right so that waste of material and time was kept to a minimum. Factory workers were considered to be just workers and operators, almost as attachments to machinery.

During the 1950s and '60s, a time when most of the world's industrial powers were rebuilding from the devastation of World War II, America enjoyed its Golden Age. U.S. manufacturers dominated their markets, controlling the major technologies in their products and processes. Moreover, they expected little change in the demands of their customers. As Prahalad and Hamel [1990] noted, a diversified firm could simply point its business units at particular products and admonish them to become world leaders.

THE ELEMENTS OF THE NEW THEME

Modern corporations are now operating in a totally different environment where static optimization is often irrelevant. Technological progress has become a matter of days and months in this age of continuous innovation. Such tremendous changes as more intense international competition, diversification of customer needs, shorter product life-cycles, and automation of factories are pervasive. Many firms' competitiveness does not derive from the price/performance attributes of existing products. Instead, competitiveness derives from an ability to build new quality products at lower cost and more timely than competitors. Firms that wish to be world-class manufacturers must produce goods of substantially higher quality with greatly reduced inventory levels, shorter set-up times and production runs, and less uncertainty in the overall production process than presently exists. Rather than constrained optimization, the mission of today's management accounting is to assist continuous innovation and the creation of a competitive tomorrow.

All employees, including factory workers, are now required to "think while they work." A priority of management is to bring employees together in the promotion of innovative activities. Today's management accounting must build a constant awareness of strategic messages in every nook and cranny of the company, assuring that employees will be involved in unified, innovative activities and thus facilitating the enactment of corporate strategies. The following elements together constitute the new theme of management accounting:

1. A behavior influencing focus (linking organizational strategies to action)
2. Market-driven management
3. A dynamic approach
4. A team-oriented approach

From Information for Decisions to A Behavior Influencing Focus

Accounting information is losing its prominence as data input for decision making in the age of innovation and strategies. The relevance of accounting information for decisions or choosing among alternative courses of action is declining. While managerial decisions always require a variety of input data of which accounting numbers are only a part, inputs to decisions other than accounting information are becoming more and more important. Moreover, management is less concerned with using information as a power base than encouraging interdepartmental brainstorming and communication.

At this point, management accountants need to change their focus in designing their systems from an information-for-decisions to a behavior-influencing focus.[2] The information-for-decisions approach was apparently stressed because management accountants wanted to recommend the optimal decision, even though the final choice always rested with the operating managers.

The primary concern of the behavior-influencing approach is to design a system to influence employees to do the desired things. This system does not necessarily try to provide a true and accurate cost and an optimal solution, but allows employees to be creative and resourceful. For instance, discounted cash flow models could be used to help focus, identify and analyze critical input assumptions or project assumptions including possible scenarios and management responses and risks, rather than to solely

[2]The information-for-decisions approach is close to what Ijiri [1975] calls the decision approach, although he contrasts it with the accountability approach.

assist managers' choices, as described in Hodder [1986]. A CAM-I CMS project study group [From the Editors, p. 3], which visited some Japanese manufacturing firms in November 1986, reported that Japanese management accounting was usually less complex and less sophisticated, including the investment justification procedure. The reason why Japanese practice is often simple can be explained by the widespread emphasis on consensus decision making in Japan. That is, "the consensus formation process usually entails discussions among a number of managers from different areas and levels within the firm. In analyzing a project, such discussions tend to include a considerable amount of ... verbal scenario analysis" [Hodder, p. 19]. For satisfactory participation in this process, managers must understand the analytical details, but that does not mean that the accounting system must become detailed and complex.

Integrating the Behavior Influencing Focus with Strategies

In the age of innovation, strategies give the direction of the innovation. As Anthony [1988, p. 10] states, strategies are guidelines for deciding the appropriate actions for attaining the organization's goals. They may be a vision of what and where you want to be, and may be the scenario of the activities that will lead to that vision.

Today's good and innovative management accounting systems are being used to encourage employees to behave in accordance with the organization's strategies. The systems are used to motivate employees to think and act strategically and to implement a chosen strategy.

Company A, for example, which will be described later, illustrates the case where a cost allocation system is used to implement a policy of parts standardization. Manufacturer A faced a situation where it had to implement a cost reduction strategy in an environment of product diversification. The manufacturer identified the number of part numbers as its key cost driver or strategic behavioral cost driver in order to better implement the chosen scenario: standardizing and reducing parts → simplifying the manufacturing process → decreasing manufacturing costs. The parts standardization was the focal point for implementing the cost reduction strategy in the environment of product diversification. (After this strategy was successfully in place, a different strategic need brought forth a different allocation scheme in Example B.)

From Technology-Driven to Market-Driven Management Systems

At this point, it is advisable to think of a firm as an interface between a technology and its market, leaving out other elements that have effects on corporate activity, such as culture, social practices, legal institutions and education systems. Business activities should be undertaken in harmony with both technological conditions and market needs.

In the tough economic situation after World War II, however, it was extremely difficult, virtually impossible, for Japanese manufacturers to survive and grow by operating at the optimal level computed taking the current marketing and technological conditions as given, as American companies did. In industries such as automobiles and consumer electronics, some companies began to look at the market first and follow a market-driven strategy and as a result finally gained international competitiveness. Many other companies in Japan have learned from those experiences, and have adopted market-driven rather than technology-driven practices especially during critical times like oil crises and skyrocketing appreciation of the yen.

The practice followed by Japanese manufacturers is what I would call market-driven[3] management as contrasted with technology-driven management. It is a way of management thinking that gives priority to market or customer requirements over technological limitations. Above all things, attention should be paid to market trends and to what customers want and need.

With a market-driven philosophy, management tries to break the current technological limitations that restrict business activities, to satisfy market and customer needs. It stresses the continual improvement of technology rather than the optimal behavior under current technological conditions.

Now in the age of continuous innovation, even the U.S. manufacturers can no longer produce and market large volumes of standard products with a relatively stable market and technological environment. There has been a shift from a manufacturing environment where markets and technologies were stable to one where markets and technologies are unstable and change quickly. To implement market-driven management across the organization, top management repeatedly and emphatically should tell employees to stay close to their customers. And they must make structural changes in the organization to accomplish this goal. Those actions are not enough, however. Measurement and control systems must be designed to motivate market-driven behavior. These systems are in essence not push systems, but pull systems, as illustrated by Figure 1 where the market rather than technology drives performance goals.

Market-Driven Cost Management Systems

Management accounting for motivating market-driven behavior that is most typically conducted at Japanese companies is based upon target costing at the pre-production (or development and design) and production stages. Target cost systems at the development and design stage are often called *genka kikaku*. Under the target cost system, activities are controlled by using a target or a market-based allowable cost that has to be realized if the company is to be profitable in the competitive market, and comparing it with the actual or actually expected cost.

From Static to Dynamic Approaches

Management accountants have traditionally used the static approach to designing and using their management accounting systems. Emphasis was on performance for the individual time period, which is analogous to focus on improved efficiency in each department.

Today's management accounting systems must be dynamic. Performance has to be judged over time without emphasis on individual time periods. Because innovation is a learning process, good management accounting today should help the organization to learn by stressing the progress of performance over time.

[3] *Market* driven or oriented is not *marketing* oriented. See Shapiro [1988].

Figure 1
Market-Driven vs. Technology-Driven
Cost Management Systems

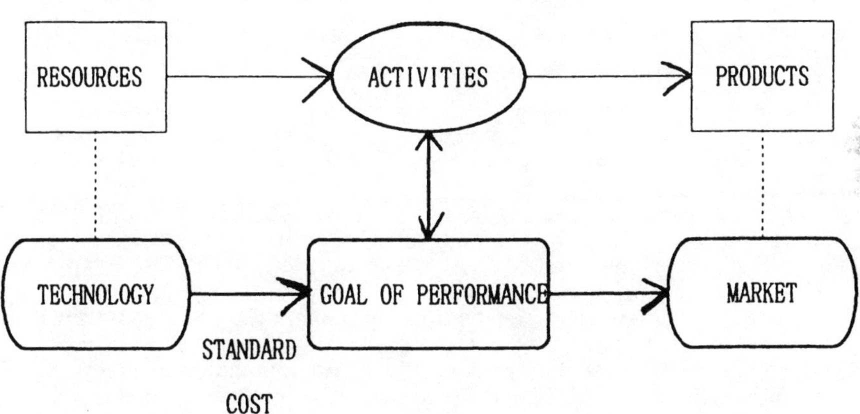

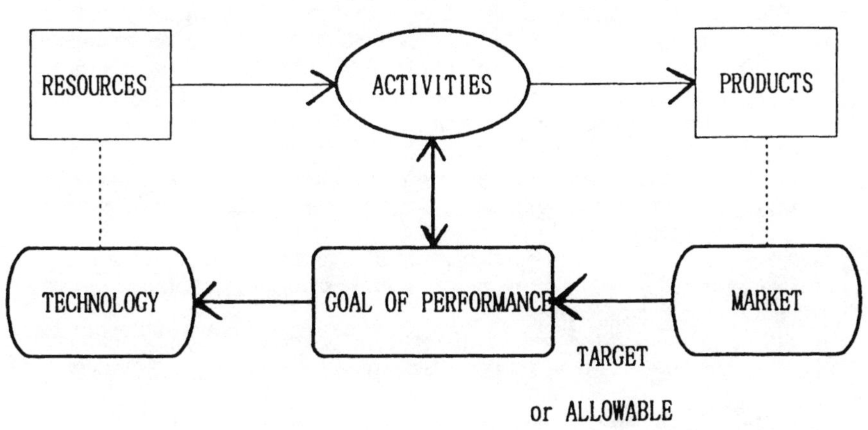

Okamoto [1989] and Hall et al. [1991] observed measuring trends in actual performance. Hiromoto [1988] described the use of moving goals of performance. Moreover, my field study observations have revealed that one of the car manufacturers in Japan that installed the genka kikaku process carried out the decomposition of target (allowable) cost per car dynamically. That is, at earlier stages of development and design, the company assigned the target cost only roughly by sections such as engine design and chassis design. Then it started comparing the targets and actual results by each design group. Finally, targets were assigned for each part and for each parts manufacturer.

From Baton-Passing to Team-Oriented Approaches

Specialization of function, which is a heritage of F. W. Taylor, is surely necessary, but within reason. Today's corporations have been overspecialized. Excessive specialization has led to a situation where independent activities "pass the baton" to get the job done [Cole, 1988].

Many authorities, including Clark [1989], Kanter [1989], and Okamoto [1989], have come to notice the disadvantages of the baton-passing or sequential approach and argued for the team-oriented approach to production process and product development.

A team-oriented approach requires that management accountants should facilitate bringing together all knowledge and experience in the organization. For example, the significance of the use of nonfinancial measures to evaluate factory performance has been widely recognized. Notable here is that such measures should be used in combination with improvement programs implemented through small-group activities. In a large Japanese company, the controller assumes the responsibility of promoting such activities. The foolishness of baton passing is illustrated by a labor variance defined at the individual production cell level creating incentives for workers in each production cell to ignore the effect of their actions on other production cells [Foster and Horngren, p. 23].

The team-oriented approach requires that management accountants are always thinking of how they can contribute to solving management problems. A management accountant should be a member of the management team through close communication with all the people in the organization. Concerning this point, Ferrara [1987, p. 20] provides a succinct description: "The management accountant does not live in a cloistered environment surrounded by books and reports and securing knowledge of the organization from the paperwork which crosses his or her desk. Even if the accountant has theoretical training or even actual experience in all phases of operations, close contact must be maintained with all staff and operating units...." Accounting is a human activity, often entailing some delicate interpersonal communication.

Actually, however, the professional tends to be overspecialized.[4] Johnson and Kaplan [1988] observed that the design of accounting systems was

[4]Goetz [1939, p.152], who had learned much from J. O. McKinsey, the author of *Managerial Accounting* (The University of Chicago Press, 1924), pointed out: "Accounting texts have been the product of public accountants or of teachers trained by public accountants.... Hardly believable, but demonstrably true, this [public accounting] point of view has so permeated the profession and the literature that private accountants and cost accountants are also forgetful of the managerial function of accounting."

often the province of accountants who had little knowledge about their firm's markets and technologies. Now is the time to change. A management accountant as a member of the team is neither the distant evaluator of performance nor the gatekeeper of the organization's financial resources.

Some Examples

Example A

Factory A deals with almost a dozen product categories, including packaged air conditioners (its major product), chiller units, fan coils, and freezers. Each product category includes various models and types that, taken together, number about 3,000.

In the late 1970s, Factory A noticed that demand was growing for a wider variety of products. It produced 466 different items in 1977; this increased to 518 in 1978 and 580 in 1979. It was obvious that product diversification made manufacturing processes extremely complicated and caused ballooned indirect manufacturing costs. Managers of the factory faced the problem of promoting diversification while preventing cost increases. After consideration, they concluded that diversification increased the number of parts used and thus made the production process complicated. At the same time, they paid attention to standardization, which was so important a theme for the company that it held company meetings on standardization. As a result, the reduction and standardization of parts used became an immediate manufacturing strategy for the factory.

Then, they looked into the next problem, determining the appropriate measurement system for implementing the strategy. As discussed in the section on "team-oriented approaches," management accountants of the factory were always thinking of how they could contribute to solving management problems.

The question was raised about how product designers could be motivated to cut the number of parts and work toward use of standard parts. The company's product designers were expected to work with the idea that their department was a profit-making part of the company. Therefore, they worked on designs to give the products better function at lower cost. After discussion, management arrived at an agreement: to find a method to allocate manufacturing overhead so that product costs increase with the number of parts used and with the number of non-standard parts used.

As described below, design and testing costs were allocated to products according to a new method called "standardization-based allocation," which was set up to motivate the new strategy. The people concerned agreed that there was a cause-and-effect relationship between design and testing costs and the number and commonality of parts used.

Under the standardization-based allocation system, design and testing costs were first allocated to each product category based on the number of the employees engaged in the category. Then, the total weighted number of parts used (TWN) was computed by product category using this formula:[5]

---

[5]The weighted values, 10, 5, and 1 were derived from an engineering study so that people would accept them as fair. These figures may be inexact, but not capricious [Anthony, 1983, pp. 126-7]. The reader may imagine intense arguments about whether it should be 10, 9, or 8, rather than an understanding of the purpose of the calculation. Note that the purpose is to calculate an influencing cost instead of the "true" cost.

$$TWN = \Sigma_i (Ni \times WNi)$$
$$= \Sigma_i \{Ni \times (UPi \times 10 + CPAi \times 5 + CPBi \times 1)\}$$

where,

NI = production quantity of model i
WNi = weighted number of parts used in model i
UPi = number of unique parts used in model i
CPAi = number of common parts among products in the same category used in model i
CPBi = number of common parts among products in different categories used in model i

Suppose a model in product category X uses 100 parts. Thirty of them are unique, 50 are shared with other models in X, and 20 are common parts also used in other models in different categories from X. Then, WN is 570 for the product.

The budgeted burden rate was obtained by dividing budgeted design and testing costs by TWN for each product category, and revised every six months. The costs were allocated to individual products at the charge rate multiplied by WN.

The new system had a substantial effect. When I asked about improvement, they gave me the following measures. They obviously stressed the progress of performance over time. The standardization rate (number of common parts / number of total parts) for all products was 60.5 percent in the first half of 1978, grew to 62.2 percent in the second half, and to 63.8 percent in the first half of 1979. The same figure for newly developed products was 11 percent in the first half and 20 percent in the second half of 1978, rising to 22 percent in the first half of 1979. The rate increased steadily despite increasing product variety, and reached almost 68 percent as of the second half of 1987 for all products.

Example B

The above-mentioned factory, Factory A, faced a new problem in the late 1980s in the form of a substantial change in the market for the factory's major product, packaged air conditioners. The market for 1.5 to 3.0 hp air conditioners began to grow rapidly and was recognized as promising. It became strategically important to invest as many resources as possible in that particular product group. The problem facing the factory was that 5 hp and 2 hp air conditioners used the same number of parts, but the ratio of retail prices was 100 to 60 or 70. Since the standardization-based allocation system allocated the same costs to the two products, it determined that the 2 hp product, which the factory should have been emphasizing, was less profitable. While it became necessary to encourage designers to work on this type of product much more than before, the allocation system of Example A became a big obstacle to the strategy.

On the other hand, the designers had learned the value of common parts so that they now naturally design products with common parts. Moreover, computer-aided design had been introduced during the last few years, which promoted the use of standard parts.

As a result, Factory A decided to abolish its standardization-based cost allocation system and introduce a new system starting from October 1988.

Under the new system, design and testing costs were first allocated (as before) to each product category based on the number of employees, and then allocated to each model in a category based on sales expressed in yen.[6] This encouraged the designers to be much more interested in the 2 hp product because the 2 hp product became more profitable under this method.

Example C

Factory C introduced a flexible manufacturing system (FMS) into a manufacturing department in 1984, based on the strategic judgment that as far as possible, in-company production of parts was preferable for cost reduction, improved quality, and shortening the delivery time as well as secure employment. However, it was not easy. Because the reported conversion cost of the newly-established FMS department was almost twice as high as that of outside manufacturers, it was more economical to order from outside manufacturers.

The problem faced by Factory C was that if decisions were made using available cost information, then the long-term manufacturing strategy for internal production by FMS could not be realized. Various alternative measures of product cost were examined, including the proposal to count the variable costs only or count only direct costs. However, agreement could not be reached about this sort of partial costing. For senior management, product cost had to be total absorption cost. The result was it seemed impossible to carry out an internal production strategy while maintaining total absorption costing.

Managers of the factory succeeded in solving the problem by changing their way of thinking. The business environment was becoming increasingly competitive internationally due to such factors as the advancement of newly industrialized economies and technological innovation had also accelerated. To survive in such a competitive environment, what needed to be asked was not "whether our current activities were economical" but "what to do in order to carry out economical activities tomorrow." If the current technological level was not economically viable, then technological innovations were required to make it economically viable. Accordingly, management accountants of the factory changed their focus in designing their cost system from an information-for-decisions to a behavior-influencing focus.

As a result, Factory C came up with an innovative cost accounting system in 1988. The factory revised its method of charging conversion costs to the product. Under the new system, the conversion cost charged to each product or job order was not based on its own currently accrued cost, but based on the cost arising from outside manufacturers, as illustrated below. Notable was that internal conversion costs charged were made equivalent to outside manufacturing cost.

For example, suppose the company has some work that takes 120 hours for outside suppliers to process, but only 100 hours for the company thanks to the FMS. The outside order charge is $25 per hour, while the conversion

[6]Sales in yen and the number of employees are often used allocation bases, since they are considered equitable. Hiromoto [1990, p. 18] illustrates an example of how influencing strategies can be incorporated in the allocation process on the basis of sales.

cost is $50 per hour. Assuming the company does 24 hours of external work in 20 hours and contracts 96 hours outside of the 120 total hours, the product costs for in-house and outside work are calculated as follows according to the new system:

Outside order		
materials cost		$2,000
cost of outside work	$25 x 120 hrs	3,000
total		5,000
In-house processing		
materials		$2,000
cost of outside work	$25 x 96 hrs	2,400
conversion cost	$30* x 20 hrs	600
total		5,000

*Equivalent value of in-house processing or $25 (120 hours/100 hours) = $30 per hour.

The above can be compared to the old system which is as follows:

Outside order		
materials		$2,000
cost of outside work	$25 x 120 hrs	3,000
total		5,000
In-house processing		
materials		$2,000
cost of outside work	$25 x 96 hrs	2,400
conversion cost	$50 x 20 hrs	1,000
total		5,400

The calculated product cost was no longer higher when done in-house than outside ($5,000 in both cases). Since the difference between the actual conversion cost and the charged cost ($1,000 – 600 or $400) was determined and highlighted as a significant variable, people were motivated to make all efforts to reduce that difference so that they could become competitive manufacturers. Note that the new system, which is in essence a form of target costing, permits the manufacturing strategy for internal production without breaking the company's cost recovery policy and leads to the long-term competitiveness of the company whose managers are no longer concerned about obtaining the optimal activities with regard to the current conditions.

Example D

Factory D was operating near full capacity in an extremely competitive situation. But it was not making satisfactory profits. Managers tried various methods to improve performance. They measured actual and standard processing hours by process more often than before and analyzed the standard-cost variances more closely. Nonetheless, they could not get satisfactory results. They began to think about whether there was something wrong with their way of thinking.

Soon thereafter, the managers of Factory D turned to the new ideas of just-in-time and optimized production technology characterized by producing products as needed and cutting lead time. They began to understand that improved efficiency in each division did not necessarily add up to greater efficiency for the factory as a whole. They knew they had wrongly believed that everything was fine if only high capacity utilization was secured.

Management started a change by explaining its new manufacturing strategy to all the people in the organization. Putting a strategy into practice required the cooperation of people in all departments.

Unfortunately, the sales department had always anticipated future possible orders and included them as well as actual orders in their information system because they feared delays in deliveries to customers. This practice obviously went against the new strategy of producing the actually required product in the required quantity. The thinking and action of the sales people had to be changed. As a starter the input code for "anticipated sales" in the sales department computer was eliminated.

In 1984, Factory D added two new performance measures, lead time and inventory turnover, and gave priority to them. In addition, it decided not to report actual processing time by division, even though modern computerization of factory operations drastically reduced the cost of detailed measurement of actual processing time. Efficiency in each division did not necessarily lead to efficiency of the whole. Reporting the actual processing time of each division encouraged actions focused on the efficiency of the division at the cost of efficiency for the overall operation, and discouraged necessary cooperation among divisions and employees.

A remarkable improvement in performance was made. Turnover days were reduced from 102 days in 1985 to 30 days in 1988. Production lead time was reduced from 108 days in 1984 to 52 days in 1988.

Allocated manufacturing overhead used to be calculated by multiplying the predetermined division rate by the actual processing time. But, since divisional actual time became unavailable, it was replaced by the division standard time, which was the sum of each work station's standard processing time.

At this point, the cost allocation system was not yet totally linked to the factory's new production strategy. In 1989, however, the new cost allocation system was devised and introduced. Under the new system, allocated costs were calculated by multiplying the division rate by the total standard "elapsed time" of the divisions.

The new system worked as follows. Assume three work stations, A, B, and C. The standard processing time of each work station is, respectively, 2 minutes, 10 minutes and 3 minutes. Then, the total standard elapsed time was computed to be 10 x 3, or 30 minutes, while the total division standard time is 15 minutes. The factory reported that the new cost system began to influence employees' behavior so that cost reduction activities were concentrated on bottleneck or constraining work stations.

CONCLUDING REMARKS

The business environment is not entirely chaotic, and at the same time it is not entirely definitive. Business activities are carried out in a mixture of optimization and innovation. However, yesterday's management accounting lost its balance. Yesterday's management accounting overemphasized supporting static optimization and helping managers plan and control optimal behavior. The questions to be asked now are "For what purpose does management accounting exist today?" and "Which role should management accounting emphasize today, 'information for decisions' or 'behavior influencing'?"

In the old, stable business environment, the keys to competitiveness were the good machines and good decisions concerning their use. The key resource to becoming an excellent company was material, and therefore the primary concern of management accountants was to see that materials and existing plant and equipment was used in an optimal manner and that the employees worked in a way that those facilities were operated most efficiently. Thus, management accounting used to be recognized as "accounting to facilitate a superior's optimal decisions." However, today when continuous innovation is the source of global competitiveness, the key resource to manufacturing excellence is creative people. Here, management accounting should be recognized as "accounting for getting people to do the desired jobs well."

Management accounting for continuous innovation presupposes an awareness of the fact that the employees of the organization are the ultimate source of improvements in quality and productivity. Its success depends on the quality and ability of employees. Top management must recognize this and utilize the management accounting system to motivate all employees to move toward the strategies developed and endorsed by top management. Thus, the most basic element of today's management accounting must be a behavioral focus.

REFERENCES

Anthony, R. N., "Cost Concepts for Control," *The Accounting Review* (April 1957).

———, *Tell It Like It Was: A Conceptual Framework for Financial Accounting* (Richard D. Irwin, Inc., 1983).

———, *The Management Control Function* (Harvard Business School Press, 1988).

Bedford, N. M., "Cost Accounting as a Motivation Technique," *NACA Bulletin* (June 1957).

Clark, K. B., "What Strategy Can Do for Technology," *Harvard Business Review* (November-December 1989).

Cole, R. E., "Inter-Departmental Coordination: A Key to Quality and Productivity Improvement," unpublished manuscript, 11/88.

Ferrara, W. L., "The New Cost/Management Accounting: More Questions than Answers," *Management Accounting* (October 1990).

———, F. P. Dougherty, and I. W. Keller, *Managerial Cost Accounting: Planning and Control* (Dame Publications, Inc., 1987).

Foster, G., and C. T. Horngren, "JIT: Cost Accounting and Cost Management Issues," *Management Accounting* (June 1987).

From the Editors, *Journal of Cost Management* (Summer 1987).

Goetz, B. E., "What's Wrong with Accounting," *Advanced Management* (Fall 1939).

Hall, R. W., H. T. Johnson, and P. B. B. Turney, *Measuring Up: Charting Pathways to Manufacturing Excellence* (Richard D. Irwin, Inc., 1991).

Hiromoto, T., "Another Hidden Edge: Japanese Management Accounting," *Harvard Business Review* (July-August 1988).

———, "Comparing Japanese and Western Management Accounting Systems," *Controllers Quarterly* (June 1990).

Hodder, J. E., "Evaluation of Manufacturing Investments: A Comparison of U.S. and Japanese Practices," *Financial Management* (Spring 1986).

Horngren, C. T., "Cost and Management Accounting: Yesterday and Today," *Journal of Management Accounting Research* (Fall 1989).

Ijiri, Y., *Theory of Accounting Measurement* (American Accounting Association, 1975).

Imai, M., *Kaizen* (Random House, 1986).

Johnson, H. T., "Professors, Customers, and Value: Bringing a Global Perspective to Management Accounting Education," in *Performance Excellence, Proceedings of the Third Annual Management Accounting Symposium*, 1990. American Accounting Association, Peter B. B. Turney, ed.

———, and R. S. Kaplan, *Relevance Lost: The Rise and Fall of Management Accounting* (Harvard Business School Press, 1987).

———, and ———, "Management by Accounting Is Not Management Accounting," CFO (July 1988).

Kanter, R. M., "The New Managerial Work," *Harvard Business Review* (November-December 1989).

Kaplan, R. S., "Measuring Manufacturing Performance: A New Challenge for Managerial Accounting Research," *The Accounting Review* (October 1983).

Okamoto, K., "Planning and Control of Maintenance Costs for Total Productive Maintenance," in *Japanese Management Accounting: A World Class Approach to Profit Management*, edited by Y. Monden and M. Sakurai (Productivity Press, 1989).

Prahalad, C. K. and G. Hamel, "The Core Competence of the Corporation," *Harvard Business Review* (May-June 1990).

Schiff, M. and A. Lewin, "Where Traditional Budgeting Fails," *Financial Executive*, (May 1968).

Shapiro, B. P., "What the Hell is 'Market Oriented'?" *Harvard Business Review* (November-December 1988).

[20]

Accounting, Organizations and Society, Vol. 12, No. 1, pp. 49–61, 1987.
Printed in Great Britain

0361–3682/87 $3.00+.00
Pergamon Journals Ltd.

MANAGEMENT CONTROL SYSTEMS AND DEPARTMENTAL INTERDEPENDENCIES: AN EMPIRICAL STUDY

N. B. MACINTOSH
School of Business, Queen's University, Kingston, Canada

and

R. L. DAFT
Department of Management, Texas A & M University

Abstract

Behavioral accounting research suggests that (1) the design and use of a management accounting system is related to overall characteristics of the organization, and (2) a management accounting system is one element in a package of control systems. The research reported here investigated the relationship between the organizational characteristic of departmental interdependence and the design and use of three elements in a package of management controls — the operating budget, periodic statistical reports, and standard operating policies and procedures. The findings support the hypothesis that departmental interdependence is related to the emphasis placed on each management control system. Standard operating procedures were an important control device when interdependence was low. The budget and statistical reports were used more extensively when interdependence was moderate. When interdependence among departments was high, the role of all three control systems diminished.

The literature on accounting control suggests that the design and focus of management accounting systems may be related to overall characteristics of the organization. From this perspective accounting systems are intertwined with the way organizations function, and they can be studied in conjunction with their organizational setting (Waterhouse & Tiessen, 1979; Otley, 1980; Ewusi-Mensah, 1981; Birnberg *et al.*, 1983; Burchell *et al.*, 1980; Merchant, 1981; Hopwood, 1983; Gordon & Narayanan, 1984; Govindarajan & Gupta, 1985). The purpose of the research reported here is to explore the relationship of one such characteristic — departmental interdependence — and control system design.

DEPARTMENTAL INTERDEPENDENCE

The design of organizations and internal systems is related to factors such as the external environment (Duncan, 1972; McCann & Selsky, 1984), technology (Fry, 1982; Daft & Macintosh, 1981) and interdependence among departments (Thompson, 1967). Although a growing body of research supports the relationship between organization design and environment or technology, interdependence among departments is an area of potential new insight into the design of control systems within organizations. Interdependence is the extent to which departments depend upon each other and exchange information and resources to accomplish their respective tasks (Van de Ven *et al.*, 1976; McCann & Ferry, 1979). The concept of interdependency is proposed as an organizational variable relevant to control systems for two reasons. First, interdependency reflects workflow and hence the amount of coordination and feedback needed among departments. The data available for coordination and feedback may be available from the management systems used to manage and control those departments (Thompson, 1967; Van de Ven *et al.*, 1976; Tushman, 1977). Second, several accounting researchers have identified interdependency across departments as a potentially important organizational variable for future management accounting studies (Watson & Baulmer, 1975; Hayes, 1977; Ginzberg, 1980; Otley, 1980; Kilmann, 1983; Emmanuel & Otley, 1985; Merchant, 1985; Chenhall & Morris, 1986).

Thompson (1967) first proposed the role of interdependence in organizational design, and defined three types that are widespread in modern organizations — pooled, sequential and reciprocal. Each of these place unique and identifiable demands on management systems and processes. Pooled is the lowest form of interdependence. Departments are relatively autonomous and little work flows between them. This occurs when departments are self-contained, or when they provide services to geographically distributed clients. Branch banks and stores are examples of units that operate independently of each other. Operating units share resources (e.g. financial, advertising) from a common pool. The low level of interdependence leads to standardized coordination through rules and procedures.

Sequential interdependence involves the linkage of organizational departments in serial fashion. The output of one department becomes a direct input to the next department. Each department completes its work by depending on work from preceding departments. Breakdowns and disruptions in this work flow do occur and place greater coordination and control demands on the organization than does pooled interdependence. Here accounting and control systems may be used to facilitate planning and scheduling, and also encourage feedback to coordinate workflow between departments.

The third and highest form of interdependence is reciprocal. It is characterized by the movement of work back and forth among departments in reciprocal fashion. Organizational departments featuring reciprocal interdependence typically work jointly on the same project or customer. Services are customized and coordinated on the basis of feedback about the project and mutual adjustment among the specialized departments. In a hospital, for example, a patient may move back and forth among departments (X-ray, surgical, psychiatric) on the basis of the most current information and feedback about the patient's health. Reciprocal interdependence places a heavy demand on management for coordination. Standardization and accounting information often are not sufficient for coordination, so face-to-face interaction and mutual adjustment may be required.

MANAGEMENT CONTROL SYSTEMS

The role of management accounting systems in organizational control traditionally has been studied in isolation from characteristics of the total organization and from other non-accounting based control systems (Young, 1979; Flamholtz, 1983; Macintosh, 1985). Recently a few researchers have argued that this narrow view is part of the reason that we still do not have a good understanding of how management accounting systems function (Gordon & Miller, 1976; Otley & Berry, 1980; Daft & Macintosh, 1984).

The reason accounting systems alone represent a narrow view is that the package of formal controls in an organization typically includes: accounting reports, the budget, formal hierarchy and supervision; job descriptions; rules and standard operating procedures; statistics for measuring performance; organization structure; employee performance appraisal systems; and corporate culture (Lawler, 1976; Flamholtz, 1983). These controls may seem an *ad-hoc* collection of techniques and mechanisms, but in many cases they are the tangible elements of a strategy to create an integrated organizational control package (Otley & Berry, 1980; Otley, 1980; Flamholtz, 1983). In this research we propose to investigate the way three control sub-systems interrelate with one another as well as the way the package fits the organizational setting.

Operating budget

The operating budget schedules and records department revenue and expenditures for salaries, noncapital equipment and other operating expenses. The budget is considered a crucial component of the control system package (Horngren, 1982; Kaplan, 1982). Usually a detailed operating budget is drawn up for the forthcoming year and then periodic budget reports are issued (usually monthly) to provide information to department managers and upper management about progress toward budget targets.

Statistical reports

In addition to the budget, most organizations rely on periodic operational reports that provide upper management with information on departmental outputs and performance (Daft & Macintosh, 1984). These reports are composed of statistical data such as number of personnel, number of new customer contracts, volume of orders received and on hand, machinery down time and other statistics relevant to the department. Most of the data in these reports are non financial and are issued in weekly, monthly or quarterly reports. The specific content of these reports may differ across departments. These reports normally originate in staff units other than accounting or finance, such as MIS or computing services.

Standard operating procedures and policies

The set of written rules, procedures, policies and operating manuals (SOPs) are used to guide managers as they administer their departments. The SOPs also include general policy guidelines, job descriptions and prescriptions for how managers should handle operational situations that might arise.

THE RESEARCH MODEL

The theoretical question to be addressed concerns the relationship between the design and use of these management control systems and the type of interdependence among departments. Control is typically a three-stage cycle that includes target setting, monitoring of performance, and feedback for correction. Management control systems should theoretically assist managers to perform the control cycle. Control systems also help managers evaluate employees and coordinate across departments. Depending upon the emphasis given to a control system within the organization, its scope and frequency may vary, and so may the emphasis given to each control function, such as target setting, monitoring, and coordination. Moreover, control systems have the potential to exert a motivational force on employees who are affected by the system (Hopwood, 1976; Brownell, 1982; Daroca, 1984; Merchant, 1985). Management control systems can vary in terms of many characteristics including: scope; reporting frequency; influence in target setting; importance for key functions (planning, coordination and measurement); emphasis, response to variances, and influence on day-to-day operations. The three interdependencies (pooled, sequential, reciprocal) are expected to be related to the design and use of budgets, statistical reports and SOPs along these dimensions. The overall research model is illustrated in Table 1. The reasons for the hypothesized relationships are as follows.

Under conditions of pooled interdependency, organizations rely on standardization for controlling operating departments (Van de Ven *et al.*, 1976; Mintzberg, 1979). Standardization makes possible the operation of the independent tasks over time by assuring that segments of the organization are operating in compatible ways. "It is in such situations that the bureaucratic techniques of categorization and impersonal application of rules have been most beneficial" (Thompson, 1967, p. 17). Thus SOPs are expected to be a primary control medium when interdependence is pooled and consequently the scope, function and motivational impact of SOPs are expected to be high. Most control and coordination needs can be met through SOPs. Other forms of control, such as budgets and statistical reports, are not expected to be important when interdependence is low. Hence budgets and statistical reports are expected to receive less emphasis than SOPs when organizational departments experience pooled interdependence. These arguments are summarized in the following hypotheses.

Hypothesis 1a. The use of SOPs for control will be positively correlated with the extent of pooled interdependence among departments.

Hypothesis 1b. The use of operating budget and statistical reports for control will be negatively correlated with the extent of pooled interdependence among departments.

For sequential interdependence, performance in a department depends on the work of other departments in the chain. Planning and scheduling are critical to ensure that departments provide necessary resources for other departments in the work flow. Measurement of output is important so that management can monitor whether activities are on schedule and can respond to any exceptions or deviations that arise. The pressure to run interdependent departments without interruption can lead to a strong control mentality from the top to coordinate differences among departments (Mintzberg, 1979). The primary control systems used by managers under these conditions are expected to be the budget and statistical reports. The budget provides for the planning and scheduling of resources into each department and statistical reports measure and monitor outputs from each department.

The greater coordination and control demand of sequential interdependence is expected to mean that budgets and statistical reports will receive greater control emphasis than SOPs as a mechanism of management control. SOPs provide standardization when interdependence is low, but they are not expected to be emphasized or to provide sufficient control when interdependence is sequential because each department in the chain is performing a different task. These relationships are reflected in the following hypotheses.

Hypothesis 2a. The use of the operating budget and statistical reports for control will be positively correlated with the extent of sequential interdependence among departments.

Hypothesis 2b. The use of SOPs for control will be negatively correlated with the extent of sequential interdependence among departments.

When departments experience reciprocal interdependence, organizational performance is based on the ability to fuse diverse departments into a joint effort. Coordination and control come from rapid mutual adjustment and face-to-face communication among departments, and feedback from the customer or client (Thompson, 1967). The transformation process is difficult to quantify, and performance tends to be based on whether the joint activities produce the best outcome rather than on schedules or ef-

TABLE 1. Proposed relationship between department interdependency and use of management control systems

Departmental interdependency	Preferred means of control	Hypothesized relationship of interdependency with use of control system
Pooled	Standardization	(+) SOPs (−) Operating budget (−) Statistical reports
Sequential	Planning and measurement	(−) SOPs (+) Operating budget (+) Statistical reports
Reciprocal	Mutual adjustment	(−) SOPs (−) Operating budget (−) Statistical reports

(+) positive relationship.
(−) negative relationship.

ficiency. Control systems such as standardization, rules, procedures, planning, budgets and formal reports are expected to be less important for control when interdependence is very high. The impersonal control of SOPs and the data in the budget and statistical reports tend not to capture the dynamic nature of mutual adjustment (Hayes, 1977). Professional norms, supervision and other forms of personal, decentralized control become more important under conditions of reciprocal interdependence. Thus the scope, function and motivational impact of formal management control systems such as SOPs, budget and statistical reports are expected to be low under conditions of reciprocal interdependence.

Hypothesis 3. The use of SOPs, budget, and statistical reports for control will be negatively correlated with the extent of reciprocal interdependence among departments.

RESEARCH METHOD

Sample

The main criterion used to guide sample selection was the need to include a wide range of departmental tasks to have variation in interdependencies. To accomplish this, twenty five firms representing each industrial and commercial category in a directory of industrial and commercial enterprises were selected at random and contacted to see if they would participate in the study. Organizations from the service and public sectors were also included to ensure that the sample represented a cross section from both the private and public sectors.

Eighty percent of the organizations contacted agreed to participate in the study. During the preliminary visits, the control systems in each organization were discussed with the corporate controller or his counterpart. Within each organization every attempt was made to obtain a diverse cross-section of departments. The main criteria for inclusion in the sample was that the department managers had a clearly defined responsibility for meeting their operating budget. In one company, for example, plant, marketing, personnel and engineering departments were selected. The final sample included 90 major departments from twenty organizations in five sectors of the economy. The organizations were located in the U.S.A. and Canada. Details of the sample are given in Table 2.

Data collection

The primary method of data collection consisted of a personal interview with each department manager. A preliminary interview format had been pre-tested on managers in several organizations, after which the final questionnaire was developed. Personal interviews were used because they eliminated some of the distortions ascribed to mail questionnaires when used to measure organizational phenomena.

The interviews were conducted in the offices of the department managers. They were asked to pull out the actual budget and statistical reports under investigation, and these documents remained in front of the managers as they responded to the interview questions. The SOPs were also on hand, usually in the manager's office or nearby.

Two types of measurements were obtained. First, actual physical counts were taken of the number of books, pages and lines of standard operating procedures and practices. The second measurement involved asking managers for their perception of how the controls were used, such as for motivational impact. The managers were asked, for example, to rate the level of difficulty of budget targets, using a nine point scale ranging from "very easy to achieve" to "almost impossible to achieve". For the interdependence variables the managers were shown diagrams (Appendix A) and asked for their perception of the work flow betweeen their department and other departments. This instrument was developed and validated by Van de Ven *et al.* (1976).

FINDINGS

The statistical tests of the hypotheses about

TABLE 2. Sample composition

Sector	Main activities of each organization
1. Manufacturing	a. Machinery (6)
	b. Electronics (6)
	c. Wood products (3)
	d. Textiles (4)
	e. Oil, gas, and petrochemicals (3)
	f. Wine (4)
	g. Spirits (7)
	h. Telephone and telecommunications equipment (5)
2. Merchandising	a. Large, general department store chain (7)
	b. Specialty department store chain (3)
	c. Clothing retail chain (3)
3. Consumer marketing	a. Food products (5)
	b. Personal, food, and grocery products (4)
4. Service	a. Advertising (3)
	b. Telephone and telecommunications (6)
	c. Bank (3)
	d. Finance (2)
	e. Trust and banking (4)
5. Health care	a. Hospital (9)
	b. Faculty of medicine (3)

Figures in parentheses represent the number of departments sampled in each organization.

the design and use of control system and the extent of interdependence are shown in Tables 3, 4 and 5. The tables report partial correlation coefficients that control for department size. The departments varied widely by size, and a substantial literature indicates that size is associated with greater use of bureaucratic rules and other forms of impersonal control (Child, 1972; Khandwalla, 1974; Bruns & Waterhouse, 1975; Waterhouse & Tiessen, 1979; Merchant, 1981;

TABLE 3. Partial correlations (controlling for size) of standard operating procedures and departmental interdependence

Characteristics of the standard operating procedures	Interdependencies Pooled	Sequential	Reciprocal
1. Number of books	0.33*	–	– 0.22†
2. Number of pages	0.31*	–	– 0.30*
3. Percentage of departmental work covered	0.29†	–	– 0.24†
4. Percentage of time necessary to follow SOP's to do work well	0.22†	–	– 0.21†
5. Adherence to SOP's used to evaluate performance	–	–	–
6. Influence of SOP's on department activities and operations	0.27†	–	– 0.32*

* $p < 0.01$.
† $p < 0.05$.
– Not significant.

TABLE 4. Partial correlations (controlling for size) of budget characteristics and departmental interdependence

Budget characteristics	Pooled	Interdependencies Sequential	Reciprocal
Frequency	0.22†	–	–
Target difficulty	– 0.26†	–	–
Influence in target setting			
Upper management	–	0.23†	– 0.23†
Department manager	–	–	– 0.32*
Department employees	–	–	0.18‡
Importance for			
Planning	–	–	–
Coordination	–	0.18‡	–
Measure and monitor	– 0.18‡	0.24†	– 0.23†
Emphasis on meeting targets	–	0.25†	– 0.19‡
Response to negative variances	–	–	–
Influence on daily activities	– 0.25†	0.29†	–

* $p < 0.01$.
† $p < 0.05$.
‡ $p < 0.10$.
– Not significant.

TABLE 5. Partial correlations (controlling for size) of statistical reports characteristics and departmental interdependence

Statistical reports characteristics	Pooled	Interdependencies Sequential	Reciprocal
Frequency	–0.33*	–	– 0.22‡
Target difficulty	– 0.37*	0.33†	–
Influence in target setting			
Upper management	–	0.19‡	–
Department manager	– 0.33*	–	0.21‡
Department employees	– 0.28*	–	0.22‡
Importance for			
Planning	–	–	0.36‡
Coordination	– 0.28*	–	0.21‡
Measure and monitor	– 0.29*	–	– 0.29*
Emphasis on meeting targets	–	0.25‡	–
Response to negative variances	–	–	–
Influence on daily activities	– 0.22†	0.20‡	–

* $p < 0.01$.
† $p < 0.05$.
‡ $p < 0.10$.
– Not significant.

Kimberly, 1983; Daft, 1986). Otley (1978) found that operating unit size had a significant impact on budget behavior. Controlling for the effect of size should provide a better test of whether systematic differences in interdependence are related to control system scope and use. The overall tendency of controlling for size is to weaken the correlations slightly, although a few small correlations for the budget and statistical reports disappeared.

The findings in Table 3 support Hypothesis 1a that the use of SOPs will have a positive correlation with pooled interdependence. Five of the six SOP characteristics are significantly associated with pooled interdependence, including the quantity and coverage of SOPs, the necessity to follow them to do the job well, and SOP influence on daily operations.

Table 3 also indicates that the extent of sequential interdependence has no relationship with standard operating procedures, but that the extent of reciprocal interdependence has a negative relationship. These findings are consistent with the theoretical argument that as the level of interdependence increases, the size and use of SOPs as a primary control device will decline.

The results in the first column of Tables 4 and 5 provide modest support for Hypothesis 1b that the operating budget and the statistical reports will be negatively correlated with pooled interdependencies. Four budget and seven statistical reports characteristics were negatively associated with pooled interdependence. The overall finding is that the use of SOPs appears to be an important control for departments having pooled interdependencies while the budget and the statistical reports are less so.

Hypothesis 2a proposed that under conditions of sequential interdependence organizations will emphasize the operating budget and statistical reports for control. The results in the second column of Tables 4 and 5 provide some support for this relationship. Five budget characteristics and four statistical report characteristics were positively associated with sequential interdependence. In general, for sequential interdependency it appears that top management have a lot of influence in setting targets, and these controls have motivational force on employees. This is consistent with Mintzberg's (1979) idea that a strong top-down control mentality prevails in sequentially interdependent departments.

Hypothesis 3 stated that managers in reciprocally interdependent departments will rely less on the three formal control systems than managers in departments with low interdependence. The data generally support this hypothesis for the SOPs and the budget. Five of the six SOP characteristics (Table 3, column 3) and four budget characteristics (Table 4, column 3) are negatively associated with reciprocal interdependence. SOPs and budgets thus are reported to be used less as the level of interdependence increases.

Contrary to Hypothesis 3 some characteristics of the statistical reports are positively associated with reciprocal interdependence (Table 5, column 3). Statistical reports appear to be used more for planning and coordination when interdependence is high. Department managers and lower level employees also have more influence in target setting. Thus SOPs and budgets are used less under conditions of reciprocal interdependence while the statistical reports seem to play an expanded role in planning, target setting and coordination. Planning and target setting also seem to entail more participation from lower level employees.

DISCUSSION AND IMPLICATIONS

The research reported here gathered data from 90 departments in 20 organizations to examine the relationship between departmental interdependence and control systems. The hypothesized pattern was that increasing levels of interdependence would be associated with differential use of SOPs, the budget and statistical reports. All three control systems were used in the organizations, but the scope and extent of use did differ by extent of departmental interdependence.

Under conditions of pooled interdependence, the organizations in the sample seemed to rely more on SOPs and less on budget and statistical reports. A requirement of pooled interdependence is that departments operate in compatible ways, but frequent adjustments are not needed. For example, Daft (1986) cites the McDonald's fast-food chain as an example of pooled interdependence where each component used procedures and reports as a way of standardizing outcomes.

For sequentially interdependent departments the findings indicated that managers tended to use budgets and statistical reports more than SOPs. The sequential linkage among departments appears to require more emphasis on resources, targets, scheduling, monitoring and feedback, which are accomplished with budgets and periodic operational reports. Management accounting systems and statistical reports are well-suited to measuring the performance of departments when internal variables are the major explanators of effectiveness (Hayes, 1977), and in large, process dominated organizations (Bruns & Waterhouse, 1975).

The findings also indicated that under conditions of reciprocal interdependence the budgets and SOPs were used less than when interdependence was low. Reciprocal interdependence increases uncertainty, and managers used statistical reports for planning and coordination. Statistical reports probably were used less for measuring and monitoring because work flow is hard to quantify and measure under reciprocal interdependence. Management accounting tools and other traditional controls seem to lose their primacy under the uncertainty and rapid adaption needed for reciprocal coordination. The findings are consistent with Mintzberg's (1979) suggestion that the need for quick response and sophisticated innovation, with different departments joining forces around specific projects, means the organization cannot rely on rules, standardization and all the regular bureaucratic trappings. Expert knowledge, mutual adjustment, and full-time project managers replace formal reporting systems, SOPs, and emphasis on hierarchical arrangements (Thompson, 1967). Formal controls are still used, of course, but more often for help with planning and coordinating by lower managers than for top level performance monitoring.

Reciprocal interdependence appears to pose the greatest challenge to formal management control systems. Financial data and budgets apparently do not play as large a role for departments such as R&D and Marketing in which reciprocal interdependence dominates (Hayes, 1977). Our findings indirectly support Govindarajan's (1984) finding that business units facing higher environmental uncertainty rely more on subjective performance evaluations than on formula-based ones. A basic tenet of management accounting is that managers should be held accountable for aspects of performance, such as costs, over which they have control. Yet this tendency may not fit reciprocal interdependence. The task of each department is highly dependent on the on-going work of several other departments (Hayes, 1977). Formal reporting systems may be used for planning, but they are not emphasized for current detailed data for coordinating or measuring the effectiveness of highly interdependent groups (Hayes, 1977). Although we did not test mutual adjustment directly, the requisite coordination and control seems to be achieved through personal interaction, frequent communication, and mutual adjustment by the various managers and employees involved (Van de Ven *et al.*, 1976; Daft & Macintosh, 1978; Cheng, 1983).

In conclusion, we want to address the questions raised at the beginning of this paper — do management control systems vary with departmental interdependence, and do accounting systems fit within a larger organizational control package? Watson & Baumler (1975), Bruns & Waterhouse (1975), Hayes (1977), Ginzberg (1980), and Otley (1980) proposed that departmental interdependence may be a design parameter that influences the use of accounting and information systems as integrating and control devices. The findings reported in this paper support this line of thinking and indicate how each of three control systems are used depending upon the level of departmental interdependence.

One interpretation of the findings is that the role of each control system reflects a fit between the need for information created by interdependence and the supply of information provided by the control system. SOPs are a standing body of knowledge that is appropriate for specifying standard behaviours across relatively stable and independent departments. Sequential interdependence creates a need for more data to schedule, plan, and monitor the flow of material and activities between departments. Budgeting and statistical reports, which can provide data on a monthly, weekly, or even a daily cycle, provide data that are more current and more relevant than SOPs for the short time horizon needed for coordination. When interdependence among departments is reciprocal, the information requirements begin to outstrip the data supplied by formal control systems. These systems may be used for planning and scheduling, but special emphasis is given to face-to-face coordination and mutual adjustment. Since managers cannot predict in advance the problems that may arise and the information required, the data contained in formal reports will not cover all problems, and hence will receive less emphasis than in the case of pooled and sequential interdependence. Thus as interdependence increases, data are needed that are current, timely, and pertain to unpredictable events. These data are supplied in turn by SOPs, budgets, statistical reports and by direct managerial involvement in face-to-face coordination.

The question of an organizational control package also seems to have received a partial answer from our analysis of the data. Although we can't say whether managers consciously designed each control system to play a different role, we did find that control systems were used in different yet complementary ways. SOPs were used to direct behaviour for stable, independent departments, while budgets and statistical reports were used to plan, monitor, and correct activities associated with resource inputs into departments and outputs from those departments. Although we focused on only three control systems, we found that all three were related to management functions, and had a good deal of motivational force. Moreover, department managers reported a high degree of satisfaction with all three control systems.

One realistic implication of the control package concept is that accounting systems designers may want to consider the management accounting system as part of a larger organizational control system. The presence of SOPs and periodic statistical reports may influence how the accounting system is used. Accountants tend to focus on the financial aspects of the organization, and pay less attention to other control information needed by managers. If management accountants are aware of the unique control problems posed by organization characteristics such as pooled, sequential, and especially reciprocal interdependence, they will be in a position to provide leadership in the selection of the requisite control framework.

In conclusion, this research attempted to increase understanding of control within the organizations by examining a package of control systems and comparing their use to departmental interdependency (Otley, 1980). Previous studies have found that forces such as environmental uncertainty, technology, business strategy and decentralization are related to overall structure and control processes. Interdependence among departments seems related to the use of control systems at the department level. Taken together the accumulated findings suggest an agenda for future research: begin to combine separate models into a larger theory, and undertake new empirical studies that integrate several organizational variables and management control systems into a unified framework. Although a single study cannot assess all variables, efforts to integrate past empirical findings may provide both new theoretical knowledge and normative applications for control system design.

BIBLIOGRAPHY

Birnberg, J. G., Turopolec, L. & Young, S. M., The Organizational Context of Accounting, *Accounting, Organizations and Society* (1983) pp. 111–129.

Brownell, P., Participation in the Budgeting Process: When it Works and When it Doesn't, *Journal of Accounting Literature* (1982) pp. 124–153.

Bruns, J. C. & Waterhouse, J. H., Budgeting, Control and Organizational Structure, *Journal of Accounting Research* (Autumn 1975) pp. 177–203.

Burchell, S., Clubb, C., Hopwood, A. G., Hughes, J. & Nahapiet, J., The Role of Accounting in Organizations and Society, *Accounting, Organizations and Society* (1980) pp. 5–27.

Chenhall, R. H. & Morris, D., The Impact of Structure, Environment, and Interdependence on the Perceived Usefulness of Management Accounting Systems, *The Accounting Review* (January 1986) pp. 58–75.

Cheng, J. L., Interdependence and Coordination in Organizations: A Role-System Analysis, *Academy of Management Journal* (1983) pp. 156–162.

Child, J., Organization Structure and Strategies of Control: A Replication of the Aston Study, *Administrative Science Quarterly* (1972) pp. 163–177.

Daft, R. L., *Organizational Theory and Design* (Saint Paul, MN: West Publishing, 1986).

Daft, R. L. & Macintosh, N. B., A New Approach to Design and Use of Management Information, *California Management Review* (1978) pp. 82–92.

Daft, R. L. & Macintosh, N. B., A Tentative Exploration into the Amount and Equivocality of Information Processing in Organizational Work Units, *Administrative Science Quarterly* (1981) pp. 207–224.

Daft, R. L. & Macintosh, N. B., The Nature and Use of Formal Control Systems for Management Control and Strategy Implementation, *Journal of Management* (1984) pp. 43–66.

Daroca, F. P., Informational Influences on Group Decision Making in a Participative Budgeting Context, *Accounting, Organizations and Society* (1984) pp. 13–32.

Duncan, R. B., Characteristics of Organizational Environment and Preceived Environmental Uncertainty, *Administrative Science Quarterly* (1972) pp. 313–327.

Emmanuel, C. & Otley, D., *Accounting for Management Control* (New York: Van Nostrand Reinhold, 1985).

Ewusi-Mensah, K., The External Organizational Environment and Its Impact on Management Information Systems, *Accounting, Organizations and Society* (1981) pp. 301–316.

Flamholtz, E. G., Accounting, Budgeting and Control Systems in Their Organizational Context, *Accounting, Organizations and Society* (1983) pp. 153–169.

Fry, L. W., Technology-Structure Research: Three Critical Issues, *Academy of Management Journal* (1982), pp. 535–522.

Ginzberg, M. J., An organizational Contingencies View of Accounting and Information Systems Implementation, *Accounting, Organizations and Society* (1980) pp. 369–382.

Gordon, L. A. & Miller, D., A Contingency Framework for the Design of Accounting Information Systems, *Accounting, Organizations and Society* (1976) pp. 59–69.

Gordon, L. A. & Narayanan, V. K., Management Accounting Systems, Perceived Environmental Uncertainty and Organizational Structure: An Empirical Investigation, *Accounting, Organizations and Society* (1984) pp. 33–47.

Govindarajan, V., Appropriateness of Accounting Data in Performance Evaluation: An Empirical Examination of Environmental Uncertainty as an Intervening Variable, *Accounting, Organizations and Society* (1984) pp. 125–135.

Govindarajan, V. & Gupta, A. K., Linking Control Systems to Business Unit Strategy: Impact on Performance, *Accounting, Organizations and Society* (1985) pp. 51–56.

Hayes, D. C., The Contingency Theory of Management Accounting, *The Accounting Review* (January 1977) pp. 22–39.

Hopwood, A. G., On Trying to Study Accounting in the Contexts in which it Operates, *Accounting, Organizations and Society* (1983) pp. 287–305.

Hopwood, A. G., *Accounting and Human Behavior* (Englewood Cliffs, NJ: Prentice-Hall 1976).

Horngren, C. T., *Cost Accounting: A Managerial Emphasis* 5th edn. (Englewood Cliffs, NJ: Prentice-Hall 1982).

Kaplan, R. S., The Evolution of Management Accounting, *The Accounting Review* (July 1984) pp. 390–418.

Kaplan, R. S., *Advanced Management Accounting* (Englewood Cliffs, NJ: Prentice-Hall, 1982).

Khandwalla, P. N., Mass Output Orientation of Operations Technology and Organizational Structure, *Administrative Science Quarterly* (March 1974) pp. 74–97.

Kilmann, R. H., The Costs of Organization Structure: Dispelling the Myths of Independent Divisions and Organization-Wide Decision Making, *Accounting, Organizations and Society* (1983) pp. 341–357.

Kimberly, J. R., Organizational Size and the Structuralist Perspective: A Review, Critique and Proposal,

Administrative Science Quarterly (1983) pp. 571–597.

Lawler, E. E., III, Control Systems in Organizations, in Dunnette, M. D. (ed.), *Handbook of Industrial and Organizational Psychology*, (Skokie, IL: Rand McNally, 1976).

McCann, J. E. & Ferry, D. L., An Approach For Assessing and Managing Inter-unit Interdependencies, *Academy of Management Review* (1979) pp. 113–119.

McCann, J. E. & Selsky, J., Hyperturbulence and the Emergence of Type 5 Environments, *Academy of Management Review* (1984), pp. 460–470.

Macintosh, N. B., *The Social Software of Accounting and Information Systems* (Chichester: John Wiley, 1985).

Merchant, K. A., The Design of the Corporate Budgeting System: Influences on Managerial Behavior and Performance, *The Accounting Review* (October 1981) pp. 813–829.

Merchant, K. A., Budgeting and the Propensity to Create Budgetary Slack, *Accounting, Organizations and Society* (1985) pp. 201–210.

Mintzberg, H., *The Structuring of Organizations* (Englewood Cliffs, NJ: Prentice-Hall 1979).

Otley, D. T., Budget Use and Managerial Performance, *Journal of Accounting Research* (Spring 1978) pp. 122–149.

Otley, D. T., The Contingency Theory of Management Accounting, *Accounting, Organizations and Society* (1980) pp. 413–428.

Otley, D. T. & Berry, A. J., Control, Organisation and Accounting, *Accounting, Organizations and Society* (1980) pp. 231–244.

Thompson, J. D., *Organizations in Action* (New York: McGraw-Hill 1967).

Tushman, M. L., Special Boundary Roles in the Innovation Process, *Administrative Science Quarterly* December 1977) pp. 587–605.

Van de Ven, A. H., Delbecq, A. L. & Koenig, R. Jr., Determinants of Coordination Modes Within Organizations, *American Sociological Review* (1976) pp. 322–338.

Waterhouse, J. H. & Tiessen, P., A Contingency Framework for Management Accounting Systems Research, *Accounting, Organizations and Society* (1979) pp. 65–76.

Watson, D. J. H. & Baumler, J. V., Transfer Pricing: A Behavioral Context, *The Accounting Review* (July 1975) pp. 466–474.

Young, D. W., Administrative Theory and Administrative Systems: A Synthesis Among Diverging Fields of Inquiry, *Accounting, Organizations and Society* (1979) pp. 235–244.

APPENDIX A. INTERDEPENDENCIES QUESTIONNAIRE FORM

How much work normally flows between your unit and other units in this manner?

	Almost none		Some		About half		A lot		Almost all
1. Independent work flow	1	2	3	4	5	6	7	8	9
2. Sequential work flow	1	2	3	4	5	6	7	8	9
3. Reciprocal work flow	1	2	3	4	5	6	7	8	9

Part V
The Organization in its Environment

[21]

Accounting, Organizations and Society. Vol. 5, No. 4, pp. 413-428. 0361-3682/80/1201-0413$02.00/0

THE CONTINGENCY THEORY OF MANAGEMENT ACCOUNTING: ACHIEVEMENT AND PROGNOSIS*

DAVID T. OTLEY

Department of Accounting and Finance, University of Lancaster, Lancaster, U.K.

Abstract

Contingency theories of management accounting have become a current vogue but have produced few significant new results. By surveying the development and content of these theories it is argued that they have been based on an inadequate and insufficiently articulated model. An improved model, based on ideas of organisational control and effectiveness, is put forward which suggests appropriate directions for future work that will be both perceptive and cumulative.

The use of a contingency framework for the analysis of management accounting information systems is a recent vogue. Although contingency formulations were developed in the organisation theory literature in the early to mid-1960's there was no reference to contingency theory in the accounting literature before the mid-1970's. However, during the past five years it has come to dominate the published work on the behavioural and organisational aspects of management accounting. This rapid rise and apparently widespread acceptance of a new theoretical framework requires examination to establish whether it represents an important advance in understanding or is merely a passing fad.

In this paper the contribution made by contingency approaches is reviewed and assessed by reference to what is considered to be a minimally necessary framework for the construction of a true contingency theory. It is argued that the contingency approach is an important development in the theory of management accounting, but that it requires both improved conceptual clarity and the use of different research methodologies to those commonly reported. Firstly, the main features of the contingency approach and its application to accounting control systems are examined by considering some situations where contingency theories have emerged from the interpretation of research data. Secondly, the content of current contingency theories of management accounting, both empirical and theoretical, is outlined and assessed by reference to a framework for evaluation based on an organisational control perspective. Finally, the implications of this perspective for research are discussed.

THE CONTINGENCY APPROACH

The contingency approach to management accounting is based on the premise that there is no universally appropriate accounting system which applies equally to all organisations in all circumstances. Rather, it is suggested that particular features of an appropriate accounting system will depend upon the specific circumstances in which an organisation finds itself. Thus a contingency theory must identify *specific aspects* of an accounting system which are associated with certain *defined circumstances* and demonstrate an *appropriate matching*.

Although the contingency framework is new, management accounting has long recognised its inter-relationship with organisational and behavioural factors, as is exemplified by Horngren's (1972) exhortation to the effect that

*An earlier version of this paper was given at the Accounting Research Workshop, University of Glasgow, May 1979 and at the European Accounting Association, Amsterdam, March 1980. I am most grateful for the many helpful comments received on those occasions.

> the design of a (management accounting) system and the design of an organisational structure are really inseparable and interdependent.

Unfortunately he gives no practical guidelines as to how this joint design task should be undertaken. A more recent text by Dermer (1977) explicitly adopts a contingency framework emphasising that:

> the design of any planning and control system is situationally specific. The intent of this text is not to tell a system designer what should be done; rather, it is to convey the fact that there are a number of possibilities that might be done in any particular situation. . . . This text squarely faces the uncertain and contingent application of most of the activities and techniques which make up the planning and control system.

But although relevant contingencies are specified and some of their implications explored, few practical guidelines are given as to their impact on accounting system design. The contingency approach is invoked, so it seems, in order to cover up some of the embarrassing ambiguities that exist in the universalist approach.

Neither is the research literature of greater help. Although empirical studies exist they are vague as to the links between specified contingencies and appropriate accounting systems design, as is demonstrated later. The radical change in emphasis observed over the past five years is thus disturbing in that the insights obtained do not appear to be capable of conversion into practical design guidelines. The idea that "it all depends" tends to be used as a means of avoiding rather than addressing design implications. The contingency approach, thus, has the appearance of being an influential but ephemeral fashion and it is particularly insidious because it occurs in a relatively immature field.

Two main lines of development can be distinguished. On the one hand, there are studies which have not explicitly attempted to use a contingency framework, but where contingent results have emerged either within the study itself or when its results have been interpreted in conjunction with those of other comparable work. On the other hand, some studies have begun with a contingency framework in mind and have explicitly attempted to assess the impact of various hypothesised contingent factors, either theoretically or by empirical testing. The first type of study will be examined in the next section, which will also serve to provide illustrations of the nature of contingency theories, whereas discussion of the second type of study will be deferred until the following section.

THE EMERGENCE OF CONTINGENCY FORMULATIONS

It might be thought that the justification for adopting a contingency theory of management accounting is that it emerged as a necessary means of interpreting the results of empirical research. This is true to a limited extent and the work reviewed in this section gives an insight into the types of hypothesis that have been put forward to explain apparently contradictory findings. However, it is also argued that this type of work does not by itself account for the rapid rise of contingency formulations; and that it is necessary to look to parallel developments in organisation theory to develop an adequate explanation.

The influence of empirical results

Conflicting results which could not satisfactorily be resolved within a universal framework, have been one source of stimulus for the development of contingency formulations. Concepts such as technology, organisation structure and environment have been invoked to explain why accounting systems have been found to differ from one situation to another. The studies discussed here are intended to illustrate the piecemeal way in which the need for a contingency theory has become established.

(a) *The effect of technology*. The simplest and longest established contingent variable used in management accounting is perhaps that of production technology. The distinction between different types of production technique [e.g. unit production, small batch, large batch, mass production and process production as defined by Woodward (1965)] is a factor that has long been recognised as influencing the design of internal accounting systems although it should be noted that it emerged in Woodward's study as a means of explaining contradictory results in what was originally intended to be an empirical confirmation of classical organisation theory. The nature of the production process determines the amount of cost allocation rather than cost apportionment that takes place. In job-order costing the measure of production is well-defined and only limited allocation and averaging are required because a large proportion of total costs can be directly associated with particular jobs; in contrast, the polar extreme of process costing requires extensive allocation and averaging because the bulk of total costs are incurred jointly by a mix of final products. Thus the level of detail and accuracy that is possible in costing unit and small batch production cannot be carried over into process production, although it should be noted that "process" type methods may be adequate and appropriate for some "job" situations where accurate costing of individual products is of minor importance. Production technology thus has an important effect on the type of accounting information that *can* be provided and more recent work has distinguished other aspects of technology that have an effect on the information that *should* be provided for effective performance. For example, Piper (1978) demonstrates that the complexity of the task faced by an organisation is relevant to defining an appropriate financial control structure and Daft & MacIntosh (1978) identify task variety and task knowledge as factors which affect the design of an appropriate management information system.

(b) *The effect of organisation structure.* There is evidence to suggest that the structure of the organisation affects the manner in which budgetary information is best used. Hopwood (1972) distinguished between a Budget-Constrained (B.C.) use of accounting information (where meeting the budget was the single most important factor in a superior's evaluation of his subordinates) and a Profit-Conscious (P.C.) style (where longer-run effectiveness was also considered). His study indicated that a rigid B.C. style was associated with high degrees of job-related tension, poor relationships with both peers and subordinates and dysfunctional behaviour such as the manipulation of accounting data, whereas the more flexible P.C. style had no such associations. He therefore concluded that the flexible style of budget use was likely to lead to more effective organisational performance (a universal result). However a subsequent study by Otley (1978), using comparable measures, yielded no such associations and appeared to suggest that the rigid style was more likely to lead to better performance than the more flexible style[1] (a contradictory universal result). But comparison of the two studies indicates an important situational difference which is suggestive of a contingent explanation.

Hopwood's study was based on responsibility (cost) centres in an integrated steel works which had extensive inter-dependence with each other. Otley's study involved responsibility (profit) centres in the coal mining industry which were, for all practical purposes, independent of each other. As Baulmer's (1971) earlier work indicated, the rigid use of defined performance measures is inappropriate where there is extensive interdependence. The (contingent) explanation that an appropriate style of budget use depends upon the degree of interdependence that exists between responsibility centres may thus be put forward. Because budgetary measures of performance become less appropriate as the degree of interdependence increases, managers tend to use budgetary information in a more flexible manner. The degree of interdependence that exists is a function of both technology and the organisational structure that is adopted, the organisational structure itself being influenced but not determined by technology (Child, 1972). Organisational structure and technology may thus be seen to have an important effect upon the way in which an accounting system functions.

(c) *The effect of environment.* Environmental factors have also been invoked to explain differences in the use made of accounting information. Khandwalla (1972) examined the effect that the type of competition faced by a firm had on its use of management controls and concluded that the sophistication of accounting and control systems was influenced by the intensity of the competition it faced. Moreover, different types of competition, for example price, marketing or product competition, had very different impacts on the use made of accounting controls in manufacturing organisations. A similar conclusion was arrived at by Otley (1978) who studied the effect of differences in the environments faced by unit managers within a single firm. By distinguishing between a tough operating environment (in which it was difficult for a unit manager to show accounting profits) and a liberal operating environment (in which it was relatively easy to maintain profitable operations) he showed that senior managers used budgetary information

[1] It should be noted that Otley's study also suggested that style of budget use is not an independent variable, but is itself influenced by environmental and economic factors.

to evaluate managerial performance in very different ways in the two situations. If budget accuracy is considered to be a desirable feature of an accounting system[2] different styles of budget use are necessary to achieve accurate budgets in the two operating environments.

The influence of organisation theory

The three preceding examples give an indication of some of the variables that have been put forward as affecting the design and use of an accounting system. The three general contingent variables of technology, organisational structure and environment were used as illustrative examples because they have been prominent in the theoretical development of contingency theories of management accounting. This movement from a universalistic approach [perhaps best exemplified by Hofstede's (1968) study of budgetary control] to a contingent approach in management accounting has been a feature of the 1970's, partly influenced by the necessity of explaining otherwise contradictory observations. But the recent popularity of the approach cannot be explained solely by the pressure of empirical findings in search of explanatory theories. The other major factor which influenced the development of the contingency theory of management accounting was the prior development of the contingency theory of organisations.

During the 1960's organisation theory underwent a major upheaval which led to the construction of a thorough-going contingency theory. This stemmed initially from the pioneering work of Burns & Stalker (1961) and was reinforced by the work of Woodward (1965), but was perhaps most strongly influenced by the stream of work that emanated from the Aston School which is summarised in the series edited by Pugh *et al.* (1976a, 1976b, 1977). In addition work by corporate strategists such as Chandler (1962) was emphasising the relationship between the strategy an organisation selected in order to achieve its goals and the organisational structure that was most appropriate for it to adopt. By early 1970 contingency theory was firmly established as the dominant approach in organisation theory (Child, 1977) although it has subsequently become subject to increasing criticism (Wood, 1979).

Simultaneously, although quite independently, the late 1960's and early 1970's saw the realisation by accounting academics that the organisational context of an accounting system was of fundamental importance to its effectiveness. This had been previously recognised to a limited extent, but accounting systems had been designed on the implicit assumption that the classical theory of organisations was an adequate representation of the circumstances in which they were used. Although behavioural research had been in progress from before 1960 it had focussed upon the impact of accounting information upon individuals rather than upon the organisation as a whole. It was not until around 1974 that these two movements came together. Accounting was tentatively developing contingency ideas and realising the importance of organisation structure;[3] organisation theory had just developed its own contingency formulation. The result was a minor avalanche of literature including Bruns & Waterhouse (1975), Sathe (1975), Watson (1975), Gordon & Miller (1976), Ansari (1977), Hayes (1977), Daft & MacIntosh (1978), Hopwood (1978), Piper (1978), Sathe (1978) and Waterhouse & Tiessen (1978).

Both empirical necessity and the availability of a ready-made theory can thus be seen to have contributed towards the sudden popularity of contingency approaches to the design of accounting information systems. It is now necessary to examine the content of these theories in more detail so as to be able to evaluate their contribution to management accounting.

THE CONTENT OF CONTINGENCY THEORIES OF MANAGEMENT ACCOUNTING

As has been shown in the preceding section, a substantial body of opinion holds that there is no universally "best" design for a management accounting information system, but that "it all depends" upon situational factors. However assent to such a general proposition does not produce consensus on what specific contingencies should result in particular configurations on accounting information. Indeed, a great variety of suggestions

[2] It is appreciated that in some circumstances other features will be of greater importance than budget accuracy, and that accuracy may well be sacrificed in order to gain other benefits.

[3] Although this latter development can be traced back to Caplan (1966) he did not include the contingency framework in his outline of modern organisational theory.

are available, some stemming from empirical work and others from theoretical speculation based on the results of work in organisation theory. In this section the content of the main contingent formulations that have been proposed is reviewed.

Empirical studies

There are few empirical studies in the accounting area that have explicitly adopted a contingency approach prior to collecting data. Further, two of the major studies [Bruns & Waterhouse (1975) and Hayes (1977)] use a factor analytic methodology which gives rise to problems in interpretation and comparison. Interpretation is difficult because the factors derived from the original variables can be related to underlying theoretical concepts only by an intuitive leap made by the researcher. Indeed, quite small differences in random errors in measurement may result in very different factors being obtained, making comparison of different studies next to impossible. Thus, although factor analysis may be a useful method of generating underlying "basic" dimensions [but see Armstrong's (1967) critique] it is of limited use in the accumulation of further knowledge.

Bruns & Waterhouse (1975) argue that a manager's "budget-related behaviour is contingent upon various aspects of organisational structure such as centralisation, autonomy and the degree to which activities are structured". This leads them to conclude that different control strategies are appropriate in different kinds of organisation. For example, they suggest that "a decentralised and structured organisation operating in a stable organisational environment seems particularly well suited to the use of budgetary control". Their analysis culminates in the description of two modes of control strategy, administrative and interpersonal, which are associated with different kinds of organisational arrangements.

Hayes (1977) suggests three major contingencies which are hypothesised to affect the performance of sub-units within an organisation; namely sub-unit interdependence, environmental relationships and factors internal to the sub-unit of interest. Sub-unit interdependence is examined in terms of Thompson's (1967) categorisation of pooled, sequential and reciprocal interdependence; environmental relationships in terms of his stable–dynamic and homogeneous–heterogeneous dimensions; and internal factors include the nature of the tasks performed, types of people, interpersonal relationships and the ability to measure and quantify functions. Hayes concludes that his data supports the hypothesis that the effectiveness of different types of sub-unit (i.e. production, marketing and research and development) is explained by the different combinations of these contingent variables.[4]

In both the above studies a large number of potentially relevant variables were measured by interview and/or questionnaire methods and the researchers were compelled to reduce the variety of data gathered by factor analysis. Piper's (1978) study stands in stark contrast to them as it is based on intensive study of just four multiple retail organisations. By an inductive methodology he concludes that the financial control structure of an organisation is affected by the complexity of the task it faces (as defined by, for example, the range of products sold, the diversity of the range, seasonal variations, and variations in type of outlet) and that task complexity affects financial control structure *via* the intervening variable of organisational structure.

Technology is specifically introduced as a major explanatory variable of an effective accounting information system by Daft & MacIntosh (1978). Following Perrow (1967), two explicit dimensions to measure work-unit technology are identified, namely the number of exceptions that arise in the conversion process and the search procedures used when exceptions arise. Together they define four categories of technology which are hypothesised to be associated with four categories of information system style. Their empirical study, based on questionnaires sent to 253 individuals in 24 different work units produced quite high correlations between technology and information system style, although it should be noted that the effectiveness of the information system is not assessed.

These empirical studies give less than clear-cut results for a number of reasons. Firstly, a wide variety of independent and dependent variables are

[4] Hayes' (1977) study has been extensively criticised by Tiessen & Waterhouse (1978) to the effect that his data does not substantiate his hypothesis. This criticism, together with Hayes' (1978) reply is worthy of close study as it indicates many of the conceptual and empirical problems which are involved in attempting to justify a contingent approach. Interestingly, the only point of agreement between the protagonists is that different methods of factor analysis would likely have produced quite different results!

hypothesised, with only general similarities between studies. Secondly the operationalisation of the variables is problematic, with the first two studies described measuring a large number of potentially relevant variables and reducing them by statistical means. Such statistical techniques do not in general, allow cumulative research results to be generated. Finally only the association between contingent variables and accounting system type is reported; no attempt is made to measure the effectiveness of the accounting system [except by Hayes (1977) and his measure is strongly criticised by Tiessen & Waterhouse (1978)]. All that can be concluded is that there is some degree of association between some hypothesised contingent variables and the existence of certain features of an accounting system. The general case for a contingency theory is thus supported, but specific findings are sparse.

Theoretical formulations

In addition to empirically based work there has also been theoretical speculation as to the nature of a contingency theory of accounting information systems. Gordon & Miller (1976) attempt to provide a comprehensive framework for the design of accounting information systems (AIS) which considers the specific needs of the organisation by drawing on the literature of organisation theory, management policy and accounting to identify variables which are critical to organisational performance. Environment, organisational characteristics and decision-making style are suggested to be the main classes of contingent variable; each contingency identified is matched with appropriate conditions of AIS variables, although the question of AIS design when faced by environmental, organisational and decision-making style conditions that yield conflicting recommendations is avoided by noting that three "archetypal" firms, representing typical agglomerations of contingent variables appear to exist. However two of these archetypes ("running blind" and "stagnant bureaucracy") have undesirable characteristics which, it is suggested, can be ameliorated by utilising an appropriate AIS. There is no explicit consideration of organisational objectives and effectiveness and the recommendations appear to be made on the basis of "common-sense" rather than being derived from any explicit theoretical framework.

A much simpler framework is proposed by Waterhouse & Tiessen (1978) to identify control requirements of various organisational types and their management accounting system implications. Two main classes of contingent variables are suggested: environment and technology. Environment is seen as having two important dimensions, the simple–complex and the static–dynamic which may both be mapped into the single dimension of predictability. The definition of technology follows that of Perrow (1967) (i.e. number of exceptional cases and the search procedure to be followed when exceptions are found), but is also reduced to the single dimension of degree of routineness. Organisational sub-units are seen as having either predominantly operational functions [defined similarly to Anthony's (1965) operational control] or managerial functions (which includes Anthony's management control and some of his strategic planning activities). It is suggested that managerial functions can be best understood by focussing on the environmental variable whereas the structure and processes of operating units will be more directly related to the technological variable. The management accounting system is thus viewed as one type of control mechanism and will be dependent upon the control needs of an organisational sub-unit, itself dependent on organisational structure which, in turn, is contingent on technology and environment. The study concludes by noting that the evidence linking organisational and managerial variables with effectiveness is weak, definitions of important contextual variables are often unclear, and that progress may be made by the development of taxonomic schemes. The authors also concur with Hopwood's (1978) comment that "the critical role played by accounting and information systems in organisations is now being more generally recognised and studied by scholars of organisational behaviour", by noting that "research on management accounting system variables may be a means of conceptualising and observing more abstract processes such as goal formation, power attempts or conflict resolution".

Amigoni (1978) develops a different framework in which the appropriateness of various accounting control tools, ranging from financial accounting and ratio analysis to financial simulation models, responsibility accounting and strategic planning, is assessed. He identifies two major contingent variables, namely the degree of structural complexity of the enterprise in its relations with the environment and the degree of turbulence and discontinuity in the environment. He concludes that increasing structural complexity can be adapted to by adding new accounting tools to those currently in use, which still retain their function, whereas increasing environmental discontinuity will often require the replacement of old tools, which have become obsolete, by new. He also notes a shortage of techniques that are useful when high degrees of complexity are combined with high levels of environmental discontinuity and suggests that the development of new tools in this area is a research priority. Thus, although organisational structure is not directly considered, the underlying variable of structural complexity is seen as explaining both the accounting control tools used and the organisational form adopted.

A further approach is that of Dermer (1977) which is somewhat different in nature as it is written as an advanced undergraduate or graduate text on management planning and control systems. No prescriptions are given; rather an approach to systems design is recommended and various contingencies identified. It is argued that the design of any planning and control system (PCS) is situationally specific in that it depends upon:

(a) the specific objectives to be achieved by the PCS in the context of organisational objectives;
(b) the particular form of differentiation and degree of decentralisation chosen (i.e. organisational structure);
(c) the nature and mix of the processes being controlled within any sub-unit, and the degree to which these are structured or unstructured (i.e. type of technology);
(d) the type of managerial style used by senior managers.

These factors are superimposed upon a three-cycle planning process closely related to Anthony's (1965) three-fold distinction of strategic planning, management control and operational control. Although not explicitly building on recent work in organisation theory, Dermer's book gives the most specific guidelines for PCS design of the theoretical work reviewed, but it relies predominantly on a "common-sense" approach rather than following from a coherent theoretical structure.

To summarise, the bulk of the empirical and theoretical work reviewed here relies heavily on a few common sources in the literature of organisation theory. Environment and technology (however defined) are seen as affecting organisational structure which in turn affects the design of an accounting information system [Sathe (1978) reviews this literature]. It is therefore not surprising that the defects of organisation theory are also incorporated into this contingency theory. In particular, contingent variables are ill-defined, the dimensions of organisational structure (and process) considered differ from study to study and the link with organisational effectiveness is largely unproven.[5] The tendency of accounting researchers to take such tentative theories at face value and to extend them into the accounting area with so little apparent awareness of their defects and weaknesses is disturbing. In addition the research methodologies used are inadequate for the task demanded of them, almost invariably being arms-length questionnaire-based techniques from which reliable results are expected to emerge by statistical analysis.

A FRAMEWORK FOR THE EVALUATION OF CONTINGENCY THEORIES OF MANAGEMENT ACCOUNTING

It is now possible to examine and evaluate the underlying model on which current contingency theories of management accounting have been based. It will be argued that all the work reviewed has implicitly utilised an inappropriately simple model and a more comprehensive model is therefore put forward.

The underlying model upon which the work described in previous sections can be seen to be based is shown in Fig. 1. The various propositions follow from each other in a simple linear fashion: some supposedly contingent variables are defined and measured; these are hypothesised to affect the structure (or perhaps the processes) of an organisation; for each type of organisation so defined it is possible to identify commonalities in their AIS which are associated (or are assumed to

[5] See Karpik (1978) for a number of articles which are critical of the current status of organisation theory; also Pennings (1975) for a review of the relevance of the structural contingency model in organisational effectiveness. Cooper (1980) reviews many of the criticisms and applies them to the accounting context and Burchell *et al.* (1980) expressly consider the problem of goals.

be associated) with effective performance. However it should be noted that no single study combines all four stages in the sequence, as is shown by the summary in Table 1. In particular, only one study (Hayes, 1977) attempts to measure effectiveness, and its methods have been seriously criticised. Yet the mere existence of particular AIS's associated with certain contingent variables is a weak basis on which to prescribe AIS design; evidently some assessment of effectiveness is highly desirable. In addition some authors (i.e. Daft & MacIntosh; Hayes; Khandwalla; Waterhouse & Tiessen) indicate direct links between contingent variables and the AIS without explicitly considering whether the intervening variable of organisational design is necessary. It is also evident that the AIS comprises only one part

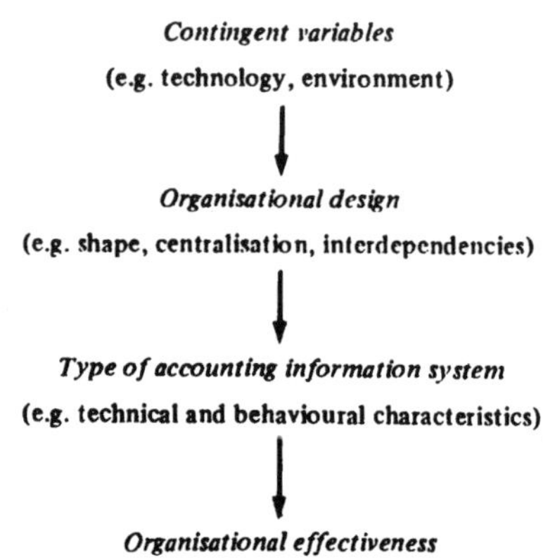

Fig. 1. A simple linear framework for AIS design.

TABLE 1. Comparison of major studies with simple linear model

Study	Contingent variables	Organisational design	Type of accounting information system	Organisational effectiveness
Bruns & Waterhouse	Organisational context (origin, size, technology, dependence)	Structuring of activities Concentration of authority	Control system complexity and perceived control leading to budget-related behaviour; interpersonal and administrative control strategies	
Daft & MacIntosh	Technology (task variety; search procedures)		I.S. style (amount, focus and use of data)	
Dermer	Organisational objectives Technology Managerial style	Decentralisation Differentiation	Choice of A.I.S. or M.C.S. techniques	
Gordon & Miller	Environment (dynamism, heterogeneity and hostility)	Decentralisation Bureaucralisation Resource availability	Technical characteristics of accounting I.S.	
Hayes	Environmental factors Inter-dependency factors Internal factors		Appropriate performance evaluation techniques	Departmental effectiveness
Khandwalla	Type of competition faced		Sophistication of accounting controls	
Piper	Task complexity (product range and diversity variability between units)	Decentralisation of decision-making	Financial control structure (e.g. use of financial planning models; frequency of reports)	
Waterhouse & Tiessen	Environmental predictability Technological routineness	Nature of sub-units – operational or managerial	Management accounting system design	

of the control structure of an organisation. An organisational control strategy will involve organisational design considerations, the provision of other management information, and planning and control systems additional to the AIS. Indeed these may be seen as partial substitutes for each other as indicated by the often expressed sentiment of industrial managers that the particular AIS used by their company is intended to cope with known weaknesses in organisational design. The "mix" of such components is probably not determined, but several different combinations may give equally good results, indicating that a wider perspective is necessary to yield a useful contingency theory for AIS design. Thus the AIS must be seen as part of a wider management information system, itself part of a management planning and control system, and all of which are but part of an overall organisational control package.

The folly of attempting to construct a contingency theory of the AIS outside of the context of an overall organisation control package is thus apparent. Firstly, what constitutes an appropriate AIS will be influenced both by what the organisation is attempting to achieve and by the other control processes that are complementary to the AIS. Secondly, there are a whole range of factors that will affect organisational performance other than its control strategy such as the entrepreneurial flair of its managers, the structure and state of its product-markets, and inter-organisational arrangements. The effect of the AIS is thus likely to be relatively small and will require carefully controlled research for it to be measured. Finally, it must be noted that what constitutes effective organisational performance must be determined, in part, by the objectives of the organisation itself rather than by an externally imposed standard. There are substantial difficulties in the measurement of organisational effectiveness (Steers, 1977) and, although it is vital for such measures to be constructed in developing a true contingency theory, it may be sensible as an interim measure to be content with the measurement of intervening variables, that is, variables which are thought to pre-dispose an organisation towards effective rather than ineffective operation.

These comments suggest that a rather more complex form of contingency framework is necessary in studying AIS design, and the minimal model required is shown in Fig. 2. Here the

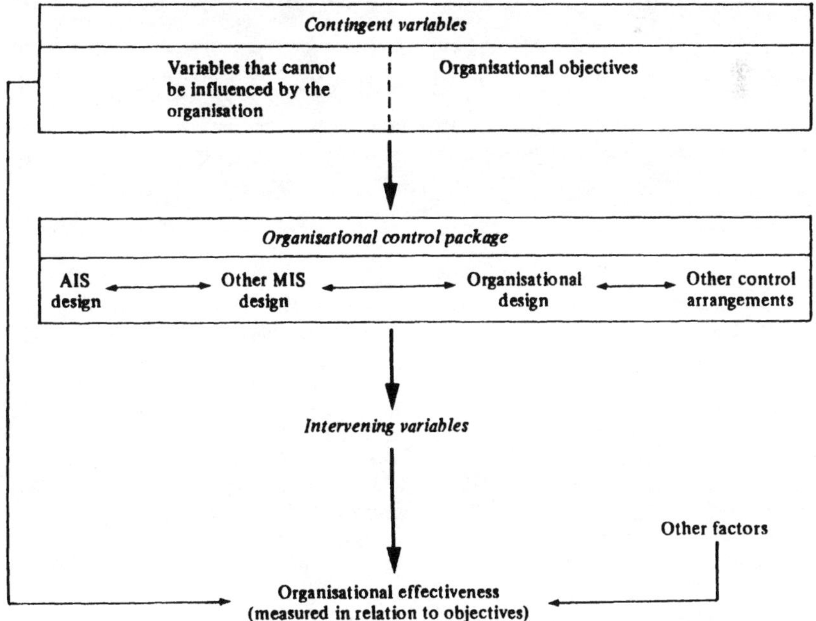

Fig. 2. The minimum necessary contingency framework.

contingent variables are considered to be outside of the control of the organisation, although it is recognised that organisations may try to influence some such supposedly exogenous variables (e.g. governmental regulations). Those variables believed to be controllable by the organisation are not considered to be contingent variables, but rather part of the package of organisational controls selected for use. The one exception is the use of organisational objectives as a contingent variable, because of their special nature as a criterion by which organisational effectiveness will be assessed. The organisation adapts to the contingencies it faces by arranging the factors it can control into an appropriate configuration that it hopes will lead to effective performance. It is, however, important to note that the level of performance potentially possible is also affected by those environmental variables that are also contingent variables for the control package. In addition, there are also a range of other factors that are likely to have an equal or more pronounced effect on effectiveness.

It is explicitly recognised that AIS design, MIS design, organisational design and the other control arrangements of the organisation (such as collective agreements, personnel selection, promotion and reward systems and external lobbying) form a package which can only be evaluated as a whole. In particular, there are extensive interdependencies between AIS design and each of the other components of the package. Organisational objectives are also explicitly incorporated, for although in certain circumstances basic similarities in objectives may be assumed (e.g. when studying firms in a single industry; but even here preferences for stability versus growth, conservatism versus innovation etc. may affect comparisons), these appear to represent a fundamental contingency so far omitted from this literature (except by Dermer).

No doubt this framework is still over-simple. Part of an organisation's control strategy may well be to influence its environment; little consideration has been given to the pattern of dependence of an organisation on important external resources and its interdependence upon other organisations. For example, Pfeffer & Salancik (1978) argue that the key to organisational survival is the ability to acquire and maintain resources, both physical and human, and the management of boundary relationships. It has also been suggested that a likely reverse loop may operate between organisational performance and objectives [Child (1972); Cyert & March (1963)]; in addition the accounting system may affect the objectives that are being used to explain its form [Burchell *et al.* (1980)].

However, it should be noted that the proposed framework takes ends as given and is concerned with the most effective means of achieving them. It is suggested that this is an entirely appropriate task for a contingency theory,[6] but that no particular ends should be *assumed* to be of predominant importance. Thus different control arrangements may well be appropriate in organisations seeking, for example, to optimise client service than in those which are seeking to maximise returns to shareholders or to create an enriching working environment for their employees.

Although the model does not seek to give a comprehensive explanation of the development of accounting information systems [see Chandler & Daems (1979) for one such attempt] it is perhaps wide enough to stimulate the development of a broad enough perspective within which assessments of the appropriateness of an AIS can properly be made. That is, it recognises that because accounting systems are an important part of the fabric of organisational life, they need to be evaluated in their wider managerial, organisational and environmental context.

IMPLICATIONS FOR RESEARCH

Accounting as part of a control system

The study of the effectiveness of management accounting information systems is intimately bound up with the study of all of the many kinds of control mechanisms used by organisations in attempting to influence the behaviour of their members and their relationships with the external world.[7] It is often impossible to separate the effect of an AIS from other controls; they act as a package and must be assessed jointly. This fact immediately widens the scope of any investigation; an indication of the range of control activities is

[6] See Otley's (1980) comments on Cooper (1980).

[7] A review of the mechanisms of organisational control from different perspectives can be found in Lawler (1976) and Salaman (1979).

given by Westerlund & Sjöstrand's (1979) list of formalised controls, shown in Table 2, although reward systems are a notable omission. In addition, different types of control can be used to achieve different purposes as Ouchi & Maguire (1975) and Ouchi (1977) have shown. The simultaneous use of a wide range of control mechanisms serving multiple purposes makes it difficult, if not impossible, to isolate the effect of any specific means of control. Perhaps an initial research strategy would be to attempt to identify those combinations of controls that appear to be particularly suited to certain circumstances.

TABLE 2. Examples of more formalized controls in an organisation [from Westerlund and Sjöstrand (1979)]

Means of control for long-range activity
Laws, rules and regulations
Collective agreements
Product and Market planning and research and development
Plans for recruitment and training
Personnel selection and promotion plans
Economic planning
Investment plans
Job descriptions
Raw materials planning
Housing plans
Means of control for short-range activity
Delegation of decision
Regulations
Accounting system
Budgets
Resource allocation
Directions, instructions
"Check lists"
Standards (consumption, price etc.)
Work flow plans
Work resources
Job descriptions

It is evident that the same contingent variables that are relevant to organisational design are likely to be important in management accounting. Unfortunately the precise nature of such variables has as yet defied definition, for although vague classes of variable have been suggested different researchers have used such disparate definitions as to make comparison between studies virtually impossible. One way forward to greater conceptual clarification lies in the utilisation of a control systems framework. Although simple mechanical models of control cannot be directly applied to organisations, Otley & Berry (1980) have identified four characteristics of controlled processes that are necessary for effective organisational control. These are:

(a) the specification of an objective;
(b) a measure of the degree of attainment of that objective;
(c) a predictive model of the likely outcomes of control actions;
(d) the ability and motivation to act.

Use of this model helps to ensure that all stages of the control process are considered. For example, although management accounting systems have traditionally been concerned with the first two characteristics of control, they have tended to neglect the development of predictive models. Such predictive models are necessary in order to determine the reasons for inadequate performance and to evaluate the likely outcomes of proposed control actions. Effective *organisational* control is possible only with adequate *organisational-level* predictive models, for as Argyris & Schon (1978) have pointed out, organisational learning is not the same as individual learning and there are many cases in which organisations appear to know less than their individual members. It is thus important to ascertain the nature and locus of organisational predictive models if the organisation is to learn how to become more effective.

It is noteworthy that, of all the contingent variables proposed, one in particular stands out, namely unpredictability (variously referred to as uncertainty, non-routineness, dynamism etc.). Even complexity and size may be important, at least in part, because of the unpredictability associated with them. Again the control framework is an aid; it is the unpredictability of those factors that are important in determining organisational success that is crucial and these factors may well differ from organisation to organisation. Thus a general theoretical framework must identify the major factors casually related to organisational effectiveness and use the unpredictability of such factors as major contingent variables.

Organisational effectiveness

The use of a control framework also reinforces the central role of organisational effectiveness and focuses attention on the nature of organisational objectives. Objectives are an essential part of a contingency framework not only because they are themselves one contingent variable that is likely to affect the nature of the accounting system but also, and more importantly, because they form the criterion against which the effects of different configurations of controls must be evaluated. That is, in order to progress beyond the mere association of particular contingencies and accounting systems, a judgement has to be made about the impact of the accounting system in aiding organisational performance.

However the terms "objectives", "performance", and "effectiveness" tend to be used as smoke-screens to hide a lack of conceptual clarity. It is necessary to question the nature of organisational objectives and study the processes by which they are arrived at and by whom they are influenced. The pre-eminence of a particular interest group cannot be assumed and it must be asked for what and for whom an organisational action is deemed effective. These are basically political questions concerning the relationships and relative powers of those involved in organisational functioning.

The empirical literature on effectiveness is of only limited assistance. Price's (1968) inventory of findings in the area notes that "most of the studies (surveyed) do not demonstrate what they assert"; indeed many do not even attempt to measure effectiveness. The problem is basically at a conceptual level rather than at an empirical level as Evan (1976) points out:

> One of the underlying causes of this state of affairs is the striking neglect – almost systematic – of the problem of conceptualising and measuring organisational performance or organisational effectiveness.

This issue is also noted by Steers (1977) in his unsuccessful attempt to derive agreed criteria of effectiveness from a review of previous research. Such problems indicate that different organisations will be effective in different ways and also that effectiveness will be perceived differently by various interest groups connected with them. Indeed the question of organisational ideologies and their effect on control arrangements also requires explicit attention. For example, Salaman (1979) argues that technologies and organisational structures are chosen for what are regarded as their control functions and benefits, and for their role in advancing class interests and conflicts. Developments in organisational control technology mean that considerable choice exists in control system design and use, although Banbury & Nahapiet (1979) observe that the majority of systems in use have been developed "in support of the more bureaucratic elements of organisations, reflecting the more mechanistic models of man and of organisations".

The evaluation of the appropriateness of particular varieties of accounting control systems must therefore take place by comparison with a range of measures of effectiveness, at both an organisational and an individual level of analysis. For example, at an organisational level of analysis, different organisations may choose to act differently because they have their own preferences regarding the distribution and timing of benefits and the levels of risk they are willing to accept. At an individual or group level of analysis an AIS may provide information that allows some groups to further their own purposes more adequately, but which is of little or no use to other groups. It is therefore important that in developing a contingency theory of accounting information systems the effect of the information on a number of dimensions of effectiveness is measured rather than an arbitrary choice of a single dimension or the issue being left implicit. A true contingency theory can only be developed as progress is made on this fundamental issue.

Research methodology

It is evident that the contingency approach is dealing with a highly inter-connected structure of control devices, of which the AIS is but one, that form an organisational control package. In particular, many of the variables which are hypothesised to affect AIS design are the same as those which are believed to explain differences in organisational structure. In these circumstances it is unrealistic to expect purely statistical methods of analysis to unravel a complex pattern of inter-action; the researcher must have a closer involvement and develop hypotheses as to likely relationships as he explores the organisations he is investigating. In addition, as causal relationships are of much greater interest than associations, longitudinal studies, where the interaction of variables over time may be observed, are of more value than cross-sectional studies. Longitudinal studies are also able to illuminate the processes by which an accounting system develops and is changed in response to organisational pressures.

However, being concerned with such fundamental organisational processes brings its own difficulties; power structures are notably difficult to observe reliably, particularly when the researcher is dependent upon one interest group (senior management) for access to individuals and information. It will usually require a considerable period of involvement for the researcher to be confident that his observations are representative and reliable (and, if not free from bias, at least containing a variety of biases).

These considerations suggest methodologies that are more anthropological in nature than the methods that have traditionally been used in accounting research, as Gambling (1978) has recommended. Such approaches require a close contact between the organisation and the researcher and the validity of the findings will be enhanced where findings are fed back to research subjects and attempts made to introduce and monitor changes based on those findings, as suggested by Argyris (1976). A multi-disciplinary approach also seems to be highly desirable as those trained in particular fields will inevitably tend to interpret their observations according to their previous experience. However multi-disciplinary research is not a panacea and the management of such research teams raises issues about the social control processes involved that are worthy of study in their own right (Tomkins, 1980). Such research methods are intended to be illuminative rather than being concerned with the rigorous testing of pre-determined hypotheses; it is however necessary for appropriate standards for this type of work to be developed to help ensure that it produces results that are both valid and cumulative (Stenhouse, 1979). There is no universal standard against which a research methodology can be judged, rather it must be evaluated in terms of its ability to produce the type of results being sought (Mitroff & Kilman, 1978). Thus Campbell (1976) draws some object lessons from previous research on organisational effectiveness and concludes that

> Firstly, it is probably counter-productive to follow the multivariate approach in the development of effectiveness measures ... Secondly, searching for so-called objective measures of organisational effectiveness is a thankless task and virtually pre-ordained to fail in the end ... Third, at this stage, it probably is a mistake to concentrate scarce research resources on attempts to develop results-oriented measures, that is, measures of the more technical outcomes of organisational functioning, such as return on investment, productivity and the like.

These comments strongly support the idea of "case studies" in the sense used by Hägg & Hedlund (1979) which involve a small number of organisations, carefully selected so as to give a range of values on chosen contingent variables whilst controlling for other variables as far as possible, and the close involvement of the researcher with the organisations over a period of time. There is an obvious conflict between this type of intensive investigation which necessarily can include only a few cases with the development of a contingency theory which requires a large number of cases to give it validity. However the disappointing results of large-scale surveys indicate that more insight is likely to be gained from the former type of study at this, essentially exploratory, stage of research.

CONCLUSIONS

A contingency theory of management accounting has a great deal of appeal. It is in accord with practical wisdom and appears to afford a potential explanation for the bewildering variety of management accounting systems actually observed in practice. In addition, the relevance of organisation theory to management accounting is being increasingly recognised and contingency formulations have been prominent in organisation theory. There thus appears to be a *prima facie* case for the development of a contingency framework for management accounting.

However, despite the strong arguments for pursuing this line of research, a number of reservations need to be expressed. Firstly, the nature of appropriate contingent variables has not yet been elucidated and requires greater theoretical, as well as empirical, attention. It is suggested that a control-based approach provides a suitable theoretical starting point. The control perspective focusses attention on the unpredictability of variables crucial to organisational success as central contingent variables. Secondly, explicit consideration of organisational effectiveness is a vital part of a true contingency theory of control system design. This has been a much neglected topic from a theoretical stance and its development is urgently needed. Thirdly, the contingency theory of organisational design is weaker than some of its own literature suggests, its links with organisational effectiveness being, at best, tentative. As the same contingent variables are likely to affect both organisational structure and accounting system design, it appears unwise to use structure as the sole intervening variable between contingent variables and the choice of the accounting information system. Finally, the highly inter-connected nature of the components that make up an organisational control package suggests that the management accounting information system cannot be studied in isolation from its wider context.

These considerations have implications for the selection of appropriate research methodologies. Initially an exploratory mode of research is necessary, possibly involving the careful observation of the operation of organisational control systems over a period of time, with the objective of inducing the major contingencies and mapping their interconnections with all parts of the organisational control package. For example the study by Murray (1970) is a very early example having many features of such an approach. Multivariate analysis based on brief questionnaire and interview surveys is unlikely to yield great insight. Because of the intensive nature of such research and its close relationship with many of the central internal policies of organisations, attention also needs to be paid to methods of securing the degree of co-operation with subject organisations necessary to yield valid observations.

The development of a theory of management accounting which explains how it is affected by various contingencies and how it is integrated into its wider context of organisational control mechanisms is an important research task. However, despite superficial indications that it is well under way, it has in fact yet to begin in earnest. Neither will it be quickly achieved for it requires painstaking work over considerable periods of time. It is therefore all the more important that such work that is attempted makes explicit the part of the theory that it is designed to illuminate and uses methods that allow cumulative knowledge to be built up.

BIBLIOGRAPHY

Amigoni, F., Planning Management Control Systems, *Journal of Business Finance and Accounting* (1978), pp. 279–291.

Ansari, S. L., An Integrated Approach to Control System Design, *Accounting, Organisations and Society* (1977), pp. 101–112.

Anthony, R. N., *Planning and Control Systems: A Framework for Analysis* (Harvard U.P., 1965).

Argyris, C., Organisational Learning and Effective Management Information Systems: A Prospectus for Research, Harvard University, Program on Information Technologies and Public Policy, Working Paper 76-4 (1976).

Argyris, C. & Schon, D., *Organizational Learning: A Theory of Action Perspective* (Addison-Wesley, 1978).

Armstrong, J. C., Derivation of Theory by Means of Factor Analysis or Tom Swift and his Electric Factor Analysis Machine, *The American Statistician* (December, 1967), pp. 17–21.

Banbury, J. & Nahapiet, J. E., Towards a Framework for the Study of the Antecedents and Consequences of Information Systems in Organisations, *Accounting, Organizations and Society* (1979), pp. 163–177.

Baumler, J. V., Defined Criteria of Performance and Organisational Control, *Administrative Science Quarterly* (September, 1971), pp. 340–349.

Bruns, W. J. & Waterhouse, J. H., Budgetary Control and Organisational Structure, *Journal of Accounting Research* (Autumn, 1975), pp. 177–203.

Burchell, S., Clubb, C., Hopwood, A. G., Hughes, T. & Nahapiet, J., The Roles of Accounting in Organizations and Society, *Accounting, Organizations and Society* (1980).

Burns, T. & Stalker, G. M., *The Management of Innovation* (Tavistock, 1961).

Campbell, J. P., Contributions Research can make in Understanding Organisations Effectiveness in Spray, S. L. (ed.), *Organisational Effectiveness: Theory-Research-Utilisation* (Comparative Administration Research Institute, Graduate School of Business Administration, Kent State University, 1976).

Caplan, E. H., Behavioural Assumptions of Management Accounting, *Accounting Review* (July, 1966), pp. 496–509.

Chandler, A., *Strategy and Structure* (MIT Press, 1962).

Chandler, A. & Daems, H., Administrative Co-ordination, Allocation and Monitoring: A Comparative Analysis of the Emergence of Accounting and Organisation in the U.S.A. and Europe, *Accounting, Organisations and Society* (1979), pp. 3–20.

Child, J., *Organization: A Guide to Problems and Practice* (Harper and Row, 1977).

Child, J., Organisation Structure, Environment and Performance – The Role of Strategic Choice, *Sociology* (January, 1972), pp. 1–22.

Cooper, D., A Social and Organisational View of Management Accounting in M. Bromwich and A. G. Hopwood (eds), *Essays on British Accounting Research* (Pitman, 1980).

Cyert, R. & March, J. G., *A Behavioural Theory of the Firm* (Prentice-Hall, 1963).

Daft, R. L. & MacIntosh, N. B., A New Approach to Design and Use of Management Information, *California Management Review* (Fall, 1978), pp. 82–92.

Dermer, J., *Management Planning and Control Systems* (Irwin, 1977).

Evan, W. M., Organisation Theory and Organisational Effectiveness: An Exploratory Analysis in Spray, S. L. (ed.), *Organisational Effectiveness: Theory-Research-Utilisation* (Comparative Administration Research Institute, Graduate School of Business Administration, Kent State University, 1976).

Gambling, T. R., Theory Construction, Empiricism and Validation in Accounting Practice, Working Paper, Department of Accounting, University of Birmingham, May 1978.

Gordon, L. A. & Miller, D., A Contingency Framework for the Design of Accounting Information Systems, *Accounting, Organisations and Society* (1976), pp. 59–70.

Hägg, I. & Hedlund, G., Case Studies in Accounting Research, *Accounting, Organisations and Society* (1979), pp. 135–143.

Hayes, D., The Contingency Theory of Management Accounting, *Accounting Review* (January, 1977), pp. 22–39.

Hayes, D., The Contingency Theory of Management Accounting: A Reply, *Accounting Review* (April, 1978), pp. 530–533.

Hofstede, G., *The Game of Budget Control* (Tavistock, 1968).

Hopwood, A. G., An Empirical Study of the Role of Accounting Data in Performance Evaluation, *Empirical Research in Accounting, Supplement to Journal of Accounting Research* (1972), pp. 156–182.

Hopwood, A. G., Towards an Organisational Perspective for the Study of Accounting and Information Systems, *Accounting, Organisations and Society* (1978), pp. 3–14.

Horngren, C. T., *Cost Accounting: A Managerial Emphasis* (3rd ed., Prentice-Hall, 1972).

Karpik, L. (ed.), *Organisation and Environment: Theory, Issues and Reality* (Sage, 1978).

Khandwalla, P. N., The Effect of Different Types of Competition on the Use of Management Controls, *Journal of Accounting Research* (Autumn, 1972), pp. 275–285.

Lawler, E. E. (III), Control Systems in Organizations, in Dunnette, M. D. (ed.), *Handbook of Industrial and Organisational Psychology* (Rand McNally, 1976).

Mitroff, I. I. & Kilman, R. H., *Methodological Approaches to the Social Sciences* (Jossey-Bass, 1978).

Murray, W., *Management Controls in Action* (Irish National Productivity Committee, 1970).

Otley, D. T., Budget Use and Managerial Performance, *Journal of Accounting Research* (1978), pp. 122–149.

Otley, D. T., The Role of Management Accounting in Organisational Control, in M. Bromwich and A. G. Hopwood, *Essays in British Accounting Research* (Pitman, 1980).

Otley, D. T. & Berry, A. J., Control, Organisation and Accounting, *Accounting, Organisations and Society* (1980).

Ouchi, W. G., The Relationship Between Organisational Structure and Organisational Control, *Administrative Science Quarterly* (1977), pp. 95–113.

Ouchi, W. G. & Maguire, M. A., Organisational Control: Two Functions, *Administrative Science Quarterly* (1975), pp. 559–569.

Pennings, J. M., The Relevance of the Structural Contingency Model for Organisational Effectiveness, *Administrative Science Quarterly* (1975), pp. 393–410.

Perrow, C., A Framework for the Comparative Analysis of Organisations, *American Sociological Review* (1967), pp. 194–208.

Pfeffer, J. & Salancik, G. R., *The External Control of Organisations* (Harper and Row, 1978).

Piper, J., Determinants of Financial Control Systems for Multiple Retailers – Some Case Study Evidence, unpublished paper, University of Loughborough, 1978.

Price, J. L., *Organisational Effectiveness: An Inventory of Propositions* (Irwin, 1968).

Pugh, D. S. & Hickson, D. J. (eds), *Organisational Structure in its Context (The Aston Programme 1)* (Saxon House, 1976a).

Pugh, D. S. & Hinings, C. R. (eds), *Organisational Studies: Extensions and Replications (The Aston Programme 2)* (Saxon House, 1976b).

Pugh, D. S. & Payne, R. L. (eds), *Organisational Behaviour in its Context (The Aston Programme 3)* (Saxon House, 1977).

Salaman, G., *Work Organisations: Resistance and Control* (Longman, 1979).

Sathe, V., Contingency Theories of Organisational Strucure, in Livingstone, J. L. (ed.), *Managerial Accounting: The Behavioural Foundations* (Grid, 1975).

Sathe, V., The Relevance of Modern Organisation Theory for Managerial Accounting, *Accounting, Organisations and Society* (1978), pp. 89–92.

Steers, R. M., *Organizational Effectiveness: A Behavioural View* (Goodyear, 1977).

Stenhouse, L., The Problem of Standards in Illuminative Research, *Scottish Educational Review* (May 1979).

Thompson, J. D., *Organizations in Action* (McGraw-Hill, 1967).

Tiessen, P. & Waterhouse, J. H., The Contingency Theory of Management Accounting: A Comment, *Accounting Review* (April, 1978), pp. 523–529.

Tomkins, C., Rosenberg, D. & Colville, I., The Social Process of Research: Some Reflections on Developing a Multi-Disciplinary Accounting Project, *Accounting, Organizations and Society* (1980).

Waterhouse, J. H. & Tiessen, P., A Contingency Framework for Management Accounting Systems Research, *Accounting, Organisations and Society* (1978), pp. 65–76.

Watson, D. J. H., Contingency Formulations of Organisational Structure: Implications for Managerial Accounting, in Livingstone, J. L. (ed.), *Managerial Accounting: The Behavioural Foundations* (Grid, 1975).

Westerlund, G. & Sjöstrand, S., *Organisational Myths* (Harper and Row, 1979).

Wood, S., A Reappraisal of the Contingency Approach to Organisation, *Journal of Management Studies* (1979), pp. 334–354.

Woodward, J., *Industrial Organisation: Theory and Practice* (Oxford, U.P., 1965).

[22]

IMPACT OF PARTICIPATION IN THE BUDGETARY PROCESS ON MANAGERIAL ATTITUDES AND PERFORMANCE: UNIVERSALISTIC AND CONTINGENCY PERSPECTIVES*

Vijay Govindarajan
(Visiting, Amos Tuck School of Business Administration, Dartmouth College)
Department of Accounting, Ohio State University, Columbus, OH 43210

ABSTRACT

Data from responsibility-center managers reveal that greater budgetary participation contributes to managerial performance and attitudes in high-environmental-uncertainty situations but hampers performance and attitudes in low-uncertainty situations. Higher budgetary participation reduces managers' propensity to create slack in high- (but not in low-) uncertainty conditions.

Subject Areas: Budgeting and Control Systems, Management Control, Managerial Accounting, and Organization and Management Theory.

INTRODUCTION

Participation in the budgetary process often has been postulated to have a positive effect on managerial performance and attitudes. The mixed results of prior empirical research led to the present study which looks at moderating effects of environmental uncertainty on the relationship between budgetary participation and certain criterion variables such as job performance, budget attitudes and motivation, and propensity to create slack.

The effect of participation in the budgetary process has been a fertile area of research for many years. Most studies have concentrated on whether high budgetary participation leads to better performance and attitudes. Results often have been conflicting. For instance, a few studies support the argument that budgetary participation leads to higher job satisfaction (e.g., [41]), higher motivation to achieve the budget (e.g., [22] and [37]), and higher performance (e.g., [24]). However, Milani [30] found only a weak correlation between participation and performance. Stedry [39] and Bryan and Locke [7] observed a *negative* association between participation and performance. To reconcile these conflicting results, this study adopts a contingency framework and attempts to identify the conditions under which budgetary participation will lead to favorable outcomes.

The particular contingency variable examined is *uncertainty* in the external environment. The original proponents of contingency theory based their arguments

*This paper benefited from the comments of Jesse Dillard, Anil Gupta, Jane Mutchler, and Ray Stephens and from research assistance provided by Joe Schlosser, Jr. Funding for this research was provided by the College of Administrative Science, Ohio State University, and the Amos Tuck School of Business Administration, Dartmouth College.

on this variable [25]. Although researchers have examined the contingency relationships among environmental uncertainty, participation in *decision making in general*, and performance (e.g., [42]), similar empirical examination has not been conducted in the specific context of participation in the *budgetary process*. This is one purpose of our research.

A second purpose is to examine the moderating effects of environmental uncertainty on the relationship between participation in the budgetary process and managers' propensity to create slack. Onsi [35] in a universalistic sense argued and found that participative budgeting reduces the need for managers to create slack in their budgets. On the other hand, Galbraith [18] made conceptual arguments to the effect that the relationship between participation in decision making and slack will not be present under all conditions; rather, the relationship will be contingent on task uncertainty.

Instead of adopting a strict contingency perspective, each hypothesis presented below leaves open the possibility of *universalistic linkages* between budgetary participation and the criterion variables *in addition to the contingency effect* of environmental uncertainty. (See Schoonhoven [36] for a more detailed examination of such a dual perspective.) Three quite different relationships are possible among the variables included in this study. First, a strict universalistic relationship would be present if budgetary participation had a *direct* positive effect on the criterion variables *irrespective of the level of uncertainty*. Second, a strict contingency relationship would be present if high budget participation, matched with high uncertainty, led to favorable performance but high budget participation, under conditions of low uncertainty, led to unfavorable performance. Third, a dual perspective is possible. This perspective would not take issue with the universalistic view; it would, however, examine the possibility that the marginal *utility* of increments in the budgetary participation might well *vary* across different levels of environmental uncertainty.

The results of this study are expected to support *one* of the above three relationships. Consistent with this expectation, the next section develops theoretical arguments for universalistic as well as contingency perspectives. This is followed by a set of hyptheses designed to test *simultaneously* predictions that reflect universalistic and contingency views.

The analytic (multiplier interaction) technique [36] used in this study has not been applied widely to contingency arguments in the past. In this analysis, partial derivatives for the complete regression equations for the criterion variables are calculated. This allows us to examine the functional form of the interaction between uncertainty and budget participation and not just the coefficients of the variables involved. Thus the partial derivatives help to determine the *direct* effects of budget participation on performance as well as any *interaction* with environmental uncertainty.

THEORY

Budgetary Participation, Environmental Uncertainty, and Managerial Performance and Attitudes

Universalistic Perspective. The universalistic view argues for the relationship between participation and performance to hold under all conditions. Coch and French [10] discovered that participation in job redesign (in a pajama manufacturing plant) was effective in increasing productivity levels over levels that occurred when employees were allowed no say in the redesign of their jobs. Similar results have been observed in studies that have focused specifically on the relationship between participation and performance in the context of budgeting [1] [2] [3] [24].

In the area of job satisfaction, Cherrington and Cherrington [9], Swieringa and Moncur [41], and Steers [40] reported results which showed a positive relationship between participative budgeting and job satisfaction.

Regarding motivation, Hofstede [22] and Searfoss and Monczka [37] found that participation increased the internalization of budgeted goals, thereby enhancing motivation.

As regards attitude, Milani [30] found that participation was associated positively and significantly with attitudes toward job and company. Collins [11] found a similar association of attitude with budgetary system.

The results of these studies point toward universalistic linkages between participation and the criterion variables. They argue that budgeted goals are more likely to be accepted when they are perceived as under personal control rather than imposed externally. Goal acceptance in turn contributes to internalization and personal commitment to the goals, thereby leading to higher motivation to achieve the goals as well as more favorable attitudes toward budgets. The internalization of goals by a manager is said to lead to more effective organizational performance, since potential conflicts between the organization's goals and the manager's goals are minimized or eliminated.

Contingency Perspective. The universalistic perspective described above has been challenged by many researchers. Milani [30], for instance, found only a weak association between budgetary participation and performance. Foran and DeCoster [15], French, Kay, and Meyer [17], and Carroll and Tosi [8] found no differences in goal attainment between participatively set and nonparticipatively set goals. Morse and Reimer [31], Stedry [39], and Bryan and Locke [7], in fact, found a *negative* association between participation and performance (i.e., nonparticipation groups outperformed participation groups).

Studies that support participation are clearly in conflict with those that do not. A contingency view that explicitly considers environmental uncertainty might help to reconcile these conflicting results. Such a view would argue that, in order to obtain favorable outcomes, high budget participation is not needed under all conditions. Instead, participation should be contingent on the level of environmental uncertainty.

Galbraith [18] and Tushman and Nadler [43] argued that, for greater effectiveness, participation in decision making should vary with task uncertainty. They viewed organizations as information-processing systems and posited that as the task environment of a subunit became more uncertain, the need for information and, in turn, for greater information-processing capacity at the subunit level would increase. When uncertainty is low, it is possible to specify behaviors, in the form of rules, in advance of task execution. When exceptions to the rules are encountered, these can be referred upward in the managerial hierarchy for centralized decision making. Centralization is possible at lower levels of uncertainty since information processed does not overburden the hierarchy. However, as the subunit's uncertainty increases, more exceptions need to be referred upward in the hierarchy and result in overloading. Serious delays develop between the upward transmission of information about new situations and response downward to that information. In such cases, the organization must develop strategies either to reduce the amount of information or to increase the capacity to process information. One strategy is the creation of lateral relations: moving the level of decision making down to where information exists rather than bringing information upward in the hierarchy. This argues for decentralization in decision making. In other words, increased influence of subunit members in decision making is a key strategy that can be used to deal effectively with environmental uncertainty and the attendant need for higher information-processing capacity.

Galbraith [18] argued further that participation in decision making does not come free. Increased participation implies greater amounts of subunit managers' time that must be spent and additional overhead expenses involved in coordination and control. Thus the benefits of participation would outweigh its costs in situations involving high uncertainty compared to situations involving low uncertainty.

Empirical support for Galbraith was provided by Lawrence and Lorsch [25]. In a field study with a variety of companies, Lawrence and Lorsch found that in companies that faced higher environmental uncertainty, successful firms designed organizational structures to facilitate the flow of information both horizontally and vertically (i.e., there was higher participation in decision making). In those companies that faced lower environmental uncertainty, successful firms were more centralized since the information required to make decisions was available to senior managers.

Although Galbraith and Lawrence and Lorsch focused on the relationship between uncertainty and participation in *decision making*, the present study extends their analyses to the specific context of participative *budgeting*. Thus, more formally:

H1: The greater the environmental uncertainty (U), the greater the positive impact of participation in the budgetary process (B) on managerial performance (P). In mathematical terms, $\partial P/\partial B$ will be greater when U is high than when it is low.

H2: The greater the environmental uncertainty (U), the greater the positive impact of participation in the budgetary process (B) on managerial attitudes and motivation (A). In mathematical terms, $\partial A/\partial B$ will be greater when U is high than when it is low.

Participation in the Budgetary Process, Environmental Uncertainty, and Budgetary Slack

Universalistic Perspective. Slack in the budget can be dysfunctional because of resulting lack of control or distortion in information used in decision making. Top management, therefore, may find it desirable to reduce slack. According to Onsi [35], participation leads to positive communication which, in turn, reduces managers' needs to create slack. Onsi found strong support for this position by noting negative and significant correlation between participation and budgetary slack.

Contingency Perspective. Collins [11] was unable to duplicate Onsi's results. In a field study of middle-level managers in seven companies, Collins failed to find a significant negative relationship between participation and propensity to create slack. Onsi's and Collins's results conflict. We suggest environmental uncertainty as a way to reconcile this conflict.

In Galbraith's [18] framework, a firm can choose one of several strategies to deal with uncertainty and the attendant increases in information-processing requirements. Organizational slack is one mechanism that can be used to reduce information-processing needs.

> The organization responds [to increased uncertainty] by increasing the resources available rather than by utilizing existing resources more efficiently...it creates additional resources by reducing performance standards. These additional resources are called slack resources. The slack resources take the form of additional time that the customer must wait, in-process inventory, under-utilized man-hours and machine time, higher costs, etc. [18, p. 24]

> Slack resources are an additional cost to the organization or the customer. However, the longer the scheduled time available, the lower the likelihood of a target being missed. The fewer the exceptions, the less the overload on the hierarchy. Thus the creation of slack resources, through reduced performance levels, reduces the amount of information that must be processed during task execution and prevents the overloading of hierarchical channels. [18, pp. 15-16]

> *The amount of slack required depends on the degree of task uncertainty.* The less the organization knows about its task, the greater the reduction in performance that is required. The performance level must be reduced until the number of exceptions is within the capacity of the organization to process them. [18, p. 25-26, emphasis added]

Higher information-processing needs also can be handled by giving subunit managers greater participation in decision making (as stated previously). Thus, the relationship between participation and slack need not be present under all conditions. Rather, the relationship will be moderated by environmental uncertainty. In situations of higher uncertainty, higher participation will reduce managers' propensity to create slack. In other words, managers need not feel they have to create slack in response to uncertainty if participation can deal effectively with information-processing needs. On the other hand, in situations of lower uncertainty, lower participation is adequate to control slack since the need of managers to create slack is not present (due to low information-processing needs). In the context of participative budgeting, the following hypothesis therefore is advanced:

H3: The greater the environmental uncertainty (*U*), the greater the impact of participation in the budgetary process (*B*) in reducing budgetary slack (*S*). In mathematical terms, ∂B will have a more negative impact on ∂S when *U* is high than when it is low.

METHOD

Sample

This study focused on the following major variables: (1) responsibility center's (functional department's) environmental uncertainty, (2) degree of participation by the responsibility-center manager in the decisions which establish and administer the budget for that center, and (3) the responsibility-center manager's performance and attitudes. It was expected that the responsibility-center manager and his/her immediate superior would be the most knowledgeable about these variables. Therefore, data were collected from both these executives. A questionnaire was used to collect data. All the measures included in the questionnaire have been used extensively in other studies with acceptable results for reliability and validity.

Given the nature of the hypotheses tested in this study, it was necessary that the sample include responsibility centers facing different levels of environmental uncertainty. This was a major consideration in the selection of 92 responsibility centers for participation in this study. The managers in charge of these responsibility centers each were sent a questionnaire. A cover letter explaining the purpose of the study assured the subjects of confidentiality. In order to minimize response bias, the participants were provided with envelopes to return the completed questionnaires directly to the researcher. A total of 80 questionnaires (87 percent) were returned of which 77 (84 percent) were usable. Respondents held middle-level management positions and were heading the following functional departments: production/operations (51 percent), sales/marketing (23 percent), accounting (15 percent), research and development (10 percent), and personnel management (1 percent). On the average, the respondents were 42 years old, had worked for their present employers for 12 years, and had held their present positions for 4 years.

Each respondent was asked to indicate the name of his/her immediate superior. Out of the 77 usable responses, superiors' names were provided on 69. A second questionnaire (along with a return envelope) was mailed to each of these superiors. The subjects were assured of confidentiality. The questionnaire sought information on the environmental uncertainty experienced by the subordinate's responsibility center. In addition, the questionnaire collected information on the subordinate's overall performance rating as well as performance relative to budget standards. It was expected that subordinates would have the most reliable information on their *own* attitudes toward the budget process. Therefore, questions relating to managerial attitudes were not asked of the superiors. A total of 60 superiors (87 percent) returned the questionnaire; 53 responses (77 percent) were usable.

Independent Variables

Participation in the Budgetary Process. This variable was defined as the responsibility-center manager's involvement and influence in budgetary matters. Following Searfoss and Monczka [37], Bruns and Waterhouse [6], and Merchant [28], this variable was extracted through a factor analysis of the budget-related behavior questionnaire developed by Swieringa and Moncur [41]. Respondents were asked to indicate, on a seven-point Likert scale, their level of agreement on each of 44 budget-related activities that take place in the budgeting for their responsibility centers. Factor analysis, using the Statistical Package for Social Sciences [32], was employed to uncover underlying patterns in the data. The decision rule for inclusion of an item in defining a factor was a factor loading of .40 or above. The resulting solution yielded six factors which accounted for 86 percent of the common variance of the 44 items. The initial principal-factor matrix was rotated orthogonally (varimax) to reach the final solution. Of the six factors, factors 2 and 3 were identified as measuring the responsibility-center managers' participation in the budgetary process. Exhibit 1 contains a description of the items loading >.40 on factors 2 and 3 as well as the percentage of variance explained by each of these factors. It is worth noting that the items loading on factors 2 and 3 closely parallel the items identified by Merchant [28] to measure budget participation. In the remainder of the paper, factors 2 and 3 (included in Exhibit 1) will be referred to as *attention* and *participation*, respectively. Higher values on these variables indicate higher budget participation.

As a check for the construct validity of the participation variables, respondents were asked two additional questions. They were asked to estimate the percentage of their time spent in budget-related activities and to indicate, on a seven-point Likert scale, the degree of influence they had in establishing the budget for their responsibility centers. If the attention and participation variables were valid, we would expect significant positive correlations between these variables, on the one hand, and the time spent on budget activities (as well as the managers' influence in establishing the budget), on the other. These construct-validity checks yielded satisfactory results as shown:

	Correlation with time spent on budget activities	*Correlation with influence in establishing the budget*
Attention	.33 ($p<.01$)	.46 ($p<.001$)
Participation	.25 ($p<.05$)	.49 ($p<.001$)

Summary statistics on the attention and participation variables as well as all other variables are given in Table 1.

Environmental Uncertainty. The present research focused on decision makers' perceptions of environmental uncertainty in their task environments rather than on any objective measures of such uncertainty. This approach is consistent with the empirical studies of Lawrence and Lorsch [25] and Duncan [14] as well as with the conceptual arguments of Weick [45] and Downey, Hellriegel, and Slocum [13].

EXHIBIT 1
Individual Items (with Respective Factor Loadings) Used to Measure Participation in the Budgetary Process ($n=77$)

Factor	Title and Items Loading>.40	Loading	Percentage of Variance
2	*Personal attention to budgeting*		15.3
	You work with your subordinates in preparing the budget for your responsibility center.	.76	
	You investigate favorable as well as unfavorable budget variations for your responsibility center.	.75	
	You discuss budget items with your subordinates when problems occur.	.66	
	You are required to submit an explanation in writing about causes of large budget variances.	.61	
	Preparing the budget for your responsibility center requires your attention to great number of details.	.60	
	You are required to prepare reports comparing actual results with budgets.	.60	
	You spend time outside of normal working hours preparing the budget for your responsibility center.	.50	
	You personally investigate budget variances in your responsibility center.	.44	
3	*Participation in the budget-setting process*		7.6
	The budget system is changed in accordance with your suggestions.	.77	
	The budget is finalized only when you are satisfied with it.	.71	
	You offer suggestions for the improvement of budget systems.	.64	
	You start preparing the budget for your responsibility center before you are asked to.	.55	

They argued that *perceptions* of uncertainty, rather than actual uncertainty, are the important determinants in decision making.

An instrument developed by Downey et al. [13] based on Duncan's [14] prior work has proved the most useful to date to measure perceived environmental uncertainty. Our study used this instrument with modifications suggested by Michlitsch [29]. Downey et al. [13] included internal as well as external components in their definition of environment; our research was concerned with the external environment only. Our research instrument, therefore, included only those components of the external task environment. Second, unlike Downey et al. [13], all our subjects responded to *all* five segments (customers, suppliers, competitors, government-political, and technological) of the external environment. This ensured that all the subjects responded to the same environmental setting, rather than one subject responding to one part of the environment and another responding to a different part.

TABLE 1
Response Structure of All Variables under Study

Variable	Mean	SD	Min	Max	Zero-Order Correlation Coefficients (n=77) 1	2	3	4	5	6	7	8	9	Coefficient Alpha	Correlation between Superior and Subordinate Responses (n=53)
1. Mahoney performance measure	5.21	.76	2	6										.78	.31**
2. Performance relative to budget	87.90	53.39	1	250	.30***									N/A	.56****
3. Budgetary slack	13.51	4.69	4	26	-.01	-.08								.74	a
4. Budget usefulness	22.74	4.76	10	33	.09	.40****	-.27***							.70	a
5. Budget relevance	4.87	1.45	1	7	.01	.36****	-.30***	.64****						N/A	a
6. Budget motivation	15.86	3.59	6	21	.05	.39****	-.31***	.60****	.77****					.90	a
7. Budget attitude	15.34	3.42	6	21	.03	.16*	-.30***	.40****	.48****	.38****				.71	a
8. Attention	37.60	9.69	9	55	.32***	.26***	-.27***	.36****	.30***	.35****	.28***			.90	a
9. Participation	16.94	4.84	5	28	.23**	.17*	-.37****	.36****	.31***	.40****	.13	.49****		.82	a
10. Environmental uncertainty	235.17	64.62	40	397	-.20**	.04	.02	.30***	.16*	.13	-.03	.13	-.09	See text	.37***

[a]Swieringa and Moncur's [41] instrument was not administered to the superiors. Hence correlations between superior and subordinate responses could not be calculated for the two participation variables, participation and attention. However, both superiors and subordinates were asked the following question: "How much influence does the focal manager have in establishing the budget for his/her responsibility center?" Correlation between superior and subordinate responses on this question was positive and significant (r=.32, p<.01).

It was expected that subordinates would have the most reliable information on their *own* attitudes toward the budget process. As such, questions relating to budgetary slack, budget usefulness, budget relevance, budget attitude, and budget motivation were not asked of the superiors.

*p<.10
**p<.05
***p<.01
****p<.001

The resulting environmental uncertainty measure had eight questions, one with two parts. The first question asked respondents to rate on a five-point Likert scale the relative importance of the five environmental segments in influencing the outcomes of typical decisions made in their responsibility centers. Subscales A (lack of information subscale) and B (lack of effect knowledge subscale) had three questions each; subscale C (ability to assign probabilities subscale) contained the two-part question. The questions for subscales A, B, and C were identical to those used by Downey et al. [13]. Each subject responded to each of the eight questions for all five segments of the environment. This produced 45 separate responses for each subject.

Following the procedures used by Downey et al. [13], internal consistency reliabilities (Cronbach's alphas) were calculated for the three subscales.

Cronbach's Alphas	*Subscale A*	*Subscale B*	*Subscale C*
Downey et al. [13]	.59	.26	.66
This study	.75	.78	.68

The three subscales were combined into an overall environmental uncertainty measure using Bourgeois's [4] method as follows:

$$(\text{Overall environmental uncertainty})_i = I_i(D_i + E_i + F_i)$$

where i = the environmental element being scored,
I = the importance of the element i,
D = lack-of-information subscale value for element i,
E = lack-of-effect knowledge subscale value for element i,
F = ability-to-assign-probabilities subscale value for element i.

Cronbach's alphas for each of the individual environmental dimensions used to construct overall environmental uncertainty varied from .72 to .86.

Dependent Variables

Managerial Performance. Two variables—Mahoney's performance measure and performance relative to budget—were used to measure managerial performance.

Mahoney's performance measure: Managerial performance was obtained using the measure developed by Mahoney, Jerdee, and Carroll [27]. Respondents were asked to rate on a seven-point Likert scale (ranging from "well below average performance" to "well above average performance") their performance on eight dimensions: planning, investigating, coordinating, evaluating, supervising, staffing, negotiating, and representing. In addition, their performance was rated globally.

The Mahoney measure offered two advantages. First, independent assessments of reliability and validity of this measure have yielded satisfactory results in other studies (e.g., [21]). Second, this measure explicitly recognizes the multidimensional nature of managerial performance while, at the same time, avoiding the problems inherent in measures with excessive dimensions. Kavanagh, McKinney, and Wolins

TABLE 2
The Mahoney Measure
($n=77$)

A. Intercorrelations among Mahoney performance dimensions

	1	2	3	4	5	6	7	8
1. Planning								
2. Investigating	.50							
3. Coordinating	.22	.26						
4. Evaluating	.47	.52	.31					
5. Supervising	.26	.34	.36	.47				
6. Staffing	.35	.32	.28	.39	.51			
7. Negotiating	.26	.30	.33	.30	.37	.29		
8. Representing	.03	.19	.11	.11	.20	.47	.25	

B. Correlations between global rating and the separate dimensions of the Mahoney measure

	Individual Performance Dimensions							
Sample	1	2	3	4	5	6	7	8
Present study	.61	.64	.47	.52	.60	.68	.48	.37
Heneman [21]	.55	.41	.39	.33	.44	.36	.40	.41

Note: $.19 \leq r \leq .25$ significant at $p<.05$; $r \leq .33$ significant at $p<.01$; $r \geq .33$ significant at $p<.001$

[23], for example, used a 20-dimension performance rating scale and obtained disappointing results on a discriminant validity test.

As a check for reliability, correlations were computed for each of the eight specific performance dimensions with each other, as well as for each specific dimension with the global rating. As shown in Table 2, each of the specific dimensions had a positive and significant correlation with the global rating, and these correlations generally were stronger than those obtained by Heneman [21]. Also, the correlations among the eight subdimensions of performance were highly significant.

As a further test of the consistency of the ratings, a multiple regression was computed by regressing the eight specific performance dimensions (independent variables) on the global rating (dependent variable). This resulted in an R^2 value of .79 with a significant F value ($p<.001$), thereby verifying that the global rating did reflect a combined measure of all eight subdimensions.

The construct validity of this variable was assessed by asking each respondent to indicate how the salary increase received by the focal manager compared with the average salary increases received by the manager's peers during the same period. Responses were obtained on a seven-point Likert scale ranging from "significantly below average" to "significantly above average." As anticipated, the Mahoney performance measure correlated positively with the "relative salary increase" variable ($r=.45$, $p<.001$).

Performance relative to budget: To compare the relative performance of two responsibility centers, we were not able to contrast their levels of costs and/or profits since these are affected by other organizational and environmental variables.

To mitigate this problem, it was decided to measure performance relative to budget standards since the latter would take into consideration the particular context of the responsibility center. First, respondents were asked how large a negative or unfavorable budget variance (a percentage of the budget) they could obtain before it became the concern of their immediate superiors. This question was used as a measure of the control limit beyond which performance would be considered unsatisfactory [22]. It was scored on a scale of 1 to 6 where 1 corresponded to the largest control limit (most flexible) and 6 corresponded to the smallest control limit (most tight). Next, respondents were asked what percentage of time during the last 12 months they had experienced unfavorable budget variances at least as large as the percentage amount specified in the previous question. This was intended to measure the frequency of unsatisfactory performance. It was scored on a scale of 1 to 10. Here, 1 corresponded to a situation where unfavorable variances beyond the control limit occurred 100 percent of the time; a score of 10 indicated the opposite.

Neither of the above two questions by itself could reflect managerial performance adequately. For instance, take two managers (A and B) who both exceed the control limit 100 percent of the time. Exclusive use of the second question would indicate that the performances of the two managers were identical. However, if the control limits of A and B were 1 (largest) and 6 (smallest), respectively, then the performance of manager B had to be better than that of manager A. It therefore was necessary to use the responses to both questions in order to construct the performance variable. Such a weighted budget-performance measure was calculated by multiplying the control limit (derived from the first question) by the frequency of falling within the control limit (from the second question). The resulting number then was weighted by the respondents' answers to another question (based on [20]) which measured the extent to which achievement of the budget captured all aspects of the responsibility centers' performance. This weighted measure was named "performance relative to budget." Higher values on this measure indicated better performance.

Managerial Attitudes and Motivation. Managerial attitudes and motivation were measured along several dimensions: budgetary slack, budget usefulness, budget attitude, budget relevance, and budget motivation.

Budgetary slack: This variable measured the managers' attitudes toward creating slack in budgets. Onsi's [35] measure was duplicated by having each manager agree or disagree (on a seven-point Likert scale) to the following four statements: (1) To protect himself/herself, a responsibility-center manager submits budgets that can be safely obtained. (2) To be safe, the responsibility-center manager sets two levels of budgets: one between himself/herself and his/her subordinates and another between himself/herself and his/her superior. (3) Slack in the budget is good to do things that cannot be officially approved. (4) In good business times, your superior is willing to accept a reasonable level of slack in your budget. The scores for the four statements were added for a combined scale. The response set was polarized so that a high score on this variable reflected an individual's propensity to create slack.

Budget usefulness: This variable was measured using the factor "usefulness of budgeting" uncovered by Swieringa and Moncur [41] and Bruns and Waterhouse [6]. Respondents were asked to rate on a seven-point Likert scale whether they believed that budgeting enabled them to (1) be more flexible, (2) be more innovative, (3) be better managers, (4) keep track of their success as managers, and (5) plan activities in their units. The scores of the five items were added for a combined scale. Managers with higher scores on this variable viewed the budget process as a more useful and worthwhile activity.

Budget attitude: While the previous variable focused on the usefulness of budgeting in specific areas, managers' overall attitudes toward the budget process were measured using the instrument developed by Hofstede [22]. Respondents were asked to indicate on a seven-point Likert scale their level of agreement with the following statements: (1) If given a chance, you would prefer to work with budgets. (2) If no budgets were set but your instruction would be to work as efficiently as possible, this would make your responsibility center's performance higher than it is now. (3) You could work as well without budgets (reverse scored). The scores on these three statements were added for a combined scale. The response set was polarized so that a high score on this variable indicated that a manager had a more favorable attitude toward the budget process.

Budget relevance: Following Hofstede [22], respondents were asked to agree or disagree (on a seven-point Likert scale) with the following statement: Budgets stimulate you to achieve better performance. Higher scores on this measure indicated greater relevance of the budget for the manager.

Budget motivation: This variable reflected the managers' intrinsic motivation derived from budget activities. Following Dermer [12], respondents were asked to indicate their agreement (on a seven-point Likert scale) with the following statements: (1) Good performance relative to budget gives you a feeling of accomplishment. (2) Attaining budgeted goals contributes to your personal growth and development. (3) You get a great sense of personal satisfaction when your actual performance compares favorably with the budget. The scores on the three statements were added to construct the total scale.

Additional Reliability and Validity Checks. As an additional test for validity, correlations were computed between the superior and subordinate ratings on a given variable. Anything approaching perfect correlation would be unlikely, of course, because of selective perception; but a reasonable relationship would tend to establish the validity of the measures employed. All the correlations were in the expected direction (i.e., positive), and all were significant at the .01 level or better (see Table 1).

Internal reliability estimates (Cronbach's alphas) for all the multi-item measures also were calculated (see Table 1). These reliability values were comfortably above the lower limits of acceptability, generally considered around .50 to .60 [33].

RESULTS

Data Analysis Technique

All three hypotheses are of the following form: $\partial Y/\partial X_1$ will be greater when X_2 is high (or low) than when X_2 is low (or high). That is,

$$\frac{\partial Y}{\partial X_1} = b_1 + b_3 X_2 \tag{1}$$

where, depending on the hypothesis, b_3 is predicted to be either positive or negative. For statistical purposes, equation (1) was integrated over X_1 and rewritten as

$$Y = c_1 + b_1 X_1 + b_2 X_2 + b_3 X_1 X_2 + \epsilon_1. \tag{2}$$

It might be noted that this specific ("multiplier interaction") model of contingency relationship also has been used by Schoonhoven [36] and Gupta and Govindarajan [19].

Southwood's [38] mathematical analysis pointed out a few other important characteristics of equation (2). If X_1 and X_2 are interval-scale (but not ratio-scale) variables, then their points of origin are totally arbitrary. As Southwood illustrated, if these origin points are changed (i.e., if X_1 and X_2 are replaced by $X_1 + k_1$ and $X_2 + k_2$, respectively), then in equation (2) the following also change: the unstandardized regression coefficients b_1 and b_2, their standard errors, their levels of significance, their standardized counterparts (β_1 and β_2), and, of course, the constant c_1. While the standardized regression coefficient (β_3) of the crossproduct term also changes, what remain invariant are the following: the unstandardized regression coefficient b_3, its standard error, its level of significance, and the R_2 and F ratio for the whole equation itself. In fact, with a suitable choice of origin points for X_1 and X_2, the coefficients b_1 and b_2 can be reduced to zero leaving only the crossproduct term with its unchanged coefficient b_3 in the equation. The net conclusion is that the only use for equation (2) is to learn about the significance and nature of the impact of interaction between X_1 and X_2 on Y and *not* about the nature of their main effects.

Test of Hypotheses

Following equation (2) as the general model, multiple regressions were conducted to test all the hypotheses. These results are summarized in Tables 3, 4, and 5. As explained in the methods section, dependent variables were grouped broadly into those relating to managerial performance (global rating and performance relative to budget) and those relating to managerial attitudes and motivation (budget attitude, budget usefulness, budget relevance, and budget motivation).

The results given in Table 3 provide clear and strong support for H1. Interaction between the variable attention and environmental uncertainty had a positive and significant effect on global rating of performance. Also, interaction between the variable participation and environmental uncertainty had a positive and significant impact on performance relative to budget.

The results contained in Table 4 provide strong support for H2. Interaction between attention and environmental uncertainty had a positive and significant effect on budget attitude. Furthermore, interaction between participation and

TABLE 3
Participation in the Budgetary Process,
Environmental Uncertainty, and Managerial Performance[a]
(n=77)

	Participation Variable	
	Attention	Participation
Performance variable (=dependent variable)	Global rating	Performance relative to budget
Unstandardized regression coefficients (standard errors)		
Environmental uncertainty[b]	-.00412	-.49177
	(.01413)	(.35257)
Participation variable[b]	-.23736*	-8.75529
	(.12950)	(6.56260)
Interaction term[c]	.00068352*	.04119**
	(.0003788)	(.02005)
R^2	.19	.10
F value	5.42***	2.51*
Inflection point	347	213

[a]Only the results of regression equations where the interaction term has a statistically significant beta are included in this table.

[b]The results (including the significance levels) given here vary with changes in the points of origin of the main independent variables. Hence, the information should be regarded as essentially meaningless. For details, see Southwood [38] as well as the results section of this paper.

[c]For the interaction terms, the values of the *unstandardized* regression coefficients, their standard errors, and their levels of significance are *independent* of the points of origin of the main independent variables. Hence, the data here do have information content.

*p<.10
**p<.05
***p<.01

environmental uncertainty was positive and significant for the following managerial attitude variables: budget attitude, budget relevance, and budget usefulness.

Table 5 contains the results to test H3. The effect of the interaction between environmental uncertainty and participation on budgetary slack was negative and significant, thereby indicating that, with greater environmental uncertainty, higher budget participation tends to reduce budgetary slack. This result supports H3.

Test for the Presence of Universalistic and Contingency Effects

The results so far show that the greater the environmental uncertainty, the greater the positive impact of budget participation on managerial performance and attitudes. But these results do not indicate whether budget participation *always* contributes positively to managerial performance and attitudes. For instance, H1 argues that higher budget participation, when coupled with higher values of environmental uncertainty, should lead to higher performance. H1 could be interpreted in two ways. The first would be that, if higher budget participation is combined with lower values of environmental uncertainty, performance should suffer since

TABLE 4
Participation in the Budgetary Process, Environmental Uncertainty, and Managerial Attitudes[a]
($n=77$)

	Participation Variable			
	Attention	Participation		
Attitudinal variable (=dependent variable)	Budget attitude	Budget attitude	Budget relevance	Budget usefulness
Unstandardized regression coefficients (standard errors)				
Environmental uncertainty[b]	-.03612*	-.02785**	-.00814	-.04207**
	(.01884)	(.01384)	(.00556)	(.01651)
Participation variable[b]	-.22958	-.42271	-.09390	-.61790**
	(.17268)	(.25766)	(.10356)	(.30727)
Interaction term[c]	.009801*	.00167**	.00062299*	.00323****
	(.005052)	(.0007872)	(.0003164)	(.0009388)
R^2	.20	.10	.18	.42
F value	5.92***	2.53*	5.22***	16.63****
Inflection point	234	253	151	191

[a]Only the results of regression equations where the interaction term has a statistically significant beta are included in this table.

[b]The results (including the significance levels) given here vary with changes in the points of origin of the main independent variables. Hence, the information should be regarded as essentially meaningless. For details, see Southwood [38] as well as the results section of this paper.

[c]For the interaction terms, the values of the *unstandardized* regression coefficients, their standard errors, and their levels of significance are *independent* of the points of origin of the main independent variables. Hence, the data here do have information content.

*$p<.10$
**$p<.05$
***$p<.01$
****$p<.001$

no congruence exists between participation and uncertainty. This implies that H1 has a *symmetrical* property because it suggests a *nonmonotonic* effect of participation on performance over the range of uncertainty. The second interpretation could be that budget participation always contributes to effectiveness in a universalistic sense irrespective of the level of uncertainty; however, increases in participation to match increases in uncertainty should lead to even higher performance. This implies a *monotonic* effect.

To determine if symmetrical or nonmonotonic effects were present, the analysis was pushed to a second stage. As suggested by Schoonhoven [36] and Southwood [38], such effects can be located by examining the partial derivative of equation (2) over X_1:

$$\partial Y/\partial X_1 = b_1 + b_3 X_2. \quad (3)$$

TABLE 5
Participation in the Budgetary Process, Environmental Uncertainty, and Budgetary Slack[a]
($n=77$)

	Participation Variable
	Participation
Dependent variable	Budgetary slack
Unstandardized regression coefficients (standard errors)	
Environmental uncertainty[b]	.03160*
	(..01284)
Participation variable[b]	.23024
	(.33210)
Interaction term[c]	-.00191*
	(.00101)
R^2	.20
F value	5.84**
Inflection point	121

[a]Only the results of regression equations where the interaction term has a statistically significant beta are included in this table.

[b]The results (including the significance levels) given here vary with changes in the points of origin of the main independent variables. Hence, the information should be regarded as essentially meaningless. For details, see Southwood [38] as well as the results section of this paper.

[c]For the interaction terms, the values of the *unstandardized* regression coefficients, their standard errors, and their levels of significance are *independent* of the points of origin of the main independent variables. Hence, the data here do have information content.

*$p<.10$
**$p<.01$

If the value of $\partial Y/\partial X_1$ is always positive or always negative over the entire *observed* range of X_1, then the relationship between Y and X_1 would be regarded as monotonic; otherwise, it would be regarded as nonmonotonic. Such a test for the presence of monotonicity was conducted for all the hypotheses and these results also are included in Tables 3, 4, and 5.

Consider the results of the regression equation used to test the interaction between attention and environmental uncertainty on budget attitude (Table 4):

$$Y(\text{budget attitude}) = -.03612(\text{uncertainty}) - .22958\ (\text{attention}) + .0098(\text{uncertainty} \times \text{attention}). \quad (4)$$

The partial derivative of equation (4) over the participation variable attention yields the following:

$$\frac{\partial(\text{budget attitude})}{\partial(\text{attention})} = -.22958 + .0098\ (\text{uncertainty}). \quad (5)$$

As can be calculated, equation (5) will be zero when environmental uncertainty has a value of 234. When uncertainty has values above 234, equation (5) will be positive; when uncertainty has values below 234, equation (5) will be negative. Thus the inflection point of the slope (or the value of uncertainty when a change in the direction of the slope occurs) is 234. This inflection point is within the range of values observed for uncertainty in the sample—40 to 397 (Table 1). In fact, the inflection point is very close to the mean value. It can be concluded therefore that budget participation has a nonmonotonic effect on budget attitude over the range of uncertainty.

The following conclusions can be drawn by focusing on the "inflection point" results in Tables 3, 4, and 5:

- The inflection points contained in Tables 3 and 4 are within the range of values for uncertainty observed in the sample—40 to 397 (Table 1). Thus, participation in the budgetary process contributes to managerial performance and attitudes when task environment is more uncertain, but budget participation hampers performance and attitudes when task environment is less uncertain. This finding does not support the position of previous researchers who argued for universalistic effects of budget participation on managerial performance and attitudes (e.g., [30]).
- The impact of budget participation on budgetary slack is nonmonotonic over the range of environmental uncertainty because the inflection point of 121 (given in Table 5) is within the observed range of values for uncertainty. This again does not support the universalistic benefits of budget participation in reducing budgetary slack as argued by Onsi [35].

DISCUSSION

While a great deal of research attention has been given to environmental uncertainty in the organizational behavior area, very little work has examined the implications of uncertainty for the design of budgeting systems. The focus of this study was the impact of environmental uncertainty on one of the design elements of budgeting, namely, participation in the budgetary process.

The results of this study support a strict contingency relationship between uncertainty and participation. More specifically, the following conclusions can be drawn based on this study:

- Greater budgetary participation contributes to managerial performance and attitudes in high-uncertainty situations but hampers performance and attitudes in low-uncertainty situations.
- Higher budgetary participation reduces managers' propensities to create slack in high-uncertainty (but not in low-uncertainty) conditions.

Much of the earlier work in this area has tended to view budgetary participation as contributing to effectiveness in a universalistic sense. Our results do not support this view. In order to obtain favorable outcomes, higher budgetary participation is needed only under high-uncertainty conditions. In fact, if high budget participation is given under low-uncertainty conditions, both performance and attitudes seem to suffer. The rationale for this conclusion is based on theoretical work in the organizational behavior area. When uncertainty is low, centralization eliminates errors, reduces the need for time-consuming information processing, and protects the decision-making process from trivial and routine matters [18]. All these benefits ultimately translate into higher performance. As regards attitudes, if uncertainty is low, most decisions are routine, and participants will be more satisfied if their time is not wasted by involvement in decisions with obvious solutions [26]. High participation in obvious decisions also may lead to fruitless disagreement. O'Connell, Cummings, and Huber [34], for example, found that, when a task was routine, less tension existed if decision making was centralized. Furthermore, French, Israel, and As [16] specified relevance and legitimacy of participation as important preconditions if participation was to produce favorable outcomes. Vroom [44] argued along similar lines and stated that intrinsic motivation is difficult to generate for activities that are not relevant to a person's self-concept. Therefore, the individual must perceive participation to be legitimate and relevant before participation will produce positive effects. These conditions are more likely to be met when uncertainty is high than when it is low. This is so since, under low levels of uncertainty, a subunit manager may not feel that he/she in fact participated or may not see the need for his/her participation in budgeting.

The results of this study have practical as well as theoretical relevance. At the level of practice, this study recommends to the designers of budgeting systems that they ought not to give high budgetary participation indiscriminately to subunit managers. Better results can be achieved, in fact, by varying budgetary participation to match variations in environmental uncertainty.

As regards theory development, the results of this study suggest the fruitfulness of considering other contingency variables in researching the effects of participative budgeting. As argued by Brownell [5], participation in the budgetary process might be contingent on four groups of variables: cultural, organizational, interpersonal, and individual. Future research should focus attention on all four groups of contingency variables in order to develop a comprehensive and integrated model specifying the conditions under which budgetary participation will produce favorable outcomes. Furthermore, future research also should explicitly consider other factors such as company policy (some firms do not allow managers to participate in goal setting, regardless of uncertainty) that might affect the variables considered in the present study. [Received: December 20, 1984. Accepted: October 28, 1985.]

REFERENCES

[1] Argyris, C. *The impact of budgets on people.* Ithaca, NY: Cornell University, Controllership Foundation, 1952.

[2] Bass, B. M., & Leavitt, H. J. Experiments in planning and operating. *Management Science*, 1963, *9*, 574-585.

[3] Becker, S., & Green, D. Budgeting and employee behavior. *Journal of Business*, 1962, *35*, 392-402.

[4] Bourgeois, L. J. Strategic goals, perceived uncertainty, and economic performance in volatile environments. *Academy of Management Journal*, 1985, *28*, 548-573.

[5] Brownell, P. Participation in the budgeting process: When it works and when it doesn't. *Journal of Accounting Literature*, 1982, *1*, 124-153.

[6] Bruns, W. J., Jr., & Waterhouse, J. H. Budgetary control and organization structure. *Journal of Accounting Research*, 1975, *13*, 177-203.

[7] Bryan, J. F., & Locke,E. A. Goal setting as a means of increasing motivation. *Journal of Applied Psychology*, 1967, *52*, 274-277.

[8] Carroll, S. J., & Tosi, H. L. Goal characteristics and personality factors in a management by objectives program. *Administrative Sciences Quarterly*, 1970, *15*, 295-305.

[9] Cherrington, D. J., & Cherrington, J. O. Appropriate reinforcement contingencies in the budgeting process. *Empirical Research in Accounting: Selected Studies* (Supplement to the *Journal of Accounting Research*), 1973, *11*, 225-253.

[10] Coch, L., & French, J. R. P., Jr. Overcoming resistance to change. *Human Relations*, 1948, *1*, 512-532.

[11] Collins, F. The interaction of budget characteristics and personality variables with budgetary response attitudes. *The Accounting Review*, 1978, *53*, 324-335.

[12] Dermer, J. D. The interrelationship of intrinsic and extrinsic motivation. *Academy of Management Journal*, 1975, *18*, 125-129.

[13] Downey, H. K., Hellriegel, D., & Slocum, J. W. Environmental uncertainty: The construct and its application. *Administrative Science Quarterly*, 1975, *20*, 613-629.

[14] Duncan, R. Characteristics of organizational environment and perceived environmental uncertainty. *Administrative Science Quarterly*, 1972, *17*, 313-327.

[15] Foran, M., & DeCoster, D. T. An experimental study of the effects of participation, authoritarianism and feedback on cognitive dissonance in a standard setting situation. *The Accounting Review*, 1974, *49*, 751-763.

[16] French, J. R. P., Jr., Israel, J., & As, D. An experiment on participation in a Norwegian factory: Interpersonal dimensions of decision-making. *Human Relations*, 1960, *19*, 3-19.

[17] French, J. R. P., Kay, E., & Meyer, H. H. Participation and the appraisal system. *Human Relations*, 1966, *26*, 3-20.

[18] Galbraith, J. *Designing complex organizations*. Reading, MA: Addison-Wesley, 1973.

[19] Gupta, A. K., & Govindarajan, V. Business unit strategy, managerial characteristics, and business unit effectiveness at strategy implementation. *Academy of Management Journal*, 1984, *27*, 25-41.

[20] Hayes, D. The contingency theory of managerial accounting. *The Accounting Review*, 1977, *52*, 22-39.

[21] Heneman, H. G., III. Comparisons of self and superior ratings of managerial performance. *Journal of Applied Psychology*, 1974, *59*, 638-642.

[22] Hofstede, G. H. *The game of budget control*. London: Tavistock, 1967.

[23] Kavanagh, M. J., MacKinney, A. C., & Wolins, L. Issues of managerial performance: Multitrait-multimethod analyses of ratings. *Psychological Bulletin*, 1971, *68*, 34-49.

[24] Kenis, I. Effects of budgetary goal characteristics on managerial attitudes and performance. *The Accounting Review*, 1979, *54*, 707-721.

[25] Lawrence, P. R., & Lorsch, J. W. *Organization and environment*. Homewood, IL: Irwin, 1967.

[26] Lorsch, J. W., & Morse, J. J. *Organizations and their members: A contingency approach*. New York: Harper & Row, 1974.

[27] Mahoney, T. A., Jerdee, T. H., & Carroll, S. J. *Development of managerial performance: A research approach*. Cincinnati, OH: South-Western, 1963.

[28] Merchant, K. A. The design of the corporate budgeting system: Influences on managerial behavior and performance. *The Accounting Review*, 1981, *56*, 813-829.

[29] Michlitsch, J. F. *Improving internal consistency reliability for perceived environmental uncertainty measures*. Paper presented at Academy of Management National Meetings, Dallas, TX, 1983.

[30] Milani, K. W. The relationship of participation in budget-setting to industrial supervisor performance and attitudes: A field study. *The Accounting Review*, 1975, *50*, 274-285.

[31] Morse, N. C., & Reimer, E. Experimental change of a major organizational variable. *Journal of Abnormal and Social Psychology*, 1956, *61*, 120-129.

[32] Nie, H. H., Hull, C. H., Jenkins, J. G., Brennel, K. S., & Bent, D. H. *Statistical package for the social sciences.* New York: McGraw-Hill, 1975.
[33] Nunnally, J. C. *Psychometric theory.* New York: McGraw-Hill, 1978.
[34] O'Connell, J. M., Cummings, L. L., & Huber, G. P. The effects of environmental information and decision unit structure on felt tension. *Journal of Applied Psychology,* 1976, *61,* 493-500.
[35] Onsi, M. Factor analysis of behavioral variables affecting budgetary slack. *The Accounting Review,* 1977, *52,* 535-548.
[36] Schoonhoven, C. B. Problems with contingency theory: Testing assumptions hidden within the language of contingency theory. *Administrative Science Quarterly,* 1981, *26,* 349-377.
[37] Searfoss, D., & Monczka, R. Perceived participation in the budget process and motivation to achieve the budget. *Academy of Management Journal,* 1973, *16,* 541-554.
[38] Southwood, K. E. Substantive theory and statistical interaction: Five models. *American Journal of Sociology,* 1978, *83,* 1154-1203.
[39] Stedry, A. C. *Budget control and cost behavior.* Englewood Cliffs, NJ: Prentice-Hall, 1960.
[40] Steers, R. M. Factors affecting job attitudes in a goal-setting environment. *Academy of Management Journal,* 1976, *19,* 6-16.
[41] Swieringa, R. J., & Moncur, R. H. *Some effects of participative budgeting on managerial behavior.* New York: National Association of Accountants, 1974.
[42] Tung, R. L. Dimensions of organizational environments: An exploratory study of their impact on organizational structure. *Academy of Management Journal,* 1979, *22,* 672-693.
[43] Tushman, M. L., & Nadler, D. A. Information processing as an integrating concept in organization design. *Academy of Management Review,* 1978, *3,* 613-624.
[44] Vroom, V. H. *Work and motivation.* New York: Wiley, 1964.
[45] Weick, K. E. *The social psychology of organizing.* Reading, MA: Addison-Wesley, 1969.

Vijay Govindarajan is Visiting Associate Professor at the Tuck School of Business Administration, Dartmouth College, and Associate Professor of Accounting at Ohio State University. He received his doctorate from Harvard University. His current research project examines how large diversified firms implement varied control systems for business units following divergent strategies. His articles have appeared in journals such as *Academy of Management Journal* and *Accounting, Organizations and Society.*

[23]

Markets, Bureaucracies, and Clans

William G. Ouchi

Evaluating organizations according to an efficiency criterion would make it possible to predict the form organizations will take under certain conditions. Organization theory has not developed such a criterion because it has lacked a conceptual scheme capable of describing organizational efficiency in sufficiently microsopic terms. The transactions cost approach provides such a framework because it allows us to identify the conditions which give rise to the costs of mediating exchanges between individuals: goal incongruence and performance ambiguity. Different combinations of these causes distinguish three basic mechanisms of mediation or control: markets, which are efficient when performance ambiguity is low and goal incongruence is high; bureaucracies, which are efficient when both goal incongruence and performance ambiguity are moderately high; and clans, which are efficient when goal incongruence is low and performance ambiguity is high.•

THE NATURE OF ORGANIZATIONS

What is an organization, and why do organizations exist? Many of us would answer this question by referring to Barnard's (1968) technological imperative, which argues that a formal organization will arise when technological conditions demand physical power, speed, endurance, mechanical adaptation, or continuity beyond the capacity of a single individual (1968: 27–28). Yet when the stone is too large or the production facility too complex for a single person, what is called for is cooperation, and cooperation need not take the form of a formal organization. Indeed, grain farmers who need a large grain elevator do not form corporations which take over the farms and make the farmers into employees; instead, they form a cooperative to own and operate the elevator.

Others would refer to March and Simon's (1958) argument that an organization will exist so long as it can offer its members inducements which exceed the contributions it asks of them. While this position explains the conditions under which an organization may continue to exist, it does not explain how an organization can create a whole which is so much greater than the sum of its parts that it can give them more than they contribute.

Most of us, however, would refer to Blau and Scott's (1962) definition of a formal organization as a purposive aggregation of individuals who exert concerted effort toward a common and explicitly recognized goal. Yet we can hardly accept this definition whole, suspecting as Simon (1945: 257–278) has that individuals within organizations rarely have a common understanding of goals.

Another point of view on the question of why organizations exist began with an inquiry by Coase (1937) and has recently been developed by Williamson (1975). In this view, an organization such as a corporation exists because it can mediate economic transactions between its members at lower costs than a market mechanism can. Under certain conditions, markets are more efficient because they can mediate without paying the costs of managers, accountants,

0001-8392/80/2501-0129$00.75

•

I am indebted to many colleagues for their constructive criticisms of this paper, particularly to Chris Argyris, Peter Blau, Larry Cummings, Charles Horngren, Joanne Martin, John Meyer, Jerry Porras, Edgar Schein, W. Richard Scott, Arnold Tannenbaum, Richard Walton, and Oliver Williamson.

or personnel departments. Under other conditions, however, a market mechanism becomes so cumbersome that it is less efficient than a bureaucracy. This transactions cost approach explicitly regards efficiency as the fundamental element in determining the nature of organizations.

MARKETS, BUREAUCRACIES, AND CLANS

Transactions costs are a solution to the problem of cooperation in the realm of economic activity. From the perspective of Mayo (1945) and Barnard (1968), the fundamental problem of cooperation stems from the fact that individuals have only partially overlapping goals. Left to their own devices, they pursue incongruent objectives and their efforts are uncoordinated. Any collectivity which has an economic goal must then find a means to control diverse individuals efficiently.

Many helpful ideas have flowed from this definition of the problem of cooperation. Some (e.g., Etzioni, 1965; Weick, 1969) have emphasized the tension between individual autonomy and collective interests which must attend cooperative action, while others (e.g., Simon, 1945) have emphasized the impossibility of achieving a completely cooperative effort. Our interest is in the efficiency with which transactions are carried out between individuals who are engaged in cooperative action.

Cooperative action necessarily involves interdependence between individuals. This interdependence calls for a transaction or exchange in which each individual gives something of value (for example, labor) and receives something of value (for example, money) in return. In a market relationship, the transaction takes place between the two parties and is mediated by a price mechanism in which the existence of a competitive market reassures both parties that the terms of exchange are equitable. In a bureaucratic relationship, each party contributes labor to a corporate body which mediates the relationship by placing a value on each contribution and then compensating it fairly. The perception of equity in this case depends upon a social agreement that the bureaucratic hierarchy has the legitimate authority to provide this mediation. In either case, individuals must regard the transaction as equitable: it must meet the standards of reciprocity which Gouldner (1961) has described as a universal requirement for collective life.

It is this demand for equity which brings on transactions costs. A transactions cost is any activity which is engaged in to satisfy each party to an exchange that the value given and received is in accord with his or her expectations.

Transactions costs arise principally when it is difficult to determine the value of the goods or service. Such difficulties can arise from the underlying nature of the goods or service or from a lack of trust between the parties. When a company is being sold by one corporation to another corporation, for example, it may not be unambiguously clear what the true value of that company is. If firms similar to the company are frequently bought and sold, and if those transactions occur under competitive conditions, then the market process will be accepted as a legitimate estimator of the true value. But if the company is unique, and there is only one potential buyer, then market forces are absent. How will the buyer and seller determine a fair price? They may call upon a third party to estimate the value of the company. Each party may in addition call upon other experts who will assist them in evaluating both the value of the company and the adequacy of the judgment of the third party. Each side may also require an extensive and complete contract which will describe exactly what is being bought and sold. Each of these activities is costly, and all of them are regarded here as transactions costs: they are necessary to create a perception of equity among all parties to the transaction.

This same argument applies to transactions in which a service, such as the labor of an individual, is the object of exchange. If one individual sells his or her services to another, it may be difficult to assess the true value of that labor. In particular, if the labor is to be used in an interdependent technology, one which requires teamwork, it may be difficult to assess the value contributed by one worker as opposed to another, since their joint efforts yield a single outcome in this case, or in a case where it is likely that task requirements will change, then the auditing and complex contracting required to create the perception of equity can become unbearably costly.

We have identified two principal mechanisms for mediating these transactions: a market and a bureaucracy. These alternatives have received the greatest attention from organization theorists (e.g., Barnard, 1968; Weber, 1968) and economists (e.g., Coase, 1937; Arrow, 1974). However, the paradigm also suggests a third mechanism: If the objectives of individuals are congruent (not mutually exclusive), then the conditions of reciprocity and equity can be met quite differently.

Both Barnard and Mayo pointed out that organizations are difficult to operate because their members do not share a selfless devotion to the same objectives. Mayo (1945) argued that organizations operated more efficiently in preindustrial times, when members typically served an apprenticeship during which they were socialized into accepting the objectives of the craft or organization. Barnard (1968: 42–43) posed the problem thus:

> A formal system of cooperation requires an objective, a purpose, an aim. . . . It is important to note the complete distinction between the aim of a cooperative effort and that of an individual. Even in the case where a man enlists the aid of other men to do something which he cannot do alone, such as moving a stone, the objective ceases to be personal.

While Barnard, like Arrow, views markets and bureaucracies as the basic mechanisms for achieving the continued cooperation of these individuals, he also allowed (1968: 141) for the possibility of reducing the incongruence of goals in a manner consistent with Mayo's view of the preindustrial organization:

> An organization can secure the efforts necessary to its existence, then, either by the objective inducement it provides or by changing states of mind. It seems to me improbable that any organization can exist as a practical matter which does not employ both methods in combination.

If the socialization of individuals into an organization is complete, then the basis of reciprocity can be changed. For example, Japanese firms rely to a great extent upon hiring inexperienced workers, socializing them to accept the company's goals as their own, and compensating them according to length of service, number of dependents, and other nonperformance criteria (see Abegglen, 1958; Dore, 1973; Nakane, 1973). It is not necessary for these organizations to measure performance to control or direct their employees, since the employees' natural (socialized) inclination is to do what is best for the firm. It is also unnecessary to derive explicit, verifiable measures of value added, since rewards are distributed according to nonperformance-related criteria which are relatively inexpensive to determine (length of service and number of dependents can be ascertained at relatively low costs). Thus, industrial organizations can, in some instances, rely to a great extent on socialization as the principal mechanism of mediation or control, and this "clan" form ("clan" conforms to Durkheim's meaning of an organic association which resembles a kin network but may not include blood relations, 1933: 175) can be very efficient in mediating transactions between interdependent individuals.

Markets, bureaucracies, and clans are therefore three distinct mechanisms which may be present in differing degrees, in any real organization.[1] Our next objective is to specify the conditions under which the requirements of each form are most efficiently satisfied.

THE MARKET FAILURES FRAMEWORK

We can approach this question most effectively by examining the markets and hierarchies approach provided by Williamson (1975), which builds upon earlier statements of the problem by Coase (1937) and others (for a more detailed description of the functioning of each mechanism, see Ouchi, 1979).

Market transactions, or exchanges, consist of contractual relationships. Each exchange is governed by one of three types of contractual relations, all of which can be specified completely. That is, because each party is bound only to deliver that which is specified, the contract must specify who must deliver what under every possible state of nature. The simplest form of contract is the "spot" or "sales" contract. This is what occurs when you walk up to a candy counter, ask for a candy bar, and pay the amount the salesperson asks. In such a transaction, all obligations are fulfilled on the spot. However, the spot market contract is, by definition, incapable of dealing with future transactions, and most exchange relationships involve long-term obligations.

A common device for dealing with the future is the "contingent claims contract," a document that specifies all the obligations of each party to an exchange, contingent upon all possible future states of nature. However, given a future that is either complex or uncertain, the bounded rationality of individuals makes it impossible to specify such a contract completely. Leaving such a contract incompletely specified is an alternative, but one that will succeed only if each party can trust the other to interpret the uncertain future in a

1
In the broader language necessary to encompass both economics and organization theory, an organization may be thought of as any stable pattern of transactions. In this definition, a market is as much an organization as is a bureaucracy or a clan. The only requirement is that, for the purposes of this discussion, we maintain a clear distinction between the idea of "bureaucracy" and the idea of "organization." Bureaucracy as used here refers specifically to the Weberian model, while organization refers to any stable pattern of transactions between individuals or aggregations of individuals.

manner that is acceptable to him. Thus, given uncertainty, bounded rationality, and opportunism, contingent claims contracting will fail.

Instead of trying to anticipate the future in a giant, once-and-for-all contract, why not employ a series of contracts, each one written for a short period within which future events can confidently be foreseen? The problem with such "sequential spot contracting" is that in many exchange relationships, the goods or services exchanged are unique, and the supplier requires specialized knowledge of how to supply the customer best and most efficiently. The supplier acquires this knowledge over time and in doing so gains a "first mover advantage," which enables him to bid more effectively on subsequent contracts than any potential competitor can. Knowing this, potential competitors will not waste their time bidding, thus producing a situation of "small numbers bargaining" or bilateral monopoly, in which there is only one buyer and seller. Under this condition, competitive pressures are absent, and each party will opportunistically claim higher costs or poor quality, whichever is in his or her interest. In order to maintain such an exchange, each party will have to go to considerable expense to audit the costs or performance of the other. If these transactions costs are too high, the market relationship will fail due to the confluence of opportunism with small numbers bargaining, even though the limitations of uncertainty and bounded rationality have been overcome.

Thus, under some conditions no completely contractual market relationship is feasible. Table 1 summarizes the conditions which lead to market failure. According to the paradigm, no one of the four conditions can produce market failure, but almost any pairing of them will do so.

The idea of market failure is an analytical device. Economists do not agree on a specific set of conditions that constitute the failure of a market; indeed one point of view argues that even monopolistic conditions may be competitive. However, the idea of market failure as expressed by Williamson (1975) is useful as a conceptual framework within which to compare the strengths of markets as opposed to bureaucracies. The technique is to contend that all transactions can be mediated entirely by market relations, and then ask what conditions will cause some of these market mechanisms to fail and be replaced by bureaucratic mechanisms. In this sense, every bureaucratic organization constitutes an example of market failure.

The bureaucratic organization has two principal advantages over the market relationship. First, it uses the employment relation, which is an incomplete contract. In accepting an employment relation, a worker agrees to receive wages in

Table 1

The Market Failures Framework*

Human factors		Environmental factors
Bounded rationality	←——→	Uncertainty/Complexity
Opportunism	←——→	Small numbers

*Adapted from Williamson (1975: 40).

exchange for submitting to the legitimate right of the organization to appoint superior officers who can (1) direct the work activities of the employee from day to day (within some domain or zone of indifference), thus overcoming the problem of dealing with the future all at once and (2) closely monitor the employee's performance, thus minimizing the problem of opportunism.

Second, the bureaucratic organization can create an atmosphere of trust between employees much more readily than a market can between the parties to an exchange. Because members of an organization assume some commonality of purpose, because they learn that long-term relationships will reward good performance and punish poor performance, they develop some goal congruence. This reduces their opportunistic tendencies and thus the need to monitor their performance.

Bureaucracies are also characterized by an emphasis on technical expertise which provides some skill training and some socialization into craft or professional standards. Professionals within a bureaucratic setting thus combine a primary affiliation to a professional body with a career orientation, which increases the sense of affiliation or solidarity with the employer and further reduces goal incongruence.[2]

In summary, the market failures framework argues that markets fail when the costs of completing transactions become unbearable. At that point, the inefficiencies of bureaucratic organization will be preferred to the relatively greater costs of market organization, and exchange relationships move from one domain into the other.

Consider one example. The 10,000 individuals who comprise the workforce of a steel mill could be individual entrepreneurs whose interpersonal transactions are mediated entirely through a network of market or contractual relationships. Each of them could also have a market relation with yet another combine which owned the capital equipment and facilities necessary to produce steel. Yet steel mills are typically bureaucratic in form and each worker is in an employment, not market, relation with the corporation. Market forces have failed because the determination of value contributed by one worker is highly ambiguous in the integrated steelmaking process, which makes the transactions cost attendant upon maintaining a market too high.

EXTENDING THE MARKET FAILURES FRAMEWORK: CLANS

Bureaucracies can fail when the ambiguity of performance evaluation becomes significantly greater than that which brings about market failure. A bureaucratic organization operates fundamentally according to a system of hierarchical surveillance, evaluation, and direction. In such a system, each superior must have a set of standards to which he can compare behavior or output in order to provide control. These standards only indicate the value of an output approximately, and are subject to idiosyncratic interpretation. People perceive them as equitable only as long as they believe that they contain a reasonable amount of performance information. When tasks become highly unique, completely integrated, or ambiguous for other reasons, then even bu-

2 Despite these desirable properties, the bureaucratic type has continually been under attack and revision. As Williamson points out, the move from U-form (functional) to M-form (divisional) organization among many large firms has been motivated by a desire to simulate a capital market within a bureaucratic framework because of its superior efficiency. By regrouping the parts of the organization, it is possible to create subentities that are sufficiently autonomous to permit precise measurement and the determination of an effective price mechanism. Although each division may still operate internally as a bureaucracy, the economies which accrue from this partial market solution are often large, offsetting the diseconomies of functional redundancy which often accompany the separation of the organization into divisions.

reaucratic mechanisms fail. Under these conditions, it becomes impossible to evaluate externally the value added by any individual. Any standard which is applied will be by definition arbitrary and therefore inequitable.

If we adopt the view that transactions costs arise from equity considerations, then we can interpret Table 1 in a different light. Simon's work on the employment relation (1957: 183-195) shows that Table 1 contains some redundancy. He emphasized that under an employment contract, the employer pays a worker a premium over the "spot" price for any piece of work. From the point of view of the worker, this "risk premium" compensates him for the likelihood that he will be asked to perform duties which are significantly more distasteful to him than those which are implied in the employment contract. The uncertainty surrounding the likelihood of such tasks and the expectation that the employer will or will not ask them determines the size of the risk premium. If the employee agreed with all the employer's objectives, which is equivalent to completely trusting the employer never to request a distasteful task, then the risk premium would be zero.

The employment relation is relatively efficient when the measurement of performance is ambiguous but the employer's goals are not. In an employment relation, each employee depends on the employer to distribute rewards equitably; if employees do not trust the employer to do so, they will demand contractual protections such as union representation and the transactions cost will rise.

Thus, the critical element in the efficiency of market versus employment relations has to do with (1) the ambiguity of the measurement of individual performance, and (2) the congruence of the employees' and employer's goals. We can now reformulate the transactions cost problem as follows: in order to mediate transactions efficiently, any organizational form must reduce either the ambiguity of performance evaluation or the goal incongruence between parties. Put this way, market relations are efficient when there is little ambiguity over performance, so the parties can tolerate relatively high levels of opportunism or goal incongruence. And bureaucratic relations are efficient when both performance ambiguity and goal incongruence are moderately high.

What form of mediation succeeds by minimizing goal incongruence and tolerating high levels of ambiguity in performance evaluation? Clearly, it is one which embodies a strong form of the employment relation as defined by Simon (1945), which is a relationship in which the risk premium is minimized. The answer is what we have referred to as the clan, which is the obverse of the market relation since it achieves efficiency under the opposite conditions: high performance ambiguity and low opportunism.

Perhaps the clearest exposition of the clan form apears in what Durkheim (1933: 365) refers to as the case of organic solidarity and its contrast with contractual relations:

> For organic solidarity to exist, it is not enough that there be a system of organs necessary to one another, which in a general way feel solidarity, but it is also necessary that the way in which they should come together, if not in every kind of meeting, at least

in circumstances which most frequently occur, be predetermined. . . . Otherwise, at every moment new conflicts would have to be equilibrated. . . . It will be said that there are contracts. But, first of all, social relations are not capable of assuming this juridical form. . . . A contract is not self-sufficient, but supposes a regulation which is as extensive and complicated as contractual life itself. . . . A contract is only a truce, and very precarious, it suspends hostilities only for a time.

The solidarity to which Durkheim refers contemplates the union of objectives between individuals which stems from their necessary dependence upon one another. In this sense, any occupational group which has organic solidarity may be considered a clan. Thus, a profession, a labor union, or a corporation may be a clan, and the professionalized bureaucracy may be understood as a response to the joint need for efficient transactions within professions (clan) and between professions (bureaucracy). Goal congruity as a central mechanism of control in organizations also appears repeatedly in Barnard:

The most intangible and subtle of incentives is that which I have called the condition of communion. . . . It is the feeling of personal comfort in social relations that is sometimes called solidarity, social integration. . . . The need for communion is a basis of informal organization that is essential to the operation of every formal organization (1968: 148; see also pp. 89, 152, 169, 273).

Descriptions of organizations which display a high degree of goal congruence, typically through relatively complete socialization brought about through high inclusion (Etzioni, 1965), are also found in Lipset, Trow, and Coleman (1956: 79–80), Argyris (1964: 10, 175), Selznick (1966), and Clark (1970). In each case, the authors describe the organization as one in which it is difficult to determine individual performance. However, such organizations are not "loosely coupled" nor are they "organized anarchies" simply because they lack market and bureaucratic mechanisms. A clan, as Durkheim points out, provides great regularity of relations and may in fact be more directive than the other, more explicit mechanisms. That clans display a high degree of discipline is emphasized by Kanter (1972) in her study of utopian communities, some of which were successful businesses such as Oneida and Amana. According to Kanter, this discipline was not achieved through contractualism or surveillance but through an extreme form of the belief that individual interests are best served by a complete immersion of each individual in the interests of the whole (1972: 41).

More recently, Ouchi and Jaeger (1978) and Ouchi and Johnson (1978) have reported on modern industrial organizations which closely resemble the clan form. In these organizations, a variety of social mechanisms reduces differences between individual and organizational goals and produces a strong sense of community (see also Van Maanen, 1975; Katz, 1978). Where individual and organizational interests overlap to this extent, opportunism is unlikely and equity in rewards can be achieved at a relatively low transactions cost. Moreover, these organizations are typically in technologically advanced or closely integrated industries, where teamwork is common, technologies change often, and therefore individual performance is highly ambiguous.

When a bureaucracy fails, then due to excessively ambiguous performance evaluation, the sole form of mediation remaining is the clan, which relies upon creating goal congruence. Although clans may employ a system of legitimate authority (often the traditional rather than the rational-legal form), they differ fundamentally from bureaucracies in that they do not require explicit auditing and evaluation. Performance evaluation takes place instead through the kind of subtle reading of signals that is possible among intimate coworkers but which cannot be translated into explicit, verifiable measures. This means that there is sufficient information in a clan to promote learning and effective production, but that information cannot withstand the scrutiny of contractual relations. Thus, any tendency toward opportunism will be destructive, because the close auditing and hard contracting necessary to combat it are not possible in a clan.

If performance evaluation is so ambiguous and goals so incongruent that a clan fails, what then? We can only speculate, but it seems that this final cell may be the case discussed by Meyer and Rowan (1977) in which control is purely ceremonial and symbolic. School systems, like other organizations, do employ a variety of mechanisms. Yet if there is no effective mechanism of mediation between individuals, the perception of equity may be purely superstitious, based on a broad, community-based acceptance of the legitimacy of the institution.

MARKETS, BUREAUCRACIES, AND CLANS: AN OVERVIEW

Having distinguished three mechanisms of intermediation, we can now summarize them and attempt to set out the general conditions under which each form will mediate transactions between individuals most efficiently. Table 2 discriminates markets, bureaucracies, and clans along two dimensions: their underlying normative and informational requirements.

Table 2

An Organizational Failures Framework

Mode of control	Normative requirements	Informational requirements
Market	Reciprocity	Prices
Bureaucracy	Reciprocity Legitimate authority	Rules
Clan	Reciprocity Legitimate authority Common values and beliefs	Traditions

Normative requirements refer to the basic social agreements that all members of the transactional network must share if the network is to function efficiently, without undue costs of performance auditing or monitoring. A norm of reciprocity, according to Gouldner (1961), is one of only two social agreements that have been found to be universal among societies across time and cultures (the other is the incest taboo). If no such norm were widely shared, then a potential trader would have to consume so much energy in setting the contractural terms of exchange in advance and in auditing the performance of the other party afterwards that the potential transaction would cost too much. Under such conditions, a division of labor is unthinkable and social existence impossible. Therefore, a norm of reciprocity underlies all exchange mechanisms.

A norm of legitimate authority is critical for two reasons. As discussed above, it permits the assignment of organizational superiors who can, on an ad hoc basis, specify the work assignments of subordinates, thus obviating the need for a contingent claims employment contract which would be either so complex as to be infeasible or so simple as to be too confining or else incomplete. Legitimate authority also permits organizational superiors to audit the performance of subordinates more closely than is possible within a market relationship. In a bureaucracy, legitimate authority will commonly take the "rational/legal" form, whereas in a clan it may take the "traditional" form (see Blau and Scott, 1962: 27–38). Legitimate authority is not ordinarily created within the organization but is maintained by other institutions such as the church or the educational system (Weber, 1947; Blau and Scott, 1962; Barnard, 1968: 161–184). While the legitimacy of a particular organization may be greater or smaller as a result of its managerial practices, it is fundamentally maintained within a society generally.

Common values and beliefs provide the harmony of interests that erase the possibility of opportunistic behavior. If all members of the organization have been exposed to an apprenticeship or other socialization period, then they will share personal goals that are compatible with the goals of the organization. In this condition, auditing of performance is unnecessary except for educational purposes, since no member will attempt to depart from organizational goals.

A norm of reciprocity is universal, legitimate authority is accepted, though in varying degree, in most formal organizations, and common values and beliefs are relatively rare in formal organizations. Etzioni (1965) has described this last form of control as being common only to "total organizations" such as the military and mental hospitals, and Light (1972) describes its role in ethnically bound exchange relationships. However, we have also noted that a partially complete form of socialization, accompanied by market or bureaucratic mechanisms, may be effective across a wider range of organizations. Mayo (1945) contended that instability of employment, which upsets the long socialization period necessary, is the chief enemy of the development of this form of control.

The informational prerequisites of each form of control are prices, rules, and traditions. Prices are a highly sophisticated form of information for decision making. However, correct prices are difficult to arrive at, particularly when technological interdependence, novelty, or other forms of ambiguity obscure the boundary between tasks or individuals. Rules, by comparison, are relatively crude informational devices. A rule is specific to a problem, and therefore it takes a large number of rules to control organizational responses. A decision maker must know the structure of the rules in order to apply the correct one in any given situation. Moreover, an organization can never specify a set of rules that will cover all possible contingencies. Instead, it specifies a smaller set of rules which cover routine decisions, and refers exceptions up the hierarchy where policymakers can invent rules as needed. As Galbraith (1973) has pointed out, under conditions of uncertainty or complexity the number of exceptions becomes so great that the hierarchy becomes overloaded and the quality of decision making suffers.

Traditions are implicit rather than explicit rules that govern behavior. Because traditions are not specified, they are not easily accessible, and a new member will not be able to function effectively until he or she has spent a number of years learning them (Van Maanen and Schein, 1978). In terms of the precision of the performance evaluation they permit, traditions may be the crudest informational prerequisite, since they are ordinarily stated in a general way which must be interpreted in a particular situation. On the other hand, the set of traditions in a formal organization may produce a unified, although implicit philosophy or point of view, functionally equivalent to a theory about how that organization should work. A member who grasps such an essential theory can deduce from it an appropriate rule to govern any possible decision, thus producing a very elegant and complete form of control. Alternatively, a disruption of the socialization process will inhibit the passing on of traditions and bring about organizational inefficiency.

SOME CONCLUDING THOUGHTS

Under conditions of extreme uncertainty and opportunism, transactions cost may rise. Indeed, Denison (1978) has observed that net productivity declined in the United States between 1965 and 1975 due to changes in "the industrial and human environment within which business must operate" (1978:21). According to Denison, output per unit of input has declined for two reasons: 78 percent of the decline is due to increased costs of air, water, and safety on the job, and the remaining 22 percent is attributable to increased needs for surveillance of potentially dishonest employees, customers, contractors, and thieves. The resources put into improvements in air, water, and safety are not a net loss to society although they may reduce corporate profitability. The increased need for surveillance in business, however, may represent the fact that the cost of monitoring transactions has risen. Mayo (1945) might have predicted this change as an inevitable result of the instability which accompanies industrialization. In our framework, we could advance the following explanation: exchange relationships are generally subject to so much informational ambiguity that they can never be governed completely by markets. Consequently, they have been supplemented through cultural, clan mechanisms. As instability, heterogeneity, and mobility have intensified in the United States, however, the effectiveness of these cultural mechanisms has been vitiated and bureaucratic mechanisms of surveillance and control have increased. Although bureaucratic surveillance may be the optimal strategy under present social conditions, it is nonetheless true that the United States is devoting more of its resources to transactional matters than it did ten years ago, and that represents a net decline in its welfare.

The degree of uncertainty and opportunism that characterize American society may be such that no mechanisms of control ever function very well. We have already observed that the conditions necessary for a pure market, bureaucracy, or clan are rare. Even a combination of these control mechanisms may be insufficient in many cases, however. In organizations using new technologies or in the public sector, the rate of change, instability of employment, or ambiguity of performance evaluation may simply overwhelm all rational control attempts.

In these cases, exchange becomes institutionalized. Meyer and Rowan's (1977) central thesis is that school systems, by their nature, evade any form of rational control. They have no effective price mechanism, no effective bureaucratic control, and no internally consistent cultures (see also Meyer et al., 1978). Thus school systems (as distinguished from education, which need not be done by large organizations) continue to grow and survive because the objectives which they are believed to pursue have been accepted as necessary by society. Since rational control is not feasible within the school, no one knows whether it is actually pursuing these goals, but an institutionalized organization (the church is another example) need not give evidence of performance (see also Ouchi, 1977: 97–98).

All work organizations are institutionalized in the sense that fundamental purposes of all viable organizations must mesh at least somewhat with broad social values (Parsons and Shils, 1951). This institutionalization permits organizations to survive even under conditions that severely limit their capacity for rational control. Ultimately, organizational failure occurs only when society deems the basic objectives of the organization unworthy of continued support.

What is an organization? An organization, in our sense, is any stable pattern of transactions between individuals or aggregations of individuals. Our framework can thus be applied to the analysis of relationships between individuals or between subunits within a corporation, or to transactions between firms in an economy. Why do organizations exist? In our sense, all patterned transactions are organized, and thus all stable exchanges in a society are organized. When we ask "why do organizations exist," we usually mean to ask "why do bureaucratic organizations exist," and the answer is clear. Bureaucratic organizations exist because, under certain specifiable conditions, they are the most efficient means for an equitable mediation of transactions between parties. In a similar manner, market and clan organizations exist because each of them, under certain conditions, offers the lowest transactions cost.

Markets, Bureaucracies, and Clans

REFERENCES

Abegglen, James C.
1958 The Japanese Factory: Aspects of Its Social Organization. Glencoe, Il: Free Press.

Argyris, Chris
1964 Integrating the Individual and the Organization. New York: Wiley.

Arrow, Kenneth J.
1974 The Limits of Organization. New York: Norton.

Barnard, Chester I.
1968 The Functions of the Executive, 30th anniversary ed. Cambridge: Harvard.

Blau, Peter M., and W. Richard Scott
1962 Formal Organizations. San Francisco: Scott, Foreman.

Clark, Burton R.
1970 The Distinctive College: Antioch, Reed, and Swarthmore. Chicago: Aldine.

Coase, R. H.
1937 "The nature of the firm." Economica, new series, 4: 386–405.

Denison, Edward F.
1978 Effects of Selected Changes in the Institutional and Human Environment upon Output Per Unit of Input. Brookings General Series Reprint #335. Washington: Brookings.

Dore, Ronald
1973 British Factory-Japanese Factory. Berkeley: University of California.

Durkheim, Emile
1933 The Division of Labor in Society. G. Simpson, trans. New York: Free Press.

Etzioni, Amitai
1965 "Organizational control structure." In James G. March (ed.), Handbook of Organizations: 650–677. Chicago: Rand McNally.

Galbraith, Jay
1973 Designing Complex Organizations. Reading, MA: Addison-Wesley.

Gouldner, Alvin W.
1961 "The norm of reciprocity." American Sociological Review, 25: 161–179.

Kanter, Rosabeth Moss
1972 Commitment and Community. Cambridge: Harvard.

Katz, Ralph
1978 "Job longevity as a situational factor in job satisfaction." Administrative Science Quarterly, 23: 204–223.

Light, Ivan H.
1972 Ethnic Enterprise in America. Berkeley: University of California.

Lipset, Seymour M., Martin A. Trow, and James S. Coleman
1956 Union Democracy. Glencoe, Il.: Free Press.

March, James G., and Herbert A. Simon
1958 Organizations. New York: Wiley.

Mayo, Elton
1945 The Social Problems of an Industrial Civilization. Boston: Division of Research, Graduate School of Business Administration, Harvard University.

Meyer, John W., and Brian Rowan
1977 "Institutionalized organizations: Formal structure as myth and ceremony." American Journal of Sociology, 83: 340–363.

Meyer, John W., W. Richard Scott, Sally Cole, and Jo-Ann K. Intili
1978 "Instructional dissensus and institutional consensus in schools." In Marshall W. Meyer and Associates (eds.), Environments and Organizations: 233–263. San Francisco: Jossey-Bass.

Nakane, Chie
1973 Japanese Society, rev. ed. Middlesex, England: Penguin.

Ouchi, William G.
1977 "The relationship between organizational structure and organizational control." Administrative Science Quarterly, 22: 95–113.
1979 "A conceptual framework for the design of organizational control mechanisms." Management Science, 25: 833–848.

Ouchi, William G., and Alfred M. Jaeger
1978 "Type Z organization: Stability in the midst of mobility." Academy of Management Review, 3: 305–314.

Ouchi, William G., and Jerry B. Johnson
1978 "Types of organizational control and their relationship to emotional well-being." Administrative Science Quarterly, 23: 293–317.

Parsons, Talcott, and Edward A. Shils
1951 "Values, motives, and systems of action." In Talcott Parsons and Edward A. Shils (eds.), Toward a General Theory of Action: 47–275. Cambridge: Harvard.

Selznick, Philip
1966 TVA and the Grass Roots (orig. ed., 1949). New York: Harper Torchbooks.

Simon, Herbert A.
1945 Administrative Behavior. New York: Free Press.
1957 Models of Man. New York: Wiley.

Van Maanen, John
1975 "Police socialization: A longitudinal examination of job attitudes in an urban police department." Administrative Science Quarterly, 20: 207–228.

Van Maanen, John, and Edgar H. Schein
1978 "Toward a theory of organizational socialization." Manuscript, Sloan School of Industrial Administration, Massachusetts Institute of Technology.

Weber, Max
1947 The Theory of Social and Economic Organization (orig. ed., 1925). A. M. Henderson and T. Parsons, trans. New York: Free Press.
1968 Economy and Society (orig. ed., 1925). G. Roth and C. Wittich, eds. New York: Bedminster Press.

Weick, Karl E.
1969 The Social Psychology of Organizing. Reading, MA: Addison-Wesley.

Williamson, O. E.
1975 Markets and Hierarchies: Analysis and Antitrust Implications. New York: Free Press.

Accounting and Organisation Change

Anthony G. Hopwood
London School of Economics and Political Science, UK

We live in a world in which there is an acute consciousness of both change itself and the necessity for it. This is no less true for business and commercial affairs than for other aspects of social and economic life. We have an awareness of shifting technologies and their organisational and social implications. A growing internationalisation of business and economic life is making us more conscious of global interdependencies and their implications for competition, for corporate decision making, for organisational structuring and management, and for the shifting location of power and authority. New knowledges are themselves suggestive of new spheres for business and economic activity, and new modes of organising them. And shifting political values and ideologies have questioned prevailing conceptions of the spheres of the public and the private, the domains of the economic and the social, and the boundaries between governmental and business life.

Such developments are mirrored in the financial sphere. Renewed attention is being given to the financing of new technologies, to the mobilisation of organisations around more financially oriented strategic postures and to the propagation of the language of efficiency and profit in spheres of life where these have been less significant to date. And of course the financial sector has been one where change has been occurring in its own right. New financial instruments have been invented and gained prominence in practical affairs. We are witnessing a growing internationalisation of the financial markets, with all that implies for the management of both business organisations and national states. The financial markets are also now significantly larger than and increasingly more independent of the markets for real goods and services which they initially sought to enable. Indeed we are living in a world where the ratio between the financial and the real sectors has increased dramatically over the last decade.

Of course we need to be cautious about emphasising the uniqueness and magnitude of such changes. I am sure that all ages have so prioritised the new, thus identifying the discontinuities rather than the continuities which shape organisational, social and economic life. And sometimes they possibly have had more reason to be concerned than we. I always think about what might have been the consciousness of change, indeed the anxiety towards it, in mid-17th century England. A citizen of that time living in London would have experienced the transition from a monarchy to a republic, and back again. A king claiming absolute rights had been decapitated. A religious revolution was in progress. And, after the return of the monarchy, a plague first exterminated vast sections of the

This article is taken from the John V. Ratcliffe Memorial Lecture, given at the University of New South Wales, 6 September 1988.

population and then a fire destroyed much of London as it was known. Perhaps that was change indeed! And perhaps compared with the magnitude of such disturbances we need to be conscious of the fact that change is appealed to both because of its presence and because of its perceived desirability, for some at least. People as frequently highlight change because of their desire for it as for the fact of it.

Recognising the very ambiguity of the concept of change is not unhelpful when reflecting on how accounting is caught up in such wider processes of transformation. For, on the one hand, both practitioners and researchers are now aware that many of the shifting patterns of organisational and economic life are impinging on accounting practices, the uses of which are made of them and the knowledges in which they are embedded. Increasingly recognising that accounting is not an autonomous phenomenon, other social, political and economic factors are now seen as being able to provide bases for accounting change, often playing a significant role in influencing the course of its transformation. On the other hand, however, attention is also being given to the need for accounting to change. Accounting, to some at least, is too rigid a discipline, protected and buffered from the pressures of the world by professional conservatism and an inadequate knowledge basis. In the name of particular new knowledges of accounting, calls are made for the practice of the craft to change, often in order to provide a new alignment between accounting and the economic, organisational and social contexts in which it is perceived to be imperfectly embedded. It is as if the very same phenomenon is subject both to the reality of change and to a rhetoric of arguing for it.

Being conscious of such a duality of involvement with change, I nevertheless want to consider in a little more detail some of the ways in which accounting is caught up in wider processes of organisational change. In so doing, I want to set aside some of the conventional ways in which accounting and change are related. I am not going to consider the ways in which accounting can provide relevant information for decision making in change situations. Nor do I want to analyse how accounting is implicated in processes oriented towards the re-establishment of control in those situations where the paths of organisational transformation have been disturbed and disrupted. Rather I would like to emphasise some quite general roles which accounting can play in processes of organisational change, initially giving particular emphasis to three such roles.

The first of these is the role which accounting plays in creating a quite particular visibility in the organisation, making things visible that otherwise would not be. Such a role is clearly not a new one. Jeremy Bentham, the early 19th century British utilitarian philosopher, recognised the role which bookkeeping, rather than accounting *per se*, can play in facilitating organisational control. In a discussion of proposals for reforming the Poor Law, Bentham noted that there were two sciences underlying control, the science of architecture and the science of bookkeeping. Architecture facilitates control by the strategic design of physical space. As was so beautifully illustrated by Bentham's proposals for the perfect prison (Bentham, 1791; see Foucault, 1977), the Panopticon, the location of walls, windows and doors can create or constrain patterns of visibility. By the careful positioning of barriers, actions and events can be opened up to a wider observation and thereby control. Equally domains of privacy can be created, where the eyes of the outside world cannot penetrate. Bookkeeping, according to Bentham, enables an indirect means of visibility to be created where the eye could not otherwise see. Records can be kept of what is happening on the other side of the wall, or indeed on the other side of the world. A possibility for an ever-present observability thereby can be created. And, what is of particular significance in an accounting context, records can even be kept of phenomena that can never be seen. No one has yet perceived a cost, or a profit for that matter. They are abstract and conceptual phenomena, creations of the human intellect, forged and shaped by economic, social and institutional forces. Not directly visible, they nevertheless can be enshrined in the books of record, thereby providing a basis for their observation, monitoring and control.

Enabling such a conceptual visibility to be created, accounting can play a powerful role in organisational and social affairs. It can influence perceptions, change language and infuse dialogue, thereby permeating the ways in which priorities, concerns and worries, and new possibilities for action are expressed.

Focusing on accounting's involvement in shifting patterns of visibility provides a powerful way of appreciating how the craft can become implicated in processes of organisational change. It is possible to probe into what a particular organisation seeks to make visible by its accounting and other information systems. Moreover, by making some things visible and other things not, an organisation can strive to exclude particular visibilities from the official organisational agenda. What, we can ask, is treated in this way, and why? And which groups have the power to influence the patterns of visibility prevailing in the organisation? What bodies of knowledge and sets of organisational practices are involved in making some things visible and other things not? How contested are dominant patterns of visibility? And from where have new visibilities emerged?

The second role of accounting which I wish to consider is its functioning as a calculative practice. Accounting is implicated in the objectification of phenomena, of making appear real and seemingly precise those things that would otherwise reside in the realm of the abstract. Profit is an example, as is cost. Economists can call profit "p", they can differentiate it and incorporate it into models of firm and market behaviour. They can even change the world in the name of it. But they do not have to be concerned with the operationalisation of the concept, with making profit into a fact rather than only an idea. Similarly for cost. For better or for worse, it has been the accountant who has been concerned with making the abstract concept into a concrete instrument of governance in organisations and society at large. The essential subjectivity of the concept of cost has been reduced by the accountant into a fact, something which strives to be a calculative embodiment of the abstract phenomenon, but which often is not.

As with visibility, the power of calculation is potentially great. When something comes into the calculative sphere, it very often enables new organisational interdependences to be created, both with other calculative phenomena and, through the establishment of more precise means-end relationships, with

AAAJ
3,1

objectives and rationales that are articulated for organisational action. Relays of more explicit interrelationships can be established. A precision is added to attempts to infuse organisational affairs with particular concerns and agendas. Couplings between accounting and other aspects of organisational life can more readily be forged. And a priority can start to be given to the seemingly factual and precise, thereby shifting forms of organisational debate and the rationales that must accompany organisational action.

The final role for accounting which I seek to emphasise is the active part it plays in creating a domain of economic action. The abstractions and objectifications in the accounting area are created in the name of the economic. They enable economic knowledges and understandings to be operationalised and thereby more readily to permeate and shape organisational agendas, concerns and choices. Through its investment in a calculative form, accounting is implicated in enhancing the visibility and salience of economic and financial phenomena. It provides a powerful means for confronting the social and the political with the economic. It facilitates the extent to which economic trade-offs can be made. And it thereby enables a precision and a seeming objectivity to be given to economic affairs that otherwise would not exist.

Whilst it would be possible to elaborate further on such roles of accounting, I hope that I have provided a sufficient insight at this stage that will enable me to build on them later. Taken together, they provide a basis for looking at the role of accounting in organisational and social functioning in rather different terms from more conventional appeals to its decision and control functions. The latter ways of perceiving and understanding accounting take for granted the centrality of its role in organisational and social affairs. Rather than trying to probe the factors implicated in the emerging significance of the craft, they unproblematically attribute quite particular functionalities to it, often then trying to provide these with a greater cohesion and organisational and technical rationality. Rather than building on such traditions of accounting enquiry, I am seeking to explore at least some of the ways in which the functions of accounting might have emerged and changed, something which I see as being of some importance if we are to understand the pressures for change which are now impinging on the craft.

Of course thoroughly to analyse accounting in such terms is a task beyond the confines of the present occasion. So I have decided to focus much of my remaining discussion on three themes illustrative of the involvement of accounting in organisational change processes. The first of these relates to some of the current ways in which accounting is being involved in bringing market pressures to bear on internal organisational affairs. Thereafter I discuss a number of the effects of technological change on the accounting craft. And finally some brief consideration is given to the relationship between accounting calculations and economic discourse.

Reweaving the Inside in the Name of the Outside

Accounting has the power to shift patterns of organisational visibility so that the concerns of the external world can permeate and influence internal organisational affairs. Used with care and forethought, accounting thereby can play a role in strategically changing managerial awareness away from the problems of just internal interdependences towards a view of the external positioning of the organisation or a particular segment of the organisation. The language, pressures and requirements of the marketplace can be infused into the organisation as a result of a strategic realignment of organisational structures, internal patterns of organisational segmentation and flows of information, including accounting information.

Such uses of accounting information are an increasingly prevalent feature of modern organisations. Enterprises are being broken down into more units than is necessary for the purposes of internal co-ordination. They are being broken down into units where the language of the market, of competitive pressures and forces and, importantly, of profit can be introduced by calculative, informational and, not least, accounting means into the internal bureaucracy of the organisation, mediating internal decision processes and the exercising of choice. New patterns of managerial accountability are thereby being forged and new performance measurements articulated. Externally driven flows of information are entering internal organisational reports through accounting means. More managers are being subjected to the need to relate to market forces. Profit is being used as a means for broadening management responsibilities in such a way that they assume a more widely conceived business form, rather than one cast in more narrowly defined functional terms.

Information increasingly is being moved across organisations rather than only up and down the bureaucratic hierarchy. Lateral linkages are being established across organisational units. Manufacturing activities are being more directly coupled with marketing spheres of influence. Retailing activities are being related to wholesaling and the eventual manufacturing process. Product oriented flows of information are superseding earlier segmented functional reports. Prices thereby can be more readily related to costs. Costs, in turn, can be related to product designs and changing patterns of component sourcing. And quality standards can be tied in with changes in consumer demand. Through the use of market rather than cost-based internal transfer prices, more competitive pressures can be brought to bear on internal decision making and the assessment of managerial performance. And the use of modes of reporting based on overall product life-cycle performance enables more general business analyses to permeate organisational debates, introducing both a longer temporal perspective and concerns with performance that, in showing the implications of competition and competitive product innovation, are also more market based.

Through such configurations of organisational and accounting changes, enterprises are in the process of being made more market oriented. More than a mere processing of new accounting information is occurring, however. The concerns of the market are more actively permeating the internal functioning of the organisation. Patterns of visibility are shifting. Information, including accounting information, is moderating managerial vocabularies, proactively shaping and changing their conceptions of what is important and what is not. The new information has at least the potential to change managerial awarenesses.

Different organisational linkages can be created and different bases thereby established for organisational action. And that is why many organisations are looking afresh at the power of accounting information.

Both to appreciate and to activate such changes, more than a merely technical view of accounting is required. To understand what is going on, accounting needs to be appreciated in its organisational context. It needs to be seen not merely as something that reflects organisational circumstances but also as a phenomenon that can play a role in changing them. Used strategically, accounting can help to make organisations what they were not.

Technological Perturbations and Organisational Ripples

Turning to my second illustration of accounting change, I wish briefly to consider the area of technology. Here too I want to argue that an appreciative organisationally grounded stance is necessary for understanding what is happening in enterprises today.

The role of new technologies in the office, seen in their widest sense, is of fundamental importance to understanding accounting processes in organisations. Indeed it lies behind not only modern management structures but also the buildings in which they function. Indeed the very skylines of our cities now testify to the powerful presence of clerical, managerial and financial functions in the business sphere. The co-ordinating managerial function is increasingly vast, one that is increasingly isolated from where actual productive and service activities take place, and one where the application and use of modern office technologies have been centrally implicated in the rise of that "management at a distance" (Latour, 1987).

The area of office technology is perhaps one where we need to be cautious about overemphasising the role of new computer-based technologies. They are important. They have resulted and still are resulting in an amazing intensification of organisational changes. But I still think that there is a need to be conscious of how they have speeded up rather than established afresh a number of existing organisational trends. The development of earlier office technologies — the filing cabinet, means for sorting, sifting, codifying and classifying information, the typewriter and the copying machine — had already resulted in the creation of the office as a sphere for managerial work where the physical realities of the organisation could be abstracted into a world of files, reports and flows of information. And these changes had already resulted in massive changes in patterns of organisational influence, power and authority.

Seen in such terms, the technologies of the office provide a basis for a powerful form of organisational cartography — a means for representing on paper (or a screen) in a coherent and abstract manner a vast array of physical circumstances and facts. Like the cartography of old (Latour, 1987), today's realm of organisational files and reports is based on a massive number of technological and organisational innovations, few of which were initially related but all of which now come together to provide a means for encapsulating the processes of the organisation in an abstract form and thereby enabling the complex activities of the organisation to be represented on pieces of paper and computer screens. And also, like the maps of old, the rise of the organisational cartographic function enables a domain of abstract decision making to be divorced from the realities of physical, concrete circumstances. It has made it possible to abstract the physical production process on to paper and thereby to schedule, to plan, and to co-ordinate in the office, with orders and instructions being given back to the physical manufacturing operations. The realm of information is now acted upon as if it was the realm of facts. The files and reports are trusted, or usually so. And, so trusted, they enable the world to be changed at a distance from where action takes place.

Accounting is, of course, centrally implicated in such processes, as is the financial sector in general. Accounting enables an assembling of complex physical processes and their abstraction into the domain of paper through the activities of planning, budgeting, costing and scheduling. More than that, however, it then provides a basis for radically changing and disrupting the physical processes in the name of criteria and concerns which are not directly implicated in the physical processes themselves, such as the economic and the financial. In such ways the power of accounting can be revealed. The abstract characterisations which it provides can provide an influential means for inducing change into organisational affairs.

Accounting, however, is not itself unresponsive to changes in the physical world which it seeks to represent. Recently, for example, attention has been placed on the implications of new manufacturing technologies for the design of accounting systems (Johnson and Kaplan, 1987). Particularly in the United States, it is now becoming almost commonplace to say that the new technologies have undermined the relevance of the accountings of old. We must, according to such views, cast the old aside and search for accountings that are more compatible with the new technological environment in which we now live.

Such arguments are interesting, but, I wish to argue, there is a danger of being too enthusiastic and too simplistic in approach, not least if we look at the organisational processes that are implicated in such technological and accounting changes. All that we know from studies of the impact of technological change in other areas of organisation and social life (e.g. Sorge and Warner, 1986) suggests that there is no simple technological determinism at work. The impact of new technologies is not singular. If such findings hold in the area of accounting, and I see no reason why they should not, there are unlikely to be any unambiguous new accountings in the name of which we can rewrite accounting textbooks. Rather the impact of new technologies on accounting is likely to be mediated and influenced by the organisational and cultural terrains into which the technologies are introduced.

An illuminating illustration of such processes at work has been provided by a comparative study of the impact of new manufacturing technologies in Germany and the United Kingdom. Sorge and Warner (1986) found that the introduction of similar changes in manufacturing technologies in the two countries had different, indeed sometimes even opposite, effects. The technological change did not have a direct effect. Its consequences stemmed from the interaction between the new organisational potential which it introduced and the very different nature of the organisational and social fabric of the two countries.

Such findings emphasise that it is not possible to understand the implications of technological changes without considering the organisational and cultural contexts in which the changes occur. Organisational consequences are not a direct result of technological changes *per se*. Rather those changes are mediated and influenced by the circumstances prevailing in the contexts in which they are introduced. It is as if a new technology represents a perturbation that is capable of creating ripples that diffuse themselves through the organisation but ripples that have consequences that reflect both the perturbation itself and the nature of the organisational terrain into which it is introduced.

Seen in such terms, we are likely, I suggest, to see a range of consequences for accounting stemming from current developments in manufacturing technology, rather than any singular effect. Therefore both to appreciate and to influence such consequences we need not only a new technical accounting understanding but also a more subtle and advanced insight into the organisational dynamics which mediate and shape accounting changes in particular contexts.

Economic Discourse and Accounting Calculations

For my third illustration I want briefly to consider another generator of accounting change. For not only can market forces, forms of organisational segmentation and new technologies influence accounting, but so also can the world of ideas and bodies of knowledge. Accounting can be and is being changed in the name of discursive developments. I particularly want to emphasise the role of economic discourse in this process.

One of the dominant features of the world in which we live is the power of economic thought — a phenomenon which I think future generations will recognise and study but one which is very much taken for granted today. Economic thought is in many senses a strange and restless phenomenon. Although claiming to provide insight into the way the world is, economics is also characterised by a dissatisfaction with the ways of the world. Even though it claims to provide a positive rather than normative knowledge of the world, economics seemingly always wants to make the world more economic than it is. Market forces are not merely present but need to be extended. Economic incentives are not merely a feature of the world but need to be reinforced. The rationality of costing needs to be enhanced in the name of an economic understanding of it. The world needs to be told what profit is even though it apparently is orchestrated in the name of it.

As the latter examples illustrate, such thinking has permeated accounting thought, not least academic accounting thought. And it is this restless, ambiguous feature of economic thought in which I am interested: the relationships between accounting and economists' claims to know not only how the world works but also how to make the world better.

Seen in such terms, economic discourse is not merely a reflective phenomenon, providing insight into the way in which the world is, but is also a constitutive phenomenon, currently playing a major role in making the world more economic than it otherwise might be, forging a reality that is more in line with our economic understandings of it.

Such a role of economic discourse is providing a powerful basis for accounting change, particularly but not exclusively in the public sector. The language of efficiency, value for money, cost effectiveness and the market has entered into political debate. Organisations are being changed in the name of such an economic vocabulary and, as this happens, new calls are being made for the extension of modes of economic calculation to objectify and operationalise the abstract concepts in the name of which change is occurring. Accounting and related bodies of techniques are important means for such operationalisation, playing thereby an often significant role in the construction rather than mere revelation of new domains of economic activity.

For much of the language of economics is rich in ambiguity when used as a basis for political action rather than a more constrained form of intellectual activity, as accountants already know only too well from their experiences with the operationalisation of economic concepts such as profit and cost.

Such ambiguity does not in and of itself constrain the practical use of economic conceptions, however. The world can be changed in the name of profit without a precise operational understanding of the concept. Indeed, the public sector in many countries is being changed in the name of efficiency without there being any precise and generally agreed definition of that concept. It might even be that the very ambiguity of the concept provides one basis for its appeal, particularly in political circles. If we knew precisely what the concept was, it most likely would be far less capable of mobilising political support.

At some stage in the practical use of such concepts, however, the specifics of operationalisation must be addressed, often by accountants. At such times it is useful to remember that the ambiguity, generality and abstractness of the concepts themselves imply that there is no one-to-one relationship between the concepts and the specific forms of operational calculus to which they give rise. One is not a mere reflection of the other. Discretion and choice exist. The technical thereby is partly independent of the abstract and the conceptual. It therefore is capable of generating its own consequences and effects, consequences that might have a complex relationship with the rationales in the name of which the new accountings were introduced.

To the extent that such forces are at work, we must always ask questions of the precise effects of changes, not least in the areas of efficiency, value-for-money and cost effectiveness, rather than presuming a mere realisation of a prior intent.

For efficiency need not be a phenomenon associated with any singular impact. Although appeals to efficiency might seem inherently sensible, the ambiguity of the concept is such that we must always look at what happens in its name, not least when the idea is appealed to in political discourse. We must consider the actual effects that occur rather than merely focusing on the seeming desirability of the intent that lies behind them. Equally in the area of economics more generally conceived, we must, I would argue, be prepared to recognise how a realm of the economic is possibly created rather than merely revealed and the role which accounting and other sources of economic and financial information can play in that process.

Just such processes can be seen at work in health care organisations in many countries in the world. In the United Kingdom, for instance, until recently there were few accountings for health. Hospitals and health management organisations had invested lightly in the accounting craft, in part because health care had not been perceived as primarily an economic phenomenon. Other visibilities had been given a priority in guiding the management function. That is now in the process of changing, however. Not least with the development of a more finely articulated knowledge of health economics (Ashmore, *et al.*, 1989) and with the political mobilisation of that knowledge, it has become possible to conceive of health care as residing in the domain of the economic. As that has occurred, given the restless and proactive nature of so much of economic thought, proposals have been made to intervene in health care organisations in the name of the economic knowledge of them. More and more economic questions have been asked of health, and investments are now starting to be made in the elaboration and intensification of economic calculating systems in the area, including accounting systems. And as this happens, there is at least the possibility that health care organisations might start to be made into organisations of more of an economic form than they otherwise would have been.

Conclusion

Albeit briefly, I nevertheless hope to have illustrated the role which appreciations of the organisational nature of accounting can play in understanding important aspects of the modern organisational world and the ways in which those relate to accounting. They can illuminate the dynamic and changing nature of accounting practices. Accounting can be seen as being actively drawn upon in the construction of new organisational forms and boundaries. Focusing on the forces that can impinge on accounting and the ways in which they can permeate accounting thought and practice, such organisational understandings have a potential to inform our views of both how accounting became what it was not and how it might become what it currently is not. For in a complex and interdependent world, accounting change is rarely easy to introduce. Although accounting can provide one of the conduits through which economic discourse enters into the world of practice, it almost invariably functions in unanticipated ways. Partial though our new organisational understandings may be, they nevertheless can provide a way of starting to come to a more adequate understanding of the ways in which accounting is embedded in processes of organisational change. Although they cannot give a new predictability and precision to the accounting craft, I nevertheless think that our understandings are now sufficient to provide a richer and more informed basis for guiding accounting in action.

References

Ashmore, M., Mulkay, M.J. and Pinch, T.J. (1989), *Health and Efficiency: A Sociology of Health Economics*, The Open University Press, Milton Keynes.

Bentham, J. (1791), *Panopticon; or The Inspection-House, Containing the Idea of a New Principle of Construction Applicable to Any Sort of Establishment, in which Persons of any Description are to be Kept Under Inspection, and in Particular to Penitentiary-Houses, Prisons, Poor-Houses, Lazarettos, Houses of Industry, Manufactories, Hospitals, Workhouses, Mad-Houses and Schools: with a Plan of Management Adapted to the Principle: 'N a Series of Letters, Written in the Year 1787, from Crecheff in White Russia to a Friend in England*, London. Reprinted in Browning, J. (Ed.), *The Works of Jeremy Bentham*, Part III (1838), William Tate, Edinburgh.

Foucault, M. (1977), *Discipline and Punish: The Birth of the Prison*, Allen Lane, London.

Johnson, H.T. and Kaplan, R.S. (1987), *Relevance Lost: The Rise and Fall of Management Accounting*, Harvard Business School Press, Boston, Mass.

Latour, B. (1987), *Science in Action: How to Follow Scientists and Engineers through Society*, Harvard University Press.

Sorge, A. and Warner, M. (1986), *Comparative Factory Organisation: An Anglo-German Comparison of Manufacturing, Management and Manpower*, Gower, Aldershot.

[25]

THE ANALYSIS OF GOALS IN COMPLEX ORGANIZATIONS *

CHARLES PERROW
The University of Michigan

An understanding of organizational behavior requires close examination of the goals of the organization reflected in operating policies. To reach a first approximation of operative goals, a scheme is proposed which links technology and growth stages to major task areas—capital, legitimization, skills, and coordination—which predict to power structure and thence to limits and range of operative goals. The major illustration of the utility of the scheme is provided by voluntary general hospitals; other voluntary and non-voluntary service organizations are discussed, in these terms, as well as profit-making organizations.

SOCIAL scientists have produced a rich body of knowledge about many aspects of large-scale organizations, yet there are comparatively few studies of the goals of these organizations. For a full understanding of organizations and the behavior of their personnel, analysis of organizational goals would seem to be critical. Two things have impeded such analysis. Studies of morale, turnover, informal organization, communication, supervisory practices, etc., have been guided by an over-rationalistic point of view wherein goals are taken for granted, and the most effective ordering of resources and personnel is seen as the only problematical issue. Fostering this view is the lack of an adequate distinction between types of goals. Without such clarification it is difficult to determine what the goals are and what would be acceptable evidence for the existence of a particular goal and for a change in goals.

It will be argued here, first, that the type of goals most relevant to understanding organizational behavior are not the official goals, but those that are embedded in major operating policies and the daily decisions of the personnel. Second, these goals will be shaped by the particular problems or tasks an organization must emphasize, since these tasks determine the characteristics of those who will dominate the organization. In illustrating the latter argument, we will not be concerned with the specific goals of organizations, but only with the range within which goals are likely to vary. Though general hospitals will be used as the main illustration, three types of organizations will be discussed: voluntary service organizations, non-voluntary service organizations and profit-making organizations.

THE OVER-RATIONALISTIC VIEW

Most studies of the internal operation of complex organizations, if they mention goals at all, have taken official statements of goals at face value. This may be justified if only a limited problem is being investigated, but even then it contributes to the view that goals are not problematical. In this view, goals have no effect upon activities other than in the grossest terms; or it can be taken for granted that the only problem is to adjust means to given and stable ends. This reflects a distinctive "model" of organizational behavior, which Gouldner has characterized as the rational model.[1] Its proponents see the managerial elite as using rational and logical means to pursue clear and discrete ends set forth in official statements of goals, while the worker is seen as governed by nonrationalistic, traditionalistic orientations. If goals are unambiguous and achievement evaluated by cost-accounting procedures, the only turmoil of organizational life lies below the surface with workers or, at best, with middle management maneuvering for status and power. Actually, however, nonrational orientations exist at all

* Some of this material was presented in a paper titled, "A Reassessment of Authority and Goals in Voluntary General Hospitals," at the Fifty-fifth Annual Meeting of the American Sociological Association (1960). I should like to thank the following for their perceptive criticisms: Morris Janowitz, Eliot Freidson, and Hanan Selvin.

[1] Alvin Gouldner, "Organizational Analysis," in Robert Merton, Leonard Broom and Leonard S. Cottrell, Jr., editors, *Sociology Today*, New York: Basic Books, 1959, p. 407.

levels, including the elite who are responsible for setting goals[2] and assessing the degree to which they are achieved.

One reason for treating goals as static fixtures of organizational life is that goals have not been given adequate conceptualization, though the elements of this are in easy reach. If making a profit or serving customers is to be taken as a sufficient statement of goals, then all means to this end might appear to be based on rational decisions because the analyst is not alerted to the countless policy decisions involved. If goals are given a more elaborate conceptualization, we are forced to see many more things as problematic.

OFFICIAL AND OPERATIVE GOALS

Two major categories of goals will be discussed here, official and "operative" goals.[3] Official goals are the general purposes of the organization as put forth in the charter, annual reports, public statements by key executives and other authoritative pronouncements. For example, the goal of an employment agency may be to place job seekers in contact with firms seeking workers. The official goal of a hospital may be to promote the health of the community through curing the ill, and sometimes through preventing illness, teaching, and conducting research. Similar organizations may emphasize different publically acceptable goals. A business corporation, for example, may state that its goal is to make a profit or adequate return on investment, or provide a customer service, or produce goods.

This level of analysis is inadequate in itself for a full understanding of organizational behavior. Official goals are purposely vague and general and do not indicate two major factors which influence organizational behavior: the host of decisions that must be made among alternative ways of achieving official goals and the priority of multiple goals, and the many unofficial goals pursued by groups within the organization. The concept of "operative goals"[4] will be used to cover these aspects. Operative goals designate the ends sought through the actual operating policies of the organization; they tell us what the organization actually is trying to do, regardless of what the official goals say are the aims.

Where operative goals provide the specific content of official goals they reflect choices among competing values. They may be justified on the basis of an official goal, even though they may subvert another official goal. In one sense they are means to official goals, but since the latter are vague or of high abstraction, the "means" become ends in themselves when the organization is the object of analysis. For example, where profit-making is the announced goal, operative goals will specify whether quality or quantity is to be emphasized, whether profits are to be short run and risky or long run and stable, and will indicate the relative priority of diverse and somewhat conflicting ends of customer service, employee morale, competitive pricing, diversification, or liquidity. Decisions on all these factors influence the nature of the organization, and distinguish

---

[2] A strong argument for considering changes in goals in made by James D. Thompson and William J. McEwen, "Organizational Goals and Environment: Goal-Setting as an Interaction Process," *American Sociological Review*, 23 (February, 1958), pp. 23–31.

[3] A third may be distinguished: social system goals, which refers to those contributions an organization makes to the functioning of a social system in which it is nested. In Parson's terminology, organizations may serve adaptive, gratificatory, integrative, or pattern-maintenance functions. See Talcott Parsons, "Sociological Approach to the Theory of Organizations," *Administrative Science Quarterly*, 1 (June–September, 1956), pp. 63–86, 225–240. This alone, however, will tell us little about individual organizations, although Scott, in a suggestive article applying this scheme to prisons and mental hospitals, implies that organizations serving integrative functions for society will place particular importance upon integrative functions within the organization. See Frances G. Scott, "Action Theory and Research in Social Organization," *American Journal of Sociology*, 64 (January, 1959), pp. 386–395. Parsons asserts that each of the four functions mentioned above also must be performed within organizations if they are to survive. It is possible to see a parallel between these four functions and the four tasks discussed below, but his are, it is felt, too general and ambiguous to provide tools for analysis.

[4] The concept of "operational goals" or "subgoals" put forth by March and Simon bears a resemblance to this but does not include certain complexities which we will discuss, nor is it defined systematically. See J. G. March and H. A. Simon, *Organizations*, New York: Wiley, 1958, pp. 156–157.

it from another with an identical official goal. An employment agency must decide whom to serve, what characteristics they favor among clients, and whether a high turnover of clients or a long run relationship is desired. In the voluntary general hospital, where the official goals are patient care, teaching, and research, the relative priority of these must be decided, as well as which group in the community is to be given priority in service, and are these services to emphasize, say, technical excellence or warmth and "hand-holding."

Unofficial operative goals, on the other hand, are tied more directly to group interests and while they may support, be irrelevant to, or subvert official goals, they bear no necessary connection with them. An interest in a major supplier may dictate the policies of a corporation executive. The prestige that attaches to utilizing elaborate high speed computers may dictate the reorganization of inventory and accounting departments. Racial prejudice may influence the selection procedures of an employment agency. The personal ambition of a hospital administrator may lead to community alliances and activities which bind the organization without enhancing its goal achievement. On the other hand, while the use of interns and residents as "cheap labor" may subvert the official goal of medical education, it may substantially further the official goal of providing a high quality of patient care.

The discernment of operative goals is, of course, difficult and subject to error. The researcher may have to determine from analysis of a series of apparently minor decisions regarding the lack of competitive bidding and quality control that an unofficial goal of a group of key executives is to maximize their individual investments in a major supplier. This unofficial goal may affect profits, quality, market position, and morale of key skill groups. The executive of a correctional institution may argue that the goal of the organization is treatment, and only the lack of resources creates an apparent emphasis upon custody or deprivation. The researcher may find, however, that decisions in many areas establish the priority of custody or punishment as a goal. For example, few efforts may be made to obtain more treatment personnel; those hired are misused and mistrusted; and clients are viewed as responding only to deprivations. The president of a junior college may deny the function of the institution is to deal with the latent terminal student, but careful analysis such as Clark has made of operating policies, personnel practices, recruitment procedures, organizational alliances and personal characteristics of elites will demonstrate this to be the operative goal.[5]

THE TASK—AUTHORITY—GOAL SEQUENCE

While operative goals will only be established through intensive analysis of decisions, personnel practices, alliance and elite characteristics in each organization, it is possible to indicate the range within which they will vary and the occasion for general shifts in goals. We will argue that if we know something about the major tasks of an organization and the characteristics of its controlling elite, we can predict its goals in general terms. The theory presented and illustrated in the rest of this paper is a first approximation and very general, but it may guide and stimulate research on this problem.

Every organization must accomplish four tasks: (1) secure inputs in the form of capital sufficient to establish itself, operate, and expand as the need arises; (2) secure acceptance in the form of basic legitimization of activity; (3) marshal the necessary skills; and (4) coordinate the activities of its members, and the relations of the organization with other organizations and with clients or consumers. All four are not likely to be equally important at any point in time. Each of these task areas provides a presumptive basis for control or domination by the group equipped to meet the problems involved. (The use of the terms control or dominance signifies a more pervasive, thorough and all-embracing phenomenon than authority or power.) The operative goals will be shaped by the dominant group, reflecting the imperatives of the particular task area that is most critical, their own background characteristics (distinctive perspectives based upon their training, career lines, and areas of competence) and the unofficial uses to which

[5] Burton Clark, *The Open Door College*, New York: McGraw-Hill, 1960.

they put the organization for their own ends.

The relative emphasis upon one or another of the four tasks will vary with the nature of the work the organization does and the technology appropriate to it,[6] and with the stage of development within the organization.[7] An organization engaged in manufacturing in an industry where skills are routinized and the market position secure, may emphasize coordination, giving control to the experienced administrator. An extractive industry, with a low skill level in its basic tasks and a simple product, will probably emphasize the importance of capital tied up in land, specialized and expensive machinery, and transportation facilities. The chairman of the board of directors or a group within the board will probably dominate such an organization. An organization engaged in research and development, or the production of goods or services which cannot be carried out in a routinized fashion, will probably be most concerned with skills. Thus engineers or other relevant professionals will dominate. It is also possible that all three groups—trustees, representatives of critical skills, and administrators—may share power equally. This "multiple leadership" will be discussed in detail later. Of course, trustees are likely to dominate in the early history of any organization, particularly those requiring elaborate capital and facilities, or unusual legitimization. But once these requisites are secured, the nature of the tasks will determine whether trustees or others dominate. The transfer of authority, especially from trustees to another group, may be protracted, constituting a lag in adaptation.

Where major task areas do not change over time, the utility of the scheme presented here is limited to suggesting possible relations between task areas, authority structure, and operative goals. The more interesting problems, which we deal with in our illustrations below, involve organizations which experience changes in major task areas over time. If the technology or type of work changes, or if new requirements for capital or legitimization arise, control will shift from one group to another. One sequence is believed to be typical.

VOLUNTARY GENERAL HOSPITALS

We will discuss four types of hospitals, those dominated by trustees, by the medical staff (an organized group of those doctors who bring in private patients plus the few doctors who receive salaries or commissions from the hospital), by the administration, and by some form of multiple leadership. There has been a general development among hospitals from trustee domination, based on capital and legitimization, to domination by the medical staff, based upon the increasing importance of their technical skills, and, at present, a tendency towards administrative dominance based on internal and external coordination. (The administrator may or may not be a doctor himself.) Not all hospitals go through these stages, or go through them in this sequence. Each type of authority structure shapes, or sets limits to, the type of operative goals that are likely to prevail, though there will be much variation within each type.[8]

Trustee Domination. Voluntary general hospitals depend upon community funds for an important part of their capital and operating budget. Lacking precise indicators of efficiency or goal achievement, yet using donated funds, they must involve community representatives—trustees—in their authority structure. Trustees legitimate the non-profit status of the organization, assure that funds are not misused, and see that community

[6] For an illuminating discussion of organizations which emphasizes technological differences, see James D. Thompson and Frederick L. Bates, "Technology, Organizations, and Administration," *Administrative Science Quarterly,* 2 (December, 1957), pp. 325–343.

[7] Many other factors are also important, such as the legal framework, official and unofficial regulatory bodies, state of the industry, etc. These will not be considered here. In general, their influences are felt through the task areas, and thus are reflected here.

[8] The following discussion is based upon the author's study of one hospital which, in fact, passed through these stages; upon examination of published and unpublished studies of hospitals; and upon numerous conversations with administrators, doctors, and trustees in the United States. Sophisticated practitioners in the hospital field recognize and describe these types in their own fashion. See Charles Perrow, "Authority, Goals and Prestige in a General Hospital," unpublished Ph.D. dissertation, University of California, Berkeley, 1960, for fuller documentation and discussion.

needs are being met. Officially, they are the ultimate authority in voluntary hospitals. They do not necessarily exercise the legal powers they have, but where they do, there is no question that they are in control.

The functional basis for this control is primarily financial. They have access to those who make donations, are expected to contribute heavily themselves, and control the machinery and sanctions for fund raising drives. Financial control allows them to withhold resources from recalcitrant groups in the organization, medical or non-medical. They also, of course, control all appointments and promotions, medical and non-medical.

Where these extensive powers are exercised, operative goals are likely to reflect the role of trustees as community representatives and contributors to community health. Because of their responsibility to the sponsoring community, trustees may favor conservative financial policies, opposing large financial outlays for equipment, research, and education so necessary for high medical standards.[9] High standards also require more delegation of authority to the medical staff than trustee domination can easily allow.[10] As representatives drawn from distinctive social groups in the community, they may be oriented towards service for a religious, ethnic, economic, or age group in the community. Such an orientation may conflict with selection procedures favored by the medical staff or administration. Trustees may also promote policies which demonstrate a contribution to community welfare on the part of an elite group, perhaps seeking to maintain a position of prominence and power within the community. The hospital may be used as a vehicle for furthering a social philosophy of philanthropy and good works; social class values regarding personal worth, economic independence and responsibility; the assimilation of a minority group; [11] or even to further resistance to government control and socialized medicine.

Such orientations will shape operative goals in many respects, affecting standards and techniques of care, priority of services, access to care, relations with other organizations, and directions and rate of development. The administrator in such a hospital—usually called a "superintendent" under the circumstances—will have little power, prestige or responsibility. For example, trustees have been known to question the brand of grape juice the dietician orders, or insist that they approve the color of paint the administrator selects for a room.[12] Physicians may disapprove of patient selection criteria, chafe under financial restrictions which limit the resources they have to work with, and resent active control over appointments and promotions in the medical staff.

Medical Domination. Trustee domination was probably most common in the late nineteenth and early twentieth century. Medical technology made extraordinary advances in the twentieth century, and doctors possessed the skills capable of utilizing the advances. They demanded new resources and were potentially in a position to control their allocation and use. Increasingly, major decisions had to be based upon a technical competence trustees did not possess. Trustees had a continuing basis for control because of the costs of new equipment and personnel, but in many hospitals the skill factor became decisive. Some trustees felt that the technology required increased control by doctors; others lost a struggle for power with the medical staff; in some cases trustees were forced to bring in and give power to an outstanding doctor in order to increase the reputation of the hospital.[13] Under such conditions trustees are likely to find that their legal power becomes nominal and they can only intervene in crisis situations; even financial requirements come to be set by conditions outside

[9] Exceptions to conservative financial policies appear to occur most frequently in crisis situations where accreditation is threatened or sound business principles are violated by run down facilities, or inefficient management. See Temple Burling, Edith M. Lentz, and Robert N. Wilson, *The Give and Take in Hospitals*, New York: G. P. Putnam, 1956, Chapters 4, 5, 6.

[10] Burling *et al.*, (*ibid.*, p. 43), note that active trustees find delegation difficult.

[11] Perrow, *op. cit.*, chapter 5.

[12] Edith Lentz, "Changing Concepts of Hospital Administration," *Industrial and Labor Relations Research*, 3 (Summer, 1957), p. 2. Perrow, *op. cit.*, p. 86.

[13] Berthram Bernhein, *The Story of Johns Hopkins*, New York: McGraw-Hill, 1948, pp. 142–148.

their control.[14] They continue to provide the mantle of community representation and non-profit status, and become "staff" members whose major task is to secure funds.

It is sometimes hard to see why all hospitals are not controlled by the medical staff, in view of the increasing complexity and specialization of the doctor's skills, their common professional background, the power of organized medicine, and the prestige accorded the doctor in society. Furthermore, they are organized for dominance, despite their nominal status as "guests" in the house.[15] The medical staff constitutes a "shadow" organization in hospitals, providing a ready potential for control. It is organized on bureaucratic principles with admission requirements, rewards and sanctions, and a committee structure which often duplicates the key committees of the board of directors and administrative staff. Nor are doctors in an advisory position as are "staff" groups in other organizations. Doctors perform both staff and line functions, and their presumptive right to control rests on both. Doctors also have a basic economic interest in the hospital, since it is essential to most private medical practice and career advancement. They seek extensive facilities, low hospital charges, a high quality of coordinated services, and elaborate time and energy-conserving conveniences.

Thus there is sufficient means for control by doctors, elaborated far beyond the mere provision of essential skills, and sufficient interest in control. Where doctors fully exercise their potential power the administrator functions as a superintendent or, as his co-professionals are wont to put it, as a "housekeeper." The importance of administrative skills is likely to be minimized, the administrative viewpoint on operative goals neglected, and the quality of personnel may suffer. A former nurse often serves as superintendent in this type of hospital. Policy matters are defined as medical in nature by the doctors,[16] and neither trustees nor administrators, by definition, are qualified to have an equal voice in policy formation.

The operative goals of such a hospital are likely to be defined in strictly medical terms and the organization may achieve high technical standards of care, promote exemplary research, and provide sound training. However, there is a danger that resources will be used primarily for private (paying) patients with little attention to other community needs such as caring for the medically indigent (unless they happen to be good teaching cases), developing preventive medicine, or pioneering new organizational forms of care. Furthermore, high technical standards increasingly require efficient coordination of services and doctors may be unwilling to delegate authority to qualified administrators.

Various unofficial goals may be achieved at the expense of medical ones, or, in some cases, in conjunction with them. There are many cases of personal aggrandizement on the part of departmental chiefs and the chief of staff. The informal referral and consultation system in conjunction with promotions, bed quotas, and "privileges" to operate or treat certain types of cases, affords many occasions for the misuse of power. Interns and residents are particularly vulnerable to exploitation at the expense of teaching goals. Furthermore, as a professional, the doctor has undergone intensive socialization in his training and is called upon to exercise extraordinary judgment and skill with drastic consequences for good or ill. Thus he demands unusual deference and obedience and is invested with "charismatic" authority.[17] He may extend this authority to the entrepreneurial aspects of his role, with the result that his "service" orientation, so taken for granted in much of the literature, sometimes means service to the doctor at the expense of personnel, other patients, or even his own patient.[18]

---

[14] For a detailed analysis of such a shift of power, see Perrow, *op. cit.*, pp. 43–50.

[15] There is a small group of doctors on the medical staff, who may or may not bring in private patients, who receive money from the hospital, either through salary or commissions—pathologists, anesthetists, roentgenologists, paid directors of the outpatient department, etc. These are members of the organization in a direct sense.

[16] Oswald Hall, "Some Problems in the Provision of Medical Services," *Canadian Journal of Economics*, 20 (November, 1954), p. 461.

[17] Albert F. Wessen, "The Social Structure of a Modern Hospital," unpublished Ph.D. dissertation, Yale University, 1951, p. 43.

[18] Wessen notes that the doctor "sees ministering

Administrative Dominance. Administrative dominance is based first on the need for coordinating the increasingly complex, non-routinizable functions hospitals have undertaken. There is an increasing number of personnel that the doctor can no longer direct. The mounting concern of trustees, doctors themselves, patients and pre-payment groups with more efficient and economical operation also gives the administrator more power. A second, related basis for control stems from the fact that health services in general have become increasingly interdependent and specialized. The hospital must cooperate more with other hospitals and community agencies. It must also take on more services itself, and in doing so its contacts with other agencies and professional groups outside the hospital multiply. The administrator is equipped to handle these matters because of his specialized training, often received in a professional school of hospital administration, accumulated experience and available time. These services impinge upon the doctor at many points, providing a further basis for administrative control over doctors, and they lead to commitments in which trustees find they have to acquiesce.

The administrator is also in a position to control matters which affect the doctor's demands for status, deference, and time-saving conveniences. By maintaining close supervision over employees or promoting their own independent basis for competence, and by supporting them in conflicts with doctors, the administrator can, to some degree, overcome the high functional authority that doctors command. In addition, by carefully controlling communication between trustees and key medical staff officials, he can prevent an alliance of these two groups against him.

If administrative dominance is based primarily on the complexity of basic hospital activities, rather than the organization's medical-social role in the community, the operative orientation may be toward financial solvency, careful budget controls, efficiency, and minimal development of services. For example, preventive medicine, research, and training may be minimized; a cautious approach may prevail towards new forms of care such as intensive therapy units or home care programs. Such orientations could be especially true of hospitals dominated by administrators whose background and training were as bookkeepers, comptrollers, business managers, purchasing agents, and the like. This is probably the most common form of administrative dominance.

However, increasing professionalization of hospital administrators has, on the one hand, equipped them to handle narrower administrative matters easily, and, on the other hand, alerted them to the broader medical-social role of hospitals involving organizational and financial innovations in the forms of care. Even medical standards can come under administrative control. For example, the informal system among doctors of sponsorship, referral, and consultation serves to protect informal work norms, shield members from criticism and exclude non-cooperative members. The administrator is in a position to insist that medical policing be performed by a salaried doctor who stands outside the informal system.

There is, of course, a possibility of less "progressive" consequences. Interference with medical practices in the name of either high standards or treating the "whole" person may be misguided or have latent consequences which impair therapy. Publicity-seeking innovations may be at the expense of more humdrum but crucial services such as the out-patient department, or may alienate doctors or other personnel, or may deflect administrative efforts from essential but unglamorous administrative tasks.[19] Using the organization for career advancement, they may seek to expand and publicize their hospital regardless of community needs and ability to pay. Like trustees they may favor a distinctive and medically irrelevant community relations policy, perhaps with a view towards moving upward in the community power structure. Regardless of these dangers, the number of administration dominated hospitals oriented towards broad medical-social goals will probably grow.

Multiple Leadership. So far we have been considering situations where one group

---

to the needs of doctors as a major function of the hospitals." (*Ibid.*, p. 328.)

[19] Charles Perrow, "Organizational Prestige: Some Functions and Dysfunctions," *American Journal of Sociology*, 66 (January, 1961), pp. 335–341.

clearly dominates. It is possible, however, for power to be shared by two or three groups to the extent that no one is able to control all or most of the actions of the others. This we call multiple leadership: a division of labor regarding the determination of goals and the power to achieve them.[20] This is not the same as fractionated power where several groups have small amounts of power in an unstable situation. With multiple leadership, there are two or three stable, known centers of power. Nor is it the same as decentralized power, where specialized units of the organization have considerable autonomy. In the latter case, units are free to operate as they choose only up to a point, when it becomes quite clear that there is a centralized authority. In multiple leadership there is no single ultimate power.

Multiple leadership is most likely to appear in organizations where there are multiple goals which lack precise criteria of achievement and admit of considerable tolerance with regard to achievement. Multiple goals focus interests, and achievement tolerance provides the necessary leeway for accommodation of interests and vitiation of responsibility. Many service organizations fit these criteria, but so might large, public relations-conscious business or industrial organizations where a variety of goals can be elevated to such importance that power must be shared by the representatives of each.

In one hospital where this was studied [21] it was found that multiple leadership insured that crucial group interests could be met and protected, and encouraged a high level of creative (though selective) involvement by trustees, doctors, and the administration. However, the problems of goal setting, assessment of achievement, and assignment of responsibility seemed abnormally high. While the three groups pursued separate and unconflicting operative goals in some cases, and were in agreement on still other goals, in areas where interests conflicted the goal conflicts were submerged in the interests of harmony. In the absence of a single authority, repetitive conflicts threatened to erode morale and waste energies. A showdown and clear solution of a conflict, furthermore, might signal defeat for one party, forcing them to abandon their interests. Thus a premium was placed on the ability of some elites to smooth over conflicts and exercise interpersonal skills. Intentions were sometimes masked and ends achieved through covert manipulation. Assessment of achievement in some areas was prevented either by the submergence of conflict or the preoccupation with segmental interests. Opportunism was encouraged: events in the environment or within the hospital were exploited without attention to the interests of the other groups or the long range development of the hospital. This left the organization open to vagrant pressures and to the operation of unintended consequences. Indeed, with conflict submerged and groups pursuing independent goals, long range planning was difficult.

This summary statement exaggerates the impact of multiple leadership in this hospital and neglects the areas of convergence on goals. Actually, the hospital prospered and led its region in progressive innovations and responsible medical-social policies despite some subversion of the official goals of patient care, teaching, research, and preventive medicine. The organization could tolerate considerable ambiguity of goals and achievements as long as standards remained high in most areas, occupancy was sufficient to operate with a minimum deficit, and a favorable public image was maintained. It remains to be seen if the costs and consequences are similar for other organizations where multiple leadership exists.

APPLICATION TO OTHER ORGANIZATIONS [22]

Voluntary Service Organizations. Other voluntary service organizations, such as

[20] As in small group analysis, there is an increasing though belated tendency to recognize the possibility that there may be more than one leader in an organization. For a recent discussion of the problem in connection with army groups, see Hanan Selvin, *The Effects of Leadership*, Glencoe, Ill.: The Free Press, 1960, Chapters 1, 7. Amatai Etizioni goes even further in discussing "professional organizations." For a provocative discussion of goals and authority structure, see his "Authority Structure and Organizational Effectiveness," *Administrative Science Quarterly*, 4 (June, 1959), pp. 43–67.

[21] Perrow, Authority, Goals and Prestige . . . , *op. cit.*, chapters 4, 10.

[22] The dogmatic tone of this concluding section is, unfortunately, the consequence of an attempt to be brief.

private universities, social service agencies, privately sponsored correctional institutions for juveniles, and fund raising agencies resemble hospitals in many respects. They have trustees representing the community, may have professionals playing prominent roles, and with increasing size and complexity of operation, require skilled coordination of activities. Initially at least, trustees are likely to provide a character defining function which emphasizes community goals and goals filtered through their own social position. Examples are religious schools, or those emphasizing one field of knowledge or training; agencies caring for specialized groups such as ethnic or religious minorities, unwed mothers, and dependent and neglected children; and groups raising money for special causes. Funds of skill and knowledge accumulate around these activities, and the activities increasingly grow in complexity, requiring still more skill on the part of those performing the tasks. As the professional staff expands and professional identification grows, they may challenge the narrower orientations of trustees on the basis of their own special competence and professional ideology and seek to broaden the scope of services and the clientele. They may be supported in this by changing values in the community. Coordination of activities usually rests with professionals promoted from the staff during this second character defining phase, and these administrators retain, for a while at least, their professional identity. Trustees gradually lose the competence to interfere.

However, professionals have interests of their own which shape the organization. They may develop an identity and ethic which cuts them off from the needs of the community and favors specialized, narrow and—to critics—self-serving goals. Current criticisms of the emphasis upon research and over-specialization in graduate training at the expense of the basic task of educating undergraduates is a case in point in the universities.[23] There is also criticism of the tendency of professionals in correctional institutions to focus upon case work techniques applicable to middle-class "neurotic" delinquents at the expense of techniques for resocializing the so-called "socialized" delinquent from culturally deprived areas.[24] The latter account for most of the delinquents, but professional identity and techniques favor methods applicable to the former. Something similar may be found in social agencies. Social workers, especially the "elite" doing therapy in psychiatric and child guidance clinics and private family agencies, may become preoccupied with securing recognition, equitable financial remuneration, and status that would approach that of psychiatrists. Their attitudes may become more conservative; the social order more readily accepted and the deviant adapted to it; "worthy" clients and "interesting cases" receive priority.

It is possible that with increasing complexity and growth in many of these voluntary service organizations, administrators will lose their professional identity or be recruited from outside the organization on the basis of organizational skills. In either case they will be in a position to alter the direction fostered by selective professional interests. Of course, the problem of coordinating both internal and external activities need not generate leadership seeking broadly social rather than narrowly professional goals, any more than it necessarily does in the hospital. Administrative dominance may stunt professional services and neglect social policy in the interest of economy, efficiency, or conservative policies.

Non-Voluntary Service Organizations. A different picture is presented by non-voluntary service organizations—those sponsored by governmental agencies such as county or military hospitals, city or county welfare agencies, juvenile and adult correctional

[23] Earl J. McGrath, *The Graduate School and the Doctrine of Liberal Education*, New York: Bureau of Publication, Teachers College, Columbia University, 1960.

[24] Robert Vinter and Morris Janowitz, "Effective Institutions for Juvenile Delinquents: A Research Statement," *Social Service Review*, 33 (June, 1957), pp. 118–122; Donald Cressey, "Changing Criminals: The Application of the Theory of Differential Association," *American Journal of Sociology*, 56 (September, 1955), p. 116; Lloyd Ohlin and W. C. Lawrence, "Social Interaction Among Clients as a Treatment Problem," *Social Work*, 4 (April, 1959), pp. 3–14.

agencies.[25] Authority for goal setting, regulation, and provision of capital and operating expenses does not rest with voluntary trustees, but with governmental officials appointed to commissions. In contrast to volunteers on the board of a private service organization, commissioners are not likely to be highly identified with the organization, nor do they derive much social status from it. The organizations themselves often are tolerated only as holding operations or as "necessary evils." Commission dominance is sporadic and brief, associated with public clamor or political expediency. On the other hand, the large size of these organizations and the complex procedures for reporting to the parent body gives considerable importance to the administrative function from the outset, which is enhanced by the tenuous relationship with the commissioners. Consistent with this and reinforcing it is the low level of professionalization found in many of these agencies. The key skills are often non-professional custodial skills or their equivalent in the case of public welfare agencies (and schools). Administrators are often at the mercy of the custodial staff if, indeed, they have not themselves risen to their administrative position because of their ability to maintain order and custody.

Nevertheless, professional influence is mounting in these organizations, and professional groups outside of them have exercised considerable influence.[26] Professionals may assume control of the organization, or administrators may be brought in whose commitment is to the positive purposes of the organization, such as rehabilitation of the clients, rather than the negative custodial functions. This appears to have happened in the case of a few federal penal institutions, a few state juvenile correctional institutions, and several Veterans Administration mental hospitals. Even where this happens, one must be alert to the influence of unofficial goals. The organizations are particularly vulnerable to exploitation by the political career interests of administrators or to irresponsible fads or cure-alls of marginal professionals. In summary, the sequence of tasks, power structure, and goals may be different in non-voluntary service organizations. The importance of administrative skills with system maintenance as the overriding operative goal does not encourage a shift in power structure; but where new technologies are introduced we are alerted to such shifts along with changes in goals.

Profit-Making Organizations. Our analysis may appear less applicable to profit-making organizations for two reasons. First, it could be argued, they are not characterized by multiple goals, but relate all operations to profit-making. Second, skill groups are not likely to dominate these organizations; owners control the smaller firms, and professional executives the larger ones. Thus power structure and possibly goals may merely be a function of size. We will discuss each of these points in turn.

If profit-making is an overriding goal of an organization, many operative decisions must still be made which will shape its character. Even where technology remains constant, organizations will vary with regard to personnel practices, customer services, growth, liquidity, an emphasis upon quality or quantity, or long or short run gains. An adequate understanding of the organization will require attention to alternatives in these and other areas.

Furthermore, it has often been asserted that the importance of profits, *per se*, has declined with the increased power of professional management, especially in large organizations. The argument runs that since management does not have a personal stake in profits, they consider them less important than stability, growth, solvency, and liquidity.[27] The impressionistic evidence of those

[25] Public schools are excluded here because of the elective status of school boards; however, with some revisions, the following analysis would be applicable.

[26] Thompson and McEwen note that the "importance of new objectives may be more readily seen by specialized segments (professionals) than by the general society" and argue that public clamor for change has not been the initiating force. *Op. cit.*, p. 29.

[27] Robert A. Gordon was perhaps the first to deal at length with this proposition, and many have subsequently argued along the same lines. See Robert A. Gordon, *Business Leadership in the Large Corporation*, Washington, D.C.: Brookings Institution, 1945, pp. 308–312, 322, 327–329, 336, 340. For similar assertions see C. E. Griffin, *Enterprise in a Free Society*, Chicago: Irwin, 1949, pp. 96–104; H. Maurer, *Great Enterprise*, New York:

who assert this is not supported by a study of James Dent.[28] When asked, "What are the aims of top management in your company?", the response of executives of 145 business firms showed no greater mention of "to make profits, money or a living" among large than small firms, nor among those with professional managers than owner-managers. Because goals stated in this form may not reflect actual policies and because of other limitations, one is somewhat reluctant to take this as a fair test of the hypothesis.

Even though his sample was not representative, and the question asked does not get at what we have called operative goals, his study provides good evidence of variations of stated goals in profit-making organizations. Responses coded under the category "to make money, profits, or a living" were mentioned as the first aim by 36 per cent of the executives; "to provide a good product; public service" by 21 per cent, and "to grow" was third with 12 per cent. When the first three aims spontaneously mentioned were added together, profits led; employee welfare tied with "good products or public service" for second place. Dent found that the variables most associated with goals were size of company and "proportion of employees who are white-collar, professional or supervisory." [29] While goals no doubt are influenced by size, this accounted for only some of the variance. Holding size constant, one might discover the effects of major task areas. The association of goals with the "proportion of employees who are white-collar . . ." supports this argument.

R. A. Gordon and others have asserted that in large corporations it is the executive group, rather than stockholders or the board of trustees, that generally dominates.[30] A study of the role of trustees, frankly in favor of their exercising leadership and control, actually shows through its many case studies that trustees exercise leadership mainly in times of crisis.[31] The generalization of Gordon, almost a commonplace today, appears to be sound: he asserts that the common pattern of evolution is for active leadership by owners in the early years of the firm, then it is passed on to new generations of the families concerned, and gradually responsibility for decision-making passes to professional executives who frequently have been trained by the original leaders.[32] Goals likewise shift from rapid development and a concern with profits to more conservative policies emphasizing coordination, stability and security of employment.[33]

But does this mean that for large, old, and stable firms that operative goals are substantially similar, reflecting professional administration? Does it also mean that for profit-making organizations in general there are only two alternative sources of domination, trustees (including owners) and professional administrators? Our theoretical scheme suggests that neither may be true, but the evidence is scanty. Certainly within the organizations dominated by professional managers there is ample opportunity for a variety of operational goals less general than, say, stability and security of employment. Even these are likely to vary and to shape the nature of the firm. (We exclude, of course, the failure to achieve these broad goals because of poor management or en-

---

Macmillan Co., 1955, pp. 77–78; and F. X. Sutton, *et al., The American Business Creed,* Cambridge: Harvard University Press, 1956, pp. 57–58. For a contrary view see G. Katona, *Psychological Analysis of Economic Behavior,* New York: McGraw-Hill, 1951, p. 197.

[28] James K. Dent, "Organizational Correlates of the Goals of Business Managements," *Journal of Personnel Psychology,* 12 (Autumn, 1959), pp. 375–376.

[29] *Ibid.,* pp. 378, 380, 383. Data on types of business, unfortunately, are not presented, except as reflected in the variable "proportion of employers who are white collar . . ."

[30] Gordon, *op. cit.,* pp. 114, 131–132, 145–146, 180, 347.

[31] M. T. Copeland and A. Towl, *The Board of Directors and Business Management,* Boston: Harvard University, 1947. For a similar conclusion and excellent discussion of these matters see R. H. Dahl, "Business and Politics," *American Political Science Review,* 53 (March, 1959), p. 6. The argument for increasing managerial control was, of course, also put forth by Burnham in 1941, but he was only faintly interested in the effects upon organizations, his thesis being that managers would supplant capitalists in the national and world power elite. See *The Managerial Revolution,* New York: John Day, 1941.

[32] Gordon, *op. cit.,* p. 180.

[33] *Ibid.,* pp. 327, 339. See his illustrations from General Motors and U.S. Rubber Company in chapter 7.

vironmental factors over which the organization has no control; we are dealing with operating policies which may not be achieved.) Gordon notes that the "historical background" of a company (he does not elaborate this phrase) and especially the training received by its leading executives may be a powerful factor in shaping management decisions. "It is the 'Rockefeller tradition' rather than the present Rockefeller holdings which actively conditions the management decisions in the Standard Oil companies. This tradition is largely responsible for present methods of management organization and internal control, use of the committee system and the domination of boards of directors by [company executives]." [34] Historical factors will certainly shape decisions, but the nature of technology in the oil industry and the trustees' awareness of the prime importance of coordination may have been decisive in that historical experience.

Domination by skill groups is possible in two ways. On the one hand, a department—for example, sales, engineering, research and development, or finance—may, because of the technology and stage of growth, effectively exercise a veto on the executive's decisions and substantially shape decisions in other departments. Second, lines of promotion may be such that top executives are drawn from one powerful department, and retain their identification with the parochial goals of that department. Gordon asserts that chief executives with a legal background are conservative in making price changes and find 'order in the industry' more appealing than aggressive price competition.[35] It is possible that engineers, sales executives, and financial executives all have distinctive views on what the operating policies should be.

Thus, goals may vary widely in profit-making organizations, and power may rest not only with trustees or professional administrators, but with skill groups or administrators influenced by their skill background. Of course, one task area may so dominate a firm that there will be no shifts in power, and operative goals will remain fairly stable within the limits of the changing values of society. But where basic tasks shift, either because of growth or changing technology, the scheme presented here at least alerts us to potential goal changes and their consequences. An ideal-typical sequence would be as follows: trustee domination in initial stages of financing, setting direction for development and recruitment of technical or professional skills; then dominance by the skill group during product or service development and research, only to have subsequent control pass to coordination of fairly routinized activities. As the market and technology change, this cycle could be repeated. During the course of this sequence, operative goals may shift from quantity production and short-run profits as emphasized by trustees, to the engineer's preoccupation with quality at the expense of quantity or styling, with this succeeded by a priority upon styling and unessential innovations demanded by the sales force, and finally with an emphasis upon the long-run market position, conservative attitude towards innovation, and considerable investment in employee-centered policies and programs by management. It is important to note that the formal authority structure may not vary during this sequence, but recruitment into managerial positions and the actual power of management, trustees or skill groups would shift with each new problem focus. Multiple leadership is also possible, as noted in an earlier section.

There are many critical variables influencing the selection of key problem areas and thus the characteristics of the controlling elite and operative goals. They will be applicable to the analysis of any complex organization, whether business, governmental, or voluntary. Among those that should be considered are capital needs and legitimization, the amount of routinization possible, adaptability of technology to market shifts and consumer behavior, possible or required professionalization, and the nature of the work force. Our analysis of profit-making organizations suggests that we should be alert to the possibility of a natural history of changes in task areas, authority, and goals which parallels that of hospitals and other voluntary service organizations. Non-voluntary service organizations may system-

---

[34] *Ibid.*, p. 188.

[35] *Ibid.*, p. 264.

atically deviate from this sequence because of the source of capital (government) which influences the commitments of appointive trustees (commissioners), and the character of the administrative tasks. The scheme presented here, when used in conjunction with the concept of operative goals, may provide a tool for analyzing the dynamics of goal setting and goal changing in all complex organizations.

[26]

Accounting, Organizations and Society, Vol. 11, No. 6, pp. 471–482, 1986. 0361–3682/86 $3.00+.00
Printed in Great Britain Pergamon Journals Ltd.

THE ILLUSION OF MANAGERIAL CONTROL

J. D. DERMER and R.G. LUCAS
Faculty of Administrative Studies, York University, Toronto

Abstract

The design and implementation of organizational control systems based on a cybernetic model stand in need of revision. The revision is required by increasing numbers of reports of system ineffectiveness and, in some cases, failure. The paper suggests that a major reason for current difficulties resides in the "illusion of control" implied by theory and implemented in practice. An alternative definition of organizational control based in the concept of "multirationality" is proposed.

The illusion of control (Dunbar, 1981; Van Gunsteren, 1976) results from managers believing that their assumptions concerning measurability, communication, and compliance are actually in use throughout an organization. More specifically, the illusion fosters the belief among managers that conventional controls such as operating standards, profit targets and budgetary criteria accurately and validly measure, and thereby help determine, behavior. The illusion reflects a presumption that management can intervene when necessary and successfully effect change. Further, the illusion provides for the belief that, by changing a given mix of existing controls, managers make necessary and sufficient functional responses to internal or external change. To those managing within an illusion of control, negative consequences of mangerial action often signify the necessity for more controls. Consequently, managerial activity often reflects the ritual application of theory and convention, while ignoring or suppressing behavior which does not fit these preconceptions (Riley, 1983; Pfeffer, 1977).

Turning to the literature of managerial control, there appears to be an ongoing difficulty in recognizing the social implications of cybernetic control models upon which much organizational control is based (Hofstede, 1978). Hofstede points out that neither the prior social conditions implied by cybernetic models nor the social consequences of the use of such models have received the attention they deserve. Management remains portrayed as the sole causal agent, and the question of the degree to which "non-managerial" agents can really influence outcomes tends to be avoided. While this is understandable where a particular concept is still in its definitional and consolidation stages, the cybernetic approach to control is now clearly beyond those developmental stages.

We suggest that managerial control theory has not really confronted the question of the illusion of control. Rather, it has often been enough to assume that control systems improve the probability of appropriate behavior and deem that sufficient to maintain the productivity of a given system, or to intervene and effect change as desired. But when setting goals proves difficult, measurements turn ambiguous, or when deviations cannot be analysed well enough to attribute causality, system designers often change the control strategies they recommend to simply reflect those influences which retain face validity (Dunbar, 1981). There is little acknowledgement that events may be emergent, that change may require an understanding of the actors involved, and that the external manipulation of existing controls may not suffice. And crucially, in our view, there is rarely any acknowledgement of the political dimensions of control.

Without this acknowledgement, management control theorists (and managers in many cases) implicitly perpetuate the use of, but not necessarily the *understanding of*, the illusion of control — the belief that the attempt to make changes through the unilateral exercise of power is control — irrespective of the effects these changes may produce.

The functionality of the illusion of control

However baseless the illusion of control may be from the viewpoint of contemporary control theory, paradoxically it is functional in many ways for both managers and organizations. That is, while theory may prescribe clarity and purposiveness, managers operate only rarely in conditions they clearly and completely understand (Wildavsky, 1979). The "multirational approach" to be described in this paper offers a means of understanding why illusions are, in fact, useful. For example, in some organizations the global vision provided by senior management is only partially adhered to in any concrete sense throughout the organization as a whole. In these organizations, where senior management is unable to impose its own vision, a system of accommodation tends to develop (Pettigrew, 1973; Simon, 1979). Put slightly differently, where one particular global vision is not implementable, but must contend with a diverse set of other visions, then a composite vision and complementary mode of control tends to emerge and become institutionalized over time (Dunbar, 1981; Weick, 1976). The resulting mode of control, while not actually implementing the vision of a senior management group in its entirety, accommodates and legitimates that vision *as well as others*.

Conventional control systems theory, reinforcing the illusion of control, ignores such possibilities. Undesirable outcomes remain linked to deficiencies in existing control practices, perpetuating the assumption that modifying control systems can correct these deficiencies (Hofstede, 1978; Wildavsky, 1979).

The illusion of control also influences the role of controls in the implementation of organizational change. In conventional conceptions of control senior management normally presumes that it is possible, if not necessarily easy, to move from one strategy to another. This is a highly useful presumption because the senior management teams of many organizations change frequently, or at the very least, tend to change strategies reasonably frequently in order to take advantgage of environmental opportunity (Clegg, 1979; Kanter, 1984). It is also highly useful to presume that the implementation of new strategies can take place using presently existing systems. Costly new implementation and control systems do not have to be designed and tested. Rather, existing systems are presumed to be reliable enough to implement new strategies.

Finally, the illusion of control allows control systems themselves to buffer the effects of internal and external change. While senior management and its strategies often change, less senior groups and the relations between them change much less frequently (Crozier, 1964; Aiken *et al.*, 1980). A buffering effect is one result of the masking of actual control relationships between officially superior and subordinate groups by existing control systems. As a consequence, existing control systems can be seen as protecting less formally powerful groups from changes which may well damage them or make them less efficient in their operations. Thus the illusion of control is useful not only to senior management, but to those at lower levels of the organization as well. Consequently, beyond their conventionally appreciated functions, control systems serve to maintain a relatively stable existing set of relations between organizational groups. They do so while reinforcing the illusion of control to those who see their mission as controlling the overall direction of the organization. It is through this ability to be many things at the same time that control systems resolve the paradox between illusion and functionality.

A MULTIRATIONAL PERSPECTIVE ON CONTROL

This paper introduces a conception of organizations which provides for multiple interest groups within organizations, carrying with it several implications for the design and implementation of control systems. It will be shown that, in addition to a need to reflect shared power, the design and implementation of effective controls depends also on the understanding of the content and the form of political processes and structures in an organization.

A "multirational" approach to studying organizations is not new. Over the last three decades several scholars have argued that political relations play a large part in determining an organization's actions and outcomes. Research findings from the literature of organizational behavior and case study analysis have strongly suggested that multiple rationalities exist in organizations (e.g. Blau, 1955; Cohen *et al.*, 1972; Crozier, 1964; Gouldner, 1954; Silverman, 1970; Strauss, 1978; Van Maanen, 1975; Weick, 1977). Hence our use of the term "multirational".

The multirational conception is based on the premise that political relationships between interest groups within an organization play a large part in determining its decision process and the outcomes of that process. Since about 1970, this line of analysis has emerged in the work of a body of researchers concerned with identifying the political realities of organizational decision process and structure (e.g. Allison, 1971; Bacharach & Lawler, 1980; Clegg, 1979; Edelman, 1971; Pettigrew, 1973; Pfeffer, 1981). Under this view, organizations are constructed out of conflict, and control systems are one means, as well as one result, of the political interaction between organizational interest groups. Individuals alone and in groups struggle to find their interests in a situation and seek to attain them. As they do so they come into conflict with other individuals and groups. With or against these others they enter into negotiations which classify and accommodate group interests (more or less well) into an equilibrium for the organization as a whole at any one point in time. One reflection of this equilibrium is the set of controls used within the organization. Consequently, organizational control systems can be seen as the sum of solutions to organizational contradictions derived from the differences between interest group activities and perceptions. A useful empirical image of such a structured equilibrium may be provided by the concept of "negotiated order" (Strauss, 1978). Under this view, organizational control emerges out of the interaction between interest groups as they define the meaning of, and then act upon, specific organizational issues such as budgets, strategic plans, plant acquisitions or manpower policies.

The essence of the political approach as we use it in this paper is its unit of analysis — the interest group. Each participating interest group is presumed to have its own perspective, to have its own rationality, and to operate consistently within that rationality. Each interest group recognizes, defines, and attempts to resolve the uncertainty it faces into limited and manageable problems (March & Simon, 1958). The interest group then seeks to articulate and legitimize those problems for which it possesses implementable solutions (Cohen *et al.*, 1972). Put slightly differently, each interest group enacts its own environment (Weick, 1977), or constructs its own rationality (March & Simon, 1958).

From the perspective of a control theory which includes political processes, each interest group resolves the uncertainty it faces into limited but functional control systems which are, at least in part, defined by its own model of what the organization is. Further, each interest group has its own set of stakeholders with whom it acknowledges relationships and whose expectations it considers. As a result, each interest group can be presumed to engage in a rational process of strategy formulation and implementation, similar to that conventionally seen as the responsibility and the right of the Chief Executive Officer.

It seems probable then, that there is more than one model of controllable reality operating in a given organization at any particular time. Multiple models imply the necessity for multiple modes of implementation, i.e. control systems.

Of course, normally only one set of such control systems is publicly acknowledged as legitimate and it is usually associated with the interests of senior management (Pfeffer, 1977). Pfeffer suggests that the impression of legitimate control is often based on reality, but it is equally possible that legitimacy is the result of the creation of an "impression of rationality" on the part of a particular organizational group. Other control systems, specific to officially subordinate groups, may not necessarily have had the benefit of consensus, and in any public confrontation, either escape notice or are placed in subordinate relation to an authorized system (Wildavsky, 1979). These other systems await their chance to exert influence, basing their capacity to do so on shifts in the balance of interest group power in complex organizations.

THE CONVENTIONAL APPROACH TO MANAGERIAL CONTROL

In contemporary theory, managerial control is the generic process of ensuring conformance to expectations (Tannenbaum, 1968), and is usually expressed in effectiveness and efficiency terms (Anthony & Dearden, 1980). The need for control arises among two or more distinguishable organizational units when achieving the goals of one unit is dependent on the behavior of others. Controls are the tools, methods, rules, agreements, accords, measurments, actions etc., used to effect control and, therefore, manage that dependence, and a control system is a set of formal elements (controls) working together to effect control (Drucker, 1964).

The technical approach to control is based on the feedback of deviance, detected by a specific mechanism, which motivates subsequent action (Eilon, 1965; Hofstede, 1978). Following the analysis of a task situation, i.e. one in which inputs are transformed into outputs through a technology or process, expectations are established and then actual events are measured. These task related data are then compared to reveal deviations, for which subsequent corrective action can be taken.

A significant revision of the technical control model included the interaction of individual personalities, abilities, and objectives with such task-based controls such as standards, measurements, budgets, and rules (Nutt, 1984). This revision helped to account for results which diverged from managerial expectations, and the design of control systems expanded to encompass behavioral factors (Child, 1973; Hopwood, 1973; Ouchi & Johnson, 1978). Typical modifications which have been applied include alternative reinforcements (e.g. varying the frequency of feedback or making compensation contingent on performance), and differing degrees of discretion allowed through de-centralization.

In contemporary managerial control theory, it is believed that a concern with human behavior has made the use of task-oriented controls significantly more effective. In response, contemporary practice now often includes such recommendations as increased participation in goal setting to elicit ego involvement and feelings of self-control for greater motivation, use of alternative report formats to overcome problems of information overload, and setting objectives of different degrees of difficulty to reflect different aspiration levels and needs for achievement. These changes in control process construction are now an accepted part of the contemporary approach to managerial control. Consequently, we suggest that the design of control systems currently consists to a large degree of balancing the interaction between task and behavioral considerations, contingent on the different requirements of various organizational functions.

The gap between the conventional and the real

We suggest that, under the assumptions of the contemporary approach to managerial control, a situation to be controlled is conceptualized in terms of a transformation model consisting of four components: inputs, process, outputs and consequences. The evaluation criteria for these are economy, efficiency, effectiveness and appropriateness. The role that each of these four components can play in control varies depending on the answers to four questions: (1) Can expectations be prescribed? (2) Can what is taking place/will take place be measured? (3) Is it possible to decompose deviations into their component parts and to attribute causality? (4) Is it possible to intervene in order to alter the nature or magnitude of the deviation? Possible control situations created by asking these questions in relation to each of the components of a control situation are depicted in the matrix presented in Table 1.

Each of the cells in the matrix depicted in Table 1 prescribes a question asked about a component of a control situation. For example, in a particular situation, can causality be attributed with regard to a deviation between expected and actual output? The question is presumed to be answerable by either a yes (Y) or a no (N). The answer depends on the degree of uncertainty associated with that component of the control situation. Assuming each cell is independent of the other, there are 256 possible variations. This provides an indication of the information capacity required, as well as the range of control situations that contemporary theory tries to accommodate. Our charting of ranges of organizational control is similar to that developed by Hofstede (1981, pp. 195–198).

The contingency approach to control (Gordon & Miller, 1976; Khandwalla, 1972; Camman & Nadler, 1976; Vancil, 1973) confronts this problem of differing situations. It holds that the type of control to be implemented depends on the situation to be controlled (Ouchi, 1977). It is further emphasized that the framework, techniques and style of implementation of the control system used in each situation must be capable of maximizing the probability of achieving goal congruence within the constraints of equity and cost effectiveness (Vancil, 1973).

We suggest that the contemporary approach is predicated on the assumed ability to exercise control as far downstream as possible, while encompassing as much information as possible (Merchant, 1982). The ideal situation under this approach is one in which all sixteen cells in the matrix can be labelled "Yes" because full and complete information is available. Control is then based on the ability to specify expectations, record events, understand the cause (s) of deviations, and to intervene as indicated. To the extent that "No" answers prevail, the ability to control is reduced, and theory prescribes that managers utilize only those cells which provide a "Yes" indication (Ouchi, 1979).

The gap between contemporary control system theory and the reality of how systems actually operate in real organizations is indicated by the theoretical response to a predominance of "No" answers. In those situations where "No" answers predominate, the amount of discretion

TABLE 1. Possible control situations

	Components of a control situation			
Questions	Inputs	Process	Outputs	Consequences
Can expectations be specified?	Y/N	Y/N	Y/N	Y/N
Is measurement possible	Y/N	Y/N	Y/N	Y/N
Can causality be attributed?	Y/N	Y/N	Y/N	Y/N
Is intervention functional?	Y/N	Y/N	Y/N	Y/N

Y = yes; N = no.

allocated to the controllee and the degree of interaction between the controller and the controllee before and during activity is "to be adjusted accordingly" (Vancil, 1973).

While this may be a quite practical response to a lack of information, causal connection, or ability to actually measure deviance, it tends to beg the question of why discretion, and therefore control, needs to be adjusted. As we have maintained earlier, the answer may well lie in the tendency of contemporary approaches to rule out the possibility of interest groups existing within the organization, their differing models of what it is that needs measuring and controlling, as well as the political process of negotiation which plays its part in resolving just which questions shall be answered under what conditions. We suggest that this tendency can be corrected through a revised conception of control.

UNIRATIONALITY, POWER AND REGULATION

The need for a revised conception of control is based on a change from a "unirational" to a "multirational" conception of organizational process, a revised conception of the role of power, and a shift away from the sole objective of regulating compliance toward an acceptance of the legitimacy of differences.

Unirationality

The conventional approach to organizational control relies on a crucial assumption of "unirationality". The organization is assumed to be made up of individuals, operating departments, and staff groups which are relatively homogeneous with regard to the criteria they use to assess the achievement of their interests. Furthermore, it is assumed that the unirationality represented by control systems of senior management is necessarily dominant and effective throughout the organization as a whole. The global vision is presumed to be the local vision. This single common rationality is expected to provide the criteria necessary for making day-to-day decisions. To the extent any individual or group is identifiable as not holding goals in common with those stated by the C.E.O. through (his) formal systems, behavioral manipulations such as participation, contingent performance rewards, and/or decreased time span of control are often used to extract compliance. Put simply, such individuals or groups are subject to negative or positive sanctions.

The assumption remains that a single vision exists and is appropriate to all parts of the organization. This perspective will be called unirational, indicative of a single rationality emanating from the senior management group which is presumed to be implemented throughout the organization using formal control systems.

Revised conception of power

One reason for re-examining the assumptions of unirationality stems from an analysis of the relationship between power and control. Uncertainty and lack of consensus have a direct influence on the power to control (Bacharach & Lawler, 1980; Pfeffer, 1981). The compliance approach to control is predicated on the legitimacy of *one* rationality. As a result, it depends on the ability to specify, measure and gain acceptance for a specified set of control variables which encompass certain objectives and constraints. However, to the extent that a given set of prescribed control variables cannot be effectively used due to inherent uncertainty difficulties of measurement, or lack of knowledge concerning causality, the application of contemporary control approaches will likely produce poor results.

Put slightly differently, the greater the number of "Nos" that appear in the matrix of Table 1, the lower the ability to apply the compliance approach because these "Nos" open a zone of discretion for the controllee. This discretionary zone has been described in spatial and temporal terms (i.e. the dimensions of behavior left unspecified), and in terms of a resource pool (the number, type and magnitude of resources available for use). These are the two subcomponents of "organizational slack" (March & Simon, 1958; Thompson, 1967).

The essence of the compliance approach is the *ex ante* preclusion of this space and/or the imposition of *ex post* consequences for its inappropriate use. However, if because of uncertainty and/or lack of consensus this cannot be done, the compliance model breaks down.

The implications of this fact are significant. Recall that unirationality and the compliance approach are predicated on the following assumptions:

The right to expect conformance to the global vision rests with senior levels of the management hierarchy.

The global vision is the local vision.

Subordinates suspend individual judgement and accept the global vision.

Those at higher levels have superior analytical insights and, as a result, are better able to prescribe the future activity of the organization.

There is a presumption of both the ability and the legitimate right to prescribe subordinate activities.

Consequently, an asymmetrical distribution of power represented by the organizational hierarchy is both expected and accepted.

Clearly the existence of shared power invalidates some of these assumptions. In many situations, total compliance is an inappropriate expectation because the controllee possesses power, arising from the sphere of discretion open to him and the increased availability of resources to be used as desired by the controllee (Child, 1973; Crozier, 1964). What exists, in reality, is a sharing of power between controller and controllee with its distribution depending on the characteristics of particular control systems.

Regulations and compliance

Conventionally, control also relies on the assumption that its objective is to condition a controllee to behave in conformance with the rationality of the controller. Extracting compliance is made possible by the ability to exercise power, and is legitimated by the existence of regulatory authority. It involves prescribing, measuring and manipulating, working through the consequences subsequent to performance which become the antecedents to future behavior (by expressing expectations, directions, and constraints to shape behavior), and/or by selecting role incumbents as the situation allows. It is exacted by constructing the best portfolio of influencing tools and processes and then combining these with with social and self control to maximize the likelihood of appropriate behavior. How best to interweave behavioral considerations into what the task requirements provide is the essence of designing control systems under conventional assumptions.

If one accepts the assumptions of shared power and multirationality, then it is possible to see that formal, authoritative control systems cannot fully prescribe or predetermine behavior. They can, at best, proscribe or constrain it. Hence, much behavior within and between organizational units is regulated by other means. Dunbar (1981) argues that such regulation is essentially *self*-control. He suggests that people in organizations do what they want in relation to the prevailing constraints and consequences. What motivates and what regulates behavior depends on the objectives pursued, the ability to effect change and the motivation to do so.

A revised conception of control signals a significant shift in the nature of the regulatory relations between units normally superior and subordinate to each other. We suggest that relationships of mutual dependence between units must be acknowledged. We further suggest that such relationships should be understood in terms of political negotiations, and the balancing of forces between units, and not in solely terms of unilateral regulations by a controller of a controllee. The role of each organizational unit is regulated, but the revised conception suggests that this regulation exists on the basis of negotiation between units. Thus, we contend that actual control systems are, in fact, the emergent results of prior political negotiation between organizational units.

One implication of all of these assertions is that the notions of unirationality and compliance which underly the way control systems design is taught and practiced do not in fact reflect the whole of organizational reality. The selection of key variables, the development of standards of performance, and the measurement and reconciliation of subsequent events all take place in an assumed situation that does not necessarily exist in the real world. Yet, we suggest, the unirational/compliance model remains the dominant approach to control in organizations.

TOWARD AN EXPANDED THEORY OF CONTROL

An alternative conception of control

It is suggested that managerial control theory include a focus on the interest group as a unit of analysis in the design of control systems. One result would be the growth of a conception of control which encompasses the means by which interest groups interact and coexist. An interest group is an organizational group whose interests are articulated as an internally consistent rationality or model of its situation. Interactions between them are multilateral processes modelled on political variables. Interest groups respond to uncertainty and a lack of consensus through negotiations. This political conception is premised on acceptance of the need to understand the allocation and use of power, that outcomes are influenced by and are conditional on the behavior of others, and that all contenders have a legitimate right to pursue their own interests.

Negotiations among interest groups yields a relatively stable order which can be observed as a combination of three general types of rationalities (Scott *et al.*, 1981):

(1) the technical rationality of task performance focusing on the objective of efficiency;
(2) the organizational rationality of communication and cooperation focusing on a coordinative effort for goal attainment;
(3) the political rationality, mediating among conflicting parties pursuing their own interests, for the objective of stability and perceived equity.

Control is itself a form of rationality, a form of behaving consistently to achieve objectives over time. The overall form of rationality implied by an organization's control system hinges on the mix of the above three rationalities which emerges as a result of negotiation and choice among interest groups within the organization.

For any interest group, multiple control relationships exist: those within the interest group; those between the interest group and others, e.g. with subordinates; those with lateral units or with superiors; and directly to units outside conventionally accepted organizational boundaries. Each set of control relations represents a mix of the above rationalities. The alternative conception of control allows for the possibility that other interest groups are not always totally subordinated to the rationality of the currently authoritative interest group and hence surbordinated to the control system which articulates it. Conceptually, the effect is to open organizational control systems to the recognition of valid disturbances, critiques and the advocacy of internally generated change.

An alternative definition of control

With the inclusion of a political perspective, the objective of control remains the same — to intervene and effect desired change at some specific point in time. Implementing control implies the ability to establish expectations, develop a plan for their realization, implement this plan, and then maintain the desired state until change is deemed necessary. Being in control implies the ability to prescribe and realize that which is in the best interests of the controller, in this case an interest group. Each interest group in an organization pursues its own ends in accordance with its own rationality in accordance with its own control capabilities. Although only the control system associated with the interests of senior management is publicly acknowledged, these other control systems are influential because of the inevitable sharing of power. In order to effect control, it is necessary to: (1) identify the elements of the illusion of control regulating relations between organizational units, and (2) distinguish the illusion from control systems actually used within units.

Some dysfunctional consequences of exposing the illusion of control

It does not necessarily follow that, because an illusion of control exists, it should be exposed. There are significant consequences in doing so, consequences which could be dysfunctional to individuals, groups and the organization as a whole. For example, exposure adversely affects any group (e.g. a dominant coalition of interest groups) which stands to lose either resources or administrative discretion should the existing mode of control in the organization actually change. Secondly, it is crucial to recognize that the stability of the organization, which depends on acceptance by those controlled (Weber, 1947), is itself at risk if the beliefs upon which control is based are called into question. To the extent that all groups realize this fact, they are somewhat less likely to attempt to expose the existing illusion . . . unless, of course, they believe they have a ready and practicable replacement and can benefit from the resultant changes.

CONCLUSIONS

The alternatives just presented suggest that the role and function of control be regarded somewhat differently. For example, overlap and redundancy among control units may be regarded in two quite different ways. From a unirational perspective an organization is a coordinated network pursuing common objectives (Landau, 1969). Overlap and redundancy are symptoms of inefficiency. Using a multirational conception, such overlaps reveal conflicts and disagreements and so stimulate action. They also provide inherent reliability in regulating the relationships between organizational units because if one relationship should prove unsatisfactory, there are additional linkages to compensate (Weick, 1976).

Implementing a multirational conception of control relies upon an image of control systems which bears a resemblance to a political federation — the key is the nature of the relationships between units. It is suggested that the structure and process of control in an organization can be characterized as a constitutional framework which is partially written (presumably agreed upon and legitimately authoritative), and partially under continuous negotiation (therefore unwritten and not yet necessarily legitimated by all groups within the organization).

Any given approach to organizational control can choose to either reflect as accurately as possible the (admittedly difficult to describe) political relationships among individual actors and groups, or to model the situation based on assumptions that prescribe a preconceived feedback process and more observable variables. We believe that the former provides for a conception more consistent with the often messy realities of organizations, while the latter represents superimposing a neater (but less situationally valid) set of preconceived control relations on an existing organization. We have referred to the two approaches as "multirational" and "unirational" respectively.

One advantage of the multirational conception is the recognition of the legitimate existence of multiple interest groups within organizations. Therefore, it warns senior management not to overestimate the effectiveness of compliance approaches and encourages them to ask some difficult questions — what is the nature of internal opposition to either proposed change or to continued maintenance of the corporate vision, and what should be done about that opposition? It asks them to acknowledge that contention and opposition may be of value to a given organization at particular times. The issue for senior management, as well as others in the organization, is to be able to know when it is valuable and when it is not.

A multirational conception of control suggests that senior management needs to ask whether organizational control systems should strive for compliance or whether an international negotiation strategy might be more effective. If unirationality actually exists within an organization, then there is no necessity for negotiation. The only requirement is for commitment to systems already in place. In this case an organization would literally be using the results of negotiation which had already occurred. However, we have pointed out that case research suggests the more common situation is one in which multirationality exists. Therefore pursuing the compliance approach alone will probably prove inappropriate.

The key question for a C.E.O. and senior management is whether the organization is, in fact, unirational or multirational. More specifically, what is the current state of the organization — who are the interest groups, what are their interests, what do the relations or bonds between them consist of, and how strong are those relations or bonds? Under contemporary conceptions of control these questions are rarely asked, as the existence of contending interest groups is not perceived. Control is, in that case, a matter of eliminating observed contention through behavioural or political manipulation. Yet, if the reality is that a firm is made up of multiple interest groups, an elimination strategy may well be expensive in the short run and risky in the longer term.

This paper has suggested that rather than being unirational, most organizations are multirational. Therefore goal congruence and behavioral sensitivity remain only a partial listing of the assumptions needed to provide an improved approach to managerial control. We suggest that control systems be designed to sustain co-existing, yet divergent, rationalities and resulting control models used by self-regulating interest groups. The relationships between controller and controllee is not a one-way exercise of authority in order to extract compliance. It is a process of commitments and constraints exercised in either direction (Blau, 1955). Control systems may benefit from being reconceptualized as a framework within which these exercises take place, as well as providing an image of the results of such negotiation. Furthermore, the inclusion of behavioral considerations to modify task oriented designs in order to influence behavior should be regarded more as tactical modifications within a political structure. What is required to more effectively implement managerial control is a combination of task, behavioral and political perspectives.

BIBLIOGRAPHY

Aiken, M., Bacharach, S. & French, L., Organization Structure, Work Process, and Proposal Making in Administrative Bureaucracies, *Academy of Management Journal* (1980) pp. 631–652.

Allison, G., *Essence of Decision* (Boston, MA: Little, Brown, 1971).

Anthony, R. & Dearden, J., *Management Control System* (Homewood, IL: Irwin, 1980).

Blau, P., *The Dynamics of Bureaucracy* (Chicago, IL: University of Chicago Press, 1975).

Cammann, C., Effects of the Use of Control Systems, *Accounting, Organizations and Society* (1976) pp. 301–313.

Cammann, C. & Nadler, D., Fit Control Systems to Your Managerial Style, *Harvard Business Review* (January 1976) pp. 65–72.

Child, J., Strategies of Control and Organizational Behaviour, *Administrative Science Quarterly* (March 1973) pp. 1–17.

Clegg, S., *The Theory of Power and Organisation* (London: Routledge and Kegan Paul, 1979).

Cohen, M., March, J. & Olsen, J., A Garbage Can Model of Organizational Choice, *Administrative Science Quarterly* (March 1972) pp. 1–25.

Drucker, P., Controls, Control and Management, in Bonini, J. *et al.* (eds) *Management Controls: New Directions in Basic Research* pp. 286–296 (Toronto: McGraw-Hill, 1964).

Dunbar, R., Budgeting for Control, *Administrative Science Quarterly* (March 1971) pp. 43–57.

Dunbar, R., Designs for Organizational Control, in Nystrom, P. and Starbuck, W. (eds) *Handbook of Organizational Design* (New York: Oxford University Press, 1981).

Edelman, M., *Politics as Symbolic Action* (Urbana, IL: University of Illinois Press, 1971).

Edstrom, A. & Galbraith, J., Transfer of Managers as a Coordination and Control Strategy In Multinational Organizations, *Administrative Science Quarterly* (June 1977) pp. 248–263.

Eilon, S., A Classification of Administrative Control Systems, *British Journal of Management Studies* (1965) pp. 3–12.

Flamholtz, E., Organizational Control as a Managerial Tool, *California Management Review* (Winter 1979) pp. 50–59.

Giglioni, G. & Bedeian, A., A Conspectus of Management Control Theory: 1900–1972, *Academy of Management Journal* (1974) pp. 292–305.

Gordon, L. & Miller, D., A Contingency Framework for the Design of Accounting Information Systems, *Accounting, Organizations and Society* (1976) pp. 56–69.

Gouldner, A., *Patterns of Industry Bureaucracy* (Glencoe, IL: Free Press, 1954).

Grimes, A., Authority, Power, Influence and Social Control: A Theoretical Synthesis, *Academy of Management Review* (1978) pp. 724–735.

Hofstede, G., The Poverty of Management Control Philosophy, *Academy of Management Review* (1978) pp. 450–461.

Hofstede, G., Management and Control of Public and Not-for-Profit Acitivities, *Accounting, Organizations and Society* (1981) pp. 193–211.

Hopwood, A., *An Accounting System and Managerial Behaviour* (Westmead: Saxon House, 1973).

Horovitz, J., Strategic Control: A New Task for Top Management, *Long Range Planning* (June 1979) pp. 2–7.

Kanter, R., *The Change Masters* (New York, NY: John Wiley, 1984).

Khandwalla, P., The Effect of Different Types of Competition on the Use of Management Controls, *Journal of Accounting Research* (1972) pp. 275–285.

Landau, M., Redundancy, Rationality and the Problem of Duplication and Overlap, *Public Administration Review* (1969) pp. 336–358.

March, J. & Simon, H., *Organizations* (New York, NY: John Wiley, 1958).

Merchant, K., The Control Function of Management, *Sloan Management Review* (Summer 1982) pp. 43–55.

Nutt, P., Types of Organizational Decision Processes, *Administrative Science Quarterly* (September 1984) pp. 414–450.

Ouchi, W., The Relationship Between Organizational Structure and Organizational Control, *Administrative Science Quarterly* (March 1977) pp. 95–113.

Ouchi, W., The Transmission of Control Through Organizational Hierarchy, *Academy of Management Journal* (1978) pp. 173–192.

Ouchi, W., A Conceptual Framework for the Design of Organizational Control Mechanisms, *Management Review* (1979) pp. 833–848.

Ouchi, W. & Johnson, J., Types of Organization Control and their Relationship to Emotional Well Being, *Administrative Science Quarterly* (1978) pp. 559–569.

Pettigrew, A., *The Politics of Organizational Decision Making* (London: Tavistock, 1973).

Pfeffer, J., *Power in Organizations,* (Boston, MA: Pitman, 1981).

Pfeffer, J., Power and Resources Allocation in Organizations, in Staw, B. and Salancik, G. (eds) *New Directions in Organizational Behavior* (Chicago, IL: St. Clair Press, 1977).

Riley, P., A Structurationist Account of Political Cultures, *Administrative Science Quarterly* (September 1983) pp. 414–437.

Scott, W., Mitchell, T. & Perry, N., Organizational Governance, in Nystrom, P. and Starbuck, W., (eds) *Handbook of Organizational Design,* (New York, NY: North-Holland, 1981).

Sihler, W., Toward Better Management Control Systems, *California Management Review* (Winter 1971) pp. 33–39.

Silverman, D., *The Theory of Organizations* (New York: NY: Basic, 1970).

Simon, H., Rational Decision Making in Business Organizations, *American Economic Review* (1979) pp. 493–513.

Streauss, A., *Negotiations,* (San Francisco, CA: Jossey-Bass, 1978).

Tannenbaum, A., *Control in Organizations* (New York, NY: McGraw-Hill, 1968).

Thompson, J., *Organizations in Action* (New York, NY: McGraw-Hill, 1967).

Vancil, R., What Kind of Management Control Do You Need?, *Harvard Business Review* (March–April 1973) pp. 75–86.

Van Gunsteren, H., *The Quest for Control* (New York, NY: John Wiley, 1976).

Van Maanen, J., Police Socialization, *Administrative Science Quarterly* (1975) pp. 207–228.

Weber, M., *The Theory of Social and Economic Organization,* trans (New York, NY: Free Press, 1947).

Weick, K., Enactment Processes in Organizations, in Staw, B. and Salancik, G., (eds) *New Directions in Organizational Behavior* (Chicago, IL: St. Clair Press, 1977).

Weick, K., Educational Organizations as Loosely-Coupled Systems, *Administrative Science Quarterly* (March 1976) pp. 1–19.

Journal of Management Studies, **19**, 1, 1982

THE IRRATIONALITY OF ACTION AND ACTION RATIONALITY: DECISIONS, IDEOLOGIES AND ORGANIZATIONAL ACTIONS

NILS BRUNSSON
Stockholm School of Economics

ABSTRACT

Irrationality is a basic feature of organizational behaviour. Organizational decision making tends to be irrational, and organizational ideologies bias organizations' perceptions. Much effort has been spent on prescribing how organizations should achieve more rationality. However, rational decision making affords a bad basis for action. Some irrationalities are necessary requirements for organizational actions. Choices are facilitated by narrow and clear organizational ideologies, and actions are facilitated by irrational decision-making procedures which maximize motivation and commitment.

THE DECISION-MAKING PERSPECTIVE AND IRRATIONALITY

A characteristic of social science is the multitude perspectives used by different researchers. The significant differences between research fields lie less often in what is described than in how it is described. One important way of developing a social science is to apply new perspectives to a part of reality, thereby highlighting new features of the reality. Perspectives determine what data are seen, what theories are developed, and what kinds of results turn up.

One of the most influential perspectives has been the decision-making perspective which conceives of human behaviour as resulting from decisions made by individuals, group, or organizations. A decision is normally described as a conscious choice between at least two alternative actions. Researchers have studied the choosing among alternatives, the generating of alternatives, and the forming of criteria for choice (goals, objectives).

The attractiveness of the decision-making perspective has several explanations. One explanation is that diverse social theories can be stated in decision-making terms. This is true for parts of microeconomics and of political science. Another explanation is that the perspective lends itself to experimentation; psychological researchers can create experimental decision situations by giving people objectives and information, and then they

Address for reprints: Professor N. Brunsson, Stockholm School of Economics, Box 6501, s-11383 Stockholm, Sweden.

study the resulting choices. In addition, social development has spawned situations where the decision-making perspective seems relevant from a common-sense point of view. The establishment and growth of large organizations have added hierarchy to society and, consequently, many actions are determined by forces outside the actors themselves (Chandler, 1977; Galbraith, 1967; Lindblom, 1977). This separates cognition from action and makes it natural to say some individuals decide and others carry out the decisions. The decision-making perspective seems almost imperative in democratic conventions. According to the existing law for industrial democracy in Sweden, for example, the employees' influence should be guaranteed by their participation in decisions. These imperatives may result from a spread of the decision-making perspective from researchers to practitioners.

Still, the decision-making perspective has derived from studies of individual behaviour rather than organizational. An individual has less difficulty going from decision to action than does an organization. This emphasis on individual behaviour might explain why the choosing of actions has received much more attention than the carrying out of actions. Organizational decision processes are described in essentially the same terms as individual decision processes, and research has often characterized organizations as being led by single powerful entrepreneurs (as in microeconomic theory) or by coalitions (as described by Cyert and March, 1963).

The decision-making perspective has been most elaborated in normative research which prescribes how decisions should be made. This kind of research sets the criteria for a 'rational' decision. Strong efforts have been devoted to prescribing how a best choice should be made, given a specific problem, specific alternatives and specific information. Typically, a problem is described as one where there is either too little information or too much. Little attention has been paid to other phases of decision-making processes or to implementing the decisions made.

Normative research has engendered an increasing consensus among researchers as to what kinds of decision making should be called rational. At the same time, empirical research has found ample evidence of decision-making processes that appear irrational by the normative standards (Cyert and March, 1963; Janis, 1972; Lindblom, 1959; March and Olsen, 1976; Nisbett and Ross, 1980; Tversky and Kahneman, 1974). What is more, the apparent irrationalities are not limited to insignificant decisions: people behave similarly when making major decisions on strategic issues. It can even be argued that the apparent irrationalities are largest in major decisions. Janis (1972) demonstrated how decisions with serious actual or potential effects—such as the decision by the Kennedy administration to start the invasion in the Bay of Pigs—were made without normative rationality. Disturbing information was suppressed, and false illusions of unanimity were built up among the decision makers, who took immense and unjustified risks.

There are three common ways of explaining the irrationality found in practice. One chauvinist explanation is that the people studied are not clever enough to behave rationally. For instance, difficulties of implementing models from operations research have been explained by managers' emotional reactions or by their cognitive styles (Huysmans, 1970; Tarkowsky, 1958). If decision makers only had the brain capacities and knowledge of scientists, they would behave as the rational decision models prescribe. Thus, decision makers ought to be selected better and trained better.

A second explanation derives from recent psychological research, which indicates that certain types of irrationality are inherent characteristics of human beings, and these characteristics are difficult to change by training (Goldberg, 1968; Kahneman and Tversky, 1973). Consequently, not even experts can be fully rational, and full rationality can only be reached by mathematical formulae or computer programs.

A third way of explaining apparently irrational behaviour is to point out practical restrictions. In realistic decision situations, values, alternatives and predictions interact; so decision makers have incomplete information, or they have more information than human beings can grasp. This view implies that normative research should design systems for gathering and processing data. Not many years ago, some people expected computer-based information systems to solve numerous management problems (Murdick and Ross, 1975). Also, recognizing that objectives may be difficult to compare with each other, normative research has produced cost-benefit analysis and multiple-criteria methods (Keeney and Raiffa, 1976; Prest and Turvey, 1965).

These traditional explanations are made within the decision-making perspective. They refer to diverse phenomena that disturb decision processes. Like the decision processes themselves, the disturbances are described as being cognitive; they arise from deficiencies in perceived information or deficiencies in decision makers' mental abilities.

These ways of explaining irrationality cannot be said to be inherently wrong, but there is much evidence that these explanations do not suffice. Computer-based information systems have not been used in the prescribed ways; recommendations given by operations-research models have not been followed; cost-benefit analyses have not been done or have been neglected even by competent and successful managers and politicians (Ackerman et al., 1974; Argyris, 1977; Churchman, 1964; Harvey, 1970).

If actual behaviour is to be understood, other explanations are needed. As long as actual behaviour is not fully understood, the recommendations of normative research may be irrelevant, confusing or even harmful.

The main purpose of this article is to argue that an action perspective will be more fruitful for understanding large areas of organizational behaviour. The action perspective explains behaviour within attempts to change and differences in abilities to achieve changes. Because organizational actions do not lend themselves to laboratory experiments, the article is based on studies of major organizational changes or stabilities in seven organizations. The organizations include industrial companies, governmental agencies and local governments. Processes of change were observed, and people's ways of describing both the changes and the general situations were measured.

The decision-making perspective fails to recognize that practitioners do more than make decisions. Making a decision is only a step towards action. A decision is not an end product. Practitioners get things done, act and induce others to act.

An action perspective makes it easier and important to observe that there exist both decisions without actions and actions without decisions. Some actions are not preceded by weighing of objectives, evaluating of alternatives or choosing; and decision processes and decisions do not always influence actions, particularly not when the actions precede the decisions. On the other hand, decision processes often comprise some of the processes associated with actions. Because managers and representatives in political bodies describe part of their work as decision making, decisions and decision making should remain important topics for study.

In fact, the very relationship between decision making and action helps explain why decisions deviate from normative rationality. Since decision processes aim at action, they should not be designed solely according to such decision-internal criteria as the norms of rationality; they should be adapted to external criteria of action. Rational decisions are not always good bases for appropriate and successful actions.

How can decisions lay foundations for actions? The next section attempts to answer this question.

DECISIONS AS INITIATORS OF ACTIONS

Making decisions is just one way among several of initiating actions in organizations. However, it is a familiar one. Actions are often preceded by group activities which the participants describe as decision-making steps. Certain issues are posed in forms that allow them to be handled by decision processes: several alternative actions are proposed, their probable effects are forecasted, and finally actions are chosen. Sometimes the decision makers even formulate goals or other explicit criteria by which the alternatives can be evaluated. The final results are called decisions.

For decisions to initiate actions, they must incorporate cognitive, motivational and committal aspects. One cognitive aspect of a decision is expectation: the decision expresses the expectation that certain actions will take place. A decision also demonstrates motivation to take action, and it expresses the decision makers' commitments to specific actions. By making a decision, decision makers accept responsibility both for getting the actions carried out and for the appropriateness of the actions.

To go from decision to action is particularly complicated and difficult when there are several decision makers and several actors and when decision makers and actors are different persons. These conditions are typical of organizations. Thus, organizations should provide motivational and social links from decisions to actions. Strong motivations, sometimes even enthusiasm, are needed to overcome big intellectual or physical obstacles. Cooperating actors should be able to rely on certain kinds of behaviours and attitudes from their collaborators, so they should construct mutual commitments: the actors should signal to one another that they endorse proposed actions, for example, by presenting arguments in favour of them or by expressing confidence in success. Actors should also elicit commitments from those who will evaluate their actions afterwards, because committed evaluators are more likely to judge actions as successful (Brunsson, 1976).

Thinking, motivation and commitment are aspects of all actions. However, the importance of each aspect might differ in various situations, depending on such variables as the actors' time horizons, the degrees of change that the actions involve, and the power relationships within the organization. Cognitive activities probably become more important where the actors expect more information to be beneficial. Motivations would be more important where actors lack information needed for predicting the consequences of acting, where the negative consequences could be great, or where great efforts are essential; motivations would be less important where the actions are highly complex and the actors must collaborate extensively (Zander, 1971). Commitments would be more important where many people are involved in actions, agreements from many people are necessary, efforts must be tightly coordinated, or results depend upon the actions or evaluations of collaborators who are accessible through communication. Since motivations and commitments represent internal pressures for action, they are particularly influential where external pressures are weak. This is true of wait-and-see situations where people think that it may be possible to take no action: the actors can reject one proposed action without having to accept another at the same time.

The stronger the expectation, motivation and commitment expressed in a decision, the more power that decision exerts as a basis for action. Insofar as the constituents of decisions are determined by decision processes, the likelihoods of actions can be influenced by designing the decision processes. However, effective decision processes break nearly all the rules for rational decision making: few alternatives should be analyzed, only positive consequences of the chosen actions should be considered, and objectives should not be formulated in advance.

The following subsections explain how irrationalities can build good bases for organizational actions.

Searching for Alternatives

According to the rational model, all possible alternatives should be evaluated. This is impossible, so the injunction is often reformulated as evaluating as many alternatives as possible.

In reality, it seems easier to find decision processes which consider few alternatives (typically two) than ones which consider many alternatives. It is even easy to find decision processes which consider only one alternative. This parsimony makes sense from an action point of view, because considering multiple alternatives evokes uncertainty, and uncertainty reduces motivation and commitment. If actors are uncertain whether a proposed action is good, they are less willing to undertake it and to commit themselves to making it succeed. For example, in order to facilitate product-development projects, uncertainty should not be analyzed but avoided (Brunsson, 1980). If people do not know which action will actually be carried out, they have to build up motivations for several alternatives at the same time, and this diffuses the motivations supporting any single alternative For the same reasons, commitments may be dispersed or destroyed by the consideration of several alternatives. Therefore, very early in decision processes, if possible before the processes even start, decision makers should get rid of alternatives that have weak to moderate chances of being chosen.

On the other hand, alternatives with no chance to being chosen do not have these negative effects: they may even reinforce motivation and commitment. One strategy is to propose alternatives which are clearly unacceptable but which highlight by comparison the virtues of an acceptable alternative. This defines the situation as not being of the wait-and-see type: rejecting one alternative means accepting another. Another and more important effect is that commitments become doublesided: commitments arise not only through endorsements of acceptable alternatives but also through criticisms of unacceptable alternatives. Thus, considering two alternatives can lay a stronger foundation for action than considering only one alternative if one of the two alternatives is clearly unacceptable.

One example is the decision process following the merger of Sweden's three largest steel companies. The merger was supposed to make production more efficient by concentrating each kind of production in one steelworks. A six-month-long decision process considered several alternative ways of redistributing production. Besides the alternative that was actually chosen, however, only one alternative was investigated thoroughly. This was the alternative to make no change at all. Because this alternative would have made the merger meaningless, no one considered it a practical action.

Estimating Consequences

Decision makers who want to make rational decisions are supposed to consider all relevant consequences that alternatives might have; positive and negative consequences should get equal attention. But such a procedure evokes much uncertainty, for inconsistent information produces bewilderment and doubt, and stimulates conflicts among decision makers (Hoffman, 1968). Also, it is difficult to weigh positive and negative consequences together (Slovic, 1966).

One way of avoiding uncertainty is to search for consequences in only one direction—to seek support for the initial opinion about an alternative. People tend to anchor their judgements in the first cues they perceive (Slovic, 1972; Tversky and Kahneman, 1974). Searching for positive consequences of an acceptable alternative has high priority, while negative consequences are suppressed. The purpose is not only to avoid uncertainty: active search for arguments in favour of an alternative also helps to create enthusiasm and to increase commitments. If negative consequences do pop up, adding more positive consequences can at least help to maintain commitment and motivation.

For example, in a company with high propensity to undertake innovative product-development projects, personnel spent most of their discussions collecting arguments in favour of specific projects. This helped them to build up enthusiasm for projects—an enthusiasm that they deemed necessary to overcome difficulties (Brunsson, 1976).

Evaluating Alternatives

The rational model prescribes that alternatives and their consequences should be evaluated according to predetermined criteria, preferably in the form of objectives. Decision makers are told to start with objectives and then to find out what effects the alternatives would have on them. This is a dangerous strategy from the action point of view because there is a high risk that decision makers will formulate inconsistent objectives and will have difficulties assessing alternatives. Data are needed that are difficult or impossible to find, and different pieces of information may point in conflicting directions.

For producing action, a better strategy is to start from the consequences and to invent the objectives afterwards (Lindblom, 1959). Predicted consequences are judged to be good because they can be reformulated as desirable objectives. The relations between alternatives and objectives are not investigated in detail, only enough to demonstrate some positive links. The objectives are arguments, not criteria for choice; they are instruments for motivation and commitment, not for investigation. The argumentative role of objectives becomes evident in situations where objectives are abandoned after data indicate that they will not be promoted by preferred actions.

For instance, the calculations in the merged steel company actually demonstrated that the no-change alternative would be at least as profitable as the alternative that was chosen. The decision makers then shifted their criterion from profitability as defined in the calculations to criteria such as access to a harbour and the age of a steelworks—criteria which favoured the alternative to be chosen.

Choosing

Within the decision-making perspective, a decision is normally described as a choice which follows automatically from preceding analysis. But when decision making initiates action, a choice is not merely a statement of preference for one alternative but an expression of commitment to carrying out an action. A choice can be formulated in diverse ways which express different degrees of commitment and enthusiasm. Which people participate in choosing influences which people participate in acting.

A local government with an unstable majority postponed for eight years a decision about where to build new houses. Yet, at every time, there existed a majority favouring one location. Majority support was not thought to be a sufficient basis for the complicated and time-consuming planning work to follow (Brunsson, 1981; Jönsson, 1982).

Making Rational Use of Irrationality

The purpose of action calls for irrationality. Some irrationalities are consistent with the prescriptions of Lindblom (1959) who argued that thorough rational analyses are irrelevant for the incremental steps in American national policy. But irrationality is even more valuable for actions involving radical changes, because motivation and commitment are crucial.

Much of the decision irrationality observed in decision processes can be explained as action rationality. The hypothesis that such may be the case is worth considering at least in situations where motivation and commitment are highly beneficial. For example, this kind of explanation can be applied to some of the strategic decisions described by Janis (1972). Much of the irrationality Janis observed in the decision of the Kennedy administration to invade Cuba can be explained by the fact that such risky and normally illegitimate actions needed extreme motivation and commitment to be adopted. Strong motivations and commitments seem actually to have arisen, and they led to very strong efforts to complete the action in spite of great difficulties and uncertainties.

According to Janis, better alternatives would have been found if the decision process had been more rational, giving room for more criticism, alternative perspectives and doubts. Perhaps so. But deciding more rationally in order to avoid big failures is difficult advice to follow. If the decisions should initiate actions, the irrationality is functional and should not be replaced by more rational decision procedures. Rational analyses are more appropriate where motivation and commitment offer weak benefits. This is true for actions which are less significant, less complicated and short-term. Lundberg (1961) observed that investment calculations are made for small, marginal investments but not for large, strategic ones. If one believes that rational decision processes lead to better choices, this observation should be disquieting. Moreover, important actions tend to be carried out with strong motivations and commitments, which make it difficult to stop or change directions if the actions prove to be mistakes.

There is also the opposite risk—that decision rationality impedes difficult but necessary actions. For actions involving major organizational changes, the magnitudes of the issues and the uncertainties involved may frighten people into making analyses as carefully as possible At the same time, the uncertainty potentials and the involvements of many people heighten the risks that rational decision making will obstruct action

One extreme and pathological case of decision making giving no basis for action is decision orientation This occurs when people regard decision making as their only activities, not caring about the actions and not even presuming that there will be actions In full accordance with the decision-making perspective, these people look upon decisions as end points. In one political organization, for instance, the politicians facilitated their decision making substantially by concentrating on making decisions and ignoring subsequent actions. Since the decisions were not to be carried out, the politicians did not have to worry about negative effects, and they could easily reach agreements. On the other hand, the lack of actions threatened the survival of the organization.

To sum up, rational decision-making procedures fulfill the function of choice—they lead to the selection of action alternatives. But organizations face two problems: to choose the right thing to do and to get it done. There are two kinds of rationality, corresponding to these two problems: decision rationality and action rationality. The one is not better than the other, but they serve different purposes and imply different norms. The two kinds of rationality are difficult to pursue simultaneously because rational decision-making procedures are irrational from an action perspective; they should be avoided if actions are to be facilitated.

How can the problem of choice and the problem of action be solved concurrently? One way is to solve the problem of choice by means of ideologies instead of by decisions. Ideologies can fulfill the function of choice without impeding actions. This is the theme of the next section.

IDEOLOGIES THAT FACILITATE ACTIONS

Recent research has stressed other cognitive aspects of organizational life than decision making. Organizational members share interests which determine their participation in an organization. They also perceive similarly the organization, its environment, its history and its future. Some shared knowledge, perspectives and attitudes persist over time (Clark, 1972; Jönsson and Lundin, 1977; Starbuck, 1976; Starbuck et al., 1978). These cognitive phenomena, or parts of them, have been given names such as frames of reference, myths or strategies; here they are called organizational ideologies.

An ideology is a set of ideas. A person's ideas about one particular object or situation is here called a cognitive structure. Because people can be more or less closely related to their ideas, it is possible to distinguish three kinds of organizational ideologies. One kind is the members' individual cognitive structures. These can be called *subjective ideologies*. The members also have ideas of the cognitive structures of their colleagues. These ideas are *perceived ideologies;* what people think other people think. Finally, *objective ideologies* are ideas which are shared by all organizational members and which afford common bases for discussion and action. These different kinds of ideologies are at least partly inconsistent.

Ideologies describe both how things are and how they should be, and these two aspects are often strongly interdependent. Both the descriptive and the normative aspects answer questions about reality. One question is *how*? How do the members act in relation to each other or to people outside the organization? Another question is *what*? What has happened (history), or what will (expectations)? Ideologies define not only what is perceived as fact but also which facts appear important. Thirdly, ideologies can answer the question *why*? Causes may be attributed to an individual member, to the whole organization (self-attribution), or to the organization's environments (environmental attribution).

Organizational ideologies interrelate closely with decisions, since they make it easier for people to agree on what objectives to pursue, on what action alternatives hold promise, and on what outcomes are probable. Ideologies afford short-cuts in decision making by enabling decision makers to omit or abbreviate some steps and by filtering out some alternatives and consequences (March and Simon, 1958).

Ideologies also substitute for decisions. Many organizational actions do not follow decision processes; agreement and coordination arise without decision making, because the actors perceive situations similarly and share expectations and general values (Danielsson and Malmberg, 1979).

In the innovative company mentioned earlier, most ideas for product-development projects clearly matched the ideology. Such proposals could be accepted and projects started without explicit decisions. Instead of carrying out decision-making processes, management engaged in supporting the proposals by arousing commitments and strengthening the expectations that the projects would succeed.

Organizational ideologies tend to arise by themselves in any organization, but according to some authors, they can also be consciously moulded by an organization's members (Ansoff et al., 1976; Lorange and Vancil, 1977;

Starbuck et al., 1978). This suggests that ideologies can be formed with the direct purpose of avoiding rational decision making, thus reinforcing the potential for taking difficult actions. In fact, organizational ideologies might reconcile the tasks of thinking and of acting, because ideologies might identify appropriate actions and also contribute to their accomplishment.

If ideologies are to take the place of rational decision making, confrontations between proposed actions and ideologies should give clear results. It should be possible to classify a proposal as acceptable or unacceptable after little analysis and discussion. There should be high consistency among the cognitive structures of individual organizational members. There should not only be common ideologies to undergird discussions, but these objective ideologies should be very conclusive—so clear and so narrow that additional filters for ideas are unnecessary.

Conclusiveness could be accomplished by objective ideologies that include just a few, precise normative statements. However, a confrontation between very simple ideologies and a nonconforming action proposal might throw the ideologies into question rather than the proposal. Complex ideologies that make contingent statements about an organization and its environments can also be conclusive, and such ideologies are unlikely to be challenged by a single action proposal.

A comparison between two companies revealed that the one with narrow, clear and complex objective ideologies was able to accomplish great changes in its product mix, whereas the company with broad, ambiguous and simple ideologies had great difficulties getting new products into production (Brunsson, 1979). Ideologies which are clear, narrow, differentiated, complex and consistent can provide good bases for action because they solve a large part of the choice problem. Such ideologies can determine what actions are right, so analysis is minimized, and efforts can concentrate on reinforcing actions. Decision rationality can be used for forming ideologies, and action rationality can be used for forming actions. Thinking can be separated from acting.

Attribution is important too. If the outcomes of action are believed to depend on environmental events, an organization should construct forecasts of the type prescribed by rational models. If the outcomes seem to depend on what members do within an organization itself, the key task is to create motivations and commitments. Thus, environmental attribution fits decision rationality, whereas self-attribution facilitates action rationality.

IDEOLOGICAL SHIFTS THAT FOSTER RADICAL CHANGES

Actions that would radically change an organization's relations to its environments are typically difficult to carry out and need strong commitments and high motivations, so ideologies should endorse these actions precisely and enthusiastically. But such ideologies constrain the possibilities for change, because only changes that match the ideologies receive ideological support.

Changes within narrow ideologies do sometimes suffice. Often, however, organizations need quick and radical changes to accommodate rapid environmental changes, and precise ideologies would rule out changes which are radical enough to cope with these situations. Yet, broad and ambiguous ideologies would not afford strong bases for action. A company which regards itself a transportation company may be no more flexible than one which considers railways its domain. There seems to be a dilemma: radical changes require conflicting qualities of organizational ideologies.

There is a solution, however. Again, the trick is to separate thinking from acting. If change actions are preceded by ideological shifts, they can attract enough support to be accomplished. This implies that change actions should wait until new ideologies have been established.

If ideologies are to serve as bases for choice, they must resist pressures for change and change slowly. In fact, the slowness of ideological shifts can explain the long time-lags before organizations respond to important threats in their environments, even when the threats seem obvious to external observers (Starbuck et al., 1978).

The need for complex and precise ideologies that shift explains the 'myth cycles' reported by Jönsson and Lundin (1977). They found that organizations jump from one dominant ideology, or myth, to another. Belief in a dominant ideology is strong under normal conditions, and the dominant ideology is questioned only during crises. When members lose faith in a dominant ideology, they replace it by another. Such myth cycles imply a strong belief in one objective ideology and a consistency between subjective and objective ideologies which seem irrational from a decision-making point of view. On the other hand, the cycles contain much action rationality. A dominant ideology maximizes an organization's ability to act. Consensus and strong adherence to one ideology are not merely results of people's analytical and perceptual deficiencies; they are necessary conditions for organizational survival.

If radical changes have to be initiated by ideological shifts, it becomes a crucial issue how ideologies can be changed. External factors—such as crises or shifts in leadership—may be important, as may the properties of ideologies themselves. What properties make ideologies apt to shift when shifts are needed? Fortunately, the same properties that make ideologies good bases for action make them apt to change. Precision and complexity facilitate both.

Because descriptive statements in ideologies can be checked against reality, changes in reality provide incentives for ideological shifts. The more factors an ideology considers, the greater is the chance that some of them will change; and the more causal links among these factors, the more repercussions a change in one of them will have. If statements are clear, they can be proved false, and they have weak chances of surviving drastic changes in reality. The most stable ideologies are simple ones which are both vague and widely applicable—such as, our goal is profitability, or we shall operate in the transportation industry.

Paradoxically, the refining and elaborating of ideologies are steps toward abandoning them. However, a situation from which a change is initiated need not have much in common with the situation in which the change occurs. Existing ideologies are threatened when their implications contradict observations. If these threats cannot be met by making ideologies more ambiguous, inconsistencies arise within both subjective and objective ideologies. If subjective ideologies change more rapidly than the objective ideologies, inconsistencies arise between the subjective and the objective ideologies, so belief in objective ideologies decreases. Diverse subjective ideologies appear, and these may correspond to social structures different from the ones founded upon the old ideologies. The result is inconsistency between an organization's social and its ideological structures, inconsistency which gives less room for compromise and authority. Differences between what people think privately and the ideologies to which they can refer publicly in their discussions give rise to misunderstandings. When people misinterpret each others' statements, conflicts arise, escalate and remain difficult to resolve. Once the objective ideologies have been questioned, many people see chances to change the organization's environments, its internal functioning and their own positions. The differences increase between what is and what should be, with regard to what goals to pursue, how things should be done, and who should control events.

Ideological shifts afford very bad contexts for action. Ideological inconsistencies increase uncertainty and make it extremely difficult to marshall commitments for organizational actions. Conflicts interfere with coordination. Simultaneous attempts to change environments, the ways things are done, and who has control may easily exceed an organization's problem-solving abilities. Thus, an ideological shift has to be completed before acting begins. In fact, an ideological shift in one organization produced a complete inability to act, a social deadlock where everyone worked for change, but their individual actions actually impeded change, and where no one understood how to break out of this frustrating situation (Brunsson, 1981). A social deadlock is a steady state: it is full of activities, but these activities stabilize the situation, reinforcing the deadlock. A productive ideological shift must be a step in a process which leads to something new.

The difference between social deadlocks and productive ideological shifts has two implications. The first implication concerns observers of organizational changes: they might mistake confused situations for productive ideological states. Since confused situations precede the actions that create radical changes, observers might infer that confused situations produce changes, and that organizations should try to remain confused in order to have high propensities to change and high abilities to adapt to changing environments (Hedberg and Jönsson, 1978). This inference neglects the transitional character of confused situations, and it mistakes processes of change for initiators of change. The confused situation during an ideological shift may resemble neither its predecessor nor its successor. On the contrary, consistent, clear and complex ideologies are both good starting points for ideological shifts and desirable results of the shifts. Consensus rather than conflict breeds change.

The second implication is more practical: ideological shifts may become steady states. Social deadlocks are created and maintained by vicious circles in which ideological confusion leads to more confusion, and conflicts lead to still more conflicts. The confusion and conflict during an ideological shift bring an organization to the brink of social deadlock. How to prevent social deadlocks is an intriguing question for research.

CONCLUSIONS

This article discusses two aspects of organizations' thinking: decision making and ideologies. Observations of organizations demonstrate that both aspects tend to be irrational in the traditional meaning of the word. Many decisions are based on biased information about a biased set of two alternatives, sometimes only one, and the information is weighed improperly. Organizational ideologies focus members' perceptions on just a few aspects of reality, and members' confidence in their biased perceptions greatly exceeds what seems justified. Organizational processes systematically reduce, rather than exploit, the multitude perceptions that numerous people could have brought in.

These irrationalities appear both harmful and difficult to explain if the main purpose of an organization's thinking is to choose the right actions. However, the main problem for organizations is not choice but taking organized actions. Decision making and ideologies form bases for action and can be fully understood only by recognizing that function. Thinking must be adapted to the purpose of action; and, in that perspective, irrational decision making and narrow, prejudicial ideologies are necessary ingredients of viable organizations inhabiting complex and rough environments.

Organizations have two problems in relation to action—to find out what to do and to do it. When confronting difficult actions, organizations separate these problems. Organizations solve the problem of choice by forming ideologies, then the activities preceding specific actions focus on creating motivations and commitments.

Getting things done is particularly problematic in political organizations. These organizations institutionalize conflict: people are recruited on the basis that they adhere to disparate ideologies, and these ideological differences persist in spite of common membership in the same organizations. The ideological differences block radical actions because each proposed action is scrutinized from diverse viewpoints. Actions are supposed to be initiated by rational decision procedures that integrate the disparate viewpoints. Thus, proposed actions that involve major changes are rejected, and the organizations move in small steps (Brunsson and Jönsson, 1979). Generally, political organizations try to generate action by forming strong majorities. Where this is impossible, the problems aggravate.

Lindblom (1959) argued that irrationalities can be accepted in national policy making because policies develop incrementally. The conclusion here is instead that the high degree of rationality in political organizations produces incrementalism. It is rationality, not irrationality, that is tied to incrementalism.

Decisions and actions can also be separated organizationally. Civil servants can take actions, while the politicians discuss and debate. This heightens the chances of powerful actions but decreases the politicians' influence over what actions to take. Strong political influence seems to hinder radical changes even if there is a strong majority.

In Sweden, the control of industrial companies is shifting from managers to groups representing diverse interests, such as unions, local governments, and regional and national authorities. The industrial companies are becoming more and more like political organizations. Finding ways to combine influence by diverse groups with ability to act is a pressing challenge for organizational research.

REFERENCE

Ackerman, B. A., Ross-Ackerman, S., Sawyer, J. W. and Henderson, D. W. (1974). *The Uncertain Research for Environmental Quality*. New York: Free Press.

Ansoff, H. I., Declerck, R. P. and Hayes, R. L. (Eds.) (1976). *From Strategic Planning to Strategic Management*. New York: Wiley.

Argyris, C. (1977). 'Organizational learning and management information systems'. *Accounting, Organizations and Society*, **2**, 113–23.

Brunsson, N. (1976). *Propensity to Change*. Göteborg, Sweden: B.A.S.

Brunsson, N. (1979). 'The fallacy of accepting everything as a strategy for change'. *Munich Social Science Review*, **2**, 29–39.

Brunsson, N. (1980). 'The functions of project evaluation'. *R & D Management*, **10**, 61–5.

Brunsson, N. (1981). *Politik och administration*. Stockholm: Liber.

Brunsson, N. and Jönsson, S. (1979). *Beslut och handling*. Falköping, Sweden: Liber.

Chandler, A. D. (1977). *The Visible Hand*. Cambridge, Mass.: Belknap.

Churchman, C. W. (1964). 'Managerial acceptance of scientific recommendations'. *California Management Review*, **7**, 31–8.

Clark, B. R. (1972). 'The organizational saga in higher education'. *Administrative Science Quarterly*, **17**, 178–84.

Cyert, R. M. and March, J. G. (1963). *A Behavioral Theory of the Firm*. Englewood Cliffs, N.J.: Prentice-Hall.

Danielsson, A. and Malmberg, A. (1979). *Beslut fattas*. Stockholm: S.A.F.

Galbraith, J. K. (1967). *The New Industrial State*. Boston, Mass.: Houghton Mifflin.

GOLDBERG, L. R. (1968). 'Simple models or simple processes? Some research on clinical judgments'. *American Psychologist*, **23**, 483–96.

HARVEY, A. (1970). 'Factors making for implementation success and failure'. *Management Science, Series B*, **16**, 312–20.

HEDBERG, B. L. T. and JÖNSSON, S. A. (1978). 'Designing semi-confusing information systems for organizations in changing environments'. *Accounting, Organizations and Society*, **3**, 47–64.

HOFFMAN, P. J. (1968). 'Cue-consistency and configurality in human judgement'. In Kleinmetz B. (Ed.), *Formal Representation of Human Judgement*. New York: Wiley.

HUYSMANS, J. H. (1970). 'The effectiveness of the cognitive style constraint in implementing operations research proposals'. *Management Science*, **17**, 99–103.

JANIS, I. L. (1972). *Victims of Groupthink*. Boston, Mass.: Houghton Mifflin.

JÖNSSON, S. A. (1982). 'Cognitive turning in municipal problem solving'. *Journal of Management Studies*, **19**, 63–73.

JÖNSSON, S. A. and LUNDIN, R. A. (1977). 'Myths and wishful thinking as management tools'. In Nystrom, P. C. and Starbuck, W. H. (Eds.), *Prescriptive Models of Organizations*. Amsterdam: North-Holland, 157–70.

KAHNEMAN, D. and TVERSKY, A. (1973). 'On the psychology of prediction'. *Psychological Review*, **80**, 237–51.

KEENEY, R. L. and RAIFFA, H. (1976). *Decisions with Multiple Objectives*. New York: Wiley.

LINDBLOM, C. E. (1959). 'The science of "muddling through" '. *Public Administration Review*, **19**, 79–88.

LINDBLOM, C. E. (1977). *Politics and Markets*. New York: Basic Books.

LORANGE, P. and VANCIL, R. F. (1977). *Strategic Planning Systems*. Englewood Cliffs, N.J.: Prentice-Hall.

LUNDBERG, E. (1961). *Produktivitet och räntabilitet*. Stockholm: S.N.S.

MARCH, J. G. and OLSEN, J. P. (Eds.) (1976). *Ambiguity and Choice in Organizations*. Bergen: Universitetsforlaget.

MARCH, J. G. and SIMON, H. A. (1958). *Organizations*. New York: Wiley.

MURDICK, R. G. and ROSS, J. E. (1975). *Information Systems for Modern Management*. Englewood Cliffs, N.J.: Prentice-Hall.

NISBETT, R. and ROSS, L. (1980). *Human Inference*. Englewood Cliffs, N.J.: Prentice-Hall.

PREST, A. R. and TURVEY, R. (1965). 'Cost-benefit analysis: a survey'. *Economic Journal*, **75**, 685–705.

SLOVIC, P. (1966). 'Cue consistency and cue utilization in judgement'. *American Journal of Psychology*, **79**, 427–34.

SLOVIC, P. (1972). *From Shakespeare to Simon*. Portland: Oregon Research Institute.

STARBUCK, W. H. (1976). 'Organizations and their environments'. In Dunnette, M. D. (Ed.), *Handbook of Industrial and Organizational Psychology*. Chicago: Rand McNally, 1069–123.

STARBUCK, W. H., GREVE, A. and HEDBERG, B. L. T. (1978). 'Responding to Crises'. *Journal of Business Administration*, **9**, 2, 111–37.

TARKOWSKY, Z. M. (1958). 'Symposium: problems in decision taking'. *Operational Research Quarterly*, **9**, 121–3.

TVERSKY, A. and KAHNEMAN, D. (1974). 'Judgement under uncertainty: heuristics and biases'. *Science*, **185**, 1124–31.

ZANDER, A. (1971). *Motives and Goals in Groups*. New York: Academic Press.

[28]

Accounting, Organizations and Society, Vol. 12, No. 3, pp. 235–265, 1987.
Printed in Great Britain

0361–3682/87 $3.00+.00
Pergamon Journals Ltd.

ACCOUNTING AND THE CONSTRUCTION OF THE GOVERNABLE PERSON*

PETER MILLER
Division of Economic Studies, University of Sheffield

and

TED O'LEARY
Department of Accounting, University College, Cork

Abstract

The concern of the paper is historical. It addresses one familiar event within the literature of the history of accounting — the construction of theories of standard costing and budgeting in the first three decades of the twentieth century. A different interpretation of this event is offered from that commonly found. This is seen to have significant implications for the relevance of historical investigation to the understanding of contemporary accounting practices. Instead of an interpretation of standard costing and budgeting as one stage in the advance in accuracy and refinement of accounting concepts and techniques, it is viewed as an important calculative practice which is part of a much wider modern apparatus of power which emerges conspicuously in the early years of this century. The concern of this form of power is seen to be the construction of the individual person as a more manageable and efficient entity. This argument is explored through an examination of the connections of standard costing and budgeting with scientific management and industrial psychology. These knowledges are then related to others which, more or less simultaneously, were emerging beyond the confines of the firm to address questions of the efficiency and manageability of the individual. The more general aim of the paper is to suggest some elements of a theoretical understanding of accounting which would locate it in its interrelation with other projects for the social and organisational management of individual lives.

Accounting has remained remarkably insulated from important theoretical and historical debates which have traversed the social sciences. Accounting history, for example, is a context in which one can begin to substantiate this lack of a problematisation of the roles of accounting. A standard concept which guides accounting history is one that sees accounting as essentially having functional roles in society, albeit ones which can change (American Accounting Association, 1970). Little or no suspicion seems to surface that different methodological starting points could be entertained, which could lead to rather different understandings of accounting's history.

There are ripples, however. Recently there

* Earlier drafts of this paper were presented at the Symposium of the Roles of Accounting in Organizations and Society, University of Wisconsin–Madison, U.S.A., July 1984, and at the Accounting Workshop of the European Institute for Advanced Studies in Management, Brussels, Belgium, December 1984. We are obliged to the participants at both gatherings for very helpful comments.

We express our thanks especially to Anthony Hopwood for ideas and encouragement, and for suggesting this collaboration. Ted O'Leary is grateful for the financial support of the Management Fund and the Development Fund, University College, Cork. We are both grateful to the Symposium Organizers, University of Wisconsin–Madison, for their financial contributions towards travel costs.

have been attempts to indicate the directions which a fully social interpretation of accounting might follow (Burchell *et al.*, 1979, 1980). These seem to us to be very useful first steps.

Our concern in this paper can be designated historical. We are concerned with the emergence of standard costing and budgeting in the early decades of this century and the way this can be related to other social practices. To identify our concern as historical is, however, to beg the question as to the meaning and significance of historical analysis. Care is needed in formulating an appeal to an historical viewpoint from which to understand changes in accounting thought and practice. There are a number of quite different ways in which to understand the contribution of an historical perspective. One request voiced from time to time is for more histories (see e.g. Parker, 1981, p. 290; Solomons, 1968, p. 17). These would, it is suggested, uncover the how and the what of accounting. What, for instance, was actually accounted for in a particular firm in the early nineteenth century? It is tempting to rally around this call. It has an innocent appeal and would appear to have undeniable force.

In one sense we have no objection to the call for more facts. However, the simplicity of the request can be misleading. We would like to propose a different agenda for the interpretation of accounting's past, one which casts a different light on the understanding of accounting practices. This is one which we feel has considerable relevance for understanding accounting today, and which enables us to develop a theoretical understanding of accounting as a social and organisational practice.

One conception of accounting history, which appears to have a significant level of acceptance at the present time, is one which sees accounting as changing, or capable of being changed, in response to demands expressed or implied by a changing environment. It is a notion of accounting history in which references to the metaphor of evolution are not infrequent (American Accounting Association, 1970; Chatfield, 1977; Littleton & Zimmerman, 1962; Lee & Parker, 1979; Kaplan, 1984). What is here required of accounting history, it would seem, is that (purely aesthetic consideration apart) it should seek to elucidate:

> the evolution in accounting thought, practices and institutions in response to changes in the environment and societal needs. It also (should consider) ... the effect that this evolution has worked on the environment (American Accounting Association, 1970, p. 53).

The utility of accounting history, its potential in relation to current theoretical and practical concerns, is that through elucidating the resolution of past incongruities of accounting with its environment, it could facilitate the more effective resolution of such issues in the present. The image to be gained is that accounting can enmesh with its context in ways that are inevitable, given some overwhelming environmental shift, and that may even be socially desirable. We do not find such an interpretation of accounting's history to be persuasive. In particular, the functional tone of the very language in which accounting history is defined significantly obliterates the possibility of accounting's location, along with a range of other social practices, in relation to modes of operation of power.

One way of countering such an approach is to invert the perspective. Accounting would then no longer be viewed as becoming, or as having capacity to become, an increasingly refined technical apparatus. It would also no longer be viewed as neutral but rather seen, once the veils of current misperception have been drawn back, to clearly reflect and to serve certain economic or political interests. Such an approach has achieved considerable currency when applied to disciplines other than accounting (see, e.g. Baritz, 1960; Scull, 1979; Stedman-Jones, 1971).

We are not persuaded by this line of argument either. Central to it is a notion that there is a more or less direct and unproblematic relation between economic and/or political interests, and the knowledges and techniques which are held to represent such interests. The terms and categories through which such interests are represented are seen to have no effects. Whether it is a thesis centered on a notion of knowledge as a "servant of power" (Baritz, 1960) or knowledge viewed as representing class interests, the difficulties remain. The notion of control in such a view comes to substitute for notions of progress or evolution in standard histories. Whereas the latter see accounting as progressing in terms of an unproblematic social utility, the former see history as the elaboration of better and more subtle forms of control.

It seems to us that there is a very real need to develop an understanding of accounting and its past which is distinct from these two approaches. This is the thrust of our attempt in this paper, undertaken through a discussion of the emergence of standard costing and budgeting within the accounting literature, and the relation between these and a number of other related social and organisational practices. Our concern is with a particular episode in the history of accounting which we see as crucial, and its relevance and implications for understanding contemporary accounting.

If our concern in this paper can be called historical, it entails an understanding of historical processes which is unfamiliar in the accounting literature. It may be useful to refer to one or two landmarks in relation to which the concerns of this paper may be identified.

The interpretation of historical processes we have utilized takes much of its inspiration from the work of Michel Foucault and his associates (Castel *et al.*, 1982; Donzelot, 1979; Foucault, 1973, 1977, 1981). In no sense would we wish to suggest that such studies offer a panacea for thinking about accounting. In any case they do not directly address accounting or for that matter economic processes. But despite the difference in the field of study we feel that there is something distinctive in such an approach which is useful in an attempt to understand accounting as a social and organisational practice. Clearly we can do no more here than point to what we see to be some important themes. A number of recent studies address these issues in much greater depth (Sheridan, 1980; Cousins & Hussain, 1984; Burchell *et al.*, forthcoming; Miller, forthcoming).

Over a period of some twenty years Michel Foucault has worked on what can be called a series of histories of the emergence of the human sciences. His studies have covered medicine (Foucault, 1973), the emergence of psychiatry (Foucault, 1967), and the prison (Foucault, 1977) to name just some of the more important. The historical focus for these has generally been on the period around 1800 which he sees as a crucial point in the formation of the modern era. Other writers in a similar vein have explored the period closer to the present day (Donzelot, 1979; Castel *et al.*, 1982). Alongside the historical studies a number of methodological issues concerning the understanding of historical processes have been addressed (Foucault, 1972, 1981). In the more recent studies an explicit concern with the issue of power has emerged.

There are three issues we would like to single out for our purposes here from this vast and still growing body of material. These concern what can be called a "genealogical" question concerning the role of historical investigation; an "archaeological" question concerning the way one goes about doing history; and a thesis concerning the interdependence of bodies of knowledge and relations of power.

The notion of genealogy is deceptively simple. It concerns centrally a questioning of our contemporarily received notions by a demonstration of their historical emergence. The point of history in this sense is to make intelligible the way in which we think today by reminding us of its conditions of formation. Whether the terms be efficiency, rationality or motivation, genealogical analysis helps us to appreciate their ephemeral character. But genealogy is not just a matter of de-bunking, a valuable enough enterprise in its own right. It concerns also a particular approach to the tracing of the emergence of our frequently unquestioned contemporary rationales. This is one which does not entail looking for a single point in history which would be the point of origin of our current practices. The emergence of our contemporary beliefs is viewed rather by reference to a complex of dispersed events. Genealogy does not lead us to solid foundations; rather, it fragments and disturbs what we might like to see as the basis of our current ideas and practices. Applied to accounting it means questioning a search for the origins of accounting in the invention of techniques, whether in recent centuries or in antiquity. Other types of events, such as the political objectives of states, but also historical contingency, particular national conditions and the development of related disciplines, all enter into the explanation. Genealogy opens out into a much less certain field than the standard histories of accounting would lead us to believe.

The archaeological question is historical also. Its focus is on our most legitimated forms of contemporary discourse, and the real historical conditions which have led to their emergence. It concerns the more sociological aspects of the emergence and functioning of discourses as well as their internal conceptual features. The status of our most legitimated forms of discourse (law and medicine, for example, but also economics and accounting) are seen to depend, amongst other things, on institutional and legal criteria as well as on pedagogical norms for their functioning. Archaeology directs our attention to these features of discourse. It also has an epistemological aspect. This concerns the relationship between discourses and the objects to which they refer. Again there is an element of de-bunking. Applied to our concerns in this paper one could for instance say that there is no obvious reason why we should have come to talk in terms of efficiency and standards. Such notions do not exist in the object itself or in limbo waiting to be discovered. They are seen rather to have been formed in a complex of relations established between a heterogeneous range of discourses and practices. This is why we talk below of the standard costing and budgeting complex, and relate it to a range of other discourses and practices which share a common vocabulary and set of objectives. Standard costing is, we suggest, intertwined with other attempts within the enterprise and outside it to embark on a vast project of standardisation and normalisation of the lives of individuals. It is, we argue, to this web of relations established between, for example, basic technical requirements and adjustments, and elaborate forms of philosophical discourse, that one should look in trying to understand redefinitions of the practice of accounting. It is the positive conditions of a complex group of relations within which accounting exists that we should address.

The third aspect of Foucault's work of relevance to this paper concerns the relationship between knowledge and power. Foucault's arguments on this question are distinctive. He suggests that we can understand the development of modern societies in terms of power, and the shift in its mode of exercise. The broadest shift he refers to is one which he suggests took place around 1800 and is from what he calls sovereign power to disciplinary power. Sovereign power is identified as a diminished form of power. Its ultimate recourse is seizure — of things, of bodies and ultimately of life. Disciplinary power is much richer and entails penetrating into the very web of social life through a vast series of regulations and tools for the administration of entire populations and of the minutae of people's lives. The calculated management of social life is one way of designating the form of operation of disciplinary power. It can be witnessed, Foucault suggests, in the fields of public health, housing, concerns with longevity, but also in the schools, workshops, barracks and prisons.

Foucault's arguments concerning power are closely linked to his investigation of the emergence of the human sciences (Foucault, 1970). The shift he identifies from sovereign to disciplinary power is intimately connected with changes in our forms of knowledge. His argument is expressed in the formula "power/knowledge" and the constitutive interdependence of the two terms of the equation — the operation of the human sciences should be understood in relation to the elaboration of a range of techniques for the supervision, administration and disciplining of populations of human individuals. This is seen to take place in particular institutions and in social relations in a wider sense. This is not to suggest that all institutions are homogeneous and coterminous with the type of administration which occurs in society at large. Viewed in terms of power and at the level of certain general principles for its operation there is nonetheless held to be an important inter-relation between a diverse range of practices.

Our attempt in this paper to understand one particular important period in accounting's history has been influenced by these three broad themes. However the historical period Foucault's researches address, the institutions they concern, and the absence of a clearly identifiable "method" mean that we cannot claim to be testing a method by transposing its field of application. We have studied a different period, namely that around the year 1900, and a different discipline, namely accounting. In our preliminary investigations we were led to formulate a number of working propositions, and it is these which directly inform the paper. These concern general methodological principles, an attempt to locate accounting within a wider set of calculative techniques, and some reflections on the level of our analysis and what we see to be its significance. It may be useful to briefly comment on the most important of these concerns.

A first and general methodological postulate can be called "constructivist". By this we mean that we have been concerned with the way accounting, in conjunction with other practices, serves to construct a particular field of visibility. Rather than view accounting as a neutral tool of observation we have attempted to examine how accounting assists in rendering visible certain crucial aspects of the functioning of the enterprise. Questions of wastage and efficiency are examples which we address in the paper.

A second point which emerged in our reading of the literature was that this process of rendering visible alighted on the individual person. More particularly it did so by surrounding the individual at work by a series of norms and standards. Through such norms and standards the inefficiencies of the person were rendered clearly visible. This was a novel step for accounting. It is significant also in relation to the issue of power identified above. At the risk of being misunderstood we shall be highly schematic to register what we see to be the significant change brought about by the emergence of standard costing and budgeting and their alliance with scientific management, topics which we address in detail below. In the nineteenth century discipline within the enterprise took the form of direct confrontations between the worker and the boss. In the early twentieth century, and through the changes we will be referring to, the employee comes to be surrounded by calculative norms and standards, interposing between him and the boss a whole range of intermediary mechanisms. With this shift discipline comes to be seen to reside not in the will of the boss but in the economic machine itself, in the norms and standards from which the worker can be seen to depart. Accounting is, we argue, an important aspect of this development of a range of calculative programmes and techniques which come to regulate the lives of individuals at work in the early twentieth century. It is for this reason that we talk of standard costing as being located within a significant reorientation of the exercise of power within the enterprise.

A third issue we wanted to address is the wider framework within which changes in accounting took place. Our concern in the paper is with the enterprise and the nation, viewing these as distinct levels for the elaboration of a range of techniques of supervision and administration of individual lives. Extending our view beyond the enterprise and beyond accounting it became clear to us that an important redefinition of the tasks and objectives of government took place around the early years of this century. Central to this redefinition was the emergence of the social sciences, in particular psychology and sociology. In conjunction with a changed conception of the role of the state, the social sciences were able to enter an alliance with the state and to undertake a quite novel form of administration and surveillance of individual lives. Central to this project was the possibility of comparing the capacities of individuals (health, intelligence, longevity) against specific standards. It is our contention that one can understand the emergence of standard costing and budgeting in the early years of the twentieth century by situating it within this more general shift in the form of administration of social life which occurs around the turn of the century.

A fourth and final issue concerns the level of analysis we have undertaken here. We have placed greatest emphasis on what we might call programmatic discourses as opposed to accounting as it was practised in particular firms. This is not because we regard the latter as unimportant. Nor is it because we view our concerns as entirely independent from this more technical level of analysis. To clarify our views it may help to identify what we see to be two distinct orders of events and the interrelation between them. The one we have concentrated on in this paper can be called the discursive programmes for the administration and calculation of activities within the enterprise and in society as a whole. The other we would call technological and concerns the actual operation of accounting practices, their elaboration through particular procedures and techniques. Our point is that these two levels are distinct, yet crucially interdependent. A discursive programme (for the calculation of individual inefficiences, say) only fulfils its vocation when it has as its counterpart an adequate technology. What the programme contributes to the technology is a more general rendering of reality in a form such that it can be known, a rendering visible of certain activities in a way which is intelligible by virtue of certain general categories. A programme is also the space for the articulation of problems, negotiation and conflict over interests. There is, of course, considerable play in the mechanism which links the programmatic level with the technological. Yet it is precisely the looseness of the linkage which makes it important to recall its existence.

These are the principle themes which inform our thinking in this paper. If they have validity for the understanding of accounting as an organisational and social practice the implications are significant. Accounting can no longer be regarded as a neutral and objective process. It comes rather to be viewed as an important part of a network of power relations which are built into the very fabric of organisational and social life. It is a constitutive element in a form of normalising socio-political management whose concern is with rendering visible all forms of activity of the individual in view of their contribution to the efficient operation of the enterprise and of society.

STANDARD COSTING AND BUDGETING

Between 1900 and 1930 there appears in the accounting literature an initial delineation of theories of standard costing and budgeting. This is a novel event within accounting. At a purely technical level the innovation brought about was nothing less than an entire re-casting of the definition of cost accounting. Its primary concern would henceforth no longer be the ascertainment of only the actual costs (Nicholson, 1913; Church, 1917; Epstein, 1978, pp. 90–120), of production or of activities. There would be an expansion of domain to permit a concern for the future as well as for the past.

The virtue of these novel practices lay in their capacity to routinely raise questions of waste and efficiency in the employment of resources, whether human, financial or material, at as many levels of analysis as required. One could, for example, routinely point to, and analyse, variances of actual from standard or plan at the level of the profit of the total firm, or at the level of material or labour use in production or, indeed, at the level of every accountable person within the firm.

The existing histories note the importance of the introduction of standard costing. For Sowell (1973) standard costing entailed the development of a set of techniques and a theoretical rationale for the "scientific" predetermination of the costs of raw material, labour and overhead, as well as for the analysis of the variance of such costs from the actual or historical costs. Solomons (1968) identifies similar themes across a range of writers, in particular Harrington Emerson (1919) and Charter Harrison (1930).

What interests us here is the way the existing histories construe the development of standard costing. They tend to narrate the emergence of standard costing and budgeting according to two distinct criteria. One of these consists in a careful and detailed exposition of the ideas and techniques in the terms of those who, at the time, had developed or articulated them. Such an approach is taken by Sowell (1973) who declares his task as that of presenting "in chronological succession, those related events, forces, individuals, and ideas that have contributed to and/or have developed into" (p. 2) a theoretical and technical complex called standard costing. That achieved, through an immense wealth of source material consulted and described, Sowell ends his work. A second approach, which Solomons (1968) adopts, is to construe these novel practices through the lens of progress, to outline the difficult and often error-prone paths whereby costing has progressed to its current level of sophistication. Thus, for example, he points to "weaknesses" in one of the early outlines of a standard costing, that of Emerson, indicating its failures in analytic power and in clarity of thought relative to writing which follows it in time.

We wish in this paper to place a different interpretation on the emergence of standard costing. We do not view the development of standard costing and budgeting as part of the unfolding of a socially useful theoretical-technical complex, whose underlying logic is one of progress. We wish to locate it rather as an important contribution to a complex of practices which consist in a form of socio-political management whose concern is with individual persons and their efficient functioning.

Standard costing and budgeting provided quite novel theorisation and technique which served to render visible the inefficiencies of the individual person within the enterprise. In routinely raising questions of waste and inefficiency in the employment of human, financial and material resources, they supplemented the traditional concerns of accounting with the fidelity or honesty of the person. Cost accounting could now embrace also the individual person and make them accountable by reference to prescribed standards of performance. With this step accounting significantly extended its domain, enmeshing the person within a web of calculative practices aimed not only at stewardship but efficiency also.

We can identify the shift entailed in the emergence of standard costing during the period 1900 and 1930 across a number of central texts of that period. Garcke & Fells (1911) make the following statement concerning the role of systematic cost accounts and their relevance for managerial action:

> it is only by means of systematic records that leakage, waste, and fraud can be prevented, and that employers can know the cost of any article of their manufacture, and be able to determine accurately and scientifically, not merely approximately and by hap-hazard, the actual profit they make or loss they sustain, not only on the aggregate transactions during a given period, but also upon each individual transaction (Garcke & Fells, 1911, pp. 3–5).

In a similar manner A. L. Dickinson (1908, cited in Garcke & Fells, 1911, pp. 7–8), states the principal objects of a modern cost system. They should comprise:

> (1) Ascertaining the cost of the same product at different periods in the same mill, or at the same period in different mills, and so to remedy inequalities in cost by reducing all to the results shown by the best.
>
> (2) The provision of an accurate, running book of inventories on hand, so facilitating reduction in stocks and capital invested to the lowest state consistent with efficiency.
>
> (3) The preparation of statistical information as to costs of parts, quantity, and variety of output, relative efficiency of different classes of labour, and relative costs of labour and material, between different mills and periods.
>
> (4) The preparation of periodical statements of profit and loss in a condensed form, readily giving directors all material information as to the results of the business.

These statements are admirable in their rigour. It is, however, what is missing from them which is significant for our purposes here. Missing from both is a clear statement of the purposes that might be fulfilled by standard or predetermined costs. Missing, as a consequence, are materials dealing with how a routine technology of standard or predetermined costs might operate.

By 1930 there had been a clear establishment, in texts on both sides of the Atlantic, of several new prominent additions to the vocabulary of costs accounts keeping. These are "the standard cost", "the variance analysis", "the budget", 'budgetary control". This is the rupture with which we are concerned and its implications. One way of designating the change would be from the "registration of costs of production" to "the rendering of all activities capable of suspicion as to their costliness".

Charter Harrison (1930) expresses most clearly the dissatisfaction with the old system and the promise of the new:

> The most serious defect of the job-order cost plan was that it failed, most utterly and dismally to achieve what should be the primary purpose of any cost system, namely, to bring promptly to the attention of the management the existence of preventable inefficiencies so that steps could be taken to eliminate these at the earliest possible moment (Harrison, 1930, p. 8).

And again:

> one of the primary advantages of standard costs . . . is that the clerical work involved in the operating of a properly designed standard cost system is very much less than that required to operate any complete job-order cost plan. That this is so is evident when it is considered that *with standard costs we are dealing with the principle of exceptions, that is to say with variations from the standards* (Harrison, 1930, p. 12, emphasis added).

For our concerns in this paper there is one crucial dimension to this innovation. The principle of standard costs made it possible to attach to every individual within the firm norms and standards of behaviour. Everyone, in relation to all activities which they directly carried out or directed, could be rendered susceptible to a continual process of judgment. This implanting of norms moreover concerned not just norms of physiological behavior for the worker at the bench, but also the mental activity on the part of the executive. Witness Charter Harrison again:

> We have increased the efficiency of the average man because we have applied the principles of scientific management to his work — instead of letting him proceed haphazardly we have set before him carefully determined standards of accomplishment rendered possible by standardization of conditions, and have given him scientific training supplemented by an efficiency reward. We have combined mechanical sciences and psychology, with the result that today every man, woman, and child in this country is reaping the harvest (Harrison, 1930, pp. 27–28).

With this step the possibility of a knowledge of every individual within the enterprise was established. A visibility and an allocation of responsibility could be attached to the individual. The person's activities were at last rendered knowable according to prescribed standards and deviations from the norm. Standard costing and budgeting made possible a pinpointing of responsibilities for preventable inefficiencies at the level of the very individual from whom they derived. The human element in production, and most importantly the individual person, could now be known according to their contribution to the efficiency of the enterprise.

The significance of standard costing and budgeting as an innovation, however, is not only internal to accounting and the organisation and management of the enterprise. We suggest that it should be located alongside the emergence of a range of discourses and practices which, in both Britain and the U.S.A. in the early years of this century, concerned themselves with the physical and mental health of the population. In their concern with efficiency these practices have a macro- and a micro-level concern. They took as their object both the health and efficiency of the nations as a whole, and detailed questions concerning the habits, life-styles and activities of the individual. The underlying preoccupation was with ways in which modifications in the latter might enrich the former, an overtly political concern in which the health and output of the individual was related to that of the collectivity. Standard costing can, we argue, be regarded as an important aspect of this broader concern with extablishing norms and standards for the activities of individuals and their implications for efficiency. At the level of the enterprise standard costing and budgeting contributed, we suggest, a facilitative technology which enabled a whole range of activites of the person to be rendered visible and accountable. Within the enterprise, one could at last literally make all individuals accountable.

The vagueness as to whether the notion of standard in the initial formulations of standard costing meant an ideal or an attainable standard, and the question of the possibility of actually locating the source of wastes (Solomons, 1968, p. 41) are not crucial for our purposes. For it is neither the truth-value of standard costing nor its practical utility which we are seeking to evaluate. Rather, we are concerned to locate such a practice as a form of social power, an important element of which is an ability to subject the individual to an increasingly detailed form of observation and scrutiny. In its purest form, such a type of power consists in the individual attending to his or her own deficiencies. It is a form of power in which the individual becomes an auto-regulated entity, but one for whom the standards according to which they judge their lives have been established for them. Standard costing and budgeting is, we suggest, central to such a process.

THE EFFICIENT NATION AND THE EFFICIENT INDIVIDUAL

Standard costing and budgeting provided a way of expressing in money terms the contribution of individuals to the collective efficiency of the enterprise. This allowed deviations from the norm to be located at the level of the individual. The collective efficiency of the nation during this period was expressed in different terms and with different objectives in mind. Nonetheless surprising parallels emerge in the attribution of a visibility to the individual (his health, intelligence) through which their contribution to collective efficiency could be detected. There is a similarity also in the manner in which such detection was to be achieved. Statistical deviations from a norm were central to this task of the individualisation of difference. And a plethora of techniques of socio-political management were developed which allowed observation to penetrate to the minutiae of the everyday lives of individuals (Armstrong, 1983) in an attempt to correct departures from the norm.

We want to identify here what seem to us to be the more important of these concerns and practices. These can be located at a number of distinct levels. One of these is what we call, following others (Searle, 1970; Hays, 1959; Haber, 1964), a discourse of national efficiency. This had an existence through popular political vocabulary, journalistic writings, as well as the state and governmental apparatuses. A second concerns philosophical and sociological writings, and the emergence in them of a notion that one could actively intervene within society and within the lives of indivuals. The general aim to which such writings saw this as contributing was the rational administration of the social and the active promotion of progress. The state was to play a central role in such a programme. A third level is that of the actual practices of socio-political management (eugenics, mental hygiene, mental testing) in relation to which such schemes operated. As noted above we do not view such practices as the simple implementation of the first two levels identified. It seems to us, however, that they can be viewed in terms of and as related to these more general sets of concerns.

The discourse of national efficiency

A number of writers have argued forcefully (Searle, 1970; Hays, 1959; Haber, 1964), that the notion of efficiency emerges in the early years of this century as a "convenient label" under which could be grouped a range of assumptions, beliefs and demands concerning government, industry and social organisation. Whilst being careful not to think that this notion of efficiency is used in the same way by all commentators, nor that it presupposes agreement on matters of social or industrial policy, it does seem to be a very common theme in the early years of this century. Of course, it is a notion which varies not just from one field of application to another, but from one national context to another.

One can begin to substantiate the existence of a discourse of national efficiency through journalistic writings, the arguments of politicians, as well as medical and para-medical writings. Thus the British writer Arnold White (1901) in his rather demagogic book *Efficiency and Empire,* most of the material of which had first appeared in newspaper articles the previous year, proclaimed the need for a thoroughgoing reappraisal of the nation's political and moral values. White was a polemicist, yet in a Britain which was stumbling through the successive revelations and disasters of the Boer War such arguments were not out of place.

Inefficiency was considered by White to derive from both physical and moral deterioration. The middle classes had, he argued, become largely "a class of pleasure-seekers" whilst the working classes "artificially restrict their labour" (p.310). Meanwhile drink exercised its despotism over all social groups. The result was a softening of the fibre of the ruled and the rulers alike. But the first element of efficiency, according to White, was health (p.95). Here the problem was seen to be most acute. "Our species", he proclaimed dramatically, "is being propagated and continued increasingly from undersized, street-bred people". (p.100). White was referring here to "Spectacled school-children, hungry, strumous, and epileptic" who "grow into consumptive bridegrooms and scrofulous brides . . ." (pp. 101–102). Outside certain institutions such as the Army, the Navy and the police, the population was seen to consist mainly in "hospital out-patients, enfeebled with bad air, sedentary lives, drink, and disease." (pp. 107–108). In short, the nation was rapidly deteriorating and the State was doing virtually nothing to prevent this deterioration.

White was only one of many journalists to suggest the need for a new political alignment, which would give expression to a programme of "national efficiency". Such themes, moreover, were not absent from the arguments and statements of politicians. Whilst an astute politician such as Roseberry shied away from White's journalistic excesses, he admitted, however, to being in "substantial agreement" with White's opinions (Searle, 1970, p.54). The question of national efficiency was, at heart, one which concerned social organisation. Central here was the utilisation of Germany and Japan as models or exemplars of a form of social organisation which promoted efficiency through the incorporation of science in the art of politics.

The improvement of the national physique was one element of a programme of efficiency. The need for this was seen to be highlighted by the physical unfitness of those who came forward for recruitment for the Boer War. Thus in Manchester in 1900, 8000 out of 11,000 would-be volunteers had to be turned away on grounds of ill-health, and of the remainder 2000 were declared fit only for the militia (Searle, 1970; Winter, 1980).

The mood that developed around the question of physical health was one of pessimism which at times shifted to hysteria. The concern was that Britain was breeding a race of degenerates, and that this became more acute the further one went down the social scale. White had suggested restrictions on marriage to alleviate the problem (1901, p.111). The eugenic movement was the more extreme version of such arguments with demands for "the sterilization of the unfit" gaining ground and appearing in political debate. This was, moreover, not a matter of party politics, eugenics appealing to Fabian socialists and Conservatives alike. The sick had to be taken in hand both for their own good and for the efficient functioning of society.

Efficiency was a key-word also in relation to the machinery of government, education, and the role of the scientific expert in government. The purpose of the State was to promote the "good life" of its citizens and to develop the moral nature of man (Dyson, 1980, p.192). To achieve this the application of scientific knowledge and training was deemed necessary. It is not altogether clear whether this meant leaving key decisions in the hands of experts, or making politics and public administration itself a science. Both lines of argument clearly existed, the latter finding its institutional form in the founding of the London School of Economics by the Webbs at the very end of the nineteenth century. The principle at work here was that "social reconstructions require as much specialized training and sustained study as the building of bridges and railways, the interpretation of the law, or technical improvements in machinery and mechanical processes" (quoted in Searle,

1970, p.85). Again this was a theme which cut across party politics. Roseberry, the leader of the "Liberal Imperialists" called for government by "scientific methods". Asquith, for his part, suggested that social reform should be carried out "not as a moral question. . . but as a question of social and imperial efficiency" (quoted in Collini, 1979, pp. 83–84).

This of course is no more than a suggestive glance at the literature which would enable one to substantiate the existence and depth of a discourse of national efficiency in Britain in the early years of this century. We feel it is enough, however, to support our arguments that the term efficiency provided a degree of coherence to the identification and expression of a diverse range of national concerns. If it is the case that this entitles us to talk of an ideology of efficiency in Britain during this period was this true also of the United States? It would appear that this can be answered in the affirmative, as long as one bears in mind the different socio-political context of American society. The progressive era, as one author has expressed it, "is almost made to order for the study of Americans in love with efficiency "(Haber, 1964, p.ix; Hays, 1959). The "efficiency craze" of the progressive era consisted in "an outpouring of ideas and emotions in which a gospel of efficiency was preached without embarassment to businessmen, workers, doctors, housewives and teachers . . ." (Haber, 1964, p.ix). Efficiency in this sense referred to a personal attribute, to a mechanical principle of the output–input ratio of a machine, to a commercial efficiency in the form of profit, and to efficiency conceived as a relationship between men. In this last, and possibly for our purposes here most important sense, efficiency meant social efficiency, which in turn meant social organisation.

If one can speak here of a "politics of efficiency", it was around the issues of democracy and expertise that this politics centred. Scientific wisdom was to be used to advance the cause of "good government", whether at the level of the municipality or the factory. "Democracy" was to mean government for the people based increasingly on questions of fact, a partnership between the expert and the citizen which was essential to good government (Haber, 1964, p.110). Efficient government was to be achieved through expert government officials acting in the interests of citizens, since the latter could no longer realistically achieve the level of expertise required:

> Citizens of larger cities must frankly recognize the need for professional service on behalf of citizen interests . . . Even efficient private citizens cannot deal helpfully with expert governmental questions. Efficient citizens will evidence their efficiency by supporting constructive efforts for governmental betterment (quoted in Haber, 1964, p.112).

The utilisation of notions of efficiency in relation to the business of government can be seen in such bodies as the Presidential Commission on Economy and Efficiency which was replaced by a Bureau of Efficiency when the Wilson administration took office (Haber, 1964, p. 113–114). This was not simply federal concern, the states soon setting up their own efficiency commissions. Winconsin began in 1911, and by 1917 at least sixteen states had formed such commissions. The achievements of such commissions seem to have consisted principally in consolidating state agencies, improving cost accounting techniques, and in granting more power to the governor (Haber, 1964, p.115).

The great merit of the notion of efficiency was, however, its pliability, or at least its ability to supply a point of focus for arguments covering a vast range of issues. It was not only *social* efficiency that was of concern in the early years of this century. The efficient utilisation of natural resources around the principle of conservation was central also. The notion of conservation, to be achieved through planned and efficient utilisation of natural resources, applied to such issues as water resource management and the conservation of forests (Hays, 1959). And the elasticity of the term "conservation" allowed it to extend back to the question of the conservation of human health. The National Conservation Congress of 1910 had organized a standing committee on "vital resources" which concerned itself with public health as well as having units on forests, lands, waters and minerals. Two years later, the Congress devoted the entirety of its annual session to "the conservation of human life" (Hays, 1959, p.176). And in 1909 the National Conservation Congress had included speeches on the conservation of the morals of youth, the conservation of children's lives through the elimination of child labour, the conservation of civic beauty, the elimination of waste in education and war, the conservation of manhood, and the conservation of the Anglo-Saxon race.

Philosophical and sociological conceptions of a rationally administered social

These were the most forceful and readily identifiable forms in which the notion of national efficiency appeared in the U.S. Again we feel they provide support to our argument that the term efficiency was a significant one in the socio-political debates of the time. We would like now to shift the perspective to the philosophical and sociological debates of the same period. At this level we argue that the emergence in the early decades of the twentieth century of a particular sociological and philosophical form of argument added legitimacy to, and provided a broad rationale for, the project of national efficiency. In particular it contributed a theoretical principle for an art of government founded on two central notions. The first of these was the affirmation of the possibility of a rationally administered and managed social order, something which was to be undertaken with the aid of a neutral and objective knowledge. The second was a specific conception of the nature of the social relations which linked the individual to society. The image here was of the individual as a part of a social machine conceived as an organism.

The sociologist Spencer (1878) had proposed a scientific study of society whose purpose would be "not to guide the conscious control of societal evolution, but rather to show that such control is an absolute impossibility, and that the best that organized knowledge can do is to teach men to submit more readily to the dynamic factors in progress" (Hofstadter, 1955, pp.43–44). In the period we have been addressing here such a resigned submission to social laws was being repudiated in sociological and philosophical debates. The literature of pragmatism was central to this repudiation. As one author has expressed it:

> Spencer's outlook had been the congenial expression of a period that looked to automatic progress and laissez faire for its salvation; pragmatism was absorbed into the national culture when men were thinking of manipulation and control. Spencerianism had been the philosophy of inevitability; pragmatism became the philosophy of possibility (Hofstadter, 1955, p.123).

Pragmatism offered philosophical legitimacy to a period that was becoming increasingly concerned with the rational, purposeful direction and control of social affairs. Particularly in the writings of James pragmatism sought to assert:

> . . . the fundamental idea of an open universe in which uncertainty, choice, hypotheses, novelties and possibilities are naturalized . . . (John Dewey, cited in Hofstadter, 1955, p.123).

In seeking to naturalize these concepts, the hope was permitted that there was a space within which human rationality could actively shape and reform the social organization.

Pragmatism was primarily an American phenomenon. In Britain a similar theme emerged through philosophers of what would become the New Liberalism in politics (Freeden, 1978). Here, one finds Hobhouse arguing that the human mind must itself be seen to lie within the overall process of evolution. In so far as mind has evolved to a complex rationality, then it is only fitting that this consequence of the evolutionary process should influence further evolution. Human rationality, in its distinctively scientific form, had provided humanity with: "the vastly increased power of controlling the conditions, external and internal, of life co. . ." (Hobhouse, 1911, p.156). For Hobhouse:

> the turning-point in the evolution of thought . . . is reached when the conception of the development of humanity enters into explicit consciousness as the

directing principle of human endeavour . . . (Hobhouse, 1911, p.155).

Social science conceived in this manner could become an instrument which would contribute to the better control and directing of human progress. Social science could serve human needs as natural science does, through being consciously adapted and harnessed to the purposeful achievement of ends. According to the American sociologist, Lester Ward:

> It is only through the artificial control of natural phenmomena that science is made to minister to human needs; and if social laws are really analogous to physical laws, there is no reason why social science may not receive practical applications such as have been given to physical science (Ward, 1918, p.352; cited in Hofstadter, 1955).

The introduction of a space for rational choice entailed the possibility for an applied social science. Knowledge could localise. Its function could become that of following human rationality, in order to improve its effectiveness, through a multiplicity of arenas or sites of action. Social scientific knowledges and practice could, as it were, form partnership with the state, assisting the latter in the purposeful, deliberate improvement of both the social organization, and the life and behaviour of the individual within it.

This changed conception of the nature of the social and the possibility of its rational administration was expressed in the conception of the social machine and the organic relations which were seen to link individuals to it. In Britain, for example, the Fabian socialist Sidney Webb would proclaim that:

> . . . we must take even more care to improve the social organism of which we form part, than to perfect our own individual developments. Or rather the perfect and fitting development of each individual is not necessarily the utmost and highest cultivation of his own personality, but the filling, in the best possible way, of his humble function in the great social machine (Webb, 1899, p.58; cited in Freeden, 1978).

And the working-out of a philosophy for what would become the New Liberalism of British politics took, as one of its important strands, the dilemma of how the more traditional liberal ideal of the freedom of the individual was to be rendered compatible with an organic conception of the social (Freeden, 1978, pp.25–75). For Hobhouse (1911), society consisted of:

> . . . individual persons and nothing but individual persons, just as the body consists of cells and the product of cells . . . (p.30).

But in the same way that one would fail to understand the life of a body by examining its separate cells, so one would also fail to understand society in terms only of individual persons.

> We must equally take into account that organic interconnection whereby the living processes of each separate cell cooperate together to maintain the health of the organism which contains them all. So, again, to understand the social order we have to take into account, not only the individuals with their capabilities and achievements, but the social organization in virtue of which these individuals act upon one another and jointly produce what we call social results . . . (Hobhouse, 1911, p.29).

An important task facing the social reformer was the redesign of the social organization so that the cooperation of individuals to produce social results could work in the least wasteful way. But unlike Webb's mechanistic imagery, in which the freedom of the individual seemed to disappear in the filling of a social role, Hobhouse argued that:

> . . . the life of the body is not perfected by suppressing the life of the cells, but by maintaining it at its highest point of efficiency. Nor is the organism developed by reducing the cells to a uniform type, but rather by allowing each type to vary on its own lines, provided always that the several variations are in the end mutually compatible. These things are applicable to society, from the widest to the narrowest form thereof (pp.90–91).

These two dimensions to the sociological and philosophical debates of the time combined well. A rationally administered social was one in which a concern with the individual could be formulated in terms of the collective goals of society. A concern with individual behaviours was a concern with society because the two were organically interdependent. Social reform could be conceived in a manner analogous to the reform of the enterprise. Both required the elimination of inefficiencies. Poverty and destitution represented losses for the entire social body. Issues of social reform might now be pressed not only upon moral grounds, but upon intensely practical ones as well (Freeden, 1978, pp.117–169). It was a matter of enhancing the efficiency of individuals, and of seeking to reconstruct the bases of their interactions so as to achieve a minimization of vital wastes (Ritchie, 1891: Hobson, 1914; Ward, 1881).

Some actual practices of socio-political management

Active intervention in the lives of individuals was a way of enhancing the resources of the nation. Such views were not just abstract theoretical formulations but had a real existence at the level of practices. Eugenics is one example of such practices. Eugenics was concerned with the deterioration of the nation's physical stock and its effect on the efficiency of the human component of the nation's resources. Eugenics provided what might be termed a strategic link between a certain theory of social administration and a certain conception of human abilities (Rose, 1979). Arguments concerning the deterioration of the national physique posed the question of the most appropriate mode of intervention in the organisation of the population. In Britain the principal contribution of the eugenics movement (Mackenzie, 1976), was, perhaps, that it provided a principle of legitimation for a series of operations on those individuals suspected of sapping the nation's vigour through their own defects, whether in the field of intelligence testing (Sutherland, 1972; Rose, 1979) or social administration. In the United States eugenics developed further as a "practical" movement. (cf. Haller, 1963; Pickens, 1968; Castel *et al.*, 1982). In 1907, after a number of attempts in the preceding decade or so, (cf. Kamin, 1974, p.10) legislation was passed in Indiana and Michigan providing for the sterilization of "confirmed criminals, idiots, imbeciles and rapists" (Castel *et al.*, 1982, p.47). Many states followed suit during the following two decades. Much debate followed such legislation, but the eugenic principle was upheld in 1927 by the United States Supreme Court, when it was held that sterilization fell within the police power of the state:

> It would be strange if it could not call upon those who already sap the strength of the State for those lesser sacrifices, often not felt to be such by those concerned, in order to prevent our being swamped with incompetence. It is better for all the world, if instead of waiting for their imbecility, society can prevent those who are manifestly unfit from continuing their kind. The principle that sustains compulsory vaccination is broad enough to cover cutting the Fallopian tubes (cited in Haller, 1963, p.139).

In a famous aphorism the judgement concluded by stating "Three generations of imbeciles are enough"(ibid). Eugenic principles continued to spread during the first three decades of this century, so that by 1931 some thirty states had passed a sterilization law at one time or another. It should be added, however, that by 1944 only 42,000 official sterilisations had actually been performed.

But it is not eugenics in and of itself that concerns us here. Eugenics is interesting, rather, as the most extreme example of a form of social management whose concern is the efficiency of the individual. Eugenics ultimately failed as a distinct strand of social management(Rose, 1979). Yet alongside eugenics, initially deriving support from it and ultimately supplanting it as a form of social management, we can see develop in the first three decades of this century a vast range of social interventions which take as their target the inefficient individual. Mental hygiene is an important example of such developments. In the United States in 1909 the National Committee for Mental Hygiene is founded with its aim being:

> To work for the protection of the mental health of the public; to help raise the standard of care for those in danger of developing mental disorder or actually insane; to promote the study of mental disorders in all their forms and relations, and to disseminate knowledge concerning their causes, treatment, and prevention; to

> obtain from every source reliable data regarding conditions and methods of dealing with mental disorders; to enlist the aid of the Federal Government so far as may seem desirable; to coordinate existing agencies and help organize in each State in the Union an allied, but independent, Society for Mental Hygiene, similar to the existing Connecticut Society for Mental Hygiene (cited in Castel *et al.*, 1982, p.34).

Rapidly obtaining financial support, the results of its first study carried out in a Baltimore school in 1913 are held to show that 10% of the school children were in need of psychiatric assistance. The war was to add considerable force to such developments, the "war neuroses" providing new material for observation and highlighting the relationship between psychic disorders and everyday living conditions. In this respect the greatest contribution of the mental hygiene movement lay in the treatment of the problems of soldiers returning home.

The mental hygiene movement in America was particularly concerned with children's problems, and played a leading role in the child guidance movement which first flourished in the 'twenties. The importance of such developments lay in the new form of social management which they permitted. In the words of one official of the child guidance movement:

> the (children's) clinic treats these problems by treating not only the child through whom they become manifest, but as well the family, schools, recreational and other involved factors and persons which contribute to the problem, and whose disorder the problem may reflect (cited in Castel *et al.*, 1982, p.35).

It was now possible to intervene in the whole range of behaviours of these individuals whose performance fell below the norm. The guiding principle was not the curing of disease and the eradication of defects, but the *improvement* of the health of the individual, the optimisation of their functioning. William White was to state this principle clearly in his inaugural address to the First International Congress of Mental Hygiene:

> Mental hygiene is on this account alone more important than ever before, and its significance can be seen to be gradually changing from one of the simple prevention of mental disease, which is a negative program, to the positive attitude of finding ways and means for people to live their lives at their best. Medicine has long enough maintained as ideals freedom from disease and the putting off of death. It is time that these were replaced by ideals of living, of actual creative accomplishment. The art of living must replace the avoidance of death as a prime objective, and if it ever does succeed in replacing it in any marked degree, it will be found that it has succeeded better in avoiding death than the old methods that had that particular objective as their principal goal. Health is a positive, not a negative concept (cited in Castel *et al.*, 1982, p.37).

The advantages were evident. One was now fully entitled, even required, to do something to individuals manifesting minor deviations from a statistical norm which two decades earlier might have passed unnoticed. One could now claim to be able to do something, for instance, to children who manifested such behaviours as "tantrums, stealing, seclusiveness, truancy, cruelty, sensitiveness, restlessness, and fears" (Castel *et al.*, 1982, p.38). At least in principle, there was henceforth no limit to those spheres of personal life which, once rendered visible, could now be regarded as potentially disruptive of the efficient functioning of the individual.

The focus for all these new forms of social intervention was the individual. What they achieved was to bring to the surface all those aspects of an individual's personal life which might be detrimental to their physical and mental health, and thereby to their efficiency, and to open these up to the possibility of a wide range of forms of social management. Intelligenge testing provided a further and important dimension to this overall strategy of rendering visible the level of functioning of the individual. The advantage of intelligence tests was that they supplied an elaborate and supposedly objective means whereby one could differentiate one individual from another. It did so with the aid of statistics which served to show the extent of the individual's deviation from the norm(Hacking, 1975; Rose, 1979). Intelligence tests were first developed in France by Alfred Binet in 1905, although as early as 1895 the principles were stated clearly:

> we must search with the present knowledge and

> methods at hand for a series of tests to apply to an individual in order to distinguish him from others and to enable us to deduce general conclusions relative to certain of his habits and faculties . . . (Binet & Henri, trans quoted from Rose, 1979, p.8).

Intelligence tests were imported to the United States by Terman at Stanford, Goddard at the Vineland Training School in New Jersey, and Yerkes at Harvard. Mental testing at that time had close connections with the eugenics movement. The problems were seen to be those of criminality, pauperism, indigence and inefficiency, all of these being a threat to a well-ordered social body. The difficulty, however, lay in detecting such insidious characteristics. For whilst a layperson could detect the most extreme and manifest forms, how was one to identify the high-grade defectives? The inexpert observer could easily mistake such individuals as entirely normal. Mental testing produced a "solution" in its provision of a means of systematically identifying the fine differentiation between individuals across huge masses of individuals. Statistics and the normal curve supplied another important ingredient in the form of a mechanism for identifying deviation from the norm (Galton, 1883; Hacking, 1975; Rose, 1979; Sutherland, 1972).

In the United States the question of immigration control offered a suitable experimental ground for mental testing. The testing of "the great mass of average immigrants" in 1912 had revealed that 83% of the Jews, 80% of the Hungarians, 79% of the Italians, and 87% of the Russians were "feeble-minded". It is well to recall that feeble-mindedness was a way of qualifying for deportation, and it appears that mental testing significantly increased the number of deportations for this reason (Kamin, 1974, p.16).

The first world war was a further powerful factor in encouraging the spread of mental testing. The testing programme, the Alpha and Beta tests, was applied to some two million men, public interest in such tests being given a stimulus when it was revealed that the "mental age" of the average whitge draftee was only 13 (Yerkes, 1921). Extrapolating such results to the entire population of the United States yielded a figure of some 50 million mentally defective citizens! (cited in Castel *et al.*, 1982, p.45). Although it appears that such figures were rapidly revised downward, they provided an important impetus for the spread of mental testing to other areas of social life.

In Britain the war also was significant for the development of psychological testing. The influence of the work of C.S.Myers is crucial here. Questions such as fitness in relation to length of working time, the selection and training of industrial workers, the estimation of "accident proneness" as a personal attribute, all showed the value in being able to identify the personal psychological characteristics of the individual. Myers devised and applied selection tests for men using listening devices for locating enemy submarines, and worked on problems of the "war neuroses". Myers insisted on the psychological nature of what was called "shell shock" and proposed and practiced psychotherapeutic methods of treatment. His position was emphatic:

> The physiological factors involved in purely muscular fatigue are now fast becoming negligible, compared with the effects of mental and nervous fatigue, monotony, want of interest, suspicion, hostility, etc. The psychological factor must therefore be the main consideration of industry and commerce in the future (Myers, 1920, pp.V–VI).

The psychological attributes of the person were, indeed, to provide the most fruitful ground for the expression of concerns to implicate the individual within the objectives of the enterprise and society.

THE FIRM AS A SITE IN THE CONSTRUCTION OF THE GOVERNABLE PERSON

The ambiguities of the word efficiency enabled it to operate across a series of dispersed strategies concerned with managing the life of the person. These ranged from broad political platforms to psychological and sociological concerns with individuals who deviated from specified norms in a variety of ways. We have argued that the standard costing-budgeting complex can be viewed in terms of such a preoccupation. Standard costing and budgeting, however, were intended to operate within a particular site — that of the firm. Our concern now is to identify the way in which standard costing and budgeting, in conjunction with scientific management and industrial psychology, came to define the firm as a very particular kind of space. It should be one in which efficiency and rationality would prevail. Such objectives would be stated not just in terms of the overall objectives of the enterprise, but at the level of the activities and ultimately motivations of the individual employee. Initially the worker on the factory floor, and finally every employee, would come to be identified in terms of their contribution to such ends. This was to require a process of continual monitoring and observation. The standard costing and budgeting complex was, we argue, a central element in such a process.

The creation of a standard costing within the accounting literature, accounting historians have acknowledged, owes a considerable debt to that movement which, originating in the U.S.A., became known as "scientific management". According to Solomons (1968, p. 37), for example, one cannot read F. W. Taylor's paper of 1903 on Shop Management without noticing that it contains many of the essential elements of what would later become standard costing. Accounting historians have drawn our attention, also, to another leading proponent of scientific management ideas, Harrington Emerson (see, e.g. Sowell, 1973, pp. 206–19; Epstein, 1978, pp. 90–120). Not only did his work on efficiency explictly envisage a requirement for something akin to a standard costing (Emerson, 1919, pp. 149–172), but apparently he exercised a strong influence on the writings of G. Charter Harrison, whose 1930 book has been taken as an early examplar of a fully-integrated and rationalised standard-costing and budgeting system (Sowell, 1973, pp. 220–70).

Taking scientific management and cost accounting as an interlinked complex, we wish to suggest an explanation as to the kind of project to which it contributed. This was one in which notions of efficiency identified at the level of the individual could come to be expressed in money terms and related to expected standards and norms.

Undoubtedly, the body of thought and practice that became known as scientific management was enmeshed within that American quest for national efficiency to which we have referred in the proceding section (Haber, 1964; Hays, 1959). According to F. W. Taylor (1913, pp. 5–7), in the introductory pages of his celebrated *Principles of Scientific Management,* the task was to advance national efficiency through remediation of those vast wastes which, going far beyond the poor use and inadequate conservation of natural resources, secreted themselves within the daily actions of everyone. Roosevelt had been prophetic, says Taylor, in regarding the conservation of natural resources as no more than preliminary to such a wider question of the efficiency of the person and, thereby, of the nation.

For Taylor the core of the issue was that, whereas wastes of natural resources have an easy visibility, wastes of human resources are hidden:

> We can see our forests vanishing, our water-powers going to waste, our soil being carried by floods into the sea. We can see and feel the waste of material things. Awkward, inefficient, or ill-directed movements of men, however, leave nothing visible or tangible behind them. Their appreciation calls for an act of memory, an effort of the imagination. And for this reason, even though our daily loss from this source is greater than from our waste of material things, the one has stirred us deeply, while the other has moved us but little (Taylor, 1913, pp. 5–6).

Scientific management would take upon itself the project of replacing that vagueness and other acts of the imagination with exact scientific knowledge of the extent of the wastes caused through inadequate human action and social organisation. And, it would also set itself the task of their systematic elimination.

We are not concerned here to contest Taylor's claims to scientificity. It is, rather, with the way in which such claims functioned that we are interested. Lay knowledges and practices of all kinds, such as trades, crafts and traditional practices, were to be placed under suspicion as to the wastefulness of their modes of operation. As the above quote shows, Taylor was in little doubt that such wastes were vast. Gilbreth also would illustrate the shocking waste through awkward and blundering movements in a trade as old as bricklaying (Drury, 1915, pp. 108–113). Taylor himself would point to the need for a science of such mundane tasks as shovelling and pig-iron handling, urgently to replace haphazard modes of work.

This rendering suspicious of the inadequacy of lay knowledges and practices is important. It helped to legitimate the attempt of scientific management to appropriate the work-life of the individual with a view to intervening in it in order to optimise its efficiency. Around the pillars of efficiency, the need to eliminate wastes, and the assuredness of science over and above informal knowledges, scientific management sought to establish for itself a right to interfere in people's lives. This right was eventually to be taken over by an army of technicians of the social and economic life of the enterprise.

Scientific management reflects the almost messianic role for the engineering profession envisaged by some of its leaders in the U.S.A.:

> To attain the high efficiency of the atomic energy of the fish, the high mechanical efficiency of the bird, the high lighting efficiency of the firefly, is not an ethical or financial or social problem, but an engineering problem; and to the engineering profession, rather than to any other, must we look for salvation from our distinctly human ills, so grievously and pathetically great (Emerson, 1919, p. 5).

Coupled with its rejection of the merit of lay knowledge and practices, the scientific management literature also reveals a belief in the possibility of actually improving the efficiency of the person. It reflects a philosophy which refuses to accept that greatness and success are solely accidents of birth. "In the future", says Taylor (1913, pp. 6–7),

> it will be appreciated that our leaders must be trained right as well as born right, and that no great man can (with the old system of personal management) hope to compete with a number of ordinary men who have been properly organized so as efficiently to cooperate.

In the later years of his career Taylor envisaged that scientific management would conquer the entire social space. While his proposals originated in the factory:

> It is hoped, however, that it will be clear . . . that the same principles can be applied with equal force to all social activities: to the management of our homes; the management of our farms; the management of the business of our tradesmen, large and small; of our churches, our philanthropic institutions, our universities, and our governmental departments (Taylor, 1913, p. 8).

To achieve such an objective within the enterprise meant constructing norms or standards of what efficiency might mean. Implanted within the task performance of the worker these were to provide a basis for observing deviations from expectations. It is in this context that we can appreciate the intersection of scientific management and cost accounting. For it seems that from an early date, scientific management writers had recognised the potential of an efficiency measure grounded in money, in costs saved and profits earned. As early as 1886, for example, H. R. Towne, then president of the American Society of Mechanical Engineers and a mentor of Taylor's, had wanted to construe the engineer as an economist (Towne, 1886). For Towne, the true significance of an engineer's efforts to promote efficiency, some special cases of vital national security apart, ought ultimately to be judged in terms of economics. Efficiencies were deemed true only if they could ultimately be shown to be so in terms of costs saved. One finds Harrington Emerson (1919) echoing these sentiments later, arguing a need for engineers and accountants to collaborate towards the meaningful exposition of inefficiencies. It is hardly surprising, then, that engineers associated with scientific management should have come to occupy such a central role in the construction of standard costing.

The work of G. Charter Harrison provides a way of identifying this bridge which was established between engineering and accounting. Harrison's claims to title span the professional bodies of industrial engineering, chartered accountancy and costs accountancy. To him has been attributed the writing of one of the earliest full articulations of standard costing, a work of which Solomons would say in 1968 that it was still part of the current literature. Harrison takes from Emerson (1919) his concept of the fundamental defect of existing cost accounting practices. Prior to its intersection with scientific management, cost accounting's prime defect was that it had:

> Failed most utterly and dismally to achieve what should be the primary purpose of any cost system, namely, to bring promptly to the attention of the management the existence of preventable inefficiencies so that steps could be taken to eliminate these at the earliest possible moment (Harrison, 1930, p. 8).

In rectifying this deficiency cost accounting would expand its domain. It would supply the engineers and their scientific management with a facilitative technology for expressing their norms and standards in terms of money. The earlier concern of cost accounting with the registration of the movements of workers and materials as they "attached" themselves to production (Epstein, 1978, pp. 90–120) would be augmented. This expansion would reflect a concept of the worker as almost certainly inefficient, needing to be enmeshed within a routinely-applicable calculative apparatus which standard costing would provide.

This alliance of cost accounting with the engineers was important in the construction of norms of efficiency. It provided a way for making the individual worker routinely knowable and accountable in terms of wasted actions. And scientific management was such an individualising endeavour *par excellence*. It was a matter of ceasing to treat of workers only in the anonymous terms of groups, classified by trade or skill. Attention was to be paid instead to the performance of each individual worker. Taylorism would insist that each worker be singled out, to be rewarded or punished on the basis of his or her individual performance (Taylor, 1913, p. 121; Haber, 1964, p. 23). When one ceases to deal with men in large gangs or groups, says Taylor (1913),

> and proceeds to study each workman as an individual, if the workman fails to do his task, some competent teacher should be sent to show him exactly how his work can best be done, to guide, help, and encourage him, and, at the same time, to study his possibilities as a workman (pp. 69–70).

But over whom was this individualisation to be exercised? It is clear that leaders of the scientific management movement had envisaged that their principles could embrace everyone, with no task at all too lowly or important to escape. Both physiological and mental work were to be embraced. But despite that hope, scientific management would remain entrapped at the level of fairly mundane, physiological tasks (Drury, 1915). Its first-hand technologies for constructing norms, such as the time and motion study, were hardly equipped for anything more.

This is precisely where standard costing again becomes significant. Together with budgeting it would seem to have provided an important escape route, allowing the principles of standardising and normalising to move away from the factory floor. At least in principle they could now embrace everyone within the firm. Harrison's (1930) standard costing text offers, in the terms of scientific management, a rationale for such an endeavour:

> We have increased the efficiency of the average man because we have applied the principles of scientific management to his work . . .
>
> Our accounting methods today are the best evidence of our failure to apply scientific management principles to the development of our executives. For the five-dollars-a-day man our accounting records clearly set up the objective and the accomplishment in comparision therewith. But when we come to our records for executives what do we find? . . . Of accomplishment, it is true that our profit and loss account tells the story of the ultimate result, but of executive objectives shown in relation to the accomplishment, our records are silent . . . (p. 27–28).

Standard costing had already enmeshed the factory worker within a calculus of efficiency. It should now move on, by means of the budget or profit plan, to do the same for executives.

> No man can realize his fullest possibilities, whether he be a five-dollar-a-day trucker in the factory or a five-

thousand-dollar-a-year executive, unless he has before him at all times (1) a carefully determined objective, (2) records showing the relationship between accomplishment and this objective, and (3) if he has failed to realise the objective, information as to the causes of such failure. Standard costs furnish the factory superintendent with this information as regard factory costs, and standard profit or budget systems give the executive this information as regards profits (Harrison, 1930, pp. 27–28).

The engineers (e.g. Emerson, 1919) had envisaged that standard costing would be no more than an appendage to their principles of scientific management. It would be a convenient calculative apparatus in respect of the core data the engineer would supply. But accounting's facility to operate in terms of money effected a surprising metamorphosis. By concentrating upon an end-result of money, accounting could standardise efficiency for a much larger group. In the case of more "mental" type of work, it could simply express expectations in terms of a money outcome, leaving uncertain the question of the means.

A line of continuity can, we suggest, be established from scientific management to standard costing to budgeting. It is a continuity which centres on the norm, on surrounding the person with expections of behaviour. While scientific management might seem to have faded into extinction, it has not done so without leaving a significant residue, in standard costing and budgeting. If Taylorism and scientific management more generally had envisaged the enterprise as machine-like, cost accounting, through the budget and budgetary control, would provide a means for rendering that image operational. Money would, as it were, become the common currency with which to integrate and aggregate the activities of individuals as components. For both brain-work and physical-work, indeed for every accountable person within the firm, standards and deviations therefrom reckoned in money could record the individual's contributions, and also their failure to contribute, to the ends of the machine as a whole. At hand was a calculative apparatus through which deep questions of responsibility could routinely be pressed upon individuals.

But the scientific management–cost accounting complex was not the only one in the early decades of the century to concern itself with the efficiency of the person and their contribution to collective efficiency. While standard costing and budgeting provided the lens through which engineers and managers might gaze at workers and managers and their inefficiencies, others were also interested to join in the process of observation. Specifically, these were the early industrial psychologists. A central figure here was Hugo Munsterberg. He formulated the task of industrial psychology as follows:

> Our aim is to sketch the outlines of a new science which is to intermediate between the modern laboratory psychology and the problems of economics: the psychological experiment is systematically to be placed at the service of commerce and industry (Munsterberg, 1913, p. 3).

What was now being addressed was how the psyche of the worker might be known and managed, so as to serve efficiency on an even grander scale than the promise of the engineers and the cost accountants. The industrial psychologists can be seen as a further group that would invade the firm, generating and applying a knowledge of the individual. With this development concerns of the mind as well as of the body would be introduced into the project of enmeshing the individual within norms of economic performance.

There seems little doubt that the early industrial psychology literature shares much in orientation with the scientific management–cost accounting complex we have just looked at. Industrial psychology would also lay claim to scientific status. And it would do so in a more careful manner than Taylorism. Relative to the "helpless psychological dilettantism" of others who would seek to motivate the worker, (Munsterberg, 1913, p. 56), it would thereby seek to establish for itself a privileged position. Now that it had moved beyond philosophical or theological speculation, psychology could offer a practical contribution to the goals of civilisation (Munsterberg, 1913). It would establish a laboratory within which to place the person as a subject upon whom experiments could be conducted. This would place it alongside the natural sciences. Its peripatetic laboratory would be the factory, industrial psychologists moving freely from the one to the other with great ease (Myers, 1920).

Industrial psychology would share with scientific management a concentration upon the individual. Indeed as Munsterberg (1913) points out, the entire project of an applied psychology, within which industrial psychology can be sited, had become possible only when psychologists came to recognise the importance of individual differences. The quest for universal laws of the mind, for all of its importance, had denied psychologists the possibility of bringing their skills to bear upon the practical world of affairs:

> In practical life we never have to do with what is common to all human beings, even when we are to influence large masses; we have to deal with personalities whose mental life is characterised by particular traits of nationality, or race, or vocation, or sex, or age, or special interests, or other features by which they differ from the average mind which the theoretical psychologist may construct as a type (Munsterberg, 1913, p. 9).

It is the individual whom the psychologist is to help. His or her particular aptitudes or skills are to be expertly ascertained, so that the psychologist can recommend a person–task fit that is congruent with individual well-being and the exigencies of efficiency (see e.g. Myers, 1920). And motivational difficulties in task performance are to be seen as stemming from mental traits which the non-expert cannot effectively diagnose. Only by such interventions of the psychologist will there be avoided that which

> social statistics show with an appalling clearness, what a burden and what a danger to the social body is growing from the masses of those who do not succeed and who by their lack of success become discouraged and embitted (Munsterberg, 1913, p. 35).

Finally, the early industrial psychologists share with Taylorism an appeal to efficiency as a transcendent purpose. They too, it seems, want their endeavour placed beyond the reach of politics:

> psychotechnics does not stand in the services of a party, but exclusively in the service of civilisation (Munsterberg, 1913, p. 20).

To any project of enmeshing the individual within norms of efficiency, an expert psychological selection process, as well as psychological intervention in interpreting task performance variables, is declared indispensable. Later, as we shall see, the body of psychological literature which would emerge in altered form from these beginnings would significantly intersect with budgeting and standard costing. In so doing, it would help to bring into particular relief the complex individuality of the person within the firm. This construct has, we shall suggest, reinforced a rationale for "behavioural scientists" to intensify their attention to managing the organisationally dysfunctional properties of the person.

A GESTURE TOWARDS THE PRESENT

In so far as the concern of this paper is historical we would like it to be read as a "history of the present". By this we mean an attempt to identify the dispersed events which intersect to establish our contemporary, and often unquestioned, rationales. This far, however, we have been pointing largely to notions and practices which have been supplanted or significantly redefined. We would like now to try schematically to identify some of the relocations and shifts which have occurred in more recent times. We cannot hope in any way to do justice to the richness of the intervening period. It is simply some of the lines which emerge out of and following the period 1900–1930 to which we wish to refer. This is undertaken with a view to locating the continuities between the present and the period we have addressed above. It also entaills registering the effect and implications of the shifts which have occurred in the accounting literature.

One issue which interests us particularly in this continuity of concerns, coupled with a redefinition of terms and objectives, is the introduction of the notion of the "behavioural" into accounting (Devine, 1960; Bedford and Dopuch, 1961; Ashton, 1983). Our suggestion is that this produced a modernisation of the accounting complex, but one which entailed a significant continuity with the concern to enmesh the individual within a complex web of calculative practices. It is not that accounting simply expands its domain through the introduction of the behavioural within its sphere. It is rather a redefinition of the terms according to which the accounting complex is understood that is at issue. This is achieved through incorporating within the domain of accounting a changed notion of the person. The change concerns the attribution to the individual of a complex set of motives and frustrations, a potential hostility to the budget, for example. The individual is viewed as a member of informal groups outside, from which can be drawn considerable support and into which there is always the danger that he or she may withdraw. In recognition of such a danger accounting comes, we argue, to redefine its territory by including within its legitimate sphere of operation precisely these concerns.

A second issue, and one we have referred to already, concerns the level at which the redefinition takes place. Stated baldly, and as a question, the issue is this: is our concern here simply with discourses? The answer is clear. The redefinition of accounting through the introduction of the behavioural was carried out in relation to very real practical problems. One of the pioneering studies in this field (Argyris, 1952) was indeed undertaken as a report to the Controllership Foundation itself. Concerned with "the point at which men and budgets meet" the foreword declared clearly the aims of the report:

> we hope the report sheds light on one of the most basic "Control" questions faced by management — how to gain acceptance — the real acceptance of standards and goals (Argyris, 1952, foreword).

The starting point for the rethinking of accounting through the introduction of the behavioural was a concrete problem. The formulation of the terms of such an issue was effected, however, within discourse. It could not be otherwise. The point we would draw from this is that important practical issues produce the conditions under which certain problems come to be expressed. They do not, however, determine the terms according to which they are expressed. Our concern here is with the latter.

A third point relates to the notions of rationality and efficiency, and the extent to which the changes we point to represent a continuation of such a concern. Our answer would be emphatically affirmative. Yet we would again wish to draw atttention to the redefinitions which occur. Rationality itself comes to be problematised. All individuals come to be viewed as decision-makers, albeit in different respects. Rationality remains as an issue of the relation between personal and collective efficiency, yet it is constructed according to a different conception of the person and a revised notion of the organisation.

Our interpretation of the introduction of the behavioural into accounting entails a slight detour. This is through the psychological and sociological formulation of an interest in the human relations aspect of organisations during the second quarter of the twentieth century. Central here are the Hawthorne investigations which extended for five years from 1927 until 1932 (Mayo, 1933; Whitehead, 1938; Roethlisberger & Dickson, 1939). The familiarity of the various commentaries on the Hawthorne researches entails the possible danger that we become inured to the novelty of their invention of an art of government for the enterprise. This would be unfortunate because the reformulation they produced in such a project was profound. The effect of the Hawthorne researches was to enable a concern to develop with the life of the person in all its dimensions as a problem for the collective ends of the total organisation. Roethlisberger & Dickson express this ambition clearly:

> In terms of the concept of an industrial organization as a social system many of the human problems of management can be reformulated. A traditional statement of these problems frequently distorts the actual human situation in the industrial plant. The workers, supervisors, or

> executives are often considered apart from their social setting and personal history and are treated as essentially "economic men". Simple cause and effect analysis of their behaviour is substituted for the richer situational context in which their lives are lived and in which the relation of mutual interdependence obtains (Roethlisberger & Dickson, 1939, p. 569).

The emphasis which emerges is on collective goals and mutual interdependence of the various component parts of the enterprise. This was to entail a reconceptualisation of what one could expect from budgets and other forms of standardisation of managerial expectations. One could no longer base budgets and performance standards solely on an assumption of rational economic personal motivations. To do so risked producing severe unintended consequences and resistances. In place of such limited views must be put the person characterised by sentiments, to whom managerial policies must be addressed in terms of their meanings to that person in their particular personal and social circumstances. The concern with efficiency and rationalisation must be articulated with an understanding of the possibilities of securing cooperation and acceptance of managerial goals. A negotiative conception of management should be substituted for one based on the crude imposition of standards. The concept of managerial control would have to be redefined so as to implicate individuals within the collective objectives of the enterprise. To achieve this one would have to attend to a quite different dimension of the enterprise to that previously:

> A great deal of attention has been given to the economic function of industrial organization. Scientific controls have been introduced to further the economic purposes of the concern and of the individuals within it. Much of this advance has gone on in the name of efficiency or rationalization. Nothing comparable to this advance has gone on in the development of skills and techniques for securing cooperation, that is, for getting individuals and groups of individuals working together effectively and with satisfaction to themselves (Roethlisberger & Dickson, 1939, pp. 552–553).

Economic ends are mediated through personal and social sentiments. One cannot hope to achieve the former if the latter are ignored. One must construct a work situation which is also a social situation. Through this one will be able to implicate the personal dimensions of the life of the worker within the economic objective of the organisation:

> Where the work situation is such that it does not allow the worker's preoccupations or attention to be socially expressed or directed by conversation or by other activities, an ideal setting is created for the development of morbid preoccupations. He is likely to spend his time brooding about his personal problems or his relations with his co-workers and supervisors. Where the social situation is such that it does allow for the social expression of preoccupation, much brooding about factors incidental to the worker's personal history can be alleviated (Roethlisberger & Dickson, 1939, pp. 573–574).

Now of course the concern with the personal dimension of the life of the worker was a much more complex issue than these brief remarks suggest. Their relevance for our concerns here, however, are in terms of the way such themes provided a basis for the redefinition of accounting which was to occur in the third quarter of this century. Put simply, the redifinition took place through the incorporation (within the domain of accounting) of just these personal and human relations concerns.

Argyris (1952) is the clearest early formulation of such a concern. The Foreword to Argyris' study reminds us of the defects of accounting techniques as previously conceived. Some of these, it is argued:

> have reached the ultimate state of dwelling within an electronic tube and emerging only to shake a mechanical finger at erring human beings (Argris, 1952, foreword).

The point of Argyris' study was that this conception of accounting must be drastically revised. He drew attention to "what people think of budgets", distinguishing between "budget people", "factory supervisors" and "employees" or "factory people". The point of this categorisation was to demonstrate that different groups of people had different views on budgets, on how they were used and why they often were not met. The negative consequences of budgets which were simply imposed on people were identified clearly by Argyris. Pressure to meet targets laid down in budgets risked increasing tension, resentment, and suspicion. This would often lead to the formation of groups as a way of combatting management pressure. The real danger, however, lay in the longer term. In the short term management may recognise the dangers and reduce the pressure. In principle the group should disappear. However the conclusion to which Argyris came was that there was a tendency for the group to remain. If it remained, it would continue to cause problems well after the initial irritant had been removed.

The remedy proposed was the introduction of a negotiative politics for the government of the enterprise. A number of terms came to operate within this broad space — cooperation, bargaining, communication. Of course as a negotiative politics it was weighted heavily in the favour of one side. The point however was clear. As far as budgets were concerned one should seek to gain acceptance of budgets by all those whom they affected. Accounting should be reformulated so as to take account of such factors. The worker as a complex person and as a member of an informal group should be incorporated within accounting's domain.

This shift to a behavioural conception of accounting can be indicated across a range of writings which have appeared over the past two decades and more (Caplan, 1966; Hofstede, 1968; Hopwood, 1974; Schiff & Lewin, 1974; Harrison *et al.*, 1981). Devine (1960) would argue that the behavioural assumptions of accounting needed drastic revision:

> Let us . . . turn to that part of accounting which is related directly to the psychological reactions of those who consume accounting output or are caught in its threads of control. On balance it seems fair to conclude that accountants seem to have waded through their relationships to the intricate psychological network of human activity with a heavy-handed crudity that is beyond belief. Some degree of crudity may be excused in a new discipline, but failure to recognise that much of what passes as accounting theory is hopelessly entwined with unsupported behaviour assumptions is unforgiveable (Devine, 1960, p. 394).

Another writer (Caplan, 1966) would argue that accounting as a management tool needed to take account of the complexity of the individual's motivations, their diverse needs and desires:

> It is possible that the failure of management accountants to consider the more complex motivating forces which organisation theory recognizes in the individual contributes to the use of accounting systems and procedures which produce "side-effects" in the form of a variety of unanticipated and undesired responses from participants. For example, many management accounting techniques intended to control costs, such as budgeting and standard costing, may virtually defeat themselves because they help to create feelings of confusion, frustration, suspicion and hostility. These techniques may not motivate effectively because they fail to consider the broad spectrum of needs and drives of the participants (Caplan, 1966, p. 506).

The clear lesson was that accountants should accept as relevant those bodies of knowledge which hitherto they had overlooked. What might have seemed to Harrison (1930) as no more than commonsense, namely that budgets ought to be set so as to encourage their achievement, was coming to be seen as itself rather a large territory for investigation, requiring the mediation of other and unfamiliar theories and concepts. Indeed, one might say, the whole meaning of cost accounting's effectiveness was being challenged. Instead of depending just upon the technical sophistication of the accounting system, effectiveness was coming to be seen as crucially dependent upon whether the system would actually impel people to achieve desired purposes (Benston, 1963; Caplan, 1966; Hopwood, 1973). The encircling of the person with calculative practices which would routinely construct or monitor his or her contributions to efficiency, as traditionally effected by budgeting, was seen to be dependent upon an inadequate psychology.

Other studies were to refine the issues at stake here (e.g. Likert & Seashore, 1963; Becker & Green, 1962). The encounter between the person and the budget was to lead accountants to observe the organizational life of the person at first hand. Questions would be asked as to the extent of the relevant psychological, sociological and organization theories which accountants ought to know, and the options which existed for collaborations with the more established "behavioural scientists" (Devine, 1960; Hofstedt *et al.*, 1970). And some substantive empirical studies would be carried out. Tending to take budgeting and standard costing as points of departure, such studies would explore the impact, both upon the psychological well-being of the person and upon his or her propensities to meet organizational efficiency or goals, of those "unintended consequences" produced by such calculative practices (see e.g. Hofstede, 1968; Hopwood, 1973). More knowledge was needed, in order that the systems and their methods of use might be redesigned, so as to enhance the well-being of person and organization. One might say that the discovery of the motivational complexity of the person revealed the inadequacy of such as budgets in procuring individual efficiency. A space was opened for fresh approaches to that endeavour. And in addition to empirical field studies, accountants would come not only to join the psychologist in laboratory observations of the organizational subject, but even to make some significant attempts to construct similar laboratories of their own (see e.g. Libby, 1981 for a review). Accountancy would enter alliances with the other behavioural sciences to gaze upon and to direct the organizational life of the person.

One particular expression of the shift we are referring to here was the re-casting of organisation theory through a notion of the person viewed as a decision-maker. For our concerns here this is an important development. It had the effect of significantly redefining the project of management and the attempt to establish mechanisms for the implication of the individual within organisational objectives. Or rather it rendered problematic the nature of the social bond within the enterprise.

The introduction of the notion of the person as a decision-maker rendered obsolete the image of the individual as a machine and substituted one of an individual capable of choice. This element of choice entailed in the notion of the decision-making individual placed the personal dimension of individual behaviour at the margins of the possibility of control. The individual, and the project of organisational management, would have to enter a perpetual series of moves and counter-moves. The project of management viewed in these terms could never terminate because the person was always seen to possess the possibilities of choice which could be organisationally dysfunctional. The decision-making person is seen to have an ineradicable element of freedom. The task of organisational management would come to be understood as the supervision and definition of this freedom, something which could always be subverted. An expanded group of "behavioural scientists", including at least some accountants, would set itself the task of attending to such questions.

One can locate such a shift through the writings of Barnard (1938), Simon (1957), March & Simon (1958) and Cyert & March (1963). These works were to be seen as having enriched the concerns of accountants with human motivation, and they achieved rapid recognition within the academic accounting literature (Devine, 1960; Benston, 1963). As early as 1937 Barnard was lecturing on the distinction between personal ends and organizational ends. He was to suggest the existence of "a sort of dual personality", one which was organisational and one which was personal. An important issue this raised was that of their congruence on matters of authority. The latter was seen to depend crucially on personal acceptance and not on purely formal criteria:

> If a directive communication is accepted by one to whom it is addressed, its authority for him is confirmed or established. It is admitted as the basis of action. Disobedience of such a communication is a denial of its authority for him. Therefore, under this definition the decision as to whether an order has authority or not lies with the persons to whom it is addressed, and does not reside in "persons of authority" or those who issue these orders (Barnard, 1938, p. 163).

Authority is interpersonal. The individual is seen to be free to decide for or against acceptance of norms, instructions and standards; at the very least they are no longer viewed as unproblematically internalised. The reactions of subordinates is seen to be mediated by varying degrees of conviction. Whereas for an organisation:

> decision is in its important aspects a social process... the process of decision in individuals . . . is a psychological process socially conditioned (Barnard, 1938, cited in Sofer, 1972, p. 165).

March & Simon (1958), Simon (1957) and Cyert & March (1963) were to develop this notion of the decision-making organisation. "Deciding" came to be viewed not as a momentary act but as a process which pervaded the entire organisation:

> Although any practical activity involves both "deciding" and "doing", it has not commonly been recognised that a theory of administration should be concerned with the processes of decision as well as with the processes of action. This neglect perhaps stems from the notion that decision-making is confined to the formulation of over-all policy. On the contrary, the process of decision does not come to an end when the general purpose of an organization has been determined. The task of "deciding" pervades the entire administrative organization quite as much as does the task of "doing" — indeed, it is integrally tied up with the latter. A general theory of administration must include principles of organization that will insure correct decision-making, just as it must include principles that will insure effective action (Simon, 1957, p. 1).

A drastic revision of the concept of "economic man" was seen to be needed. The revision meant incorporating the environment and the psychological attributes of individuals within a new conception of the individual human being. Cyert & March (1963) were to formulate this shift in a "behavioural theory of the firm" within which such a notion of the person and of decisions were central. The budget and its ability to define organisational objectives was central to understanding the firm in such a manner. The issue was expressed simply. Individuals have goals; collectivities do not. A means of generating collective goals so that they are congruent with personal goals was seen to be required.

The elaboration of organisational goals came to be defined in a way which saw them as inherently conflictual. The organisation was, after all, only a "coalition" of individuals, some of them organized into subcoalitions (Cyert & March, 1963, pp. 27–29). Cooperation was a process of negotiation, of bargaining. But human beings have limited capacities. Control-systems are needed to identify the considerations relevant to members of the coalition. One such control-system is the budget:

> The budget in a modern, large-scale corporation plays two basic roles. On the one hand, it is used as a management control device to implement policies on which executives have decided and to check achievement against established criteria. On the other hand, a budget is a device to determine feasible programs. In either case, it tends to define — in advance — a set of fixed commitments and (perhaps more important) fixed expectations. Although budgets can be flexible, they cannot help but result in the specification of a framework within which the firm will operate, evaluate its success, and alter its program (Cyert & March, 1963, pp. 110–111).

The budget may set organisational objectives. But it is nonetheless constrained by the more general constraints of the motivational complexity of individuals. What is interesting for our purposes here is the proposed resolution to this difficulty. One no longer seeks only to force people into the structures of the budget. Rather one redefines the accounting side of the equation through the incorporation of a concept of the person as motivationally complex. The budget and standard costing come to be displaced in favour of a task of seeking to engineer the rationality of the person. The implication and normalisation of the individual within calculative practices is no longer to be achieved through single-minded pursuit of budget requirements (Hopwood, 1973).

Let us try and express what we see to be at issue here, for it is not simply a matter of definitions. What we see to be occurring in the texts we have cited is a reconceptualisation of the boundaries of the accounting complex through an inclusion within it of a revised notion of the person and the firm. With this shift accounting comes to function as an interdependent element in a range of operations whose concern is with the implication of the individual within organisational objectives. What we are suggesting, admittedly by merely gesturing towards some relevant examples, is that an important reformulation of the objectives of accounting occurs through the introduction of the notion of the behavioural within its terms of reference. It is not just a broadening of the concerns of accounting. It is a significant redefinition of the terms and objectives of accounting as a social practice. Accounting would seek to work more closely with psychology within a complex of human sciences whose object was defined as the person and his or her life within the organisation. The redefinition which takes place, however, does not obliterate the concerns of accounting we have identified above as emerging in the early decades of this century. To adapt March's (1978) useful analogy, accounting continues to be concerned with the active engineering of the organisationally useful person. It comes to possess, however, a much more promising set of concepts, techniques and mechanisms with which to achieve such an objective.

IMPLICATIONS AND CONCLUSIONS

We have pointed in this paper to a number of events occurring roughly within the first three decades of this century which we see to be significant for the understanding of accounting as a social and organisational practice. These events have been the conspicuous emergence of different bodies of expert knowledge and practice, as well as political, journalistic and philosophical discourses, all of which share as a point of convergence the active management of the life of the person in its varied facets. Clustering around the word efficiency, we have suggested, one can witness within this period a diverse group, including engineers, psychologists, accountants, medical practitioners, proponents of eugenics, journalists and politicians, propose various projects for improving the life of the person and, thereby, of the nation. At stake, it seems, is an urgent felt need to identify and to eliminate shortcomings in such matters as people's mental and physical health, and the quality of their offspring, as well as their contribution to the economy, the protection of the empire, and public life generally. A theme running through all the discourses and practices we have looked at is a positive concern to take and to improve the life of the person. Quite literally, the person was to be worked upon, to be managed through a series of interventions into an enhanced state of life.

We have suggested that the firm can be seen as one of the sites in society towards which such projects would address themselves. Specifically, we have looked at scientific management, at the birth of industrial psychology and of modern cost accounting.

Viewed in terms of a concern with national efficiency, the project of scientific management helped to render apparent and remediable the waste lying deep within the every move of the worker. Norms or standards were to be constructed for the doing of work of every kind. Those norms, reflecting as they would an increased level of efficiency, were expected to yield that extra output and prosperity which would render class conflict obsolete. Such a congruence of self-interest of worker, employer and the social body alike, joined to the assurance of science, was to render the worker acquiescent in this "taking hold" of his or her physiology, in order to experiment with it and to improve its productive capabilities.

We have noted the alliance of scientific management and costing. From its earliest beginnings, it seems, the scientific management literature had recognised the power of an efficiency measurement grounded in costs and profits. And we have noted the influence of scientific management on the construction of standard costing, which itself merges into budgeting. The resultant calculative apparatus was to entail the possibility for going beyond a routine rendering visible of only the factory-floor worker's efficiency. We have viewed the superimposition of a notion of standardized magnitudes upon the traditional accounting statements of income and financial position as facilitating the normalization (in terms of economic accomplishment) of everyone within the firm. Budgeting, one might say, would serve as an escape-route by which standards could leave the factory floor and enmesh, potentially, everyone in the firm. Without effacing the notion of the person as potential thief, that longer-standing stewardship concern of accounting, standard costing and budgeting would render accessible to various expert and authoritative interventions the individual as "almost certainly inefficient". Cost accounting would expand its domain, to enmesh the person in a calculus of expectations. In thus constructing a notion of the person we have argued that standard costing and budgeting provided a facilitative technology whereby, in time, various interventions to improve the person's performance would become possible. For the whole project of enmeshing the person within norms of efficiency, once begun, came quickly enough to be seen as a complex, sophisticated endeavour.

Important in bringing about such a sense of complexity was industrial psychology, to whose birth we have briefly attested. More or less simultaneously with the emergence of scientific management and standard costing, psychologists began to argue the inadequacy of such endeavours' concept of the person. Wastes and inefficiencies, for their detection and elimination, were now argued to require the expertise of those who can know the person's mind. A project would be initiated which establishes the individual's psyche as the key mediating force in matching person and task and in interpreting task performance variables. And we have pointed out, albeit too sketchily and briefly, how a redefined industrial psychology comes, later in the century, to significantly intersect with accounting. By the 1950s, we have suggested, the person as machine has been replaced by the motivationally-complex decision-maker. This adds greatly to the complexity of rendering efficient his or her economic performance, and produces a redefinition of what we have called the accounting complex.

In looking at such processes in this manner we have wanted to suggest a way of viewing accounting as having contributed to a more general project of socio-political management. This is one which operates through a variety of expert knowledges and practices. The efficiency of individual persons and their contribution to collective efficiency is central to such processes. But the efficiency of the person in the firm, as we have seen Taylor point out, is not something which can be observed with the naked eye. Indeed, one might say, it cannot exist until what is to be regarded as normal or standard has first been constructed. But once a norm is to hand, and especially when it gains expression within a routinely applicable calculative apparatus like standard costing or budgeting, the person can become a subject for various human sciences. The deviations of the person from a norm, with all of their possible causes and consequences, become available for investigation and for remedial action. And, we would suggest, one distinctive contribution of standard costing, hitherto apparently ignored, is its contribution to a much wider process, whereby the life of the person comes to be viewed in relation to standards and norms of behaviour.

Now of course the processes which we have been referring to here are of a greater complexity than we have been able to indicate. But what we wanted to do was to at least make a start in untangling some of the strands of the contribution of accounting to a mode of operation of power in our societies which, we argue, emerges in its distinctive form at the beginning of this century. This is one which, we feel, cannot be explained adequately by over-zealous adherence either to a notion of economic determination and interests, or to an explanation which hinges on a desire on behalf of the professions to continually extend their field of operations. Of course this is not to imply that economic pressures and professional influences are unimportant. It is, rather, to suggest what we see to be a different line of investigation for the understanding of accounting in relation to power in our societies. This is one which locates it as an important part of that complex of interventions which can be given the name the human sciences. We have outlined briefly how our thinking on these matters has been significantly influenced by the work of Michel Foucault and his associates.

We do not feel that our concerns in this paper can be adequately captured by referring to a general process of rationalisation of Western industrial societies (Weber, 1978). In talking of projects for social and organisational management we have wanted to give weight to the actual construction of such projects, and to the terms in which they are constructed. We have sought tentatively to explain how accounting supplies an important contribution to a complex of interventions directed at providing mechanisms for the implication of individuals within the life of the organization and of society. The general principle operative here has been well expressed by Rexford Tugwell, government advisor, economics professor, and staunch advocate of the applications of scientific management to the wider society:

> Is it possible that, instead of appealing to sets of emotions of an immediate and piecemeal sort, the problem of motivation might be resolved by fixing in each individual mind a rationale of ends to be tried for, and of the means available? For if this cannot be done, it seems very little use to hope that group action will ever become coherent and cooperative in a larger, a genuinely social sense; . . . (Tugwell, 1933).

In defining our concern as with the "construction of the governable person" we would not want to imply an image of a totally obedient individual. We wanted rather to examine the programmatic frameworks and power relations in terms of which the lives of individuals are viewed, measured and supervised. In gesturing towards recent developments within accounting we wanted to suggest ways of interpreting the construction of the notion of the complex person as a rationale for a series of practical interventions. To put this rather provocatively, one could say that what is at issue in these more recent developments is a form of power which operates through freedom: a freedom for the individual to have an informal life within the organization, to deviate from criteria of rationality, to brood on personal problems, and to be influenced by the environment outside the firm. In its more recent development accounting has provided for such a freedom in its attempt to incorporate the behavioural and the decisiontaker within its sphere. In so doing we would suggest that accounting today can be viewed as in continuity with, albeit in a considerably modified form, a mode of exercise of power which was installed in the early decades of this century.

BIBLIOGRAPHY

American Accounting Association, Report of the Committee on Accounting History, *Accounting Review*, Supplement to vol. XLV (1970).

Argyris, C., *The Impact of Budgets on People* (New York: Controllership Foundation, 1952).

Armstrong, D., *Political Anatomy of the Body* (Cambridge: Cambridge University Press, 1983).

Ashton, R. H. (ed.), *The Evolution of Behavioural Accounting Research* (New York: Garland, 1983).

Baritz, L., *The Servants of Power* (Westport, CT: Greenwood Press, 1960).

Barnard, C., *The Functions of the Executive* (Cambridge, MA: Harvard University Press, 1938).

Becker, S. & Green, D., Budgeting and Employee Behavior, *Journal of Business* (October 1962) pp. 392–402.

Bedford, N. & Dopuch, N., Research Methodology and Accounting Theory — Another Perspective, *Accounting Review* (July 1961) pp. 351–61.

Benston, G., The Role of the Firm's Accounting System for Motivation, *Accounting Review* (April 1963) pp. 347–54.

Burchell, S., Clubb, C. & Hopwood, The Development of Accounting in its International Context, *Seminar on an Historical and Contemporary Review of the Development of International Accounting*, Atlanta (August 1979).

Burchell, S., Clubb, C., Hopwood, A., Hughes, J. & Nahapiet, J., The Roles of Accounting in Organizations and Society, *Accounting, Organizations and Society* (1980) pp. 5–27.

Burchell, G., Gordon, C. & Miller, P. (eds), *The Foucault Effect:* Studies in the History of Government Rationality (Brighton, Sussex: Harvester Press, forthcoming).

Caplan, E. H., Behavioral Assumptions of Management Accounting, *Accounting Review* (July 1966) pp. 496–509.

Castel, R., Castel, X. & Lovell, X., *The Psychiatric Society* (New York: Columbia University Press, 1982).

Chatfield, M. (ed.), *Contemporary Studies in the Evolution of Accounting Thought* (Belmont, CA: Dickenson, 1977).

Church, A. H., *Manufacturing Costs and Accounts* (New York: McGraw Hill, 1917).

Collini, S., *Liberalism and Sociology* (Cambridge: Cambridge University Press, 1979).

Cousins, M. & Hussain, A., *Michel Foucault* (London: Macmillan, 1984).

Cyert, R. & March, J., *The Behavioral Theory of the Firm* (Englewood Cliffs, NJ: Prentice Hall, 1963).

Devine, C. T., Research Methodology and Accounting Theory Formation, *Accounting Review* (July 1960) pp. 387–399.

Donzelot, J., *The Policing of Families* (London: Hutchinson, 1979).

Drury, H. B., *Scientific Management* (New York: Columbia University Press, 1915).

Dyson, K., *The State Tradition in Western Europe* (Oxford: Martin Robertson, 1980).

Emerson, H., *Efficiency as a Basis for Operation and Wages* (New York: Engineering Magazine Co., 1919).

Epstein, M. J., *The Effect of Scientific Management on the Development of the Standard Cost System* (New York: Arno, 1978).

Foucault, M., *Madness and Civilisation* (London: Tavistock, 1967).

Foucault, M., *The Order of Things* (London: Tavistock, 1970).

Foucault, M., *The Archaeology of Knowledge* (London: Tavistock, 1972).

Foucault, M., *The Birth of the Clinic* (London: Tavistock, 1973).

Foucault, M., *Discipline and Punish* (Harmondsworth: Allen Lane/Penguin, 1977).

Foucault, M., *The History of Sexuality*, vol 1 (Harmondsworth: Penguin, 1981).

Freeden, M., *The New Liberalism* (Oxford: Oxford University Press, 1978).

Galton, F., *Inquiries into Human Faculty and its Development* (London: J. M. Dent, 1883).

Garcke, E. & Fells, J. M., *Factory Accounts*, 6th ed. (London: Crosby Lockwood, 1911).

Haber, S., *Efficiency and Uplift: Scientific Management in the Progressive Era, 1890–1920* (Chicago: University of Chicago Press, 1964).

Hacking, I., *The Emergence of Probability* (Cambridge: Cambridge University Press, 1975).

Haller, M. H., *Eugenics* (NJ: Rutgers University Press, 1963).

Harrison, G. C., *Standard Costing* (New York: Ronald Press, 1930).

Harrison, R. H., Harrison, G. L. & Watson, D. J. H. (eds), *The Organizational Context of Management Accounting* (London: Pitman, 1981).

Hays, S. P., *Conservation and the Gospel of Efficiency* (Cambridge, MA: Harvard University Press, 1959).

Hobhouse, L. T., *Social Evolution and Political Theory* (New York: Columbia University Press, 1911).

Hobson, J. A., *Work and Wealth: A Human Valuation* (London: Macmillan, 1914).

Hofstadter, R., *Social Darwinism in American Thought* (Boston: Beacon Press, 1955).

Hofstede, G., *The Game of Budget Control* (London: Tavistock, 1968).

Hofstedt, T. R. & Kinard, J. C., A Strategy of Behavioral Accounting Research, *Accounting Review* (January 1970) pp. 38–54.

Hopwood, A., *An Accounting System and Managerial Behaviour* (London: Saxon House, 1973).

Hopwood, A., *Accounting and Human Behaviour* (London: Haymarket, 1974).

Kamin, L. J., *The Science and Politics of I.Q.* (Potomac, MD: L. Erlbaum Associates, 1974).

Kaplan, R., The Evolution of Management Accounting, *Accounting Review* (July 1984) pp. 390–418.

Lee, T. A. & Parker, R. H., *The Evolution of Corporate Financial Reporting* (London: Nelson, 1979).

Libby, R., *Accounting and Human Information Processing* (Englewood Cliffs, NJ: Prentice Hall, 1981).

Likert, R. & Seashore, S. E., Making cost control work, *Harvard Business Review* (November–December 1963) pp. 96–108.

Littleton, A. C. & Zimmerman, V. K., *Accounting Theory: Continuity and Change* (Englewood Cliffs, NJ: Prentice Hall, 1962).

Mackenzie, D., Eugenics in Britain, *Social Studies of Science*, (1976) pp. 499–532.

March, J. G., Ambiguity, Bounded Rationality and the Engineering of Choice, *Bell Journal of Economics* (1978) pp. 587–608.

March, J. G. & Simon, H. A., *Organizations* (New York: John Wiley, 1958).

Mayo, E., *The Human Problems of an Industrial Civilisation* (New York: Macmillan, 1933).

Merkle, J., *Management and Ideology* (Berkely, CA: University of California Press, 1981).

Miller, P., *Domination and Power* (London: Routledge, forthcoming).

Munsterberg, H., *Psychology and Industrial Efficiency* (London: Constable, 1913).

Myers, C. S., *Mind and Work* (London: University of London Press, 1920).

Nicholson, J. L., *Cost Accounting* (New York: Ronald Press, 1913).

Noble, D., *America by Design* (New York: Galaxy Books, 1977).

Parker, R. H., The Study of Accounting History, Hopwood, A. and Bromwich, M. (eds), *Essays in British Accounting Research* (London: Pitman, 1981).

Pickens, D., *Eugenics and the Progressives* (Nashville, TN: Vanderbilt University Press, 1968).

Ritchie, D. G., *The Principles of State Interference* (London: Swan Sonnenschein, 1891).

Rose, N., The Psychological Complex: Mental Measurement and Social Administration, *Ideology and Consciousness* (Spring 1979) pp. 5–68.

Roethlisberger, F. J. & Dickson, W. J., *Management and the Worker* (Cambridge, MA: Harvard University Press, 1939).

Schiff, M. & Lewin, A. Y. (eds), *Behavioral Aspects of Accounting* (Englewood Cliffs, NJ: Prentice Hall, 1974).

Scull, A. T., *Museums of Madness: The Social Organization of Insanity in 19th Century England* (London: Allen Lane, 1979).

Searle, G. R., *The Quest for National Efficiency* (Oxford: Blackwell, 1970).

Sheridan, A., *Michel Foucault: the Will to Truth* (London: Tavistock, 1980).

Simon, H. A., *Administrative Behavior* (New York: Free Press, 1957).

Sofer, C., *Organizations in Theory and Practice* (London: Heinemann, 1972).

Solomons, D., The Historical development of costing, in Solomons, D. (eds) *Studies in Cost Analysis* (London: Sweet and Maxwell, 1968).

Sowell, E. M., *The Evolution of the Theories and Techniques of Standard Costs* (Alabama: University of Alabama Press, 1973).

Spencer, H., *The Study of Sociology* (London: Kegan Paul, 1878).

Stedman-Jones, G., *Outcast London* (Harmondsworth: Penguin, 1971).

Sutherland, G., The Magic of Measurement: Mental Testing and English Education, 1900–40, *Transactions of the Royal Historical Society* (5th series, 1977) pp. 135–153.

Taylor, F. W., *The Principles of Scientific Management* (New York: Harper and Brothers, 1913).

Towne, H. R., The Engineer as Economist, *Proceedings of the American Society of Mechanical Engineers* (1886).

Tugwell, R., *The Industrial Discipline and the Governmental Arts* (New York: Columbia University Press, 1933).

Ward, L., The Scientific Basis of Positive Political Economy (1881), in Ward, L., *Glimpses of the Cosmos*, (New York: Putnam, 1913).

Weber, M., *Economy and Society* (eds Roth, G. and Wittich, C.) (Berkeley, CA: University of California Press, 1978).

White, A., *Efficiency and Empire* (London: Methuen, 1901).

Whitehead, T. N., *The Industrial Worker* (Cambridge, MA: Harvard University Press, 1938).

Winter, J. M., Military Fitness and Civilian Health in Britain During the First World War, *Journal of Contemporary History* (1982) pp. 211–244.

Yerkes, R. M., *Psychological Examining in the U.S. Army* (Washington, DC: Memoirs of the National Academy of Sciences, vol. 15, 1921).

AAAJ
4,2

Symbolism, Collectivism and Rationality in Organisational Control

Shahid L. Ansari and Jan Bell
California State University, Northridge

> . . . and what made her write this was not entirely guilt, but also something untranslatable, a law which obliged her to pretend that Raza's words meant no more than they said. This law is called *takallouf*. To unlock a society, look at its untranslatable words. *Takallouf* is a member of that opaque worldwide set of concepts which refuse to travel across linguistic frontiers . . . (Salman Rushdie, *Shame*).

This article reports on a study which examines the influence of societal culture on accounting and control practices. It attempts to understand how culture shapes the values and meaning frames of organisational participants and provides them with interpretive schemes for processing experiences. In turn, the study illustrates how such interpretive schema affect accounting and control practices in organisations. This is achieved by focusing on four generic issues:

(1) How do organisations initiate accounting and control systems?

(2) How do such systems evolve over time?

(3) What roles do they play in an organisational crisis?

(4) How does organisational action become disconnected from such systems?

These four issues capture the emergence and evolution of accounting *and* control practices over time in a dynamic setting. Control, as used here, refers to all organisational arrangements, formal and informal, designed to accomplish organisational objectives. It includes formal structure, operational controls, rewards, budgeting, planning and other similar activities. We are interested in examining organisational practices in areas such as strategic planning, organising, measuring performance, setting incentives, rewarding and motivating participants. Since accounting is a key element in mediating many of these activities (for example, by measuring performance and distributing rewards), we are particularly interested in what role it plays in control and the way in which the larger cultural context mediates this role.

We are grateful to the management of International Foods and their consultants for providing us with the data for our study and for reviewing and providing feedback on our analysis. Comments by participants at the International Conference on Research in Management Control Systems at the London Business School and at the Research Workshops of Macquarie University, Sydney, and the University of California, Irvine, on earlier versions of this article are gratefully acknowledged. Comments of two anonymous referees have also greatly improved it. Needless to say we remain responsible for any omissions or errors in the article.

Accounting Auditing & Accountability Journal, Vol. 4 No. 2, 1991, pp. 4-27, © MCB University Press, 0951-3574

Our research vehicle is a longitudinal field study of International Foods, a holding corporation for a group of companies located in Pakistan. We observed many of the practices and events reported here during the period 1967-1989; therefore, this is ***not a historical*** study. Consequently, we did not start with an *a priori* model to guide data collection. Rather, our study is an exercise in making sense of data, or what later became data, in the light of our model. We came to use the cultural perspective to examine and critically evaluate the practices observed only after failing to explain many of the practices using existing models of control. Using a cultural perspective has supplemented and enriched our understanding of the events. Our purpose, therefore, is to argue that existing approaches for studying the emergence of accounting and control systems in organisations need to incorporate the cultural context.

The need to reassess current thinking about the genesis of accounting and control practices in organisations has been requested by a number of scholars in recent years. These writers reject the traditional view of accounting/control systems as arising from and being shaped by "technical-rational" demands of environment and technology (Meyer and Rowan, 1977; Burchell *et al.*, 1980; Boland and Pondy, 1983; Meyer, 1983)[1]. Studies in recent years have begun to show the power implications and/or the rationalising and ceremonial roles of accounting/control systems in organisations (Tinker, 1980; Ansari and Euske, 1987; Covaleski and Dirsmith, 1988). However, very few studies have attempted to understand the influence of symbolic and cultural processes on accounting and control. (Some notable exceptions that have incorporated culture are Hofstede, (1980, 1983); Gambling (1984, 1987); Czarniawski-Joerges and Jacobsson (1989).)

The discussion which follows is divided into five main sections. The first section explains the use of a symbolic, cultural perspective and contrasts it with existing approaches used to address accounting/control systems. The next section describes the field-study approach we have utilised in addressing the issues of concern. This is followed with a description of the details of the organisation studied. The fourth section contains an analysis of the issues. This analysis is used to identify areas where traditional approaches to control fail to explain organisational action. The final section contains a summary and the implications of our findings.

Existing Perspectives on Control

A central assumption underlying existing work on accounting/control systems is that the industrial environment is the primary determinant of industrial structures. The assumption that environment and technology are key determinants of accounting/control systems has its genesis in the works of general systems theorists. It is a cornerstone for two dominant ways of viewing accounting/control systems. The first of these, the *technical-rational* view, originates in economics, particularly the economics of industrial organisation. Three key ideas characterise this perspective:

(1) Environmental determinism, or the idea that organisational survival requires the development of internal structures that best meet the needs of the organisation's environment;

(2) Economic efficiency, or the idea that organisations develop structures that minimise transactions cost;

(3) Economic rationality, or the idea that behaviour in organisations is purposeful, self-interested, and driven by a calculus of the most efficient means to accomplish given ends.

Frameworks on management control (e.g. Anthony, 1965; Pfeffer and Salancik, 1978), theories of industrial organisation (Williamson, 1975), and agency theory (Alchian and Demsetz, 1972; Mirrlees, 1976; Baiman, 1982) are prominent exemplars of the technical-rational viewpoint applied to control systems. These approaches rely heavily on Chandler's (1977) historical work of industrial development in the US in the late 19th century. His central thesis was that changes in organisational structures were caused by changes in their strategic objectives. Strategies, in turn, had to respond to changes in industrial environment caused by the introduction of mass communication and railroads. The attempt of authors such as Anthony (1965) was to use Chandler's thesis to provide a guide for practice. Williamson, however, tried to use Chandler's evidence to provide a conceptual understanding of how organisational structures change in response to the needs of economic efficiency. His central argument was that the evolution of organisational forms from functional to divisional to modern multidivisional conglomerates, and the accompanying development of certain types of control and performance measurements systems, such as the return on investment (ROI), are natural outgrowths of the pursuit of efficiency. (Agency theory also uses the concept of minimising transactions cost to develop optimal incentive and reward sharing contracts in organisations.)

Viewed from a technical-rational perspective, accounting and control systems become instruments in the service of rationality and efficiency. A clear separation between value-rationality (selection of ends) and instrumental-rationality (selection of means) is assumed. The problem with this view is that, in its extreme form, it leads to the prediction that, given comparable endowments of economic resources and similar states of economic development, organisations would tend to evolve similar accounting and control systems. Stated in this form, the prediction runs counter to most empirical observations of national and international organisations. International accounting is replete with instances of how industrially similar Western European countries have different accounting systems and practices (Arpan and Radebaugh, 1981). Similarly, studies of Japanese management systems (Ouchi, 1981; Pascale and Athos, 1981; Schein, 1981, 1985) show that reward structures and incentives in such systems may be markedly different from those in Western societies.

While the technical-rational perspective is an outside-in (environment to structure) view of control systems, the other tradition in control, the *collectivists*, view control inside-out (structure to environment). From the collectivist perspective, an organisation is primarily a co-operative system designed to overcome the limitations of individuals — biological, perceptual and others. The view that organisations are designed to overcome the physical and biological limitations of man precedes the collectivist viewpoint described in this article.

It was first explicitly recognised by Barnard (1938) and is implicit in the works of certain economists such as Alchian and Demsetz (1972) and Marschak and Radner (1972).) Instead of the black box approach of environmental determinism, the collectivist approach provides a rich description of the social interaction inside an organisation that makes adaptation possible. No longer are organisations seen as being driven by the dual engines of individual economic rationality and productive efficiency. These are replaced with the dynamics of social interaction. Processes of power and influence, as exhibited through the dynamics of coalition formation, inducements and rewards, become central in the collectivist view. (For a more detailed discussion of the technical-rational and collectivist viewpoints in control, see Ansari and Bell, 1991).

The collectivist tradition in accounting and control moves from the rational to the rationalising and hegemonic roles of accounting and control systems. Studies such as Ansari and Euske (1987); Covaleski and Dirsmith (1988), provide empirical data that show that control systems sometimes are used as *post hoc* rationalisations for decisions made. This line of research casts serious doubt on the separability of means and ends common to the technical-rational perspective. A different but related set of studies uses the political economy perspective to examine the role of accounting/control systems in establishing and perpetuating hegemony for privileged groups in organisations (for example, see Tinker, 1980). The strength of the collectivist approach is that it provides a richer description of how individual and social action comes to define, refine and shape control systems, and the way in which concepts of rationality and efficiency come to be employed as a means of exerting power and influence.

There are three weaknesses in relying solely on *traditional* collectivist perspectives to understand the roles of accounting and control systems. The first is that viewing such systems as mere pawns in power struggles fails to consider the technical and economic forces outside an organisation that influence its control structures. (This is not to imply that collectivist work is ahistorical. However, the historical factors of prime concern for collectivists have been the social, cultural and political forces, not economic and technological ones.) Explanations based solely on struggles for power and influence do not capture the dynamic ways in which control systems have changed both over time in a given society and across societies. (This is attested to by historical works in managerial accounting such as Miller and O'Leary (1987); Kaplan (1984); and Johnson (1983).) A second and related weakness is that this viewpoint does not account for the way in which changes in the technical environment can shift internal power distributions. External economic and technical demands placed on an organisation can put certain groups within it in a strategically advantageous position to exert power. Finally, this viewpoint is based on theories of motivation that fail to consider the role of symbolic processes in organisation.

For a student of accounting/control systems, these two approaches offer two somewhat extreme and incomplete descriptions of organisational reality. While the technical-rational approach offers the image of an organisation buffeted, shaped and moulded by an all-powerful environment, the collectivists see an all-powerful organisation that can shape and mould its environment. During the last decade, there has been a growing awareness that neither diversity nor similarity of control systems can be explained solely by relying on either the economic environment or individual social action. The popular literature on control systems (Peters and Waterman, 1982), as well as studies of comparative management (Ouchi, 1981), have brought forth the idea that the values and norms embedded in the culture of an organisation and/or a society influence its accounting and control practices. The cultural perspective treats organisational or national culture as the *context* within which *local* practices can be explained. Compared to the other two perspectives, this view is interested in explaining how culture supplies the interpretations that individuals use to make sense of their experiences.

Some recent collectivist work has attempted to deal with such symbolic issues. These attempts have taken two different forms. First, is the "critical history" approach (exemplified by Merino and Niemark, 1982) which takes a socio-historical look at the hegemonic role of accounting. The effort here is to flesh out the way in which certain interest groups have used accounting to maintain power. While important in its own right, this approach is motivated more by class distinctions than cultural distinctions. The other is the "symbolic interaction" approach (exemplified by Covaleski and Dirsmith, 1983; Colignon and Covaleski, 1988) which looks at the way in which participants give meaning to actions. (This is not to imply that Covaleski and Dirsmith's work ignores that organisations are embedded within larger contexts. Their works provide considerable background to the Wisconsin history. However, we have classified them as primarily focusing on the symbolic interactions which took place.) Again, the focus has been on the meaning frames of people as organisational participants and not as members of a culture.

Our approach to understanding symbolic processes in organisations is to emphasise the role of national culture. It is therefore a study of the symbolic processes through which people produce and reproduce social order. A critical feature of the approach is the emphasis on the "native's viewpoint" as it unfolds in the linguistic categories that are used to organise experience and give meaning to it. Culture is neither a *monolith*, as sometimes portrayed in studies that are cross-cultural, nor is it *invariant* over time. It is the dynamic processes of social change that are at the heart of cultural studies. The field study reported here uses the cultural perspective to explain how and why certain types of accounting/control systems existed in the organisation under consideration at various stages in its life. It also shows the sundry and changing roles of the accounting/control system over time. The cultural perspective attempts to capture the symbolic dynamics of change in a local, time-specific context.

Theoretical Frame and Method

The cultural perspective, as used in this study, is embedded in the works of cultural anthropologists, most notably Clifford Geertz (1973; 1983; 1988). The central thrust of what Geertz calls "interpretive anthropology" is to understand institutions and events in their socio-historical context. Along with music, art and literature, social institutions, such as accounting and control systems, are seen as symbolic forms through which a society expresses its collective world view. To understand these institutions, we must first understand how the acquired world views used by individuals shaped such systems and what they come to symbolise for them. (For an excellent discussion of world views and their ability to explain empirical observations in labour conflict, see Sabel, 1982).

The cultural perspective of "interpretive anthropology" used in this study has three key features. First, it relies on the linguistic categories and idiom peculiar to a culture to explain symbolic processes of meaning construction. There are four key categories in the Urdu language that will drive our explanations: *takallouf, rakh rakhao, biradari* and *bhai*. They are introduced and explained later in the article. It is important to note that, while our own narrative may sound very "scientistic" and driven by Western concepts of accounting and control, this by no means represents the "native's view". The need to communicate to a Western audience in the English language forces us to use terminology that is familiar to our readers.

A second key feature of the cultural analysis is that it uses kinship and clan structures to explain events. We will attempt to show how these structures explain accounting/control systems in our case study, and how they are different from family and clan structures in Western societies.

Finally, consistent with the requirements of the cultural perspective, the research method used is a case study in the ethnographic tradition. Accordingly, we make no claim of objectivity in the sense of being distant and neutral from the phenomena we describe. Our insights have been gained from being deeply immersed in the organisation studied. We have been personally involved in the events described here from their *very inception*. That is, it is not an ex-post study of the 22-year period described. (One of the authors was responsible for the preparation of the financial package submitted to obtain the initial funding of International Foods. Since then, both have provided the organisation with consulting advice on the various issues discussed in this article.) Our data consist of personal observations; conversations and interviews with key personnel at International Foods and their outside consultants; review of loan applications and documents related to the projects; internal memos, correspondence and minutes; financial, legal and other pertinent operational documents; review of generally accepted accounting practices in Pakistan; and various other items. Our personal observations include visits to the various plants, observing meetings of the board of directors, and general operations first-hand. We have used a strategy of employing convergent data in which this "hard" evidence is combined with impressionistic data to provide a coherent explanation.

The study attempts to explain the events in our case study by using all three frameworks discussed earlier: the technical-rational, collectivist, and symbolic. While pointing out efficiency and power explanations for many observed features, we give prominence to the symbolism in the design and functioning of the accounting/control systems. We show how such systems, as symbolic forms, provide both a model *for* making sense of the world as well as a model *of* the world (Sabel, 1982), thereby dissolving the distinction between facts and values.

AAAJ
4,2

10

Additionally, this study is an effort to explain accounting/control systems not as timeless and placeless phenomena, but as organisational, societal and time-specific. We feel that we have a unique ability to do this because of the composition of the research team. One of the researchers is a "native" of the culture in which the organisation under discussion is situated, while the other is not. Both have in-depth knowledge of the company, gained through frequent encounters over many years. By having a "native" and a "non-native" on the research team, we were able to identify unique expressions of culture in the accounting/control system and the role of that system in the culture. The remainder of this article presents the field-study results which elaborate on these themes.

International Foods: History and Background

International Foods represents a group of companies involved primarily in the manufacture and sale of food products: ice cream and other frozen treats, long-life conservation juices and milk, and chocolates and other confectionery items (a chronology of the key events in the group's history is given in the Appendix). The first company in the group started business in 1972 as a regional manufacturer and seller of ice cream and frozen treats in Lahore, Pakistan. By the end of the 1970s, manufacturing facilities were started in Karachi and in Sharjah, UAE. Vertical integration had been accomplished by expanding into the production of packaging materials. In the mid-1980s horizontal integration added long-life milk and juices, and chocolates and confectionery to the company's product line. At this time, International Foods ranked among the top 50 corporations in Pakistan, as measured by sales and assets.

The company is a closely held family corporation. Most of its shares are held by three brothers: Ali, the eldest; Masood, the middle brother; and Zabi, the youngest brother[2]. Ali, trained as an engineer, worked his way to become the managing director of the Pakistani subsidiary of a British multinational entertainment company. Masood, trained in dairy technology, worked for an ice cream company located in Bangladesh (then East Pakistan). Zabi, an electrical engineer, started his own electrical contracting business in Bangladesh. The family had moved to West Pakistan in 1947[3] at the time of Partition, and had lost all its assets. The idea of starting an ice cream company in West Pakistan (Pakistan) was conceived in 1967 by Masood.

To understand why it took five years from conception to the formation of International Foods, it is important to appreciate the business and economic conditions in Pakistan. The period 1958-1968 had been a decade of rapid industrialisation and relative political stability. One consequence of this rapid development was that most of the wealth of the country was concentrated in what was popularly referred to as the "22 families". This made it extremely difficult for others who lacked the political and economic resources of those families to start industries.

To start a new industry in Pakistan, three requirements had to be met. First, the industry had to be on a government-approved list of desired projects. Second, one of two lending institutions authorised to make foreign currency loans for equipment purchases had to have a line of credit in the currency in which the

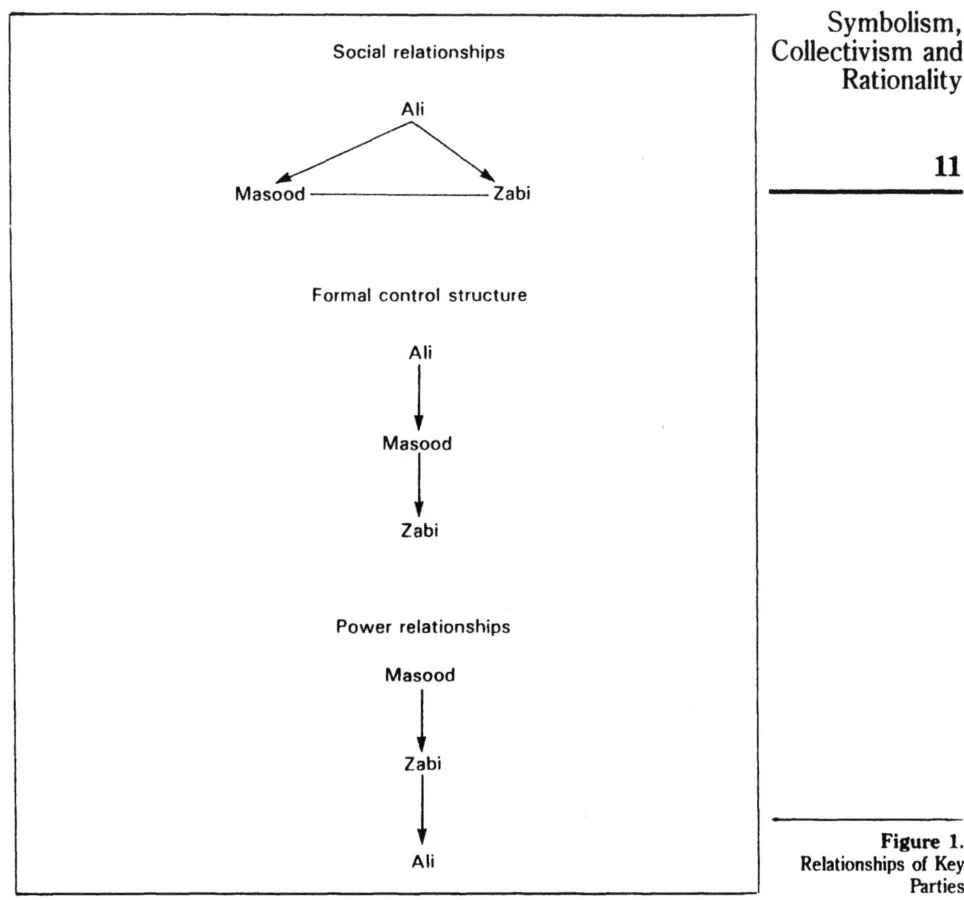

Figure 1. Relationships of Key Parties

equipment was to be purchased. (The Industrial Development Bank of Pakistan financed foreign currency loans for projects needing less than US$300,000. Larger amounts were financed by Pakistan Industrial Credit and Investment Corporation, the employer of one of the authors of this study. Both banks were subsidiaries of the World Bank (IBRD). Commercial banks financed only local currency components of the project such as working capital, land and buildings.) Third, the project had to meet the normal guidelines of profitability and debt service capability, and its principals had to have business competence. Since International Foods wanted to import ice cream manufacturing equipment from Denmark, the equipment had to be on the government's approved list, and the authorised bank had to have an available Kroner line of credit. If these two preconditions

AAAJ
4,2

12

were met, the banks would consider the applicant's credit-worthiness and business competence.

This created substantial obstacles for International Foods. First, ice cream manufacturing equipment was not on the approved list. While milk processing equipment was approved, milk had failed to prove profitable, and therefore a dairy plant to produce both milk and ice cream could not be imported. Second, ice cream was deemed a "luxury" product and financing was difficult to obtain. Finally, two multinational corporations, Foremost-McKesson and Lyons of the UK, had previously failed in their separate attempts to sell ice cream in West Pakistan.

These difficulties were overcome through the help of a network of friendships developed by Masood and Zabi in the "clubs" of Bangladesh. Some of these friends, who were working for the two industrial banks, helped to persuade the higher-level bank officials of the "catch 22" nature of the milk versus ice cream issue. Also, since they knew that the ice cream company where Masood worked in Bangladesh was successful, they thought that the project was feasible. The project was thus approved "in principle" through informal channels. The decision was ***legitimated*** by generating a business plan to show that a combined milk and ice cream plant would be profitable, would meet the government's import guidelines, and would be run by competent business executives. Accounting here came to be employed as a way to "rationalise" a decision that was made at lower levels and had to be approved on a "rational" basis at the upper levels.

The project was formally approved in 1970 using the bank's typical formula of a 50-50 debt to equity ratio. The equity was to be raised in local currency. However, the country plunged into a civil war which culminated in a war with India. In the aftermath, the Rupee was devalued by 100 per cent. Not only did this create a higher local equity requirement, it also doubled the amount of cash flow needed to repay foreign currency loans. This created two new challenges: one, convincing bank officials to fund the loan; and, two, determining how to manage the operations in a way which would generate enough cash flow to service the increased debt. These challenges took two additional years to resolve.

The Early Years

International Foods formally commenced manufacturing operations in June, 1972, in Lahore. Masood hired a plant manager; two close friends agreed to assume the roles of sales and operations managers at no salary. At the outset, sales were restricted to two territories: Lahore and Rawalpindi. Lahore was the site of the manufacturing facility, and this territory was managed by Masood. Rawalpindi, 350 miles away, was Zabi's territory. Both cities are located in Northern Pakistan. Temperatures in the summer are typically in excess of 100 degrees Fahrenheit (38 degrees centigrade). Ice cream deliveries were made by imported Volkswagen refrigerated vans.

As mentioned previously, a rudimentary form of management accounting and planning system had evolved to meet the needs of the project evaluation phase.

The main function of that system was to legitimate the project with senior bank officials and government agencies. When International Foods began operations, no prior thought had gone into the design of a control system. The organisation faced a completely changed environment from the time when the idea was first conceived. Political stability had given way to a socialist government that seemed unable to quell the growing demands of labour and students. The economy was staggering from the loss of Bangladesh as a market and the currency devaluation. Banks had been nationalised, and local currency credit was not easily obtained.

The first formal accounting and control systems that emerged at International Foods were influenced both by the technical-rational demands of the environment as well as the cultural milieu in which the company existed. The external environment created two main demands on the organisation: to preserve working capital and to meet the reporting requirements of the tax authorities. A system of book-keeping was instituted to maintain tax records, and a tax consultant was hired to do tax planning and to file necessary reports. Accounting as a rational response to external demands was created.

A managerial accounting system was devised to facilitate the generation of working capital. This system was focused on evaluating dealer sales performance. Since ice cream was being distributed through a network of dealers, each of whom had to purchase a freezer from the company, advance payments from dealers provided working capital for the company. Since freezers were an imported item, only International Foods could sell them because it had the necessary government approval and foreign currency loans. Individual dealers were not in a position to import these items directly. The limited number of freezers available were being rationed by International Foods, using sales performance of a dealer as the criterion. A formal system to evaluate dealer sales performance was developed. Again, accounting came into being as a response to environmental concerns.

While there were also technical-rational reasons to develop authority and responsibility structures, and to spell out rewards and incentives, no formal control system was developed for these areas. In a culture that values family and friendship ties over formal relationships, no-one felt the need to develop formal authority and responsibility structures. It was felt that since all agreed on the objectives to be achieved, actions taken by each member would be beneficial to the organisation. Hence a team form of management developed; whenever a problem arose, whoever was best suited and/or available dealt with it.

The absence of formal rewards and incentives can be explained by cultural variables. Four of the five top executives of the company were now working without any knowledge of their salary or potential shareholding. The initial arrangement was to provide one company house, car and servants, shared by the three executives and their families in Lahore. Zabi provided for his own living expenses from personal funds. Payments to these executives were based initially on personal need and of funds availability and not on the level of their contribution to International Foods. No discussions of shareholding or employment contracts occurred during this period because of a cultural norm, *takallouf*.

The concept of *takallouf* prevents parties in a social interaction from openly stating their needs, wants or desires. Thus the person who needs something is obligated to deny that need, while the person providing for that need is obligated to recognise it as a form of social propriety. For example, *takallouf* requires a guest at dinner to refuse a second helping of food, while the host is required to insist and fill the guest's plate. *Takallouf* does not imply refusal or resignation in some hierarchical sense. Rather, it is a norm of social behaviour that expects a giver to recognise that a lack of demand on a receiver's part does not relieve the giver of his obligation. In the case of International Foods, it was *takallouf*, rather than formal incentive systems and contracts, that bound together the organisation and allowed it to function effectively during a very critical phase of its existence.

In discussions with the principals of International Foods, in 1972, we learned that in the absence of a formal shareholding agreement, all shares were in the name of the father of Ali, Masood and Zabi. He was the family patriarch and was *not* actively involved with the company. When questioned about the "rationality" of this arrangement, coupled with the lack of formal structures in the organisation, the participants were hesitant to question the social and cultural basis for the arrangements in place. Clearly, they felt that formal structures were poor substitutes for personal trust and reciprocity. We observed, first-hand, the operation of *takallouf* in practice. The equilibrium was being maintained by using the head of the family as the symbolic holder of all power and privileges, thereby eliminating any possible source of dissension.

This informal control system, which lacked any defined reward and incentive schemes, continued through 1977. During this period the organisation functioned primarily with Masood focusing on opportunities and threats, while Zabi and others dealt with day-to-day operating matters. This proved to be a very effective arrangement as attested to by the events in 1975. That year, faced with the possible entry of a well-financed and politically well-connected competitor in Karachi, Masood responded by sending Zabi to open a plant in Karachi. Finding no help from the industrial banks this time, Zabi proceeded to work around them. With great ingenuity, International Foods was able to sell ice cream two weeks before its competition and thus secure the largest share of the bigger Karachi market. What the 1967-75 period demonstrated was that both Masood and Zabi were successful in the roles they performed; later it became clear that both had internalised these organisational experiences differently.

In the early years formal accounting and control systems played an important but unobtrusive role in organisational life. It gave legitimacy to governmental approval of the project, met the technical-rational demands of the environment (mostly for tactical problems), but had little influence on managerial and strategic decision making or rewards. Distributions of rewards were based on needs and cash availability and not on calculations of contribution.

Maturity and Expansion

The years 1975-7 were watershed years in the history of International Foods. Establishing and operating the Karachi plant in a very competitive environment, and succeeding in capturing a large market share, had established the company as a leader in ice cream sales nationwide. For the first time there was cash flow that exceeded the needs of the company. Payments to key executives had to be reconsidered. Also, these internally generated funds had to be invested to avoid being taxed as dividends. Expansion was therefore necessary. The Karachi plant, being 1,000 miles away and managed by other executives, created *de facto* decentralisation.

Externally, the nationalisation of key sectors of the economy, such as banking, insurance and automobiles, by Zulfiqar Ali Bhutto's government had created a poor investment climate. This caused economic stagnation. Also, driven by higher oil prices following the Arab oil embargo of 1974, inflation was another problem plaguing the economy. International Foods faced an economic environment which was worsening. Its planning and control system had to evolve. That evolution is described next.

The first area in which formal control and accountability was instituted was the management of ice cream deliveries to dealers. The nature and structure of these operational controls can be best explained as a technical-rational response to the needs of the environment. The delivery of ice cream creates the following problems: drivers may use the vans for personal errands; reckless driving can damage refrigerated vans, causing disruption of deliveries and the loss of a scarce resource; and drivers may chat with dealers while the van doors are open, creating a quality control problem. Since two-way radios are prohibited by security laws, this means of auditing when and where a van is cannot be used. A physical audit procedure in which a supervisor made spot checks of time on deliveries was instituted. Also, a monthly report summarising each driver's delivery performance and repair data was collected and analysed to evaluate the reliability of individual vans and drivers.

A second area in which technical-rational demands influenced controls was decentralisation. With a new manufacturing plant now located in Karachi, Zabi was given the responsibility for the southern operations. Masood continued to function in the role of the strategic planner, and one of the three founding executives remaining in Lahore was named managing director of the northern operations. The formal system of authority and responsibility was also supplemented with a formal system of compensation. A system that spelled out a base salary and fringe benefits of the various executives was adopted. No shareholding agreement, however, was drawn up and executives were not offered any profit-sharing scheme.

Financial controls, the third evolving area of controls, was where the technical-rational demands were moulded and shaped by the peculiar demands of the culture. Accounting systems had been introduced for tax purposes. However, no internal controls of the type common in the West were instituted. For instance, no separation of the controllership function from the treasury function was made. The individual performing the multiple roles of cash collection, bill payments and bank deposits was also doing the book-keeping for these items. A long-time family friend, he was not the one best qualified for the position. When queried about this lack of separation of duties and qualified personnel, Zabi responded, "In our environment this role requires *bharosa* (trust) more than qualifications. If we found someone qualified on whom we had *bharosa*, we would hire them. Until then *bharosa* is more important". As the comment indicates, the Western concept of checks and balances was not suited to the peculiar needs of that culture. Even for less sensitive areas, such as bill payment, duties were not separated. This was not due to a lack of understanding about checks and balances; it was a cultural preference for *bharosa* over formal controls.

Personnel selection practices, the fourth area, is where the cultural concept of *biradari* played an important role. Pakistani relationships are invariably bound by the concept of extended families. Unlike the West, where everyone out of the immediate blood line is considered a cousin, even first and second cousins of one's parents are considered uncles and aunts. This ever-expanding network of aunts, uncles and cousins forms an extended family called the *biradari*. Many members of the *biradari* are often unable to trace their specific lineage to another member of the *biradari* but have to accept the norms of behaviour of the group. One such norm is the need for providing for the economic wellbeing of members of the *biradari*. In practice, therefore, many of those hired are members of a family. In International Foods several positions, both at executive and lower levels, were filled by members of the extended family or *biradari*.

The final area, strategic planning, is where we begin to see the influence of the acquired world views of the participants. Strategic planning was primarily the focus and responsibility of Masood. His decisions were shaped in large part by the way in which he had internalised two key experiences. First, the migration to Pakistan had stripped the family of their assets and social position; the loss of Bangladesh had reinforced the lesson of the transient nature of nations. He stated his strongly felt belief that, "we should never again put all our eggs in one basket. Who knows where this socialist experiment will lead. . .we should be ready to leave at a moment's notice if necessary". Second, the difficulties of establishing the first ice cream company had shown him the advantage enjoyed by the privileged "22 families". As he saw it, "status and prestige comes from being an industrial family. . .we need a project that will make us one of the big boys".

The two key strategic decisions that were made in 1976-7 show the influence of these world views. First was a decision to set up an ice cream plant in Sharjah, UAE, to take advantage of the prosperity in the Persian Gulf states that followed the oil embargo of 1974. This was a first step towards diversification out of Pakistan. Second, it was decided to integrate vertically by setting up a packaging materials plant. This plant was going to be larger than any prior manufacturing facility set up by the group. It used, what was by Pakistani standards at the time, sophisticated technology. Managing this plant would provide the necessary respectability to join the select group of privileged families. It is important to note that these decisions were not arrived at by considering the strategic "fit" in a technical-rational sense; however, they were not necessarily arational or irrational.

During this phase there was a rich interplay of both rational and cultural variables that shaped the accounting and control systems in place in the organisation. Accounting played a rational role as well as rationalising the world views of participants in the guise of strategic planning. Also, accounting controls were substituted by cultural requirements of ***bharosa*** (trust). Personnel decisions came to be determined by the norms of behavour of ***biradari*** rather than by Western standards of hiring.

Organisational Crisis

In mid-1977 the Bhutto government was overthrown and replaced by a military government. With separatist movements in two of the four provinces, there was a great deal of political and economic uncertainty surrounding the future of Pakistan. The ensuing years (1978-84) were years of organisational crises for International Foods. With the packages plant under construction in Karachi, Masood had moved corporate headquarters there in 1978. By 1979, the necessary groundwork for opening an ice cream plant in Sharjah had also been completed, and construction of manufacturing facilities was well underway.

The packages plant brought with it several changes in the organisation. If it was to help the family be recognised as one of the foremost industrial families in Pakistan, it was important symbolically to have Ali involved. Instead of working as a managing director for a Pakistani subsidiary of a British company, Ali's talents should be required by his own family's ventures. Because packages was the "status" project of the group, Ali, the eldest brother, was asked to head the company. He was also named as chairman of the board for the ***entire*** group.

This decision again reflects the demands of the culture. Families in Pakistan are characterised by a "hierarchical" structure much more so than in Western societies. This is formalised in the language by the use of the suffix ***bhai*** when referring to an older brother. The word ***bhai***, literally translated, means brother. However, unlike in the West, it is not a symbol of equality but a mark of respect for family hierarchy. In the current instance the formality was extended to a point where Ali was simply referred to as ***bhai***, without his name prefixed, to indicate that there was only one older brother and authority figure in the family.

Ali introduced a series of formal control mechanisms similar to the centralised controls used by his former employer, a multinational corporation. The control system thus went from being informal and team oriented to more formal and bureaucratic. The internal controls and decision structures introduced were more suited to the needs of a remote central headquarters controlling geographically dispersed operations.

The new formal control system supplanted the informal control processes that had served the organisation so well in the past. In particular, the smooth teamwork between Masood and Zabi broke down and things began to unravel. The harmony which had characterised the organisation was replaced by disputes in three areas. First, shareholding and profit sharing became a contentious topic since Zabi was no longer willing to accept the ambiguous arrangements. Second, Zabi, who had always been an intuitive manager, was unwilling to accept the formal system of operational and managerial controls that Ali had introduced into the organisation. Finally, he expressed strong reservations about the strategy of diversifying out of Pakistan.

The reason the disputes arose was because Zabi viewed the new control system as symbolising values he found unacceptable. He stated his position as follows:

> I had contributed ***khoon*** (blood), ***pasina*** (sweat) and ***paisa*** (money) to get the Lahore plant off the ground. . . Masood and I have always been very close. . . and so I did what anyone in my position would have done for a brother. Why did I not ask for a ***quid pro quo***? The answer is ***takallouf***. I expected him to reciprocate in kind by setting up the Karachi plant for me. Now as you can see I find that after working against heavy odds to set up this plant, I am relegated to the number three position. . . It is painful to see that the staff know that I have no ***waqat*** (status) in the new pecking order. . . It is difficult to work with Ali. His style is to run the organisation as if he expects London to audit him. I suppose after 25 years of working with a multinational this is to be expected. For a small company, we document more than we act!. . . I also object to the future direction we are taking. Pakistan is our home and we cannot afford to leave it. It is up to ***all of us*** to ensure that it survives. We can't run all our lives — India to Pakistan to Bangladesh, back to Pakistan and now Sharjah. What next!

On the other hand, Masood had agreed to the new control structure since it symbolised his values. From the five-year struggle to establish the Lahore plant, he had internalised that entrepreneurship, capital and risk taking were the most important elements of business success. As he stated:

> It has been a long hard and lonely road to get the Lahore plant started. Without capital and status, we had no ***pooch*** (ability to get an audience). Lahore has bought us the status and credibility we lacked. From now on we can spin off from this success. . . We need to professionalise the company. Zabi is a great troubleshooter but he is not trained as a professional manager. . . I am happy to bring him into the business because they are family. . . Why should they be paid anything more than a professional manager?

The term "professionalising" was used often in later conversations. It symbolised Masood's belief that managerial talent is a commodity that can be bought once other elements were in place. Organisations did not fail from a lack of managerial talent. It was entrepreneurship, his contribution, that made International Foods successful. What Zabi and Ali did was no more than what was required of brothers in that culture. Masood felt that he had reciprocated under the norm of ***takallouf*** by bringing his brothers into a successful business. They, in turn, were performing managerial functions for which they were being compensated in excess of their market rate.

While Ali had no desires regarding this issue, Zabi had expectations. He had contributed everything he had to get Masood started in North Pakistan. He had given all the personal and business resources he had accumulated, as well as all of his time. He felt that the northern operations should be Masood's to control and own, and that southern operations should be his under the norms of ***takallouf***. Although he was aware of Masood's difficulty in getting the original project approved, he had not experienced Masood's frustration because of the family's lack of industrial status. His contributions to International Foods had largely been as a crisis manager and a problem solver — a set of skills that Masood seemed to lack.

Between 1978 and 1980, the control system at International Foods, far from facilitating the organisation's work, became implicated in a clash of competing world views. Zabi found himself in a very weak economic and cultural position to assert his beliefs. Having no formal shareholding nor profit sharing, he could not afford to leave the organisation. Also, as he put it:

> ***Bhai*** is a father figure to us. I cannot question his policies . . . he means well. Besides everyone around would make my life ***mushkil*** (difficult) if they felt I was doing things to question his ***izzat*** (respect/status/position). It is an extremely discouraging situation, it will hurt us financially.

Frustrated, he withdrew from all operational and strategic decisions concerning the group.

By the end of 1980, Ali's control system was creating tensions for people used to working informally and autonomously. The professional managers were reportedly upset with the centralised decision making and "paper shuffling". There were operational problems in the packages plant: difficulties were being encountered in producing quality products and meeting production schedules, costs of production were higher than competition leading to transfer pricing disputes with the ice cream companies, and the plant had operated at a loss for two years. Zabi, known for his skills as a crisis manager, was called in to help.

Finding his position strengthened, he asked that the current control system be revamped. The key changes he wanted were decentralisation of decision making to operating managers, profit sharing, clarification of shareholding, and a formal voice in all future expansion decisions. In return he would assume control of the ice cream companies in Pakistan and nurse the packaging plant back to health so it could be sold. This was agreed to and the operation in Pakistan temporarily reverted to the way it was prior to 1978.

To modify the accounting/control system, Masood hired a management consultant who was sympathetic to his world view. That consultant worked out a formal plan of shareholding which gave Zabi and Ali each 20 per cent of the company. However, all earnings and assets for the prior seven years of operations were attributed to Masood. To pay this, a dividend was declared to Masood. The size of this dividend left little cash in the companies. To allow the Pakistani companies to operate, Masood agreed to pledge the cash as collateral for bank loans to the company[4]. In addition, a three-member board comprised of the three brothers was formed. Operational decisions were vested with Zabi for Pakistani operations, and with Masood for abroad. Ali retained his position as chairman of the board, but was to focus on external relations with banks and government institutions.

There are two interesting aspects of this plan. First, it was couched in highly technical-rational terms, but appealed to familial relationships for acceptance. For instance, the preamble to the plan stated that "it was the wish and desire of the father that henceforth all three brothers should be treated *de facto* and *de jure* the partners in the business which was previously *de facto* entirely owned by Masood". The reference to the family patriarch was designed to pressure all parties to consent to the plan which explicitly stated that "these arrangements had the tacit approval and blessings of the father". Second, a valuation method was selected and accounting was done in a way that not only created a loan (for dividends from the previous seven years), but left Masood (not the corporation) in charge of the cash. The plan thus gave Masood what he felt belonged to him but did so in the name of technical rationality by invoking accounting. Zabi, who did not feel comfortable with the arrangement, was unable to protest since he did not understand accounting and did not have the technical background to challenge it. Accounting was thus successfully used to impose Masood's world view and values. (We do not mean to suggest that incorporating Masood's values in the control system was incorrect. Our point is simply to show the way in which accounting came to be invoked on behalf of values and to support world views.)

The reason why accounting and family hierarchy came to be employed jointly is again explained by the culture. The influence of 200 years of the British Raj has left some lasting influences on business practices in that culture. Business is "scientific" and no businessman wants to think of business decisions as being driven by emotional considerations. Accounting occupies a central place of rationality in this scheme because to be a chartered accountant (CA) from England was a mark of great accomplishment for a *desi* (native). The other cultural concept was that of ***rakh rakhao***. This implies a social obligation to behave in a way that is roughly the Western equivalent of not washing one's dirty laundry in public and to keep appearances so outsiders are unaware of conflicts. Zabi's decision to accept Masood's accounting was justified by an appeal to rationality. The use of paternal authority curtailed his ability to challenge the accounting since a public challenge would violate the norm of ***rakh rakhao***.

In this stage of International Foods' life we see accounting and control shift from rational concerns to become implicated in power distributions. The primary use of accounting was to appeal to it as a rational authority to consolidate one's power and control over the organisation.

Dissolution

The 1979 control system changes temporarily gave both Zabi and Masood what they wanted. Masood was able to get the cash out of Pakistani operations and invest it in Sharjah. His attitude at the time he left Pakistan was that "the companies are cancer patients". He felt that Pakistan had no economic future, and he wanted to go to a place that was booming. Zabi, on the other hand, was left to run things in Pakistan his way. However, he felt that he had been called in when the companies were in trouble and that this huge debt is "like a millstone around my neck".

The changes in the control system were instituted in December 1979, the same month in which the Russian troops invaded Afghanistan beginning a ten-year conflict. In 1980, the Reagan administration took over in the US and avowed to increase the pressure on the Russians to get out of Afghanistan. Pakistan's strategic location made it a natural ally of the US which wanted to funnel arms and financial aid to Afghan ***mujahadeen***. The country began to receive large amounts of aid as well as generous credit terms from various world financial institutions. The economy began to recover with a healthy rebound. Zabi's operations in Pakistan, freed of the problems of the packaging plant, began to show healthy profits.

In the Middle East the economic situation took the opposite turn during this time. The Iran-Iraq war caused a substantial drop in oil prices resulting in a recession in the Persian Gulf. States such as Sharjah began experiencing a loss of people as expatriate workers, out of jobs, began to go home. With the shrinking market, the short-term economic outlook for International Foods' operation in Sharjah became bleak.

These events reinforced the acquired world views of both Masood and Zabi. Masood was further convinced that the economic environment and taking risk at the right time is what makes businesses succeed or fail. The troubles in

Sharjah, he believed, were a combination of an unfavourable economic environment and bad timing. Zabi was more convinced of the importance of good management. He saw the success in Pakistan as good crisis management and the poor results in Sharjah as bad management by Masood. As he viewed it, the fruits of good management in Pakistan, while inadequately recognised, were being used to pay off Masood's loan and keep his operation in Sharjah afloat.

By 1984 the control system of 1979 had become irrelevant. Both Masood and Zabi made strategic decisions independently. In 1983 Zabi proceeded with plans to open a chocolate and confectionery manufacturing plant. During this same period, Masood proceeded with plans to build a long-life milk and juices plant in Karachi. Neither was discussed nor formally approved by the board of directors as required by the control system.

Zabi, with newly found power and confidence, hired a financial consultant to address two areas: first, the historical accounting which was the basis for Masood's dividends; second, an evaluation of group operations, which required foreign currency translations. His financial consultant revised the capital accounts attributable to partners for the 1972-9 period using market-based valuations for assets contributed. The revised valuation technique suggested that Masood's contribution had been greatly overvalued. The new consultant thus provided a technical-rational explanation of why the loan was an unjustifiable burden. In the area of evaluating group operations, he prepared financial statements in US dollars (compared to Masood's consultant, who used Deutschmarks) which made Sharjah operations show a substantial loss. Zabi's consultant had better credentials than Masood's, thereby bestowing great rationality and legitimacy on the revised interpretation. (Both currencies were reasonable units of measure for International Foods. The Sharjah operations were tied to a Deutschmark loan, while the Pakistani rupee is tied to the US dollar.)

In 1985 the differences between the principals escalated when Masood returned to Karachi to start the long-life milk and juice plant. As Zabi put it:

> Being a younger brother is hard. . . It seems that history is about to repeat itself. I have to move to the sidelines so Masood can claim the *Gaddi* (chair used as a symbol of power) by exercising his privileges as elder brother and majority shareholder.

With memories of Masood's prior move from Lahore to Karachi in 1978 guiding his actions, he saw the move as usurping of his power. Masood saw it differently:

> I do not know what has come over Zabi. He seems not to want any input from me or *Bhai* on running the operations. We want this operation professionalised and less personal.

Given the different world views about the meaning of events, difficult discussions about the ownership of the two new proposed plants ensued. Reflecting his belief that the two key factors of success are capital and risk, Masood felt that all future expansion originated from the success of the Lahore plant. Therefore, he insisted that the existing 60-20-20 ratio be continued for all future expansions.

Zabi, who had performed both the entrepreneurial and managerial functions for the chocolate plant, was unwilling to accept this. In addition, he wanted both the dividends and loans to Masood from the ice cream operations reviewed, as well as the "foreign" Sharjah operations, managed by Masood, declared unsuccessful. The clash in world views was backed by technical-rational arguments on both sides. Since their meaning frames were irreconcilable, and technical-rationality could no longer come to the aid of one side exclusively, the two brothers decided to proceed separately on all future plans. Masood took over control of the ice cream operations in Pakistan from Zabi, who devoted his time exclusively to chocolate and confectionery manufacturing. In 1986, International Foods, rationally positioned to take advantages of synergies and the favourable economic climate in Pakistan, ceased to operate as a group.

The final stage in the group's life is marked by a complete disregard for accounting. Having become a party to a dispute, accounting lost its authority as a rational system of last resort. The control systems also became impotent since the strain of the dispute caused many of the cultural categories of restraint to fall apart also. The struggle over whose world view would prevail, Zabi's or Masood's, that was previously implicit in "rational" discourses over accounting now became an open struggle. The discussions turned more to establishing who had violated the norms of culture rather than whose accounting was right.

Discussion

The evidence presented in the prior pages shows the rich and varied ways in which organisations adopt, change, use and discard control systems. The four stages in the 22-year history of International Foods attest to the important role that culture plays in this process. We show the influence of culture by the way it shapes the world view of participants, their meaning frames and their expectations of reciprocity.

The early years of International Foods were marked by an absence of formal controls. Yet the organisation functioned effectively due to the cultural forms of control that were present. It is important to point out that the cultural controls to which we are referring are not the same as the "clan" form of control (Ouchi, 1981). The key individuals who ran International Foods in its early years were a "natural' community. As defined by Geertz (1983), these were people whose lives were bound together by more than the exigencies of economic survival. The bonds of brotherhood and friendship between them preceded the formation of the formal organisation. The organisation was simply a different arena in which to pursue the social relationships already in place. The culture had defined the roles and expectations that the parties had. A formal control system was not necessary to invent these expectations. The only controls needed were to legitimate the organisation with outsiders, and that was put into place in these early years.

During the ***growth and maturity*** phase, both the technical-rational demands of the environment and the culture influenced the control system. Most of the operational controls and the decentralisation of decision making were in response to the needs of the environment. However, the technical-rational system was shaped by the unique requirements of the culture. This was clearly evident in the area of financial controls in which "trust" rather than "checks and balances" were the guiding principles. Ideas and forms of control do travel across cultural boundaries, but do not end up in the same form in which they started. They also coexist with the forms of control peculiar to a culture.

The ***crisis and conflict*** stage in the history of International Foods attests to the symbolic role of accounting and control systems in organisations. It is here that we see how such systems come to embody world views of participants. The crisis was caused by introducing a technical-rational system that embodied a world view and values alien to a key member of the organisation. For the first time a technical-rational system, instead of coexisting with cultural controls, began to clash with them. The technical-rational system was also responsible for a shift in power in the organisation. Culture in the norm of ***rakh rakhao*** provided a temporary respite from conflict by appealing to values of restraint and reason allowing rationality to work. In the longer term, however, rationality was no substitute for the cultural glue that had bound the organisation together.

The last stage in the history, ***dissolution***, demonstrates the difficulty of separating value rationality from instrumental rationality. This distinction fell apart when both key individuals in International Foods had the power to employ accounting and, therefore, appear rational. With two forms of rationality present, it was clear that the differences were over world views and values. The control system became irrelevant, and the organisation dissolved.

Concluding Remarks

At the start of this article we asked four questions: How do control systems get initiated in organisations? How do they evolve over time? What roles do they play in organisational life? Why does action become disconnected from such systems? Our purpose in posing these questions was to make sense of our field experience. We discovered that traditional theories of control, such as the technical-rational or collectivist, did not fully explain or capture the existence of certain practices and the dynamics of some events, while culture did. In addition, we discovered that culture also has interesting implications for understanding the limitations of traditional models of control.

Turning first to the power of ***culture as an explanatory variable***, there are clearly many accounting and control practices at International Foods that are the result of the culture and world views of the individuals. For example, some instances in which culture rather than economic rationality or power played a key role are: the lack of a shareholding agreement; rewards based on need not on performance; the bowing to family hierarchy in appointing a chairman of the board; the lack of separation of treasury and control functions; the strategic decisions to acquire a packages plant and the geographical expansion to UAE; and the inability to confront perceived inequities in reward sharing.

The strength of culture as an explanatory variable is particularly evident in the dissolution of the group at the height of its power and potential. The sequence of events that lead up to this action can be understood as a "Greek tragedy". This is because each party to the conflict, Zabi and Masood, was fully aware that both collective and individual economic rewards would be higher if they were to co-operate. In addition, the emotional cost of family conflict would be avoided. Their consultants had arrayed all alternatives and calculated payoffs to demonstrate that co-operation between the two would lead to higher returns. (A correct assessment as later events demonstrated.) As in a Greek tragedy, each side also fully understood and appreciated the position of the other party. However, the fundamental clash of world views, shaped largely by culture through traditions such as ***takallouf*** and family hierarchy, prevented either from finding

AAAJ
4,2

a solution. Inevitably dissolution followed. An analogy that comes to mind here is the Greek tragedy, ***Antigone***. In this classic play Princess Antigone clashes with her father, the King, over the burial of her brother (the King's son) executed for treason. Antigone's sense of duty to her brother and the King's responsibility to uphold the law of Greece result in Antigone's own execution. This, by today's standards, "irrational" outcome could have been avoided by the exercise of utility maximising calculus or by having the key players in family therapy. However, what the play depicts is that the outcome makes sense within the system of beliefs supplied by the Greek culture. Bounded by the culture, both Antigone and the King understand each other's imperatives and yet are helpless to avoid the inevitable consequences. In the case of Zabi and Masood neither the imperatives of economic rationality nor power or the psycho-dynamics of the individuals involved explain the decision to separate.

The second set of insights focuses on the role of *culture as a critique* of existing models. It shows that existing explanations for adoption and evolution of control systems in organisations fail to appreciate the *interplay* rather than exclusivity of symbolic, collectivist, or rational concerns. Environments do dictate certain forms of accounting/control systems, but not in the deterministic fashion suggested by the environment-strategy-structure model of control. The way in which culture moulds and shapes control systems also calls into question the contingency theory idea of technological determinism. Accounting/control systems, it seems, are not uniquely fashioned by either the environment, technology or power distributions in an organisation.

Another limitation of existing approaches highlighted by the study is that efficiency and rationality are beliefs that cannot be arbitrated independent of the system of values in which they exist. Power comes to play an important role in what is considered efficient, therefore creating hegemony for certain values and world views. Formal systems can be used to discipline the powerless (as Zabi was at one time) but the "disciplinary power" (Foucault, 1980) of rationality and efficiency falls apart when the party being disciplined can also invoke these concepts in the defence of its values. The acceptance of a control system rests, therefore, *not* on how rational it is, but on how well it reflects the value system of its participants and the belief system within which it operates.

Our insights rely on a study of the familial relationships between members of one family within the Pakistani culture. It is by no means suggested that their behaviour is typical, or that their experience will be replicated by others in that culture. However, the case does serve to highlight some of the important underlying cultural concepts that Pakistanis in general use to organise social behaviour and give it meaning. By using these cultural constructs to question and critique received wisdom in the area of accounting and management control, we add to the small but growing body of empirical field research in this area. Prior studies by Tinker (1980), Covaleski and Dirsmith (1983), Berry *et al.* (1985), Ansari and Euske (1987), Hopwood (1987), Birnberg and Snodgrass (1988), Colignon and Covaleski (1988) and Czarniawska-Joerges and Jacobsson (1989) have all examined some of the issues discussed here. We used a cultural form of analysis to evaluate critically what is taken for granted as rational or logical. Our aim was not to demonstrate why certain practices do not work in other cultures, but rather to expose the cultural or local nature of rationality. Undoubtedly, as other such studies are undertaken, we will begin to develop a richer understanding of the practice of accounting and control in organisations.

Notes

1. The term rational in the label "technical-rational" is not intended to privilege this approach to control over others discussed in this article. It is simply a way of labelling a set of assumptions and views about management control.
2. At the participants' request, we are using fictitious names for both the company and the principals. Western readers should note that the first letter of the alphabet in each fictitious name is representative of that person's position in the family hierarchy, e.g. A for eldest, M for middle, and Z for youngest.
3. In 1947, Pakistan consisted of two geographically separate parts, West and East. In 1971 East Pakistan seceded to become Bangladesh and the West is now Pakistan. After initially moving to the West from India, the brothers Masood and Zabi started their working careers in East Pakistan. Events after 1971 refer to Pakistan; those before 1971 refer to East and West Pakistan.
4. We recognise that with the sketchy details about loan size, banking arrangements, etc., it may be difficult for the reader to follow this discussion. We apologise for this fuzziness, since to clarify this discussion would require us to disclose sensitive company information which we are not at liberty to disclose.

References

Alchian, A.A. and Demsetz, H. (1972), "Production, Information Costs, and Economic Organization", *American Economic Review*, Vol. 62 No. 5, December, pp. 777-95.

Ansari, S.L. and Bell, J. (1985), "Accounting from a Cultural Perspective", Working Paper Series, California State University, Northridge, CA.

Ansari, S.L. and Bell, J. (1990), "Symbolic Behavioral and Economic Roles of Control in Organizations and Societies", in Bell, J. (Ed.), *Accounting Control Systems: A Technical, Social and Behavioral Integration*, Wiener Publications, New York.

Ansari, S.L. and Euske, K. (1987), "Rational, Rationalizing and Reifying Uses of Accounting Data in Organizations", *Accounting, Organizations and Society*, Vol. 12 No. 4, pp. 549-70.

Ansari, S.L. and Bell, J. (1991), "Symbolic, Behavioral and Economic Roles of Control in Organizations and Society", in Bell, J. (Ed.), *Accounting Control Systems: A Technical, Behavioral and Social Integration*, Markus Wiener, New York.

Anthony, R.N. (1965), *Planning and Control Systems*, Harvard University Press, Cambridge, MA.

Arpan, J.S. and Radebaugh, L. (1981), *International Accounting and Multinational Enterprises*, Warren, Gorham and Lamont, New York.

Baiman, S. (1982), "Agency Research in Managerial Accounting: A Survey", *Journal of Accounting Literature*, Spring.

Barnard, C.I. (1938), *The Functions of an Executive*, Harvard University Press, Cambridge, MA.

Berry, A.J., Capps, T., Cooper, D., Ferguson, P., Hopper, T. and Lowe, E.A. (1985), "Management Control in an Area of the NCB: Rationales of Accounting Practices in a Public Enterprise", *Accounting, Organizations and Society*, Vol. 10 No. 1, pp. 3-28.

Birnberg, J. and Snodgrass, C. (1988), "Culture and Control: A Field Study", *Accounting, Organizations and Society*, Vol. 13 No. 5, pp. 447-64.

Boland, R.J. and Pondy, L.R. (1983), "Accounting in Organizations. A Union of Natural and Rational Perspectives", *Accounting, Organizations and Society*, Vol. 8 No. 2/3, pp. 223-34.

Burchell, S., Clubb, C., Hopwood, A., Hughes, J. and Nahapiet, J. (1980), "The Roles of Accounting in Organizations and Society", *Accounting, Organizations and Society*, Vol. 5 No. 1, pp. 5-28.

Chandler, A.D. Jr (1977), *The Visible Hand: The Managerial Revolution in American Business*, Harvard University Press, Belknap Press, Cambridge, MA, 1977.

Colignon, R. and Covaleski, M. (1988), "An Examination of Managerial Accounting Practices as a Process of Mutual Adjustment", *Accounting, Organizations and Society*, Vol. 13 No. 6, pp. 559-80.

Covaleski, M.A. and Dirsmith, M.W. (1983), "Budgeting as a Means for Control and Loose Coupling", *Accounting, Organizations and Society*, Vol. 8 No. 3, pp. 323-40.

Czarniawska-Joerges, B. and Jacobsson, B. (1989), "Budget in a Cold Climate", *Accounting, Organizations and Society*, Vol. 14 No. 1/2, pp. 29-39.

Deal, T.E. and Kennedy, A.E. (1982), *Corporate Cultures*, Addison-Wesley, Reading, MA.

Foucault, M. (1980), in Gordon, C. (Ed.), *Power/Knowledge, Selected Interviews and Other Writings 1972-1977*, Harvester Press, Brighton.

Gambling, T. (1984), *Positive Accounting: Problems and Solutions*, Macmillan Press, London.

Gambling, T. (1987), "Accounting for Rituals", *Accounting, Organizations and Society*, Vol. 12 No. 4, pp. 319-30.

Geertz, C. (1978), *The Interpretation of Cultures*, Basic Books, New York.

Geertz, C. (1983), *Local Knowledge*, Basic Books, New York.

Geertz, C. (1988), *Works and Lives*, Stanford University Press, Stanford, CA.

Hofstede, G. (1980), *Culture's Consequences, International Differences in Work-related Values*, Sage Publications, London.

Hofstede, G. (1983), "The Cultural Relativity of Organizational Practices and Theories", *Journal of International Business Studies*, pp. 75-89.

Hopwood, A. (1987), "The Archaeology of Accounting Systems", *Accounting, Organizations and Society*, Vol. 12 No. 3, pp. 207-34.

Johnson, H.T. (1983), "The Search for Gain in Markets and Firms: A Review of the Historical Emergence of Management Accounting Systems", *Accounting, Organizations and Society*, Vol. 8 No. 2, pp. 139-46.

Kaplan, R. (1984), "The Evolution of Management Accounting", *The Accounting Review*, Vol. LIX No. 3, July.

Marschak, J. and Radner, R. (1972), *Economic Theory of Teams*, Yale University Press, New Haven, CT.

Merino, B. and Neimark, M. (1982), "Disclosure Regulation and Public Policy: A Socio-Historical Reappraisal", *Journal of Accounting and Public Policy*, pp. 33-57.

Meyer, J.W. (1983), "On the Celebration of Rationality: Some Comments on Boland and Pondy", *Accounting, Organizations and Society*, Vol. 8 No. 2, pp. 235-40.

Meyer, J.W. and Rowan, B. (1977), "Institutionalized Organisations: Formal Structure as Myth and Ceremony", *American Journal of Sociology*, Vol. 83, pp. 340-63.

Mirrlees, J.A. (1976), "The Optimal Structure of Incentives and Authority within an Organization", *Bell Journal of Economics*, Vol. 7 No. 1, Spring, pp. 105-31.

Miller, P. and O'Leary, T. (1987), "Accounting and the Construction of the Governable Person", *Accounting, Organizations and Society*, Vol. 12 No. 3, pp. 235-65.

Ouchi, W.G. (1981), *Theory Z: How American Business Can Meet the Japanese Challenge*, Addison-Wesley, Reading, MA.

Ouchi, W. (1979), "A Conceptual Framework for the Design of Organizational Control Mechanisms", *Management Science*, Vol. 25 No. 9, September, pp. 833-48.

Pascale, R.T. and Athos, A.G. (1981), *The Art of Japanese Management; Application for American Executives*, Simon and Schuster, New York.

Perrow, C. (1972), *Complex Organizations: A Critical Essay*, Scott Foresman, Glenview, IL.

Peters, T.J. and Waterman, R.H. Jr (1982), *In Search of Excellence: A Lesson from America's Best Run Companies*, Harper & Row, New York.

Pfeffer, J. and Salancik, G.R. (1978), *The External Control of Organizations: A Resource Dependence Perspective*, Harper & Row, New York, NY.

Sabel, C.F. (1982), *Work and Politics*, Cambridge University Press, New York.

Schein, E.H. (1981), "SMR Forum: Does Japanese Management Style Have a Message for American Managers?", *Sloan Management Review*, Fall, pp. 55-68.

Schein, E.H. (1985), *Organizational Culture and Leadership*, Jossey-Bass, San Francisco, CA.

Tinker, A.M. (1980), "Toward a Political Economy of Accounting", *Accounting, Organizations and Society*, Vol. 5 No. 1, pp. 147-60.

Williamson, O.E. (1975), *Markets and Hierarchies: Analysis and Antitrust Implications*, Free Press, New York, NY.

Appendix: Chronology of Key Events

1931 Ali, birth year.
1940 Masood, birth year.
1943 Zabi, birth year.
1947 India gains independence and is partitioned into East and West Pakistan. Hindus and Moslems flee across borders amidst savage communal riots.
1947 Family migrates to Pakistan, leaving all assets behind.
1954 Ali graduates, joins major British multinational.
1963 Ali promoted to managing director of Pakistani subsidiary.
1964 Masood joins ice cream company in East Pakistan.
1965 Zabi starts electrical contracting business in East Pakistan.
1967 Masood submits loan application for ice cream plant in Lahore with Industrial Development Bank of Pakistan (IDBP).
1968 IDBP rejects proposed ice cream plant.
1969 Loan application filed with Pakistan Industrial Credit and Investment Corporation (PICIC), and is rejected.
1970 Political unrest in East Pakistan; mobs target West Pakistanis.
1971 Zabi loses business in East Pakistan and moves to Rawalpindi, West Pakistan.
1971 PICIC approves loan application; Masood moves to West Pakistan.
1971 Civil war in East Pakistan, war with India. East Pakistan becomes Bangladesh.
1972 Bhutto government takes power. Rupee devalued 100 per cent. Major labour unrest in all industries.
1972 Lahore plant commences operations.
1973 Bhutto government nationalises banks, insurance and key industries.
1974 Arab oil embargo causes major jump in oil prices and spurs worldwide inflation.
1975 Karachi plant commences operations two weeks prior to major competitor entering the market.
1977 Political unrest results in overthrow of Bhutto government. Economy in shambles.
1978 Masood moves corporate headquarters to Karachi. Ali joins as chairman of the board.
1979 Packaging materials plant commences operation. Formal control system introduced and shareholding agreement reached.
1979 Russia invades Afghanistan.
1980 Sharjah ice cream plant commences operations; Masood moves to Sharjah.
1980 Reagan administration decides to funnel arms and economic aid to Afghan *mujahadeen* through Pakistan.
1981 Zabi takes control of Packaging from Ali. Plant breaks even and is sold.
1982 Iran/Iraq war breaks out. Oil prices begin to fall.
1984 Economic prosperity in Pakistan. Ice cream plants show large profits.
1984 Zabi gets approval for chocolate and confectionery plant in Karachi; Masood applies for loan for long-life conservation plant in Karachi.
1985 Masoood returns to Karachi. Attempt to restructure the formal control system fails. Long-life conservation plant approved.
1986 Zabi separates chocolate plant from International Foods; Masood separates long-life conservation plant and assumes control of International Foods from Zabi.
1987 Chocolate and long-life conservation plants commence operations.

Part VI
Epilogue

[30]

RESEARCH AND CONTROL IN COMPLEX ORGANIZATIONS: AN OVERVIEW

Kenneth A. Merchant and Robert Simons*
Harvard Business School

ABSTRACT

In this paper, we provide an overview of six types of research efforts, all of which are concerned to a significant extent with issues relevant to managers who are trying to effect and maintain control in complex organizations:

- principles of management;
- cybernetic control theory;
- agency theory;
- psychological research on control;
- contingency research (large data base sociological research);
- case (and small sample) sociological research.

One purpose of this paper is to show the parallels that exist among these types of research. Then, for purposes of comparison and contrast, we discuss the above types of works in terms of three criteria that we believe are useful both for deriving practical control-related findings and for having confidence in those findings. The first criterion is the extent to which organizational context variables are included in the research. The second is the clarity of the linkage between control variables and the achievement of organizational goals. The third is the reliability of evidence offered in support of the findings. Through this review, we hope to provide both an historical perspective for researchers new to the field and our views on opportunities for the integration of existing and future research.

INTRODUCTION

Purpose of Paper

The purpose of this paper is to provide an overview of the disparate bodies of research literature that relate to the problems of effecting and maintaining control in complex organizations.[1] Although the control-related literature is voluminous, there is no dominant research paradigm,[2] and, as a result, the works are often difficult to compare, contrast, and integrate. There are several reasons for this difficulty.

First, the choice of problem scope can vary significantly among studies. For example, some authors consider planning as a necessary component of the control process, while others discuss control processes as separable from planning. Sec-

---

* We gratefully acknowledge the suggestions and comments provided by Bob Anthony, Stan Baiman, Robin Cooper, Julie Hertenstein, Bob Kaplan, Krishna Palepu, and Al Schick.

[1] Etzioni [1975] defines organizations as social units devoted primarily to the attainment of specific goals; complex organizations have many of the characteristics of bureaucracy described by Weber. See Perrow [1979] and Etzioni [1975] for a full discussion.

[2] Paradigms represent coherent and consistent laws, theories, applications, and methodologies that enjoy general acceptance in the scientific community. See Kuhn [1970] for a more complete discussion.

ond, it is possible to discuss control at different levels of analysis, including control of individuals, organizations, assets, quality, and/or production. Third, control systems and issues can be considered at different levels of aggregation. Some authors have focused, for example, on specific control techniques (e.g., variance analysis) or control system characteristics (e.g., degree of formality), while others have attempted to identify commonly occurring clusters of control mechanisms that characterize a particular control strategy or control-system archetype. Finally, research methods often utilize different technical language. For example, what are known as superior-subordinate and owner-manager relationships in the organizational behavior literature, and as owner-steward relationships in some early accounting works,[3] are now referred to as principal-agent relationships in the economics and accounting literature.

Some fundamental similarities do exist, however, in the control-related research literature. Definitions of control generally encompass two key concepts: a focus on the behavior of organizational participants and a concern with the effect of this behavior on organizational outcomes [Horngren, 1982; Flamholtz, 1979; Lawler and Rhode, 1976; Benke, 1975]. Thus, understanding the control process in complex organizations ultimately requires study of (1) the actions of organizations and their members and (2) the processes by which desirable outcomes or goals are elaborated and achieved. We shall use these key concepts in our review of the following six research areas that have findings relevant to the understanding of the control purposes of accounting in complex organizations:

- principles of management;
- cybernetic control theory;
- agency theory;
- psychological research in control;
- contingency theory (large data base sociological research);
- case (and small sample) sociological research.

These six areas represent, in our opinion, the major ongoing research efforts in control. Clearly, some of these areas are gaining momentum (e.g., agency theory), while the interest in other areas appears to be waning (e.g., cybernetic control theory). However, unlike topics that have proven to be of transitory interest, (e.g., human resource accounting), each of these six areas has generated and continues to sustain current research interest.

Criteria for Evaluating Control Research

We shall employ three criteria to discuss and critique past and present research efforts related to the problems of controlling behavior in complex organizations. The first criterion describes the extent to which potentially important contextual variables are included in the research model. In simple models, the context of the organization[4] is exogenous to the analysis; i.e., the relationships

---

[3] See Chatfield [1974] for a review of stewardship in accounts since Roman civilization.

[4] By organizational context, we refer to firm-specific conditions that are relevant in understanding the manner in which the firm is organized and managed to achieve its objectives.

being studied are assumed to be independent of organizational settings. At the other extreme are complex models in which the organizational setting is a conditioning factor in control outcomes; i.e., the attributes of the organization are endogenous variables in the control model.

We believe that research on control in complex organizations must eventually attempt to specify the organizational conditions under which the relationships being studied will be obtained. If the relationships are unique to particular activities or situations, as we believe many are, then it follows that fruitful research should provide descriptions of the relevant organizational context and analyses using these descriptions.

The second criterion is the clarity of the linkage between control variables and the achievement of organizational goals. However elegant our models and research designs, the ultimate aim of our research should be to understand how managers can use control mechanisms to further organizational goals. Some research, which is at the desirable extreme of this dimension, clearly specifies the relationship between control actions and the goals of the firm. This tight linkage is evident in control research models that functionally relate the outcomes undertaken by organizational participants with the firm's objective function, usually stated in terms of utility.

At the other extreme are loosely coupled control models. In some of these models, the relationship between control actions and the goals of the firm are unspecified. In other models, one or more mediating variables are chosen as a proxy for important organizational outcomes, with the assumption that the relationship between the proxy and the desired outcome is known and fixed. Examples are studies that use employee attitudes, instead of company performance, as the dependent variable.

The third and final criterion we use to discuss the control research concerns the reliability of the findings or conclusions of the study. While nothing can be proved scientifically [Kerlinger, 1973, p. 155], we can and must evaluate the quality of the reasoning and evidence gathered to support propositions about controlling behavior in complex organizations. In some cases, mathematical analyses and experiments are conducted with careful attention to the rigor of scientific inquiry (i.e., internal reliability is high), while in other instances only anecdotes and casual reasoning are offered as evidence. Accordingly, the evaluation of any research endeavor must consider the likelihood, based on the evidence, that the findings and conclusions are valid.

Since control research is conducted with a view to widening our knowledge base and ultimately to improving practice, we believe that these three criteria are useful for reviewing the extant literature in control. That is, these criteria provide a means to evaluate our progress toward unambiguous prescriptions of proven value to practicing managers and accountants.

In the following sections, we provide a brief overview of the six types of control-related research efforts listed above and discuss each in terms of the three criteria we have just described. We then conclude the paper with some thoughts about future opportunities for research on control in complex organizations.

MAJOR CATEGORIES OF CONTROL RESEARCH

A. Control as a Principle of Management

The oldest conception of control in organizations is as a discrete function of management.[5] Giglioni and Bedeian [1974] trace the development of this literature in the twentieth century and note numerous listings of prescriptive management principles and techniques. These writings all discuss some basic control needs or tasks, particularly as related to production areas or accounting functions. For example, among his "twelve principles of efficiency," Emerson [1912] included "reliable, immediate and adequate records," (principle 8) and "written standard-practice instructions" (principle 11). Church [1914, p. 8] identified five "organic functions of administration," which included "control," meaning supervision (number 3) and "comparison" (number 4). And Fayol [1916] identified control as one of the four functions of management, together with planning, organizing, and coordinating.

More recently, and indicative of similar works published in the last 30 years, Koontz et al. [1980] present a list of 13 "especially important" control principles. Szilagyi [1981] offers a similar, but shorter, list of "keys to success with control systems."

In our opinion, the popularity of the principles of management approach stems from pedagogical rather than theoretical strengths. Clearly, management principles have proven to be useful checklists for introductory management courses. Moreover, recent best-sellers such as Peters and Waterman's [1982] checklist for effective managerial action have addressed our first two criteria to some extent. That is, first, these works do consider organizational context (e.g., history, structure, environment, and leadership style) and, second, the authors clearly identify linkages between control actions and results, and a recipe for action is offered as a panacea to organizational ills.

However, this research is very weak in terms of our third criterion — reliability of support for conclusions — and that is why most academic researchers have been slow to embrace the principles of management literature. In these works the supporting evidence is generally anecdotal, superficial, and incomplete, so it is difficult to evaluate the power and generalizability of the managerial actions suggested. Further, due to the lack of control of related variables, the link between action and results has not been demonstrated in either the classical management principles or the new wave of management "how-to" books.[6] To remedy

---

[5] In fact, Sayles [1972, p. 21] noted that "the subject of management controls is one of the oldest in the field of administration." Garner [1954] and Wells [1978], for example, survey control systems back to the 18th century

[6] In fact, in a follow-up article, *Business Week* [November 5, 1984, pp. 76-78] noted that 14 of the 43 firms identified by Peters and Waterman two years previously as excellent companies are experiencing significant business and management problems. The *Business Week* analysis concludes, "the more important lesson is that good management requires much more than following any one set of rules."

this situation, accounting researchers have focused on better specified models of managerial action, which we review in the following sections.

B. Cybernetic Control

An enduring effort to capture the processes of planning, comparison, and evaluation in a rigorous fashion can be seen in cybernetic models of control. Cybernetic models are dynamic models (i.e., a sequence of recursive relationships) with one or more correcting feedback loops.[7] These models implicitly assume that management control is "essentially the same basic process as is found in physical, biological and social systems" [Koontz et al., 1980, p. 725]; the only change is that human regulators (e.g., managers) are substituted for mechanical regulators (e.g., thermostat).

Twenty-five years ago, Forrester [1960, p. 1] stated that use of feedback control systems by management represented a "new frontier in our society,"[8] and, indeed, some cybernetic models of control have been shown to have practical management applications. For example, the notions of accounting variance analyses and "management-by-exception," which appear in every management accounting textbook [e.g., Horngren, 1982; Kaplan, 1982], are consistent with the basic cybernetic view of control. More advanced cybernetic control models involving, for example, feedforward loops have been applied to management problems such as controlling cash, inventories, and new product development by a number of authors, including Koontz and Bradspies [1972], Amey [1979], Buckley and O'Sullivan [1980], and Lebas [1980].

As the complexity of modern organizations increases, tne modeling of interrelations and causal patterns becomes increasingly important to control research. To the extent that these models are rigorously solved in relation to an objective function specified in terms of organizational outcomes, they meet our second and third criteria of having a tight linkage between controls and objectives and providing sound support for the conclusions. However, they fail in terms of our first criterion, since there has been little attempt to date to incorporate organizational context in the models due in large part to limitations in existing modeling techniques. Because of this limitation, we must conclude that the ability of cybernetics to provide the tools to expand our understanding of control in complex organizations beyond a few limited settings remains an open question.

C. Agency Theory

Agency theory involves the application of economic principles and tools to the problems of organizational control. The focus of the agency theory models is

---

[7] In this simple model, output, z, is a function of inputs, x, a transformation process, y, and a negative feedback process, f, based on a preset standard such that the system's output is,

$z = yx + yfz$

or, $z = yx / 1\text{-}yf$.

[8] More globally, general systems theory [von Bertalanffy, 1968], of which cybernetics is a part, has been proposed as a means of unifying science across diverse disciplines.

on achieving a commonality of interest between principals and their agents. An agency relationship exists whenever one party (a principal) delegates to another party (an agent) a service to be performed for compensation. Hence, top management can be considered to be the agents of the shareholders and, throughout the organizational hierarchy, subordinates can be considered to be the agents of their superiors.[9] An organization is viewed as a nexus of contracts between principals and agents.

The models that are developed using the agency theory paradigm explore how to minimize total agency costs in different settings. Agency costs are, "the sum of the costs of the incentive compensation plan, the costs of monitoring the manager's actions, and the remaining costs of actions taken by managers that diverge from the preferences of the owners" [Kaplan, 1982, p. 568]. The models typically include a small set of variables that describe characteristics of principal-agent relationships and the environments in which they function. Some examples of specified variables are the relative attitudes of the principal and agent toward risk, the degree of symmetry or asymmetry of information between principal and agent, the range of possible actions by either party, the costs of monitoring agent behaviors, and a range of possible states of nature and outcomes.

Theoretical agency models are developed to explore rigorously the conditions that will maximize the objective function of the principal and the agent. Thus, the linkage to organizational objectives is tight. However, these models do not generally consider much of the context of the organizational setting in which principals and agents contract. Little attention is given to differences in organization strategy, structure, technology, culture, or leadership style in conditioning contracting behavior.[10] Furthermore, with only a few exceptions (e.g., Baiman and Demski [1980], Baiman and Evans [1983], the agency theory papers focus on only one control mechanism (e.g., incentive payments, communication, supervisor monitoring), and there is little exploration of tradeoffs or interactions among the types of control mechanisms and/or control mechanisms and organizational characteristics. This is natural at this early state of research; over time the models may become more complex in order to investigate these relationships.

Empirical testing of the findings from the agency models is in its infancy, but this is a growing area of research.[11] Since the agency models ignore potentially important contextual factors, and since they are built on assumptions that may not accurately reflect conditions found in the real world, the findings in these papers must be considered tentative until they are tested against empirical evidence.

---

[9] Baiman [1982] provides an excellent review of agency research in managerial accounting.

[10] Contextual variables are often embedded in the production function in abstract form. However, current modeling technology does not allow precise specification and differentiation of these variables.

[11] For example, see recent studies by Chow [1983], Antle and Smith [1985, 1986], and Waller and Chow [1985].

D. Psychological Research in Control

Unlike agency theory, where the focus is on generic processes such as contracting and monitoring, psychological research in control is concerned with the cognitive variability and cognitive limitations of individuals. This research views organizations as coalitions of decision-making individuals, each of whom has distinct aspirations, expectations, and personal feelings apart from and interacting with the larger organizational entity. The behavior of individuals in organizations is believed to be a function of (1) individual psychological variables and (2) individual abilities to process information accurately.

This literature can be roughly divided into two categories. The first category of behavioral research takes decision accuracy as its dependent variable. The second category includes research in which the dependent variable is a constructed measure of individual psychological well-being or duress: job satisfaction and role conflict are examples. We shall first consider the vein of research that focuses on aspects of human information processing, since it is well developed in the behavioral accounting and control literature.[12]

The objective of inquiries into human information processing is to model individual decision making in order that decision accuracy can ultimately be improved. In terms of control, such studies will provide better understanding of cognitive processes, and this understanding should allow managers to alter information structures and decision environments to enhance the probability of effective decision responses. The research designs take into account characteristics of the cues (information set provided), the decision maker (personal and decisional characteristics), and the quality of the decision outcome [Libby and Lewis, 1977]. Most of the studies are structured using Brunswick's lens model, Bayes' theorem, or subjective expected utility maximization.[13]

The second category of psychological research encompasses an eclectic assortment of studies based on psychological constructs. One approach has been to draw on theories from other disciplines; e.g., applications of expectancy theory to control problems [Rockness, 1977; Ronen and Livingstone, 1975]. Also of continuing interest to control researchers are the conditions related to dysfunctional control behaviors. Hirst [1983], for example, studied the effect of individual perceptions of task uncertainty and reliance on accounting performance measures on dependent variables of individual stress and social withdrawal. The effects of the budget process on employee satisfaction and other behavioral variables have been reported in a number of studies [Brownell 1981, 1982a, 1982b; Kenis, 1979; Onsi, 1973; Lowe and Shaw, 1968].

---

[12] Indeed, Dyckman and Zeff [1984] tabulated 88 studies concerned with human information processing published in *The Accounting Review*, *Journal of Accounting Research*, and other accounting journals. This literature is summarized by Libby [1981] and Ashton [1982].

[13] Dyckman and Zeff [1984] count 52 studies based on Brunswick's lens model and 36 studies based on a subjective expected utility criterion in their tabulation of recently published behavioral accounting studies.

Psychological research in accounting and control has two main strengths. First, this research is often grounded in well-developed theory borrowed from other disciplines, so the research designs and hypotheses can be well specified. Further, much of this research is conducted by means of controlled laboratory experiments, which produce a desirable environment for validating and building on previous work and for directly testing theories of causality. The quality of evidence in support of findings, therefore, is potentially high. However, the artificial nature of laboratory settings and the frequent use of students as subjects limits real world applicability.

Notwithstanding the laboratory settings of many of these experiments, researchers undertaking studies in behavioral accounting are increasingly aware of the need to include organizational context in their analyses. This is evidenced by a recent tendency to use real decision makers (e.g., practicing managers and auditors) in experiments rather than students [Ashton, 1982, p. 185] and to conduct experiments that attempt to mirror real working environments (Cooper [1982]; Ashton [1984]).

For purposes of understanding control processes in complex organizations, a major weakness of the psychological studies is due to the fact that much of this research is framed around improving individual decision accuracy or improving feelings of worker satisfaction, while there is little evidence to date that these conditions necessarily improve organizational performance. The unstated assumption that improved individual decision accuracy in simplified settings leads to increased organizational welfare is unproven given the dynamics of decision making in complex settings [Allison, 1971; Mintzberg et al., 1976]. Furthermore, it is an open question whether employee satisfaction and other measures of emotional well-being are systematically correlated with the achievement of organizational objectives [Greene and Craft, 1979]. Thus, psychological research suffers from difficulties in linking behavioral conditions with organizational objectives.

E. Contingency Theory (Large Data Base Sociological Research)

In the last decade, control research rooted in the sociology of organizations has become increasingly prevalent. Researchers in control have argued that control system structures and processes are influenced by, for example, environmental uncertainty [Burns and Stalker, 1961], uncertainty [Galbraith, 1977], production technology [Woodward, 1965; Hayes, 1977; Merchant, 1984], shared organizational knowledge of goals and throughput mechanisms [Thompson, 1967], and organizational size [Bruns and Waterhouse, 1975; Merchant, 1981]. The overall consensus is that the design and use of control systems and procedures clearly is (and should be) contingent upon the context of the organizational setting in which these controls operate.[14]

---

[14] Structural contingency theory has been the dominant school of organizational thought influencing control research. Other perspectives in organization theory are reviewed in Burrell and Morgan [1979], Pfeffer [1982], and Astley and Van de Ven [1983]. These competing theories have received, to date, little attention in empirical testing by control researchers.

The general contingency theory approach to organizational design holds that the effectiveness of an organization is positively related to the goodness-of-fit between structure (of which control systems are a key component) and contextual variables such as the work performed and environment. An interaction is proposed such that the interactive effect of independent variables (e.g., technological uncertainty, control system structure) is functionally related to a dependent variable of firm effectiveness. However, as Schoonhoven [1981] points out, several problems have surfaced repeatedly in empirical tests of contingency hypotheses due to the underspecification of the functional form of the hypothesized relationship; lack of clarity results from ambiguous theoretical statements; interactions are not properly specified and tested; and models and tests rely on invalid assumptions of linearity. Thus, contingency research, while incorporating increasingly sophisticated measures of organizational context, has generally failed to demonstrate that the hypothesized relationships benefit the organization.

Contingency research appears to offer the potential for an increase in our knowledge of control in complex organizations, but, since much of this research is conducted by analyzing questionnaire data, the possibility of respondent bias and the potential superficiality of questionnaire data remain problems. Organizational context is often a construct of the researcher rather than a description of perceived reality in the terms used by the organizations under study. The small sample research described in the next section attempts to deal with this latter problem.

F. Case (and Small Sample) Sociological Research

A distinct body of control-related works can be grouped as case research. These works are unique in that they provide a rich description of a significant part of the control system and all (or most) of the relevant context at one or a few field sites. Thus, case research scores very highly in terms of one of our criteria: specification of organizational variables. Case research usually does not present data that can be used for formal statistical analyses, but the researchers do provide real-life stories and quotes from people with whom they have talked to provide support for their findings.

In case research, heavy reliance is placed on gathering evidence through interviews and direct observations and, to a lesser extent, questionnaire surveys. Organizations are often studied over a multiple-year period to provide an understanding of the history of the firm and the effects of major changes made in the firm's control system. Case researchers are interested not only in typical firms; they are also particularly interested in unusual situations — what some researchers would call "outliers" — to try to understand how important relationships operate under extreme conditions and how broadly the current understanding of relationships can be generalized.

Case research tends to explore areas that are not well understood. Conducting case research involves specifying area of interest in order to identify the variables that are important and how they vary with one another in unique organizational settings. In describing the setting and outcomes, case researchers try to understand why and how things operate as they do.

Researchers who choose the case study method of research tend to believe that the effects of control systems are produced by many significant interactions among control system variables and any of a number of firm-specific contextual factors. This was well expressed in a case study commissioned by the National Association of Accountants [Caplan and Champoux, 1978, p.55]:

> [The] effectiveness of even the most advanced accounting procedures rests on the appropriateness of their selection given the needs, attitudes and abilities of specific managers in a specific organization at a specific point in time.

Case research, however, has two serious drawbacks. One is a severe limitation in the number of sites that can be studied because case research is very time consuming and costly. Table 1 shows examples of some control-related case studies and highlights the small numbers of organizations studied. Case researchers often draw generalizations from the findings of their research, but if the contextual variables are important, then one can be confident about the findings only in the specific and limited settings that were being studied. Thus, generalization of findings to other sites may be flawed.

A second drawback is that the findings and the evidence itself are highly dependent on the researcher. Both are subject to bias and misinterpretation if the researcher is not perceptive, inquisitive, and open-minded. Since these researcher qualities are difficult to judge *ex post,* critiquing case research is also difficult. Therefore, the reliability of evidence of case research is always suspect.[18]

OVERVIEW AND CONCLUSION

Table 2 summarizes the focus, research methods, and major assumptions of the six research areas in control, and Table 3 provides a critique of each of the six areas in terms of three criteria that we consider to be important to good research in control. The six categories of research differ markedly across these three criteria. We recognize that tradeoffs are often necessary among competing research aims, but we suggest that future research in control should endeavor to combine the desirable features of each type of research.

As stated at the outset of this paper, one of our objectives is to provide an opportunity to reflect on the possibilities for convergence among areas of research

---

[18] An important point that is not always well understood is that despite their surface-level similarities, cases written to describe research findings are quite different from those written for teaching purposes. Teaching cases, which have formed a critical part of the instruction given to advanced students of management control for many years (e.g., the Anthony and Dearden textbook — now Anthony, Dearden and Bedford [1984] — has been used for 20 years), are written for pedagogical purposes, not necessarily to document advances in the state of knowledge. A teaching case is written to give students insights about how something works and to bring sometimes dry subjects to life. Casewriters developing teaching cases often do gain insights from writing cases, but any such benefits are above and beyond the primary goal of producing a useful teaching vehicle. Case research, on the other hand, is designed first and foremost to give the researcher/case writer insights into phenomena previously not well documented or understood.

that are often not recognized as being related to one another. Numerous control typologies have been developed in attempts to integrate this literature. However, these typologies generally focus on the integration of concepts within a single research area; little attempt has been made to tie together findings across the six research areas identified in this paper.

Table 4 presents an overview showing the great variance in the focus, level of aggregation, choice of control-system descriptors, and level of analysis among some of the control-typology writings. Given this variance, it is often difficult to relate one typology to another. Further, the lack of empirical testing of typologies precludes an assessment of their predictive power. A good typology, in addition to codifying phenomena, allows the observer to predict relationships that do not seem connected in any obvious way [Tiryakian, 1968, p. 178]. Prediction should be a first step in developing and testing hypotheses. Unfortunately, with a few exceptions (e.g., Ouchi [1977]), there has been little attempt to test hypotheses developed from existing control typologies.

The research directions we propose present new challenges. For example, tightening theoretical and empirical linkages between organizational objectives and control variables poses questions about both the nature of organizational goals and valid measures of effectiveness. The debate around the nature of organizational goals remains unresolved. Some believe that organizations do not have goals [Georgiou, 1973]. Others conceptualize organizational goals as coalitions of individual goals [Cyert and March, 1963], as constraints [Simon, 1964], or as objective functions to be maximized.

The measurement of effectiveness is also problematic. In addition to the profit-oriented goals with which accountants are familiar, goals may be specified in terms of survival, efficiency, control, growth, or mission [Mintzberg, 1983]. Thus, the validity of return on investment or other easily quantifiable profit measures as surrogates of organizational success may be open to challenge [Dalton et al., 1980; Goodman and Pennings, 1980].

Similarly, attempts to incorporate notions of organizational structure and process in our control models produce uncertainties concerning the convergent validity of scales and other measures commonly used in organization research. For example, reviews of operational measures of organizational technology reveal that different scales have similar names, variables often overlap conceptually, and instruments are seldom validated [Withey et al., 1983].

Notwithstanding these difficulties, we maintain that control research must continue to study opportunities for organizational improvement in complex settings. Accordingly, major research efforts should focus on problems that are widely appreciated by managers to be costly in organizational terms, on problems where benefits and costs can be considered simultaneously, and on problems where organizational variables can be specified to aid in subsequent generalizations and possible implementation.

To some extent the disparate nature of the control literatures has been an advantage, because different approaches have identified different sets of variables that are likely to be important. For example, the agency literature has demonstrated the importance of variables such as risk aversion, effort aversion, and information asymmetry, while the psychological research has directed useful attention at perception, cognition, and personality variables.

However, identifying and summarizing the unambiguous conclusions that have emerged from control studies published to date is an important task that remains to be accomplished. Especially useful would be a summary of empirical and analytic findings that are replicated across areas of control research. Such a summary could help provide both a foundation and an improved agenda for future research in control.

Table 1

EXAMPLES OF CASE RESEARCH

Study	Focus of Study	Research Site(s)
Simon et al. [1954]	Controller's department.	7 large, multilocation companies.
Van Voorhis [1957]	Internal auditing in smaller businesses.	8 small companies.
Hekimian [1965]	Management planning and control process.	3 life insurance companies.
Bower [1970]	Resource allocation process.	1 large, diversified company.
Caplan and Champoux [1978]	Management accounting.	1 apparel firm.
Young [1979]	Management.	2 human service agencies.
Umapathy [1980]	Budgeting processes.	2 large, decentralized manufacturing firms.
Hertenstein [1984]	Management control: adoption of inflation accounting.	4 large, diverse manufacturing firms.
Eccles [1985]	Transfer pricing.	13 large companies.

Table 2

OVERVIEW OF RESEARCH AREAS IN CONTROL

	Focus	Primary Research Methods	Major Assumptions
1. Principles of Management.	Normative management and control practices.	Personal experiences of author/researcher.	Good management techniques are generic across organizations.
2. Cybernetic Control Theory.	Recrusive information flows.	Mathematical modeling.	Feedback induces self-correcting behavior.
3. Agency Theory.	Effects of controls and monitoring on individual behavior.	Mathematical modeling.	Individual behavior is self-interested.
4. Psychological Research in Control.	Emotive and cognitive traits of individuals.	Laboratory experiments.	Emotions and cognitive limitations are a key input to behavioral outcomes.
5. Contingency Research (Large Data Base Sociological Research).	Relationships among organizational characteristics, controls, and performance.	Questionnaire data analysis.	Organizations can be custom designed to facilitate performance in a variety of settings.
6. Case (and Small Sample) Sociological Studies.	Control processes in unique organizational settings.	Participant observation and interviews.	Processes can be best understood with a detailed knowledge of an organization's unique circumstances.

Table 3

EVALUATION OF RESEARCH AREAS IN TERMS OF THREE CRITERIA

	Specification of Organizational Variables	Linkage to Firm Objective Function	Reliability of Evidence
1. Principles of Management	Moderate	High	Low
2. Cybernetic Control Theory	Low	High	Moderate
3. Agency Theory	Low	High	Moderate-High
4. Psychological Research in Control	Low	Moderate	Moderate-High
5. Contingency Research (Large Data Base Sociological Research)	Moderate	Variable	Moderate
6. Case (and Small Sample) Sociological Studies	High	Variable	Low

Table 4

SELECTED CONTROL FRAMEWORK STUDIES

Reference	Scope of Concern	Control System Descriptors			Level of Analysis
		Focus	Number	Example	
Anthony [1965]	broad	archetypes	2	management control.	activity
Eilon [1966]	cybernetic control	characteristics	12	rigidity of standards.	unspecified
Reeves and Woodward [1970]	broad	archetypes	4	unitary-personal.	organization
Child [1973]	work roles/ organization structure	characteristics	12	centralization.	organization
Hellriegel and Slocum [1974]	broad	tools	6	policies and rules.	individual and activity
Newman [1975]	cybernetic control	tools	3	steering controls.	individual and activity
Lawler and Rhode [1976]	cybernetic control	characteristics	11	objectivity of measures.	individual
Ouchi [1979]	broad	archetypes	3	bureaucracies.	organization
Kerr and Slocum [1981]	broad	tools	11	leader initiation of structure.	individual
Hofstede [1981]	broad	archetypes	6	intuitive control.	activities
Simons [1982]	broad	tools	7	programmed feed-back.	unspecified
Merchant [1982, 1985]	broad	tools	3	results controls.	individual, activity and organization
Flamholtz et al. [1985]	cybernetic control	elements	6	measurement ele-ment.	individual, activity and organization

REFERENCES

Allison, G. T. (1971), *Essence of Decision: Explaining the Cuban Missile Crisis* (Boston: Little, Brown, and Co.).

Amey, L. R. (1979), *Budget Planning and Control Systems* (London: Pitman).

Ansari, S. L. (1979), "Towards an Open Systems Approach to Budgeting," *Accounting Organizations and Society*, pp. 149-61.

Anthony, R. N. (1965), *Planning and Control Systems: A Framework for Analysis* (Boston: Division of Research, Graduate School of Business Administration, Harvard University).

__________, J. Dearden, and N. M. Bedford (1984), *Management Control Systems* (Homewood, Ill.: Richard D. Irwin).

Antle, R., and A. Smith (1985), "Measuring Executive Compensation: Methods and an Application," *Journal of Accounting Research* (Spring), pp. 296-325.

__________ (1986), "An Empirical Investigation into the Relative Performance Evaluation of Corporate Executives," *Journal of Accounting Research*, forthcoming.

Ashton, A. H. (1982), *Human Information Processing*, Studies in Accounting Research #17 (Sarasota, Fl.: American Accounting Association).

__________ (1984), "A Field Test of Implications of Laboratory Studies of Decision Making," *The Accounting Review* (July), pp. 361-75.

Astley, W. G., and A. Van de Ven (1983), "Central Perspectives and Debates in Organization Theory," *Administrative Science Quarterly* (June), pp. 245-73.

Baiman, S. (1982), "Agency Research in Managerial Accounting: A Survey," *Journal of Accounting Literature* (Spring), pp. 154-213.

Baiman, S., and J. S. Demski (1980), "Economically Optimal Performance Evaluation and Control Systems," *Journal of Accounting Research* (Supplement), pp. 184-220.

Baiman, S., and J. H. Evans III (1983), "Pre-Decision Information and Participative Management Control Systems," *Journal of Accounting Research* (Autumn), pp. 371-95.

Benke, R. L., Jr. (1975), "Human Behavior and Control," *Managerial Planning* (July/August), pp. 18-23.

Bower, J. L. (1970), *Managing the Resource Allocation Process: A Study of Corporate Planning and Investment* (Boston: Division of Research, Graduate School of Business Administration, Harvard University).

Brownell, P. (1981), "Participation in Budgeting, Locus of Control, and Organizational Effectiveness," *The Accounting Review* (October), pp. 844-60.

__________ (1982a), "A Field Study Examination of Budgetary Participation and Locus of Control," *The Accounting Review* (October), pp. 766-77.

__________ (1982b), "The Role of Accounting Data in Performance Evaluation, Budgetary Participation and Organizational Effectiveness," *Journal of Accounting Research* (Spring), pp. 12-27.

Bruns, W. J., and J. H. Waterhouse (1975), "Budgetary Control and Organization Structure," *Journal of Accounting Research* (Autumn), pp. 177-203.

Buckley, J. W., and P. O'Sullivan (1980), "Control Theory and Management Accounting" *Management Accounting 1980: Proceedings of the University of Illinois Management Accounting Symposium*, H. P. Holzer (Ed.), Department of Accountancy, University of Illinois at Urbana-Champaign, pp. 55-78.

Burns, T., and G. M. Stalker (1961), *The Management of Innovation* (London: Tavistock).

Burrell, G., an G. Morgan (1979), *Sociological Paradigms and Organizational Analysis* (London: Heinemann).

Caplan, E. H., and J. E. Champoux (1978), *Cases in Management Accounting: Context and Behavior: The Ralin Company — An Exploratory Study* (New York: National Association of Accountants).

Chatfield, M. (1974), *A History of Accounting Thought* (Hinsdale, Ill.: The Dryden Press).

Child, J., (1973), "Strategies of Control and Organizational Behavior," *Administrative Science Quarterly* (March), pp. 1-17.

Chow, C. W. (1983), "The Effects of Job Standard Difficulty and Compensation Schemes on Performance: An Exploration of Linkages," *Accounting Review* (October), pp. 667-85.

Church, A. H. (1914), ***The Science and Practice of Management*** (New York: Engineering Magazine Co.).

Cooper, R. (1982), "The Cognitive Biases in Business Decisions; The Base Rate Effect and Software Project Approval," DBA Dissertation, Harvard Business School.

Cyert, R. M., and J. G. March (1963), ***A Behavioral Theory of the Firm*** (Englewood Cliffs, N.J.: Prentice-Hall.

Dalton, D. R., Todor, W. D., Spendolini, J. J., Fielding, G. J., and L. W. Porter (1980), "Organization Structure and Performance: A Critical Review," ***Academy of Management Review*** pp. 49-64.

Driver, J. J., and T. J. Mock (1975), "Human Information Processing, Decision Style Theory, and Accounting Information Systems," ***The Accounting Review*** (July), pp. 490-508.

Dyckman, T. R., and S. A. Zeff (1984), "Two Decades of the Journal of Accounting Research," ***Journal of Accounting Research*** (Spring), pp. 225-97.

Eccles, R. G. (1985), ***The Transfer Pricing Problem: A Theory for Practice*** (Lexington, Mass., Lexington Books).

Eilon, S. (1966), "A Classification of Administrative Control Systems," ***The Journal of Management Studies*** (February), pp. 36-48.

Emerson, H. (1912), ***The Twelve Principles of Efficiency*** (New York: Engineering Magazine Co.).

Etzioni, A. (1975), ***A Comparative Analysis of Complex Organizations***, 2d ed. (New York: The Free Press).

Fayol, H. (1949), ***General and Industrial Management***, translated by C. Storrs (Pitman). Originally published in French in 1916.

Flamholtz, E. G. (1979), "Behavioral Aspects of Accounting/Control Systems." In ***Organizational Behavior***, S. Kerr (Ed.) (Columbus, Ohio: Grid), pp. 289-316.

Flamholtz, E. G., T. K. Das, and A. S. Tsui (1985), "Toward an Integrative Framework of Organizational Control," ***Accounting, Organizations and Society*** pp. 35-50.

Forrester, J. (1960), ***The Impact of Feedback Control Concepts on the Management Sciences***, Foundation for Instrumentation Education and Research.

Galbraith, J. R. (1977), ***Organization Design*** (Reading, Mass.: Addison-Wesley).

Garner, S. P. (1954), ***Evolution of Cost Accounting to 1925*** (University Al.: University of Alabama Press).

Georgiou, P. (1973), "The Goal Paradigm and Notes Toward a Counter Paradigm," ***Administrative Science Quarterly*** (September), pp. 291-310.

Giglioni, G. B., and A. G. Bedeian (1974), "A Conspectus of Management Control Theory," ***Academy of Management Journal*** (June), pp. 292-305.

Goodman, P. S., and J. J. Pennings (1980), "Critical Issues in Assessing Organizational Effectiveness," in ***Organizational Assessment: Perspectives on the Measurement of Organizational Behavior and the Quality of Work Life***, E. E. Lawler, D. A. Nadler, and C. Cammann (Eds.), (New York: Wiley), pp. 185-215.

Greene, C. N., and R. E. Craft (1979), "The Satisfaction-Performance Controversy — Revisited," in ***Motivation and Work Behavior***, R.M. Steers and L.W. Porter (Eds.), 2d ed. (New York: McGraw Hill), pp. 270-87.

Hayes, D. C. (1977), "The Contingency Theory of Managerial Accounting," ***The Accounting Review*** (January), pp. 22-39.

Hekimian, J. S. (1965), ***Management Control in Life Insurance Branch Offices*** (Boston: Division of Research, Graduate School of Business Administration, Harvard University).

Hellriegel, D., and J. W. Slocum, Jr. (1974), ***Management: A Contingency Approach*** (Reading, Mass.: Addison-Wesley).

Hertenstein, J. H. (1984), Innovation in Management Control: A Comparative Study of Inflation Adjusted Accounting Systems in Diversified Firms, DBA diss., Harvard Business School.

Hirst, M. K. (1983), "Reliance on Performance Measures, Task Uncertainty, and Dysfunctional Behavior: Some Extensions," ***Journal of Accounting Research*** (Autumn), pp. 596-605.

Hofstede, G. H. (1981), "Management Control of Public and Not-For-Profit Activities," ***Accounting, Organizations and Society***, pp. 193-226.

Horngren, C. T. (1982), ***Cost Accounting: A Managerial Emphasis***, 5th ed. (Englewood Cliffs, N.J.: Prentice-Hall).

Kaplan, R. S. (1982), *Advanced Management Accounting* (Englewood Cliffs, N.J.: Prentice-Hall).

Kenis, I. (1979), "Effects of Budgetary Goal Characteristics on Managerial Attitudes and Performance," *The Accounting Review* (October), pp. 707-21.

Kerlinger, F. N. (1973), *Foundations of Behavioral Research* (New York: Holt, Rinehart and Winston).

Kerr, S., and J. W. Slocum, Jr. (1981), "Controlling the Performance of People in Organizations," in *Handbook of Organizational Design*, P.C. Nystrom and W.H. Starbuck (Eds.), (London: Oxford University Press), pp. 116-34.

Koontz, H., and R. W. Bradspies (1972), "Managing Through Feedforward Control," *Business Horizons* (June), pp. 25-36.

Koontz, H., C. O'Donnell, and H. Weihrich (1980), *Management*, 7th ed. (New York: McGraw Hill).

Kuhn, T. S. (1970), *The Structure of Scientific Revolution*, 2d ed. (Chicago: University of Chicago Press).

Lawler, E. E., and J. G. Rhode (1976), *Information and Control in Organizations* (Pacific Palisades, Calif.: Goodyear Publishing).

Lebas, M. (1980), "Toward a Theory of Management Control: Organizational Information Economics, and Behavioral Approaches," working paper, Centre d'Enseignement Superieur des Affaires (Jouy-en-Josas, France).

Libby, R. (1981), *Accounting and Human Information Processing: Theory and Applications* (Englewood Cliffs, N.J.: Prentice-Hall).

Libby, R., and B. L. Lewis (1977), "Human Information Processing Research in Accounting: The State of the Art," *Accounting, Organizations and Society*, pp. 245-68.

Lowe, E. A., and R. W. Shaw (1968), "An Analysis of Managerial Biasing: Evidence From a Company's Budgeting Process," *Journal of Management Studies*, pp. 304-15.

Merchant, K. A. (1981), "The Design of the Corporate Budgeting System: Influences on Managerial Performance and Behavior," *The Accounting Review* (October), pp. 813-29.

——— (1982), "The Control Function of Management," *Sloan Management Review* (Summer), pp. 43-55.

——— (1984), "Influences on Departmental Budgeting: An Empirical Examination of a Contingency Model," *Accounting, Organizations and Society*, pp. 291-307.

——— (1985), *Control in Business Organizations* (Boston: Pitman).

Mintzberg, H. (1983), *Power in and Around Organizations* (Englewood Cliffs, N.J.: Prentice-Hall).

Mintzberg, H., D. Raisinghani, and A. Theoret (1976), "The Structure of 'Unstructured' Decision Processes," *Administrative Science Quarterly*, pp. 246-75.

Newman, W. H. (1975), *Constructive Control* (Englewood Cliffs, N.J.: Prentice-Hall).

Onsi, M. (1973), "Factor Analysis of Behavioral Variables Affecting Budgetary Slack," *The Accounting Review* (July), pp. 535-48.

Ouchi, W. G. (1977), "The Relationship Between Organizational Structure and Organizational Control," *Administrative Science Quarterly*, (March), pp. 95-113.

——— (1979), "A Conceptual Framework for the Design of Organizational Control Mechanisms," *Management Science* (September), pp. 833-48.

Perrow, C. (1979), *Complex Organizations: A Critical Essay*, 2d ed. (New York: Random House).

Peters, T. J., and R. H. Waterman (1982), *In Search of Excellence* (New York: Harper & Row).

Pfeffer, J. (1982), *Organizations and Organization Theory* (Boston: Pitman).

Reeves, T., and J. Woodward (1970), "The Study of Managerial Controls," in *Industrial Organization: Behavior and Control*, J. Woodward (Ed.) (Oxford).

Rockness, H. O. (1977), "Expectancy Theory in a Budgetary Setting: An Experimental Evaluation," *The Accounting Review* (October), pp. 893-903.

Ronen, J., and J. L. Livingstone (1975), "Expectancy Theory Approach to the Motivational Impacts of Budgets," *The Accounting Review* (October), pp. 671-85.

Sayles, L. (1972), "The Many Dimensions of Control," *Organizational Dynamics* (Summer), pp. 21-31.

Schoonhoven, C. B. (1981), "Problems with Contingency Theory: Testing Assumptions Hidden within the Language of Contingency 'Theory'," *Administrative Science Quarterly* (September), pp. 349-77.

Simon, H. A., (1964), "On the Concept of Organizational Goal," *Administrative Science Quarterly* (June), pp. 1-22.

Simon, H. A., G. Kozmetsky, H. Guetzkow, and G. Tyndall (1954), *Centralization vs. Decentralization in Organizing the Controller's Department*, reprinted in 1978 by Scholar's Book Co., Houston.

Simons, R. (1982), "Control in Organizations: A Framework for Analysis," *Proceedings of the Canadian Academic Accounting Association Conference*, pp. 101-13.

Szilagyi, A. D., Jr. (1981), *Management and Performance* (Glenview, Ill.: Scott, Foresman).

Thompson, J. D. (1967), *Organizations in Action* (New York: McGraw Hill).

Tiryakian, E. A. (1968), "Typologies," *International Encyclopedia of the Social Sciences*, Vol. 16, D.S. Sills (Ed.) (New York: MacMillan).

Umapathy, S. (1980), The Process of Budgeting in Decentralized Firms, DBA diss., Harvard Business School.

Van Voorhis, R. H. (1957), *How the Smaller business Utilizes Internal Auditing Functions* (New York: The Institute of Internal Auditors).

von Bertalanffy, L. (1968), *General System Theory* (New York: George Braziller).

Waller, W. S., and C. W. Chow (1985), "The Self-Selection and Effort Effects of Standard-Based Employee Controls: A Framework and Some Empirical Evidence," *The Accounting Review* (July), pp. 458-76.

Wells, M. C. (1978), *Accounting for Common Costs* (Urbana, Ill.: Center for International Education and Research in Accounting, University of Illinois).

Withey, M., R. L. Daft, and W. H. Cooper (1983), "Measures of Perrow's Work Unit Technology: An Empirical Assessment and a New Scale," *Academy of Management Journal* (March), pp. 45-63.

Woodward, J. (1965), *Industrial Organization: Theory and Practice* (London: Oxford University Press).

Young, D. W. (1979), *The Managerial Process in Human Service Agencies* (New York: Praeger Publishers).

SELECTED ANNOTATED BIBLIOGRAPHY

1. Control as a principle of management: Peters, T. J., and R. H. Waterman, *In Search of Excellence* (Harper & Row, 1982).

The authors of this best-selling book conducted interviews in 33 companies they rated as having had excellent or close-to-excellent performance over a twenty-year period. They distilled their observations into eight principles of management. One control-related principle is to try to establish "simultaneous loose-tight properties." The authors suggest that by cultivating corporate value systems, managers can rigidly control organizations and still allow autonomy, entrepreneurship, and innovation.

2. Cybernetic control theory: Ansari, S. L., "Towards an Open Systems Approach to Budgeting," *Accounting, Organizations and Society* (1979), pp. 149-61.

Using a systems theory distinction, Ansari distinguishes between open and closed systems in organizations. He argues that business firms operate as open systems, yet budgetary controls are designed with a closed system perspective. This misalignment, Ansari argues, causes suboptimization and an inappropriate focus on certain categories of costs, and it inhibits organizational learning. An open system approach to variance analysis is advocated and described that recognizes the fundamental interdependencies in organizational activity and allows for improved managerial performance.

3. Agency theory: Baiman, S., "Agency Research in Managerial Accounting: A Survey," *Journal of Accounting Literature* (Spring 1982), pp. 154-213.

This article reviews the agency literature and provides a critique of the agency model as a possible foundation for a normative theory of managerial accounting. The article first discusses the basic model and three major categories of extensions: multiple agents, endogenous labor market, and multiple periods. Then the agency literature is related to two central and related questions: (1) the ex ante value of information and (2) optimal use of information. Baiman concludes that it is premature to translate the results of agency research into normative guidelines for the choice and design of information systems because they are based on very limiting assumptions. But he also notes that the agency-theory approach seems to be a potentially fruitful research approach.

4. Psychological research in control: Driver, M. J., and T. J. Mock, "Human Information Processing, Decision Style Theory, and Accounting Information Systems," *The Accounting Review* (July 1975), pp. 490-508.

The authors set out to test hypotheses concerning interactions between the decision style of an individual and the way in which that person uses information. Fifty-four student subjects were tested and grouped into five categories of decision making style. An experimental, decision making task allowed subjects to purchase different types and amounts of information in simulated marketing and production environments. The behaviors of the subjects are analyzed and described in terms of information purchasing and the time taken to complete the decision. An example of the conclusions presented by the authors is that decision makers appear to become rapidly overloaded in complex, structured tasks and cannot use complex feedback effectively.

5. Contingency research: Bruns, W. J., Jr., and J. H. Waterhouse, "Budgetary Control and Organization Structure," *Journal of Accounting Research* (Autumn 1975), pp. 177-203.

Using data collected from 25 diverse organizations, this study shows significant relationships between two important types of control devices: budgets and organization structure. Relatively large, technically sophisticated, decentralized organizations tended to make greater use of standardized operating procedures and formal processes, including budgeting, to control managerial behaviors, but the managers in these firms perceived themselves and others as having a significant amount of control over their operations. Smaller firms, or those that are dependent on other organizations, tended to be based on simple or narrowly defined measures of performance, and superiors often did not accept their superiors' methods of attaining the budget goals. Bruns and Waterhouse label the former situation as an Administrative Control Strategy and the latter as an Interpersonal Control Strategy.

6. Case research: Eccles, R. G., *The Transfer Pricing Problem: A Theory for Practice* (Lexington Books, 1985).

Eccles interviewed 150 managers in 13 companies to try to understand transfer pricing in practice. He concludes that there are two principal determinants of transfer pricing practices: strategy and the administrative processes used to make transfer pricing decisions. Eccles concludes that transfer pricing practices should be evaluated both in terms of whether the practices lead to economic decisions that positively affect corporate performance and in terms of whether the managers feel they are being fairly rewarded for the contribution they are making to the company.

7. Conceptual typologies: Anthony, R. N., *Planning and Control Systems: A Framework for Analysis* (Division of Research, Harvard University, Graduate School of Business Administration, 1965).

In this oft-cited framework, Anthony identifies three differentiable planning and control processes: strategic planning, management control, and operational control. He describes each and observes that they differ in many ways, including the organizational level of the personnel involved, the amount of judgment involved, the time space of their consequences, and the importance of a single action taken.

Name Index

Abernathy, W.J. 173, 176, 178, 179
Ableggan, James C. 346
Ackerman, B.A. 397
Aiken, M. 52, 384
Alchian, A.A. 445, 446
Aldrich, H.E. 45, 52, 190
Allen, R.G. 191
Allison, G.T. 385, 476
Amey, L.R. 112, 473
Amigoni, F. 310
Andrews, K.R. 174, 175
Ansari, Shahid L. xxiv, 104, 308, 443–68, 488
Ansoff, H.I. 404
Antle, Rick xvii, 115–33
Anthony, Robert N. xv, xvi, xvii, xviii, xx, 11, 12, 19–36, 37, 38, 39, 40, 42–53 *passim*, 78, 105, 173, 174, 231, 274, 277, 310, 386, 445, 483, 489
Argyris, Chris xix, 38, 78, 84, 85, 183, 199, 315, 317, 350, 397, 432, 433
Ariss, S.S. 192
Armstrong, D. 419
Armstrong, J.C. 309
Arpan, J.S. 445
Arrow, Kenneth J. 108, 345
Ashby, W.R. 105
Ashmore, M. 366
Ashton, A.H. 476
Ashton, R.H. 432
Asplund, Ingemar 11, 12
Athos, A.G. 445
Avison, D.E. 151

Bacharach 385, 388
Baiman, S. 445, 474, 488
Banbury, J. 316
Baritz, L. 412
Barnard, Chester I. 103, 175, 343, 344, 345, 350, 352, 435–6
Bass, B.M. 18
Baumler, J.V. 290, 297, 307
Bayton, J.A. 204
Becker, Selwyn xix, 82, 84, 197–207, 434
Bedeian, Arthur G. xv, 3–16, 37, 472
Bedford, N. 39, 40, 42–53 *passim*, 274, 432
Beer, Stafford xvii, xviii, 49, 104, 105, 137–50
Bell, Jan xxiv, 443–66
Benke, R.L. jr 470
Benston, G. 434, 435
Bentham, Jeremy 358, 359
Berry, A.J. xvii, xxv, 101–14, 290, 463
Bertalanffy, Ludwig von 105, 152, 241
Beynon, I.L. 107
Binet, Alfred 425–6
Birnberg, Jacob G. 84, 289, 463
Blake, Robert R. 86
Blau, Peter M. 343, 352, 385, 392
Boland, R.J. 444
Bonini, C.P. xx, 71
Boulding, K.E. 105, 152, 241
Bower, J.L. 187, 480
Bradspies, Robert W. 11, 473
Braybrooke, D. xxiii
Brech, E.F.L. 9, 12, 38
Broadbent, J. xxv
Brownell, P. 291, 339, 475
Bruns, William J. jr 84, 294, 297, 308, 309, 327, 333, 476, 489
Brunsson, Nils xxiv, 395–410
Bryan, J.E. 321, 323
Buckley, Adrian xvii, 75–88
Buckley, J.W. 473
Burchell, S. 289, 314, 412, 413, 444
Burgelman, R.A. 182, 191
Burns, T. 48, 93, 95, 109, 308, 476

Camman, C. 387
Campbell, Andrew xviii, 161–71
Campbell, J. 190, 191
Campbell, J.P. 317
Caplan, Edwin H. 75, 77, 78, 84, 112, 209, 434, 478, 480
Carroll, S.J. 323, 330
Castel, R. 413, 424–5, 426
Champoux, J.E. 478, 480
Chandler, Alfred D. jr 308, 314, 396, 445
Chatfield, M. 412
Checkland, Peter B. xviii, 151–9
Chenhall, R.H. 290
Cherrington, D.J. 323
Cherrington, J.O. 323
Child, J.L. 82, 83, 203, 294, 308, 386, 389, 483
Chorley, R.J. 152
Christy, D.P. 191

Chua, Wai Fong 52
Church, A. Hamilton 5, 12, 37, 416, 472
Churchman, C.W. 397
Cilignon, R. 463
Clark, Burton R. 350, 371, 404
Clegg, S. 384, 385
Coase, R.H. xxii, 343, 345, 346
Coch, L. 78, 201, 323
Cohen, M.D. 183, 385
Coleman, James S. 350
Collini, S. 421
Collins, F. 323, 325
Cooper, R. 476
Copley, Frank B. 3
Cornell, William B. 8, 12
Cousins, M. 413
Covaleski, M.A. 444, 446, 447, 463
Craft, R.E. 476
Crozier 384, 385, 389
Cummings, L.L. 339
Cyert, Richard M. xxix, 68, 76, 211, 212, 314, 396, 436, 479
Czarniawski-Jerges, B. 444, 463

Daems, H. 314
Daft, R.L. xxi, xxii, 289-301, 307, 308, 309, 312
Dale, E. 210
Dalton, D.R. 479
Dalton, M. 212
Danielsson, A. 404
Daroca, F.P. 291
Davies, L. 151
Davis, Ralph C. 7, 8, 10
Dearden, John 19-36, 38, 39, 40, 42-53 *passim*, 386
DeCoster, D.T. 323
Deming, Robert H. 11, 12
Demsetz, H. 445, 446
Demski, Joel S. xvii, 115-33, 473
Denison, Edward F. 353
Denning, B.W. 89, 90
Dent, James K. 379
Dent, Arthur G.H. 9, 12
Dermer, J.D. xxiii, xxiv, 39, 306, 311, 314, 333, 383-94
Deverell, Cyril S. 12
Devine, C.T. 432, 434, 435
Dewey, John 422
Dickinson, A.L. 417
Dickson, W.J. 432-3
Diemer, Hugo 5, 12, 37
Diggory, J.C. 203
Dimock, Marshall E. 8
Dirsmith, M.W. 444, 446, 447, 463
Donnelly, James R. jr 10
Donzelot, J. 413
Dopuch, N. 432
Dore, Ronald 346
Downey, H.K. 190, 327, 328, 330
Driver, M.J. 488
Droge, C. 192
Drucker, Peter F. 4, xvi, xx, xxiii, 103, 209-18, 386
Drury, H.B. 428, 429
Dugdale, D. xxiv
Dunbar, R. 383, 384, 389
Duncan, R.B. 45, 190, 191, 289, 327, 328
Durkheim, Emile 346, 349-50
Dutton, J.E. 191
Dutton, Henry P. 6, 12
Dyckman, Thomas R. 84
Dyson, K. 420

Eccles, R.G. 480, 489
Edelman, M. 385
Eilon, S. 382, 479
Emerson, Harrington 5, 12, 416, 427, 428, 429, 430, 472
Emery, F. 48
Emmanuel C.R. xxv, 110
Epstein M.J. 416, 427, 429
Etzioni, Amitai 102, 103, 344, 352
Euske, K.J. 39, 444, 446, 463
Evan, W.M. 316
Evans, J.H. 474
Ewusi-Mensah, K. 176, 289

Fayol, Henri 5, 6, 9, 10, 12, 33, 38, 210, 472
Feldman, M.S. 183
Fells, J.M. 417
Ferrara, W.L. 274, 280
Festinger, L. 203
Filipetti, George 8
Filley, A.C. 104
Finkelstein, S. 192
Fiol, C.M. 183
Fish, Lounsbury S. 8, 12
Flamholtz, E.G. 290, 470, 483
Flood, R.L. 151
Follett, Mary P. xxiv, 4
Foran, M. 323
Forbes, P. 156
Forrester, J.W. 109, 473
Foster, G. 280
Foucault, Michel 358, 413, 414, 438, 463
Fouraker, L. 204
Franklin, Benjamin A. 12
Freeden, M. 422, 423

Freeman, J. 190
French, J.R.P. 78, 201, 323
Friesen, P.H. 173, 176, 187, 192
Fry, I.W. 289

Galbraith, Jay K. 322, 324, 325, 353, 396
Galbraith, J.R. 476
Galton, F. 426
Gambling, T.R. 317, 444
Garcke, E. 417
Geertz, Clifford 447, 461
Georgiou, P. 479
Gerard 152
Gibson, James L. 10
Giddens, A. 191
Giglioni, Giovanni B. xv, 3-16, 37, 472
Ginzberg, M.J. 290, 297
Glover, John G. 8, 12
Goetz, Billy E. 10, 12
Goldberg, L.R. 397
Goodman, P.S. 479
Goodwin, E. Sidney L. 6
Goold, Michael xviii, 161-71
Gordon, L.A. 104, 176, 289, 290, 308, 310, 387
Gordon, Robert A. 379, 380
Gouldner, Alvin W. 344, 351, 385
Govindarajan, V. xxii, 173, 177, 187, 289, 297, 321-41, 334
Gray, Barbara xix, 190-93
Gray, W. 152
Green, D. xix, 82, 434
Greene, C.N. 476
Gupta, A.K. 173, 177, 187, 289, 334

Haber, S. 419, 421, 427, 529
Hacking, L. 425, 426
Hage 52
Hägg, I. 237, 317
Hall, R.W. 280
Haller, M.H. 424
Hambrick D.C. 192
Hamel, G. 275
Hamermesh, R.G. 175
Hannan, M.T. 190
Harrison, G. Charter 416, 418, 427, 428, 429-30, 434
Harrison, R.H. 434
Harvey, A. 397
Hayes, D.C. 104, 290, 293, 297, 308, 309, 310, 476
Haynes, Michael G. xviii, 151-9
Hays, S.P. 419, 421, 422, 427
Hedberg, B.L.T. 105, 176, 183, 408
Hedlund, G. 317
Hekimian, James S. 11, 12, 480
Hellriegel, D. 327, 483
Heneman, H.G. 331
Hertenstein, J.H. 480
Herzberg, Frederick 79-81 *passim*, 82
Hicks, M.J. 151
Hiromoto, Toshiro xxi, 273-87
Hirst, M.K. 475
Hobhouse, L.T. 422-3
Hobson, J.A. 424
Hodder, J.E. 277
Hofer, C.W. 174, 175
Hoffman, P.J. 401
Hofstadter, R. 422, 423
Hofstede, Geert H. xx, 52, 78, 80, 81, 82, 83, 102, 112, 231-42, 308, 323, 333, 383, 384, 386, 387, 434, 435, 444, 483
Hofstedt, T.R. 435
Holden, Paul E. 8, 12
Holmstrom, B. 129
Hopf, Harry A. 8
Hopwood, Anthony G. xxii, xxiii, 104, 105, 289, 291, 307, 308, 310, 357-67, 386, 434, 435, 436, 463
Horngren, C.T. 105, 274, 280, 291, 305, 470, 473
Hrebeniak 191
Huber, G.P. 339
Hussain, A. 413
Huysmans, J.H. 397

Ijiri, Y. 73
Ivancevich, John M. 10, 102

Jackson, M.C. 151
Jackson, S.E. 191
Jacobsson, B. 444, 463
Jaeger, Alfred M. 350
Jaedicke, R.K. xx
Janis, I.L. 396, 402
Jerdee, T.H. 330
Jerome, William T. 4, 11, 12
Johnson, H.T. xxi, 274, 275, 363, 446
Johnson, Jerry B. 350, 386
Jonas, H. 234
Jones, C. xxiv
Jönsson, S.A. 105, 176, 402, 404, 406, 408, 409
Joyce 191

Kahn, Robert L. 104, 246
Kahneman, D. 396, 397, 401
Kamin, L.J. 424, 426
Kanter, Rosabeth M. 280, 350, 384
Kaplan, R.S. xxi, 275, 291, 363, 412, 446, 473, 474

Karpik, L. 45, 52
Kast, Fremont E. 4, 104
Katz, Daniel 104, 246
Katz, Ralph 350
Kay, E. 82, 323
Keeney, R.L. 397
Kenis, I. 475
Kennedy, B.A. 152
Kerlinger, F.N. 471
Kerr, S. 483
Khandwalla, P.N. 187, 294, 307, 312, 387
Kiesler, S. 191
Kilman, R.H. 317
Kimberly, J.R. 295
Knight, K. 262
Koestler, A. 155
Koontz, Harold D. 10, 11, 12, 42, 472, 473

Landau, M. 391
Lane, D.C. 153–4
Latour, B. 362
Lawler, E.E. 104, 290, 385, 388, 470, 483
Lawrence, Paul R. 45, 48, 264, 324, 327
Lawson, Francis M. 6, 12
Leavitt, H.J. 78, 205, 210
Lebas, M. 473
Ledington, P. 151
Lee, T.A. 412
Leifer, E.M. 182
Lewin, Kurt 202
Lewin, Arie Y. xix, 83, 209–18, 274, 434
Lewis, B.L. 475
Libby, R. 435, 475
Lichtner, William O. 6, 12
Light, Ivan H. 352
Likert, Rensis 77, 83, 84, 434
Lindblom, C.E. xxiii, 109, 396, 401, 402, 409
Lipset, Seymour M. 350
Litterer, Joseph A. 4
Littleton, A.C. 412
Livingstone, J.L. 475
Locke, E.A. 321, 323
Lorange, P. 174, 404
Lorenzi, P. 190
Lorsch, Jay W. 45, 48, 264, 324, 327
Lowe, E.A. 46, 47, 63–74, 83, 105, 108, 109, 212, 217, 247, 475
Lowe, Tony xvi, 37–54
Lucas, R.G. xxiii, xxiv, 383–94
Lundberg, E. 403
Lundin, R.A. 404, 406
Luneski, Chris 4
Lyles, M.A. 183

McCann, J.E. 289
McCaully, Harry J. jr 8
McClelland, D.C. 79–81 *passim*
McGregor, Douglas 77, 78, 84
Machin, John L.J. xx, 243–71
McInnes, J.M. 46, 247
Macintosh, N.B. xxi, xxii, 289–301, 307, 308, 309, 312
McKenna, Eugene xvii, 75–88
MacKenzie, D. 424
McMahon, J.T. 102
McNamara, Robert 239
McRae, T.W. 83
Maguire, M.A. 315
Mahoney, T.A. 330, 331
Malmberg, A. 404
March, James G. xxiv, 38, 68, 76, 102, 183, 210, 211, 212, 314, 343, 385, 389, 396, 404, 435, 436, 437, 479
Marschak, J. 446
Maslow, Abraham H. 79–81 *passim*
Mayo, Elton 344, 345, 352, 353, 432
Maze, Coleman L. 8, 12
Mechanic, D. 103
Merchant, Kenneth A. xxv, 289, 290, 291, 294, 327, 387, 469–89
Merino, B. 447
Meyer, H.H. 323
Meyer, John W. 351, 354, 444
Meyer, M.W. 182
Milani, K.W. 321, 323
Miles, R.E. 83, 173, 175, 176, 177, 178, 179
Miller, D. 104, 173, 176, 187, 192, 290, 308, 310, 387
Miller, Peter xxiv, 411–41, 446
Mills, A.E. xvii, 89–100
Mintzberg, Henry 104, 111, 173, 175, 176, 178, 179, 181, 183, 291, 292, 296, 476, 479
Mirrlees, J.A. 445
Mitroff, I.I. 317
Mock, T.J. 488
Mockler, Robert J. 4, 11, 12
Moncur, R.H. 323, 327, 333
Moncza, R. 323, 327
Morris, D. 290
Morse, N.C. 323
Moulton, Jane S. 86
Mueller, R.A.H. 205
Mundel, Marvin A. 11, 12
Munn, N.L. 205
Munsterberg, Hugo 430–31
Murdick, R.G. 397
Murray, G. 51
Murray, W. 318

Muth, John F. 11, 12
Myers, C.S. 426, 431

Nadler, D.A. 324, 387
Nahapiet, J.E. 316
Nakane, Chie 346
Narayanan, V.K. 176, 289
Nath, Raghu 84
Newman, William H. 9, 483
Nichols, T. 107
Nicholson, J.L. 416
Niemark, M. 447
Nisbett, R. 396
Nutt, P. 386

O'Connell, J.M. 339
O'Donnell, Cyril J. 10, 42
Okamoto, K. 280
O'Leary, Ted xxiv, 411-41, 446
Olsen, J.P. 396
Onsi, M. 322, 325, 332, 475
O'Sullivan, P. 473
Otley, David T. xvii, xxi, xxii, xxv, 101-14, 289, 290, 295, 297, 298, 305-20
Ouchi, William G. xxii, 315, 343-55, 386, 387, 445, 447, 461, 479, 483

Paik 11, 12
Parker, L. 104
Parker, R.H. 412
Parsons, Talcott 102, 354
Pascale, R.T. 445
Patching, D. 151
Paul, R.J. 270
Pennings, J.J. 52, 479
Perrow, Charles xxiii, 309, 310, 369-81
Peters, Tom J. 447, 472, 488
Pettigrew, A, 384, 385
Pfeffer, Jeffrey 45, 191, 314, 383, 385, 386, 388, 445
Pickens, D. 424
Pinfield, L.T. 182
Piper, J. 307, 308, 309
Pondy, L.R. 444
Popper, Karl xx
Porter, Michael E. 173, 175, 176, 178, 179, 187
Prahalad, C.K. 275
Prest, A.R. 397
Price, J.L. 316
Pugh, D.S. 308
Puxty, Tony xvi, 37-54

Quinn, J.B. 192

Radebaugh, L. 445
Radner, R. 446
Raiffa, H. 397
Rapoport 152
Rathe, A.W. 101
Reeves, Tom K. 4, 483
Reid, Samuel R. 76
Reimer, E. 323
Rhenman, E. 45, 50
Rhode, J.G. 470, 483
Rice, William B. 10
Riley, P. 383
Ritchie, D.G. 424
Rizzo, N.D. 152
Robinson, Webster R. 6-7, 12
Rockness, H.O. 475
Roethlisberger, F.J. 432-3
Ronen, J. 475
Roosevelt, F.W. 427
Rose, N. 424, 425, 426
Rose, Thomas G. 9, 12
Rosenszweig, James E. 4, 104
Ross, J.E. 397
Ross, L. 396
Rowan, Brian 351, 354, 444
Rowe, Alan J. 4
Rowland, Floyd H. 8
Roy, D. 103
Rushdie, Salman 443

Sabel, C.F. 452
Salaman, G. 316
Salancik, G.R. 45, 191, 314, 445
Sappington, D. 129
Sathe, V. 307, 311
Schachter, S. 201
Schäfer, G. 151
Schein, Edgar H. 353, 445
Schell, Erwin H. 8
Schendel, D.E. 174, 175
Schiff, Michael xix, 83, 209-18, 274, 434
Scholes, J. 151, 154, 155, 157
Schön, D.A. 183, 315
Schoonhoven, C.B. 322, 334, 336, 476
Schreiber, Norman B. 8
Schultze, C.L. 239
Scott, W. Richard 343, 352, 389
Scott-Morton, M.F. 174
Scull, A.T. 412
Searfoss, D. 323, 327
Searle, G.R. 419, 420
Seashore, S.E. 434
Selsky, J. 289
Selzniick, Philip 350

Senge, Peter 153
Shaw, R.W. 212, 217, 475
Sheridan, A. 413
Shillinglaw, Gordon 78, 212
Shils, Edward A. 354
Shrivastava, P. 174
Siegel S. 204
Silverman, D. 102, 385
Simon, Herbert A. 38, 40, 76, 102, 103, 104, 108, 181, 210, 343, 349, 384, 385, 388, 404, 435, 436, 480
Simons, Robert xviii, xix, xxv, 173-89, 190-92 *passim*, 469-89
Sisk, Henry L. 10
Sjöstrand, S. 315
Slocum, J.W. 327, 483
Slovic, P. 401
Smircich, L. 190, 191
Smith, Hubert L. 8, 12
Smith, Robert D. 11, 12
Snodgrass, C. 463
Snow, C.C. 173, 175, 176, 177, 178, 179
Sofer, C. 436
Solomons, D. 412, 417, 419, 427, 429
Somervell, Brehon B. 8
Sord, Burnard H. 11, 12, 199
Sorge, A. 363
Southwood, K.E. 334
Sowell, E.M. 417, 427
Spence, M. 182
Spencer, H. 422
Sproull, L. 191
Stalker, G.M. 48, 93, 95,109, 307
Starbuck, W.H. 191, 404, 405, 406
Staw, B. 191
Stedman-Jones, G. 412
Stedry, Andrew C. 82, 203, 206, 321, 323
Steers, R.M. 313, 323
Stenhouse, L. 317
Stokes, Paul M. 11, 12
Strauss, A. 385
Strong, Earl P. 11, 12
Stubbart, C. 190, 191
Sutherland, G. 424, 426
Sutherland, J.W. 236
Swieringa, R.J. 323, 327, 333
Szilagyi, A.D. jr 472

Tannenbaum, Arnold S. 4, 102, 107, 390
Tarkowsky, Z.M. 397
Taylor, Frederick W. 10, 12, 38, 210, 234, 427-8 *passim*, 429, 430
Terreberry, S. 45
Terry, George R. 10
Thompson, J.D. 289, 290, 291, 292, 309, 388, 476
Thurston, John B. 8
Tiessen, P. 105, 289, 294, 308, 310
Tinker, A.M. 47, 108, 444, 446, 463
Tiryakian, E.A. 479
Tocher, K. xvii, 106, 108
Tosi, H.L. 323
Towne, H.R. 428
Townsend, Robert 84
Tricker, R.I. 75
Trist, E. 48
Trow, Martin A. 350
Trundle, George T. 10
Tugwell, Bernard 439
Turvey, R. 397
Tushman, M.L. 290, 324
Tversky, Amos 396, 397, 401

Umapathy, S. 480
Urwick, Lyndall F. 6, 7, 10, 12, 38
Utterback, J.M. 173, 176, 178, 179

Vancil, R.F. 38, 231, 387, 388, 404
Van de Ven, A.H. 289, 290, 291, 293, 297
Van Gunsteren, H. 383
Van Maanen, John 350, 353, 385
Van Voorhis, R.H. 480
Vergin, R.C. 83
Vickers, Sir Geoffrey xvi, 55-61, 104, 106
Villers, Raymond 12
Vroom, V.H. 81, 339

Wagner, H.W. xx
Ward, Lester 423, 424
Waring, A. 151
Warner, M. 363
Wartick, S.L. 191
Waterhouse, J.H. 105, 289, 294, 297, 308, 309, 310, 327, 333, 476, 489
Waterman, Richard H. 447, 472, 488
Waters, J.A. 175
Watson, D.J.H. 290, 297, 308
Webb, Sidney 423
Weber, Max 38, 345, 352, 391, 437
Weick, Karl E. 52, 190, 191, 327, 344, 384, 385, 391
Weiner, N. 104
Weirich, H. 42
Welsch, Glenn A. 11, 12, 199
Westerlund, G. 315
Wharton, Kenneth J. 10
White, Arnold 419, 420
White, H.C. 182

White, Percival 7
Whitehead, T.N. 432
Whiting, J.W.M. 82, 83, 203
Wiener, Norbert 40, 232
Wildavsky, A. 102, 109, 240, 384
Williams, John H. 7, 12
Williamson, Oliver E. xxii, 181, 211, 212, 343, 346, 347, 445
Wilson, B. 151
Winter, J.M. 420
Withey, M. 479
Wolstenholme, E. 153
Wood, S. 308
Wood-Harper, A.T. 151
Woodward, Joan 4, 93, 306, 308, 476, 483

Yerkes, R.M. 426
Young, D.W. 290, 480

Zander, A. 399
Zimmerman V.K. 412